Terrorism in Africa

The International Library of Terrorism

Series Editors:
Yonah Alexander and Alan O'Day

Titles in the Series:

Terrorism: British Perspectives
Paul Wilkinson

Dimensions of Irish Terrorism
Alan O'Day

European Terrorism
Edward Moxon-Browne

Terrorism in Africa
Martha Crenshaw

Middle East Terrorism: Current Threats and Future Prospects
Yonah Alexander

Terrorism in Africa

Edited by

Martha Crenshaw

Wesleyan University, Connecticut

G.K. Hall & Co.
An Imprint of Macmillan Publishing Company
New York

Maxwell Macmillan Canada
Toronto

This American edition published in 1994 by G.K. Hall & Co.,
An Imprint of Macmillan Publishing Company

G.K. Hall & Co.
An Imprint of Macmillan Publishing Company
866 Third Avenue
New York, NY 10022

Maxwell Macmillan Canada, Inc.
1200 Eglinton Avenue East, Suite 200
Don Mills, Ontario M3C 3N1

First published in Great Britain by
Dartmouth Publishing Company Limited
Gower House
Croft Road
Aldershot
Hampshire GU11 3HR
England

Macmillan Publishing Company is part of the Maxwell Communication Group of Companies.

Library of Congress Catalog Card Number: 93-38368

PRINTED IN GREAT BRITAIN

printing number
1 2 3 4 5 6 7 8 9 10

Library of Congress Cataloging-in-Publication Data
Terrorism in Africa / edited by Martha Crenshaw.
     p. cm. -- (International library of terrorism : 4)
  Includes index.
  ISBN 0-8161-7336-2 (alk. paper)
   1. Terrorism-- Africa. 2. Terrorism--South Africa. 3. Insurgency-
-Africa. 4. Insurgency--South Africa. 5. Africa--Politics and
government. 6. South Africa--Politics and government.
I. Crenshaw, Martha. II. Series.
HV6431.I546 1994 vol. 4
[HV6433.A35]   93-38368
303.6'25'096--dc20   CIP

The paper used in this publication meets the minimum requirements of American National Standard for Information Sciences—Permanence of Paper for Printed Library Materials.
ANSI Z39.48—194.∞TM

ISBN 0-8161-7336-2

Contents

PART III   SOUTH AFRICA: STATES, TERRORISM, AND RESISTANCE

General

Legal Dimensions of the Issue

Acknowledgements

The editor and publishers wish to thank the following for permission to use copyright material.

Blackwell Publishers for the essay: Paul Rich (1984), 'Insurgency, Terrorism and the Apartheid System in South Africa', *Political Studies*, **32**, pp. 68–85.

Brooklyn Journal of International Law for the essay: Elisabeth Love Goot (1989), 'Should South Africa Be Named a Terrorist State?', *Brooklyn Journal of International Law*, **15**, pp. 801–41.

Canadian Journal of African Studies for the essay: Cora Ann Presley (1988), 'The Mau Mau Rebellion, Kikuyu Women, and Social Change', *Canadian Journal of African Studies*, **22**, pp. 502–27.

Conflict Quarterly for the essay: Femi Otubanjo (1980), 'African Guerrillas and Indigenous Governments', *Conflict Quarterly*, **1**, pp. 32–41. Copyright © Centre for Conflict Studies.

Council for Social & Economic Studies for essays: F. McA. Clifford-Vaughan (1987), 'Terrorism and Insurgency in South Africa', *Journal of Social, Political and Economic Studies*, **12**, pp. 259–75, and Samuel T. Francis (1986), 'Communism, Terrorism, and The African National Congress', *Journal of Social, Political and Economic Studies*, **11**, pp. 55–71.

Foreign Policy Research Institute for the essay: J. Bowyer Bell (1974), 'Endemic Insurgency and International Order: The Eritrean Experience', *Orbis*, **17**, pp. 427–50. This article originally appeared in the Summer 1974 issue of Orbis: A Journal of World Affairs, published by the Foreign Policy Research Institute.

Nkosinathi Gwala (1989), 'Political Violence and the Struggle for Control in Pietermaritzburg', *Journal of Southern African Studies*, **15**, pp. 506–24. Copyright © Nkosinathi Gwala.

Heather Hughes (1987), 'Violence in Inanda, August 1985', *Journal of Southern African Studies*, **13**, pp. 331–54. Copyright © Heather Hughes.

Heldref Publications for the essay: Adeoye A. Akinsanya (1982), 'The Entebbe Rescue Mission: A Case of Aggression?', *Journal of African Studies*, **9**, pp. 46–57. Reprinted with permission of the Helen Dwight Reid Educational Foundation. Published by Heldref Publications, 1319 Eighteenth Street, N.W., Washington, D.C. 20036–1802. Copyright © 1982.

International Journal of Comparative and Applied Criminal Justice for the essay: Patrick Edobor Igbinovia (1986), 'Terrorist Aircraft Hijacking and Sabotage in African States', *International Journal of Comparative and Applied Criminal Justice*, **10**, pp. 73–93.

The John Hopkins University Press for the essay: Timothy M. Shaw (1984), 'Unconventional Conflicts in Africa: Nuclear, Class and Guerrilla Struggles', *The Jerusalem Journal of International Relations*, **7**, pp. 63–78.

Christina Murray (1987), 'The ANC in Court: Towards International Guidelines in Sentencing', *Journal of Southern African Studies*, **14**, pp. 140–46. Copyright © Christina Murray.

Oxford University Press for essays: Steven Metz (1986), 'The Mozambique National Resistance and South African Foreign Policy', *African Affairs*, **85**, pp. 491–507, and D.W. Throup (1985), 'The Origins of Mau Mau', *African Affairs*, **84**, pp. 399–433.

Sage Publications Incorporated for essays: Elaine A. Friedland (1982), 'South Africa and Instability in Southern Africa', *Annals of the American Academy of Political and Social Science*, **463**, pp. 95–105, and Zeev Maoz (1981), 'The Decision to Raid Entebbe: Decision Analysis Applied to Crisis Behavior', *Journal of Conflict Resolution*, **25**, pp. 677–707.

Social Justice for essays: John Dugard (1991), 'Movement and State Strategies: The Role of International Law in the Struggle for Liberation in South Africa', *Social Justice*, **18**, pp. 83–94, and Eliphas G. Mukonoweshuro (1991), 'The Basis of Structural Violence: Between Verwoerd and the ANC: Profiles of Contemporary Repression, Deprivation, and Poverty in South Africa's "Bantustans"', *Social Justice*, **18**, pp. 171–85.

Third World Quarterly for the essay: Ali A. Mazrui (1985), 'The Third World and International Terrorism: Preliminary Reflections', *Third World Quarterly*, **7**, pp. 348–64.

University of Pennsylvania Law Review and Fred B. Rothman and Company for the essay: Sydney Kentridge (1980), 'The Pathology of a Legal System: Criminal Justice in South Africa', *University of Pennsylvania Law Review*, **128**, pp. 603–21. Copyright © University of Pennsylvania Law Review.

Every effort has been made to trace all the copyright holders, but if any have been inadvertently overlooked the publishers will be pleased to make the necessary arrangement at the first opportunity.

Series Preface

The International Library of Terrorism puts into book form a wide range of important and influential academic articles on contemporary terrorist political violence. The articles were initially published in English-language journals or have previously appeared in English. Each volume in the Library is devoted to a specific geographical region which has been afflicted by political terrorism during the past two decades.

Political terrorism has been a concern of national policy in numerous states and received the attention of international bodies including the United Nations. At the same time it has gripped public imagination, on occasion causing disruption in patterns of transnational tourism or influenced international investment decisions. Not surprisingly political terrorism has found a place in the academic programmes of universities and other educational establishments. In the present series no line of inquiry or ideological outlook is deliberately favoured or excluded - the aim of the Library is to constitute a useful and representative sampling of quality work on terrorism. As the contributions are drawn from previously published studies in periodicals this imposes perimeters on the sorts of material included. All volumes then have an incompleteness resulting from lacuna in the literature. Nevertheless, the series aims to bring into wider accessibility materials scattered through many periodicals, some having only limited circulations. Indeed, in no volume can all of the articles selected be located in a single repository including even the great national and famous university libraries of Great Britain and North America.

Each volume's articles have been chosen by a recognized authority on the political terrorism of the region. In no instance does the omission of a specific article or category of material imply a value judgement for the selection process has been governed by relevance to a theme, space and similar considerations. The general editors are grateful to the individuals who compiled each book and prepared the introductions. Their efforts and scholarly judgement are the cornerstone of the series. We wish to express our thanks to John Irwin of Dartmouth Publishing Company, from whom the idea of the Library originally sprang, and who brought the project through some dark hours to fruition. Also, we appreciate the kindly efforts of Sonia Hubbard.

YONAH ALEXANDER
The George Washington University
Washington DC

ALAN O'DAY
University of North London, England
and Concordia University, Montreal, Canada

Introduction

Terrorism as we generally conceive it – violence of relatively low magnitude employed by small underground groups against civilians for purposes of intimidation, typically practised to the exclusion of other methods – has not been a distinct characteristic of political violence in Africa. In that region terrorism has usually been an aspect of insurgencies, civil wars, communal conflict or government repression. It has not been an isolated phenomenon. Thus the essays chosen for inclusion in this volume both connect terrorism to the complex and varied incidents of political violence in Africa and also stress a broad range of causes and effects. The events discussed here deal mainly with the transition from colonialism and the post-independence period and with subSaharan Africa. Naturally a great deal of attention is devoted to the problems of South Africa.

Part I deals with the general issue of the potential for political violence in Africa. Ali Mazrui, writing in 1968 just as terrorism was becoming an international phenomenon, argues in Chapter 1 that in the independent African states, political violence, especially assassinations of leaders, reflects a crisis of national integration and legitimacy. The prevalence of assassinations in the early post-independence period was a result of an inadequate popular consensus supporting the government and a tendency to personalize authority. Secessionism was often the context for violence. By 1985, however, Mazrui's analysis of terrorism had changed; he now explicitly describes it as 'the manipulation of fear as a mechanism of combat' and as a strategy for maximizing anxiety rather than sympathy (Chapter 2, p. 26). He discusses the background to the 1976 hijacking that led to the Israeli intervention to rescue hostages held at Entebbe (Uganda) and notes the links between Africa and the Arab-Israeli conflict. 'Aerial terrorism', he finds, is especially well suited for issues that require international intervention; these events are fundamentally different from the forms of domestic terrorism, both state and insurgent, that accompanied the conflicts in Zimbabwe, Angola and Mozambique. He also concludes that kidnappings are more common in Francophone Africa than elsewhere on the continent.

Igbinovia (1986) also analyses aircraft hijackings as well as sabotage. He covers the period from 1931 to 1983 and includes North Africa and Egypt in a broadly descriptive and factual survey (Chapter 3). He notes that the extent of such incidents in Africa was small compared to the rest of the world, and that most hijackings and hijacking attempts targeted North Africa. The preferred landing sites for hijackers were Libya, Egypt and Algeria. He advocates improved security measures in Africa, as well as a solution to the underlying problems that have led to this 'modernization of barbarism' (p. 61).

In Chapter 4, Akinsanya examines at length the case of the Israeli intervention at Entebbe in 1976. After admitting the seriousness of the problem of hijackings and noting its recognition as a source of disorder by the international community, he considers the reasons for the Israeli intervention and its possible justification under international law. He finds that although Uganda was in violation of international law (including her own treaty obligations) and did not effectively exercise sovereignty over her own territory, still Israel's reliance on the doctrine of self-help in resorting to the use of force was not justified. The Israeli hostages were not in the degree of danger that Israel claimed, and the amount of force used was disproportionate.

Whereas Akinsanya approaches the problem of intervention against international terrorism from the perspective of international law, Maoz examines the Israeli action from the point of view of foreign policy decision making during crises. After first analysing alternative explanations for crisis decision making, he then reconstructs the Israeli decision-making process. He concludes that Israeli leaders perceived a high threat to the lives of the hostages, that the credibility of the Israeli counter-terrorism policy was at stake, and that the government's stability was at issue. The decision to intervene was reached only after a careful assessment of the credibility of the hijackers' threats, based on their previous as well as current behaviour. The Israeli decision makers did believe that the hostages were likely to be killed if the hijackers' ultimatum was not met or if negotiations failed.

Part II deals with the relationship between terrorism and insurgency or guerrilla warfare, opening with two general overviews. First, Otubanjo in Chapter 6 argues that Africa has been fertile ground for guerrilla warfare, a strategy that has proved very attractive to resistance movements since its inception in Kenya in 1952. The Mau Mau rebellion was an example of a successful war against a colonial power. Other types of conflicts included guerrilla wars against white-dominated minority regimes, as in Zimbabwe and Namibia, wars of national self-determination, including the Sudan and Eritrea, and wars against indigenous authority, such as in Chad, Zaire and Angola. The last two types of war were much less likely to be successful than the first two.

Shaw confirms in Chapter 7 that unconventional conflict is more typical of Africa than traditional warfare. He foresees increasing authoritarianism and militarism in African regimes, developments that will lead to more repression and more counter-violence. Shaw correctly predicts that the routes to end the conflicts in Namibia and South Africa will be through compromise rather than escalated warfare. But otherwise his view of Africa's future is pessimistic. Indigenous conflict will grow, especially as outside powers begin to lose interest in the region. Violence will target the African ruling classes. Secessionism will increase.

The remainder of the selections in Part II provide case studies. J. Bowyer Bell begins by offering an early (1974) analysis of the conflict in Eritrea, a case that involved the use of external terrorism by domestic secessionists. Bell notes the endemic quality of insurgencies and the stubborn persistence of the Eritrean Liberation Front (ELF), which was established in 1961. (In 1991, the Eritrean People's Liberation Front, which was formed in 1970, defeated the Ethiopian army.) The ELF was an early user of terrorism ('spectacular external operations') against Ethiopian targets abroad, including civil aviation. It is worth noting that the war also involved a conflict between 'African' and 'Arab' interests, which was one cause of the ELF's separatist drive.

In Chapter 9, Throup provides a detailed history of the Mau Mau rebellion, which he blames on the deficiencies of the British administration. Africans and settlers in Kenya had been on a collision course since the 1930s. Despite the fact that the British government labelled the Mau Mau as 'terrorists', most Mau Mau violence targeted African 'collaborators' rather than settlers – a pattern that is typical of anti-colonial conflicts. Throup argues that Mau Mau was never a truly nationalist movement and that resistance to the British was weakened by internal power struggles.

Presley follows by calling attention to an often-neglected dimension of both terrorism and insurgency: the role of women. Although over 34,000 women were imprisoned during the Mau Mau rebellion, their contribution to the struggle has been ignored. The government regarded them as more fanatical and more violent than the men engaged in Mau Mau, but dismissed their motivations for participation as non-political. (These attitudes remain typical of some contemporary analysts of terrorism as well.) Presley concludes that the British military victory in the struggle against Mau Mau was dependent on its success against the women involved in the war.

Writing on Zimbabwe in Chapter 11, Jakonya stresses the damaging effects of violence on peasant life. The Rhodesian regime, which labelled the African resistance 'Terrs' for terrorists, conducted a counter-insurgency campaign that was excessively brutal towards civilians. The 'guerrillas' in turn attempted to disrupt the civil administration, using assassination as an important weapon. As a consequence of these practices, the war resulted in the extensive displacement of rural populations.

All the selections in Part III address the vast problem of South Africa. The first two chapters contend that the responsibility for terrorism lies with the African National Congress (ANC) and its military wing, Spear of the Nation. Clifford-Vaughan (1987) considers terrorism a vital part of the ANC's campaign of revolutionary war. He argues that in the mid-1980s the ANC shifted to attacking both urban and rural 'soft targets' by means of car bombs, limpet mines in shopping centres and other random violence against civilians. He is extremely supportive of the government's response to the ANC, which he considers generally successful. He condemns as misguided the international image of the ANC as 'freedom fighters'. In his view, the ANC's continued terrorism was likely to lead to disaster and chaos.

Francis (1986) held similar views, considering the ANC as primarily a terrorist organization to be defeated at almost any cost. He repeatedly emphasizes the links between the ANC and the Communist bloc, the ANC in his opinion being no more than a Soviet satellite. He also interprets the ANC's resort to terrorism in the 1980s as a sign of weakness rather than strength.

Goot asks quite a different question in Chapter 14. In 1988 the American Democratic Party labelled South Africa a 'terrorist state'. Would it have been useful to add South Africa to the list of 'state supporters' of terrorism under the terms of the Export Administration Act? Although she feels that apartheid had to be opposed and that the ANC resorted to violence only after peaceful means of resistance to apartheid were exhausted, she thinks that labelling South Africa a terrorist state was not the best way to apply pressure to end apartheid. State repression does not fit the definition of international terrorism as used by the US Department of State. In addition, South Africa's military incursions into neighbouring states posed a tricky problem since the US had undertaken similar interventions. To condemn South Africa for the same behaviour would be hypocritical. Finally, the sanctions already imposed against South Africa were much more stringent than any of the normal penalties associated with being listed as a 'supporter of terrorism'.

In his brief remarks in Chapter 15, Howe takes an opposite approach to that of Clifford-Vaughan and Francis. In his view, the South African government itself was responsible for a regime of terror. He adds that the government has exacerbated differences among black groups, especially by tolerating violence from the Zulu movement, Inkatha.

Rich tends to use the term 'terrorism' in quotation marks in Chapter 16, perhaps because he feels the distinction between terrorism and guerrilla warfare has become blurred. He sees the ANC's ideology as an amalgam rather than the monolithic Leninism that Francis fears.

The purpose of ANC violence, he believes, is to disrupt the economy, demoralize white elites and the regime, and raise black consciousness. The state's response, which became increasingly militarized with the shift to a 'total national strategy' after South Africa's neighbours became independent and capable of providing sanctuary for the ANC, was, however, fully capable of containing the threat. The greater danger was the development of a legal regime of terror from above.

In looking at the future prospects of terrorism in Chapter 17, Campbell (like Rich) tries to distinguish terrorism from guerrilla warfare. He argues that guerrilla warfare is directed against a military occupation that is both recent and foreign, whereas terrorism is intended to overturn long-term indigenous structures. Thus the targets of guerrilla warfare are military; those of terrorism civilian. As a result, he thinks it fair to say that the ANC, as well as SWAPO (the South-West Africa People's Organization in Namibia, which achieved independence in 1990) and FRELIMO (the Mozambican Liberation Front, victorious against the Portuguese in 1975), are terrorists. Like Clifford-Vaughan, Campbell is an apologist for the South African government, which he feels to have been unjustly maligned and in need of more vocal public support at home. He defends South Africa's cross-border raids against 'terrorist' sanctuaries in the frontline states. Israel, after all, follows such a policy. He concludes, with other authors included here, that the South African state is in no danger of succumbing to an ANC takeover. Rather, at the time he found the ANC's prospects 'bleak'.

Herbst looks at the prospects for revolution (rather than terrorism) in Chapter 18 and concurs that they too are bleak. The fate of Iran had made people think of regimes as inherently fragile in the face of rebellion, but the South African state was too strong and its repressive policies too efficient to crumble before ANC pressure. Furthermore, the ANC's key problem, never resolved, was how to organize the masses. For example, the popular uprisings of the 1980s caught the ANC by surprise. In the long run, Herbst argues, a military solution could not be the answer, as proved by events of the early 1990s.

A serious problem in contemporary South Africa is black-on-black violence, which reached alarming proportions after the movement towards compromise between the ANC and the South African government. Mukonoweshuro, writing in 1991 after the ANC was granted legal status and Nelson Mandela released from prison, examines South Africa's homelands policy (Chapter 19). He predicts that the collapse of authority in the homelands as well as impoverished conditions will encourage future political violence.

Gwala next provides a detailed case study of township violence in Natal, focusing on the disruptive role of Inkatha in the context of extreme social and economic deprivation. Before 1985, Natal province was not generally affected by political violence, but the growing activism of the labour movement and Inkatha's attempt to swell its ranks through forcible recruitment led to the establishment of a 'regime of terror' by Inkatha vigilantes. The community then mobilized against Inkatha, which in turn led to a cycle of violence, pitting Inkatha against supporters of the United Democratic Front. Gwala also suggests that the South African government supported Inkatha in its bid for political power.

Hughes provides additional analysis of political violence in Natal in Chapter 21, in this instance discussing African violence against the Indian population of an area of Durban. She explains that 'the state widened every faultline' (p. 449) in a society that was already divided not only along Indian-African lines but between Pondo and Zulu groups. Violence was precipitated by the assassination of the black activist Victoria Mxenge, which led to a school boycott that put large numbers of youths on the street. Events quickly spun out of control. However, no Indians were hurt or killed although they suffered serious property damage.

The next cluster of articles is concerned with the legal dimensions of violence in South Africa. Kentridge, a South African lawyer, argued in 1980 that South Africa's response to violence, chiefly the 1967 Terrorism Act, represented a distortion of the traditional legal system. Terrorism became a new form of treason, defined broadly as any act that intends to endanger law and order. The act permitted indefinite detention without trial. Prisoners were held incommunicado without the right to see a solicitor. The procedures that had formerly guaranteed the right to a fair trial were abandoned. These regulations may have contributed to defeating the ANC, Kentridge argues, but their effect was to undermine even the idea of an independent judiciary and due process. He concludes that the judiciary was a poor bulwark against the government: the law in South Africa became an instrument of political power.

In Chapter 23, Murray analyses a specific trial – that of four members of the ANC's Spear of the Nation wing in 1985. They refused to accept the jurisdiction of the court and demanded prisoner-of-war status. She argues that South African court procedures should have used the Geneva Conventions, and specifically the 1977 Protocols, as a guide to sentencing. The fact that Spear of the Nation considered itself a legitimate national liberation movement should have been a mitigating factor.

Dugard, a professor of law at the University of Witwatersrand who testified in some of the trials Murray refers to, also analyses the role of international law and the UN in trying to end apartheid. Writing in 1991 after the regime had begun to move to dismantle apartheid and to reach a compromise with the ANC, he concludes that international pressure was effective, especially the imposition of sanctions (Chapter 24).

The last two essays in this collection are concerned with South Africa's military interventions in neighbouring states. Friedland (1982) describes South Africa's use of resistance organizations in Mozambique, Angola and Zimbabwe to destabilize their respective governments. These groups were properly defined as 'terrorist organizations' dependent on South African support. The purpose of South Africa's surrogate warfare was to prevent the frontline states from aiding the ANC or SWAPO.

Metz (1986) focuses on the case of the Mozambique National Resistance (MNR), which was originally a creation of the government of Rhodesia, picked up by South Africa after 1980. The MNR's tactics consisted of 'random violence, sabotage, and intimidation' (p. 518), including killing foreign technicians. South Africa's involvement in Mozambique was part of the 'total national strategy' that reflected the view that domestic terrorism within South Africa was part of a Communist plot, not the expression of local discontent or reaction to the injustices of the apartheid system.

Part I
Assassinations, Hijackings and International Terrorism

General

[1]

Thoughts on Assassination in Africa*

ALI A. MAZRUI
Makerere University College
University of East Africa

Perhaps no international treaty betrays a greater sensitivity to the risk of assassination than does the Charter of the Organization of African Unity. The Charter consecrates its disapproval of this phenomenon in Article III, in which it expresses its "unreserved condemnation, in all its forms, of political assassination, as well as of subversive activities on the part of neighboring States or any other State."[1]

Independence is a beginning. So is the month of January every year, sometimes spilling over into February. For some reason a disproportionate number of the historic acts of violence in Africa since independence have tended to happen in the months of January and February. It was in January 1961 that Patrice Lumumba was handed over to Moise Tshombe, his enemy in Katanga. That was the prelude to one of the most significant assassinations in Africa's history. The following month the death of Lumumba was announced.

In January 1963 President Sylvanus Olympio of Togo was as-

*This paper was written for the panel on "Consensus and Dissent, with Special Reference to the Developing Countries" at the Seventh World Congress of the International Political Science Association in Brussels in September 1967.

[1] The Charter is available in Boutros Boutros-Ghali, "The Addis Ababa Charter," *International Conciliation*, No. 546 (Jan. 1964), Appendix, 53-62.

sassinated. And it was with Olympio's fate in the background that the Charter of the Organization of African Unity was signed a few months later.

In January 1964 the Zanzibar revolution exploded in East Africa, with vital consequences for the region as a whole. Among the immediate effects were the army mutinies of Tanganyika, Uganda, and Kenya which happened later the same month.

In January 1965 the prime minister of Burundi was assassinated. The heads of neighboring Kenya, Uganda, and Tanzania discussed the event and jointly expressed their sense of shock.[2]

Within the same period Kenya had its first assassination since independence—the killing of Mr. Pinto, a prominent member of Parliament.

In January 1966 came the Nigerian coup, which cost the lives of Federal Prime Minister Balewa and the premiers of the northern and western regions. The following month Nkrumah fell. His regime was overthrown while he was on his way to Peking. From the point of view of the theme of assassination the Ghanaian coup had a different kind of significance; it seems to have been a studied policy of the soldiers to avoid the risk of assassinating Nkrumah. That seems to have been one reason why the coup was timed to take place after his departure for Peking.

Is there any special reason why the opening months of January and February from year to year should have had such a disproportionate share of Africa's great acts of turbulence? Other months have had their events, too. But the deaths of Lumumba, Olympio, Balewa, and the Sardauna of Sokoto; the regionally transformative Zanzibar revolution; the East African mutinies; and the fall of Nkrumah are almost in a class by themselves as events which shook Africa. Yet, while sharing January and February for their anniversaries, the events provide little evidence for a Montesquieu-like hypothesis about the effect of climatic changes on major political events. Our collection of events is too

---

[2] This was the second prime minister of Burundi to be assassinated. The first was Prince Rwagasore, who was shot dead with a hunting-gun as he sat in a restaurant in Usumbura, less than a month after his Lumumbist Uprona party had swept the polls in September 1961. That, however, was before Burundi's independence. For an account of the trial and retrial of those accused of complicity, see, for example, Clyde Sanger's article in *The Guardian* (Manchester), Jan. 12, 1963.

widely distributed to be correlated with weather conditions in January and February. The most that one can hope for is a symbolic correlation—a new year; a new nation; a new manifestation of instability.

What is of greater interest than the month in which it occurs is, of course, the phenomenon of assassination itself. Everything considered, there might easily have been many more assassinations in Africa than we have had so far. The potentialities of this and other forms of political violence have been there from the start. What this paper hopes to analyze are, in part, precisely those potentialities. But it will be a postulate of mine that the risk of assassination was not only objectively there, but was keenly felt to be there by many of the leading participants in African politics. African leadership soon developed a conscious or subconscious fear of the assassin. This fear exerted an important influence not only on their personal behavior from day to day, but also on their policies and ideologies.

In our analysis we shall first place the issue of assassination within the context of the problem of legitimacy in a newly invented state. We shall then link this up with different levels of consensus, and examine these in relation to personal leadership as a functional alternative to weak legitimacy. Where authority is too personified, challenge to authority also tends to take the form of personal violence. The possibilities of assassination are maximized. Ideology, however, tries to mitigate these possibilities. And in any case there are assassinations which, in their impact, produce the kind of retrospective hero-worship which is itself a contribution to national identity. We shall conclude with an examination of the influence of assassination on certain aspects of Pan-African behavior and diplomatic thought.

But, first, a definitional problem has to be tackled.

What is "Assassination"?

An alternative rendering to the term "assassination" is sometimes supposed to be "political murder." But this rendering only shifts the definitional problem. When is a murder "political"? If the answer is "When it is committed for political reasons," then not every political murder is an assassination. In the course of the Zanzibar revolution thousands of people were killed, and many

of these were killed for reasons which, in their racial implications,
could only be described as "political." Yet the killing was at the
grass-roots level—a petty Arab shopkeeper killed by his African
neighbor; a petty landlord killed by a tenant. One of the curious
things about the Zanzibar revolution—in contrast to, say, the
Cuban, with which it has often been compared—was the relative
toleration shown toward leading members of the previous regime
under the Sultan. The Zanzibar revolutionaries showed little immediate desire to "make a public example" of their predecessors
in power. Not only were there no executions, but a special effort
was apparently made by the revolutionaries to spare Sheikh Ali
Muhsin, the leader of the overthrown Nationalist party, any public indignity. Even John Okello, the temperamental Ugandan who
appeared to have spearheaded the coup, made threats on Zanzibar
radio against anyone who had "violent designs" against Ali Muhsin. A long detention awaited him and his kind, but there was a
marked reluctance to sentence them to a physical penalty.

Yet this tolerance of the revolutionary leaders toward their predecessors was in marked contrast with the outbreak of racial ven-
detta at the grass-roots level—neighbor against neighbor, farmer
against farmer. Many of these were politically-inspired killings.
But were they "assassinations"? It is possible to argue that the
Zanzibar revolution unleashed a large number of "political murders"—but not a single "assassination." For the term "assassination" does not merely mean "killing for political reasons." In
fact, the reasons can be quite irrelevant. For example, in November
1963 headlines in different parts of the world proclaimed "Kennedy
Assassinated"—before we knew who had killed him, let alone for
what reasons. Perhaps we still do not know for what reasons. Yet
the death of John F. Kennedy remains a case of assassination.

What seems more plausible is that the term "assassination" derives its meaning less from the motives of the killing than from
the political importance of the victim. The victim need not be a
professional politician, nor hold a formal office of state. Neither
Mahatma Gandhi in 1947 nor Malcolm X in 1964 was a politician or state official in this professional sense. Yet we think of
their deaths as instances of "assassination."

Victor T. LeVine prefers to base the definition of "assassination" on the role of the killer rather than the status of the victim.

LeVine would also add the element of surprise to his definition. As he himself put it, "the difference between assassination and political murder is admittedly a tenuous one; I would contend that it lies in two areas, the role of the killer, and the element of surprise. Assassins are usually hired or delegated, and they generally strike without warning to the victims."[3]

That assassins usually carry out their purpose "without warning their victims" can surely be taken for granted. Assassins do not normally warn the police, either. As for the claim that "assassins are usually hired or delegated," surely this—even if it were statistically true—could have no bearing on the definition of assassination. A king can be assassinated by his own prospective successor.

As for the element of surprise, again this is at best an accompanying characteristic of assassination rather than a defining one. What if the killer is "theatrical" enough to telephone his victim anonymously and tell him that he has only until Thursday the following week to live? And what if on that Thursday the man is indeed killed? Was the theatrical forewarning enough to deprive the killing of the status of an assassination?

What about Lumumba when he was handed over to his enemies in Katanga? The news of his death was announced a month later. Many people were "shocked" without really being "surprised." The phenomenon of "surprise" implies a high degree of unexpectedness. And yet Lumumba already bore the marks of a violent beating even before he was handed over to his worst enemies. He was being publicly manhandled as he was being transported to Katanga, and the press informed the world with photographs of an abused Lumumba being dragged about by soldiers. There followed the weeks of mystery and speculation. Was Lumumba still alive? When the answer came in February 1961 many people, especially in the Third World, were indeed shocked that the worst had come to the worst. Any yet somehow it was the shock of anger, and perhaps of political anguish, rather than the shock of surprise.

From this it can be concluded that neither the speed of killing

[3] See Victor T. LeVine, "The Course of Political Violence," in William H. Lewis (ed.), *French-Speaking Africa, The Search for Identity* (New York, 1965), 59-60; 68; 241, n. 15.

nor the role of the killer is crucial in defining assassination. What is crucial is the status of the victim. The core or minimal definition is that an assassination is the killing of someone politically important by an agent other than himself or the government—for reasons which are either political or unknown.

Legitimacy Versus Integration

Perhaps the most fundamental problems confronting African countries are reducible to two crises—the crisis of national integration and the crisis of political legitimacy. For our purposes, the crisis of integration may be seen as a problem of horizontal relationships. It arises because different clusters of citizens do not as yet accept each other as compatriots. The sense of a shared nationality has yet to be forged.

The crisis of legitimacy, on the other hand, is a problem of vertical relationships. It arises not because one citizen does not recognize another as a compatriot, but because significant numbers of citizens are not convinced that their government has a right to rule them. Integration is a problem of neighbor against neighbor, legitimacy a problem of the ruled against their rulers.

Assassinations arise both in situations of inadequate national integration and in situations of weak legitimacy or accepted authority. But it would be a mistake to assume that the crisis of integration and the crisis of legitimacy need necessarily go together. It is possible for a country to have attained a high degree of integration or sense of nationhood while its capacity for accepting shared authority remains underdeveloped. The reverse phenomenon is also quite possible, and has perhaps even more examples in history.

Assassinations are often symptomatic of both crises. But here again it is not necessary that both crises be present. Recurrent assassinations have been known to happen in countries with a highly developed sense of shared nationality. Japan provides one dramatic example. Robert E. Ward has argued that Japan's history as a whole is a strange mixture of docility and violence:

Violence and the use of armed force to accomplish political ends have a long and honourable tradition, which is by no means limited to pre-Restoration times. The phrase "government by assassination" gained broad currency in Japan as late as the 1930's and with considerable justification.[4]

Ward points out that the fourteen-year period of 1932-45 marked a reversion to this form of political behavior. The period began with the assassination of Prime Minister Inukai Tsuyoshi on May 15, 1932: "This was merely the most conspicuous of a number of such incidents that represented protests against widespread economic—especially agrarian—distress . . . and a foreign policy held to be insufficiently nationalistic and aggressive."[5]

Here were a people with a marked degree of national consciousness. Indeed, many of the killings were widely regarded as *"patriotic* assassinations," carried out for the sake of national honor. And yet the widespread approbation of many such acts in the country was an indication that the successful creation of national identity in Japan had not been accompanied by a successful tradition of governmental legitimacy. It is true that the emperor himself had more than political acceptance. He commanded mystical reverence as well. But in the final analysis the emperor was perhaps more a symbol of nationhood than of secure governmental authority.

In Africa the crises of both integration and legitimacy are still acute. And political violence is often symptomatic of both. Assassination itself as a political solution was rare during the colonial period. One can almost say that—in the light of our definition of it as "the killing of someone politically important, by an agent other than himself or the government, for reasons which are either political or unknown"—assassination comes near to being a post-independence phenomenon in Africa. Rival political groups in colonial Africa might have killed each other before. But the kind of political importance which a victim had to have if the killing was to be defined as an "assassination" was, to some extent, camouflaged by the colonial situation. Thus, if Patrice Lumumba had been killed mysteriously before the Congo became independent and afforded him a chance to be prime minister, the killing would have appeared less obviously as an assassination than it did when it took place some months after the country's independence.

[4] "Japan," in Robert E. Ward and Roy C. Macridis (eds.), *Modern Political Systems: Asia* (Englewood Cliffs, N.J., 1963) 60.

[5] *Ibid.*, 30.

But reasons of definition are not the only ones which make the killing of politically important African figures a post-independence phenomenon in the main. More weighty reasons are tied up with problems of the crises we have mentioned.

British colonial governors were hardly ever killed in office whereas within a few years of independence African heads of governments found themselves victims or near-victims of assassins. Why the difference? One possible answer is that the British colonial governor was well guarded. Another answer is that he mixed less with the general populace, and therefore exposed himself less to possible assassination. Both these statements might be true, and yet as *reasons* they might be of only marginal relevance.

We might get nearer the real reasons if, first, we reflected on this hypothesis: That there had been few attempts on the lives of colonial governors in Africa for the same reason for which there had been few mutinies by African soldiers under the colonial regime—the range of possible retaliatory signals was wider in the British power-spectrum than in that of the new regimes.

And yet the range of possible changes in the situation which could result from an assassination was seemingly narrower in a colonial situation than in a post-independence one. An assassin asks himself in a colonial situation what will happen if he kills the British governor. On the one hand, British power seemed great enough to be able to inflict a whole range of possible acts of revenge on the assassin alone, or on the assassin and others as collective punishment.

On the other hand, British power also seemed great enough to prevent any fundamental change in the political situation being brought about by the mere assassination of a governor. A replacement could be sent, and the colony would remain a colony under basically the same policy. British capacity for varied forms of revenge could put off an assassin through fear of credible consequences. British capacity for maintaining the political *status quo* despite the loss of a governor could put off an assassin through fear of futility.

But in a post-independence situation, getting rid of a prime minister could cause a more significant change in a country's orientation—just as an army mutiny after independence can effect an important change, unless it is thwarted by appeal to the former colonial power.

And even when thwarted it could—on issues like the Africanization of the officer corps in the army—prove to be a victory of the vanquished. The fluidity of the basis of legitimacy in a post-independence situation maximizes the temptation to revolt— and both military insubordination and attempted assassinations become a more common phenomenon than in pre-colonial days.

That is one reason why African independence and increased African violence are often companions—at least for a time.

Consensus, Primary and Secondary

Linking this up with more traditional categories of political analysis, we may say that the problem of legitimacy is the old problem of "political obligation" in political philosophy. It is the problem of why and when one obeys or ought to obey the government. Where legitimacy is fully secure, the citizens do not question the government's right to govern, though they may question the wisdom of this or that governmental action. When it is not secure, challenges to authority may allow little differentiation between dissent, insubordination, rebellion, and outright treason.

In traditional political theory, the problem of political obligation involves a shifting balance between the area of consent in government and the area of compulsion. And the area of consent itself has different levels. To take Uganda as an example, one might note that there is a difference between consenting to being ruled by President Obote's government and consenting to this or that *policy* of his government. It is possible for an opponent of Dr. Obote's regime to be in favor of this or that policy pursued by the regime. Thus there were many Ugandans outside Obote's party who supported his toughness against the kingdom of Buganda although they would not vote for Obote in a general election. In this case they accept the policy though, given a choice, they would not accept the government.

But even the idea of accepting Obote's government, or consenting to be ruled by it, has two levels. The more obvious level is in the sense of having voted for Dr. Obote's party at the last election. Yet there is a sense, of course, in which even the Democratic party, although in *opposition*, consented to be ruled by

Obote's Uganda People's Congress. The very idea of a loyal opposition implies consenting to be ruled by the constitutional government in power, although reserving the right to disagree with
almost everyone of its policies.

The problem in Africa in the first few years of independence
was of trying to ensure that every Opposition remained a loyal
opposition. It was a quest for a situation in which one could challenge decisions of the government and not the government's right
to execute them.

In the final analysis, this was the ultimate problem of *consensus*—not a consensus on policies (that is, secondary consensus),
but a consensus on legitimate methods of policy-making and legitimate methods of implementation (primary consensus). Thus
even those who did not vote for the majority party in Uganda
but took advantage of the elective principle concede the right of
governance to their rival party.

In this primary sense, consensus is that which makes it possible
to have *compulsion by consent*. It is what makes citizens accept
a certain degree of force from the government, or even complain
about that force, without feeling that the government lacks the
right to govern them at all.

But the degree of compulsion needed is sometimes in inverse
proportion to the degree of secondary consensus already achieved.
This secondary consensus, or agreement behind certain policies,
is sometimes known as "national unity" at a particular moment
in time. There are occasions when we have to think of compulsion
as that which we have to put into a governmental system in order
to make up for deficiencies in unity. The Congo is less united than
Uganda; therefore the Congo needs more coercion or compulsion
in its system than does Uganda. Mainland Tanzania is more united
than Uganda. Therefore mainland Tanzania or Tanganyika needs
less coercion for minimal system-maintenance than does Uganda.
Coercion and consensus are sometimes functional alternatives for
system-maintenance.

But secondary consensus is not necessarily agreement behind
policies; it can sometimes be agreement behind a leader, almost
regardless of the policies he pursues.

African countries, faced with inadequate primary consensus,
have sometimes invoked diverse devices in order to consolidate

at least secondary consensus behind the leader. There is a tragic paradox involved in the process. On the one hand, the absence of primary consensus creates the danger of assassination because of the very inadequacy of legitimacy. On the other hand, the attempt to create secondary consensus leads to the personification of government. "Nkrumah is the CPP; the CPP is Ghana; Nkrumah is therefore Ghana." This is the syllogism which, in its conclusion, legitimates African equivalents of Louis XIV. But the doctrine of "I am the State," by personifying government, can be an invitation to regicide in conditions of primary dissensus. To challenge the leader is to challenge the state. The transformation of the state therefore "requires" the elimination of its present embodiment.

African attempts to promote "leader-worship" are, therefore, caught up in this contradiction. The whole idea of promoting it is partly inspired by a desire to mitigate the potential for regicide inherent in primary dissensus. And so leader-worship sometimes verges on being almost literal. Nkrumah was the clearest example in recent African history, though by no means atypical. He permitted himself to be portrayed as a messiah. But he needed to be a political Christ without a political crucifixion. Indeed, the reason for portraying him as a messiah was to avert the danger of crucifixion. But the sacralization of authority has entailed a personification of authority as well. And it is this which leads to the personification of opposition as well.[6]

Death and Hero-Worship

Then there are occasions when it is, in fact, the "crucifixion" which achieves the leader-worship so vainly sought by propaganda. The clearest example is probably the place of Lumumba in the Congo. Before his death Lumumba was perhaps more a hero of Pan-Africanists outside the Congo than of the Congolese themselves. It is true that he was "the nearest thing" to a national leader that the Congo had; but that was not all that "near." Lumumba stood for Congolese unity, but he was not himself popular enough or strong enough to ensure that unity without exter-

[6] See Ali Mazrui, "The Monarchical Tendency in African Political Culture," *British Journal of Sociology*, XVIII (1967), 231-50. See, also, David E. Apter, "Political Religion in the New Nations," in Clifford Geertz (ed.), *Old Societies and New States* (New York, 1963), 82-84.

nal help. Perhaps the forces against unity were in any case greater than any single leader could cope with. Lumumba might well have been a casualty of circumstances. Yet one thing was clear: while he lived he was essentially a factional hero rather than a national one.

But after his death the myth of Lumumba was rapidly nationalized. His death was announced in February 1961. By the summer of the same year a coalition government was formed under the premiership of Cyrille Adoula, with Kasavubu still president. When the new Prime Minister Adoula ventured into Stanleyville, he made a point of placing flowers at a temporary monument of Lumumba and he exclaimed: "We have achieved what Lumumba wanted: one Congo, one Congo, one Congo."

Commenting on this situation, Henry Tanner said:

> The gesture . . . showed that Lumumba's place in Congolese politics has undergone a subtle but far-reaching change. Before the formation of the coalition government, the Lumumba legend had been the exclusive tool of one political faction. Now it is being invoked, with different shades of meaning and enthusiasm, by both parties in the coalition . . . even a politician who owes his power to Kasavubu, Lumumba's earliest rival, may find it wise to worship at the shrine.[7]

In July 1964, to the astonishment of the world, Moise Tshombe, the former secessionist of Katanga, was invited by President Kasavubu to succeed Adoula as prime minister of the Congo. Tshombe was widely regarded as the man behind the murder of Lumumba. Yet he had now come back from his exile in Europe to take over the reins of national power. On July 19, 1964, he addressed an enthusiastic crowd of 25,000 at the Baudoin Stadium in Leopoldville and proclaimed: "Give me three months and I will give you a new Congo."

On July 26 he was in Stanleyville, the Lumumbist stronghold. He repeated his theme of "give me three months" to a major rally. And as one more step toward that goal of a "new Congo," Moise Tshombe laid a wreath at the monument of Patrice Lumumba.[8]

Yet instability continued in the Congo. Tshombe scored a victory over the rebels, but the entire political regime ended with

[7] Henry Tanner, "Over the Congo, Lumumba's Ghost," New York *Times Magazine*, Oct. 29, 1961.

[8] *Africa Report*, IX (1964), 20.

General Mobutu's coup in December 1965. On the first Independence Day anniversary following the coup a great crowd assem-
bled in the capital to celebrate the occasion. The day was June
30, 1966, and President Mobutu was delivering a speech. Suddenly
he made an unexpected statement:

> Glory and honour to an illustrious citizen of the Congo, to a great
> African, and to the first martyr of our independence. Patrice Emery
> Lumumba, who was the victim of the colonialist plot. In the name of
> the Government, we proclaim his name on this national heroes' day. . . .

Mobutu also declared a new policy toward the Belgian mining
interests in the Congo, implying a greater assertion of Congolese
control over the country's economy. Opposition to the autonomy
of mining interests in the Congo was certainly in the tradition of
Lumumbist thought in the Congo.[9]

Not long after, George Penchenier devoted one of four articles
on the Congo in *Le Monde* to Mobutu's move in proclaiming
Lumumba a hero. Penchenier pointed out that it was not merely
in the rebel-held areas that Lumumba was regarded in such terms.
"The three short months in which he held power were enough to
make him a legend, and the circumstances of his death made him
a martyr." Penchenier went on:

> Six years have passed. . . . The old street named Leopold III will be
> known in future as Patrice Emery Lumumba and a monument will
> be erected to his memory. The Congolese welcome these acts without
> stopping to think about the strange fate of a man who was followed,
> then betrayed, and now rehabilitated. General Mobutu has taken a
> political step. After having defeated the Lumumbist rebellion, he is
> trying to create a united Congo. Who better to help him than Patrice
> Lumumba?[10]

It looks as if the *memory* of Lumumba may contribute more to
the "oneness" of the Congolese than anything Lumumba himself
actually did while he was still alive. It all depends upon whether
shared heroes constitute one of the factors which help to create
national consciousness.

[9] *Africa Digest*, XIV (1966), 22-23.
[10] *Le Monde*, Sept. 1, 5, 1966. The English rendering of the quotation is from
Africa Digest, XIV (1966), 22-23.

But why should Lumumba be a hero for reasons other than what he actually accomplished for his country while he lived? This takes us back to the place of violence in political mythology at large. Criteria for heroism in relation to violence can take one of three main forms. First, a person can be a hero because of some accomplishment in a violent activity like war. These are, of course, the war heroes. Secondly, a person can be a hero because of his capacity for non-violence in the face of provocation. Mahatma Gandhi and Jesus Christ fall within this second category. And, thirdly, a person can be a hero simply by being a victim of someone else's violence in a particular set of circumstances. It is within this third category that Patrice Lumumba falls.

Young nations often feel a need to have an antiquity. The desire to be old becomes part of the quest for identity. And dead heroes even of the immediate past are history personified. In that lies their relevance for the development of national consciousness. Hero-worship when the heroes are alive is at best a case of secondary consensus; hero-worship when the heroes are dead might well be a contribution to primary consensus.

But the secret both of national pride and national cohesion is to know what to forget. The desire to be old and wrinkled as a nation must be accomplished by a determination to have a failing memory. In Kenya, for example, this phenomenon is tested against what happened during the Mau Mau insurrection. On the one hand, there is a desire that yesterday's villains—the Mau Mau fighters—should become today's heroes. On the other hand, there is a determination that yesterday's heroes—the "loyalists" who fought against the Mau Mau—should not become today's villains. A similar selectivity will be demanded of the memory of the Congolese. In the case of the legend of Lumumba, it is a selectivity which has already taken place.

As we have argued before, the very idea of a nation can sometimes be a little too abstract, and hence a little too cold, to command ready human allegiance. To give the idea of a nation warmth, it is often necessary either to personify it metaphorically, or, more effectively, to give it specific human form in national heroes. This is why ancestor-worship is important not only among tribes but also within nations. And this is indeed why the assassination of Patrice Lumumba remains one of the most important single contributions to the development of primary consensus in the Congo.

Pan-Africanism and the Assassin

The distinction between national consensus and regional consensus in Africa is not always easy to draw. The same factors which make nationalism and Pan-Africanism in the continent so intimately connected have also produced an overlap between problems of domestic territorial identity and problems of continental racial identity. The very fact that Lumumba was a Pan-African hero before he became a Congolese national hero emphasizes this overlap.

Problems of separatism in Africa often get into a paradoxical relationship with problems of Pan-regionalism. The old issue of Katanga's secession, the continuing difficulty of secessionist Somalis in Kenya and Ethiopia, and even the isolation of Biafra, have in their different ways exemplified the tense connection between the politics of African separatism and problems of Pan-Africanism at large.

In what way is seccessionism on the one hand and pan-regionalism on the other related to the phenomenon of assassination in Africa? A step toward an answer can be taken by asking yet another question: What sort of issues in such areas of political experience arouse the kind of passions which produce assassins?

One major category is of issues which imply a great sense of finality once a decision is taken. And these are issues which command such a degree of emotional involvement among those affected that the apparent finality of the decision, once it is taken, seems almost unbearable to the loser. This category of issues can produce assassins even though the immediate reason for killing a public figure might be a mere side-effect of the central factor which set the passions free.

Pre-eminent among the breeding grounds of assassins is a situation involving territorial partition—prospective, accomplished, or thwarted partition. Partition can take different forms. The term is normally used to apply to a case like that of Ireland or India where a foreign power was involved in the partitioning. But in-

ternally-generated secessionism is also a quest for partitioning a
country.

Mahatma Gandhi lost his life in a situation involving separatist passions. Abraham Lincoln lost his life after frustrating a bid
to partition the United States. More recently the issue of the separation of Algeria from France let loose emotions which resulted
in a number of political murders, including several attempts on
the life of de Gaulle.

The situation in the Algerian case was indeed complex. But to
people like Jacques Soustelle, Algerian independence was at the
time synonymous with the partition of France. The assassinative
emotions generated were in part derived from the dread of partition, while the FLN was regarded as a secessionist movement.

When one considers this relationship between separatism and
assassination, the prospect in Africa can be very disquieting. It
was, after all, in Africa that Europe practiced the art of partition
at its most elaborate. Where Europe attempted to unify those who
were distinct, it left the seeds of future separatism—and Patrice
Lumumba was assassinated in a secessionist province. Where
Europe divided, it sometimes left behind latent passions for reunification—and political killings at the grass-roots level have resulted from such division. In short, balkanization is a breeding
ground of political violence, including the phenomenon of assassination. And balkanization is what Africa is burdened with for
the time being.

Pan-Africanism is often an attempt to grapple with the consequences of balkanization. One early assassination which had Pan-
African significance, as well as being somewhat connected with
Africa's fragmentation, was the assassination of Sylvanus Olympio, first president of independent Togo. In this regard, we might
begin by noting that, from the point of view of Pan-Africanism,
there are three types of assassinations. There is the kind of assassination which might harm the cause of Pan-Africanism; secondly, the kind which might conceivably help the cause of Pan-
Africanism; and thirdly, of course, the kind which has had little
relevance for Pan-Africanism.

The assassination of Sylvanus Olympio remains perhaps the
most dramatic case of a continentally divisive assassination which
Africa has had so far. Olympio happened to be a pre-eminently

"bicultural" or "tricultural" African leader in his upbringing. He was at home both among French- and English-speaking colleagues. And his country, Togo, under his leadership, was expected to be an important inter-lingual link between the two sectors of Westernized Africa.

However, a border dispute between Togo and Ghana marred this picture of potential amity. Nkrumah had become a champion of the reunification of the Ewe on the two sides of the border, hoping thereby to enlarge the boundaries of Ghana. Because of this border dispute and of personality factors in the relations between Olympio and Nkrumah, Ghana became a little too hospitable in the refuge it gave to discontented Togolese "at war" with the regime of their own country.[11]

When, therefore, Olympio was assassinated in January 1963, there was immediate suspicion in some circles that Ghana under Nkrumah was, either directly or indirectly, implicated. Nigeria's Foreign Minister at the time, Jaja Wachuku, articulated his suspicions perhaps a little too quickly. He regarded Olympio's assassination as "engineered, organized, and financed by somebody." He warned that Nigeria would intervene militarily if "the contingent of armoured Ghanaian troops lined up on the Ghana-Togo border" attempted to cross the border.[12]

Observers outside shared similar suspicions. Even the pro-Ghana American periodical at the time, *Africa Today*, saw a connection between a frontier dispute of that kind and the danger of assassination. In its own words:

> It is not the opposition which takes to the hand grenade but usually the neighbouring country whose leaders have taken up the cause of the opposition. . . . Africa balkanised will continue to be fertile ground for senseless political rivalries.[13]

But apart from the issue of frontiers, there was the issue of diplomatic recognition. With the murder of Olympio, African states were faced for the first time with the whole problem of "legitimate succession" following a case of regicide. West African

[11] For a comprehensive recent treatment of the border problem and its ethnic implications, see Claude E. Welch Jr., *Dream of Unity* (Ithaca, 1966), especially Chaps. II, III.
[12] See Helen Kitchen, "Filling the Togo Vacuum," *Africa Report*, VIII (1963), 9.
[13] "Conspiracies and Balkanisation," *Africa Today*, X (1963), 3.

governments were divided on the issue of whether or not to recognize the new Togolese government under Mr. Nicolas Grunit-
zky. From the east coast of Africa came the voice of Tanganyika,
then almost alone as an independent state in its area. Tanganyika
cabled the secretary-general of the United Nations in the following terms:

> After the brutal murder of President Olympio, the problem of rec-
> ognition of a successor government has arisen. We urge no recogni-
> tion until satisfied first that the government did not take part in Olym-
> pio's murder or second that there is a popularly elected government.[14]

The first condition concerned the issue of whether assumption
of power was by legitimate means. The second concerned a possible subsequent legitimation of what was originally an illegitimate method of assuming power. Subsequent elections were, in
other words, capable of giving a stamp of moral dignity to a regime which originally acceded as a result of assassination or insurrection. It was like de Gaulle coming into power in 1958 as a
result of military insubordination—and then organizing a ref-
erendum throughout the French community in order to validate
his standing.

The year of Olympio's murder was also the year of the formation of the Organization of African Unity. Only a few months
separated the two events. The ghost of Olympio virtually dictated
that dramatic part of Article III of the Charter of the new Organization: "unreserved condemnation, in all its forms, of political
assassination, as well as of subversive activities on the part of
neighbouring States or any other State."

Lumumba's martyrdom had perhaps, on the whole, been a positive contribution to Pan-Africanism. It gave Africa a shared hero
as the memory of nationalism indulged in unifying selectivity.
Olympio's murder, on the other hand, at first deeply divided the
continent, as suspicion and recrimination reigned supreme. But
history is beginning to reveal Olympio as essentially the first
major victim of a military coup in independent Africa. His death
now appears to have been an omen of things to come. Whether
this prophetic symbolism of his assassination would convert
Olympio into a continental African hero depends very much upon

[14] *Tanganyika Standard* (Dar-es-Salaam), Jan. 26, 1963.

whether Africa will experience a fundamental disenchantment with military regimes—and turn back with nostalgia to the first casualty of the wave of militarism.

If that were to happen, othcr heroes, too, of pre-military Africa—from Lumumba to Balewa—may contribute the vague mystique of their ancient names to the slow growth of primary consensus in the consciousness of Africa.

[2]

ALI A MAZRUI

The Third World and International Terrorism: preliminary reflections

Raymond Aron once analysed contemporary warfare in terms of a triad of violence. The three types of warfare were symbolised by the hydrogen bomb, the tank, and the Sten gun. The most comprehensive of these three types of warfare was, of course, nuclear war, with its power of massive destruction and capacity to encompass widely dispersed areas. The age itself is called the nuclear age, and yet the warfare represented by it is the least experienced within that age. Numerous outbreaks of violence and a variety of battles have erupted in different parts of the globe since World War II. The range is from the Vietnam war in the Far East to the football war in Latin America early in 1970. Yet a nuclear war as such is still outside direct human experience. It is the fear of nuclear war, rather than its experience, which has affected the age.

By contrast, warfare symbolised by the tank and by the Sten gun has been very much part of the post-World War II period. The tank signified what is sometimes called conventional warfare, though what is conventional is itself subject to the mutations of time. The most important outbreaks of conventional wars since World War II include the Korean War, the Suez adventure of 1956 when Israel, Britain and France attacked Nasser's Egypt, and the June war of 1967 between Israel and the Arabs, the more recent Iran-Iraq conflict, the clashes between India and China and India and Pakistan, the Israeli intrusions into and invasions of Lebanon over the years, the Vietnamese occupation of Kampuchea and the Soviet occupation of Afghanistan.

An even older form of conventional warfare is civil war. African experiences include Chad, Nigeria, Eritrea, Sudan, Angola and others. Many of these are conventional both in being intra-territorial and in the armaments they used.

A third type of warfare in Aron's triad of violence are guerrilla and terrorist movements. These are symbolised by the Sten gun, the stealthy steps in the stillness of the forest, the sudden spurt of fire on an unsuspecting target.

TWQ 7(2)April 1985/ISSN 0143-6597/85. $1.25

THE THIRD WORLD AND INTERNATIONAL TERRORISM

It should be noted from the start that the term 'terrorism' in this essay is value-free in the same way in which the term 'war' is. As far as this analysis is concerned, terrorism is a form of warfare and can be 'perpetrated' either by private individuals or by governments. 'Terrorism' is the deliberate creation of specialised terror among civilians, through the use of violence, in order to promote political ends.

But what are the purposes of politicised conspicuous terrorism? Here we must distinguish between ultimate goals and immediate targets. The ultimate goals include an ambition to gain a hearing for causes which would otherwise go unheard, and to make a contribution towards the realisation of those causes. The immediate target is the manipulation of fear as a mechanism of combat in the context of wide publicity. This is particularly so in the case of terrorism 'perpetrated' by individuals instead of by governments. The more sensational of terrorist initiatives by private individuals relates to the use of the skies as a battlefield. Let us turn to this area of guerrilla warfare.

Terror in the skies: a retrospect
A new version of this last type of warfare was initiated by the Palestine commandos in the 1970s. This was the tactic of attacking civil aircraft, sometimes on the ground, but more sensationally in mid-air. A more timid adventure tried in 1970 was that of planting bombs in aircraft. One blew up in mid-air, killing a number of people, many of whom had nothing to do with the issue of Palestine. But on 6 September 1970 Palestine commandos took this strategy a stage further. They hijacked four planes—two American, one Swiss, and one Israeli. According to some reports, the hijacking of the Israeli plane was thwarted by a somersault trick performed by the pilot, which threw the hijackers off balance and by the intervention of the plane's steward, resulting in one hijacker being killed and the second wounded. One of the American aircraft was taken to Cairo, where, after the passengers had been permitted to disembark, it was blown up in one dramatic explosion.

The remaining two planes went to Beirut and Amman, and passengers were for a while held as hostages as demands were made for the release of other Palestinians held prisoner in different parts of the Western world. Three of these were being held in Switzerland, after being sentenced to serve seven years on charges of attacking an Israeli airliner at Zurich. The Swiss Government, after urgent and decisive domestic consultations, agreed to release the three Palestinians in exchange for all the passengers from the Swiss airliner held by the terrorists.

For the remaining passengers, especially the male passengers from the United States, Britain and West Germany there were additional demands. Among stipulations reportedly made by the hijackers was the release of Sirhan Sirhan, under sentence of death in the United States for the murder of Robert Kennedy, though this demand was later withdrawn, if it was ever made.

What did these hijacks carried out by the Palestinians really mean in terms of the history of combat tactics? We have to go further back than the skyjack which resulted in the Entebbe raid in 1976.

What the world was witnessing from September 1970 until the Entebbe raid was guerrilla warfare transferred from the forests to the skies. This is what we mean by aerial terrorism. As in the case of guerrilla tactics in a domestic situation, the purpose of aerial terrorism was to manipulate fear as a mechanism of combat. The grand design was to undermine morale, not only among the soldiers but also the civilian body. An atmosphere of general insecurity, promoted by spectacular acts of destruction or specially dramatised acts of brutality, was contrived in order to drive the enemy into a desperate readiness to seek a settlement. What the Palestine commandos were doing in September 1970 was to use the international skies as fair ground for terrorist activities, since the streets of Israel were not accessible to them for domestic terrorism.

This fact itself brings us to another important different between aerial terrorism and domestic guerrilla tactics. Aerial terrorism as so far illustrated in its initial phases was by the very nature of things, international. Either the plane itself might be travelling across territorial boundaries, or the passengers on board might be nationally mixed, or both these forms of internationality might be present.

Aerial terrorism was in some important respects, symbolic both of the communications revolution and of the conversion of the world into a global village. The communications revolution played its part in the degree to which a hijack attained spectacular publicity, and with regard to the very increase in air traffic and the greater reliance of influential sectors of humanity on air transport. The news aspect of the communications revolution made aerial terrorism a useful device for attracting world attention to a particular grievance. The travelling aspect of the communications revolution meant heavy air traffic and therefore a wide choice of planes for hijacking. Among the passengers on such

THE THIRD WORLD AND INTERNATIONAL TERRORISM

planes were men and women in influential countries of the world, who were now forced to worry about the implications for their holidays or for their business of this new phenomenon in the skies.

The publicity side of aerial terrorism relied in part on the sensational-ism of political piracy. By 'political piracy' we mean the forceful takeover of a vessel at sea or in the air for such purposes as attracting publicity, carrying out political revenge, or preparing for a political deal. In 1961 a Brazilian seized control of a Portuguese ship on the high seas in a dramatic assertion of solidarity with the colonised peoples of Angola and Mozambique. This was political piracy in the tradition of tactical publicity.

Will aerial terrorism increase since it is such a guaranteed way of getting international and media attention for otherwise obscure causes? Two trends are pulling in opposite directions. The fact that air traffic in the world will almost certainly continue to increase should expand opportunities for political piracy in the skies. Even more obscure causes may take to the skies—such as the grievances of North Yemenis against Saudi Arabia as manifested in the takeover of a Saudi plane by Yemenis in November 1984. The skyjackers were later overwhelmed by Iranian troops with the help of passengers when the aircraft was at Teheran airport. The international obscurity of the cause was perhaps the most ominous aspect of the whole episode.

But although the expansion of air traffic in the world has increased opportunities for aerial piracy, there have also simultaneously been improvements in the technology of detecting metal weapons. There is thus a race between the opportunities provided by expanding air traffic and the controls afforded by improved technology.

Within the Third World it is the expansion of air traffic which is winning. Technological improvements are significantly slower than multiplication of air passengers and aircraft. At least in the immediate future, aerial terrorism is most likely to increase within the Third World or on aircraft which start in the Third World or pass through it.

There have of course always been Third World revolutionaries (including Palestinians) who have been opposed to hijacking. Some have felt that such tactics were bound to be counterproductive and to alienate international opinion. Those who have favoured such tactics have sometimes echoed Machiavelli's advice to The Prince—It is better to be feared than to be loved! The international community was more likely to want a problem resolved if it threatened its own safety and comfort. The international community might hate the terrorists—but it would still prefer a world without terrorism. Complete abolition of all kinds of terrorism was impossible—but the solution of certain fundamental international problems (like the dispersal of Palestinians or apartheid in South Africa) could reduce the number of situations which inherently generate terrorism and violence.

And yet at least the Palestinian movement seems to have shelved the skyjacking option for the time being. The question arises: Why?

It seems likely that three shocks helped to paralyse this particular arm of the Palestinian struggle. One was the shock of the Entebbe raid—a spectacular display of Israeli organisational superiority. Israel's reach exceeded its grasp—as the long arm of the Jewish state stretched itself from Jerusalem to the source of the Nile. The blow against Palestinian morale was devastating. The blow against the 'legitimacy' of skyjacking as a mode of Palestinian struggle was even more direct.

After the Entebbe raid, the second great shock for the Palestinian struggle was Anwar Sadat's visit to Jerusalem and the ensuing events which culminated in the Camp David Accords. Again it was a major blow to Palestinian morale and inaugurated fundamental agonising about priorities. Should the struggle redirect itself against 'the enemy within' the Arab nation (eg Sadat) or 'the enemy without' (namely 'the Zionist entity'). Skyjacking was not appropriate as a method of inter-Arab infighting, so it was widely assumed among Palestinians. Skyjacking against 'the enemy without' was also suspended for the time being.

The third great shock for Palestinians (after Entebbe and the Sadat initiative) was, of course, Israel's brutal invasions of Lebanon, especially the devastating one of 1982. The invasion destroyed much of the military infrastructure of the Palestine Liberation Organisation. Did this mean it also destroyed the PLO's capacity for skyjacking and other terrorist activities? It is too early to be sure. Sometimes terrorism increases precisely because other military options have been weakened. About Israeli arrogance it may be true to say that 'power tends to corrupt and absolute power corrupts absolutely'. In the case of the Palestinians the fear is that they will be forced to more extreme measures precisely because of weakness. It is after all equally true (in spite of Lord Acton) that *powerlessness* corrupts—and absolute powerlessness corrupts absolutely. New levels of desperation may in time force segments of the Palestinian movement to return to the days prior to the Entebbe raid—if not worse!

THE THIRD WORLD AND INTERNATIONAL TERRORISM

Political kidnapping

Then there is the piracy involving the kidnapping of a specific individual or individuals. This is where political piracy ties in with the more recent phenomenon of political abduction, especially the abduction of foreign diplomats in Latin America. The abduction of foreign diplomats in Latin America involved the diversion not of aeroplanes in mid-air, but quite often of cars in the street. A car is stopped, the victim forced out, and taken away in another car; or alternatively an uninvited passenger enters the victim's car, and, at gun-point, 'hijacks' the vehicle to another part of the city.

The kidnapping of diplomats of other powers is distinctive of recent times; but the kidnapping of specific individuals as a form of political vengeance or as a prelude to civic justice is part of an older tradition of political behaviour.

In Africa—north and south of the Sahara—abduction has tended to be preeminently a Francophone style of gamesmanship and intrigue. This is not to suggest that there has been no abduction in the politics of English-speaking Africa. It is merely to point out that, whether by accident or not, Francophone Africa has had a more consistent 'tradition' of kidnapping than other parts of the world.

Sometimes, France herself has been implicated in this phenomenon. In the course of the Algerian war, for example, there were cases of dramatic abduction conducted with the full connivance of French authorities. Then there was the kidnapping of Ben Barka, the Moroccan radical, from a street in Paris in 1965—a kidnapping and suspected killing which again compromised the French police itself.

In French-speaking black Africa there was in 1967 the forceful restriction of Guinea's Foreign Minister by the Ivory Coast, after a whole Guinean delegation from the United Nations had been virtually hijacked from a plane. The only difference in this case was that the plane carrying the minister and the delegation was not 'hijacked' in the sky but when it had momentarily landed at an airport in the Ivory Coast on the way home to Guinea.

But the most dramatic abduction in the history of modern Africa involved Moise Tshombe, the late Congolese (Zairean) political figure, once self-styled President of breakaway Katanga, and later Prime Minister of Zaire (then the Congo) as a whole. In July 1967 the plane on which he was travelling was hijacked, and brought to Algiers the capital of Algeria. The government of the Congo at the time requested Tshombe's extradition to the Congo so that he could face the death sentence which had been passed on him in his absence for treason. The Algerian Supreme Court sat to decide whether the offences with which Tshombe had been charged were political or not. They decided that some of the offences were criminal, and Tshombe was therefore extraditable. It was then left to the Algerian Government itself to decide whether or not Tshombe was to be extradited.

Curiously enough, even in regard to the abduction of Tshombe, the issue of Israel and the Arabs was somewhat in the background either as a direct political factor or by analogy. Just a month before Tshombe was abducted, the Arabs had sustained a humiliating defeat in the June 1967 war against Israel. There was widespread speculation at the time of Tshombe's abduction as to whether the Algerians, then holding Tshombe, would attempt, in diplomatic circles, to extract extra support against Israel from the Congolese Government in exchange for Tshombe's extradition to the Congo.[1]

By analogy the Jewish question was also present behind that abduction. The kidnapping of Tshombe was interpreted as an opportunity for an African Nuremberg. Nuremberg was, of course, the great international trial of Hitler's collaborators which established in current international law that there were such things as legal crimes against humanity for which it was no defence to say that one was obeying the orders of one's government.[2]

If Hitler's henchmen were charged with crimes against the human race, Tshombe and his henchmen were now to be considered for possible charges of crimes against the African race. And yet an African Nuremberg could have made sense only if it were held under the auspices of the Organisation of African Unity or a comparable pan-African umbrella. Only if Tshombe had been handed over by Algeria to the OAU or to a comparable pan-African body could his trial have become sufficiently internationalised to bear an adequate comparison with the phenomenon of Nuremberg.

But the real analogy of Tshombe's 'judicial abduction' was not Nuremberg but another event connected with the Jews—the kidnapping of Eichmann by Jews and his trial in Israel. Eichmann, who had helped Hitler to exterminate hundreds of thousands of Jews, was outwitted in a dramatic abduction from Argentina, and made to face

---

[1] These points are discussed more fully in Mazrui, 'Moise Tshombe and the Arabs: 1960–1968', *Race*, January 1969. Reprinted as Chapter 11 in Mazrui, *Violence and Thought: Essays on Social Tensions in Africa*, London: Longmans, 1969, pp 231–54.
[2] For the analogy with Nuremberg see *East African Standard* (Nairobi) 24 July 1967.

trial in Israel more than fifteen years after the presumed death of Hitler, within the legal jurisdiction of a state which had not been in existence at the time when he had committed the crimes.

Political relations between Africans and Arabs in the post-colonial world have often included the principle of a *quid pro quo*. African support against Israel and Zionism have sometimes been exchanged for Arab support against white minority rule in the old Rhodesia or against *apartheid* in South Africa. The abduction of Tshombe and his imprisonment in the Arab world was to some extent an exercise in Afro-Arab exchange. Arab action against the enemies of Africa (eg Tshombe) was apparently asking to be rewarded by African diplomatic action against the enemies of the Arabs (the Israelis).

The abduction of Eichmann, the kidnapping of foreign diplomats in Latin America, the hijacking of Moise Tshombe's plane to Algiers in 1967, and the hijacking of civil aviation planes by Palestine commandos in the 1970s, all these fall into place as a pattern of political combat, at once very old in its links, and very new in some of the manifestations it has recently taken.

Towards globalising grievance

And yet, of course, there are differences between the abduction of Eichmann and Tshombe, the abduction of foreign diplomats in Latin America, and the hijacking of planes for purposes of holding hostages. The abductions of Eichmann and Tshombe were specific—they concerned particular individuals wanted for acts of betrayal or brutality by those who regarded themselves victimised. This kind of abduction is at a high point of specificity.

The second type of abduction, that of kidnapping foreign diplomats, is less specific but still retains particular individuals as targets. The reduction in particularity arises out of the fact that the kidnapped have no direct link with the grievances for the dramatisation of which they are being diverted from their daily routines. A German diplomat or a Japanese diplomat in Latin America could hardly be regarded as having a very immediate bearing on the clash of views between a Latin American government and its domestic antagonists. And yet the men abducted are nevertheless purposefully chosen as specific individuals.

The hijacking of aeroplanes by Palestine commandos in September 1970 was general in regard to the people, but specific in regard to the vehicle. In the kidnapping of a particular diplomat, the car in which he is travelling is usually irrelevant. In the abduction of Moise Tshombe, the

355

national ownership of the plane was a factor in the politics which followed, but it was incidental to the motives behind the kidnapping. The real target was Tshombe, regardless of the plane in which he was travelling.

But in the hijacking of aeroplanes it can often be the nationality of the plane, rather than the passengers on the plane, which is the critical variable. The planes hijacked in September 1970 illustrated this quite clearly. Two of them were American planes, one was Swiss, and the fourth was Israeli. The grievances of the Palestine commandos against Americans included not only the general American sympathy with Israel, but, more recently, the American initiative in persuading Egypt to start negotiating an *ad hoc* settlement with Israel, without necessarily seeking the concurrence of Arab Palestinians.

The fact that this kind of hijacking is specific as to the nationality of the vehicle but general as to the nationality of the people within the vehicle is an important element to be borne in mind in assessing the general implications of this new form of combat. The hijackers have no way of telling in advance the precise international composition of the passengers inside the aircraft they intend to seize: that composition must, therefore, remain at the level of presumed generality. But the very random nature of the passenger list could be important in terms of creating a general sense of insecurity among air travellers from different parts of the world.

The specificity of the nationality of the plane implies that a hijacking of this kind is not simply a matter of kidnapping individuals but also a matter of violating territory. Hijacking is an instrument of the weak; it enables a couple of Palestinians to engage in an activity which is almost tantamount to the violation of the territorial jurisdiction of, say, the United States.

But from the angle of attracting publicity, does aerial terrorism attract the right kind? Does it not succeed only in alienating world opinion?

Questions of this kind miss the whole point of the exercise. In a propaganda campaign to win sympathy in the more influential parts of the world, the Arabs are no match for the Jews. Quite apart from the greater sophistication of Jewish communities in the Western world, and indeed of Israel itself as compared with the more underdeveloped capacities of the Arab world, there is also the question of access to the influential media of the international system. C Eric Lincoln refers to stereotypes which black Americans have about different categories of whites—'The Anglo-Saxons are diplomats and statesmen; the Italians are criminals and racketeers; the stupid Irishmen are cops; the Germans are good scientists; the Jews are the brains of the white race'.

Lincoln draws attention to the disproportionate Jewish presence among writers and intellectuals in the United States. He also refers to the financial resources which enable the Jews to exercise considerable influence on mass media:

The Jews are believed to have a stronger hold on public opinion through their control of mass communication. They are said to own the radio and television stations, along with many magazines and newspapers. They hire Gentiles to 'front' for them so as not to antagonise the public; but on crucial issues such as the Suez Canal, they control the thinking of the people. And they use this power to forward the Zionist cause.[3]

It is quite clear that black American images of Jews include, in some cases, strong anti-Semitic tendencies. The images can, therefore, become hostile stereotypes. But one cannot escape the issue of comparative Jewish access to the media of communication. Indeed, without such success, Israel itself might never have been created. From the point of view of racial equality, there is little doubt that the Jews have been among the privileged groups of the human race. When we divide the world into the haves and have-nots, it is quite clear where world Jewry belongs—and it does not belong in the ranks of the indigent.

Terrorism and the establishment: competitive publicity

Zionism as a movement to create a national home for the Jews would not have got very far if it had lacked access to immense financial resources for its implementation as a movement. Even the establishment of a political party in one country needs considerable financial support. The establishment of a movement to create a home for the Jews, the necessary economic resources for their transportation, and the necessary propaganda and financial power to create a national climate favourable to such a move, was something which only a group happily privileged in monetary influence could have undertaken. We might therefore say that discrimination against the Jews in Europe helped the creation of Israel in two ways. One way was in arousing the conscience of Europe in the twentieth century to the need for some form of protection for this racial minority. But a way with a longer history

[3] Eric Lincoln. *The Black Muslims in America*. Boston: Beacon Press, 1968 edition. pp 165–9.

behind it was the role of medieval European anti-Semitism in forcing Jewish minorities in the Western hemisphere over the years to specialise in business techniques and financial enterprises. This enabled them to acquire an impressive base of economic and political initiative. The Armenians may have been oppressed in Turkey and Russia over the ages, and the Kurds have been oppressed in the Arab world, with special reference to Iraq, but no national home for them has emerged. As minorities they have differed from the Jews in one fundamental respect; they have not specialised in wealth.

If Jewish access to these media was effective enough to result in the very creation of Israel, it remains effective enough in the Western world, especially in the United States, to create a climate of opinion favourable to the Israeli cause. Any competition by Palestine commandos for sympathy is handicapped from the start by the massive disproportion between them and Israel in terms of access to mass communications.

The purpose of Palestinian aerial terrorism in the 1970s was, therefore, not a quest for sympathetic publicity, but an attempt to arouse popular anxieties. Sympathy does sometimes help in mobilising international opinion, and could result in changes in a particular situation. Sympathy for Biafra, and the starving Ibo, for example, was escalating at a pace which might sooner or later have resulted first in the French recognition of Biafra, and then recognition by many states in French-speaking Africa. This, in turn, could have transformed the Nigerian situation, and perhaps made it more difficult for the war to end in favour of the Federal side.

Of course, French recognition of Biafra would not have been simply a case of sympathy. There were important economic and diplomatic assets to be gained by France in a Biafra separate from the rest of Nigeria. But there were enough inhibitions to such a move arising out of diplomatic non-intervention that the French government had to move carefully before making a decision on recognition. The escalation of sympathy for Biafra made it increasingly unlikely that the French government could do such a thing without alienating too many friends. French military and financial help for Biafra is already a matter of record, though the documentation is incomplete. It is speculative whether the regime in France after de Gaulle would indeed have gone the whole way towards according diplomatic recognition. All we are arguing at this stage is the relevance of sympathetic escalation for important moves in the diplomatic sphere.

THE THIRD WORLD AND INTERNATIONAL TERRORISM

A related question to be borne in mind in assessing the place of propaganda for sympathy in the case of both Biafra and Israel lies simply in the psychological impact of a David versus Goliath confrontation. Such a confrontation gives potentialities for sympathetic exploitation in propaganda by the smaller unit. Thus Biafra, quite apart from being more sophisticated than the Federal side in techniques of propaganda, was substantially aided in mobilising international sympathy by the simple image of a courageous David defying an aggressive Goliath. All the innate tendencies of empathising with the underdog were effectively mobilised to the side of Biafra.

The same kind of image can be teased out of the human imagination by the predicament of Israel. That is, the image of Israel as a courageous and industrious immigrant community, defying a hostile environment of nature and of neighbours, and surviving with honour. Other communities elsewhere, anxious about a hostile environment, have drawn inspiration from the Israeli predicament. A Minister of Defence in South Africa once extolled Israel in the following terms: 'They stand alone in the world, but they are full of courage.'

The South African publication *Die Burger* has drawn similar inspiration from Israel's example of triumphant loneliness:

We in South Africa would be foolish if we did not at least take account of the possibility that we are destined to become a sort of Israel in a preponderantly hostile Africa, and that fact might become part of our national way of life. . .[4]

Then, there was the response of white Rhodesians to Israeli successes against the Arabs. Certainly in June 1967, following the swift victory of Israel, there was clear evidence in Rhodesia (as it then was) of empathetic identification with Israel. Israel was small; the Arab countries and their populations were large. And yet the Arabs had proved to be militarily impotent in the face of Israel. By the same token, Rhodesia was small; the African continent was large and its population impressive. And yet Africans were militarily impotent in the face of Ian Smith's government. The white Rhodesians did identify themselves as 'the Israelis of Africa' surrounded by hostile, but less distinguished, neighbours.

In the face of these handicaps in the propaganda game for sympathy,

---

[4] Cited by Colin and Margaret Legum, *South Africa: Crisis for the West*, London: Pall Mall Press 1964, pp 107, 108. On the other hand, Afrikaner nationalism has often suspected sections of the local Jewry in South Africa of having leanings towards Communism. See for example Muriel Horrell, (Compiler) *A Survey of Race Relations in South Africa*, Johannesburg: South African Institute of Race relations, 1965, pp 22–54.

it was for a while rational for the Palestinians to pursue a strategy of maximising anxiety rather than promoting popularity. Aerial terrorism alienated much of world opinion even further away from the Palestinian cause. But their cause could be less popular and yet nearer to fulfillment at the same time. The Palestinian commandos were forcing more and more people—ordinary travellers on civil aircraft—to develop a vested interest in a solution of the Middle Eastern problem. They might hate the tactics that were being used; they might dislike the Arabs more than ever; they might be drawn closer to Israel in sympathy; and yet all these tendencies were not inconsistent with a growing desire by more and more of the jet-set of the world to see this whole Middle Eastern mess sorted out once and for all.

Terrorism and the global island

This is what brings in the issue of the world as a global village into relevance. The Sten gun approach in the skies globalises guerrilla tactics. The Middle Eastern problem has never been purely local. Moreover, the original cause of the present problem—the creation of Israel—was an act of the international community rather than an outcome of the domestic balance of forces between localised Jews and localised Arabs. If the creation of Israel was itself an act of the international community, the consequences which have followed can never be shrugged off as merely a regional difficulty. The world was involved in the mess from the start. The aerial tactics of Palestinian commandos in September 1970 were effective in reminding the world that it was still part of the mess.

In fact, two unhealthy partitions have caught up with those who brought them into being, at roughly the same period. One was the partition of Palestine; the other the partition of Ireland. The world entered the decade of the 1980s with sharper reminders of the repercussions of these partitions than it had ever had before.

But, as a new development in international violence, how does terrorism relate to older systems of combat? We are back here to Raymond Aron's triad of violence. There are important differences between the thermo-nuclear weapon, the tank, and the Sten gun as symbols of three types of combat. Among the differences is, quite simply, the ultimate requirements for making them feasible. At a broad level of generality, we might say that the hydrogen bomb is capital-intensive, the tank is labour-intensive and the Sten gun is secrecy-intensive.

THE THIRD WORLD AND INTERNATIONAL TERRORISM

Capability in nuclear warfare does, of course, presuppose considerable economic resources. It also presupposes technological sophistication, but this itself could be bought either by rapid training internally or by importing scientists from other countries. The whole phenomenon of the brain-drain to the United States is an example of economic determinism in distribution of expertise.

The tank as a symbol of conventional war implies availability of armies and mobile troops and fighting equipment, with something meaningfully called a 'war front'. This kind of military engagement is evidently labour-intensive, and conscious of the size of armies in an assessment of military strength. The People's Republic of China has linked this demographic dimension to nuclear war itself. China's strength is seen partly in the conventional terms of numerical superiority. This view has continued to be emphasised even after China's successful entry into the world of nuclear weaponry. Indeed, an article published in the *Peking Review*, not long after China's successful explosion of a nuclear weapon, argued that precisely because modern warfare kills extremely large numbers of people the resources of manpower have become more important. In the words of the article:

Once a war breaks out, we have to have powerful reserves which can ensure a continuous supply of manpower and materials to meet our needs. The existence of a large-scale peoples' militia provides an inexhaustible source of replacements for the army.[5]

What is important here is not whether Chinese reasoning is sound, but how far it affects her outlook on world affairs. There seems little doubt that China's conception of her role in the world is affected by her consciousness of the massive size of her population. As K S Karol reported to a British weekly at about the same time, 'In all their diplomatic notes, as in their public speeches, Chinese leaders insist on their numbers: "We are 650 million and we are one " '.[6]

But although conventional warfare is labour-intensive, and demographic factors affect military superiority, numbers alone are clearly not enough. The most dramatic example has, in fact, been precisely in the Middle East, where the vastly superior number of the Arabs has still

---

[5] Liu Yun-Chang, 'Peoples' militia in China', *Peking Review* 8(6)5 February 1965, pp 19–20.
[6] See *New Statesman* (London) 19 February 1965, p 267. Previous works by Mazrui which include a discussion of terrorism and guerrilla warfare include *A World Federation of Cultures: An African Perspective*, New York: The Free Press, 1976, and *Africa's International Relations: The Diplomacy of Dependency and Change*, London: Heinemann Educational Books and Boulder: Westview Press, 1977. This article has of course been influenced by Mazrui's previous work on 'deviancy' and violence.

been unable to match up to the organisational and technological sophistication of the Israelis. The attack, as a weapon, is particularly vulnerable to air power. Again the Middle Eastern situation has been a spectacular illustration of the implications of air differentials. Conventional warfare on land is affected more by mere numbers and sizes of armies than is warfare through the skies where skills and organisational calculations assume extra relevance.

The great irony of aerial terrorism in the 1970s lay precisely in the simple proposition that just as it had been the control of the skies which had made the Arabs totally unequal to Israeli sophistication, so also was it now the use of the skies by hijackers which was providing Arab Palestinians with a mode of desperate retaliation.

But the success of hijacking tactics depends on well-guarded secrecy. Secrecy is a characteristic of guerrilla tactics both in the forests of individual countries and in the international open skies. Domestic terrorism relies on well-guarded movements, on hit-and-run tactics, and very often on the profound primeval secrecy of dense bushes and deep jungles. Symbolically, there is also the important difference that terrorist fighters abjure the uniform. Other kinds of fighters are at least non-secret enough to wear the uniform of their country and pronounce their national identity in visual conspicuousness. But the guerrilla fighter has had to learn the skills of disguise and general subterfuge in order to survive. A major reason for the mobilisation of secrecy is the relative conventional or technological weakness of movements which have to resort to guerrilla warfare for the pursuit of their aims. The North Vietnamese and the Vietcong, confronted with the military pre-eminence of the United States, had to rely on disruption and general secrecy as military resources. With those two resources they succeeded in denying military victory to a power which, by other criteria of military preeminence, is regarded as the strongest in the world.

As terrorism is transferred from the jungles to the skies an important aspect of secrecy is, almost by definition, eliminated. The skies are the open skies; the airlines traverse continents according to specified schedules; a diverted aeroplane soon arouses curiosity among those who might follow its unexpected route or seek an explanation for its unexpected delay in arriving at its scheduled destination. Sometimes to ensure traffic safety contact has to be maintained with stations on the ground. And in order to land, an elaborate system of communication and guidance often needs to be set in motion. All these factors are, fundamentally, a denial of secrecy. In this limited sense, terrorism

THE THIRD WORLD AND INTERNATIONAL TERRORISM

transferred from the jungle to the skies is terrorism disrobed and laid bare.

And yet skyjacking at the preparatory stage has to rely overwhelmingly on secrecy. In fact, the great problem before civil aviation as a whole is how to devise ways of detecting potential hijackers among passengers. New attempts are already being made to detect whether certain firearms are being carried by passengers. And yet so far a certain delicacy has had to be observed, partly out of respect for the privacy of passengers, and partly out of the fear that systematic searches before every boarding are likely to increase alarm among passengers rather than to create a sense of security.

A hijack could be perpetrated by a single individual; though it has sometimes been a collaborative venture involving two or three people. These three have to pass as legitimate passengers until the plane is airborne. Any exposure of their intentions before the actual moment of action is almost bound to thwart the entire exercise.

Once again the point to remember is that terrorism is a tactic of the weak. The tactic itself is highly vulnerable unless the preliminary subterfuge is carried out with accuracy and precision.

Behind it all, is again the simple fact that aerial terrorism is specially suited for issues which cannot be resolved without international intervention. In the case of the Nigerian civil war, it is possible that the end was delayed because of international intervention. The massive aid provided to each side kept on raising hopes about imminent triumph. The efforts made by the Organisation of African Unity to bring the two sides to some agreement might have succeeded sooner had there not been extra-African participation in that violent adventure in Nigeria.

Indeed the next major frontier of international terrorism generally is not necessarily poor against rich, or South against North. What is on the horizon for the rest of this century may well be South-South international terrorism, though by no means exclusively.

The atrocity in Burma in 1983 against South Korean visitors (attributed to North Koreans) is one illustration. Libya's activities in a number of different countries amount to a cluster of terrorist diplomacy. Air piracy between Iran and Iraq in the course of their conflict is a third illustration.

This is quite apart from domestic terrorism within individual Third World societies. Opponents and supporters of Robert Mugabe's government in Zimbabwe have been 'guilty' of competing acts of terrorism. The Philippines has had a variety of terrorist activity—involving regime militarists, Muslim separatists, radical revolutionaries, and Marcos' supporters. Iran and Ethiopia have been hanging near the abyss of political disintegration since their respective revolutions. Central America is torn assunder with domestic terrorism and superpower interventionism. Uganda under Milton Obote is still agonising over the terrorising anarchy unleashed by the legacy of Idi Amin. Angola is suffering under the challenge of UNITA under Savimbi against the ruling Marxist regime of MPLA. Mozambique under the rule of FRELIMO has been forced to compromise with the racist government of South Africa—and all because of the terrorist pressures exerted by the dissident Mozambique Resistance Movement.

On the other hand, Argentina has begun to emerge from a 'dirty war' of governmental and semi-official terrorism. Ghana under Jerry Rawlings may also have left its worst terroristic record behind it, though the risk of a relapse in both Ghana and Argentina is real.

The Middle East question, on the other hand, seems, for the time being, to be of the kind where no speedy solution could be reached without international intervention. They used to say with John Donne 'No man is an island, entire of itself'. Yet the critical lesson of the communications revolution of the space age might well be that humanity as a whole is contained on a planetary island, for better or for worse. No single man is an island but humanity resides on an island. If the world is a global village in the face-to-face relationships which are coming with increased communications, it is a village in splendid isolation within the cosmos. The Middle Eastern situation becomes one of those irritating reminders that few wars from now on are ever likely to be purely local wars, unless the whole international system is changed.

If we are to take John Donne a step further, it is simply to remind ourselves that the alarm bells are ringing in places like the Middle East—'And therefore never send to know for whom the bell tolls; it tolls for thee'. Terrorism in the Third World is a bell tolling for thee. No man is an island—but every man lives on one.

[3]

INTERNATIONAL JOURNAL OF COMPARATIVE AND APPLIED CRIMINAL JUSTICE
SPRING 1986, VOL. 10, NO. 1

Terrorist Aircraft Hijacking and Sabotage In African States

PATRICK EDOBOR IGBINOVIA
University of ILorin, Nigeria

> But the revolution does require of the revolution-
> ary class that it should attain its end by all methods at
> its disposal; if necessary by an armed uprising; if re-
> quired by terrorism.
>
> Leon Trotsky

Introduction

The hijacking and sabotage of civil aircraft is a serious international crime. It endangers the safety, regularity, and efficiency of civil aviation. Indeed, unlawful interference with civil aviation has been of concern to world governments and bodies for a long time. This concern is expressed in the following documents: (1) The Geneva Convention for the Prevention and Punishment of Terrorism of 16 November 1937; (2) The United Nations General Assembly Resolution 2645 (xxv) of 1970; (3) The United Nations Security Council Documents/10705 of June 20, 1972; (4) The 1970 Resolution of the Assembly of the Council of Europe which condemns all acts of hijacking, sabotage, and the taking of hostages; (5) The 1971 Organization of American States Convention to Prevent and Punish Acts of Terrorism Taking the Form of Crimes Against Persons and Related Extortion that are of International Significance; (6) The Tokyo Convention on Offenses and Certain Other Acts Committed on Board the Aircraft (1963); (7) The Hague Convention for the Suppression of Unlawful Seizure of Aircraft (1970); (8) The Montreal Convention for the Suppression of Unlawful Acts Against the Safety of Civil Aviation (1971); and (9) The 1970 Resolution of the Council of Ministers of the Organization of African Unity condemning "all attempts and acts of hijacking and sabotage of civil aircraft."

Bodies like the Council of the International Civil Aviation Organization (ICAO), Interpol General Assembly, the Airport Association Coordinating Council (AACC), the International Air Transport Association (IATA), and the International Federation of Air Line Pilots Association have also adopted resolutions requiring members to take appropriate domestic and international measures to prevent hijacking of civil aircrafts and sabotage of aircraft facilities.

In spite of these efforts, the problem persists. Examination of Interpol, ICAO, and U.S. Federal Aviation Authority (FAA) reports on hijacking and sabotage of civil aircrafts reveal certain principal trends. Reports reaching ICAO in 1983 showed that the number of unlawful seizures of aircrafts had continued at about the same level for ten years. In addition, between 1970 and August 1983, there were 533 threats to seize aircrafts worldwide; from 1969 to August 1983, 636 aircrafts were seized worldwide; from 1970 to August 1983, 194 acts of aircraft sabotage were reported worldwide; from 1969 to August 1983, a total of 1,299 persons were injured and 1,363 persons killed in aircraft hijackings; from 1969 to August 1983, 49,601 persons were taken as hostages by hijackers worldwide; from 1971 to 1982, a total of 91,263 firearms/ammunition/explosives were found on passengers embarking at airports worldwide; and from 1971 to 1982, a total of 153,514 "other weapons" (knives, etc.) were found on passengers at airports around the world.[1] Similarly, from January to December 1983, eighty-four criminal acts involving civil aviation occurred worldwide. These acts resulted in 292 deaths and 82 injuries. Of these, 34 (40%) were cases of hijacking; 28 (33%) consisted of explosions (one on board an aircraft, six at airports, and 21 at airline offices); 7 (8%) were live or hoax explosive devices discovered at airports or airline offices; one "terrorist attack," and 14 "other" criminal acts against civil aviation.[2] In addition, from 1949 to 1983 there were 76 explosions on board aircrafts worldwide. The explosions resulted in the death of 1,037 persons. Finally, from 1931 to January 1, 1984, there were 403 successful hijackings, 59 incomplete hijackings (i.e., hijacker was killed or apprehended as a result of "hot pursuit"), and 262 unsuccessful hijacking attempts worldwide.[3]

Criminal acts against civil aviation have existed for more than 53 years. The figures cited above illustrate the seriousness of the problem and the continuing vulnerability of air transportation to attacks by terrorists, criminals, and other disgruntled or demented individuals. The number of hijacking incidents and of hijackers and victims killed or injured illustrates the hijackers' determination and the danger they represent. In spite of the measures that have been adopted by many countries and world bodies to protect and safeguard civil aviation from criminal attacks, the problem continues to persist.

Hijacking and sabotage of aircrafts are not limited to the countries of Europe, America, and the Middle East. The countries in Africa are also affected. Therefore, this paper is concerned with presenting a descriptive evaluation of the evolution, causes, rationale, nature, trend, legal aspects, and modus operandi of aircraft hijacking and sabotage in Africa. Data from February 1931 to July 1983 are marshalled in an eclectic manner to provide what is hoped would be useful information on the phenomenon.

Extent of Hijacking

The first recorded incident of hijacking in contemporary times occurred in February 1931 when a Peruvian airliner on a domestic flight was seized.

TERRORIST AIRCRAFT HIJACKING AND SABOTAGE   75

Thirty years after this incident, the first hijacking of an aircraft occurred in Africa. On November 10, 1961, six men diverted a domestic Portuguese aircraft to Tangier in Morocco. Although the hijackers were expelled and sent to Senegal, they eventually were granted political asylum in Brazil. In another hijacking incident, a man by the name Riya Kamal Hajjal seized a domestic Egyptian aircraft on February 7, 1967. The plane was diverted to Jordan where the hijacker escaped to Sweden and received a long prison sentence for other crimes.

Similarly, at the height of the Nigerian Civil War in April 1963, five men who were identified as sympathizers of the Republic of "Biafra," commandeered a Nigerian aircraft whose normal flight plan was from Benin City to Lagos. They diverted the aircraft to Enugu, the capital of the self-styled "Republic of Biafra." Furthermore, on June 30, 1967, a Belgian national seized an airliner bearing the former Congolese Prime Minister, Moise Tshombe. The aircraft was flying from Iviza to Palma de Mallorca in Spain when it was diverted to Algiers. At Algiers, Mr. Moise Tshombe was arrested and held until his death on June 29, 1969. The hijacker of the aircraft left Algiers in 1969 and lived for a number of years in France and Belgium. While in Belgium, he was arrested in November 1979 on non-related charges and extradited to Spain on April 16, 1980.

In addition, a Greek airliner with 102 passengers and crew was diverted to Cairo by a Greek national in February 1969. In April 1969, three men hijacked an Angolan aircraft and forced it to land in Pointe Noire, Congo; in August 1969, seven Ethiopian male students armed with knives and revolvers commandeered an Ethiopian aircraft and diverted it to Khartoum in the Sudan where they held the airliner stewardess hostage. On surrender, the Sudanese police returned the hijackers to the Ethiopian authorities. In the same month, an Egyptian aircraft enroute to Luxor was diverted by three men (the passengers included the wife and three children of one of the hijackers) with pistols to El Wagah, Saudi Arabia. The hijackers were returned to Egypt on board the same aircraft by the Saudi Arabian authorities. In September, 1967, three armed men seized an Ethiopian aircraft with 70 passengers and forced it to Aden in South Yemen where one of the offenders was shot and the others taken into custody. In December, two Arab men attempted to seize an Ethiopian aircraft at Athens but were slain by security guards on board the aircraft.

In May 1970, a young Italian student diverted an Italian aircraft with 35 passengers from Genoa, Rome, to Cairo, Egypt, with a toy pistol. In June, a Pan American airliner with 144 persons on board was seized with a pistol by a 32-year old man and forced to Cairo where the hijacker was detained. Similarly, six Arab men with guns and handgrenades, seized a Greek aircraft on a Beirut-Athens route in July 1970 and diverted it to Cairo. At Cairo, the hijackers took the passengers hostages and demanded for the release of seven political prisoners in Athens. When the demands were met by the Greek government, the hijackers released the hostages and surrendered to the Egyptian authorities. In August 1970, three Algerian males seized an Algerian airliner on domestic flight with pistols and grenades. The aircraft was refused landing rights in Albania and so was subsequently diverted to Dubrovnick, Yugoslavia, where the hijackers asked for asylum. On September 6, 1970, three Arab men seized another Pan-American airliner in Amsterdam. They forced the aircraft to refuel in Beirut, picked up seven men, and diverted the airplane to Cairo, Egypt. The aircraft was blown up by the hijackers minutes after the 169 passengers and crew disembarked. The hijackers were eventually held for questioning by the Eqyptian authorities. Four days later, three Arab men seized an Egyptian aircraft in Beirut but were apprehended by security officers on board the aircraft shortly after the hijacking attempt was initiated. In a separate incident, a Chadian national seized an Egyptian airliner in Tripoli on September 12, 1970. The hijacker was apprehended by security officers on board the aircraft while it was airborne. Similarly, armed hijackers were disarmed by security officers on board another domestic Egyptian airliner on September 16, 1970.

Furthermore, an Ethiopian airliner on the Bahar-Dar-Gondar route was diverted by four armed men to Libya via Khartoum on January 22, 1971. In June 1971, two males commandeered an Angolan Air Taxi at gun point and forced it to Pointe Noire in the Congo. In August, a man attempted to hijack an Egyptian aircraft on the Cairo-Amman route to Israel but was overpowered by Sky Marshalls. Similarly, in September a Jordanian airliner was hijacked between Beirut and Amman and forced to land in Benghazi, Libya. At Benghazi, the offenders were taken into custody.

In addition, 2 Lebanese men diverted a South African airliner between Salisbury and Johannesburg to Blantyre, Malawi, in May, 1972. Malawian troops freed the 66 passengers and crew on board the aircraft. On surrender, the hijackers were sentenced to 11 years in prison and deported to Zambia in May, 1974. On January 5, 1972, two Americans seized a B-727 aircraft on the Los Angeles-Seattle route and forced it to San Francisco. They threatened to blow up the aircraft, and demanded a ransom of $500,000. On receiving the money, the hijackers changed from the B-727 to a B-720 aircraft and requested to be flown to Algiers, Algeria, where they asked for asylum. The Algerian authorities obtained the ransom from the hijackers and turned it over to the American airliner. Similarly, on July 12, 1972, an attempt to seize a French airliner before it touched down at Abidjan was foiled when the male hijacker was shot and apprehended after he had shot at his wife. In addition, on July 31, 1972, two women and three men accompanied by three children seized an American aircraft at gun-point in Detroit, Michigan, and demanded a ransom of $1 million. On receiving the money, the hijackers allowed the 94 passengers on board to disembark. After refueling in Boston, the hijackers with eight of the aircraft's crew flew to Algeria. In Algeria, the authorities obtained the $1 million ransom from the hijackers and turned it over together with the children accompanying the hijackers to the U.S. authorities. In August, two unidentified males and a woman seized a South

TERRORIST AIRCRAFT HIJACKING AND SABOTAGE   77

Yemeni aircraft with 61 persons at gun-point. The aircraft was refueled at Cyprus and was diverted to Benghazi, Libya, where the three hijackers deplaned. In September 14, 1972, an East African airliner was stolen at night in Dar Es Salaam by unknown persons. The aircraft was recovered at Kilimanjaro with burst tires and other damages. On October 29, 1972, two Arab males seized a West German aircraft. Threatening to blow up the plane and its passengers, they demanded the release of three Arab males imprisoned for involvement in the slaying of 11 Israelis at the Munich Olympics. After successfully securing the release of the prisoners, the hijackers diverted the aircraft with passengers on board to Tripoli, Libya. Furthermore, on December 8, 1972, five men and two women attempted to hijack a domestic Ethiopian aircraft. When the intention of the hijackers was announced, security guards on board the airliner opened fire killing six of the hijackers. One of the hijackers, however, successfully detonated a hand-grenade which tore the engine and rudder of the aircraft, and resulted in injuries to seven passengers, two flight attendants, and the only surviving female hijacker. The airliner with 100 passengers and crew landed safely in Addis Ababa.

Similarly, on March 20, 1974, a married couple armed with pistols seized an East African airliner on the Nairobi-Malindi route. The hijacker ordered the pilot to take the aircraft to Libya after refueling at Entebbe, Uganda. At Entebbe, President Amin was able to persuade the offenders to surrender to the Ugandan authorities. In September, 1974, an airliner was forced by a male hijacker from Angola to South West Africa where he turned himself over to the South African authorities. In addition, on November 6, 1974, three Arab men forced a Royal Jordanian domestic airliner to Benghazi, Libya. The hijackers released the passengers and crew unharmed. Sixteen days later, four men with automatic weapons forced their way into a British airliner at Dubai and inflicted wounds on two persons. After refueling in Tripoli, the hijackers diverted the aircraft to Tunis, Tunisia. In Tunis, the hijackers demanded the release of 13 terrorists in Egypt and two in the Netherlands. While waiting for their demands to be met, they killed one of the 47 passengers on board the aircraft. This action forced the Dutch and Egyptian governments to turn-over to the hijackers some of the prisoners in their countries. The hijackers were subsequently detained by the Tunisian authorities.

On October 7, 1975, a Philippine aircraft was seized in Davao. An attempt was made to divert the aircraft to Benghazi, Libya. However, the airliner was forced into Manila where the hijackers surrendered to the authorities. On April 7, 1976, another Philippine airliner was seized by three armed men at Cagayan de Oro. They asked for $300,000 and the release of numerous political prisoners. In Manila, the hijackers exchanged 72 passengers for another set of hostages and $300,000 in cash. For six days, the hijackers flew to Kota Kinbalu and Juala Lampur, Malaysia; Bangkok, Thailand; Karachi, Pakistan; and Benghazi, Libya. At Benghazi, the hijackers released the remaining hostages and asked for political asylum.

The most spectacular hijacking incident involving an African country occurred on June 27, 1976. A France Airbus was seized by four to seven men shortly after departure from Athens. The aircraft refueled at Benghazi, Libya, and diverted to Entebbe, Uganda, where the 258 passengers/crew were taken into the airport building and held hostage. The hijackers asked for the release of 53 pro-Palestinian prisoners in numerous countries in exchange for the hostages. Negotiations resulted in the release of approximately 150 passengers; leaving as hostages the crew and passengers with Israeli passports. On the evening of July 3, 1976, Israeli Commandos launched a rescue operation at the Entebbe airport. Three hostages were killed and the rest rescued. The hijackers, some Ugandan troops, and one Israeli Commando officer were killed in the operation. Similarly, on July 6, 1976, a man with two replica pistols and two knives hijacked a Libyan airliner on domestic flight and diverted it to Tunis where the aircraft with 78 passengers was denied landing. As a result, it had to be diverted to Palma de Majorca, Spain, where the hijacker surrendered. On August 23, 1976, three armed men seized a domestic Egyptian aircraft. However, the hijacking was terminated in Luxor when the hijackers were overpowered by security forces. In a separate incident, three armed Arabic-speaking men commandeered a Dutch aircraft which was enroute from Spain to Amsterdam. The aircraft was enrouted to Tunisia, Cyprus, and Israel where it circled off shore. The airliner was returned to Cyprus where the hijackers surrendered and were turned over to the Libyan Embassy. In a similar incident, a domestic Ethiopian aircraft was hijacked in April, 1977, by two gun-wielding men shortly after takeoff from Meleke. The hijackers were overpowered by security guards and killed. Furthermore, on August 27, 1977, a French airliner with 242 persons on board was seized in Nice and diverted to Benghazi, Libya, where it was refused landing rights. Permission to land in Athens, Greece, was also denied. However, because the aircraft was low on fuel, the Italian authorities allowed it to land at Brindisi-Casale Airport where the hijackers were arrested. Similarly, five Japanese men seized a Japanese airliner with 155 persons shortly after departing Bombay in September 1977. The airliner was diverted to Dacca, Bangladesh, for refueling. In addition, the hijackers asked for $6 million ransom and the release of prisoners in Japan. On October 1, 1977, the money and six prisoners were exchanged for 59 hostages. Forty-seven more hostages were later released. However, the aircraft took off from Dacca for Algiers with approximately 36 hostages making refueling stops in Kuwait and Damascus. In Damascus, the hijackers released some of the remaining hostages. The rest of the hostages were freed on the airliner's landing in Algeria; and the hijackers taken into police custody.

A spectacular hijacking incident occurred on October 13, 1977, when four hijackers with pistols and plastic explosives took control of a German airliner with 87 persons near Majorca. The aircraft was diverted to Rome for refueling where the hijackers asked for the release of comrades held in German and Turkish prisons, and $15 million. Refueling stops were made in Cyprus,

TERRORIST AIRCRAFT HIJACKING AND SABOTAGE   79

Bahrain, Dubai, United Arab Emirates, and Aden. At Aden, the pilot was killed by the leader of the hijackers and the aircraft forced to depart for Mogadishu, Somalia. While the aircraft was on the ground in Somalia, German commandos blasted open the emergency exits and rushed into the passenger cabin killing two of the hijackers. A third hijacker died in hospital while a female hijacker, nine passengers, and a German commando officer were injured. In April, 1978, the injured female hijacker was sentenced to 20 years and 30 years in prison in absentia by courts in Somalia and Rome respectively. On January 12, 1979, three or four Tunisian men seized an aircraft on the Tunis-Djerba route. The men were armed with two starter pistols, blanks, batteries (strapped together to resemble explosives), ten pairs of handcuffs and a non-operational shotgun (which was altered to resemble a machine gun). The hijackers demanded the release of a Tunisian Union leader and a former Tunisian Foreign Minister. The aircraft was refused permission to land in Malta and was diverted to Tripoli, Libya, where discussions were held with the leader of the hijackers. At Tripoli, the aircraft was refueled and took off only to return to Tripoli where the hijackers surrendered and requested political asylum. On August 24, 1979, a domestic Libyan aircraft on the Tripoli-Benghazi route was hijacked by a man brandishing a pistol. He ordered the aircraft to be flown to a non-Arab country. Permission to land at Larnaca, Cyprus and other places was denied. However, because the aircraft was low on fuel, it was allowed to land at Larnaca where the hijacker gave his pistol to the pilot, surrendered, and requested political asylum and was turned over to a Libyan delegation who sent him to Libya where he was executed. On October 16, 1979, another Libyan aircraft was diverted to Malta by three armed men. The men, who were armed with homemade gasoline bombs and knives, demanded to be flown to Switzerland but later agreed to land in Malta where they surrendered after being promised a press conference. The Syrian hijackers indicated at the press conference that the hijacking was carried out to express anger about unsettled financial problems and lack of Libyan travel passports.

In addition, on January 4, 1980, a hijacker entered the cockpit of an Italian aircraft with 89 persons in Rome. He announced that an accomplice had explosives and was ready to blow up the aircraft if 25 prisoners in Tunisia together with several union leaders were not released and arrangements made to fly them to Tripoli, Libya. Since the aircraft was unable to land at Tripoli because of poor weather conditions, it had to be diverted to Palermo, Sicily, where after ten hours of negotiations the hijacker surrendered and requested political asylum. He indicated that he was acting on behalf of a group called "Les Vivants" (the Living), described as a Tunisian political renewal organization.

In a separate incident, 44 armed men boarded an Air Indian aircraft on the ground at Seychelles. The hijackers asked to be flown to Durban, South Africa, where, after six hours of negotiations, the hijackers surrendered and the aircraft crew and 79 passengers were released. The hijackers were part of a group who had arrived at Seychelles Airport from Swaziland in November, 1981. They had forcefully taken the aircraft in an effort to escape capture by security forces. The hijackers received various prison terms for air piracy. Furthermore, on December 7, 1981, a Libyan Arab Airlines B-727 was hijacked during flight from Zurich to Tripoli. The three armed lebanese hijackers diverted the aircraft to Beirut, Lebanon, where they demanded the release of their Shiite Moslem spiritual leader, Imam Musa Sadr, who had disappeared while on a trip to Libya in August, 1978. At Beirut, the hijackers threatened to blow up the aircraft and kill all the passengers on the aircraft if it was not refueled. They shot a male passenger in the foot and after refueling, two male accomplices boarded the aircraft. The airliner was diverted to Athens where it was grounded for three hours before it was flown to Rome where it was again refueled and rediverted to Beirut. At Beirut, the accomplices of the hijackers on the ground seized and held 30 passengers on another airliner as hostages until the hijacked aircraft was refueled and provisioned. After the demands were met, the aircraft took off from Beirut for Tehran where the hijackers restated their demands, refueled, and departed only to return to Beirut for the fourth time. During negotiations, one of the hijackers fired two shots into the air and threatened to blow up the aircraft at various times. However, after 5½ hours of negotiations, the hijackers surrendered on December 10, 1981, to officials of the Arab Deterrent Force in Lebanon. The aircraft took most of the freed passengers and crew to Damascus, Syria.

On February 26, 1982, four or five men seized a domestic Tanzanian airliner 20 minutes after take off. The pilot was forced to divert the aircraft to Nairobi, Jedda, Athens (where the plane was refueled and supplied), and Stansted, England. The hijackers who claimed to be members of the Tanzanian Revolutionary Youth Movement, demanded the resignation of the President of Tanzania. They threatened at various times to blow up the aircraft, kill the 99 persons on board; and even claimed to have killed some of the passengers. During some 26 hours of negotiations at Stansted, the hijackers talked to Tanzanian and British officials restating their demands and threats. However, negotiations were instrumental in the gradual release of all passengers/crew and the surrender of the hijackers and the members of the families accompanying them to the Essex Police. Search by the police revealed that explosives were wired to the doors and restrooms of the aircraft and the hijackers were armed with a pistol, a fake pistol, and a wooden hand grenade. No passenger was killed but the co-pilot was shot in the leg. Similarly, on May 27, 1982, a Moroccan airliner with 100 passengers was seized. The male hijacker boarded the aircraft at Damascus 45 minutes after it left Athens. He commandeered the aircraft by placing a pistol to the head of a flight attendant and demanding to see the captain. At the cockpit, the hijacker who was armed with a gun and grenade, ordered the captain to divert the plane to Tunis, Tunisia. After making various demands for improved morality and strict Islamic faith observance in Morocco, the hijacker allowed

TERRORIST AIRCRAFT HIJACKING AND SABOTAGE   81

the passengers to deplane. An hour of negotiations resulted in the surrender of the hijacker to the Tunisian officials.

Furthermore, on January 20, 1983, an Alyemda Democratic Yemen airliner with 146 persons on board was diverted to Djibouti by three men while enroute from Aden to Kuwait. Two persons on board the aircraft sustained injuries in a gun battle which erupted inside the aircraft while it was on the ground at Djibouti. Negotiations by Djibouti authorities resulted in the surrender of the hijackers. In mid-November, 1983, the hijackers were convicted of air piracy and sentenced to six months in prison. The sentence was later suspended and the culprits set free and placed under surveillance.

Furthermore, a domestic Libyan Arab airliner with 161 persons was hijacked on February 20, 1983, by two men while enroute from Sabha to Benghazi and forced to land at Valletta, Malta. The aircraft was surrounded by Maltese army and police vehicles to prevent it from taking off. During negotiations with Maltese authorities, the hijackers threatened to blow up the aircraft if it was not refueled for a flight to Morocco. The refusal of the Moroccan authorities to accept the hijackers and assurances by Prime Mintoff of Malta that they would be allowed to go to any country of their choice and would not be prosecuted or turned over to the Libyan authorities, convinced the hijackers to release all passengers unharmed. In addition, on June 22, 1983, while enroute from Athens, Greece, to Trysoli, Libya, a Libyan Arab airliner on lease from the Tarom (Romanian) Airline, was hijacked with 23 passengers and 11 crew while enroute from Athens to Trysoli, Libya, by two young men identified as Shiite Moslems. The hijackers were armed with a pistol and a package that appeared to contain explosives. The aircraft was forced to Tehran, Iran. However, on refueling, the aircraft took off instead for Beirut but was not allowed to land. The airliner was subsequently allowed into Larnaca, Cyprus, because it was low on fuel. Seven hours of negotiations resulted in the surrender of the hijackers to the Cyprus authorities. A search of their baggages revealed that a bomb was hidden inside a camera. It was also revealed that the aircraft was seized because the Shiite Moslems in Lebanon believed that Libya was responsible for the disappearance of their Imam (spiritual leader) during a visit to the country in 1978. The two hijackers were sentenced on August 2, 1983, to seven years in prison for hijacking and three years for possession of explosives; all to be served concurrently.

Similarly, on August 27, 1983, four hijackers seized an Air France B-727, Flight 781 with guns and grenades. They demanded the release of Lebanese in French prisons and the withdrawal of French troops from Chad and Lebanon. Finally, on July 5, 1984, a fugitive former Nigerian minister was found by the British police in a crate allegedly bound for Nigeria on a Nigerian airliner on the ground at Stansted airport; and in June, 1985, TWA airline Flight 847 was seized in Turkey and diverted to Beirut and Algiers, back to Beirut and Algiers, and finally to Beirut where the ordeal ended after two weeks.

Extent of Sabotage

The first act of sabotage against an African aircraft occurred in 1969 when two explosions occurred in the tourist class passenger compartment of an Ethiopian airliner at Frankfurt. Although the passengers of the aircraft had deplaned, several women cleaners were injured in the explosions. In June 1969, two armed Eritrean men attacked another Ethiopian aircraft with grenades and submachine guns at Karachi.[5] In the same month, a bomb was discovered in Rome in the lavatory of another Ethiopian aircraft with 39 persons on board. Police authorities used the emergency chute to throw the bomb into a nearby field.[6]

In March 1970, an explosion occurred in the landing gear well of an Egyptian aircraft near Alexandria. The aircraft was extensively damaged and two persons were slightly injured. Similarly, on September 6, 1970, two Popular Front for the Liberation of Palestine guerrillas hijacked a Pan American World Airways aircraft at gun-point at Amsterdam and diverted it to Beirut, Lebanon. A third man boarded at Beirut with demolitions. Following emergency evacuation of crew, passengers, and hijackers, the aircraft was demolished on the ground at Cairo. Several persons were injured in the melee. Furthermore, an attempt to hijack an Ethiopian airliner as it approached Addis Ababa in December, 1972, resulted in the exchange of gun shots between Ethiopian security guards and seven hijackers. Six of the hijackers were killed. The seventh hijacker was seriously wounded but was still able to detonate a hand grenade which tore a 12 to 15-inch diameter hole in the floor of the first class cabin section of the aircraft. The aircraft landed safely but electrical wires/control cables on the airliner were damaged and 11 passengers wounded. In addition, an explosion occurred in a Japanese aircraft in July, 1973 as it was flying over German territory. The woman hijacker was killed and a person wounded. After making stops at Dubai and Damascus, the aircraft landed at Benghazi, Libya, on July 24, 1973. After the passengers and crew were released, an explosion in the cockpit destroyed the entire aircraft.

In another incident, lumps of metal were discovered behind turbo-fan engines of two Nigerian Airways aircraft in April, 1974, in a London airport.[7] In April, 1975, a South African aircraft was hit by bullets as it was landing at the Luanda Airport. Actual damage to the aircraft with 287 passengers was light.[8] Similarly, in December, 1977, members of the Eritrean Liberation Front shelled the Asmara airport. The rebels who are seeking independence from Ethiopia maintained a sporadic bombardment to prevent restoring traffic with Addis Ababa.[9] In May, 1978, a bomb was planted in a Kenyan aircraft at Entebbe Airport. The bomb exploded enroute to Nairobi killing all four persons on board.[10] On February 14, 1979, a Rhodesian aircraft on domestic schedule with 59 passengers was shot at during the flight by unidentified persons.[11] A similar incident occurred the next day resulting in some damage to the aircraft. In March 1979, another Rhodesian aircraft was destroyed by unknown persons at Middle Sabie.[12]

TERRORIST AIRCRAFT HIJACKING AND SABOTAGE 83

Furthermore, an explosion occurred in the early hours of July 7, 1980, at the office of the Libyan Arab Airlines office in Valleta, Malta. The blast completely destroyed the interior of the office and caused substantial damage to the windows and shops adjoining the office. Five months later, a firebomb exploded in the doorway of the Libyan Arab Airlines office in London causing property damage. In both of these incidents, no injuries were reported and no group claimed responsibility for the blasts.[13] Similarly, two parcels exploded in the baggage compartment of an Air Malta aircraft shortly after it arrived at Cairo International Airport on October 13, 1981, killing two persons, injuring eight and severely damaging the baggage compartment of the aircraft. An undetonated bomb was also later discovered.[14] In November, 1980, 44 men seized the control tower in Seychelles and gave landing clearance to an Air Indian Flight. On landing, the armed men entered the aircraft and demanded to be flown to Durban, South Africa.[15]

Similarly, on February 24, 1981, a group of Libyan men opened fire with pistols and machine guns on passengers who had arrived at the customs inspection section at the Fiumicion Airport in Rome from Algiers on a Kuwaiti airliner. Four of the arriving passengers were wounded, one critically. Airport security forces returned fire, wounding one of the alleged assassins and capturing another. The hijackers claimed they were supposed to kill a certain individual but this individual was not on the flight manifest. Obviously, the wounded passengers were victims of mistaken identity as the attack was to be directed against opponents of the Libyan leader, Colonel Qadhafi. The Libyan diplomatic mission in Rome denied that their government was involved in the shooting[16] Similarly, a bomb was discovered on board an Air Tanzania jet at Kilimanjaro airport in March, 1982;[17] and on August 9, 1983, a bomb seriously damaged an Air Algerian office in Marseilles, France. Although there were no injuries reported, a rightist anti-immigration organization called the Charles Martel Group claimed responsibility. Finally, in the early hours of September 17, 1983, a truck bomb exploded at the Leabua Jonathan Airport destroying a cargo building. Although no group claimed responsibility for the bombing, Lesotho officials believed that the Lesotho Liberation Army was responsible.[18]

In sum, from June 1949 to August 1983 there were 92 acts of sabotage directed against aircrafts worldwide. Of these 22 or 23% occurred or impacted on civil aviation in Africa and resulted in the death of more than 1,050 persons worldwide.

Characteristics of Hijacking and Sabotage

The U.S. has the unique distinction of being the country whose aircrafts are most often hijacked and/or sabotaged. For example, of a total of 724 successful/unsuccessful and incomplete hijackings reported worldwide from 1931 to January 1, 1984, 275 (38%) were in the United States alone. In addition, from 1973 to 1983 there were almost 29,000 firearms detected on board U.S. aircraft and 12,000 related arrests.[19]

Acts of sabotage and criminal interference against civil aviation in Africa is small when compared to those directed against countries in the Americas, Western Europe, Asia, and the Middle East. Aircraft hijacking and sabotage incidents involving or impacting African countries/civil aviation show the following trends. In 55 hijacking incidents which impacted on Africa from 1961 to June 22, 1983,[20] ten were terminated or aborted by security forces, 45 were successful. Of the 45 successful hijackings, two required commando attacks to neutralize the hijackers and liberate the hostages; and four required payment of ransom. Of the ten aborted hijackings, four were terminated by security forces in Egypt, three by Ethiopian security authorities and the rest by security officers on aircrafts owned by France, Italy and Philippines. In three of the unsuccessful hijackings, the aircrafts were to be diverted to Libya.

Of the 55 hijackings/attempted hijackings affecting African countries from 1961 to June 22, 1983, seven were directed against aircraft registered in Egypt, six against those registered in Libya and Ethiopia, four against aircraft registered in the U.S., three against airliners registered in Angola and France; and two against aircraft registered in Jordan, Philippines, England, Italy, South Yemen, West Germany, Greece, and the East African Airways. The remaining aircraft were registered in Algeria, Japan, South Africa, Nigeria, Portugal, Morocco, Tanzania, India, Tunisia, and the Netherlands. Indeed, it appears that most hijackings/attempted hijackings which impacted on Africa for the period were directed against aircraft owned or registered in the Arabized States of North Africa and/or aircraft registered in North African countries by Arab-speaking nationals.

Furthermore, of the six hijacking incidents in which the culprits announced plans for diversion before the hijacking was aborted by security forces, Libya was suggested on two occasions. The other countries mentioned were Greece, Israel, Saudi Arabia, and the Ivory Coast. Overall, in 51 hijackings/attempted hijackings in which the hijackers specified the ultimate destinations of aircraft, Libya was specified in ten cases, Egypt in seven, Algeria in four, and Cyprus on three occasions. Malta, Saudi Arabia, Uganda, Tunisia, and the Congo were each mentioned on two occasions; while Morocco, South Yemen, Djibouti, South West Africa, South Africa, Somalia, Spain, Tanzania, Ivory Coast, Malawi, Israel, Yugoslavia, Sudan, Nigeria, Jordan, Lebanon, and the United Kingdom were each specified once as destination of hijacked aircraft.

It appears that Libya, Egypt, and Algeria have the unenviable distinction of being the preferred landing points for hijacked aircrafts. Tripoli and Benghazi in Libya, Cairo in Egypt, and Algiers in Algeria are notorious cities which serve as sanctuaries for hijackers/hijacked aircrafts. For example, in 45 successful hijacking incidents which impacted on Africa from 1961 to June 22, 1983, eight landed in Libya, six in Egypt, four in Algeria, three in Cyprus, two in Malta, the Congo, and Tunisia. The other hijacked

TERRORIST AIRCRAFT HIJACKING AND SABOTAGE 85

airliners landed in Uganda, Morocco, South Africa, Somalia, Tanzania, Ivory Coast, Malawi, Sudan, and Nigeria. Paradoxically, it appears that in recent years most of the hijacking/sabotage of aircraft/aircraft facilities is directed more often against Libya than any other country in Africa.

Furthermore, of the 55 aircraft involved in hijacking incidents in Africa from 1961 to 1983, 30 were registered in African countries, 18 in Europe and North America, two in Jordan, South Yemen and the Philippines and the others in Japan and India. The likelihood that aircraft registered in African countries would be diverted to countries outside the continent is high. For example, 23 aircraft registered in Africa were hijacked successfully from 1961 to 1983. Of these, 12 were diverted to countries in Africa, and 11 to other countries. During the same period, 22 foreign registered airliners were successfully diverted to African countries. Indeed, most foreign registered airliners whose hijacking/attempted hijacking impacted on Africa from 1961 to 1983 were diverted to and from the African continent by Europeans and Arab-speaking nationals.

Records for the period (1961-1983) indicate that African hijackers tended to seize airliners belonging to their countries, and were less likely to take and/or harm hostages than their Arabized/Europe counterparts. In addition, the overwhelming majority of persons involved in hijacking/attempted hijacking which affected Africa from 1961 to 1983 were men. Women accomplices accounted for less than 1%. However, 94% of the hijackers were men with Arab-sounding names.

Furthermore, in 25 recorded incidents of aircraft sabotage which impacted on Africa from 1961 to June 1983, five were directed against Ethiopia, three against Libya and Rhodesia (Zimbabwe), two against Malta, Kenya and Nigeria, and the others against Algeria, Egypt, Lesotho, Tanzania, Seychelles, South Africa, Japan, and the United States. Sabotage was more often directed against airliners registered in Africa than aircraft registered in foreign countries. In addition, sabotage of African aircraft/aircraft facilities occurred were more frequently in Africa than in foreign countries. For example, 15 of 25 acts of sabotage which affected African civil aviation from 1961 to 1983 occurred in African countries, three in London, two in Rome and West Germany and the others in Malta and Karachi. In addition, of the 25 acts of sabotage, 21 were directed against facilities and/or aircrafts owned by African countries and four against foreign aircrafts. The bombs which exploded on board the four foreign aircrafts were planted by non-Africans living outside the continent. However, three of the four explosions on board the four foreign owned aircraft occurred in Cairo, Egypt. Furthermore, sabotage of African aircraft/aircraft facilities occurred more frequently in Africa than in foreign countries. For example, in 21 acts of sabotage against African civil aviation from 1961 to 1983, 12 occurred in Africa and nine in countries outside the region.

Finally, pistols and grenades were the weapons most often used in hijackings/attempted hijackings/sabotage which impacted on Africa from 1961 to 1983. For example, grenades were employed in 16 of 25 acts of sabotage which affected Africa during the period. Some of the other weapons which were used in hijacking incidents include knives, watches, revolvers, dynamites, bombs and nitro-gylcerin.

The motives for hijacking and sabotage of aircraft/aircraft facilities are numerous. These terrorist acts may be committed for personal or private objectives: by a fugitive from justice, the military deserter, the disgruntled spouse, the forlorn adolescent, the escapee from an oppressed society, the real and alleged political offender, the homesick political refugee, and the mentally deranged person. It appears, however, that the hijacking of aircraft and the sabotage of civil aviation facilities in Africa is politically and ideologically motivated. Indeed, the hijacking/attempted hijacking and sabotage incidents which impacted on Africa from 1961 to 1983 were used to accomplish the following purposes: to make politico-ideological statements, as a platform to demand the release of political prisoners, or to call public attention to the culprit's causes, and/or for publicity. The hijacking of a Greek B-727 on July 7, 1970, the German aircraft on October 29, 1972, a Philippine airliner on April 7, 1976, a Tunisian aircraft on January 12, 1979, and January 14, 1980, a Libyan aircraft on December 7, 1981, among others, were used as platforms to demand the release of jailed comrades or other political prisoners. In addition, a Tanzanian airliner was seized on February 26, 1982, by persons claiming to be members of the "Tanzanian Revolutionary Youth Movement" who demanded the resignation of the President of Tanzania. Similarly, the hijackers who seized a Moroccan airliner in May, 1982, called for improved morality and strict Islamic faith observance in the country. Furthermore, most of the hijackers whose activities affected African civil aviation from 1961 to June, 1983, asked for political asylum.

Note must be made that the use of terrorism for attention-getting political objectives is not new to Africa. Indeed, the opening phase of the international terrorist threat we face today is traceable, in part, to Africa. In commenting on this, Fearey said:

> Terrorism as a form of violence for political ends is as old as history, probably older. It is said to have acquired its modern name from the French Reign of Terror of the mid-1790s. The first use of international terrorism is hard to pinpoint. However, . . . historians . . . recall the Moroccan rebel Raisuli's kidnapping of an American and an Englishman in 1904 in a successful attempt to force the American and British governments to pressure France into compelling the Sultan of Morocco to comply with Raisuli's ransom, prisoner release, and other demands.[21]

However, extortion for money does not appear to be a motivating factor for hijacking incidents in Africa. Indeed, hijackers demanded sums of money (ranging from $300,000 to $6 million) on four occasions from 1961 to 1983. The hijackers involved in these cases were non-Africans who made

TERRORIST AIRCRAFT HIJACKING AND SABOTAGE   87

their demands on airliners owned by the United States, the Philippines, and Japan. Note must be made that the money in these cases was recovered from the hijackers and returned to their owner by the authorities in Africa.

The hijacking of aircraft to Africa has resulted in the use of foreign commando forces for the purpose of hostage extraction on only two occasions. These were West German Border Protection Group 9's raid on the aircraft runway in Mogadishu, Somalia, on October 18, 1977; and Israel General Intelligence and Reconnaissance Unit 269's rescue operation at the airport at Entebbe, Uganda, during the first hours of Sunday, July 4, 1976. It appears from these two hijacking incidents that some of the world's most notorious terrorist groups are associated in a loose coalition which has slashed a trail of violence around the world. For example, the seizure and diversion of a Lufthansa airliner to Mogadishu, Somalia, was the joint operation conducted by West German's Red Army Faction (Baader-Meinhof Gang) and a splinter of the Popular Front for the Liberation of Palestine (PFLP) called the "Special Operations Group." Similarly, the Israeli raid onEntebbe, Uganda, was necessitated by the holding of hostages by terrorists associated with the PFLP and the Red Army Faction and linked to "Carlos," an internationally sought terrorist. The group headed by "Carlos the Jackal." a Venezuelan by birth, is a classic example of international terrorist cooperation as it includes Germans, Dutchmen,. Latin Americans, and Arabs.[22]

Prevention and Control of Hijacking/Sabotage

Civil aviation is currently threatened by acts of terrorism in the form of bomb threats, forceful seizure and diversion of aircrafts to places they were not originally scheduled to go. The human, material, and financial cost of aircraft hijacking, and sabotage of civil aviation facilities is enormous. In an attempt to tackle the problem, the governments in Africa have adopted measures to reduce the number of unlawful interference with civil aviation.

African governments are now parties to international conventions (particularly those signed in Tokyo in 1963, Hague in 1970, and Montreal in 1973) which defines acts against international civil aviation as offenses and recommends arrest. investigations, extraditions, and transfer of proceedings from one country to another as measures for combating them. These conventions (see Tables I-III) have paved the way for many of the countries in Africa to pass anti-hijacking, sabotage laws, to refuse landing rights to hijacked aircrafts; to implement airline screening procedures to detect firearms/explosives and/or other incendiary devices; to introduce armed personnel on board aircrafts (especially in Egypt and Ethiopia), and to acquire the necessary technical and scientific knowledge in aviation security. For example, nationals of 23 African countries participated in the first major International Civil Aviation Organization sponsored security technical assistance project in 1983. In addition, fellowships were also

TABLE I: AFRICAN CONTRACTING STATES:
CONVENTION ON OFFENSES AND CERTAIN OTHER ACTS COMMITTED ON BOARD AIRCRAFT
SIGNED AT TOKYO ON 14 SEPTEMBER 1963* AND AS
NOTIFIED TO ICAO UP TO 30 JUNE 1983

States	Date of Signature	Date of Deposit of Instrument of Ratification or Accession	Effective Date
Botswana		16 January 1979	16 April 1979
Burundi		14 July 1971	12 October 1971
Chad		30 June 1970	28 September 1970
Congo	14 September 1963	13 November 1978	11 February 1979
Egypt		12 Feburary 1975	13 May 1975 (1)
Ethiopia		27 March 1979	25 June 1979 (1)
Gabon		14 January 1970	14 April 1970
Gambia		4 January 1979	4 April 1979
Ghana		2 January 1974	2 April 1974
Ivory Coast		3 June 1970	1 September 1970
Kenya		22 June 1970	20 September 1970
Lesotho		28 April 1972	27 July 1972
Liberia	14 September 1963		
Libyan Arab Jamahiriya		21 June 1972	19 September 1972
Madagascar	2 December 1969	2 December 1969	2 March 1970
Malawi		28 December 1972	28 March 1973
Mali		31 May 1971	29 August 1971
Mauritania		30 June 1977	28 September 1977
Mauritius		5 April 1983	4 July 1983
Morocco		21 October 1975	19 January 1976 (2)
Niger	14 April 1969	27 June 1969	4 December 1969
Nigeria	29 June 1965	7 April 1970	6 July 1970
Rwanda		17 May 1971	15 August 1971
Senegal	20 February 1964	9 March 1972	7 June 1972
Seychelles		4 January 1979	4 April 1979
Sierra Leone		9 November 1970	7 February 1971
South Africa		26 May 1972	24 August 1972 (2)
Togo		26 July 1971	24 October 1971
Tunisia		25 February 1975	26 May 1975 (1)
Uganda		25 June 1982	23 September 1982
Upper Volta	14 September 1963	6 June 1982	4 December 1969
Zaire		20 July 1977	18 October 1977
Zambia		14 September 1971	13 December 1971
United Republic		12 August 1983	10 November 1983

*Entered into force on 4 December 1969, in accordance with Article 21, paragraph 1.

(1) Reservation: does not consider itself bound by Article 23, paragraph 1, of the convention.

(2) "In case of a dispute, all recourse must be made to the International Court of Justice on the basis of the unanimous consent of the parties concerned."

given to appropriate African officials to attend training courses at the East African School of Aviation (EASA) in Nairobi and the L'Ecole Africaine de Me'te' rologie et de l'Aviation Civile (EAMAC) in Niamey, Niger.

Despite these provisions, unlawful interference in civil aviation is still a problem in African countries. (Witness the hijacking of TWA Flight 847 to Beirut and Algiers in June, 1984.) The problem of hijacking in Africa has been compounded by lack of technological know how, outmoded security/surveillance equipment, human failure during aircraft/passenger inspection/screening, inadequate training of crew to be able to respond to unlawful interference; and inappropriate facilities in African airports.[23] Therefore, if any meaningful improvement is to be made in Africa against

TERRORIST AIRCRAFT HIJACKING AND SABOTAGE 89

TABLE II: AFRICAN CONTRACTING STATES:
CONVENTION FOR THE SUPPRESSION OF UNLAWFUL SEIZURE OF AIRCRAFT
SIGNED AT THE HAGUE ON 16 DECEMBER 1970* AND AS
NOTIFIED TO ICAO UP TO 30 JUNE 1983

States	Date of Signature	Date of Deposit of Instrument of Ratification or Accession	Effective Date
Benin	5 May 1971	13 March 1972	
Botswana		28 December 1978	
Burundi	17 February 1971		
Cape Verde		20 October 1977	
Chad	27 September 1971	12 July 1972	
Egypt		28 February 1975 (1)	
Ethiopia	16 December 1970	26 March 1979	
Gabon	16 December 1970	14 July 1971	
Gambia	18 May 1971	28 November 1978	
Ghana	16 December 1970	12 December 1973	
Ivory Coast		9 January 1973	
Kenya		11 January 1977	
Lesotho		27 July 1978	
Liberia		1 February 1982	
Libyan Arab Jamahiriya		4 October 1978 (2)	
Malawi		21 December 1972 (1)	
Mali		29 September 1971	
Mauritania		1 November 1978	
Mauritius		25 April 1983	
Morocco		24 October 1975 (1)	
Niger	19 February 1971	15 October 1971	
Nigeria		3 July 1973	
Rwanda	16 December 1970		
Senegal	10 May 1971	8 February 1978	
Seychelles		29 December 1978	
Sierra Leone	19 July 1971	13 November 1974	
South Africa	16 December 1970	30 May 1972 (1)	
Sudan		18 January 1979	
Togo		9 February 1979	
Tunisia		2 December 1981	
Uganda		27 March 1972	
Zaire		6 July 1977	
United Republic of Tanzania		9 August 1983	

*This convention entered into force on 14 October 1971. This list is based on information received from depository states.

(1) Reservation made with respect to paragraph 1 of Article 12 of the convention.
(2) The instrument of accession deposited by the Libyan Arab Jamahiriya contains a disclaimer regarding recognition of Israel.

air-piracy and sabotage, it is imperative that the following steps be intensified:

(1) Inspection and screening of all passengers and cabin baggage prior to departure of all scheduled and non-scheduled flights;

(2) Reduction in the number of cabin baggage alloted to each passenger;

(3) Prohibiting contact and mixing of controlled passengers/uncontrolled persons after security control gates at airports have been passed (i.e., prior to embarkation). If mixing of contact has taken place before the passengers board the aircraft, their persons/cabin baggage should be rechecked;

TABLE III: AFRICAN CONTRACTING STATES:
CONVENTION FOR THE SUPPRESSION OF UNLAWFUL ACTS AGAINST THE
SAFETY OF CIVIL AVIATION SIGNED AT MONTREAL ON
23 SEPTEMBER 1971* AND AS NOTIFIED TO ICAO
UP TO 30 JUNE 1983

States	Date of Signature	Date of Deposit of Instrument of Ratification or Accession	Effective Date
Botswana	12 October 1972	28 December 1978	
Burundi	6 March 1972		
Cape Verde		20 October 1977	
Chad	23 September 1971	12 July 1972	
Congo	23 September 1971		
Egypt	24 November 1972	20 May 1975 (1)	
Ethiopia	23 September 1971	26 March 1979 (1)	
Gabon	24 November 1971	29 June 1976	
Gambia		28 November 1978	
Ghana		12 December 1973	
Ivory Coast		9 January 1973	
Kenya		11 January 1977	
Lesotho		27 July 1978	
Liberia		1 February 1982	
Libya Arab Jamahiriya		19 February 1974	
Malawi		21 December 1972 (1)	
Mali		24 August 1972	
Mauritania		1 November 1978	
Mauritius		25 April 1983	
Morocco		24 October 1975 (2)	
Niger	6 March 1972	1 September 1972	
Nigeria		3 July 1973	
Rwanda	26 June 1972		
Senegal	23 September 1971	3 February 1978	
Seychelles		29 December 1978	
Sierra Leone		20 September 1979	
South Africa	23 Setpember 1971	30 May 1972 (1)	
Sudan		18 January 1979	
Togo		9 February 1979	
Tunisia		2 December 1981 (1)	
Uganda		19 July 1982	
United Republic of Cameroon		11 July 1973 (3)	
Zaire		6 July 1977	
United Republic of Tanzania		9 August 1983	

*This convention entered into force on 26 January 1973. This list is based on information received from depository states

(1) Reservation made with respect to paragraph 1 of Article 14 of the convention.
(2) "In case of a dispute, all recourse must be made to the International Court of Justice on the basis of the unanimous consent of the parties concerned."
(3) "In accordance with the provisions of the Convention of 23 September 1971, for the Suppression of Unlawful Acts directed against the Security of Civil Aviation, the Government of the United Republic of Cameroon declares that in view of the fact that it does not have any relations with South Africa and Portugal, it has no obligation toward these two countries with regard to the implementation of the stipulations of the convention."

TERRORIST AIRCRAFT HIJACKING AND SABOTAGE 91

(4) Guarding and locking all entry points to airport; and strict control of all persons/vehicles requiring access to the facility;

(5) Instituting identification procedures for all personnel/crew/ passengers and others within the vicinity of airport;

(6) Availability of armed guards at all times at the gates and airport terminals;

(7) Frequent and aggressive patrols of airports;[21]

(8) Use of dogs to complement/supplement security devices/personnel in detecting explosives or incendiary materials;

(9) Updating equipment and upgrading air carrier personnel training programs;

(10) Cooperating with and sharing of responsibilities among airlines, airport authorities, governments, and the passengers in order to meet current security needs and respond to threats to civil aviation;

(11) Establishing in each country a "third force"—a specialized unit capable of launching operations to neutralize hijackers and/or available to supplement local law enforcement efforts. The "third force" could be similar to the U.S. Army strike force (the Delta Force) and the FBI Special Weapons Tactics Teams (SWAT).

Finally, the governments in Africa must maintain and train a team of hostage negotiators and post-trauma psychiatrists/psychologists. Hostage negotiators must be multilingual.

Conclusion

There has been some improvement in the security of civil aviation in Africa in the past several years. In spite of this improvement, a myriad of solutions is needed to meet the challenge of aircraft piracy and unlawful interference in civil aviation. Although helpful, engineering and mechanical improvements generally do not provide a complete solution. Therefore, efforts must be made to resolve the socioeconomic and political problems which may have been, in part, responsible for the criminal acts perpetrated against civil aviation. Until this is done, efforts designed to stem the wave of hijacking/sabotage would be largely in vain. We should expect, therefore, that civil aviation will remain a desireable and vulnerable target for the political zealot, the self-styled crusader, the religious fanatic, the mentally disturbed, the fugitive offender, the holy warrior, and other criminal and terroristic elements. The world community must catch up with this modernization of barbarism before it is victimized by acts of terrorism and hijacking as yet only imagined.

ACKNOWLEDGMENT

I wish to acknowledge the assistance of John Marrett (Chief, Aviation Security Section, International Civil Aviation Organization, Montreal, Canada) and Alan W. Read (Manager, Aviation Security Division, Office of Civil Aviation Security, Federal Aviation Administration, U.S. Department of Transportation, Washington, D.C.) for their assistance in data collection from which this manuscript was developed.

NOTES

[1]"The ICAO Programming for Safeguarding International Civil Aviation Against Acts of Unlawful Interference." Fourth Asia/PAC Aviation Security Seminar, Bangkok, November 14-18, 1983, pp. 4, 38-42.

[2]"Worldwide Significant Criminal Acts Involving Civil Aviation," U.S. Department of Transportation, Federal Aviation Authority, Office of Civil Aviation, U.S. Department of Transportation, Federal Aviation Authority (FAA), January-December, 1983, May 1983, p.1.

[3]"Explosion Aboard Aircraft," U.S. Department of Transportation, FAA, Office of Civil Aviation, Updated January 1, 1984, p. 13.

[4]Except otherwise stated, the materials used in this section of the paper were drawn from: (1) "International Civil Aviation Organization: Chronology of Unlawful Interference with Civil Aviation 1969-1983," International Civil Aviation Organization, Montreal, Canada, 1969-1983; (2) "Chronology Hijackings of U.S. Registered Aircraft and Legal Status of Hijackers, 1961-1983," Department of Transportation, FAA—Office of Civil Aviation Security, Updated: January 1, 1984; (3) "U.S. and Foreign Registered Aircraft Hijackings 1947-1983," Department of Transportation, FAA—Office of Civil Aviation Security, Updated: January 1, 1984; (4) "Worldwide Significant Criminal Acts Involving Civil Aviation, January-December 1980-May 1984," Department of Transportation, FAA-Office of Civil Aviation Security, Washington, D.C. 1947-1983; (5) "Aircraft Hijackings and Other Criminal Acts Against Civil Aviation Statistical and Narrative Reports 1961-1983," Department of Transportation, FAA—Office of Civil Aviation Security, Washington, D.C.; Updated to January 1, 1984, May 1984; and (6) "Semiannual Report to Congress on the Effectiveness of the Civil Aviation Security Program," July 1-December 31, 1983, April 1984.

[5]"International Civil Aviation Organization: Chronology of Unlawful Interference with Civil Aviation," ICAO, Montreal,Canada, 1969, p. 6.

[6]Ibid., 1970, p. 2.

[7]Ibid., 1974, p. 3.

[8]Ibid., 1975, p. 2.

[9]Ibid., 1977, p. 9.

[10]Ibid., 1978, p. 4.

[11]Ibid., 1979, pp. 1, 2.

[12]Ibid.

[13]"Worldwide Significant Criminal Acts Involving Civil Aviation," January-December 1980, Department of Transportation, FAA—Office of Civil Aviation Security, 1980, pp. 10, 23.

[14]"International Civil Aviation Organization: Chronology of Unlawful Interference with Civil Aviation," ICAO, Montreal, Canada, 1981, p. 12.

[15]Ibid., p. 14.

[16]"Worldwide Significant Criminal Acts Involving Civil Aviation," January-December 1981, p. 3.

[17]"International Civil Aviation Organization: Chronology of Unlawful Interference with Civil Aviation," ICAO, Montreal, Canada, 1982, p. 9.

[18]"Worldwide Significant Criminal Acts Involving Civil Aviation," January-December 1983, pp. 15, 18.

TERRORIST AIRCRAFT HIJACKING AND SABOTAGE 93

[19]"Semiannual Report to Congress," pp. 7-9, and 12.

[20]See note #4 for data sources.

[21]Robert A. Fearey, "International Terrorism," in J.B. Wolf, *Fear of Fear: A Survey of Terrorist Operations and Control in Open Societies,* New York: Plenum Press, 1981, p. 202.

[22]John W. Wolf, "Anti-Terrorism: Operations and Controls in a Free Society," *Police Studies: International Review of Police Development,* Volume 1, No. 3, 1978, p. 35.

[23]International Criminal Police Organization-Interpol, 46th General Assembly Session, Committee on International Civil Aviation, Stockholm, September 1-8, 1977, p. 6.

[24]"Resolutions Adopted by the International Civil Aviation Organization Council on 2 December 1971," Fourth ASIA/PAC Aviation Security Seminar," The ICAO Programming for Safeguarding International Aviation Against Acts of Unlawful Interference, Bangkok, November 14-18, 1983, p. 18.

The Entebbe Hijacking
and Rescue

[4]

The Entebbe Rescue Mission:
A Case of Aggression?

ADEOYE A. AKINSANYA

The Entebbe Rescue Mission and the Stanleyville Rescue (Peace Mercy) Mission have similar parallels in the history of Africa's international relations. First, both missions were staged and launched by foreign powers. Second, both missions were condemned and applauded in many quarters. With respect to the latter mission Radio Algiers was very blunt: "The premeditation [was] obvious and the distinctive aggression against the people of the Congo cannot otherwise be hidden by hypocritical statements."[1] Radio Cairo contended that "the question of the white hostages was only a farce and an excuse for aggression." To Nkrumah's Ghana, the "sneak attack" appeared to be designed to maintain the West's hold on the Congo's mineral wealth. In the same vein, the Government of Benin Republic (Dahomey) issued a communique accusing "Belgian and American parachutists" of "indisputable aggression." The communique continued:

> The humanitarian motives do not appear very convincing to us. The true reason . . . was undoubtedly the existence of deposits of uranium. Without supporting in any way the massacre of the hostages by the rebels in Stanleyville, the government finds it difficult to understand why civilized countries, which have remained indifferent before the corpses of millions of black Congolese citizens for four years, have suddenly taken the initiative to alert international opinion and put

---

Adeoye A. Akinsanya teaches both at the University of South Carolina in Columbia, and at the University of Lagos, Nigeria.

0095-4993/82/0902-0046·$1 00

forward humanitarian motives to justify a carefully prepared aggression, just because the fate of a few Europeans was involved.[2]

On the other hand, several African countries, notably, Nigeria, Liberia and West and Equatorial African states were full of praise and sympathy for the so-called Peace Mercy Mission, regarding it as a good humanitarian gesture.[3] Member-states of the Organization of African Unity, attending an urgent meeting of the United Nations Security Council on the matter,[4] not only regarded the mission as an outrage, indeed, a criminal act and a violation of the sovereignty and territorial integrity of Uganda, but also a naked act of aggression. The Western Powers and press, however, were full of support for the Entebbe Mission. They regarded the mission as "a timely rescue conducted within the confines of international law to save absolutely innocent people from suffering and death arising from international terrorism.[5] The third parallel is that both missions were staged and launched to release hostages held by terrorist groups.

This paper, which attempts to examine some issues raised by the Entebbe Rescue Mission, is divided into five parts: Part I looks at the circumstances leading to the Israeli action; Part II considers the incidence of aircraft hijacking and international efforts at controlling aircraft hijacking; Part III focuses on intervention, while Part IV attempts a justification of the Israeli action; Part V examines the view that the Rescue Mission was essentially a "naked act of aggression."

I

On Sunday morning, June 27, 1976, a French Jumbo Jet (Flight 139) with 245 passengers and 12 crew left Tel-Aviv for Paris, stopping in Athens, Greece. On leaving

Athens, it was announced over the plane's internal communications system that Air France was under the *control* of members of the "Che Guevara Group" and the "Gaza Unit" of the Popular Front for the Liberation of Palestine (PFLP), led by Dr. Wadi Hadad.[6] Put simply, Air France had been hijacked, apparently because of lax security measures at the Athens Airport. Some time later the plane landed at Benghazi, Libya. It left after more than six hours on the ground, presumably because the authorities would not provide sanctuary to the hijackers, but more likely because Uganda invited it, although the Ugandan authorities contended that the hijacked plane was allowed to land at the Entebbe Airport only on "humanitarian considerations." According to Heyman,[7] the hijackers were "armed." They were alleged to have had high explosives ("placed at exit doors of the aircraft"), hand grenades and automatic weapons. Shortly after taking over command of the plane, they collected the passports of all passengers.

On June 29, the price of freedom of the hostages was set and announced by the terrorists. They requested the release of fifty-three convicted terrorists—40 in Israel, 6 in the Federal Republic of Germany, 5 in Kenya and 1 each in France and Switzerland. July 1st, at 2 p.m. East African Time or 1100 hours GMT was set as a deadline for the release of the convicted terrorists to the custody of the Ugandan authorities. Otherwise the plane would be blown up, the hostages with it. On June 30, the hijackers released 47 hostages including the old, the sick and some children, and on arrival in Paris late that night, they gave real warning of the danger to the lives of the remaining hostages. After much persuasion, the hijackers released 101 hostages who were non-Jews and extended the deadline to July 4th, 2 p.m. East African Time or 1100 hours GMT. In essence, only passengers with Israeli nationality or Jewish connections remained in terrorists' hands. While the Israeli Government declared its readiness to release convicted terrorists in Israeli prisons, the hijackers made further demands. They announced that Israel would be held responsible for the release of all convicted terrorists, including those not held in Israel. They also refused to allow the exchange to be made in France or on a neutral territory outside Uganda. It has been alleged that the Israeli Government gave the impression of negotiating but prolonged the process so that it had time to plan a rescue mission. This may well be true. This is not the point of controversy. It would appear that the Israeli Government had no other option than to launch a rescue mission because it was concerned about the imminent danger to the lives of its nationals. More importantly, it had convinced itself that terrorism was war without formal declaration, and that other nations preferred to shy away from taking precautions and frustrating international terrorism.

On July 4 at 2120 hours GMT three transport planes

with Israeli paratroopers and a Special Military Commando Unit landed by surprise at Entebbe, and in a 36-minute operation released all the remaining 110 hostages held by the terrorists, killing a number of Ugandan soldiers and seven hijackers, and destroying a number of Ugandan military planes, perhaps to prevent any possible "hot pursuit."

II

Undoubtedly, civil aviation is currently threatened by acts of terrorism, ranging from bomb threats against aircraft in flight to seizures of aircraft and their diversion to destinations other than those for which they were originally scheduled.[8] Table 1 shows that there were 343 successful and unsuccessful acts of international and domestic hijacking between 1961 and 1972. If attempted hijackings in the United States and abroad are added, 396 flights were endangered during this period. In 1968 alone, twenty seven aircraft carrying 1,490 passengers were diverted from their scheduled routes by threat or force. During 1969 to 1970, eighty nine aircraft involving 4,519 passengers were hijacked. In fact, the data shows a marked increase from 1968 to 1972. The record for the first eight months of 1973 shows that there were five attempts at hijacking in the United States, two hijacking attempts abroad, eight successful international and domestic hijackings abroad, and one unsuccessful domestic hijacking, bringing the number of flights endangered during this period to sixteen. Table 2 indicates that the United States has been the principal victim of air hijacking between 1961 and 1972. During this period, 157 aircraft of United States registration were successfully or unsuccessfully hijacked. These included 91 flights diverted from the United States to foreign countries. Outside the United States, over two hundred aircraft were successfully or unsuccessfully hijacked between January 1961 and August 1973. Among countries that have had 5 or more hijackings are: Argentina 8, Brazil 10, Canada 5, Colombia 25, Cuba 5, Czechoslovakia 6, Ecuador 5, Egypt 5, Ethiopia 5, Greece 5, Japan 5, Mexico 10, Poland 7, Soviet Union 8, and Venezuela 7. As to the ultimate destinations for hijacked flights, Cuba topped the list, having given 149 hijacked flights landing permits. Forty-five other states and four areas have provided sanctuaries for hijackers' but four hijacked aircraft were refused landing permits in the state of first choice and had to find another destination.[10]

What are the motives for air hijacking? According to one observer:

Where the acts had been committed almost entirely for what may be described as "personal" or "private" objectives—by the fugitive from justice, the military deserter, the disgruntled

Table 1.—Air Hijackings Worldwide

	International	Domestic	Total
1961	6	4	10
1962	1	2	3
1963	1	0	1
1964	1	1	2
1965	0	5	5
1966	2	2	4
1967	5	1	6
1968	28	7	35
1969	75	13	88
1970	60	23	83
1971	29	19	48
1972	28	30	58
1961-1972	236	107	343

Source: A. E. Evans. "Aircraft Hijackings: What Is Being Done," in *International Terrorism and Political Crimes,* edited by M. C. Bassiouni (Springfield, Ill.: Charles C. Thomas, 1975), p. 211.

Table 2.—Hijacking of United States Aircraft

	International	Domestic	Total
1961	2	2	4
1962	1	1	2
1963	0	0	0
1964	1	0	1
1965	0	4	4
1966	0	0	0
1967	1	0	1
1968	17	3	20
1969	31	6	37
1970	15	8	23
1971	12	11	23
1972	11	19	30
1961-1972	91	54	154

Source: Alona, p. 222

Table 3.—Comparisons of Hijackings

	U.S.A.	Abroad
1968	20	15
1969	37	51
1970	23	60
1971	23	25
1972	28	28

Source: A. E. Evans. "Aircraft Hijackings: What is Being Done," in *International Terrorism and Political Crimes.* ed. be M. C. Bassiouni (Springfield, Illinois: Charles C. Thomas, 1975), p. 234, note 50.

spouse, the forlorn adolescent, the escapee from an oppressive society, the real or alleged political offender, the homesick political refugee, the mentally deranged person—from 1968 on, hijacking evolved into the weapon or the platform, of persons acting for 'public' or 'political reason.'"[11]

Thus, the reasons for air hijacking are legion, but a majority are ideologically or politically motivated.

Terrorist or guerilla and left-wing groups have used hijacking as an avenue for the extortion of money, or the release of "political" prisoners, or for publicity for their causes. The Popular Front for the Liberation of Palestine (PFLP), which hijacked Air France (Flight 139) on June 27, 1976, initiated the use of hijacking for blackmail when they diverted an El Al (Israeli) airplane to Algeria in July 1968. After forty days' detention, twelve Israeli passengers and crew members and the aircraft were released by Algeria in exchange for sixteen convicted members of Al-Fatah and other Arab guerilla groups in Israeli prisons. The PFLP has been able to secure the release of seventy eight of its members, of whom 16, convicted of terrorism including murder, assault and wilful destruction of aircraft and related ground facilities, were imprisoned in Greece, Switzerland, and the Federal Republic of Germany. More important, the hijacking of El Al in July 1968, was followed over the next eight years by more than sixteen successful and unsuccessful hijackings by the PFLP.

By the late sixties, hijacking was being used as a vehicle for financing international terrorism. What we are saying here is that hijacking was being used for the purpose of extorting money from the carrier, and in some instances, aircraft have been hijacked for the purpose of robbing the passengers and the crew or because the hijackers had advance information that an aircraft was being used to convey large sums of money.[12] In any event, none of the twenty-two hijacking incidents during the period 1970-1972 in the United States appeared to have been politically motivated:[13]

Hijackers demanded sums of money ranging from $50,000 to $2,000,000. In one instance the demand included fifteen pounds of gold (then valued at about $8,000). In eight instances, the extortionists asked for parachutes and bailed out of the hijacked aircraft; seven were subsequently captured with their loot. In four instances, the extortionists successfully hijacked the aircraft to a foreign destination.[14]

In 18 out of these 22 extortion-related hijackings the hijackers surrendered, were overpowered, captured or killed, and the money recovered in 20 instances. Overseas, extortion was the principal motive for successful or unsuccessful hijacking of aircraft of foreign registration between May 1971 and January 1975. Of the groups which organized three of these hijackings, only the Popular Front for the Liberation of Palestine (PFLP) was successful in keeping what it demanded and received from Lufthansa Airlines in February 1972, $5 million. In one instance, a $15 million ransom for a hijacked JAL plane by the PFLP was rejected by the carrier, and as a result the plane was blown up on the runway of Benghazi Airport.

Undoubtedly the costs of hijacking, in terms of human lives lost and properties destroyed, have been enormous. More than 200 persons—passengers, crew, ground personnel, police and hijackers—have been killed or injured in the United States and abroad in the course of efforts to thwart a hijacking or apprehend the hijacker. Human lives have been lost as a result of mid-air collisions or crashes in the course of hijacking attempts. Hijacked aircraft have been blown up because of slow or negative responses to hijackers' demands. For example, to demonstrate their determination to secure the release of its convicted members in many countries and dramatize their cause, the PFLP destroyed four aircraft of U.S., Swiss, and United Kingdom registration in *one* week in September 1970, and in July 1973, it also destroyed a JAL Boeing 747 at Benghazi, apparently because the carrier rejected a ransom of $15 million. In 1970 alone, some $60 million worth of property damage was suffered due to destruction of aircraft. While the losses suffered following the diversion of aircraft and crew from commercial service are staggering, the anguish imposed on innocent passengers was, by any measure, incalculable. Other problems were personal injury to passengers and crew, interruption to communications, changing flight paths and alteration of landing destinations.

Just what efforts are made at the international level to combat the dangers of air hijacking? Until 1969, when hijackings abroad exceeded those originating in the United States (see Table 3), air hijacking appeared to be treated as a manifestation of the strained relations between the United States and Cuba.[15] When the Popular Front for the Liberation of Palestine hijacked and destroyed four aircraft within a week in September 1970 nations felt an urgent need for international measures at dealing with the grave dangers of hijacking. Within three months a Convention for the Suppression of Unlawful Seizure of Aircraft was signed at The Hague (December 16, 1970), and entered into force on October 14, 1971.[16] That the States Parties to the Convention were conscious of the grave dangers of air hijacking and also of the urgent need to deter air hijacking and punish perpetrators of such acts was reflected in the Preamble to the Convention:

THE STATES PARTIES TO THIS CONVENTION CONSIDERING

that unlawful acts of seizure or exercise of control of aircraft in flight jeopardize the safety of persons and property, seriously affect the operation of air services, and undermine the confidence of the peoples of the world in the safety of civil aviation;

CONSIDERING that the occurrence of such acts is a matter of grave concern;

CONSIDERING that, for the purpose of deterring such acts, there is an urgent need to provide appropriate measures for punishment of offenders.

Article 1 of the Convention states that

Any person who on board an aircraft in flight:
(a) unlawfully, by force or threat itself, or by any other form of intimidation, seizes, or exercises control of that aircraft, or attempts to perform any such act, or
(b) is an accomplice of a person who performs or attempts to perform any such act commits an offense (hereinafter referred to as "the offense").

Several provisions of the Convention are germane to our study here. Article 2 provides that "Each Contracting State undertakes to make" hijacking "punishable by severe penalties." Article 6(1) which states, *inter alia:*

Upon being satisfied that the circumstances so warrant, any Contracting State in the territory of which the offender or the alleged offender is present, shall take him into custody or take other measures to ensure his presence. The custody and other measures shall be provided in the law of the State but may only be continued for such time as is necessary to enable any criminal or extradition proceedings to be instituted.

If the hijacker is not extradited to the State of registration of the aircraft, Article 7 of the Convention states that

The Contracting State in the territory of which the alleged offender is found shall . . . be obliged, without exception whatsoever and whether or not the offense was committed in its territory, to submit the case of its competent authorities for the purpose of prosecution. Those authorities shall take their decision in the same manner as in the case of any ordinary offense of a serious nature under the law of that state.

Most significant is article 9 which provides thus:

1. When any of the acts mentioned in Article 1(a) has occurred or is about to occur, Con-

tracting States shall take all appropriate measures to restore control of the aircraft to its lawful commander or to preserve his control of the aircraft.

2. In the cases contemplated by the preceding paragraph, any Contracting State in which the aircraft or its passengers or crew are present shall facilitate the continuation of the journey of the passengers and the crew as soon as practicable, and shall without delay return the aircraft and its cargo to the persons lawfully entitled to possession.

Essentially, the Hague Convention for the Suppression of Unlawful Seizure of Aircraft is punitive in focus, directing States to extradite and/or prosecute hijackers.[17] In a situation involving an individual's search for political asylum, the State providing political asylum has a hard decision to make about the disposition of the hijacker, particularly if such a state is a party to the Hague Convention and/or the 1951 Convention Relating to the Status of Refugees, and given the fact that "wars of national liberation" serve as an excuse for and as the genuine *raison d'etre* for political hijackings.

Because the Hague Convention for the Suppression of Unlawful Seizure of Aircraft or the Montreal Convention for the Suppression of Unlawful Acts Against the Safety of Civil Aviation (not yet entered into force) has not reduced the incidence or the spate of hijackings,[18] many States have resorted to bilateral agreements, unilateral actions of *self-help* to deter hijackers, and enacted legislation providing severe penalties for hijackers. Following a spate of hijackings of aircraft of United States registration. the following actions were taken to combat the dangers of hijacking:

1. The 1958 Federal Aviation Act was amended. making "aircraft piracy" punishable by penalties ranging from a minimum of 20 years imprisonment to death.
2. Aircraft carriers are authorized by the Civil Aeronautics Board to deny transportation to any person refusing to permit a search of his person or luggage. This regulation applies to persons entitled to diplomatic immunity.
3. Airport ticket counters and boarding areas post notices to the effect that hijacking and the carrying of concealed weapons on board aircraft are federal crimes. and that passengers are liable to search.
4. Electronic surveillance was instituted by aircraft carriers while airport personnel were taught in the use of a "behavioral profile" or compilation of psychological characteristics devised by the Federal Aviation Administration as a way of identifying potential hijackers.

5. Under the "sky marshal" program, federal officers were placed on duty in aircraft on long-distance flights.[19]

Some of these measures had positive results, namely, in reducing the number of successful international and domestic hijackings of United States aircraft. The presence of "sky marshals" did not effectively deter hijacking because of the dangers of shoot-out in mid-air between the hijackers and "sky marshals." In one instance, a passenger who fitted a psychological profile devised by the FAA, and who was searched before boarding, hijacked an aircraft to Honduras, having concealed a weapon in a book.

In the Peoples Republic of China, an Aviation Law calling for the death penalty for hijackers includes the following provisions: (a) hijacking of airplanes is punishable by penalties ranging from life imprisonment or twenty years' imprisonment to death; (b) interference with aviation by means of violence or threat is punishable by death, life imprisonment, prison detention or a fine of NT $15,000; (c) damage to aircraft and airport facilities is punishable by at least five years' imprisonment; (d) riding aircraft with concealed weapons or other items endangering aircraft is punishable by at least a year's imprisonment, detention, or a fine of NT$6,000; and (e) death or injury due to hijacking is punishable by penalties ranging from death, life imprisonment to ten years' imprisonment.[20]

The United States and some other countries have not only become strong proponents of a "sanction convention" providing for a Commission of Experts to hear complaints against States detaining hijacked planes or failing to prosecute or extradite hijackers. More often than not they have advocated the use of *limited* force on humanitarian grounds for the protection of one's own nationals from an imminent threat of injury or death in a situation where the State in whose territory a hijacked plane is allowed to land is either unwilling or unable to protect them. From a cursory look, it would appear that the foundation for the Entebbe Rescue Mission was laid on this policy.

III

Intervention. to Richard A. Falk of Princeton University, refers to conduct with an external *animus* that credibly intends to achieve a fundamental alteration of the state of affairs in the target nation.[21] It is, according to another scholar,

organized and systematic activities across recognized boundaries aimed at affecting the political authority structures of the target.[22]

Thus, interventions occur across State's borders with the goal of affecting the state of affairs in the other. Absent from these definitions are more specific features such as a statement of objectives, post-hoc justifications for actions or any time dimension. This void is filled by Urs Schwarz who defines "intervention" as actions in which:

> a superior power, a nation or an international organization, transcends the framework of the existing relations and attempts to impose its will on a weaker nation in defence of some concept of political, moral or legal action, and with a limited duration in mind.[23]

In essence, states have intervened in the affairs of one another for a myriad of reasons: self-preservation; redressing wrong-doing; protecting the lives and property of its nationals; redeeming national honor; intervention on humanitarian grounds; invitation to the intervening state, among others.

Intervention is a very old concept in international law, and it is traceable to Vattel, the eighteenth century Swiss jurist in his *Le Droit des Gens*, published in 1758. Although Hugo Grotius (1583-1645) did not make mention of the term in his classic work, *De Jure Belli ac Pacis*, published in 1625, this was probably because to him there could be no midway between war and peace, and therefore, "intervention" is *war*. Over the years, the technical meaning which intervention has come to acquire, is

> dictatorial interference by a state in the affairs of another state irrespective of the will of the latter, for the purpose of either maintaining or altering the condition of things.[24]

In general, intervention, being a violation of another state's independence and territorial integrity, is contrary to international law. Thus, any act of intervention must be justified as a legitimate act of reprisal, self-defence, protection of nationals abroad or it is authorized under a treaty with the state concerned.

Three types of intervention have been distinguished by classical international law. Internal intervention, takes place when State A intervenes in the internal politics of State B with a view to carrying out operations which State B is *disabled* from performing. In the case of external intervention, a state interferes in the hostile relations of two or more states without any invitation. Punitive intervention is a form of reprisal by one state against another, the purpose being to seek redress for a wrong done either to the nationals of the intervening state, or for a breach of treaty obligations, or to protect national honor which had been called into question.

IV

Undoubtedly, intervention is a violation of the independence and territorial inviolability (or integrity) of

another state, and therefore, contrary to international law. Nevertheless, traditional international law permitted the right of intervention or the resort to the use of armed force in certain circumstances. Intervention involving the use of armed force is permissible where there is an armed attack by one state against another. Article 51 of the United Nations Charter is very explicit:

> Nothing in the present Charter shall impair the inherent right of individual or collective self-defence if an armed attack occurs against a member of the United Nations until the Security Council has taken measures necessary to maintain international peace and security.

Thus, a state atacked by another state has a right to retaliate by force in self defence. Intervention involving the use of armed force is permissible when the United Nations takes collective action against any member-state committing acts of aggression. The Security Council, acting under Article 39 of the Charter, must determine the

> existence of any threat to the peace, breach of the peace, or act of aggression and shall make recommendations, or decide what measures shall be taken in accordance with Articles 41 and 42 to maintain or restore international peace and security.

Where the Security Council is unable to exercise the powers of collective self-defence because of veto power exercised by any of the "big five," the General Assembly, under the "Acheson Plan" (Uniting for Peace Resolution), has residual responsibility to recommend military measures which members can or may take in the exercise of the right of self-defence under Article 51 of the United Nations Charter.

It would appear then that a State may resort to the use of armed force only in *two* circumstances. Does it mean that a State has no recourse to the use of armed force under any other circumstances? The right of a State to intervene by the use or threat of force for the protection of its nationals abroad whose lives and property are imperilled is generally admitted in international jurisprudence, the writings of publicists, and in the practice of states. In the *Spanish Moroccan Claims* (1925) the Rapporteur of the Commission, Judge Max Huber, has noted:

> However, it cannot be denied that at a certain point the interest of a state in exercising protection over its nationals and their property can take precedence over territorial sovereignty, despite the absence of any conventional provisions. This right of intervention has been claimed by all states; only its limits are disputed.[25]

In the same vein, Oppenheim has stated:

> The right of protection over citizens abroad,
> which a state holds, may cause an intervention by
> right to which the other party is legally bound to
> submit. And it matters not whether the protection
> of the life, security, honor or property of a citizen
> is concerned.[26]

Since it is the duty of every sovereign State to protect
nationals and aliens alike,

> In certain cases, where diplomatic protection in
> the sense of diplomatic interposition or of the
> presentation of a claim on behalf of a national by
> his State has either failed or is inadequate to pre-
> vent an immediate danger to life or property
> which would otherwise be irremedial, states have
> resorted to the threat or use of force as a means of
> protection.[27]

One authority has observed:

> We now envisage action by the protecting State
> which involves a prima facie violation of the in-
> dependence and territorial inviolability of the ter-
> ritorial State. In so far as this action takes effect in
> derogation of the sovereignty of the territorial
> state it must necessarily be *exceptional in
> character and limited to those cases in which no
> other means of protection are available.* It presup-
> poses the inadequacy of any other means of pro-
> tection against some injury, actual or imminent,
> to the persons or property of nationals and,
> moreover, an injury which results either from the
> acts of the territorial State and its authorities or
> from the acts of individuals or groups of in-
> dividuals which the territorial state is unable, or
> unwilling to prevent.[28]

What Bowett seems to be saying here is that in exercis-
ing its rights of intervention to protect its nationals
whose lives are imperilled, the degree of physical force
employed in the protection of such nationals must be
proportional to the situation.

Other writers have recognized the right of a state to
take military action in defence of its nationals in mortal
danger. For example, Brierly has this to say:

> Whether the landing of detachments of troops to
> save the lives of nationals under imminent threat
> of death or of serious injury owing to the
> breakdown of law and order may be justifiable is a
> delicate question. Cases of this form of interven-
> tion have not been infrequent in the past and,
> when not attended by suspicion of being a pretext
> for political pressure, have generally been re-

> garded as justified by sheer necessity of instant ac-
> tion to save the lives of innocent nationals, whom
> the local government is unable or unwilling to pro-
> tect.[29]

He added:

> Every effort must be made to get the United Na-
> tions to act. But if the United Nations is not in a
> position to move in time and the need for instant
> action is manifest, it would be difficult to deny the
> legitimacy of action in defence of nationals which
> every responsible government would feel bound to
> take, if it had the means to do so; this is, of
> course, on the basis that the action was strictly
> limited to securing the safe removal of the
> threatened nationals.[30]

Writing on the same issue, O'Connell makes the point
that:

> Traditional international law has not prohibited
> States from protecting their nationals whose lives
> or property are imperilled by political conditions
> in another State, provided the degree of physical
> presence employed in their protection is propor-
> tional to the situation. When the Sixth Interna-
> tional Conference of American States at Havana
> attempted to formulate a legal notion of interven-
> tion in 1928, the United States pointed out that in-
> tervention would need to be clearly defined, for
> the United States would not stand by and permit
> the breakdown of government to endanger the
> lives and property of American citizens in
> revolution-ridden countries. Interposition of a
> temporary character would not, in such cir-
> cumstances, it was argued, be illegal.[31]

He maintained, and this is very significant:

> Article 2(4) of the United Nations Charter should
> be interpreted as prohibiting acts of force against
> the territorial integrity and political independence
> of nations, and not to prohibit a use of force
> which is limited in intention and effect to the pro-
> tection of a State's own integrity and its nationals'
> vital interests, when the machinery envisaged by
> the United Nations Charter is ineffective in the
> situation.[32]

Once again, the degree of physical violence employed in
the process of protecting nationals in *mortal* danger
must be proportional to the situation.

It has been asserted that the protection of the nationals of the state is in effect the protection of the state
per se. By implication, an injury to the nationals of the
state is an injury to the state itself; thus, the protection
of nationals, whether within or without the territorial

jurisdiction of the state, is in *essence* the defence of the state itself, and an essential function of the state. To be sure, writers have deduced the right of protection from the fundamental right of self-preservation or defined an attack on the state as including "all violations of the legal rights of itself or its subjects."

However, the view that an injury to the nationals of the state is an injury to the state *per se*, however attractive theoretically, tends to obscure the real basis of the right of self-defence. While it cannot be claimed that a threat to the safety of nationals abroad constitutes a threat to the security of the state,

yet there may be occasions when the threat of danger is great enough, or wide enough in its application to a sizable community abroad, for it to be legitimately construed as an attack on the state itself.[33]

However,

The measures of self-defence, or protection, must be proportionate to the danger, actual or imminent, to the nationals in need of protection. It follows, therefore, that action in self-defence must be conditioned by respect for the equal rights of states, and . . . must not be . . . 'unreasonable or excessive . . . [but] justified by the necessity of self-defence . . . limited by that necessity and kept clearly within it.'[34]

Although a large-scale naval demonstration or the landing of paratroopers could never be justified as action in the defence of a *single* national, since such action would be to totally disregard the rights of the territorial state by the disproportionate exercise of the rights of the intervening state, such action would be justified if the lives of a large number of its nationals are in *imminent* and *mortal* danger, and then the magnitude of the danger to its nationals would have satisfied the requirement of proportionality. In essence, if the intervening state is motivated by factors other than the need for protection, the measures of protection cease to be within the concept of self-defence.

The practices of the United States, Great Britain and France provide the greatest sources of instances of the use of force in the protection of the lives and property of their nationals. For example, a few months before the Entebbe Rescue Mission, thirty French children in a school bus were held as hostages by a group of terrorists on the Somali border. They announced the price of freedom for these children, threatening to cut their throats if their demands were not met. As a result, French forces took action against the terrorists on the Somali border, killing them and freeing the hostages. The right of self-defence was asserted in the well-known *Caroline Case (1837), and the Mayaguez* incident (1975).

In effect, the Entebbe Rescue Mission could be justified on many grounds. The first is the need to protect Israeli nationals whose lives are in *imminent* and *mortal* danger, a duty which the territorial state either denied or found impossible to fulfill. Second, international precedent seems to justify the Israeli action. Third, by failing to secure the release of the passengers, and indeed, by failing to protect foreign nationals on its territory, Uganda violated a basic tenet of international law. By failing to protect the hostages held by the terrorists who hijacked the French airliner, the Ugandan Government made it clear that it did not exercise sovereignty over its territory. Much more significant, by resorting to the use of force to release all the remaining 110 hostages held by the terrorists, Israel may *well* be contributing to the development of law against international terrorism. Air hijacking, a new form of international terrorism, has been condemned by members of the international community, as reflected in the following resolutions or documents:

1. The Geneva Convention for the Prevention and Punishment of Terrorism, November 16, 1937.
2. United Nations, General Assembly Resolution 2645 (XXV) of 1970.
3. United Nations Security Council Document S/10705, June 20, 1972.
4. The 1970 Resolution of the Assembly of the Council of Europe condemning all acts of hijacking, sabotage and the taking of hostages.
5. The 1971 Organization of American States Convention to Prevent and Punish the Acts of Terrorism Taking the Form of Crimes against Persons and Related Extortion that are of International Significance.
6. The Tokyo Convention on Offences and Certain Other Acts Committed on Board Aircraft (1963); The Hague Convention for the Suppression of Unlawful Seizure of Aircraft (1970); and the Montreal Convention for the Suppression of Unlawful Acts Against the Safety of Civil Aviation (1971).
7. The 1970 Resolution of the Council of Ministers of the Organization of African Unity condemning "all attempts and acts of hijacking and sabotaging of civil aircraft."

As we have noted, the General Assembly and the Security Council of the United Nations adopted resolutions expressing grave concern at the increase in hijackings of aircraft, and calling on member-states to take appropriate domestic and international measures to prevent such acts and to deal with perpetrators of such acts. Thus, under the auspices of the International Civil Aviation Organization, one of the Specialized Agencies of the United Nations, the Conventions for the Suppression of Unlawful Seizure of Aircraft, and Unlawful Acts Against the Safety of Civil Aviation were adopted at The Hague and Montreal respectively. At the United Nations, the General Assembly, by a vote of 76 to 35 (including the United States) with 17 abstentions, rejected the United States Draft Convention for the Prevention and Punishment of Certain Acts of International Terrorism and its accompanying draft resolution, and adopted Resolution 3034 (XXVII) on December 18, 1972.[35] The Resolution, while expressing *"deep concern* over increasing acts of violence which endanger or take innocent human lives or jeopardize fundamental freedoms," and inviting states to become parties to existing conventions on international terrorism, and to take appropriate measures at the national level to eliminate terrorism, focuses its primary attention on "finding just and peaceful solutions to the underlying causes which give rise to such acts of violence." The Resolution

> *Reaffirms* the inalienable right to self determination and independence of all peoples under the colonial and racist regimes and other forms of alien domination and upholds the legitimacy of their struggle. *(Emphasis in original.)*

In essence, Resolution 3034 (XXVII) is a condonation rather than a condemnation of international terrorism.

Finally, by not apprehending the hijackers and putting them on trial for their acts, and by not taking appropriate measures to facilitate the continuation of Flight 139 after it had been granted permission to land at the Entebbe Airport on "humanitarian grounds," Uganda acted in gross violation of her treaty obligation under Articles 2, 6, 7 and 9 of the Hague Convention for the Suppression of Unlawful Seizure of Aircraft. The Ugandan Government would have been justified in granting the hijackers "political asylum" if they had been arrested and prosecuted, and their prosecution had resulted in conviction or acquittal.

V

We have now come to an examination of the view that the Entebbe Rescue Mission was essentially a "naked act of aggression." We have stated that traditional international law permitted the right of intervention by states and that most states with military capability to intervene have always alluded to various aspects of intervention recognized in international law. Such states, for instance, claim that although the Kellog-Briand Pact of 1928, and the United Nations Charter generally enjoin states to "refrain in their international relations from the threat or use of force," their provisions do not impair the right of self-defence which is recognized by

general international law, of which the Pact and the Charter are a part.[36]

This, in our view, is a charitable interpretation of the two instruments referred to above. More specifically, it does not conform with present day norms of international behavior which the United Nations Charter seeks to obtain, and indeed, to maintain. Article 51 of the United Nations Charter has stipulated the *two* circumstances under which a state may resort to the threat or use of force: individual and/or collective self-defence. In the light of this basic principle of intervention as permitted by the Charter, it has been claimed that Israel acted under the hallowed doctrine of *self-help* which generally includes self defence or reprisals. The core meaning of the principle of self-help is that if a state is threatened or grievously injured but the international community (i.e. the United Nations) is incapable of giving a timely redress, the injured or threatened state may take necessary but proportionate measures to protect itself. It is also claimed that self-defence is not limited to the actual defence of the state *per se* but that it includes the defence of the nationals of the defending (intervening) state wherever they are found. The inference here is that the nationals of the intervening state who are abroad still remain part of that state. A protection, therefore, of these nationals abroad is the protection of the state.[37]

However, those who asssert the right of a state to intervene on "humanitarian grounds" or on the basis of self-defence, as Israel appeared to have done, do not seem to recognize the potential *abuse* to which this right will be put. One would have expected, for instance, an imminent danger to the lives and/or property of the nationals to the extent that it would *reasonably* be concluded that only some form of military action could save them. From the detailed accounts of the events during the hijacking and the raid itself, there is nothing to suggest that the lives of the hostages were in extreme danger.[38] In fact, the stories narrated by the released hostages about the separation of non-Jewish from Jewish passengers, and the stories about the dangers to the lives of the remaining hostages may well have been exaggerated, but they were used by the Israeli Government as an excuse to justify military intervention. Furthermore, the 103 Israeli hostages were rather too many to be put to death, as the hijackers threatened to do. One could talk of one or two diplomats but certainly not 103 hostages. This is not to say that the actions of the hijackers were being condoned or that President Amin could not escape blame for appearing to collaborate with the hijackers to press their demands. Nor do we suggest that Israel, or any other country, should submit to blackmail. In fact, the Israeli statement to the effect that

The State of Israel was created to ensure that

THE ENTEBBE RESCUE MISSION

never again should Jews perish for lack of home and haven, that there can be no concession to terrorism.

showed clearly that Israel was certainly not in any mood to give in to the terrorists. According to the Israeli Defence Minister, Shimon Peres, "if Israel means anything, it means Jews can go anywhere as free men without fear. We can't give in to blackmail."[40] In any event, the force unleashed by the Israelis to rescue the hostages was not proportionate to the danger with which the hostages were allegedly faced.[41]

From all available evidence and the existence of international norms guiding the use of force, other than the practices of states, we find no justification for the Israeli action. It is an incontrovertible fact that Israel not only abused the right of self-defence within the context of Article 51 of the United Nations Charter (if that was the premise on which the Mission was carried out), but has violated one of the cardinal principles of international law, namely, sovereignty and territorial integrity of States. Article 2(4) of the Charter enjoins all member states of the United Nations to

refrain in their international relations from the threat or use of force against the territorial integrity or political independence of any State, or in any manner inconsistent with the Purposes of the United Nations.

The framers of the Charter must have recognized that the preservation of a peaceful international system rests solely on the respect states accord or are expected to accord each other's sovereignty and territorial integrity.

Apart from the Charter itself, the United Nations has reemphasized the principle of sovereignty and independence of states on many occasions. On December 21, 1965, the General Assembly adopted Resolution 2131 (XX), which in an uncompromising manner, specifically stressed the inadmissability of intervention in the domestic affairs of states and the protection of their sovereignty and independence:

No state has the right to intervene directly or indirectly, for any reason whatever, in the internal or external affairs of any other State. Consequently, armed intervention and all other forms of interference or attempted threats against the personality of the State or against its political, economic and cultural elements are condemned.[42]

And, on October 24, 1970, the General Assembly, *vide* Resolution 2625 (XXV), reaffirmed the principle of non-intervention as one of the cardinal principles of friendly relations and cooperation among states. The Resolution declares, *inter alia*, that:

a threat or use of force constitutes a violation of international law and of the Charter of the United Nations and shall never be employed as a means of settling international issues.

The importance of the prohibition of intervention has always been recognized and other regional organizations had inserted it in their Charters: Article 15 of the Charter of the Organization of American States; Article 8 of the Charter of the League of Arab States; and Article III (c) of the Charter of Organization of African Unity. All this reinforces the view that armed intervention by any state on behalf of its nationals abroad to rescue, enforce reparation or punish has not received international acceptability, and, therefore, should be regarded as illegal.

Let us for the moment assume that Israel extends the definition of self-defence or the right of *interposition* (intervention) to disguise her action.[43] Could the landing of Flight 139 at the Entebbe Airport and the holding of the passengers as hostages thereafter be regarded as an armed attack against Israel by Uganda for which Israel was to defend itself? Again, was the force used commensurate with the "imminent danger" confronting the hostages? It must be noted that the Israeli paratroopers and commandos not only rescued the hostages but also destroyed eleven Ugandan Air Force planes that were parked nearby. These planes, according to them, were destroyed to prevent any possible "hot pursuit."

The fact is that there is no body of law that would justify the Israeli action. The evidence, as far as the international legal order is concerned, weighs heavily against the Rescue Mission. We submit that humanitarian intervention or the right of self-defence used to justify the Israeli action is nothing but a doctrine adopted by the relatively powerful nations, the exact content of which is determined by the intervening nations themselves. To date, if every nation were to be its own judge of humanitarian intervention or if more and more nations were to possess enough military power to go into the act of intervention, the result would be *chaos*. By then, those who cite this principle as part of recognized international law would undobtedly conclude that things had really gone too far. Any support given to it would permit

outside powers to invade sovereign states for all sorts of spurious reasons.[44]

It is therefore appropriate to treat the Israeli action as a violation of Uganda's sovereignty and territorial integrity, and a clear breach of international peace, for which the United Nations stands.

VI

In concluding this paper, let us examine the politics of the Entebbe Rescue Mission. As expected, Uganda availed herself of the normal procedure open to her under the United Nations Charter to lodge complaints against Israel at the Security Council. This was done with a view to seeking redress against Israel in accordance with Article 39 of the Charter. Were the Security Council to adhere strictly to the spirit of the Charter, Israel would have been condemned in no uncertain terms, and she would also have been required to make reparations to Uganda for the loss of lives and property. It is a matter of regret that the Council was unable to make reparations to Uganda for the loss of lives and property. It is a matter of regret that the Council was unable to make any decision. First, a Resolution sponsored by Tanzania, Libya and the Republic of Benin, which would have condemned Israel for "flagrant violation" of Uganda's sovereignty and territorial integrity, was withdrawn when it was clear that it could only receive eight of the nine required votes in the Security Council. Even if the resolution were to receive enough votes, the United States or any of the Western Powers in the Security Council would have vetoed it. Second, the United States and Great Britain submitted another Resolution which condemned hijacking generally, called on states to prevent and punish terrorist acts, and reaffirmed the sovereignty and territorial integrity of all states in accordance with the United Nations Charter and international law. This resolution was also withdrawn when the supporters of Uganda served on the Security Council a notice that they would not participate in the debate on the Anglo-American sponsored resolution.

Thus, the event in the Security Council reveals the disproportionate power and influence of the Great Powers in the United Nations, to the detriment of small and medium powers. Undoubtedly, the small and medium powers may enjoy numerical advantages at the General Assembly, but the voting procedure in the Security Council ensures that the will of the Great Powers shall prevail at all times, whenever their interest or that of their *protege* is affected. Let us assume that the Security Council condemned Israel and asked her to pay compensation to Uganda. The fact still remains that neither the Security Council nor the General Assembly could enforce that decision. This strengthens the belief that the international community is not in a position to redress wrongs committed by one State against the other. Apart from the statement from the United Nations Secretary-General to the effect that Israel has violated the sovereignty and territorial integrity of a member-state of the United Nations, the whole episode has since been swept under the carpet in the United Nations.

To sum up, while the Entebbe Rescue may be defended on "humanitarian grounds" or on the basis of self-defence, from the available evidence and the existence of norms governing the use of force, we do not find much justification for the Israeli action. In any event, it is now common knowledge that international law itself is honored more in the breach than the observance. Consequently, weak nations will have to strengthen their capabilities as it is clear that their chances of securing redress for wrong committed against them are very slim if the organization that is vested with the power to compel reparation is unwilling to do so. Finally, without in any way denigrating the importance of understanding the causes giving rise to various forms of international terrorism, it is our view that the use of forms of violence especially against innocent passengers are illegitimate, and member-states of the United Nations, through bilateral treaties, national legislation and international conventions, should take appropriate measures against air piracy and punish the perpetrators of such acts.

NOTES

The author acknowledges the assistance of Arthur Davies, one of his graduate students at the University of Lagos, in the course of preparing this paper. Mr. Davies, however, is not responsible for any of its shortcomings.

This paper was presented at the 22nd Annual Convention of the International Studies Association at Benjamin Franklin Plaza, Philadelphia, March 18-21, 1981.

1. K. W. Grundy, "The Stanleyville Rescue: American Policy in the Congo," *The Yale Review* (Winter 1967):242.

2. Ibid., p. 243.

3. Ibid., p. 244. See also L. A. Jinadu and A. Akinsanya, "Nigeria's African Policy With Special Reference to the Congo Crises 1960-1965," *Africa Quarterly*.

4. Art. 29 of the United Nations Charter.

5. See M. A. Ajomo, "The Entebbe Affair: Intervention in International Law," A Public Lecture Delivered Under the Auspices of the Nigerian Institute of International Affairs, Victoria Island, Lagos, October 25, 1976, p. 2.

6. Various accounts put the number of hijackers at four (one German and three Arabs) or five (two Germans and three Arabs).

7. Patricia Heyman was holding a British passport but her home was in Petach Tikva, Israel. She persuaded the terrorists to release her at Benghazi, Libya, because she was in advanced pregnancy and risked giving premature birth. According to her, "Benghazi was described as stop over only. Central Africa appears to be final destination." See W. Stevenson, *90 Minutes at Entebbe* (New York: Bantam Books, 1976), p. 10.

8. Except otherwise stated, the materials used in this portion of the paper are drawn from A. E. Evans, "Aircraft Hijacking: What is Being Done," and A. Lee, "International Suppression of Hijacking," in *International Terrorism and Political Crimes*, edited by M. C. Bassiouni (Springfield, Ill.: Charles C. Thomas, 1975), p. 219-256.

9. Evans, p. 223, n. 7.

10. Ibid., p. 223, n. 8.

11. Ibid., pp. 223-4.

12. Ibid., p. 226, n. 19.

13. Ibid., p. 226, n. 19.

14. Ibid., pp. 226-7.

15. Akinsanya, *The Expropriation of Multinational Property in the Third World* (New York: Praeger, 1980), pp. 121-7.

16. The parties to the Convention included: Argentina, Brazil, Bulgaria, the Byelorussian Soviet Socialist Republic, Canada, Chad, Chile, Costa Rica, Cyprus, Czechoslovakia, Dahomey (Benin Republic), Ecuador, Fiji, Finland, France, Gabon, the German

THE ENTEBBE RESCUE MISSION

Democratic Republic. Hungary, Iran, Iraq, Israel, Japan, Jordan, Mali, Mexico, Mongolia, the Niger, Norway, Panama, Paraguay, Poland, Republic of China, Rumania, South Africa, Sweden, Switzerland, Trinidad and Tobago, the Ukraine Soviet Socialist Republic, the Soviet Union, the United Kingdom, the United States and Uganda.

17. Other conventions dealing with the dangers of air hijacking are the Convention on Offences and Certain other Acts Committed on Board Aircraft and the Convention for the Suppression of Unlawful Acts Against the Safety of Civil Aviation. The former, signed on September 14, 1963, entered into force on December 4, 1969 while the latter, signed on September 23, 1971, has not yet entered into force. See M. C. Bassiouni (ed.), *International Terrorism and Political Crimes*, pp. 257-266, 274-281.

18. At the time of writing three terrorists were holding a PIA plane (Boeing 720) and demanding the release of fifty-five detainees in Pakistani prisons in exchange for more than 100 hostages being held in Damascus, Syria. See "Fathers of Hijackers Try to Win Hostages' Release," *The State* (Columbia), March 12, 1981, p. 1.

19. Evans, pp. 228-31, 233, 235-7.

20. Lee, p. 256.

21. R. A. Falk, *Legal Order in a Violent World* (Princeton, N.J.: Princeton University Press, 1968), p. 343.

22. O. Young, "Intervention and International System," 20 *Journal of International Affairs* (1968):177-8.

23. Urs Schwarz, "Intervention: The Historical Development II," in *Intervention in International Politics*, edited by L. G. M. Jaquet (The Hague: Martinus Nijhoff, 1971), p. 32.

24. L. F. L. Oppenheim, *International Law*, Vol. 5 (New York: David McKay, 1955), pp. 306-9.

25. D. W. Bowett, *Self-Defence in International Law* (Manchester: Manchester University Press, 1958), p. 88.

26. Ibid.

27. Ibid.

28. Ibid., emphasis added.

29. J. L. Brierly, *The Law of Nations*, Sixth Edition (New York and Oxford: Oxford University Press, 1963), p. 427.

30. Ibid., pp. 427-8.

31. D. P. O'Conneil, *International Law*, Second Edition (London: Stevens, 1965), p. 303.

32. Ibid.

33. Bowett, p. 93.

34. Ibid.

35. J. F. Murphy, "United Nations Proposals on the Control and Repression of Terrorism," in *International Terrorism and Political Crimes*, pp. 493-506.

36. Bowett, pp. 184-5.

37. Ibid., p. 92.

38. Stevenson, *90 Minutes At Entebbe, et seq.*

39. *Keesings Contemporary Archives* 1976.

40. Stevenson, p. 10.

41. See I. Brownlie, *International Law and the Use of Force By States* (London: Clarendon, 1963), pp. 261-4.

42. See 5 *International Legal Materials* (1966):374.

43. The term "interposition" was first used by the United States at the Havana Conference in 1928 when Mr. Hughes noted: "What are we to do when government breaks down and American citizens are in danger of their lives? . . . Now it is a principle of international law that in such a case a government is fully justified in taking action—I would call it interposition of a temporary character for the purpose of protecting the lives and property of nationals. I could say that that is not intervention. One can read in text books that that is not intervention." Brownlie, p. 293; Bowett, pp. 99-100.

44. T. M. Franck and N. S. Rodley, "After Bangladesh: The Law of Humanitarian Intervention By Military Force," 67 *American Journal of International Law* (1973):277.

[5]

The Decision to Raid Entebbe

DECISION ANALYSIS APPLIED TO CRISIS BEHAVIOR

ZEEV MAOZ

Department of Political Science
University of Michigan, Ann Arbor

Despite the variety of theories of crisis behavior, increasing agreement exists regarding one proposition: Rational choice models do not fit the actual decision processes that take place under crisis-induced stress. This proposition is examined in the case of Israel's decision during the Entebbe crisis. Two major models of choice are introduced, and testable propositions are deduced from each model for the individual choice level and for the group level. A discriminating test among these models is established and applied to the decision processes during the Entebbe crisis. The findings support the analytic (rational) model of choice at both the individual and the group level. Two important propositions are derived from the empirical analysis: (1) SOPs may positively affect the quality of choice processes to the extent that they are comprehensive and flexible, and (2) intragroup conflict and uniform distribution of authority within groups enhances, rather than constrains, the quality of group decisions.

OVERVIEW

Studies of decision-making under crisis conditions have become a booming enterprise over the last two decades (Tanter, 1978: 347-360). In recent years, some studies have made a major step toward a unified theory of crisis behavior through synthesis of existing knowledge in the field (for example. Snyder and Diesing, 1977; Brecher, 1979, 1980; Stein and Tanter, 1980). However, the state of the art is still one of competing paradigms, whose proponents claim to provide the "best" approxima-

AUTHOR'S NOTE: I am indebted to Rami Benbenishti, Ran Segev and Yaacov Schul for research and coding assistance, to Robert Axelrod and Eugene Burnstein for their perceptive comments on earlier drafts, and to Raymond Tanter who has been an invaluable source of inspiration and encouragement. The errors, nonetheless, are all mine.

JOURNAL OF CONFLICT RESOLUTION. Vol. 25 No. 4. December 1981 677-707
© 1981 Sage Publications. Inc.

678   JOURNAL OF CONFLICT RESOLUTION

tion to the actual processes that take place under crisis conditions. Despite this diversity, a consensus seems to be forming around one theme: Rational choice models do not fit the empirically observable choice processes under crisis-induced stress (Hermann, 1972; Holsti and George, 1975; Snyder, 1978). It is hypothesized that search for options is reduced; information processing is constrained and biased; value tradeoffs are avoided; and choice is based on satisficing or analogizing principles.

It is precisely this proposition which the present study attempts to examine by (a) deducing empirically observable predictions from two major decision-making models for both the individual choice and the group decision levels, (b) suggesting a set of discriminating tests for the evaluation of the relative fit between these models and actual decision processes, and (c) applying these tests to Israel's decisions during the Entebbe crisis.

While findings based on a single case can hardly constitute firm support or refutation for any given model, they can accumulate into a growing body of codifiable knowledge and provide readily accessible data for comparative projects, as well as shed light on subtle characteristics of decision processes which are not readily apparent in comparative studies of decisions (George, 1979).

ALTERNATIVE APPROACHES TO CHOICE

Two major models of choice seem to have dominated the literature on foreign policymaking in recent years. Although most scholars agree that real-world decision processes are marked by a mix of the procedures postulated by these models (Horelick et al., 1975: 53; Stein and Tanter, 1980: ch.3), these models are often presented as alternative, rather than complementary, explanations of choice processes (Snyder and Diesing, 1977: 340-361; Allison, 1971). Thus, the task in this section is to generate empirically observable predictions for each of these models both at the level of individual choice and at the group level.

INDIVIDUAL CHOICE

The Analytic (Rational) Model

(1) Exhaustive search. When faced with a decision problem, an individual explores all possible options that are relevant for solving this

problem. The individual then assigns to each option a set of outcomes that may result from the implementation of this option. The set of outcomes for each of the options should be mutually exclusive and logically exhaustive. That is, it should be so defined that no two outcomes can occur at the same time, and that no outcome which does not belong to the perceived set can occur (Holsti and George, 1975: 271; Braceley et al., 1977).

(2) Optimal revision. This stage consists of two steps. First initial estimates (preferably explicitly probabilistic ones) are generated regarding the likelihood of occurrence of each of the perceived outcomes. During this step, use is being made of all relevant information. That is, background information (base rates) and current indicators are combined to produce estimates. Second, estimates are revised as new information enters the system through a similar combination of base rates—in this case, initial estimates—with the additional data received. The magnitude of revision depends primarily on the perceived diagnosticity of the incoming data (Stein and Tanter, 1980: ch. 2).

(3) Comprehensive evaluation. Analytic decision makers specify all value dimensions or goals affected by the decision problem. A relative weight score is then assigned to each value dimension according to its perceived importance. All outcomes are ranked separately on each value dimension and are assigned partial utility scores according to the relative preference distance between pairs of outcomes. This process is repeated for all value dimensions. Finally, an integrated utility function is generated by summing across partial utility scores for each outcome, discounted by the relative weight score of corresponding value-dimensions (Coombs et al., 1970: 122-137).

To clarify this somewhat complex evaluation procedure, a formal presentation is in order. Let 0 [0 = 1,2. . .,n] be the set of outcomes assigned to each of the options identified. Let VD[VD = 1,2. . .,m] be the set of value dimensions perceived to be affected by the decision. Now we can generate a Search-Evaluation (SE) matrix of order m x n that tells us how each outcome is ranked on any given value dimension. Thus, each entry O_iVD_j in the SE matrix reflects a partial utility score for outcome i on value dimension j. Let WV be a column vector of order m, where each entry WV_j represents a relative weight score for value dimension j. The integrated utility function is obtained by the formula U = SE*WV. This is illustrated graphically in Figure 1.

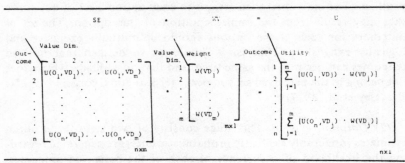

Figure 1: Analytic Evaluation

(4) Optimizing choice. The subjectively expected utility (SEU) for each option is obtained by summing across all outcome utilities discounted by their corresponding probabilities, such that:

$$SEU_k = \sum_{i=1}^{n} [U(O_i) * P(O_i)]$$

The analytic decision maker chooses that option which yields the highest SEU (Raiffa, 1968).

The Cybernetic/Cognitive Model

Cybernetic and cognitive theorists argue that average decision makers lack the computational skills required by analytical procedures, or the time and resources that are needed even for intuitive and nonrigorous analytic decision-making (Simon, 1957; Steinbruner, 1974: 48-56). Moreover, the analytic model is criticized for ignoring or discounting the role of cognitive mechanisms which constrain the quality of search, revision, and evaluation processes. Decision makers cannot be treated as formal scientists because they all too often deviate from scientific inference criteria (Nisbett and Ross, 1980).

Although they are often discussed as distinct models, and although they emphasize different mechanisms that force decision makers to deviate from the analytic mode,[1] the cybernetic and cognitive models

1. Cybernetic theorists emphasize the pressures emanating from environmental complexity and uncertainty, as well as the organizational settings in which foreign policy decisions are made (Allison, 1971; Allison and Halperin, 1972; Steinbruner, 1974). Cognitive theorists emphasize the role of psychological variables such as belief systems and consistency-maintenance constraints (Holsti, 1976: 29-30; Art, 1973; Shapiro and Bonham, 1973).

will be integrated for the purpose of this analysis. The main reason underlying this integration is that both models specify very similar predictions with respect to the observed decisional procedures at the individual and group levels—in fact, they may supplement each other empirically (Steinbrunner, 1974: 138-139).

The general idea underlying the cybernetic cognitive approach is that individuals are able to impose meaning and structure on their complex environment through a highly consistent and stable belief system (Holsti, 1962), which serves as a dominant base for individual decision processes. In organizational settings, standard operating procedures (SOPs) serve a similar function of reducing environmental complexity and as a general guide for behavior (Allison, 1971). The cybernetic/cognitive model starts its predictions one step prior to that of the analytic model.

(1) Identification and diagnosis. A problem is identified when some event in the external environment is perceived to be "discrepant from an ideal or expected state" (Burnstein and Berbaum, 1979: 10-11). The magnitude of the decision problem is a direct function of this discrepancy. Once identified, the problem is diagnosed and categorized within available cognitive schemas or organizational programs (Axelrod, 1973: 1949-1950; Allison, 1971). The most common cognitive diagnosis technique is that of analogizing—that is, search for past events which share some features with the problem at hand. Diagnosis by analogy is often dominated by the availability, representativeness, and vividness heuristics (Tversky and Kahneman 1974; Nisbett and Ross, 1980: 17-62). Decision makers tend to select "the most recent and dramatic analogy drawn from an event which had important personal or national consequences" (Stein and Tanter, 1980: 51), while paying little attention to the actual base rates or to the fit between the analogized case and the problem at hand. This process simplifies the definition of the situation and serves as a general guide for subsequent decisional stages (Pruitt, 1965).

(2) Deductive search. Search is sequential and limited to such options which are consistent with the major normative components within the belief systems or with predesigned programs. Options which proved to be disasterous in the past are rejected (Jervis, 1976: 275-281), and additional exploration occurs only if the initial option fails to satisfy some level of preset aspiration (Simon, 1969: 84-118).

(3) Biased and conservative revision. Prior theories emanating from the belief system are highly resistant to change and to discrepant

evidence (Nisbett and Ross, 1980: 169-187). These categories generate single hypotheses (that is, null hypotheses are ignored), against which current information is contrasted. Supporting evidence is assigned high reliability weights, and discrepant evidence is ignored or discredited regardless of its diagnosticity (Axelrod, 1973; Jervis, 1976: 117-202). Revision in organizational settings is limited to such variables specified in existing SOPs.

(4) Single-value evaluation. People tend to avoid conflict among values, or to employ various repressive mechanisms if value conflict becomes evident. Conflict-reducing strategies involve ignoring or discrediting the importance of conflicting value dimensions (McGuire, 1966: 9-14). Value integration, particularly under crisis conditions, almost invariably involves value conflict, since an option that ranks highly on one dimension is likely to rank poorly on another dimension. Thus, in order to maintain cognitive consistency while reducing complexity caused by value integration, outcomes are evaluated on a single, most important or salient value dimension. Additional value dimensions, if considered, are confronted in a sequential "elimination by aspects" manner (Tversky, 1972). Incorporation of utilities and probabilities is limited to nominal terms (Gallhofer and Saris, 1979: 429; Kahneman and Tversky, 1979).

(5) Satisficing choice. Given the early elimination of options due to analogizing and consistency-maintenance strategies, the first option which satisfies the individual or organizational acceptability threshold is selected.

GROUP DECISION

Foreign policy decision-making is by and large a collective enterprise, hence requiring the models to extend their predictions to the process by which individual preferences are transformed into a group decision. Both the analytic model and the cybernetic/cognitive model acknowledge the fact that individuals enter the group setting with preestablished preferences and that these preferences may change in the course of the group discussion[2] (Collins and Guetzkow, 1964; Pruitt, 1971a, 1971b; Cartwright, 1971). The models differ in their predictions, however, with

2. Initially assumed by psychologists to be a "risky shift." Subsequent research, however, suggests that group-induced shifts can be toward more moderate as well as toward riskier options (Cartwright, 1971).

respect to the factors that account for group-induced shifts and with respect to the dominating group decision scheme (Davis, 1973).

(1) The analytic model. This model postulates a group process of argumentation, coalition formation, and persuasion attempts. Individual preferences change as a result of exposure to new arguments and additional information which are exchanged during the group discussion (Burnstein et al., 1971; Vinokur and Burnstein, 1974; Kaplan, 1977; Kaplan and Miller, 1977; Axelrod, 1977). Consequently, the analytic explanation emphasizes the differential influence by individuals on the group decisional outcome.[3] Two important determinants of individual influence are conviction and formal authority, which are particularly relevant in political, and thus hierarchical, settings.[4] The group decision scheme is defined as weighted aggregation of preferences. Individual preferences are discounted by relative influence scores, and the option whose aggregated weighted score is the highest would emerge as the group decision.

Formally, this process looks as follows: Let GP be a matrix of order m x n, in which rows stand for the m options considered by the group, and the columns represent the n participants. Each entry GP_{ij} represents the SEU attached to option i by individual j. Let RI be a column vector of order n, in which each entry RI_j represents a relative influence score for individual j. The group decision is obtained by the highest entry in a vector of order m, where:

$$0 = GP*RI$$

The matrix representation of this deduction is displayed in Figure 2.

(2) The cybernetic/cognitive model. Despite single-value evaluation at the individual level, interindividual differences in terms of preference orderings may emerge at the group level because of different value criteria employed by individuals or by different organizations (Allison, 1971; Allison and Halperin, 1972). However, the potential group conflict caused by disagreement regarding the most appropriate value dimension for group evaluation (Axelrod, 1976: 90) is checked by two

3. The bureaucratic politics model is viewed here as an extension of the analytic model to the group level, since both emphasize argumentation, intragroup bargaining, and coalition formation processes (Snyder and Diesing, 1977: 408).
4. Conviction can be operationally defined as the gap in SEUs between the most preferred option and the second-ranked option for each individual. Conviction is a major determinant of individual influence, in that the relative shift required in utilities for a highly convinced individual will be greater than for less convinced individuals (Collins and Guetzkow, 1964).

684   *JOURNAL OF CONFLICT RESOLUTION*

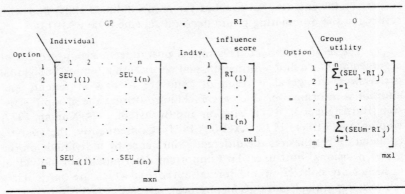

Figure 2: The Analytic Model's Solution for Group Decisional Outcomes

complementary group decision schemes. The "elimination by aspects" scheme allows for sequential introduction of value dimensions which lead to sequential elimination of options that fail to satisfy these dimensions (Tversky, 1972). Second, "groupthink" tendencies generate concurrence-seeking patterns by individuals and lead them to shift their initial preferences to support that option which is advocated by the group leader, or in accordance with the perceived "group consensus" (Janis, 1972; Janis and Mann, 1977: 129-134). In general, the group process postulated by the cybernetic/cognitive model involves little argumentation and suggests that the leader's preference or the group's norms are likely to determine the decisional outcome.

THE MODELS COMPARED

Several points should be made regarding the models specified above. First, these models are not mutually exclusive, nor are they clearly distinguishable. For instance, an option selected as a result of programmed search, limited revision, unidimensional evaluation and satisficing choice may still be the one with the highest SEU, had an analytic process taken place. Moreover, even if choice at the individual level can be best accounted for in terms of a single model, there is no theoretical or practical reason why the same model will also account for group decisions (Axelrod, 1976: 243).

With these caveats in mind, we can now compare the predictions of the three models at the individual and group levels. This is displayed in Table 1.

TABLE 1
Three Models of Choice[a]

	Analytic	*Cybernetic*[b]	*Cognitive*
Search	Exhaustive: across all relevant options	Sequential: programmed consideration of a preselected number of options	Deductive: through the general system of beliefs
Revision	Optimal: combination of base-rate information with current indicators	Incremental and conservative	Deductive and Categorical: unequal reliability weights assigned to evidence compatible with prior beliefs relative to discrepant items
Evaluation	Comprehensive: cost-benefit analysis of outcomes across all relevant value dimensions; multiple value integration	Single-Value Analysis: sequential elimination by aspects for additional value dimensions	Conflict Reducing: undimensional analysis of costs and benefits to avoid value conflict
Choice	Maximizing: incorporation of utilities and probabilities for SEU maximization	Satisficing: application of acceptability thresholds for choice	Analogizing: single-value maximization
Main Features of Group Process	Weighted Aggregation of Preferences: argumentation and coalition formation; exercise of formal and informal influence	Elimination by Aspects: sequential elimination by aspects; limited argumentation; limited exercise of influence	Groupthink: concurrence-seeking; little dissidence; limited or no argumentation; leader's preferences or group norms major determinants of decisional outcomes

a. Individual choice comparisons are partially adapted from Stein and Tanter (1980).
b. The cybernetic/cognitive model is decomposed to illustrate the contribution of the component-models to the set of integrative predictions.

686   *JOURNAL OF CONFLICT RESOLUTION*

METHOD

Attempts to discriminate among these models (for example, Snyder and Diesing, 1977: 340-407; Gallhofer and Saris, 1979) were primarily concerned with search processes or with ways in which values are ranked and estimates are made—that is, nominal versus interval revision and evaluation. The method suggested below is a mix of qualitative assessments and quantitative formal analysis. Such a mix seems necessary, given the lack of formal specification for the cybernetic and cognitive models and given the lack of hard evaluation criteria with respect to rational search and revision[5] (Janis and Mann, 1977: 11).

In general, the method consists of a set of discriminating questions for each of the decisional stages. These questions were submitted to three coders reviewing independently interview materials with principal decision makers during the Entebbe crisis, as well as secondary accounts of the decision process. The questions were decomposed into specific sections, corresponding to the decisional stages specified above. After answering the questions for each of these sections, coders were asked to evaluate which model best describes the actual procedures applied by decision makers for this stage.

For the evaluation stage, coders were asked to specify all value dimensions mentioned by each decision maker and to arrange them on a 100-point scale according to perceived importance. Then they were asked to rank outcomes on each value dimension and to determine preference distances across all pairs of outcomes. Partial utilities were assigned to each outcome according to the mean preference distance between pairs. Similarly, coders were asked to assign subjective probabilities for each outcome, as perceived by each decision maker.[6]

For the group decision process, coders were asked to evaluate the group authority structure on the basis of case-specific as well as background information relating to Rabin's government. They were also required to scale relative authoritativeness of the three principal decision makers.

Overall coders' agreement was .88 (p $<$ .01), whereas pairwise agreement rates ranged between .79 and .92.[7] Such a rate of agreement is

---

5. Attempts to formalize cybernetic choice models focus exclusively on the incremental nature of decision outputs rather than on the characteristics of the choice process. See for example Tanter (1974).

6. Conversion of verbal estimates and value or preference judgments into numerical values (that is probabilities and preference-distances) was done by the coders using the Stein and Tanter (1980) method. See also Braceley et al. (1977).

7. Computation of intercoder agreement rates was done in two forms. Answers to questions requiring categorical identification (for example, identification of options,

surprisingly high given the elusiveness of the source material. However, when agreement tests were broken down into subsets of answers regarding the behavior of individual decision makers, the results reflected the relative availability of information regarding each individual participant in the decision-making process. Agreement on Rabin's considerations, which are by far better documented, ranged between .89 and .92, agreement on Peres's considerations ranged from .85 to .89, and for Allon, these rates ranged from .79 to .83.

On the basis of this method we can now reconstruct the decision process of Israel's decision makers during the Entebbe crisis. This will be done first by outlining a brief narrative description of the crisis, and second by analyzing the decision process step-by-step.

THE ENTEBBE DECISIONS

NARRATIVE DESCRIPTION

On Sunday, June 27, 1976, an Air France plane en route from Lod (Israel) to Paris was hijacked several minutes after leaving Athens airport. On board were 160 passengers, of whom 103 were Israeli citizens. The hijackers were two Germans and two Palestinians, later identified as members of an extremist Palestinian organization headed by Dr. Wadie Hadad, a former deputy of George Habbash of the Popular Front for the Liberation of Palestine. As soon as the Israeli government was notified of the hijacking, it ordered a high state of alert in Lod airport in case the hijacked plane was brought back to Israel. At the same time, the government appointed a special ministerial team to deal with the problem. This team consisted of Prime Minister Rabin; Defense Minister Peres, Foreign Minister Allon, and Gallilli, minister without portfolio.

---

outcomes, value dimensions), and categorical evaluation (such as yes/no questions, or evaluation of fit between a given model's predictions and the actual procedures employed) generated a response matrix of order 150 x 3. In this response matrix, rows represent questions and columns represent coders. Thus each entry represents the answer that coder i has given for question j, and was coded either as 1 (yes) or 0 (no). Agreement was measured by the proportion of cases of discrepancy among coders to the total area of the matrix, where discrepancy is observed in cases where row entries are not uniform. For questions requiring scaling and interval estimation (for example, probabilities assigned to outcomes), where answers generate numerical values, partial correlations were computed for all pairs of coders, and multiple correlation—for all three coders.

After a brief stop at Benghazi airport in Libya, the hijacked plane landed at Entebbe Uganda. The passengers were brought into the old terminal building of the airport, and two additional guerrillas joined the hijackers. The demands of the hijackers were announced on Tuesday, June 29, and included the release of 52 Palestinians held in prisons in Israel, West Germany, Kenya, and France, by Thursday, July 1, at 2:00 p.m. The decision makers had little doubt regarding the credibility of the hijackers' threat to execute hostages if their demands were not met by the time the ultimatum expired. In a previous incident involving Hadad's people in 1974, the American ambassador to Sudan was killed even before the expiration of the ultimatum.

On Wednesday, June 30, it became clear that all the non-Israeli hostages would soon be released. The Israeli hostages were separated from the other hostages, and the latter were told to prepare for departure. Information about the separation of the Israeli hostages and the release of non-Israelis acted as an electrical shock on Israel's decision makers. The analogy that clearly came to their mind was that of the "selection" of Jews by the Nazis before they were shipped to the gas chambers.

On Wednesday, however, most efforts were invested in gathering information on the situation at Entebbe and in exploring options for response. The Israeli government contacted all the other governments concerned in an attempt to coordinate response to the hijackers' demands, and was assured of their cooperation. In addition, a telephone contact was established with Idi Amin, Uganda's ruler. Baruch Bar-Lev, a former Israeli military envoy to Uganda, attempted to persuade Amin that it was in his best interest to bring about the peaceful release of hostages. However, this attempt proved futile. Furthermore, the discussion with Amin confirmed Israeli suspicion that Amin fully cooperated with the hijackers. At the same time, military teams were working on a variety of plans for rescue operations.

The release of the non-Israeli hostages also had some important advantages. First, the Israeli government was relieved of moral responsibility for the lives of non-Israeli citizens. Second, the release of hostages provided an excellent opportunity to acquire essential information regarding the number, location, and shifts of the hijackers in the terminal. The Israeli ministerial team met for a concluding session on Thursday morning, several hours before the expiration of the ultimatum. Rabin reviewed the available information and consulted the Army Chief of Staff regarding the feasibility of a military rescue operation. The latter responded that at the moment none of the options reviewed by the military planning teams had a good chance to succeed, due to lack of information regarding some critical details. Rabin went on to argue that given the low likelihood of success attached to a military option, he recommended that the government decide to negotiate with the hijackers on the release of the Palestinians held in prison. He pointed out that previous Israeli governments had agreed to release prisoners in exchange for hostages in similar cases when there was no feasible military option. Peres dismissed Rabin's analogies, arguing that Israel could not afford to capitulate in the face of blunt blackmail. Such an exchange would severely damage Israel's capacity to fight terrorism in the future and would lead to an increased number of terrorist attacks on Israeli citizens. Rabin asked Peres whether he had specific recommendations; Peres suggested that the decision to negotiate be kept secret and that his own reservations be put on the record.

While debate in the government continued, Rabin left the room to brief the Defense and Foreign Affairs Committee of the Knesset. He told senior opposition leaders that the government was about to make the decision to exchange the hostages with Palestinian terrorists held in Israeli jails. The opposition leaders, Begin and Rimalt, assured Rabin of their party's support. Rabin then returned to the government meeting and announced the opposition's support for the negotiation option. Allon pointed out that a decision to negotiate with the hijackers would probably lead to an extension of the ultimatum and would allow time for acquiring additional information and for exploring additional courses of action. The government then decided unanimously to negotiate with the hijackers on the release of Palestinian prisoners.

Allon's prediction proved to be accurate. As soon as the hijackers in Entebbe heard about Israel's decision, they decided to extend the ultimatum until Sunday, July 4. In Israel, activity continued in two parallel avenues. Preparations on the substantive and technical details of negotiations were already under way. The general principle adopted was that Israel would not release those terrorists who took active part in operations where Israeli citizens had been killed. A special envoy was appointed to coordinate negotiation plans with the French government. At the same time, the non-Israeli hostages who were released and arrived in Paris were interrogated by Israeli intelligence agents, and military planning activities continued. A military rescue plan started to take shape during the early hours of Friday. On Friday noon, Rabin was presented with the military plan by Defense Minister Peres and Chief of Staff Gur. However, on being asked about the likelihood of success of such a plan, Gur replied that he could not estimate this likelihood before seeing a mock-up exercise by the forces designed to carry out this operation. In addition, one crucial issue had to be clarified. At this point

in time, no one knew whether the hijackers had wired the terminal in
Entebbe with explosives. The government was confronted with conflict-
ing reports on this issue. Rabin discussed it with the head of the
"Mossad," Israel's civilian intelligence agency, and the latter assured
Rabin that definite information would be available by Saturday
morning.

The military exercise on a model of the old Entebbe terminal on
Friday night convinced the Chief of Staff that as far as the raiding force
was concerned, the operation was feasible. In addition, by Saturday
morning, final details arrived and were reassuring with regard to the
likelihood of success of a rescue operation. Thus when the ministerial
team met on Saturday morning, both Peres and Gur argued that the
military operation had a high likelihood of success.

Rabin opened the special governmental session by reviewing the
available options. "We now have a military option with a high
probability of success," he said. "I ought to stress, however, that success
cannot be assured with certainty. Even if the military force can
overcome the terrorists, we should expect between 15 to 20 fatalities
among the hostages and the raiding forces. However, a failure would
have grave consequences: the death-toll would be enormous, Israel may
be charged of violating Uganda's sovereignty, and domestically, the
government would have to resign. In spite of the risks, I recommend that
we take the military option, because I believe that it has a good chance of
success" (Rabin, 1976, 1978, 1979a, 1979b; Ben Porat et al., 1976: 261-
263, 284-285). After this review, Rabin insisted on an open debate and
wanted every minister to be given a chance to speak. Rabin also required
that any decision in favor of the operation be unanimous. While the
debate continued, Rabin went to brief the opposition leaders and once
again was assured of their support. After a brief debate, the government
decided unanimously to carry out the military raid.[8]

ANALYSIS OF INDIVIDUAL CHOICE PROCESSES

All the characteristics of a crisis situation were present in the Entebbe
case. The decision makers perceived a high threat to basic values: loss of
a considerable number of human lives, a severe challenge to Israel's
antiterrorism policy, and a domestic threat to the government. The

---

8. The narrative description of the decision process is based on the following sources
(Allon, 1978; Ben Porat et al., 1976; Ofer, 1976; Rabin, 1976, 1978, 1979a, 1979b;
Williamson, 1976).

government also faced a short time situation defined by the hijackers' ultimata. Most important, the hijacking created for the decision makers an unavoidable tradeoff situation: they had to choose between "highly valued, but mutually incompatible goals" (Morse, 1972: 127). The following section attempts to account for the substantive and procedural characteristics of the three principal decision makers who coped with these stressful conditions.

Individual Search

Exploration of options was comprehensive for all three principal decision makers. Overall, four options were explored, but only three were given serious consideration. A "do nothing" option was brought up by Gallili on Wednesday, but after brief consideration it was dropped. All three decision makers believed that inaction was inferior on all value dimensions to the other options. Another option which was explored and given somewhat more consideration was to induce Amin to bring about the release of the hostages. Although Peres and Allon found this option preferable to direct negotiations with the hijackers, by Wednesday night it became clear from the testimony of the released hostages that Amin cooperated with the hijackers. Thus, by Thursday morning, the decision makers dealt with only two options: negotiation with the hijackers and a military rescue operation. With regard to the military option, a variety of plans were briefly considered but dropped because of the high likelihood of detection and because of the need for political coordination with foreign governments.

Although the search for options was comprehensive, it was consistent with preexisting guidelines for dealing with "bargaining raids" by Palestinian guerrillas. According to Rabin (1978; 1979a), one of his first undertakings as prime minister was to establish a set of guidelines dealing with various contingencies of bargaining raids. If such an event took place in Israel, the army was instructed to operate immediately without entering into negotiations with the terrorists. If the raid occurred in a friendly country, the policy was to urge the authorities of that country to take military action and to provide all the aid and advice required for such an operation. However, if the raid occurred in a hostile state, only if an independent military rescue was unfeasible was the government to consider negotiation with the terrorists. Thus, although there is substantial support for the analytic predictions regarding search, the observed search process in the Entebbe case is compatible with cybernetic predictions.

The outcomes assigned to the various options satisfy the mutual exclusiveness and logical exhaustiveness criteria. Options were discussed and considered in terms of success and failure, success meaning ability to release most—but not necessarily all—of the hostages. Failure was referred to in terms of inability to bring about hostage-release, or considerable loss of human life.

Revision Processes

The revision process at the individual and intraorganizational level is the most remarkable feature of the Entebbe decision process. Initial estimates regarding the credibility of the hijackers' threats were generated by utilizing background information concerning the behavior of Hadad's men in previous incidents, as well as current indicators emanating from released hostages' reports of the hijackers' behavior toward the hostages. On the basis of this information, it was established that the hijackers were likely to release the hostages if their demands were met, and likely to massacre the hostages if the ultimatum was not met or negotiation failed. Accordingly, the probability of release of the hostages as a result of a capitulation to the hijackers demands was estimated at about .77. Information received from released hostages further substantiated this estimate. Rabin viewed with skepticism the possibility of inducing Amin to bring about the release of the hostages. His estimate of the probability of success for this option averaged .20 throughout the crisis period. Allon and Peres were slightly more optimistic, Allon estimating this outcome to have a probability of .33 and Peres, .40. However, both Allon and Peres reduced their estimates to an average of .20 by Thursday morning, when it became apparent that Amin cooperated closely with the hijackers. Despite the low likelihood assigned to successful inducement of Amin, and despite the fact that Amin—even if successfully induced—had still to cope with the terrorists, this option was continuously pursued until the moment of the final decision.

The most dramatic shift in probability estimates concerns the outcomes assigned to the military rescue operation. On Thursday, July 1, the probability of success assigned to the military option averaged .32 for the three principal decision makers. On Saturday, however, this estimate changed to a .62 probability of success. To explain this substantial shift in estimates, a brief account of the revision process is in order. Given the complexity involved in estimating the success or failure of a military operation, the general outcomes were decomposed into distinct elements. Military planners perceived that the outcome of a rescue operation depended on two major clusters of factors: (1) factors concerning the ground operation which affect the release of the hostages by the commandos, and (2) factors concerning the safety of the planes on the ground and the safe take-off from Entebbe after the hostages were released.

The factors affecting the ground operation were (1) ability to land by surprise at the Entebbe airport; (2) ability to cover the distance between the landing track and the old terminal without being detected; (3) ability to overcome the hijackers and the Ugandan troops in the terminal.[9] The probability of surprise landing was estimated at best as .50 on Thursday. This was due mainly to the fact that the Entebbe airport was closed to all flights, and unidentified planes above the airport would have immediately raised suspicion.

Apparently reassured by the Israeli decision to negotiate, Amin allowed the reopening of the Entebbe airport to international flights. This increased the probability of surprise landing to .80, because it appeared possible to sneak in between civilian flights. The probability of undetected arrival to the terminal given surprise landing was estimated as .60 on Thursday, but increased to .80 by Saturday due to an innovative idea of one of the commanders of the raiding force. He suggested that the first unit of the raiding force would drive to the terminal in a black Mercedes, the standard vehicle of high-ranking Ugandan officers, and that the rest of the commandos be driven by Landrovers, which were used by the Ugandan army. Undetected approach to the terminal, given failure to land by surprise, was estimated as .20 throughout the planning stages. The probability of overcoming resistance in the terminal, assuming surprise break-in, was estimated at best as .50 on Thursday, due to the lack of definite information regarding wiring of the terminal with explosives. It was not until early Saturday that the Israeli Premier received assurance on this issue. At this point the probability of this conditional outcome was revised to .80. On the other hand, the probability of overcoming resistance within the terminal, in case of no surprise break-in, was estimated as .20 throughout the planning stages. The integration of these conditional outcomes is illustrated in Figure 3.

9. These factors are not independent and were not perceived as such by the military planning teams. Surprise landing was perceived to be the key to the entire operation and a precondition for the following stages on the ground. The ability of the commandos to overcome resistance in the terminal depended on the surprise element—the ability to cover the distance between the point where the planes stop and the terminal rapidly and without being detected en route.

694   *JOURNAL OF CONFLICT RESOLUTION*

Thursday's Estimates				Saturday's Estimates		
SGO	FGO			SGO	FGO	
.32[a]	.68			.61[a]	.39	

	ORT	NORT			ORT	NORT
AUD	.50 (.32)	(.68)[b] .50		AUD	.8 (.61)[b]	(.39) .2
AD	.20	.80		AD	.2	.8

	AUD				AUD	AD
SL	.60 (.40)	(.60) .40		SL	.80 (.68)	(.32) .20
NSL	.20	.50		NSL	.20	.8

	SL	NSL			SL	NSL
	.50	.50			.80	.20

Where: SGO = Success of Ground Operation
           FGO = Failure of Ground Operation
           ORT = Overcoming Resistance within the Terminal
           AUD = Approach (to terminal) Undetected
           AD = Approach (to terminal) Detected
           SL = Surprise Landing
           NSL = No Surprise Landing

Figure 3: Bayesian Integration of Outcomes Related to Success of the Ground Operation

a. Probabilities were calculated using Bayes's theorem. See Bracely et al. (1977) for detailed explanation of hierarchical inference procedures. For instance:

$$P(AUD) = P(SL) \cdot P(AUD|SL) + P(NSL) \cdot P(AUD|NSL)$$

$$P(ORT) = P(AUD) \cdot P(ORT|AUD) + P(AD) \cdot P(ORT|AD)$$

b. Numbers in parentheses signify revised probabilities.

The factors relating to the safety of the planes on the ground and the safe takeoff consisted of two independent elements. First, the parked planes, waiting for the hostages and the commandos, could have been an easy target for heavy weaponry that may have been located in the airport. On Thursday there was no definite information regarding the existence of heavy weapons in Entebbe; thus the probability of securing the planes was estimated at best as .50. By Saturday, however, it was firmly established that no such heavy weapons existed in the airport; thus the probability of securing the parked C-130 planes was revised to .90.[10]

Second, it was known to the military planners that several Mig-17 and Mig-21 jets were parked in Entebbe.[11] The risk was that those jets

10. Actually, one antitank cannon was located in the airport, but this fact was not known to the Israelis. Both Rabin and Allon indicated in their interviews with the author that had this fact been known, the probability of success would have been much lower.
11. The exact numbers were 7 Mig-21s and 4 Mig-17s.

would chase the Israeli heavy planes after the evacuation and destroy them in the air—they had to be destroyed by the raiding force to assure safe evacuation. However, on Thursday, it was unknown to what extent these jets were guarded and how difficult it would be to overcome resistance by Ugandan guards. Thus the probability of safe evacuation was determined as .40. But in this case, too, reassuring information arrived by Friday noon; the Migs were virtually unguarded. The probability of safe evacuation was revised to .80.

At this point, probabilistic estimates of the distinct elements had to be integrated to produce an overall estimate of the likelihood of success of the military rescue operation. Figure 4 illustrates this integration process.

Analysis of the revision process provides support for the analytic model's predictions concerning this decisional stage. It is not contended that the individuals or the intraorganizational teams performed the detailed calculations that have been illustrated above. Rather, the analysis of individual and intraorganizational revision suggests that both individuals and planning teams closely approximated, in an intuitive fashion, Bayesian approach to revision of opinion in light of new information. The evidence suggests that complex outcomes were decomposed into distinct elements, that conditions of dependence and interdependence among elements were determined and processed accordingly, and that the combination of those elements into an overall estimate intuitively approximated optimal methods such as Bayesian analysis. Although search for and processing of additional information was done according to predesigned programs, the outcome of the revision process was far from conservative. This is due to the fact that much was done beyond the prescriptions of available SOPs in terms of collecting information and processing available evidence. Not only is the way in which information was processed quite impressive; considerable efforts were invested in acquiring missing information.

The propositions of the cognitive model regarding revision processes are unsupported. Base rates were not ignored; on the contrary, they were clearly incorporated into the estimation process. This is best illustrated by the use of background evidence regarding previous operations of Hadad's organization in combination with current evidence regarding the behavior of the hijackers toward the hostages. This combination allowed the decision makers to assess the credibility of the hijackers' threats. Moreover, there is no evidence to suggest that unequal weights were assigned to data supporting favorable outcomes relative to data supporting unfavorable outcomes. The decision makers were equally

696   *JOURNAL OF CONFLICT RESOLUTION*

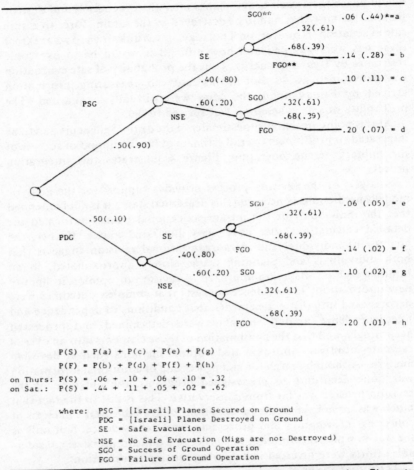

$$P(S) = P(a) + P(c) + P(e) + P(g)$$
$$P(F) = P(b) + P(d) + P(f) + P(h)$$

on Thurs: P(S) = .06 + .10 + .06 + .10 = .32
on Sat.:   P(S) = .44 + .11 + .05 + .02 = .62

where: PSG = [Israeli] Planes Secured on Ground
        PDG = [Israeli] Planes Destroyed on Ground
        SE = Safe Evacuation
        NSE = No Safe Evacuation (Migs are not Destroyed)
        SGO = Success of Ground Operation
        FGO = Failure of Ground Operation

Figure 4: Integration of Probability Estimates Assigned to Independent Elements Which Affect the Overall Success of the Military Operation

*All numbers in parentheses signify the revised estimates provided to the principal decision makers on Saturday morning.
**Probabilities relating to the success or failure of the ground operation are adapted from Figure 3.

receptive to "bad news"—for instance Amin's refusal to cooperate with Israel—as they were with respect to "good news."

Given the enormous time pressure the decision makers experienced, and given the overwhelming quantity of information they were required to process, the quality of the revision process was remarkably high.

Evaluation Processes

So far, interindividual differences in terms of perceptions of options and outcomes, and in terms of probabilistic estimates, were marginal. The evaluation process, however, is the key in explanations of interindividual differences. The same value dimensions were identified by all three decision makers as relevant for the cost-benefit considerations. These dimensions were loss of human life, credibility of Israel's antiterrorism policy, domestic support for the government, and Israel's diplomatic status. The first significant differences among decision makers emerge regarding their evaluation of the relative importance of the various dimensions. The WV vectors in Figure 6 illustrate clearly these different evaluations.

Rabin's and Allon's rank ordering of the value dimensions is identical. However, when translated into interval scores, differences clearly emerge. Rabin considered the human factor to be much more important relative to the credibility factor. However, these differences become marginal when compared to Peres's evaluation. For Peres, by far the most important factor was the credibility factor. Furthermore, Peres evaluated the diplomatic factor to be more important than the domestic one, whereas Rabin and Allon evaluated the domestic factor to dominate the diplomatic one.

As indicated earlier, by Thursday morning only two viable options were perceived by the principal decision makers. However, our analysis will include the option to attempt to induce Amin to cooperate.[12] How did these options rank on the value dimensions identified above? Figure 5 describes qualitatively the decision problem in terms of the implications for the various value dimensions which were identified by the decision makers.

The most salient feature of the decision problem is the tradeoff between human life and the credibility of Israel's antiterrorism policy. There is no outcome which was perfect on both value dimensions. A less salient—but nevertheless important—tradeoff is that between domestic support and diplomatic support. This tradeoff situation is of particular significance because it demonstrates the difficulty and complexity of the decision, and because it suggests that no option clearly dominated all of the other options. It seems obvious, therefore, that the decision makers were forced into a situation requiring value integration which is compatible with the propositions of the analytic model. Figure 6

12. This option is included in the analysis, since it was continuously pursued even beyond the Thursday decision. Also, it enables us to examine whether it was rationally justified to drop it from the group deliberation process.

698   JOURNAL OF CONFLICT RESOLUTION

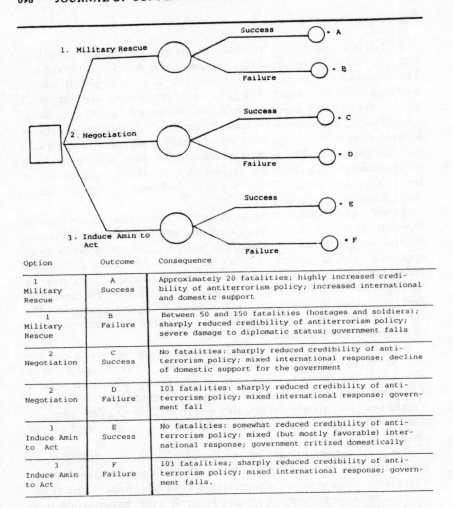

Option	Outcome	Consequence
1 Military Rescue	A Success	Approximately 20 fatalities; highly increased credibility of antiterrorism policy; increased international and domestic support
1 Military Rescue	B Failure	Between 50 and 150 fatalities (hostages and soldiers); sharply reduced credibility of antiterrorism policy; severe damage to diplomatic status; government falls
2 Negotiation	C Success	No fatalities: sharply reduced credibility of antiterrorism policy; mixed international response; decline of domestic support for the government
2 Negotiation	D Failure	103 fatalities: sharply reduced credibility of antiterrorism policy; mixed international response; government fall
3 Induce Amin to Act	E Success	No fatalities: somewhat reduced credibility of antiterrorism policy: mixed (but mostly favorable) international response; government critized domestically
3 Induce Amin to Act	F Failure	103 fatalities; sharply reduced credibility of antiterrorism policy; mixed international response; government falls.

displays the analytic solution to the Entebbe decision for all three
principal decision makers, as was derived from the coders' judgments.[13]

    13. Utility transformations for coders' scaling of outcomes on the various value-
dimensions was conducted in the following way: (a) on each value-dimension mean coders'
estimates were computed; (b) the outcome with the highest score received a value of 100,
and the lowest-scaled outcome received a score of 0; (c) outcomes were arranged from
highest to lowest scaled, and distances between each pair of outcomes were computed; (d)
the total utility distance—that is, 100 was divided by the sum of between-pairs distances to
solve for the preference function; (e) the sum of distances between any given outcome and
the highest-ranked outcome was multiplied by the preference function value and the
product was subtracted from 100; (f) an arbitrary indifference point was determined—in
this case, 50—and the utility for each outcome was subtracted from this value to signify

TABLE A
Utility Transformation for the Human Value Dimension: An Example

Outcome	Value	Between-Pair Distances	Utility	Transformation to Pos. & Neg. Utilities
2.C	0 fatalities		100	100 − 50 = 50
3.E	0 fatalities	0	100	100 − 50 = 50
1.A	− 20 fatalities	20	100- 20 * .67 = 86.7	86.7 − 50 = 36.7
2.D	−103 fatalities	83	100-103 * .67 = 31.1	31.1 − 50 = 18.9
3.F	−103 fatalities	0	100-103 * .67 = 31.1	31.1 − 50 = −18.9
1.B	−150 fatalities	47	100-150 * .67 = 0	0 − 50 = −50
		150		

$$(x) = \frac{100}{150} = .67$$

As was indicated earlier, we do not claim that the decision makers actually performed these complex calculations, but rather that they intuitively, and in a qualitative fashion, approximated the kind of logic required by analytic procedures. So far, nothing has been said about the risk dispositions of the decision makers. Our analysis implicitly assumes that the decision makers were risk-neutral, but this does not necessarily need to be the case.[14] It is usually assumed by proponents of rational choice models that people are risk-averse with respect to positive utilities and risk-acceptant with respect to negative utilities (Kahneman and Tversky, 1979: 253-255). To take into account risk disposition, a logarithmic transformation of the utilities was performed for each decision maker.[15] The results indicate one major difference from the

positive and negative utilities. An example for the application of this method is shown in Table A. For a more elaborate discussion of the procedure, see Braceley et al. (1977) and Stein and Tanter (1980: appendix).

14. I am indebted to Bob Axelrod for bringing up this issue.

15. The logarithmic transformation of utilities was conducted by transforming the formula

$$U_i = \sum_{j=i}^{m} [U(O_i, VD_j) * W(VD_j)]$$

into a logarithmic form which yields

$$(U_i) = \sum_{j=1}^{m} [U(O_i, VD_j)^{W(VD_j)}]$$

$$\log (U_i) = \sum_{j=1}^{m} [\log(O_i, VD_j) * \log(VD_j)]$$

700   *JOURNAL OF CONFLICT RESOLUTION*

I. Rabin's "Calculations"

Outcome	The SE Matrix[a] Value Dimension Human	Cred.	Dom.	Int.	The WV Matrix Weight for Value Dim.		The U Matrix Utility for outcome		
1.A	36.7	50	50	50	Hum. 42.7		1.A 4417.1	P=.32(.62)[b]	
1.B	-50	-33.6	-50	-47.6	Cred. 27.3		1.B -4508.2	P=.68(.38)	
2.C	50	-21	-16	1.2	• Dom. 17.6	=	2.C 1294.6	P=.77(.77)	
2.D	-18.9	-50	-46	-34.8	Int. 12.1		2.D -3402.7	P=.23(.23)	
3.E	50	6.3	-6	1.2			3.E 2215.9	P=.20(.20)	
3.F	-18.9	-43.1	-36	-25.2			3.F -2922.2	P=.80(.80)	

SEU (Military Rescue) = -1652.1(1025.5)[c]
SEU (Negotiation) = 214.1(214.1)
SEU (Induce Amin) = -1894.5(-1894.5)
Threshold Probability for Military Rescue[d] = .52

II. Peres' "Calculations"

Outcome	Human	Cred.	Dom.	Int.	Weight		Utility		
1.A	36.7	50	50	50	Hum. 27		1.A 4640.9	P=.32(.62)	
1.B	-50	-20	-41.3	-38.9	Cred. 42		1.B -3416.3	P=.68(.38)	
2.C	50	-12	-12.5	-18.8	• Dom. 13	=	2.C 345.1	P=.77(.77)	
2.D	-18.9	-50	-50	-50	Int. 18		2.D -4160.3	P=.23(.23)	
3.E	50	8	-23.3	4.5			3.E 1464.1	P=.20(.20)	
3.F	-18.9	-20	-44.9	-48.4			3.F -2805.2	P=.80(.80)	

SEU (Military Rescue) = -838.9(1579.2)
SEU (Negotiation) = -691.1(-691.1)
SEU (Induce Amin) = -1951.3(-1951.3)
Threshold Probability for Military Rescue = .34

III. Allon's "Calculations"

Outcome	Human	Cred.	Dom.	Int.	Weight				
1.A	36.7	50	50	50	Hum 34.7		1.A -538.5	P=.32(.62)	
1.B	-50	-35	-44.4	-50	Cred. 32		1.B -4419.8	P=.68(.38)	
1.C	50	-12.5	-7.9	1.6	• Dom. 17.9	=	2.C 1215.2	P=.77(.77)	
1.D	-18.9	-50	-50	-35.8	Int. 15.4		2.D -3702.2	P=.23(.23)	
1.E	50	15	16.4	-0.6			3.E 2499.3	P=.20(.20)	
1.F	-18.9	-15	-3.2	-33.8			3.F -2250.6	P=.80(.80)	

SEU(Military Rescue) = -1553.1(1134.4)
SEU(Negotiation) = 86.5(86.5)
SEU(Amin) = -1300.6(-1300.6)
Threshold Probability for Military Rescue = .50

Figure 6: The Analytic Solution for the Entebbe Decision

a. See Figure 1 for formal specification.
b. P = probability of the given outcome. Probabilities outside the parentheses represent Thursday's (July 1) estimates. Probabilities within the parentheses represent Saturday's (July 3) estimates.
c. Utilities in parentheses represent Saturday's (July 3) evaluation.
d. Threshold probability refers to the probability of success—in our case, of the military operation—under which the decision maker would be indifferent between negotiation and military rescue. It is calculated by the following formula:

$$SEU (Neg.) = U(1.A) \cdot P + U(1.B) (1-P)$$

Solving for P: $SEU (Neg.) = U(1.A) \cdot P + U(1.B) - U(1.B) \cdot P$
                   $SEU (Neg.) - U(1.B) = [U(1.A) - U(1.B)] P$

$$P = \frac{SEU (Neg.) - U(1.B)}{U(1.A) - U(1.B)}$$

linear version: threshold probabilities drop significantly for all decision makers. For Rabin, the threshold probability drops from .52 to .38; for Allon it drops from .46 to .35, and for Peres it drops from .34 to .30. Thus Peres was supposed to have preferred the military option even on Thursday, July 1. Whatever the version of risk disposition we adopt, it seems to be supported by evidence. Rabin clearly preferred the negotiation option on Thursday, July 1, when the likelihood of success of the military option was low, and shifted to support of the military option on Saturday, July 3, when the probability of success for the military raid increased markedly. Allon, whose threshold probability of success for the military option was slightly lower, and hence was less convinced of the absolute necessity of negotiation, still supported the negotiation option but pointed out that the delay of the ultimatum by the hijackers would allow an opportunity to acquire additional information. Peres, whose threshold probability of success for the military option was very close to the actual probability of success (slightly higher according to the linear version and slightly lower according to the logarithmic version), had severe reservations regarding the adoption of the negotiation option on Thursday. When additional reassuring information began to pour in by late Thursday night and early Friday, he shifted his preference strongly toward the military option and began pressing both the chief of staff and other government ministers to add their support to that option. For Rabin, however, much more information supporting success of a military operation was necessary before he could shift his preferences. Indeed, it was only on Saturday morning that Rabin became convinced that a military operation had sufficient prospects of success to shift his preferences.

It is also clear that the option of attempting to induce Amin to bring about the release of the hostages was rationally dropped. For Rabin and Peres, the Amin option was dominated by both the military and the negotiation options by Thursday. For Allon, it was dominated only by the negotiation option on Thursday and by both the military and negotiation options by Saturday.

The analysis of the evaluation stage provides support for the propositions of the analytic model. Decision makers were aware of and willing to make value tradeoffs among highly valued but mutually incompatible goals. In particular, they were willing first to sacrifice severe loss of credibility regarding their antiterrorism policy for the sake of saving human life, but when they were sufficiently convinced that a military option had a reasonable chance of success, they were willing to sustain some loss of innocent human life (hostages) to preserve credibility. Moreover, they were aware that even a successful completion of the military rescue operation may well have some diplomatic ramifications.[16] Although the existing SOPs of coping with bargaining raids suggest built-in tradeoff calculations regarding credibility and human factors, the actual evaluation process included a higher degree of multivalue integration than prescribed by those guidelines. There is no evidence of attempts to ignore or discount certain value dimensions so as to establish cognitive consistency. There exists, however, evidence regarding the use of analogies as a means of bolstering policy preferences. This is demonstrated by Rabin's use of previous decisions to negotiate with hijackers as an argument supporting his preference of the negotiation option. But this did not seem to have impressed other decision makers. There is also some evidence which suggests predecisional bolstering (Janis and Mann, 1977: 82-85). The likelihood of success of the military option was presented by Rabin and Peres to the other decision makers as slightly higher than it actually was, but the key to the government decision was the preferences of the three principal decision makers.[17]

GROUP DECISION PROCESS

Group deliberations took place in two formal settings. The first was the small ministerial team appointed by the government to cope with the crisis; the second was the large cabinet session. Within the small ministerial setting, the interindividual dynamics can be accounted for best in terms of the analytic model's predictions of argumentation, persuasion attempts, and multiple advocacy (George, 1972). The ministerial team had reviewed most—if not all—of the options considered at intraorganizational levels, including a variety of military plans and negotiation plans. Participants were presented with most of the information required for the various options and made numerous tactical decisions such as instructing the special envoy sent to Paris to conduct negotiations. However, intragroup conflict was mostly checked within the ministerial team. Rabin and Peres, with a history of strained relationships, were able to make the best of their differing attitudes. Whereas Peres continuously pushed for the military option, Rabin cast a prudent eye on the numerous technical and substantive problems involved in its execution. Allon, for his part, dealt with the diplomatic

---

16. Foreign ministry aides pointed out the fact that an anti-Israel motion would occur at the UN as a result of violating Uganda's territorial sovereignty by the military raid.

17. Here we adopt the logarithmic version of the evaluation process, which seems to account better for the Peres-Rabin debate at the Thursday session.

	The GP Matrix			The RI Vector		0 Vector	
SEU of Options:	Rabin	Individual Peres	Allon	Authority Score for Individual[b]		Group Preference for Option	
Military	-5.3	-3.1	-3.1	Rabin	0.41	Mil	-4.0
Negotiate	-2.3	-3.7	-2.6	Peres	0.34	Neg	-2.9
Amin	-5.7	-5.8	-4.7	Allon	0.25	Amin	-5.5

Figure 7: The Distribution of Preferences and Authority Across Individuals During Thursday's Session[a]

a. Logarithmic version of SEUs.
b. Authoritativeness scores are derived by averaging individual coders' scores of authoritativeness for each decision maker.

aspects of the crisis, and also served as a "balancer" between the two other principal decision makers.

The differences between Rabin and Peres emerged, however, in the broader context of the cabinet meetings, especially during the Thursday session when Peres expressed his reservations regarding the negotiation option Rabin had previously advocated. Given the difference in individual preferences, and given the almost uniform distribution of authoritativeness among decision makers, a weighted aggregation of preferences would predict the acceptance of the negotiation option, but not as a consensus decision. This situation is well described in Figure 7. Rabin's ultimate success to achieve a unanimous vote in favor of the negotiation option during the Thursday session and on the military option during the Saturday session was largely due to his success in securing the opposition's support. On Thursday, his announcement that the major opposition party would back the decision to negotiate with the hijackers sharply reduced the domestic ramifications attached to the negotiation option and may have been the ultimate cause behind Peres's vote in favor of this option. On Saturday, the same factor—namely, the opposition's support of the military option—again impressed minor government ministers and led them to vote unanimously in favor of the rescue operation.

Although there is no evidence of concurrence-seeking behavior among the principal decision makers, minor governmental participants may have displayed such a tendency. Rabin, however, insisted on an open debate despite the time constraints, and in both decisional occasions required unanimous decisions. In both group settings, tradeoffs were acknowledged and considered, and there is no evidence to support strongly either a concurrence-seeking pattern or an "elimination by aspects" process. Thus, group decision processes in the Entebbe case strongly support an analytical model of argumentation, influence, and persuasion processes.

CONCLUSION

Several propositions can be made as a result of the analysis of the Entebbe decisions. First, it is possible to discriminate empirically between various models of individual and group decisions on the basis of clear differentiation among the testable predictions deduced from each model. Second, although a certain decision may be compatible with the propositions of several models, the relative plausibility of different explanations can be clearly established. In this particular case, the predictions of the analytic model fit much better the observed choice processes at both the individual and group levels. The Entebbe case demonstrates that individuals can be vigilant explorers of multiple options, competent information processors, and comprehensive evaluators of multiple values under the most stressful circumstances. The evidence suggests awareness of and willingness to accept highly sensitive value tradeoffs and efficient revision of opinion in light of new information. These findings run contrary to most of the evidence regarding choice processes under crisis conditions, and may suggest that decision-making in the Entebbe crisis is the exception rather than the rule.

Why this is the case is not entirely clear, but some speculations can be made at this stage. First, existing SOPs, instead of constraining the decision makers, provided a useful guide for the exploration of multiple options, had a built-in element of value tradeoffs, and were sufficiently flexible to allow on-the-spot improvisations. Second, the distribution of authoritativeness across decision makers was sufficiently uniform to turn interindividual conflict into an asset rather than an obstacle. Interindividual conflict contributed to the quality of group choice, in that it allowed for argumentation and multiple advocacy. Such processes could not have been observed in highly differential authority structures where the leader always prevails. Finally, the openness of the decision-making group to advice and information from advisory groups, as well as their willingness to secure support from competing political elites, may have allowed a high-quality decision process under the most stressful crisis conditions.

REFERENCES

ALLISON, G. T. (1971) Essence of Decision: Explaining the Cuban Missile Crisis, Boston: Little, Brown.

—— and M. H. HALPERIN (1972) "Bureaucratic politics: a paradigm and some policy implications," pp. 40-79 in R. Tanter and R. H. Ullman (eds.) Theory and Policy in International Relations. Princeton: Princeton Univ. Press.

ALLON, Y. (1978) Interview with the author, Jerusalem, May 23, 1978.

ART, R. J. (1973) "Bureaucratic politics and American foreign policy: a critique." Policy Sciences 4, 4: 467-490.

AXELROD, R. (1977) "Argumentation in foreign policy settings: Britain in 1918, Munich in 1938, and Japan in 1970." J. of Conflict Resolution 21, 4: 727-743.

——— [ed.] (1976) The Structure of Decision: The Cognitive Maps of Political Elites. Princeton: Princeton Univ. Press.

——— (1973) "Schema theory: an information processing model of perception and cognition." Amer. Pol. Sci. Rev. 67, 4: 1248-1266.

BEN-PORAT, Y., E. HABER, and Z. SCHIFF (1976) Tissa 139 [Flight 139]. Tel-Aviv: Zmora, Bitan, Modan. (Hebrew)

BRACELEY, S. et al. (1977) Handbook of Decision Analysis. McLean, VA: Advanced Research Projects Agency, Decisions and Designs Inc.

BRECHER, M. (1980) Decisions in Crisis: Israel, 1967 and 1973. Berkeley: Univ. of California Press.

——— (1979) "State behavior in international crisis: a model." J. of Conflict Resolution 23, 3: 446-480.

BURNSTEIN, E. and M. BERBAUM (1979) "Policy decisions by governmental groups: an information-processing analysis." University of Michigan. (mimeo)

BURNSTEIN, E., H. MILLER, A. VINOKUR, S. KATZ, and J. CROWLEY (1971) "Risky shift is eminently rational." J. of Personality and Social Psychology 20, 3: 462-471.

CARTWRIGHT, D. (1971) "Risk taking by individuals and groups: an assessment of research employing choice dilemmas." J. of Personality and Social Psychology 20, 3: 361-378.

COLLINS, B. E. and H. GUETZKOW (1964) A Social Psychology of Group Processes for Decision Making. New York: John Wiley.

COOMBS, C. R., R. M. DAWES, and A. TVERSKY (1970) Mathematical Psychology: An Elementary Introduction. Englewood Cliffs, NJ: Prentice-Hall.

DAVIS, J. H. (1973) "Group decision and social interaction: a theory of social decision schemes." Psych. Rev. 80: 92-135.

DESTLER, I. M. (1972) Presidents, Bureaucrats and Foreign Policy. Princeton: Princeton Univ. Press.

GALLHOFER, I. N. and W. E. SARIS (1979) "Strategy choices and foreign policy decision makers: the Netherlands 1914." J. of Conflict Resolution 23, 3: 425-445.

GEORGE, A. L. (1979) "Case studies and theory development: the method of structured, focused comparison," in P. G. Lauren (ed.) Diplomacy: New Approaches, in History, Theory and Policy. New York: Free Press.

——— (1972) "The case for multiple advocacy in making foreign policy." Amer. Pol. Sci. Rev. 66, 3: 751-794.

706   *JOURNAL OF CONFLICT RESOLUTION*

HERMANN, C. F. [ed.] (1972) International Crises: Insights from Behavioral Research. New York: Free Press.

HOLSTI, O. R. (1976) "Foreign policy formation viewed cognitively," pp. 18-54 in R. Axelrod (ed.) The Structure of Decision: The Cognitive Maps of Political Elites. Princeton: Princeton Univ. Press.

——— (1962) "The belief system and national images: a case history." J. of Conflict Resolution 6, 3: 244-252.

——— and A. L. GEORGE (1975) "The effects of stress on the performance of foreign policy makers." Pol. Sci. Annual 6: 255-319.

HORELICK, A. L., A. R. JOHNSON, and J. D. STEINBRUNER (1975) The Study of Soviet Foreign Policy: Decision-Theory Related Approaches. Beverly Hills, CA: Sage.

JANIS, I. L. (1972) Victims of Groupthink. Boston: Houghton & Miffin.

——— and L. MANN (1977) Decision Making: A Psychological Analysis of Conflict, Choice and Commitment. New York: Free Press.

JERVIS, R. (1976) Perception and Misperception in International Politics. Princeton: Princeton Univ. Press.

KAHNEMAN, D. and A. TVERSKY (1979) "Prospect theory: an analysis of decision under risk." Econometrica 47, 2: 263-291.

KAPLAN, M. F. (1977) "Discussion polarization effects on modified jury decision paradigms: informational influences." Sociometry 40, 3: 262-271.

KAPLAN, M. F. and C. E. MILLER (1977) "Judgments and group discussion: effects of presentation and memory factors on polarization." Sociometry 40, 4: 337-342.

McGUIRE, W. J. (1966) "The current status of consistency theory." pp. 1-46 in S. Feldman (ed.) Cognitive Consistency: Motivational Antecedents and Behavioral Consequences. New York: Academic Press.

MORSE, E. L. (1972) "Crisis diplomacy, interdependence, and the politics of international economic relations." pp. 123-150 in R. Tanter and R. A. Ullman (eds.) Theory and Policy in International Relations. Princeton: Princeton Univ. Press.

NISBETT, R. E. and L. ROSS (1980) Human Inference: Strategies and Shortcomings of Social Judgment. Englewood Cliffs, NJ: Prentice-Hall.

OFER, Y. (1976) Operation Thunder: The Entebbe Raid. Harmonsworth, England: Penguin.

PERES, S. and M. GUR (1976) "Excerpts from a press conference." Ma'ariv, July 4, 1976.

PRUITT, D. G. (1971a) "Choice shift in group discussion: an introductory review." J. of Personality and Social Psychology 20, 3: 339-360.

——— (1971b) "Conclusions: toward an understanding of choice shifts in group discussion." J. of Personality and Social Psychology 20, 3: 495-510.

——— (1965) "Definition of the situation as a determinant of international action," pp. 391-432 in H. C. Kelman (ed.) International Behavior: A Social Psychological Analysis. New York: Holt, Rinehart & Winston.

RABIN, Y. (1979a) Pinkas Sherut [Personal Service File]. Tel-Aviv: Ma'ariv. (Hebrew)

——— (1979b) "How long are you going to play roulette with our children's life?" (excerpts from Rabin's memoirs). Ma'ariv, August 10, 1979, pp. 13-14.

——— (1978) Interview with the author, Tel-Aviv, July 6, 1978.

——— (1976) "Interview with the prime minister." Ma'ariv, July 5.

RAIFFA, H. (1968) Decision Analysis: Introductory Lectures on Choices Under Uncertainty. Menlo Park, CA: Addison-Wesley.

SHAPIRO, H. J. and G. M. BONHAM (1973) "Cognitive process and foreign policy decision making." Int. Studies Q. 17, 2: 147-176.

SIMON, H. A. (1969) The Sciences of the Artificial. Cambridge: MIT Press.
——— (1957) Models of Man: Social and Rational. New York: John Wiley.
SNYDER, G. H. and P. DIESING (1977) Conflict Among Nations. Princeton: Princeton Univ. Press.
SNYDER, J. L. (1978) "Rationality at the brink: the role of cognitive processes in failures of deterrence." World Politics 30, 3: 345-365.
STEIN, J. G. and R. TANTER (1980) Rational Decision Making: Israel's Security Choices, 1967. Columbus: Ohio State Univ. Press.
STEINBRUNER, J. D. (1974) The Cybernetic Theory of Decision. Princeton: Princeton Univ. Press.
TANTER, R. (1978) "International crisis behavior: an appraisal of the literature." Jerusalem J. of Int. Relations 3 (Winter-Spring): 340-374.
——— (1974) Modeling and Managing International Conflicts: The Berlin Crises. Beverly Hills, CA: Sage.
TVERSKY, A. (1972) "Elimination by aspects: a theory of choice." Psych. Rev. 79: 281-299.
——— and D. KAHNEMAN (1974) "Judgment under uncertainty: heuristics and biases." Science 185: 1124-1130.
VINOKUR, A. and E. BURNSTEIN (1974) "Effects of partially shared persuasive arguments on group-induced shifts." J. of Personality and Social Psychology 29, 3: 305-315.
WILLIAMSON, T. (1976) Counterstrike Entebbe. London: Collins.

Part II
The Relationship between
Terrorism and Insurgency in Africa

General

[6]

AFRICAN GUERRILLAS AND INDIGENOUS GOVERNMENTS

by

Femi Otubanjo

The Theory of Guerrilla Warfare

The acceptance of guerrilla warfare as 'sui generis' can be traced to the remarkable use by Mao's Communist Party of guerrilla tactics to wrestle power from the Kuomintang and impose on China a new socio-political structure. Hitherto, guerrilla warfare was treated in theoretical writings on war and strategy as mere adjuncts of conventional warfare. In pre-Mao writings on small wars, guerrilla warfare was perceived as standing no chance of success when fought independently of regular warfare. As Laqueur reported, Jomini, the famous French military thinker of the nineteenth century, saw no prospect of success for wars fought by partisans alone: "popular uprising without the support of a disciplined and regular army would always be suppressed".[1]

It is not surprising, therefore, that writings relating to guerrilla tactics were, for the most part, concerned with the amount of scope to be given to small roving bands of irregular soldiers or partisans in a war or wars involving engagements between massed armies. The use of guerrilla tactics was also, significantly, thought appropriate only for small units of professional soldiers operating to undermine the enemy's war capabilities by selective acts of sabotage or for bands of partisans, that is, civilians committed to the defence of their values, institutions or beliefs.

Paradoxically, Karl Marx and Engels, whose works have formed the legitimising creed of nearly all of the major guerrilla movements in the 20th century and have become essential reading for guerrilla activists, shared the general scepticism about the utility of guerrilla action, although for different reasons. For Marx, guerrilla training and practices were ill-suited to the attainment of the discipline and uniformity of purpose essential for a successful revolution. Guerrillas, having been conditioned to free-roving habits, looting and revenge raids were likely to transform, in peace time, into thugs and lawless bands which can be easily attracted to banditry, intimidation, blackmail and such other lawless acts which are bound to defeat the purpose of a revolution — the liberation of oppressed peoples from domination and exploitation.[2]

Although Engels was less sanguine than Marx in his assessment of the utility of guerrilla tactics, he was, nonetheless circumspect in his estimation of its value. Engels believed that guerrilla war was essential for bringing about revolutionary change for he saw guerrilla warfare as the only means by which a small or weak people can defeat a bigger or more powerful people. Engels, however, believed that there was very little prospect of success for guerrilla warfare in Europe, his reason being that "the fanaticism and national

32

enthusiasm" needed for a sustained programme of guerrilla action are not customarily exhibited by "civilized people". Besides, Europe with its developed interior, well-spread urban connurbations and efficient communication systems offered little or none of the inaccessible terrain which guerrillas require as sanctuaries. Guerrilla warfare was, consequently, in Engel's view best suited for those areas of the world in which the terrain, the forest and jungle offer excellent sanctuaries to guerrilla fighters. As far as the European theatre was concerned, Engels shared the popular view that guerrilla tactics could only be meaningfully employed in conjunction with the action of regular forces.[3]

Although Engels perceived guerrilla warfare as a veritable instrument of revolution and social change in those areas which offer excellent sanctuaries to guerrilla fighters, in the form of large expanses of jungle and inaccessible terrain, he was rather sceptical about the prospects of guerrilla warfare in these "backwaters" of the world. His scepticism was informed by the total absence in these areas of an industrial proletariat which, in the Marx-Engels dynamics of revolutionary process, only can provide the leadership and organizational opportunities required for a successful revolution. The abundance of a placid and traditionally conservative peasantry did not, in Engels' view, provide the best context for generating revolutionary zeal and prosecuting a guerrilla war against an oppressive and exploitative ruling class.

The history of guerrilla warfare since the second world war has had the paradoxical consequence of proving pre-Mao assessments of the relative utility of guerrilla warfare both right and wrong. It has shown quite clearly that in the European theatre, from which the factual framework for the evaluation of guerrilla warfare in pre-Mao writings was derived, guerrilla warfare has very limited utility. The general disposition of the civil population to accept the rule of law, the democratization of affluence,[4] the efficiency of communicative systems, the existence and efficacy of complex and highly developed intelligence networks, the presence of well-organized, well-armed and adaptable armed services, and the de-ruralization of the interior have combined with other factors to rob the guerrilla activist in Europe and North America of both the physical and popular support which are crucial to his survival and the success of his mission. The experience of the Basque separatists of Spain, the Red Army Faction of Germany (better known as the Baader-Meinhof Group), the Red Brigades of Italy, the Quebec Liberation Front of Canada and various groups in the United States of America have shown that in the developed parts of the world the value of guerrilla activities resides in keeping issues alive rather than in effecting the restructuring of society which most guerrilla movements see as their primary objective. Carlos Marighella's urban slums[5] are yet to prove impregnable and resilient enough in these parts of the world to provide the sanctuary in which urban guerrillas could weather the sustained and superior counter-attacks of the forces of the establishment and move on from a state of strategic defensive or tactical defence to that of strategic offensive.

In Asia, Latin America and Africa the gap between pre-Mao theories of guerrilla warfare and practice has been considerably wide. The victories of the Communist Party in China, the Fidelistas in Cuba, the Viet Cong in Vietnam through the success of liberation movements in Southern Africa to the triumph of the Sandinistas in Nicaragua have repeatedly undermined the general premise that guerrilla warfare can only be meaningfully prosecuted within a war or wars involving regular armies. Rather than being a dependent variable in the context of conventional warfare, guerrilla warfare has in the last three and a half decades become a major instrument of structural change outside the geographical reaches of the NATO and Warsaw Pact sub-systems.

The credit for extending the role of guerrilla warfare in political and social change and establishing it as a unique and comprehensive mode of warfare goes to Mao Tse Tung and the Communist Party of China. Under Mao's leadership the Communist Party shifted from the orthodox Marxist-Leninist dependence on the urban proletariat and the strategy of attaining political power and structural changes in socio-economic relations through urban uprisings and popular revolt to a policy of retreat (tactical mutation) from the urban centres to the rural areas and reliance on the peasantry. Consequently, Mao and his men acquired, between 1927 and 1934, bases in various parts of Central China and sought to mobilize the peasantry against the oppressive feudal system in which they lived. Mao, indeed, considered the peasantry as appropriate instruments for revolutionary change principally because of their large numbers; but the all-powerful tide of peasantry which he predicted would sweep away the exploitative feudal system in China failed to materialize in the 1930s.

However, Mao's faith in the usefulness of the peasantry did not diminish nor did circumstances enable him and the Communist Party to dispense with the support of the peasantry. Between 1933-34 the Communist policy of fighting an "open war" against the Kuomintang was clearly shown to be unwise for the Communists were defeated in successive battles. The Kuomintang decimated their numbers and alienated their support by evacuating the rural population in large numbers and training a vast army of anti-Communist militias. Consequently the Communists were forced to move their army and the core of their support to a safer part of China, hence the legendary *Long March* in which about one hundred thousand men and women embarked on a journey from the South-West of China to the Northern Province of Shensi.

The remote, barren and inaccessible terrain of Shensi provided for Mao and his men a safe base from which they built up a formidable army and expanded the Communist Party's political base. In these tasks they were helped by the Japanese invasion of China. The Communist Party identified itself with the nationalistic fervour and general antipathy against the Japanese and, indeed, signed an agreement with the Kuomintang to co-operate in expelling the Japanese from Chinese soil. But while the KMT dissipated its resources on fighting the Japanese, the Communist Party steadily built up its forces and support as well as expanding the area under its control in preparation for the confrontation with the Kuomintang which they as well as the KMT knew would eventually come. Mao perceived the Japanese invasion as a transitory stage in Chinese history for he saw no prospect for Japanese imperialism. Japan was, in his view, simply too small to impose its hegemony successfully on China and all of South-East Asia and cope with British, American and Russian military power at the same time.

While the Japanese invasion gave the Communist Party the opportunity to consolidate its gains and demonstrate its administrative and political skills in the areas in which it controlled, it exposed the inadequacies and decadence of the Kuomintang's administrative and military machineries. Thus, when the confrontation finally came, after the Japanese surrender, the Communist Party had established itself as a better alternative to the KMT. In the civil war, Mao and his men dug themselves into the countryside in readiness for a protracted war. The Communist Party gradually gained control of the rural areas and the support of the rural population. The KMT retreated and concentrated their forces in the urban centres where they were gradually surrounded and systematically overpowered by Mao's revolutionary army. The revolutionary tide of peasantry which had failed to evolve in the '30s finally sprung into life and swept away the KMT from power in China.

The success of the Communist Party in China undermined some assumptions about the nature and utility of guerrilla warfare. In the first place it showed that guerrilla warfare can have a life of its own and be used independently to attain specific political/socio-economic objectives. Mao and his men conducted their struggle first against the Japanese and then against the Kuomintang mostly through guerrilla tactics particularly after the failure of the policy of "open war" against the KMT. The Red Army was only progressively transformed into regular formations in the final stages of the civil war when it became necessary to meet the enemy on his own territory — the urban centres — and demolish his last resistance in a decisive way. The transformation of the Red Army from a guerrilla force into a regular army later formed the basis of Mao's prescription that all guerrilla armies must be transformed into regular armies in the final stages of the revolution not only for the purposes of eliminating the enemy in a final and decisive assault but also for the purposes of preparing the ground for effective control of the state after a successful revolution.*

The transformation of the Red Army into a regular army demonstrated that guerrilla bands can be organized and managed in the post-revolution period in such a way that the tendency towards individualism and lawlessness which Marx saw as a major flaw in the use of guerrilla warfare for revolutionary purposes is, for the most part, eliminated or effectively controlled.

Besides, the success of Mao and the Communist Party in China showed that the peasantry can be mobilized for revolution. Although it is true, following Marx, that peasants being generally gullible and conservative are usually resistant to change, the experience of China's revolution pointed to the possibility of harnessing the stability, sturdiness and the numerical strength of the peasantry for revolutionary change.

Finally, the revolution in China showed, in contradiction to Engels' assessment, that people outside the "civilized world" — in Asia, Africa and Latin America — were capable of taking advantages which their environment offered to overthrow oppressive and unwanted socio-economic structures. This has been demonstrated in Cuba, in Vietnam, in Algeria, in Portuguese Africa and more recently in Nicaragua.

Guerrilla Warfare in Africa

The African continent has proved a very fertile ground for guerrilla warfare. There have been no less than ten attempts, since the second world war, to force political or socio-economic changes in various parts of Africa through guerrilla warfare. The attraction of guerrilla warfare to African liberation and nationalist movements is not altogether surprising. Most of Africa offers excellent sanctuaries — either in the form of inhospitable desert or inaccessible jungle — to guerrilla fighters. The demographic distribution of population and the pattern of development in Africa also favour the guerrilla activist. With most of the population of Africa residing in primitive rural conditions the guerrilla is presented with both a deprived, alienated population and a deprived environment, both of which are excellent conditions for revolution.

There is, indeed, a general acceptance on the African sub-continent of the selective utility of guerrilla war as a means for achieving political and socio-economic changes. This acceptance is institutionalized in the African Liberation Committee of the Organization of African Unity, a committee charged with the duty of co-ordinating and supporting revolutionary wars directed against colonial powers and white-dominated minority regimes on the African continent.

It must be pointed out that the acceptance of the idea of guerrilla war in the highest levels of African politics is much less the result of mere enchantment with and admiration for the ideas and successes of men like Mao Tse Tung, Vo Giap or Che Guevara than it is of the failure of non-violent means in the attempt to achieve desired political and socio-economic changes in some parts of Africa. Put differently, the setting up of the "African Liberation Committee" in 1963 meant the rejection of Gandhi's idea of passive resistance' which had dominated the thinking of African nationalists in the forties, fifties and early sixties in favour of Frantz Fanon's call for revolutionary violence.' The presence of an intransigient colonial power (Portugal) and the existence of defiant white minority regimes (South Africa; Rhodesia) were the obvious catalysts for such a conversion.

This is by no means to suggest that guerrilla struggle only began in sub-Saharan Africa with the establishment of the African Liberation Committee. On the contrary, as early as 1952 the Kikuyu tribe of Kenya in East Africa had found in guerrilla war a very useful weapon for ending British colonial rule in Kenya and for creating a political vacuum which they sought to fill. The "Mau Mau" Movement as the Kikuyu rebellion came to be known dented the myth of the invincibility of the colonial military machinery and pointed to the possibility of achieving political change in Black Africa through violence. But rapid decolonization in the late fifties and early sixties meant that the great majority of sub-Saharan colonies did not have the need nor the opportunity to follow the example of Kenya.

If the Mau Mau movement in Kenya was the first dramatization of guerrilla war in sub-Saharan Africa it was also the least sophisticated, in ideological terms that is, of such wars. It was fought for very limited objectives; simply, the replacement of a British-controlled political structure with that of a Kikuyu-controlled structure; it was, in other words, a war to change the materials which made up the structure rather than the structure itself. Hence the "Mau Mau" movement was more in the tradition of inter-tribal competition for control of distributive power (political power). The movement's strategy was, consequently, very simple; it was to kill as many of the settlers as would not only make continued settlement in Kenya a dangerous gamble but also create antipathy, in the Mother country, towards continued imperial relations with Kenya. Besides, the locus of recruitment of fighting men was primordial; the Mau Mau Movement was essentially a Kikuyu Movement hence the Kikuyu, awakened to the chance of pre-eminence in post-colonial Kenya, provided the support and sanctuary as well as the fighting men for the movement. "Mau Mau" recruiters administered an "oath of unity" based upon Kikuyu solidarity and demanding strict secrecy and total commitment.'

Although it can be suggested that the "Mau Mau" rebellion was inspired by the example of Mao Tse Tung in China, it is doubtful whether Mao's thoughts had any significant influence on the organization and mode of operation of the movement. Any manifestation of Mao's prescriptions in the operation of the movement, such as reliance on the peasantry (Kikuyu peasants, for the most part) and the use of sanctuaries (remote Kikuyu villages), must have come through accidental approximation rather than design. This cannot be said for the subsequent guerrilla struggles which the sub-continent has witnessed or is currently witnessing.

The many guerrilla struggles that have taken or are taking place in Africa can be classified into four main categories. The first category is that with which the "Mau Mau" movement in Kenya has already been identified, that is, *Wars against colonial Powers*. This specie of guerrilla war has been the most successful on the African continent as witnessed by the dramatic victories of revolutionary movements in Angola, Mozambique and Guinea-Bissau against a Portugal reluctant to relinquish its Imperial status. The second category embraces *Wars against white-dominated minority regimes*: this is the specie of guerrilla war which currently pre-occupies the African Liberation Committee and such wars have been or are being fought out in Rhodesia and in Namibia (South West Africa). The third category may be described as *Wars for National self-determination*: this specie of guerrilla war has been dramatized in Southern Sudan and is currently being fought out in Eritrea (Ethiopia). The fourth and last category encompasses *Wars to overthrow Indigenous governments or Indigenously-controlled socio-economic or political structures*; the Republic of Chad, Zaire and Angola are the three most obvious arenas where this kind of guerrilla war has been or is being dramatized. It is possible to reduce the categories to two in which case the variant which has been described above as *wars against white-dominated minority regimes* may be subsumed under the category of *Wars against colonial Powers*. In the same way, the variant which we describe as *Wars for National self-determination* may be included in the category of *Wars to overthrow Indigenous Governments or Indigenously-controlled socio-economic/political structures*.

Wars in these two categories have common antecedents in the colonial history of Africa and borrow considerably from the pool of guerrilla experience, tactics and doctrine. However, there is a noticeable disparity in the pattern of results attending wars in the two categories. Whereas, *Wars against colonial Powers* have been attended by almost total success, the efforts of revolutionary and nationalist groups to enforce new political arrangements or overthrow existing socio-economic structures have met with little or no success.

The Pattern of Resistance to Indigenous Governments

The various wars which emanate from attempts by groups to alter existing political arrangements in Africa and create new states, as in Eritrea, or overthrow indigenous governments in pursuit of a new vision of socio-political order have certain features in common:

1 they have tended to occur in multi-ethnic or multi-racial states;

2 they have tended to occur in states where race or tribe is a major instrument in the control and distribution of political and economic power as well as a decisive element in the exclusion of certain groups from the economic and political process;

3 these wars have tended to represent the attempts by a racial or ethnic group to alter what is perceived as the monopoly of political and economic power by another racial or ethnic group;

4 these wars have generally been motivated by primarily nationalistic as distinguished from revolutionary objectives.

These general propositions are more or less true of the sixteen-year civil war in the Sudan, the Eritrean War of Seccession in Ethiopia, the Civil War in Chad, the invasions of Zaire and the guerrilla war being waged by UNITA against the MPLA-controlled government of Angola.

In the Sudan, Eritrea and Chad racial differences have combined with cultural and religious differences to produce disaffection and violent revolt against the state whilst in Zaire and Angola tribalism is the principal source of political instability and insurrection. In the Sudan the domination of political and economic power by the North and its Arabic elements and the exclusion of the Negroid population of the three Southern provinces prepared the grounds for communal distrust and the outbreak of civil violence in 1955.[10] The revolt in the South which lasted for sixteen years represented the rejection of the structure of power and privileges in the Sudan by the South and the attempt to redress the imbalance inherent in this structure. Significantly, the civil war in Chad was catalysed by the same phenomenon with the exception that the imbalance in the structure of power and privileges was in favour of the Negroid South. The Negroid tribes of Southern Chad by virtue of their education and assimilation of French culture dominated the apparatus of state power and the economy much to the exclusion of the larger Nilotic tribes of the Sahel and Tibesti Mountains with their Arabic antecedents and Islamic orientation. In Ethiopia, as well, racism and religion have been potent factors in social disequilibrium and communal violence. The Eritreans with their claim to Arabic antecedents and their Islamic religion have been ill at ease in an Ethiopia whose political and economic institutions are dominated by Christians of the Coptic faith.

In Zaire and Angola the pattern of tribal or racial domination and exclusion is not so clear-cut. In Zaire, Mobutu's reliance on men from his home province

38

of Equateur and the formidable presence of elements from this province in the bureaucracy and the business circle have given rise to resentment on the part of other tribes. It is doubtful, however, whether there has been an organised and systematic attempt to exlude men from other tribes from political power and the economy as Albert Ndele, a former Governor of Zaire's Central Bank, would like the world to believe:

> "Men from Kasai, Katanga and Bakongo have been systematically put aside in the new state system, systematically deprived of positions and maltreated. Young officers, even those trained overseas, come back to find that if they are not from Equateur there is no possibility of advancement. The most influential people in the administration are now also from this region . . . Beyond that the whole of commerce, at least in consumer goods, is in the hands of the President's own family. What Mobutu has done is to tribalise and regionalise all the key posts in public administration."[11]

The presence of men like Karl i Bond in the top hierarchy of power and of Ndele himself before his disenchantment and retreat from Zaire suggests a conscious, if not successful, attempt to encourage national representation in the hierarchy of political, bureaucratic and economic power. This is by no means to suggest that tribalism is not an important element in the calculus of power in Zaire. The suggestion here is that Zaire's problems cannot be explained simply in terms of the resentment on the part of other tribal groups at the dominance of the President's tribesmen in the economy and the apparatus of state power. Tribalism in the absence of nationally accepted channels for articulating interests remains the most important form of social organisation in Zaire and the most important source of social disequilibrium. The invasions of Shaba province in 1977 and 1978 represent this articulation of interests through tribal groupings.

In Angola, UNITA's continuing guerrilla war against the force of the MPLA-controlled government is motivated by both the reluctance of UNITA to accept the sovereignty of the MPLA-controlled state over the largest ethnic group in Angola — the Ovimbundu — which it represents and from which it draws its support, as well as the desire to enforce Ovimbundu participation, on equal terms with other tribal groups (the Bakongo and the Mbundu), in the political and economic processes in Angola.

The Roots of Failure

Whatever their causes and tactics guerrilla groups have not been too successful in altering the structure of power in indigenously controlled systems. The reason for this general lack of success lies basically in the factor of racism and tribalism. The success of guerrilla or nationalist groups in uprooting colonial regimes derives essentially not from actual military defeats but in psychological victory over the Imperial power. Most colonial wars have ended in favour of the nationalist movements principally because the nationalists succeeded in making the territory in dispute "too unprofitable and politically difficult for the colonial power".[12] In the case of indigenous regimes there is little prospect for such a psychological victory because the regime or the tribe which it represents is often psychologically committed to the territory in dispute. The race or tribe under siege often has nowhere to go and must fight to the bitter end. In Chad, where the forces of Goukoni Waddaye and Hissen Habré succeeded in forcing Felix Malloum to hand over power, their achievement was due essentially to the collapse of Malloum's military support rather than any attenuation in the psychological resolve of Malloum and the tribal groupings whose interests he represented and protected.

Another major factor responsible for the relative lack of success of guerrilla wars directed against indigenous governments is that in Africa the advantage is always on the side of incumbent governments. The Charter of the Organisation of African Unity disavows interference in the internal affairs of fellow member states. Consequently, the African Liberation Committee has no place within its statutory responsibilites for revolutionary or nationalist movements aiming to overthrow African regimes, however morally justified their case may be. This reluctance on the part of African states to get involved in domestic wars in African states has tended to detract from the legitimacy of insurrectionist movements. Indeed, the OAU is more often inclined to encourage national reconciliation with its implication of restoring the status quo which the insurrectionists would like to overthrow in the first place.

African apathy to domestic insurrections has also tended to affect the volume and intensity of external support for insurrectionist movements. The big powers have generally been reluctant to give overt support to anti-government forces. More often than not, the incumbent governments have been more successful in attracting foreign support in the proportion required to swing the balance of war in their favour. The Government of Sudan at one time or another received support from the Soviet Union and the United States in its efforts to suppress the insurrection in the South. In Ethiopia, American support for Haile Sellassie's government and the massive airlift of Russian arms to the govenment of Mengitsu have helped successive Ethiopian governments to withstand the pressure of the Liberation groups in Eritrea. In Zaire, Morroccan, French and Belgian support proved helpful in Mobutu's counter-attacks against the invaders of Shaba, as did the support of the Pan-African Security Force constituted after the second Shaba invasion.

The power play between the two major ideological blocs in the world has also tended to act as a stumbling block in the way of attempts to change domestic governments or structures. Where the super-powers have pitched their support with opposing domestic groups, as in Ethiopia-Eritrea, the tendency has been for the insurrection to slide into a stalemate which is often broken in favour of the incumbent government with its greater access to support and resilience.

A final cause of failure of guerrilla wars directed against indigenous governments is disunity among liberation movements. In Chad, Eritrea and Zaire, the liberation efforts have been handicapped by the failure of the various groups to unite their efforts and concentrate their energies against a common foe. This lack of unity is most clearly demonstrated in Chad where in spite of their apparent success in achieving the goal of ending Southern domination of power in Chad both the Waddaye and Habré's factions of FROLINAT are engaged in a fratricidal struggle to the detriment of their primary objective.

Footnotes

1. W. Laqueur, *Guerrilla Warfare* (London, 1977).

2. Karl Marx, in W. Laqueur, *op. cit.*, pp. 142-145.

3. Engels in W. Laqueur, *op. cit.*, pp. 142-145.

4. In the case of Eastern Europe the democratization of access to the basic elements of the good life.

5. Carlos Marighella, *Minimanual of the Urban Guerrilla*, published as an appendix to Robert Moss "Urban Guerrilla Warfare" in *Adelphi Papers*, no. 79 (1971).

6. Mao Tse Tung, *Selected Military Writings* (Peking, 1963).

7. Kenneth Kaunda's recent book, *Kaunda on Violence* attests to this disenchantment with Gandhi's method.

8. Frantz Fanon, *The Wretched of the Earth* (Harmondsworth, 1976).

9. K. Grundy, *Guerrilla Struggle in Africa* (New York, 1971).

10. By 1955 only about 6 out of a total of 800 senior government posts went to Southerners during the Sudanisation of posts vacated by the British.

11. Interview with Albert Ndele reported in *Sunday Times* (London) 28 May 1978, p. 12.

12. John Baylis, "Revolutionary War" in John Baylis et al *Contemporary Strategy* (London, 1975). South Africa presents a major problem for our typology (i.e. the two main categories) of guerrilla warfare in Africa. A guerrilla war against the white minority regime in Pretoria can be seen simultaneously as an instance of *Wars to overthrow Indigenously-Controlled Socio-economic/political structures*, if one accepts the thesis that Afrikaaners are Africans, and as an instance of *Wars against Colonial Powers* if one shares the popular African perception of the Afrikaaners as colonizers. (I owe this point to Professor Seth Singleton of Rippon College, Wisconsin.)

[7]

Unconventional Conflicts in Africa: Nuclear, Class and Guerrilla Struggles

Timothy M. Shaw

Despite the assertions of orthodox analyses, conventional conflict in Africa has never been a major factor in the continent's international relations. By contrast unconventional conflict continues to grow in importance as development declines and inequalities intensify. Contemporary changes in Africa's political economy are suggestive of future unconventional conflict in the mid-term future.

Prevalent orthodox approaches characterize internal politics in Africa as consisting of more cooperation than conflict, whereas prevalent realist approaches characterize international politics on that continent as consisting of more conflict than cooperation. This paper argues that both these modes of analysis are inappropriate for contemporary Africa and that internal conflict and international cooperation both affect the character the continent's political economy. The theme is that given Africa's inheritance of dependence and underdevelopment, "conventional" conflict as conceived among the idustrialized states is quite insignificant historically and at the present time, and it is likely to remain so until the end of this century. Conversely, "unconventional" conflict has already become a major factor in Africa's security. Given projections of ineluctable inequalities, unconventional violence — nuclear, class and guerrilla struggles — is likely to appear with increasing frequency, posing challenges to African statesman and to scholars of Africa. Binen (1982) has already responded positively to such challenges: "There are good reasons to predict that Africa faces more, not less, interstate conflict ... military factors in Africa can no longer be seen as just matters of domestic politics; they play a vital role in Africa's international relations" (pp. 964-65).

BEYOND THE CONVENTIONAL: RADICAL ANALYSIS CONFLICT

Africa was incorporated in the world system through violence. As Rodney (1982) indicates:

> Before the 19th century, Europe was incapable of penetrating
> the African continent, because the balance of force at their disposal
> was inadequate. But the same technological changes which created
> the need to penetrate Africa also created the power to conquer
> Africa [p. 151].

Yet despite the massive application of direct and latent force in the imposition, extension and perpetuation of colonialism, nationalist movements only occasionally resorted to counter-violence. The socialization of
Africa's embryonic bourgeoises is remarkable given the degree of "structural
violence" which they and their societies endured. Only when settler interests
resisted change — e.g., Algeria, Angola, Kenya, South Africa and Zimbabwe
— did violence become an integral part of the nationalist struggle (and,
as I will suggest below, one which is of decreasing importance as the border
of black Africa moves steadily southwards). And even in these cases the
degree of radicalization which lasted through the transitional period has been
shown to be limited: Africa's cultural and psychological dependence and
conservatism is ubiquitous.

Indeed, the locus of Africa's powerlessness lies in such dependence and
underdevelopment: most regimes simply cannot afford, even if they wished
to do so, conventional confrontation using the bulk of their national product.
Moreover, those few states which are at present rich enough to develop
their strategic capabilities — e.g., Egypt, Libya, Nigeria and South Africa
— may lack the infrastructure needed to launch any sustained military
attack (on the Nigerian case see Shaw and Aluko 1982).

NUCLEAR AGE AND NON-ALIGNMENT

Despite the prospect of at least the last of these relatively richer states
becoming a nuclear power (see Shaw and Dowdy 1982), in general most
African regimes are too preoccupied by national threats and global
linkages to engage in regional, let alone global, conflict. Their definition
of non-alignment — non-partisanship in bipolar nuclear conflict — remains,
yet their partisanship in sub-nuclear strategic issues and alliances has
increased as the world has become more complex. Indeed, the only way
in which most African regimes can sustain a battle is through "externaliz-
ation" (i. e., by seeking extra-continental support) rather than by "internationalization" (i. e., by accepting extra-continental intervention). Complex
and changeable coalitions characterize Africa's current strategic situation,
especially since the mid-1970's, although the amount of extra-continental
commitment is really quite limited and constrained. As Legum notes in his
own review of Africa's future strategic position:

UNCONVENTIONAL CONFLICTS IN AFRICA   65

> Looking back to the Berlin Treaty of 1884 and the carving out of
> separate spheres of influence by the colonial powers, Africans began
> to speak uneasily in 1977 about "a new scramble" for the
> continent ... the colonial memory persists, reinforcing the associ-
> ation of foreign power rivalries in Africa with the subjugation of
> the continent ... But in the 1970s, the foreign powers had to take
> the interests of competing African states and groups fully into
> account in order to promote their own national interests. Only by
> offering themselves as allies to particular interest groups could they
> expect to expand their infulence on the continent [1979a, p. xx].

Elsewhere, Legum has reflected the contemporary consensus — that African
conflicts will increase — and related this to continuing extra-continental
interest and intervention.

> ... Africa is at a most difficult and volatile stage of development.
> During the 1980s quarrels within one country or between hostile
> neighboring countries are likely to erupt into violent conflicts ...
> Such conflicts will affect not only the localities or countries directly
> involved, but in many cases also will provoke foreign intervention.
> This is not to say that Africa will be the passive victim of inter-
> ventional power politics. On the contrary, African factions will
> actively seek foreign military and economic assistance to bolster
> fragile positions ... [1976b, pp. 23-24].

Protectionist Era and Underdevelopment

This fragility is a central aspect of Africa's political economies and is
related to a major contradiction, one which limits the development of
Africa's own capabilities and perpetuates its dependence on external
support : exploitation. On the one hand, metropolitan countries and corporations extract as much surplus as possible from African economies,
while, on the other hand, they expect strategic stability. Without sufficient
resources remaining at the national level, African regimes are unreliable
allies at the international level. Metropolitan interests may contradict
each other, with economic profitability undermining strategic reliability.
Alternately, such a combination of relations serves to perpetuate Africa's
economic and strategic dependence, recognizing the interrelatedness between
the two.

This contradiction may be expected to intensify over the next few years
as protectionism further undermines the economic prospects of most
African states, making them even more vulnerable to internal and external
pressures. A few countries — the middle powers — may benefit from the

high price of oil, but most will be further impoverished. The inability of
most African regimes to satisfy basic human needs, let alone basic human
rights, will result in increasing pressures to change internally, with embattled
regimes having to appeal for economic and strategic assistance exernally.
Africa in the 1980s, like Africa in the 1960s, may be more vulnerable to
global, great power politics as the politics of debt, food, inflation and
recession erode the minimal infrastructures and industrial capacities of many
countries.

From Pre-Colonial to Post-Colonial Conflict

The intensification of dependence and underdevelopment on most of the
continent may, then, lead to three different outcomes, each with distinctive
implications for conflict in Africa. First, the few middle powers, with
relatively large and still expanding economies, may establish themselves as
important regional powers on an impoverished and vulnerable continent.
As Zartman (1976) suggests in his revisionist work on the distribution of
power in Africa:

> By the 1980s, the spread in the level of power sources is certain to
> increase, even dramatically. Within the decade, Algeria or Nigeria
> may be more developed economically than South Africa ... several
> effects are likely to ensue. First, the more developed members may
> become more attractive to outside influence, even if greater amounts
> of influence will now be required in order to have an effect. Second,
> at this stage of development, internal gaps between socio-economic
> levels are likely to be magnified, as are also gaps between the states
> which have surged forward and those many others which have been
> unable to do so ... the chances for regional leadership are increased
> [p. 593].

Second, in some middle powers and most peripheral states, inequalities will
increase between the minority in the bourgeoisie and the majority in the
proletariat or peasantry. The result will be either increased antagonism or
increased repression. Ake (1978) warns about the latter prospect as the
global recession and contraction intensifies, with important implications
for conflict control and character on the continent:

> ... [One] historic possibility which lies before Africa is a march to
> fascism. This could come about in a situation where there was
> protracted economic stagnation but not yet revolution ... one thing
> that would surely be needed in ever-increasing quantities in this
> situation would be repression .... It would appear that the choice

UNCONVENTIONAL CONFLICTS IN AFRICA 67

for Africa is not between capitalism and socialism after all, but between socialism and barbarism [p. 107].

And finally, the combination of domestic demands and external protectionism may lead some African leaders to a dramatic departure : from dependence to self-reliance. In this case, established assumptions and equations about inequalities and conflict would have to be revised. As Langdon and Mytelka (1979) argue — particularly in relation to change in Southern Africa, an issue which permeates the present paper — disengagement may be the prerequisite of economic development and strategic stability in the 1980s :

> We expect the contradictions of periphery capitalism in Africa to become more acute in most countries on the continent in the next decade, and we expect the struggles for change in such countries to become more bitter as a result. We are confident, however, that out of such conflict can come more equitable and self-reliant development strategies that benefit the great majority of Africans [p. 211].

This potential shift in development planning has strategic as well as economic implications : post-colonial conflict may be more complex and comprehensive than the rather simple and external character of pre-colonial struggle. Indeed, notwithstanding the general poverty of Africa, a few states clearly have nuclear potential, even if not current capability.

NUCLEAR POWER IN AFRICA

Despite the overall pattern of short, unconventional forms of conflict on the continent, a few states may be considered potential nuclear powers. Moreover, despite schemes to declare Africa a nuclear-free zone, some statemen and scholars insist on Africa retaining the right to achieve nuclear status if apartheid South Africa acquires nuclear weapons ; some Arab African leaders may use the same argument vis-à-vis Israel, too. Although Egypt and one or two other Arab states may fall into the latter category, Nigeria is the leading contender in the former group. Moreover, in a continuing quest for alternative energy sources as well as for the latest technology, some African countries are interested in nuclear energy as well as in nuclear power.

South Africa v. Nigeria as the nth Powers

Although both Nigeria and South Africa are interested in acquiring nuclear energy technology, the major tension between them is nuclear weaponry. South Africa clearly needs nuclear energy more urgently than Nigeria, with its considerable, though by no means inexhaustible, petroleum and gas reserves; yet its acquisition of energy technology and enriched uranium is inseparable from its weapons potential.

It now seems to be generally recognized that South Africa already has the capacity to develop and detonate a nuclear bomb, probably using highly accurate 155 mm. howitzer shells. After all the previous research and exposes (see, especially, Cervenka and Rogers 1978), the superpower alert of July-August 1977, about a potential nuclear test in the Kalahari and the Vela satellite recording of a probable nuclear flash in the southern oceans in September 1979 both corroborate the evidence. Moreover, South Africa has publicly prided itself on its ability to enrich its own uranium cheaply by using an adopted gas-infusion method. Finally, while the strategic gain of nuclear capability is problematic, the pride and potential of such status is not inconsiderable for an isolated and embattled people (*Africa News* 1982).

However, South Africa's nuclear power has its antithesis in Nigeria's quest for nuclear status. Though Nigeria's present power base is limited, its potential military-industrial complex is considerable. Nuclear power would reinforce its claim to being *primus inter pares* in black Africa, while also satisfying its need for both image and influence. As Henderson (1981) suggests, "Nigeria's political leaders can point to a nuclear program as a symbol of national power and national identity . . . it reinforces their claims to regional power status as well as their claims to speak for the independent states of black Africa" (p. 421). In short, South Africa's nuclear capacity constitutes a challenge to Nigeria's security and status, one which it is determined to meet through its own nuclear program. But unlike South Africa's nuclear research at Valindaba and Pelindaba, which makes it a relative "nuclear independent" despite significant European and American inputs over the years, Nigeria is considerably more "nuclear dependent" (Paneman 1981), relying extensively on external inputs for its peaceful and strategic programs. Moreover, South Africa is already several years ahead of Nigeria and has a scientific and technological infrastructure to support such research and development. Finally, the reaction of Africa in general and Nigeria in particular to South Africa's growing military link (perhaps nuclear as well as conventional) with Israel — part of the "pariah international" in terms of Harkavy's (1981, pp. 155-157) analysis — constitutes one further reason for the idea of developing a continental deterrent capability.

Nuclear Capability/Energy or Appropriate Technology?

Aside from the questions of nuclear safeguards and the considerable capital required, there is a debate over the appropriateness of such massive technological tranfers and transitions : should Nigeria and/or South Africa use alternative technologies for both defense and industry? In both instances, hydro, coal, gas, sun and wind are available as alternative sources of energy, and guerrilla and conventional strategic capabilities are present. Apart from general concerns about nuclear proliferation and pollution, the utilization of scarce resources for high-technology nuclear developments is controversial because more appropriate forms of energy and defense might be devised.

Nuclear-Free Zone as the New Paternalism

In response to such global concerns, African (and, perhaps, Afrikaner) nationalists tend to be fearful of new imperialisms, respecting the Maoist argument that the multilateral Nuclear Non-Proliferation Treaty and unilateral nuclear safeguards are merely attempts to divide the world into two — the nuclear "haves" and "have-nots." This preemptive rejection of any new paternalism has been most clearly articulated by Mazrui (1980b) and Adeniran (1981).

CLASS CONFLICT IN AFRICA

If the debate about Africa's nuclear status is "unconventional" because it involves high technology and massive destructive potential, that about class conflict is unconventional because it involves apparently "domestic" and "economic" phenomena. However, given Africa's inheritance of incorporation within the world system. class struggles on the continent have "international" connections and implications. Moreover. the treatment of class challenges by African regimes has relevance for human rights everywhere. and certainly the treatment of color differences in South Africa has general implications for the rest of the continent. Furthermore, the growth of inequality and inflation has already exacerbated tensions, leading to a rise of crime and corruption. the former often associated with gang violence.

The Transnational Bourgeoise v. National Proletariats

Class analysis has often been rejected as inappropriate for Africa because of the alleged embryonic character of classes on the continent. Leaving aside the pre-colonial origins of African classes. it is increasingly clear that classes are both in formation and in antagonism. Dialectical relations have grown exponentially as the African crisis has intensified. Nevertheless, classes remain somewhat tenuous because of other social linkages and because the bourgeoisie has been largely external or transnational. As Roxborough (1979) suggests:

> The class structures of the Third World differ from those of the advanced nations in two principal ways: they are more complex, and the classes themselves are usually much weaker....Not only are the class structures of the under-developed nations complex and weak, they are frequently 'incomplete' in the sense that the dominant class, or one fraction of the dominant class is absent. This is the case where the dominant class or fraction thereof is foreign...[pp. 72-73].

Both class politics and class analysis are developing in Africa, with one result being that more national factions are coming to challenge the more transnational or comprador factions. I turn to this issue in the following section, dealing here only with the established transnational bourgeoisie's role in African conflict.

In a classic neo-colonial situation, the "new class" in Africa has strong external links: the bourgeoisie is part-indigenous and part-foreign. So for the first years of independence the indigenous element came to challenge, as well as to cooperate with, the external, leading to a more balanced, if not equal, relationship within the transnational bourgeoisie. Strategies of indigenization and partial nationalization produced characteristic "state capitalist" relations in which the only changes that occurred took place within and not outside this nexus. Non-bourgeois forces were either weak or suppressed: African ruling classes shared interests and communication whereas the proletariats were divided into national organizations with minimal transnational contact. As Amin (1973) laments in his *Neo-Colonialism in West Africa*:

> ...the deadlock...will...continue...until new social forces appear, open to the future rather than dominated by the past, and capable of conceiving a strategy for liberation that goes beyond the narrow horizons of minor ex-colonial civil servants [p. 226].

One factor which has already broken this deadlock somewhat lies within rather than outside the bourgeoisie: the national faction as opposed to the transnational or comprador element.

National and Comprador Factions: Nationalization and Indigenization

Twenty years after independence some of the results of Africanization are beginning to show. The old assumption about the essential equality of

UNCONVENTIONAL CONFLICTS IN AFRICA 71

African states is being replaced by divergent rates of growth and accumulation. And the characteristic pattern of neo-colonialism is being replaced by new sets of tensions, particularly within the indigenous bourgeoisie between more national and more transnational elements. Indigenization has meant that local capitalisms of the pre-colonial era have been revived and have come to challenge the more comprador fractions.

This tension has extra- as well as intra-continental implications: the transnational bourgeoisie could call upon neo-colonial strategic linkages for support whenever necessary. The national faction is more autonomous, although still incorporated within the global capitalist system: any strategic support for it is contractual rather than intrinsic or automatic. Moreover, the development of national capitalism may be related to the trend towards militarism on the continent as national factions come to protect their own surplus and status. Finally, the intensification of class conflict as inflation and floating exchange rates erode the real incomes of the workers and peasants poses another challenge to embattled regimes, again calling forth an authoritarian response.

Authoritarian Impulse v. Human Needs and Rights

The tendency towards authoritarianism and militarism in Africa is not simply a function of the rise of military regimes: rather it is a function of ruling classes fearful of popular pressures. Such demands for the economic fruits of independence have increased as the post-independence period has lengthened and as the post-war expansionist period has given way to recession and contraction. While such antagonism may still be contained in those few countries with relatively high growth rates and/or vestigial confidence in the efficacy of ethnicity, in many others they are contained only by latent or actual coercion. Moreover, in many states populist pressures lack coherence, which makes them vulnerable to state retaliation.

The trend towards exclusive corporatism and increasing militarism in Africa constitutes an attempt by indigenous bourgeois interests to contain opposition and extend accumulation. It has serious implications for human rights in a continent in which such rights are embryonic and fragile; it also retards progress towards the satisfaction of basic human needs (Shaw 1982b). While such repression may receive international support or disinterest, it will drive opposition into counter-violence, despite Africa's awareness of the need for such violence in executing its own anti-colonialist and anti-racist struggles in Kenya, Algeria and southern Africa.

Paradoxically, the rise of guerrilla conflict in independent Africa coincides with its disappearance as a tactic against white-ruled states, although South Africa may foment anti-regime forces in Angola and Mozambique.

Moreover, indigenous leaders should recall the transformation of such movements from nationalist to socialist in response to regime intransigence. Therefore, it is imperative to replace repression with a more informed and sophisticated response.

GUERRILLA STRUGGLES IN AFRICA

One result of Africa's characteristic poverty is that many of the contemporary conflicts have used an unconventional type of force : guerrilla struggle. In addition to its use by both Africans and Afrikaners against the expansion of the British Empire, it has been employed in contemporary times as a strategy by which to overthrow colonialist and racist rule. However, with the passing of such regimes, except for Namibia and South Africa, this form of resistance has been revived and refocused to challenge repressive rule in independent Africa. Guerrilla activity in increasingly impoverished systems is one aspect of their decline into an anarchic state.

From Nationalisms to Socialisms

White rejection of black demands in Africa, Kenya and southern Africa led to the reluctant but inevitable adoption of guerrilla tactics by nationalist movements. While in some parts of Africa independence was negotiated between colonized and colonizer, in settler states a significant degree of counter-violence was necessary to create the conditions for successful negotiotion. The resultant escalation of violence not only endangered established infra-structures, but also produced liberation movements committed to socialism as well as to nationalism : economic as well as political independence and restructuring were demanded.

So the successor regimes in Angola and Mozambique (and possibly in Zimbabwe) are different from those in neighboring Botswana or Zambia. The appearance of such radical rule has upset the rather benign character of the Organization of African Unity consensus and revived debates and coalitions reminiscent of the pre-OAU Brazzaville, Casablanca and Monrovia grouping. Hence the transition from acceptance of dependence to assertion of self-reliance as the motif of the OAU. Disengagement from the world system constitutes a form of diplomatic-cum-economic conflict, a redefinition of non-alignment (see Shaw and Fasehum 1982).

After South Africa : Guerrilla Against Indigenous States

With the successes of FRELIMO (Frente de Libertaçáo de Moçambique), MPLA (Popular Movement for the Liberation of Angola), and now

UNCONVENTIONAL CONFLICTS IN AFRICA 73

ZANU (Zimbabwe African National Union) aided by the Front Line States (i. e., those states bordering South Africa) and the OAU Liberation Committee, the years of guerrilla struggle in southern Africa will begin to come to an end : SWAPO (South West Africa People's Organization) will soon achieve power and ANC's (African National Congress) long-postponed accession cannot be too far behind. However, at the same time that anti-colonialist and anti-racist conflict is coming to an end, the use of guerrilla tactics against African regimes is increasing : guerrilla movements in, for instance, Eritrea, Sudan and Uganda are merely instances of a wider phenomenon.

Guerrilla struggles against indigenous governments do not have the same unambigous goal or support as those against settler states ; they combine ethnic and economic ambitions. Moreover, they have not always been as successful as the liberation movements in southern Africa. Nevertheless, they have achieved control over liberated areas and have led to new political arrangements (e. g., Sudan) or leaders (e. g., Uganda). And Polisario (the Front for the Liberation of Sagvia al-Hamra and Rio de Oro) has secured OAU recognition for the Saharawi Arab People's Republic even if the Eritreans cannot shrug off Ethiopia's embrace.

Such guerrilla conflicts may be based on historical injustices or contemporary impoverishment. As the latter comes to be more prevalent than the former, the continuing decline of African economies becomes more important. Indeed, the guerrillas and gangs may form an alliance at times to play "Robin Hood" in the countryside, and together their activities challenge and undermine the logic of the post-colonial state, accelerating its decline.

Towards an Anarchic Condition? The Logic of Withdrawal

The collapse of the national economy in a few African territories — e. g., Chad, Ghana, Uganda, Zaire and now, perhaps, Tanzania — has accelerated the rate of decay with profound implications for the stability and survival of certain African authorities. This trend towards anarchy is likely to accelerate as most African economies experience minimal or negative growth. It is also likely to be exacerbated as advanced industrialized states, under the pressures of recession and protectionism, lose interest in a global reach and decrease their investments in the African periphery.

One result of this economic and political decay has been withdrawal of the peasantry from the cash economy and its return to subsistence agriculture, which is a form of effective but unplanned regional or familial self-reliance with profound implications for the viability of the national economy. Such a reaction serves to exacerbate the national crisis as commodity exports decline, foreign exchange reserves vanish and black-market-smuggling takes over the remnants of the economy. This process leads not only to domestic tensions between the bourgeoisie in the city and the peasantry in the countryside, but also to the demise of the neo-colonial transnational structure: if the North is in retreat and the South in decline, then the transnational linkage withers. This enables African regimes to be more "self-reliant" whether or not they wish to be. The post-neo-colonial situation is marked by more domestic than external conflict, although a revival in the world economy might reinvigorate neo-colonial relationships. Furthermore, the semi-periphery of Nigeria, Egypt, Ivory Coast, Kenya and Zimbabwe remains important to countries and corporations in the North. In the longer term, however, outlook for the real periphery is not bright. Until the end of this century Africa is no more likely to be conflict-free than nuclear-free.

FUTURE STRUGGLES IN AFRICA: TOWARDS A POLITICAL ECONOMY OF VIOLENCE

Conflict is likely to increase in Africa in the mid-term future because of the continent's unsatisfactory rate of economic growth. There will be insufficient resources to redistribute to ameliorate antagonisms. The few rich countries and classes — particularly the semi-periphery and the national bourgeoisie respectively — will be increasingly challenged in their relative access to affluence and accumulation by the real periphery and the non-bourgeoisie. Hence the attempts by the OAU and the International Bank for Reconstruction and Development to propose alternative development strategies (see Shaw and Fasehun 1982). As Adedeji has warned on numerous occasions: "Africa, more than any other third world region, is faced with a development crisis of great portent" (1977, p. 8). This crisis includes minimal or negative economic expansion, rapid population increases, declining food production, indebtedness and inflation and associated inter- and intranational inequalities (see Shaw 1982c); all this within a world system characterized by contraction, protectionism, and competition. It is difficult, therefore, to accept the conventional wisdom based on conventional analysis, as articulated by Copsar: "While large-scale armed international violence does not appear likely in most of Africa, it can occur at any of Africa's flashpoints. In the Horn and the Maghrib, conflict may not be an immediate prospect, but the underlying bases for conflict remain" (1982, p. 923).

Given Africa's increasing marginalization, it is likely to lack the financial and physical infrastructure necessary for establishing an effective and credible nuclear force. Notwithstanding all the rhetorical flourishes

UNCONVENTIONAL CONFLICTS IN AFRICA

about Africa needing to counteract South Africa's nuclear potential and to flout racist assumptions about its technological capacities (see Mazrui 1980a), unless a continental "high command" is established by which to harness a nuclear deterrent, nuclear status will remain a chimera.

It is possible that one or two states at the semi-periphery (e. g., Algeria, Egypt or Nigeria) might expand their arsenal to include nuclear weaponry (see Shaw and Fasehun 1980), but their delivery system would be primitive and the effect might be counter-productive; i. e., it might lead to counter-coalitions in their regions rather than to deterrence against South Africa. The more salient aspects of Africa's depressing future as related to non-conventional forms of violence lie in intranational rather than international relations, recognizing that impoverishment and inequity can be exploited by extracontinental interests.

Class Formation, Coalition and Containment

Although class formation has been retarded and complicated in Africa, it has, nevertheless, accelerated since independence, particularly since the economic shocks of the mid-1970s onwards, and projections of declining *per capita* income in most states at the periphery are likely to exacerbate such tensions. Class relations at the semi-periphery may be ameliorated somewhat by continued expansion, but such growth is likely to be uneven both between classes and over time. Moreover, the rise of a national bourgeoisie at the semi-periphery will intensify internal rather than trans-national contradictions, although the several factions in the "triple alliance" — national, international and state capitals — may collaborate as well as conflict, provided that the "national cake" is growing at a sufficiently fast rate (see Shaw 1982a). As a general strategy of containment, Africa's ruling classes are likely to move towards adoption of the Lagos Plan of Action for the Economic Development of Africa, expecting that national and collective self-reliance will improve rates of development and enhance political control.

A further global trend may exacerbate domestic tensions even as it relieves external ones: the tendency towards economic protection and isolation in the North. Recession among industrialized countries has not only reduced their demand for African products; it has also eroded the logic of neo-colonialism. In essence, only a few African states — largely those at the semi-periphery — have significance for OECD (Organization for Economic Cooperation and Development) countries and corporations. The rest are increasingly marginal, and so minimal political or strategic support is available to save such regimes. Ake's (1978) formulation about the patron-client relationship of African and metropolitan classes is now only relevant to the semi-periphery:

The African ruling class is the political power while the ruling class of the bourgeois countries is the economic power. The reality of economic dependence limits the political power of the African ruling class, while the reality of the political power of the African ruling class may to some extent limit the economic power of the ruling class of the bourgeois countries to manipulate and exploit Africa. The limitations frustrate both sides and the parties involved strive to overcome them. So, despite the fact that the interests of the African ruling class coincide in some respects, the two classes are also in struggle [pp. 27-28].

But this struggle becomes more complex as: a) the real periphery is marginalized; and b) the semi-periphery is factionalized with the emergence of national as well as transnational and state capital. One result of impoverishment in the periphery and prosperity in the semi-periphery is the rise not only of class antagonism but of guerrilla struggle.

Guerrillas Against Authoritarianism and Accumulation

As Namibia and then South Africa are liberated in the short- to mid-term future, guerrilla attacks will concentrate increasingly on the African ruling class both in systems in decay (e. g., Chad, Ghana and Tanzania) and in expansion (e. g., Morocco and Zambia). In the former case, the guerrillas may claim to be acting in the national interest, whereas in the latter they will be clearly acting in their class interest. There will also, of course, be secessionist and irredentist movements (e. g., Eritrea, Somalia and Polisario) with implications for border conflict and continental cohesion. The map of Africa, status quo attitudes and action notwithstanding, may continue to change as it has done over the last decade or so (e. g., Senegambia and Tanzania).

Guerrilla attacks on indigenous regimes may lead to extra- and intra-continental support (e. g., coalitions of the socialist states to aid Angola and Ethiopia and of the capitalist states to aid Chad and Zaire). They are also likely to lead to increasingly authoritarian responses as the ruling class seeks to protect its territory, people and profit. As basic human needs are decreasingly met, so human rights are likely to be decreasingly respected as indigenous regimes attempt to maintain their power, profit and accumulation.

Such unattractive scenarios notwithstanding, it is possible that self-reliance in Africa will generate a new situation in which political struggles will be played out. Self-reliance, although of distinctive forms and degrees, may be advanced in the immediate future in three ways. First, as political and economic decay continues in the real periphery, the peasantry may retreat from cash crop production to food and cottage industries, thus increasing local self-reliance. Second, as recession and protection are extended in the advanced industrialized states, the semi-prephery as well as the periphery may come to advocate collective and national self-reliance, albeit with differences of emphasis and expectation. And finally, the OAU-ECA (Economic Commission for Africa) nexus may, through the Lagos Plan of Action and related deliberations and declarations, provide the framework and ideology for such forms of self-reliance throughout the continent. In short the very gloominess of projections and imminence of unconventional conflict may call forth innovative indigenous responses which may prevent conventional violence on the continent up to the year 2000.

REFERENCES

Adedeji, Adebayo. 1977. Africa: the crisis of development and the challenge of a new economic order. Address to the Fourth Meeting of the Conference of Ministers and Thirteenth Session of the Economic Commission for Africa, February-March, Kinshasa, Addis Ababa: ECA, July.

Adeniran, Tunde. 1981. Nuclear proliferation and black Africa: the coming crisis of choice. *Third World Quarterly* 3, no. 4 (October): 673-83.

Africa News. 1982. US/South Africa: House study probes causes of arms embargo breakdown. 18, no. 17 (26 April): 6-10.

Ake, Claude. 1978. *Revolutionary pressures in Africa.* London: Zed.

Amin, Samir. 1973. *Neo-colonialism in West Africa.* Harmondsworth: Penguin.

Bienen, Henry S. 1982. Military aide and military order in Africa. *Orbis* 25, no. 4 (Winter): 949-65.

Bozeman, Adda. 1976. *Conflict in Africa concepts and realities.* Princeton: Princeton University Press.

Cervenka, Zdenek. 1982. The conspiracy of silence. *Africa* 125 (January): 12-15.

————, and Barbara Rogers. 1978. *The nuclear axis: secret collaboration between West Germany and South Africa.* New York: Times Books.

Cospon, Raymond W. 1982. African flashpoints: Prospects for armed international conflict. *Orbis* 25, no. 4 (Winter): 903-23.

Harkavy, Robert E. 1981. Pariah states and proliferation. *International Organization* 35, no. 1 (Winter): 135-63.

Henderson, Robert D'A. 1981. Nigeria: future nuclear power? *Orbis* 25, no. 2 (Summer): 409-23.

Langdon, Steven and Lynn K. Mytelka. 1979. Africa in the changing world economy. In *Africa in the 1980s: a continent in crisis*, ed. Colin Legum, et al., pp. 121-211. New-York: McGraw-Hill.

Legum, Colin. 1979a. The year in perspective. In his *African contemporary record: annual survey and documents*, volume 10, 1977-78, pp. xx-xxiv. New York: Africana.

————. 1979b. Communal conflict and international intervention in Africa. In *Africa in the 1980s: a continent in crisis*, ed. Colin Legum, et al., pp. 21-66. NewYork: McGraw-Hill.

Mazrui, Ali A. 1980a. *The African condition: a political diagnosis*. London: Heinemann.

————. 1980b. Africa's nuclear future. *Survival* 22, no. 2 (March-April): 76-79.

Paneman, Daniel. 1981. Nuclear policies in developing countries. *International Affairs* 57, no. 4 (Autumn): 568-84.

Rodney, Walter. 1982. *How Europe underdeveloped Africa*. Harare: Zimbabwe Publishing House.

Roxoborough, Ian. 1979. *Theories of underdevelopment*. London: Macmillan.

Shaw, Timothy M. 1982a. Beyond neocolonialism: varieties of corporatism in Africa. *Journal of Modern African Studies* 20, no. 2.

————. 1982b. The political economy of self-determination: from decolonisation to self-reliance. SUNY-Buffalo Conference on Human Rights in Africa, May.

————, ed. 1982. *Alternative futures for Africa*. Boulder: Westview.

————, and Olajide Aluko, ed. 1982. Nigerian foreign policy: alternative perceptions and projections. London: Macmillan.

————, and Lee Dowdy. 1982. South Africa. In *Security policies of developing countries*, ed. Edward A. Kolodziej and Robert Harkavy, pp. 305-27. Lexington: Heath Lexington.

————, and Orobola Faschun. 1980. Nigeria in the world system: alternative approaches, explanations and projections. *Journal of Modern African Studies* 18, no. 4 (December): 551-73.

————, and Orobola Fasehum. 1982. Beyond any NIEO: ECA and IBRD strategies for African (under) development. Ife Conference on Africa and the NIEO, June.

Smith, Dan. 1980. *South Africa's nuclear capability*. London: Anti-Apartheid Movement.

Spence, J. E. 1981. South Africa: the nuclear option. *African Affairs* 80, no. 321 (October): 441-52.

Zartman, I. William. 1976. Africa. In *World politics: an introduction*, ed. James N. Rosenau, et al., pp. 569-594. New York: Free Press.

Eritrea

[8]

ENDEMIC INSURGENCY AND INTERNATIONAL ORDER: THE ERITREAN EXPERIENCE*

by J. Bowyer Bell

FOR the rebel who can neither sweep through the streets to instant power nor fashion a conventional army to challenge the regime in open battle, the remaining option has been to wage armed struggle covertly, with tactics that are unconventional if not illicit. Denied legitimacy by the center, unrecognized at first by any validating authority, he has embarked either with enthusiasm or despair, and sometimes as a matter of local habit, on a course easily recognizable from afar as insurgency. In some cases the rebels may be bound by little cohesion beyond a traditional reluctance to accept rule from the center, a preference for the comfortable disorder of the past. Other insurgents are highly sophisticated contemporaries who have adopted the appropriate revolutionary stratagems, planned their campaign coherently, and are articulate concerning their expectations. But whether insurgencies betoken the endemic disorder of the bush or the honed calculation of an urban *foco*, they usually share certain characteristics, impose on the center certain alternatives, can be met and countered in similar ways, and, most important, are by definition protracted.

If the insurgency has bled into the countryside or contaminated the ghetto, if the rebel has found support or toleration, if the revolt cannot be killed in embryo or with swift kindness, the threatened regime faces a long process of pacification no matter how organized it may be to meet what could be a lethal challenge. Such a task may not be novel to centers inured to disorder on the distant fringe. Wild places still exist where control from the center

*This analysis is largely based on the author's several trips to the Horn of Africa, first under the auspices of the Center for International Affairs, Harvard University, and then while at the Massachusetts Institute of Technology's Center for International Studies, through the generosity of the Earhart Foundation and the John Simon Guggenheim Memorial Foundation. Given the delicate nature of research on insurrectional matters, only three of those who aided his investigations can be thanked — and even they are named with some reluctance: H. E. Raz Asrate Kassa, former American Consul General Murray Jackson and his successor, A. A. Rabida.

ORBIS

— even an imperial center replete with elegant weaponry and skilled administrators — has been a mere formality. In North Burma or South Arabia, in the far bush or along the desert's edge, at the interface of old arguments or the fault lines between races and religions, at the fringe of events, violence has been and is often endemic. There the structure of politics, or war, reflects earlier and often more brutal times. Unless there is intervention by powerful outsiders for their own distant and intricate purposes, the habits and practices of the past are scarcely disturbed except for the importation of more effective tools of banditry — witness tribes out of the thirteenth century bearing AK-47's. For these men insurgency is not a carefully formulated mix of violence and politics orchestrated to liberate the nation and endow the rebel with power, but rather a way of life. Pride matters more to them than the power that comes out of the barrel of a gun. Yet, versed as they are in the outlawry of their ancestors, these offspring of a violent past may be co-opted into the ideological quarrels of the present. Simple or sophisticated, those who engender disorder also open the way for exterior manipulation that may in turn produce escalated violence and international turmoil.

Although insurgencies are by nature protracted, the conventional assumption is that in the fullness of time either order will be restored or the center will collapse, usually the former. In much of the world, however, insurgency is at best contained, never eliminated. Those advanced industrialized democracies that can accommodate all dissent but separatism, and the authoritarian industrialized states with the will and capacity to crush any rebel rising are largely invulnerable to an extended rebel threat. But elsewhere — in the Third World — the center lacks the capacity to accommodate or crush dissent, especially when such dissent has led to open revolt. Only the commitment of resources of major proportion can eradicate entrenched insurgency. Nevertheless, though these long-lived rebellions isolated on the fringes of concern may warp the development of small nations, increase regional tension, and add to the troubles of the times, in a more perfect world they would hardly trouble the international balance. The danger is that protracted insurrection has regularly attracted those who for ideological considerations or pragmatic advantage have seized the opportunity to gain on the flank of a major opponent. Since such involvement can be engineered at minimum cost and with denied responsibility — a satchel of Maria Theresa thalers or a crate of RPG-7 rocket launchers — even those with limited

ENDEMIC INSURGENCY: THE ERITREAN EXPERIENCE

resources can fish in troubled waters. Consequently, simply to contain an insurrection, assuring the center's control and the regime's continuation, may still leave a potential threat to regional and international stability. Final success seems beyond the power of many of the threatened, for their complete commitment to pacification might well create more serious problems than the low-intensity violence of an insurrection contained but not cured.

II

For over a decade the imperial Ethiopian government has had to contend with an insurrection in the northeastern province of Eritrea, an insurrection that, drifting through cycles of violence and quiescence, has increased tension within the African Horn and involved the interests of major powers.[1] International complications aside, such a challenge from the frontier is by no means novel to Ethiopia; for a millennium the essence of imperial history has been the effort to buttress the center, absorb the diverse — particularly Moslem converts and pagan tribes — and defend the edges of empire. The Amhara elite, who constitute a minority in Ethiopia, have justifiably felt besieged in their all-but-impenetrable highlands of the Horn, under repeated attack by alien forces in the service of false if alluring gods. They have forgiven and forgotten little, for since the rise of Islam Ethiopia has been under regular threat from the fanatics of the lowlands. At one point in the sixteenth century the Moslems, under the Somali Ahmed Gran, nearly decimated the ancient Christian empire and almost won the highlands for Islam. As late as 1889 Emperor Yohannes IV was killed at Metemma while defending the empire against the depredations of zealous followers of the Sudanese

[1]There is not now, or likely to be in the immediate future, an authoritative study of the Eritrean insurrection. ELF exiles are not particularly knowledgeable, and the *shifta* are not inclined to written records. The Ethiopians generally prefer to discuss other matters and it is doubtful if a definitive internal chronicle exists. In Asmara, Ato Mammo Wodineh, head of the Research and Public Relations Department, is engaged in research but his publication has so far been in Amharic. An excellent survey of Eritrean events and implications up to 1969 was provided by the late John Franklin Campbell in "Rumblings Along the Red Sea: The Eritrean Crisis," *Foreign Affairs*, April 1970, pp. 537-548. One of the few scholarly approaches is Frank Boyce, "The Internationalizing of Internal War: Ethiopia, the Arabs, and the Case of Eritrea," *Journal of International and Comparative Studies*, Vol. 5, No. 3, 1972, pp. 51-73. With due note of the source, there is a sound and revealing survey by Fred Halliday, entitled "The Fighting in Eritrea," in the *New Left Review*, May-June 1971, pp. 57-67. In general the printed word is the result of transient exposure to the crisis, often excellent but seldom analytical: cf. André Fontaine in *Le Monde*, Graham Taylor in the *New Middle East* (April 1971), Frederic Hunter in the *Christian Science Monitor*, Marvine Howe in the *New York Times*, Jim Hoagland in the *Washington Post* (June 4, 1972).

ORBIS

Mahdi who sought to convert the Ethiopians with the sword. Thus in Ethiopian eyes the new rebels in Eritrea have a long and iniquitous history. Are they not largely Moslem? Are they not aided by the circling border states, Arabic and Islamic? Do they not make use of misguided or corrupt men, confused by "revolutionary" appeals, who are as in the past little more than adventurers bent on subverting the imperial system? No matter that the rebels purport to be nonsectarian and advocate modernization and revolution in seeking the liberation of the Eritrean nation. From the capital at Addis Ababa, the insurrection has been considered simply an age-old threat clothed in contemporary fashion.

The modern history of the Eritrean province began in 1885 with the arrival of the Italians along the Red Sea. Pushing inland, they had by 1890 carved a colony out of the Red Sea coast, the lowlands stretching across to the Sudan, and the northern tip of the Ethiopian highlands. Only the epic Ethiopian victory at Adowa in 1896 set bounds to the new colony and a limit, for the time being, on further annexation. The Italians were left with the stark and brutal desert lowlands, a country crossed by primitive nomads, who were often Islamic, always martial, and dedicated to brigandage and the tribal habits of the past; but they also held the fertile highlands inhabited in large part by a Christian population speaking Semitic languages akin to that of the Amharas to the south in Ethiopia.

Ethiopian claims to Eritrea, based on endless genealogies and an ancient heritage, were ignored by the Italians dedicated to creating their own African empire. Eritrean development was visible, if halting; mostly the colony remained in the doldrums until the second Italian invasion of Ethiopia in 1935 required the construction of a more extensive infrastructure. Then, roads and bridges were hastily thrown up, the port of Massawa was transformed, and expanded emigration from Italy raised the total of resident Europeans from 4,000 to 40,000. The capital at Asmara, with its pleasant stuccoed buildings, an opera house, and palm-lined streets, appeared to have been moved intact from Sicily. There was a railroad from Massawa out into the bush toward the Sudanese border, and passable roads elsewhere. Modern agricultural projects were fostered and an active commercial life centered on Asmara continued to be dominated by the new Italian settlers. Much remained to be done, and the fruits of development had been spread unevenly and largely to Italian advantage, but certainly in material matters Eritrea benefited from the Italian occu-

ENDEMIC INSURGENCY: THE ERITREAN EXPERIENCE

pation — at least more so than the Ethiopian provinces of the new
and brief Italian East African empire.

In 1941 the British arrived in Eritrea, nominally as Ethiopian
allies, and Italy's African adventure ended.[2] Emperor Haile
Selassie I, back in Addis Ababa and chafing under the restrictions
of a British "occupation," made it abundantly clear that Eritrea
was an integral part of his empire, had been seized by brute force,
and must be returned. There were those who disagreed, insisting
that the Christian Tigreans had never been incorporated in an
Ethiopian empire, even in the early Christian kingdom centered
at Axum, but had always existed as a separate realm. Some thus
wanted either an independent Eritrea or even the annexation of
the allied Tigré province of Ethiopia — a Greater Eritrea. The
large Moslem population, hereditary enemies of the empire, preferred independence or annexation of the Islamic areas by the
Sudan. In any case the more perceptive and sophisticated Eritreans
had grave doubts about being absorbed into a primitive, feudal
monarchy that would rule from the distant capital at Addis
Ababa, but until the end of the war speculation about the future
was muted.

Eventually the Eritrean issue reached the United Nations.
There, in 1950, the decision was reached to permit Ethiopia to fed-
erate the province with the empire. The British withdrew. On
September 15, 1952, Eritrea became part of Ethiopia with federal
guarantees, rendering the radical and separatist arguments against
union largely academic. "Politics" continued to exist only for the
few, the educated, urban elite.

However, it soon became clear that for a variety of reasons Addis Ababa found Eritrean separatism and the federal arrangement
unsatisfactory. Eritrean political parties were banned. The
Eritrean General Union of Labor Syndicates, directed by a Christian, Woldeab Woldemariam, was suppressed. Both the Eritrean
Muslim League of Ibrahim Sultan Ali and the Christian separatists
of Woldemariam came under severe suspicion. Opposition went
underground or into exile. Appeals to the United Nations produced nothing. In February 1958, a general strike in Asmara and
Massawa was quelled with great rigor. In 1959 the Eritrean flag
was abolished. Amharic became the official language.[3] It was sim-

---

[2]The standard source for the British period and much else in Eritrea is G. K. N.
Trevaskis, *Eritrea, A Colony in Transition, 1941-1952* (London: Oxford University
Press, 1960).

[3]Under the Federation the two authorized languages had been Tigrinya and
Arabic.

ORBIS

ply a matter of time before the husk of federation was discarded.

The opposition's rational options appeared to be graceful acquiescence to the inevitable or recourse to violence, since indigenous political protest and agitation had been put down and international appeals had met with indifference. Most dissenters acquiesced; a few did not. Out of the Eritrean Democratic Front, formed in Cairo by Sultan Ali and Woldemariam, came the Eritrean Liberation Front dedicated to a strategy of national liberation through armed struggle. The rebels managed to raise £500, purchased some elderly Italian rifles, and in September 1961 launched their revolt. The following year Emperor Haile Selassie announced the dissolution of the Federation and Eritrea's acceptance of imperial union instead. The United Nations took no note and the rebels were left to their own resources.

While there was strong sentiment for some form of federal solution, even after 1962, just as there were activists for complete union, the number of those advocating independence, much less seeking it through open revolt, could not be easily determined. Rebels seldom poll their avowed constituents ahead of time, and in this the leaders of the new ELF ran true to form. Their cause seemed valid, and not only in their own eyes: the liberation struggle of a long-submerged nation unfairly occupied by an alien regime in violation of international agreements. They proposed democratic government, not authoritarian monarchy. They wanted an advanced social and economic system, not the imposition of feudalism. They insisted on no established church and no authorized language — i.e., Amharic. The ELF leadership in exile felt that it represented the wave of the future. In the Ethiopian view the ELF was simply the old Islamic enemy allied with the disruptive forces of contemporary revolution and flourishing a new script.

III

The ELF's armed struggle began in obscurity in 1961 and for some time continued inconspicuously.[4] The United Nations took no notice of Ethiopia's annexation of Eritrea. Incidents and ambushes went unreported, and even an attempt to assassinate the Emperor's representative in Asmara in 1962 failed to stir general interest. The founding of the Organization of African Unity in 1963 brought the Eritreans no relief; with the exception of

[4]Early arms dribbled in across the Red Sea, sold by a sympathetic sultan in South Arabia, and when the Yemen civil war began in September 1962, weapons flooded the area.

ENDEMIC INSURGENCY: THE ERITREAN EXPERIENCE

Somalia, the new African states were wary of opening the Pandora's Box of boundary changes or tribal separatism. Ethiopian strategy was to ignore the ELF "campaign" entirely. Queries about it were parried or reference was made to the traditional *shifta* (bandit) activity of the bush. The imperial government recognized the potential challenge of a separatist insurrection all too well, but never in public. Disproportionate investment in Eritrea, largely to the benefit of the Christian population, could, if necessary, be explained on grounds of nation-building, as could a long, quiet series of promotions, awards, concessions and scholarships. In the subtle and delicate inner world of the Amhara elite, the concessions to the Tigreans were recognized as part of a general response to the ELF challenge, yet the rebel movement continued to be ignored — a curious but largely effective stratagem.

Nevertheless, the ELF challenge, combined with a variety of other factors, vastly increased tensions in the African Horn. In the Sudan a sporadic but persistent insurrection had begun the year before independence in 1955 and had spread through the three southern provinces. The southern Sudan, black, pagan or Christian, tribal or English-speaking, long exploited by the Islamic, Arab North, could neither be pacified nor absorbed by a variety of regimes in Khartoum. The result was an African insurrection in the Sudan to balance the "Arab" insurrection in Eritrea, a situation that repeatedly led to interference, manipulation, and the employment of proxy rebellion by Addis Ababa and Khartoum. Ethiopia also had a serious problem to the east, where soon after independence in 1960 the new Somali government opened both a diplomatic and a paramilitary campaign for a Greater Somalia that would include the Ethiopian Ogaden.

Potentially, therefore, the ELF had two regional allies in the Sudanese and the Somalis, but the implications of the clash of aspirations in the Horn stretched beyond the *shifta* and the wild places. In an era of intense East-West confrontation, the Arabs had turned for aid to Moscow, so that the Ethiopians saw the ELF not only as the old Islamic-Arab foe but as the tip of the communist lance: "The glove is Arab nationalism; the fist inside is communism."[5] This was a most congenial posture for them because it reflected the suspicions of many Americans — the new ally. In 1953 the United States and Ethiopia had signed a mutual defense agreement and a special treaty that permitted Washington to

[5]*Christian Science Monitor,* March 19, 1971.

ORBIS

establish a substantial radio-communication facility outside Asmara at a cost of $65,000,000. This, Kagnew Station, was manned by 1,500 American military specialists. Increasingly, too, the Ethiopians depended on the aid and friendship of Israel, thereby engendering further Arab uneasiness.

Far from the high ground of clashing international ideologies and great-power concerns, the ELF seemed content, or doomed, to wage an obscure *shifta* struggle. Seldom did it engage in visible operations — and many of those could have been simple, endemic brigandage. There was no effort to attack the Kagnew Station, which represented an economic boon to the province, or to bring the armed struggle to the cities. Much of the wild lowlands had never been patrolled and could be ignored. The roads were mostly open and the plantations could avoid difficulties with small payments to the outlaws. The position of the large Beni Amer tribe and the loyalties of the villagers remained uncertain and apparently unimportant. Abroad, the ELF was somewhat more visible: the exiles circulated through congenial capitals, and offices sprang up in Mogadishu and Damascus, Cairo and Baghdad. Aid and comfort were forthcoming from a variety of sources. The Saudis gave for Islamic purposes, but later ended the subsidy because of the presence of Christians in the ELF[6] and the exiles' contacts with radicals, particularly Chinese. The Chinese on their part ignored religious matters and contributed for revolutionary purposes. Nasser was sympathetic. Nkrumah encouraged the rebels. Syria was particularly enthusiastic.[7] The ELF claimed that five *wilayats*, each based on a liberated area, had been established in Eritrea; but there was no hard evidence to that effect and little real continuing interest in Eritrean developments even in Arab capitals. In December 1965, ELF General Secretary Osman Saleh Sabbe publicly called on Arab states to aid the revolution. The ELF seemed to be waging one of Africa's forgotten wars.

In 1965 the Ethiopian government accused Syria of intervening in Ethiopian affairs but still insisted that basically the problem was a *shifta* matter. This posture had produced certain benefits. The army had not gobbled up disproportionate resources in an anti-insurgency campaign or alienated the local population, an almost certain prospect given the attitudes of the largely Christian Amhara army. The Eritrean province had benefited from development money and from the Kagnew Station. The *shifta* raids had

⁶Halliday, *op. cit.*, p. 65.
⁷Syria has remained the most loyal advocate of the ELF cause, supplying radio facilities, training, arms and funds.

ENDEMIC INSURGENCY: THE ERITREAN EXPERIENCE

caused little trouble and there was rarely other evidence of the "armed struggle," although in 1966 the ELF slipped into Asmara and shot the CID chief. Then, too, the Ethiopian position in the Horn had improved. The Somali *shifta* campaign had dwindled to a close, leaving the Mogadishu regime in disarray. In Khartoum the cost and futility of the southern insurrection had introduced a new reality into the Sudan's passing enthusiasm for the ELF. Increasingly, if haltingly, Khartoum was willing to take steps against the ELF in return for Ethiopian neutrality vis-à-vis the southern rebels.

Thus, the ELF seemed to be more isolated. Yet astute observers suspected that large areas of Eritrea had been alienated and now supported or tolerated the ELF out of fear or faith. Instead of being an illusion fostered by foreign funds and traditional tribal habit, the Front might be an actual threat. Guerrillas might really be creeping in toward Asmara, about to squeeze a province unprepared for serious fighting. As the army patrolled the roads and went through the formal motions of control, Asmara was rife with rumors of expanding ELF actions and growing Ethiopian anxiety.

Publicly, at least, Governor General Raz Asrate Kassa, a shrewd and highly intelligent aristocrat, remained convinced that the ELF was ephemeral. He regarded efforts to extend the anti-insurgency campaign with suspicion, as a policy that would prove counterproductive. His policy of benign neglect aroused little enthusiasm in the military, which during 1966 and 1967 began to think that a serious threat was brewing. Moreover, Ethiopian diplomatic initiatives in Khartoum indicated Addis Ababa's awareness that the ELF was more than a simple *shifta* problem.

Then, during the summer of 1967, when the Israeli victory in the June war devastated the Arab world, the entire Ethiopian position grew stronger. No one had time for or interest in the obscure problems of the Eritreans. Funds trailed off and arms-running came to a halt. In August, Haile Selassie visited Khartoum to discuss a variety of matters but in effect to add his personal prestige to the fragile détente. As a result Khartoum closed down or restricted many ELF activities, and in the following year the Governor of Kassala ordered the important ELF headquarters near the Eritrean border shut. On the other flank the Somali economy was devastated by the closure of the Suez Canal and the necessity for an agreement with Ethiopia was obvious — the Somali *shifta* war was all but over.

In Eritrea the Ethiopian army, at last unleashed, swept through suspected ELF areas, and a stream of refugees flowed into the

ORBIS

Sudan. The ELF found no means to respond effectively. Indigenous leadership was limited, out of touch with the exile centers, and dependent on shipments of arms and money that no longer materialized. Even the triumph in Aden of the sympathetic National Liberation Front in November 1967 brought no immediate relief from across the Red Sea. Although in 1968 some Chinese arms started down the pipeline and some Arab regimes had a moment to spare for the ELF, to most observers the insurrection appeared nearly over.

Ethiopian spokesmen were delighted to inform transient journalists that the back of the ELF had been broken, with nothing left but the *shifta*. Most local diplomatic personnel concurred. Increasingly the ELF seemed to be running a revolution on the installment plan. The exile leaders, who never appeared in Eritrea, would sweep through the radical Arab capitals pleading for funds with revolutionary rhetoric and then swing back through the mosques to seek aid for the persecuted faithful in the name of Islam. With the new investment capital thus acquired, additional *shifta* could be hired to undertake new raids that would again permit the spokesmen of revolution to collect further funds. Certainly with offices in Damascus, Khartoum, Baghdad, Aden and Algeria, with friends in Somalia and Libya, with contacts in China and Cuba, with access to Radio Damascus for broadcasts by the Voice of the Eritrean Revolution, with agents present at the United Nations and international conferences, the ELF appeared far more visible abroad than in the *wadis* and *jebels* of Eritrea.

At the same time the shift in ELF ideology was causing concern in international revolutionary circles, for in September 1968 a policy statement had announced that Eritrea's future was tied to the Arab people — this for a province that might barely muster a Moslem majority but most assuredly was not Arab.[8] However pleasing such a declaration may have been to some Arab patrons, elsewhere it went far to undermine the legitimacy of the ELF as a genuine liberation movement,[9] which was fine with the Ethiopians.

[8]There are no authoritative figures on the percentage of Moslems in Eritrea — or elsewhere in Ethiopia. Ethiopian spokesmen, reluctant to discuss the matter, have suggested as few as 14 per cent, while the ELF claims over 70 per cent. Addis Ababa is adamant that there is not a Moslem majority.

[9]For example, the ELF observer sent to the Rabat summit suggested that the question of an independent Eritrea joining the Arab League would be a "difficult" one. This uncertain posture by revolutionaries seeking to liberate a nation demonstrably non-Arabic confused ideological colleagues untouched by the charms of Pan-Arabism.

ENDEMIC INSURGENCY: THE ERITREAN EXPERIENCE

IV

But Ethiopian gratification changed to chagrin in 1969 when the ELF suddenly reappeared in a variety of unpleasant and unexpected forms. Pre-eminently, the balance in the Middle East shifted as new men came to power, some determined to strike somewhere, somehow at the Arab world's enemies. In May in Khartoum, a group of officers under the direction of Gaafar al-Nimeiry seized power, motivated to attain radical reform, Arab unity, and an end to the southern insurrection. The Sudanese-Ethiopian détente appeared to be in shreds. In September even younger officers under the leadership of Muammar el-Qaddafi deposed King Idris of Libya. Qaddafi proved enthusiastic about Islamic causes, particularly those damaging to Israel — and was not the ELF engaged in an armed struggle against Ethiopian forces trained and advised by the Israelis? On the other side of the Red Sea, the NLF in Aden was willing to continue aid to the rebels despite Ethiopian pressure. The pipeline began to fill up. Libyan weapons arrived on the South Yemeni island of Kamaran,[10] far north on the Yemeni coast opposite Massawa, and to the west the Sudanese border was again open. But beyond the slow buildup in the bush, what was now occupying Ethiopian concern and attracting world attention was the employment of a new ELF tactic against new Ethiopian targets.

On March 11, 1969, a time bomb detonated in an Ethiopian airliner on the ground at Frankfurt, causing considerable damage. On June 18, three members of the ELF attacked an Ethiopian Boeing 720 jet on the ground at Karachi. In an interview with UPI, two of the men explained that the operation was to let the world know of the Eritrean movement. The series of skyjackings that followed began with the seizure of a DC-3 on August 12. On September 13, another plane was skyjacked between Addis Ababa and Djibouti and flown to Aden. Ethiopian security soon improved, however. Two hijackers who attempted to seize a plane between Madrid and Addis Ababa were shot and had their throats cut by security officers on December 12. On the ground a bomb was found in an airliner in Rome in March 1970, and in the same year a student was killed while constructing a bomb to use against

[10]During the September 1972 border war between the two Yemens, forces of the San'a regime occupied the island and seized Libyan arms destined for the ELF valued at £1,000,000. The complexity of Qaddafi's policies was thus revealed, for these arms had been turned over for transshipment to the National Front regime in Aden at almost the same time that other Libyan arms were given to Adenese exiles to oust the National Front — all in the name of Islam.

ORBIS

the Ethiopian Embassy in Rome. Africa's most "forgotten" war
had surfaced at last.

These spectacular external operations continued to keep the Eritrean cause in the newspapers no matter what was happening back
in the province. The ELF kept up the pressure. In January 1971,
a DC-3 was seized on an internal flight and eventually diverted to
Tripoli. A failed attempt occurred in December 1972 over Addis
Ababa when all seven ELF agents, five men and two women, were
killed in a barrage of gunfire a few seconds after they had announced their hijacking intentions. In the Horn an attack was
made on the Ethiopian Embassy in Djibouti as well as on the
railway line from the coast to Addis Ababa. In Eritrea, meanwhile,
the level of fighting increased — it was hardly a *shifta* operation
when the ELF managed to blow up the electric generator in
Asmara.

Nevertheless, throughout 1969 the Ethiopians maintained that
air piracy was a sign of weakness, and that the ELF was in-
substantial, composed of the same old *shifta* paid from abroad.
Very little hard information about internal security leaked out,
and Governor General Raz Asrate's public view of the situation
was still sanguine. It was quite possible to travel from one end of
the province to another with no trouble.[11] It was also possible to
encounter bad luck. An American servicemen's July 4 picnic party
was held in place for several hours by an ELF band, who seemed
to feel that the United States supported their revolution. The incident was hushed up. Later in the year the American Consul
General, Murray Jackson, heretofore as sanguine as the Governor
General, was detained and lectured by another band.[12]

Increasingly Raz Asrate's policy of holding army sweeps to a
minimum in order not to alienate the population appeared to be
allowing the ELF to intimidate or co-opt a growing number of
villages — or so it seemed to the Ethiopian army that had to deal
with more and more mines on the roads and ambushes in the hills.
In April 1970, the army was at last permitted to mount a major
sweep including air strikes. The Second Imperial Division swept
through the Danakil depression, the Massawa backlands and the

[11]In August 1969, I traveled without event in an unmarked car from Asmara to
the Sudanese border and back. At approximately the same time, a free-lance jour-
nalist crossed the Sudanese border and traveled with an ELF band to the edge of
Keren. See Jack Kramer, "Africa's Hidden War," *Evergreen Review,* December
1971, pp. 25-29, 61-64.
[12]In keeping with the Ethiopian policy of discretion, Jackson's kidnaping in
September was not revealed until December and then was buried in most
newspapers.

ENDEMIC INSURGENCY: THE ERITREAN EXPERIENCE

western lowlands — all areas of high endemic violence in the best of times. *Shifta* attacks declined briefly, but the ELF could still respond with an attack on the Esposito restaurant in the middle of Asmara.[13] With the arrival of the rains, the situation appeared stable if confused. Raz Asrate remained confident, the army wanted to undertake further operations, and the ELF's intentions were still unknown. Ethiopian spokesmen insisted that the population had been alienated by the terrorists; the ELF was "an organized syndicate of bandits, a Mafia with Marxist cadres."[14]

In August incidents of violence increased again. One of the district governors was killed in Serae while pursuing a group of eight ELF guerrillas. Ambushes continued along the roads and there was trouble in many of the villages. The culminating 1970 incident occurred on November 21, when Major General Teshome Erghetu, commander of the Second Imperial Division, was ambushed and killed outside Asmara on the Keren road.[15] Outraged, the army "cleared" both sides of the Keren road to a depth of ten kilometers.[16] Then as the military — and apparently the Emperor at last — felt that further stern measures were necessary, the army moved out into the lowlands supported by air strikes on suspect villages. Raz Asrate was replaced as Governor General by Lieutenant-General Debbebe Hailemariam. A state of emergency was declared, putting all of the province except the areas around Asmara, and Massawa and Assab on the Red Sea, under martial law. The ELF blew three bridges on the Asmara-Keren-Agordat highway. The Ethiopian air force bombed and destroyed a suspected village near Keren, producing another stream of refugees. The ELF seized a train and photographed its destruction. The army continued to sweep the countryside. Corpses of ELF men were trucked into Keren and tossed out in the main square. In January a U.S. serviceman driving up from Massawa was killed; no one knew by whom, but strict restrictions on travel out of Kagnew were immediately enforced. Ethiopian efforts to minimize the fighting were no longer successful —

[13]The ELF burst through the door of Esposito's, shot up the diners, killing six, but missed their targets, who had not shown up. The management subsequently decided to move the location of the restaurant to regain lost business.

[14]*New York Times,* August 18, 1970. The quotation is attributed to Raz Asrate.

[15]It is still not certain that the ELF had planned the ambush beside a blown bridge in a narrow canyon specifically with General Teshome as the target. The general had decided to leave Asmara only four hours before he met his death.

[16]The best estimate of casualties is 400 killed in the first army rampage along the road.

ORBIS

everyone in Asmara knew that military casualties were flooding into the army hospital.[17]

In a most unusual move, the Emperor in an interview accused "outside nations and groups" of fomenting trouble.[18] The Ethiopians thought the major culprit was the Syrian government, which, according to spokesmen, was a "manufacturer and storehouse of ridiculous lies and allegations."[19] In any case, the insurrection was out in the open. Although the ELF claim to control three million people in "liberated" zones was typical bombast, there could no longer be any doubt that the Front had recovered from the 1967-1968 setbacks. For several months the army concentrated on chasing down ELF bands, punishing guilty villages and imposing order on the countryside. The military felt justified that their earlier analysis of the situation had been accurate. So might Raz Asrate, though, for the Ethiopian army's excesses justified his concern. The Imperial Army, largely Amhara, was contemptuous of the people in the Eritrean province and apparently regarded the Moslems especially with suspicion and distaste. Discipline was poor and much of the exercise appeared, even to the sympathetic, as brutal repression with potentially unappetizing results, as a *Time* correspondent was told: "All we're doing is alienating the countryside, making the population more bitter than it was before."[20]

V

A substantial shift in policy was an intricate matter that required imperial enthusiasm and the balancing of various forces within the military establishment and the government elite. In time both the Emperor and the Governor General were committed to a program designed to win the hearts and minds of villagers equally fearful of ELF retaliation and army repression. Bombed and burned out villages were rebuilt by the army, development projects were undertaken, and soldiers were disciplined for indiscriminate brutality. The Moslem population was assured of their role in the empire. In Asmara and Addis Ababa there was some grumbling about the concessions, about the dilution of the army's real mission, but the new Governor General

[17]There is no way of telling the number of ELF casualties. The dead are often removed and buried elsewhere. The seriously wounded die or are killed to avoid capture. Even the identification of abandoned ELF dead is difficult, since decapitation is practiced to maintain rebel anonymity.

[18]*New York Times,* January 19, 1971.

[19]*Irish Times,* January 5, 1971.

[20]*Time,* March 10, 1971, p. 35.

ENDEMIC INSURGENCY: THE ERITREAN EXPERIENCE

pushed the program on in constant touch with the Palace, whence all power flows in Ethiopia.

The combination of civic action and continued army patrols and sweeps began to have a noticeable effect during 1971, and once more the Emperor managed to isolate the ELF. In an era of détente, he flew to Peking in October 1971, and subsequently the Chinese showed less interest in exporting revolution. The regime in Aden was persuaded toward discretion by the threat of expelling the large Yemeni population from Ethiopia and putting an end to their remittances, which would be a devastating blow to the Adenese economy. Most important, it became clear that Nimeiry intended to turn the Sudan from Arab to African matters and solve the southern problem by concession.[21] Haile Selassie offered his auspices to this effort and by the end of the year it was apparent that an accommodation between Khartoum and the southern rebels would be found, and with it an end to Sudanese support for the ELF. At no place in the Horn was there any longer active support for the ELF; even the truculent Somalis continued to maintain correct relations with Addis Ababa.

More devastating to the Eritrean rebels than their increasing isolation had been the collapse of internal ELF unity. There had long been strains between Christians and Moslems, both among the exiles and within the guerrilla bands,[22] as well as frictions born of various personalities and persuasions, and competition for limited resources. After 1969 the differences became irreconcilable and the ELF splintered. At the end of 1971, Idris Mohammed Adum announced the formation of a General Command and attacked Osman Saleh Sabbe as timid for his refusal to join the fighters in Eritrea. Saleh in turn formed the Popular Front and accused the General Command of tribalism and the assassination of two Christian members of the ELF. Inside Eritrea the two factions fought each other, Moslems attacking Christians, and tribal factions resorting to a shooting match. There suddenly seemed to be five or six squabbling *shifta* bands bent on vengeance and the unequal division of limited resources. The lofty ideological pronouncements of the exiles, which produced Iraqi support of the "correct" position of the General Command and Syrian support of the "proper" posture of the Popular Front, bore little relation to

[21]A. J. Bowyer Bell, "The Sudan's African Policy: Problems and Prospects," *Africa Today*, Summer 1973, pp. 3-12.

[22]It was often difficult to get Christian and Moslem "cadres" to eat together. Increasingly the bands became religiously monolithic — and after the split they were in open conflict.

ORBIS

the ambushes and assassinations in the bush. By 1972 even the guerrillas' momentum had dissipated. Isolated, intent on narrow advantage, without charismatic leadership, without unity, increasingly without arms or supplies, the ELF did come to resemble a Mafia with Marxist cadres — but the Marxists grew rarer as the revolution's prospects ebbed.

The ebbing proceeded slowly through 1972 into 1973. By the time of the rains in mid-1972, the days of big sweeps and major fire-fights had passed. ELF bands had become fewer and more elusive. Army casualties had dropped. Although the state of emergency was maintained, the roads were generally safe. Few in Asmara could tell whether the scattered fighting that continued was caused by banditry or the ELF. In September, for example, an Ethiopian column arrived at the village of Adi Hannes, near Sifunia in the Atlas Mountains, to sort out the theft of 168 cattle, which was a serious matter. Walking directly into an ambush, the soldiers lost twelve killed and twenty wounded. No one knew whether the tribesmen involved had close contact with the ELF or were responding to external interference by traditional means. The same was true of a similar incident near Agordat, also in September. In October during Ramadan, when the tribesmen seldom stir themselves to attack, only isolated shooting was noted and army casualties dropped to no more than ten, the lowest losses in a great many years.

With Ramadan over, attacks resumed. One along the Keren road wounded nine soldiers on November 6. A clumsy hand-grenade booby trap wounded a policeman in front of the Municipality Building in Asmara, but this was nothing like the ELF Asmara venture of the previous March, when the collection of captured "display" weapons was stolen from the financial police just before an imperial visit. Generally, serious army casualties were now running about fifty a month, mainly as the result of hit-and-run ambushes and an occasional mine. Defectors indicated that the rebels no longer had a real link with the ELF exiles and were short of arms and matériel. There were also regular reports of fighting between rival bands in the wilds. ELF claims out of Damascus, while still shrill, now and then touched on reality with the mention of past errors but still assured all that the armed struggle was continuing. Certainly the failed hijacking over Addis Ababa in December 1972 indicated that a few cadres were willing to take risks for the cause if they would not go into the bush. Thus, although the ELF was badly mauled, the insurrection had

ENDEMIC INSURGENCY: THE ERITREAN EXPERIENCE

become endemic. By 1973 it was plain that it could be contained but not closed down.

During the remainder of 1973 and on into 1974, little changed. ELF *shifta* bands surfaced from time to time. There were minor incidents, including a bomb in Asmara, but the hearts-and-minds program continued and attention was focused elsewhere. Insurgency was largely forgotten in the press of more important matters — famine, plagues, corruption, palace intrigue, and the great African drought. But beginning on February 25, 1974, Ethiopia was shaken by a remarkable train of events, more startling, perhaps, than the failed coup of 1960.

VI

Until 1974 many of the pressures for rapid political and social change had been muted in anticipation of a change of monarch, since Haile Selassie is an octogenarian. Then the rise in the cost of living, strikes and demonstrations, the continued revelation of incompetence if not corruption at the center, and the special ambitions of the moment triggered a mutiny in Asmara. Neither the senior officers in Eritrea nor the government in Addis Ababa knew what to make of the challenge. More disturbing to the conservatives, neither did the Emperor. The capacity to impose order by palace decree or personal charisma or resort to traditional loyalties had gone. A series of violent demonstrations and further mutinies engendered modest, yet unprecedented, concessions. After several months the end was still not in sight.

In the midst of the turmoil, the ELF from exile promised that its Eritrean cadres would take full advantage of the disorder to press the armed struggle. To this effect, guerrillas seized five foreign oil geologists after their helicopter had crash-landed. But the ELF and the hostages disappeared into the bush and efforts at ransom aborted — some people thought because the *shifta*, only nominally ELF, were truly isolated savages practicing habits of the past. In any case the backlands clearly had not been fully pacified and might not be for some time, given the chaos at the center. Although it was unlikely that any future Amhara elite would tolerate serious guerrilla escalation, it appeared that the endemic ELF insurgency would continue and expand once more if the center at Addis Ababa began to crumble.

As the uncertainty at the center continued, ELF operations grew more daring while the Ethiopian army concentrated on internal politics and the pace of reform. On June 30, the army once

ORBIS

more intervened by arresting and detaining those officials who had apparently been reluctant to transform the Ethiopian system. Swept up or put on wanted lists were many of the Emperor's closest advisers, senior government officials and army officers, and members of parliament. One of the key new appointments, announced on July 1, was that of General Beharane Teferra, former police chief of Eritrea, who was installed as governor of the province. Since he had been dismissed as police chief because of his insistence that a settlement could be reached only by dialogue, not by force, Teferra's appointment was widely thought to open a new phase of Eritrean-Ethiopian relations. In Rome an ELF spokesman indicated that a negotiated settlement might be possible. The military's choice of a new chief of staff, Major-General Aman Andom, seemed to strengthen this prospect: he is an Eritrean, born in Khartoum, who speaks fluent Arabic. After a decade out of power, he suddenly emerged as a dominant figure.

The views of the ELF operating inside Eritrea were not immediately known, but on July 13 gunmen assassinated Hamid Feraeg Hamid, former president of the Eritrea Assembly, while he prayed in a mosque in Agordat. Hamid had opposed independence and favored federalism, so it might be assumed that there had been no moderation in ELF ambitions.

The situation, however, remained vague. As much as anyone could be, the military officers were in effective control of the country, but as the maneuvering and arrests continued, so did reports of strains among various services and units. Until there was calm and stability in Addis Ababa, a new initiative on the Eritrean issue seemed unlikely and the extent to which any Amhara regime could make concessions without opening several other separatist doors remained uncertain. Moreover, the dissension within the ELF leadership, the isolation of its spokesmen, and the lack of internal discipline would pose serious problems for any negotiations.

VII

The unstable situation in the last few years has reflected the Eritrean potential for violence coupled with the limitations on effective repression and further pacification hampering the Ethiopian government. The martial, Islamic nomads were certain to opt for traditional skills and careers as long as their society remained nomadic and martial, Islam aside. The goal of a rifle and life as a *shifta* was too tempting, authorized by history and habit, to be permanently discarded simply because of an Ethiopian

ENDEMIC INSURGENCY: THE ERITREAN EXPERIENCE

pacification campaign. To settle the mobile tribes and erode their commitment to raids and ambushes is therefore beyond the capacity of the state, at least in the immediate future. Except for accomplishing a rise in order, such an investment would produce only minimal returns, while investment elsewhere would pay swift economic benefits far outweighing road safety in the Eritrean outback. Even if the Eritrean problem merely meant suppressing bandits there would be difficulties in maintaining absolute order. The Italians with 50,000 troops in the province, and making use of 200,000 native "militia" — in some cases rented *shifta* — largely eliminated the bandit problem. The Ethiopian army had only 40,000 troops all told. Addis Ababa committed approximately 10,000 men to Eritrean security forces beyond the normal police, frontier guards, and militia. Even so, this proved adequate to contain the *shifta* when coupled with the new hearts-and-minds pacification program.

The Eritrean problem, however, was not simply a case of controlling the *shifta;* the imperial center could hardly afford accommodation on the two major Eritrean demands — separatism and political liberalization — for one might lead to the state's fragmentation and the other to the collapse of the imperial system. Addis Ababa hoped that quiet concessions to the Christians and the promise of liberalization later on would buttress the province's loyalty, but not much more could be done swiftly enough to be effective. Thus, if the economic development of the entire empire was not to be warped or the very nature of the state changed, a certain level of disorder had to be tolerated. In any case, such disorder was hardly novel in Ethiopia. The Gojjami Amhara have long resisted the center and in 1968 undertook a tax revolt sufficiently successful to force Addis Ababa to give in to local demands. Faced with a similar revolt by the Muslim Galla of Bale province, the government opted for force that largely suppressed an open tribal rebellion. In another area, throughout the 1960's the Somali tribesmen of the Ogaden repeatedly engaged in *shifta* activity, usually with the aid and encouragement of Mogadishu. Yet, while tribal dissidence, armed rebellion, separatism and violent disorder on the imperial periphery have been the norm for a millennium, the manifold disorders during 1974 bode ill for continued tranquillity or stability at the center.

The Ethiopian response to insurrection in Eritrea has had the benefit of centuries of experience and the skill and talent of a central authority which in this case need not be modernized to react

445

ORBIS

effectively. The two continuing Ethiopian stratagems, adjusted and balanced once the ELF armed struggle began in 1961, have been (1) not to overreact and (2) to isolate the rebels. In the first instance the policy of Raz Asrate was most appropriate to imperial tradition, and even the response to the assassination of General Teshome relied on unleashing existing resources, not the sudden commitment of others. The policy of isolation as manipulated from Addis Ababa revealed the Emperor at his most effective, formed as it was by a combination of diplomatic initiatives, proxy revolution, veiled threats, the exploitation of his own image, others' fears, and shifts in the international climate. Ethiopia repeatedly closed off the ELF, not only in the forums of the United Nations and the Organization of African Unity, but also along the wild borders of the Sudan and across the Red Sea. Simultaneously, whenever possible, Ethiopia simply denied the existence of the ELF insurgency and rarely indicated publicly that allied help, i.e., American or Israeli, would be welcome.[23] As a result Ethiopian development was not unduly warped, nor was the potential for internationalization of the problem encouraged.

Despite all this, the Eritrean problem did much to poison Ethiopia's relations in the Horn for a decade. No matter what occurred in Eritrea, the Mogadishu regime, dedicated to incorporating all Somalis into one state, would clash with Ethiopia; in the case of the Sudan, normal relations with Khartoum could hardly be fashioned in face of the recurring "Arab" rebellion in Eritrea and the "Africa" rebellion in the southern Sudan. In addition, all the various Pan-Islamic currents, revolutionary or radical, found it necessary to focus on the Eritrean confrontation: Nasser had African ambitions and could not remain aloof, and Qaddafi was committed to Islamic revolution. That Ethiopia had long been a traditional enemy of Islam and was allied with Israel only made the Eritrean cause more appealing to the Arabs. The old jagged edges between Islam and Africa grated anew because of the tensions caused by the Israeli presence. Then, too, the establishment of the Kagnew Station brought the United States into the Eritrean situation by implication.[24] Revolutionary

[23]From time to time the Ethiopian military has requested special consideration because of the Eritrean problem — asking, for instance, for M-16 automatic rifles as a response to ambushes that American and Israeli advisers feel could be more effectively countered by tactical changes distasteful to Ethiopian officers. In general the Ethiopians continue to see the Eritrean challenge as a much less serious matter than that posed by Somalis allied to the Soviets.

[24]In response to the potential ELF challenge to American communication operations, in December 1970 the United States announced plans to build a facility on the isolated island of Diego Garcia, south of India.

ENDEMIC INSURGENCY: THE ERITREAN EXPERIENCE

spokesmen of varying hues painted Ethiopia as an American pawn and urged support of the ELF even though Eritrean issues were poorly understood. The growing Soviet presence in Somalia, counterbalancing the Americans in Ethiopia, gave further physical weight to the Horn's ideological differences. What is more, in this situation the Indian Ocean was adding to the concerns of distant strategists. A new generation of nuclear submarines would open vast new ocean areas to maneuver, and even if the closure of the Suez Canal continued, the oil conduits out of the Persian Gulf abutted on the Horn.

That the Eritrean problem "begs not for intervention but restraint, . . . admits of solution by the people directly concerned without complicating recourse to big-power involvement,"[25] may be a truism, but to date those maneuvering on the edge of Eritrean events have been reluctant to stay their hand. The United States (and Israel until the Yom Kippur War) has supported the Ethiopian military and has been at best but once removed from Eritrean operations. The Chinese have in the past favored the ELF. The Soviets at one time had as intimate relations with the ELF ally in Khartoum as they now have with Somalia. The French, mindful of their presence at Djibouti, are not unconcerned with Ethiopian events. But remarkably, given the clash of ambitions and aspirations within the Horn, the long-lived disorders in the southern Sudan, the Ogaden and Eritrea, the interests of major powers and the confrontation between the Israelis and Arabs on the southern flank of the Middle East crisis, the "internationalization" of the Eritrean insurrection has been relatively muted. In large part this can be credited to the skill of the Emperor and the Ethiopian elite in responding to the challenge in traditional terms. Others involved in countering endemic insurrections may not be so inclined.

VIII

In a world beset by SALT and Triton and MIRV, the fallout from the Yom Kippur War, global inflation, Cyprus, and Sino-Soviet border clashes, the problem of endemic insurgency is certainly marginal. Still, these small wars at the edge of the desert or out in the bush continue to offer the opportunity for exterior intervention and, perhaps, escalation into major confrontation. Equally distressing, if less serious, is the prospect of persistent regional involvement as the local insurgency absorbs neighboring

[25]Campbell, *op. cit.*, p. 548.

ORBIS

interest and gives weak regimes an opportunity to play the same games the big nations do.

In South Arabia in 1972, for example, the revolutionary ambitions of the radical regime in Aden engendered qualms throughout the peninsula and led to a border war. The Omani were concerned with the Dhufar insurrection supported by Aden, the Saudis with the center of communism and atheism on their borders, the North Yemeni with subversion, the exiles from the South with old ambitions, the Libyans with the Adenese apostates. That the border "war" fizzled to a stop in a negotiated agreement to seek Yemeni union can hardly disguise that South Arabia's endemic disorder threatens the stability of the oil regimes.

While even in an era of détente, major-power confrontation cannot be ruled out in marginal areas such as the Horn or Bangladesh or the Congo, we can more probably expect the continued involvement of small states in small local wars. The National Front in Aden can afford to pursue revolutionary aspirations in Dhufar at a minimal investment. Qaddafi can strike at imperialism in Northern Ireland or atheism in Aden or Zionism in Uganda without seriously depleting Libya's oil revenues. The African states followed their sentiments in aiding the rebels in Angola or Mozambique, much as the Portuguese did in showing considerable sympathy for the rebels of Biafra. But no matter under what banner, intervention disturbs the equilibrium of the region, just as insurrection warps the development of the nation involved. In an uncertain world, who can tell whether a major power may see more advantage in a war in the outback than the prudent would credit?

In sum, the Eritrean experience indicates that for an insurrection to become both endemic and internationalized several factors must exist. Of foremost importance, there must be an indigenous basis for disorder, a basis of habit and wont largely unrelated to broader ideological or political issues but firmly grounded in time-honored attitudes. Yet without the injection of a contemporary political content, traditional disorder alone is subject to conventional repression if the regime opts to invest the necessary resources. Many regimes have neither the resources nor the inclination to suppress disorder of this type, and in that case it is likely to continue at a low but tolerable intensity. If, however, a political component — Marxist cadres, black nationalism, modern separatism, Pan-Arabism — exploits the disorder under a fashionable banner, inevitably the rebels with their new image

ENDEMIC INSURGENCY: THE ERITREAN EXPERIENCE

will attract or repel distant observers. More to the point, their cause will receive some minimal exile-aid, will at least in a limited sense become "internationalized," and if it appears sufficiently promising may gain substantial support. The Eritrean rebels fall some place between the officially supported liberation movements in southern Africa and the almost completely ignored Karen separatists in northern Burma. One must conclude that it has become difficult for local activists to foment disorder, no matter how limited or how primitive the tactics or how isolated the rebel, without in time attracting outside interest. Even the Karens are not without external sympathizers.

Contemporary revolutionary strategies designed to inspire and spread disorder without recourse to traditional habits have often, if not always, been remarkably ineffectual. In most of Latin America the rural *focos* — the fashion of the 1960's — sputtered on in isolation, almost entirely ignored by the surrounding peasants or Indians. On the other hand, Colombia's ill-structured violence continued for years, the rural chaos protecting rebels who in turn could not manipulate anarchy to revolutionary advantage. When order was restored and the Colombian revolutionaries shifted their attention to the cities, the *Ejército de Liberación Nacional*, despite spectacular operations, was unable to threaten the regime seriously.

The capacity of the sophisticated rebel to mimic the local bandit, wittingly or no, as Fidel Castro did in the Sierra Maestra, can create a satisfactory rebel base far more effectively than ideologically proper campaigns of peasant education. Seizing the moment of spontaneous disorder may permit the initiation of a real insurrection, as MPLA and GRAE demonstrated in Angola in 1961. As a beginning step at least, manipulation of tribal rivalries, religious prejudice, linguistic fears or martial habits, even when such a stratagem must be denied in public, has been profitable for rebel strategists. Moreover, a reverse process seems equally possible as the sophisticated rebel, waging a long and losing conflict in the bush, passes beyond the fringe of rational revolution, enters the world of endemic insurrection, and becomes a skilled *shifta*, a sophisticated bandit. The once rigorously disciplined, keenly optimistic Malayan Races' Liberation Army, driven deep into the jungle, continued to resist. In July 1960, almost as an afterthought, twelve years after the revolt began, the British declared the Malayan Emergency legally ended, but some 500 surviving rebels held out in the jungle to reappear from time to

ORBIS

time. The history of the Hukbalahap in the Philippines was in many ways parallel, and the remnants of a Chinese Kuomintang division in northern Burma in time became a bandit army largely dependent on smuggling and theft. Each of these outfits can provide a foundation for a more highly integrated rebellion, but for years they remain moribund, brigands waiting for an injection of ideology.

Protracted disorder beyond the control of the center is a relatively common phenomenon, not only in the rural wilds but also in the circling slums of new cities and the ghettos of the old. There are always those who can apply banditry to specific advantage, see tribal atrocities through the appropriate ideological spectacles, co-opt riot for distant gain. Consequently, endemic insurgency seasoned with contemporary slogans seems certain for a time to disturb the stability of the international system, although if minimal care is exercised by the responsible it should have only limited effect. The potential battlegrounds are relatively obscure, the prizes less than dramatic. Still, given recent experience, the capacity of modern strategists to overvalue the distant domino cannot be completely ignored.

Kenya

[9]

THE ORIGINS OF MAU MAU

D. W. THROUP

THE SECOND WORLD WAR transformed the economic and political situation throughout Britain's African colonies.[1] This was particularly true in the settler colonies of East and Central Africa, where the economic depression of the 1930s had severely shaken the confidence of the local European communities as the prices they received for their agricultural products plummeted and the terms of trade moved sharply against them. In Kenya, the colonial government had attempted to preserve the fiscal basis of the colonial state by encouraging Africans, for the first time since before 1914, to increase their production for the export market. With lower production costs, unfettered by heavy mortgage debts to the commercial banks, for a short period in the late 1930s African peasant production had appeared to be essential to the economic survival of Kenya. The depression caused the Kenya Government to question the unquestionable, and to ponder whether Kenya really was a 'White Man's Country', as the settlers had so confidently proclaimed. Governor Byrne was keen to promote African interests. The Agricultural and Veterinary departments, which had been concentrated in the settler enclave of the White Highlands, began to operate in the African reserves and experimented with the introduction of more remunerative cash crops, such as coffee, on closely supervised African plots.[2]

The outbreak of war slowed the pace of this restructuring of the political economy of Kenya. Financially, settler agriculture prospered as never before from the increased demand for their agricultural exports. By 1942 a major transformation had occurred in the world economy, ending the long years of restricted demand for East Africa's exports and marking the

Dr Throup is a Bye-Fellow elect of Magdalene College, Cambridge, and thanks Drs Lonsdale, Anderson and Waller for their encouragement and comments.

1.   See I. Spencer, 'Settler dominance, agricultural production and the second world war in Kenya', *Journal of African History* 21 (1980), pp. 497–514; J. M. Lee, 'Forward thinking and war: the Colonial Office during the 1940s', *Journal of Imperial and Commonwealth History*, 6 (1977), pp. 64–79; R. D. Pearce, *The turning point in Africa: British colonial policy 1938–48*, (Cass 1982) pp. 1–89; R. von Albertini, *Decolonisation: The administration and future of the colonies, 1919–1960*, (Garden City, New York, 1971), pp. 158–78; A. R. Prest, *The war economies of primary producing countries*, (Cambridge, 1948), chs. 1, 5 and 9; N. J. Westcott, 'The impact of the second world war on Tanganyika, 1939–49', (unpublished Cambridge Ph.D. thesis, 1982) pp. 1–186; and G. Kitching, *Class and economic change in Kenya: the making of an African petite bourgeoisie 1905–70*, (Yale University Press, 1980), pp. 108–121.
2.   G. Bennett, 'Settlers and politics in Kenya, up to 1945', V. Harlow and E. M. Chilver (eds.) *History of East Africa*, vol. 2 (Oxford, 1965) pp. 322–326, for the standard account of the relations between Governor Byrne and the settlers. For the economic basis of the government's policy see Kitching, *Class and economic change*, pp. 57–107.

beginning of a new era of commodity shortages. Even the domestic market expanded as eighty thousand Italian prisoners of war, captured in Ethiopia, and Polish refugees were billeted in Kenya, while allied troops in the Middle East were fed Kenya wheat, maize and vegetables. The Japanese advance into the Philippines and Java benefited the sisal plantations, Kenya's single most important export crop, by disrupting allied supplies of hard fibres, reducing the quantities available to Britain and the United States from 530,000 tons to 245,000—half of which came from East Africa.[3]

European prosperity was ensured by the preferential terms guaranteed by the settler-dominated Agricultural Production and Settlement Board, which organized the war economy to benefit European farming interests. The high, guaranteed price for settler produced maize and the new breaking and clearing grants paid to those farmers, who increased their cereal cultivation, produced a dramatic expansion of the acreage of maize cultivated on European land from 80,000 in 1941 to 131,563 at the end of the war, while wheat production rose from 103,000 to 184,500 acres over the same four years.[4]

The war also brought major political gains for the settlers. One-third of the Administration was absorbed into the armed forces and a mere skeletal force was left in charge. The Kenya Administration had already suffered a decade of severe retrenchment, falling from a force of 136 in 1930 to 112 nine years later. After the new intake of 1932, no one else was recruited for the next three years.[5] With the outbreak of war and the military calls upon an already stretched administrative cadre, the Kenya government had to fall back on the utilization of settler manpower within the state apparatus and the incorporation of settler bodies such as the Kenya Farmers' Association as legitimate 'governing institutions' within the colonial state. This was especially true in the economic sector. While only Colonial Service officers could be entrusted to police the reserves, the settlers were, after all, adept in commercial dealings and farming and could, therefore, be trusted to operate the war economy.

It was because of this retreat from the citadels of power by the Colonial Service that the settlers were able by 1945 to become so much more powerful than they had been before the war. It was in the political and constitutional effects of the war that, in the short term, the Europeans found their greatest advantage. The economic consequences of high commodity

---

3. N. J. Westcott, 'The politics of planning and the planning of politics: colonialism and development in British Africa, 1930–60', (unpublished paper to Development Studies Association Conference 1981) pp. 4–9 and his thesis, pp. 62–3.
4. Food Shortage Commission Evidence, p. 84; Dept. of Agriculture Annual Report, 1945, (Government Printer, Nairobi, 1946) p. 11; and I. Spencer, 'Settler dominance', p. 503.
5. A. H. M. Kirk-Greene, 'The thin white line: the size of the British colonial service in Africa', *African Affairs* 79, (1980) p. 27 and table viii, p. 35.

THE ORIGINS OF MAU MAU   401

prices benefited Africans almost as much as Europeans. The reason why Kenya was to prove almost impossible to control during Mitchell's governorship was that during the war the settlers had come to occupy crucial positions within the colonial state and it was virtually impossible to dislodge them from these newly secured redoubts.

Mitchell's Failure to recoup Metropolitan Power

When Mitchell visited the Colonial Office early in December 1944 on his way from Fiji to Kenya, three main issues were discussed. The decisions reached at these meetings provide a key to understanding the priorities pursued during the Mitchell years. The three problems analysed were: post-war African economic development; the Closer Union question; and how the colonial government should reassert its authority over the Kenya state.[6] To varying degrees all three objectives were to prove impossible to achieve; but the quickest reversal of policy came over the issue of settler paramountcy. When he arrived in Nairobi on 12 December 1944, Mitchell soon perceived that it was completely impolitic to attempt directly to reduce settler power back to the position it had occupied in the late 1930s following Sir Joseph Byrne's six-year onslaught. A more ambiguous approach had to be devised.

The rationale for this temporizing with Colonial Office policy was that the Administration feared any tampering with the newly secured European political privileges would undermine the plans for African social and economic advance which were dependent upon the settler taxpayer and his private investments. Without the acquiescence, albeit largely from ignorance, of the settler communities, the whole basis of progress in the African reserves would be undermined, dependent as they were on European and Asian funding of social welfare and education programmes. Given the ideology of Colonial Development and Good Government, such schemes were also deemed to determine the pace of African political advance. The government therefore had to tax the settler communities to be able to meet African aspirations. The post-war African settlement schemes and the attempt to develop secondary industry both of which were designed to ease the increasing population pressures inside the African

6. N. J. Westcott, 'Closer Union and the future of East Africa, 1939–48: a case study in the Official Mind of Imperialism', *Journal of Imperial and Commonwealth History* 10 (1981), pp. 67–88, for an alternative view. For a diplomatic interpretation more sympathetic to my analysis see W. R. Louis, *Imperialism at bay: the United States and the decolonisation of the British Empire, 1941–1945* (Oxford University Press, 1977). See also Cranborne to Gater, 18 June, 1942 and Sir Arthur Dawe to Gater 27 July, 1942 in CO 967/57/46709, in which he contrasted the Kenya settlers to 12th century barons with their '. . . strong bulwarks against the power of the central government'. Dawe commented, 'Magna Carta year for the settlers was 1923. During that year the settlers delivered a blow at the prestige of the British Government in Kenya from which it has never recovered'. For similar comments from Dawe see CO 822/111/46705, 30 April 1942; and the minutes of the meeting on 10 June 1942, in CO 822/108/46523/32.

reserves which were threatening to destroy the stability of the colonial regime, also required their willingness to be milched. The whole programme for African advance was therefore found to be conditional upon the settlers preserving their war-time political gains. To oust Cavendish-Bentick from his control over the agricultural sector would have produced uproar and seriously impaired, if not irreparably damaged, the schemes for African economic and social progress. A frontal attack on the settler political redoubts would have had catastrophic consequences. Instead, a gradual sapping operation had to be devised. The trouble with this approach, which was frequently used during the Mitchell regime to avoid a direct confrontation with the settlers, was that it was ambiguous, and unless one was a party to government thinking, liable to misinterpretation.[7]

Cavendish-Bentick, the settler leader, was formally coopted into the administrative structure as Member for Agriculture, thereby diverting settler attention from the gradual sapping of their war-time powers over production and marketing of crops, African as well as European.[8] One dramatic concession which could not be prevented enabled the government to regain much lost ground, whilst the tradition of collective responsibility gagged Cavendish-Bentick, the most intelligent and influential of the settler politicians. Unfortunately, given the inherent suspicions of Kenya's racial politics, this step attracted all the attention and criticisms of Africans and Asians, and they failed to perceive that in many respects by 1946 the settlers had lost many of their wartime political gains, and that the Colonial Service had once again secured control over the state. The Field Administration grew from 117 in 1945 to 149 by 1950 and reached 213 full-

7. For one outstanding case of African misunderstanding see R. A. Frost, 'Sir Philip Mitchell, Governor of Kenya', *African Affairs* **78**, pp. 542–544, for the furore over Glancy's 'Report of a commission of inquiry appointed to review the Registration of Persons Ordinance 1947', (Government Printer, Nairobi, 1950). Similar misunderstandings arose over the Kenya Government's policies on the preservation of the White Highlands and with Col. 210 on East African Closer Union. For African settlement in the Ithanga Hills see Mitchell to Cohen, 17 March, 1948 in CO 533/557/38678 (1948–9) and ibid. Mitchell to Lloyd, 27 September, 1949. See also Mitchell to Cohen, on 7 September, 1949, and to Creech Jones on 13 September, 1949, both in CO 533/558/38678.2 (1949). For Closer Union Cohen to Lockhart 25 January, 1946 and Rennie to George Hall, 6 March, 1946 both in CO 822/114/46523. For Creech Jones's view of the possibility of settler opposition to the revamped proposals in Col 210 see CO 822/114/46523 for his comments of 25 September, 1946 and 30 May, 1947.
8. Mitchell to Creasy, 30 December 1944, in CO 533/536/38598 and 18 February, 1945, in CO 533/537/38628. During the war 'C–B' had acquired considerable power over the agricultural sector of the economy, serving as member of the East African Production and Supply Council; as a member of its executive board; and on its production, storage and machinery sub-committees; as controller of stock feed and fertilisers; machinery controller; East-African timber controller; and as controller of the Ziwani and Taveta irrigation schemes. He was also chairman of the Kenya Agricultural Production and Settlement Board; and a member of the Highlands Board and the Land Advisory Board. At the same time he was chairman of the Kenya Association, and of the East African Publicity Association. He also served on both the Kenya Legislative and Executive Councils. For a discussion of the Kenya Government's formal co-option of 'C–B' see J. M. Lonsdale, 'The Growth and Transformation of the Colonial State in Kenya, 1929–52', forthcoming in *Kenya in the Twentieth Century* ed. B. A. Ogot (Nairobi).

THE ORIGINS OF MAU MAU 403

time officers by 1957. Kenya also saw a considerable expansion in the size of the professional departments, agriculture expanding from 298 in 1945 to 2,519 in 1958, and the Veterinary Department grew from 291 to 892 over the same period. Colonial rule was transformed in the immediate post-war period. Manpower problems ceased to be a major factor facing the government until the outbreak of Mau Mau. The need to mobilize settler manpower had ended.[9]

The East African melodrama over Colonial Papers 191 and 210 provides an example of misplaced administrative guile; apparent concessions were made to the settlers which Africans and Asians denounced; and attention was diverted from the fact of Colonial Service resistance to settler demands.[10] The problem was that the settlers were simply too powerful to resist by a head-on confrontation. Their role in Kenya society as the essential 'steel frame' for African progress and milch cow for economic development meant that they could not simply be ignored. They had to be reconciled and led up the garden path. It was not long, however, before the settlers perceived this sleight of hand.

Kenyatta and African Politics

The main problem of post-war Kenya politics was that Africans never did see through the rhetoric of the Administration and each apparent concession to the European (over Cavendish-Bentick, 210, the Kipande Affair) was taken at face value. This was not always their fault. African and Asian constitutional leaders were never incorporated into the state structure which, seen from the outside, appeared to be an exclusive European preserve, however chilly the atmosphere might have been inside. Mitchell's initial willingness to co-opt Mathu, as Member for African Education—a crucial position, given the complexities of Local Native Council finances and their dependence on central government grants, and an appointment for which he was singularly well qualified—ran into the unwavering resistance of Carey Francis, who loathed Mathu.[11] Kenyatta's return and the close relationship which he quickly built up with Mathu seemed to prove Francis correct. Mathu was basically unsound. He was no different from Kenyatta. What Kenyatta said on the stump,

9. A. H. M. Kirk-Greene, 'The thin white line' pp. 27–9 and 34–5, especially tables i, ii, iii and viii. This surge of manpower into Africa, both in the colonial service and the technical departments, has been called the Second Colonial Occupation by J. M. Lonsdale and D. A. Low in the *Oxford History of East Africa*, vol. 3, (Oxford University Press, 1976) pp. 12–16, edited by D. A. Low and A. Smith.

10. Cohen to Gater, 10 September, 1946, in CO 822/114/46523 for the Colonial Office's determination to resist settler pressure and Davies to India Office 19 May, 1947 in CO 822/132 46523 refuting the allegation that Col 210 represented a retreat from the policy outlined in Col 191.

11. See B. E. Kipkorir, 'Carey Francis at the Alliance High School, Kikuyu, 1940–62' in B. E. Kipkorir, ed. *Biographical essays on imperialism and collaboration in colonial Kenya*, pp. 133–147, (Kenya Literature Bureau Nairobi, 1980) and acting Governor Rennie to Mitchell, 31 October, 1945 in CO 533/541/38032/5.

Mathu said in the Legislative Council, and *vice versa*: and on this the administration were indeed more correct than much early post-*Uhuru* historical writing.   The gulf was not between Mathu, the government stooge, and Kenyatta, the great leader; but between Mathu and Kenyatta, the constitutionalists, and those 'wild, uncultured minds' of the militants, so eloquently denounced by Kenyatta.[12]

Mitchell's initial reaction was invariably one of co-option; and so it was with Kenyatta upon his messianic return from Europe.   He was not simply fobbed off, refused a place on the Legislative Council and told to gain experience on the Kiambu Native Council, as has been suggested. He was in fact offered a place on the African Settlement Board and, as an acknowledged authority on Kikuyu tradition, the author of *Facing Mount Kenya*, was considered as a suitable President of the Kiambu Tribunal when the post became vacant.   These were not minor positions.   In the government's eyes they were central posts from which he could assist in policy formulation, and indeed such they could have been.[13]   But whilst at this stage, 1946/early 1947, the Secretariat was willing to 'sup with the devil', albeit with a long spoon, the Field Administration saw him as a threat to their pre-eminence in the reserves.   Any concession to Kenyatta would, they argued, be interpreted as a signal for KCA activists, in their guise as leaders of KAU, to begin agitation.[14]   Although the doctrine of Indirect Rule may never have taken root in the barren soil of Kenya's acephalous societies, nevertheless, after fifty years of colonial rule, a distinct class of 'collaborators' had emerged: a group whose pre-eminent political, social and perhaps most importantly economic position was dependent upon their relationship with the colonial authorities, i.e. the chiefs and their supporters, who were incorporated as the bottom rung of the colonial state.   To legitimize Mathu, and even more so Kenyatta was to cut the ground from underneath not only the District Commissioner but the very foundation of British rule, the chief and his headmen policing the maize *shambas*.[15]

12.   For a similar contemporary view see N. Farson, *Last Chance in Africa*, (Victor Gollancz, 1949) p. 115, and for the militants' perspective B. Kaggia, *Roots of Freedom*, 1921–63, (East African Publishing House. Nairobi, 1975), p. 82.   His old friend Peter Abrahams also noted Kenyatta's despair at his declining political power, see P. Abrahams, 'The Blacks', in L. Hughes, *An African Treasury* (Victor Gollancz, New York, 1960), especially p. 59.
13.   For Mitchell's willingness to co-opt Kenyatta onto Government advisory boards see his diary, 11 December 1946, Rhodes House Mss. Afr. r. 101, and Mitchell to Creech Jones 14 April, 1947, in CO 533 549/38232/15.
14.   Mitchell to Creech Jones 28 February, 1949, CO 533/543/38086/38 (1949), and Rankine to Creech Jones 28 December, 1948, *ibid*.   For Mitchell's growing suspicion of Kenyatta, see Mitchell to Creech Jones. 11 December, 1948 in CO 533/540/38032 and November, 1946 in CO 533/543/38086/5.
15.   The effects of the second colonial occupation upon the authority of the chief can be seen most clearly in Murang'a.   See KNA DC/FH 1/26, Fort Hall Annual Report, 1947, pp. 1–7, and DC/FH 1/28 Fort Hall Annual Report 1948, pp. 5–6.   For the Administration's views of the effectiveness of the Murang'a chiefs, see DC/FH 4/6, 'Chiefs and Headman. 1937–54'.

THE ORIGINS OF MAU MAU 405

Certain fundamental questions had to be answered: Did the British want to overturn the order established in the 1890s and incorporate the 'young men', the disgruntled political activists? Could it be done without threatening complete anarchy or was it not preferable to sit on the lid of rising African political consciousness and hope that it would subside, rather than explode? Was this not, in the last analysis, a less risky option than 'turning the world upside down', however much this may have been desired by the theorists in Whitehall of the new Labour Government, Creech Jones and Andrew Cohen? Did these academic idealists, as Lord Milverton queried from his fastness in Nigeria, really know what their policies of local government reform would actually entail? It was all very well for London to say that Indirect Rule was obsolete, and that controlled political development should be encouraged amongst the educated new elite; but was this possible? Could the process be controlled? Was it not in fact knocking the props away from British Imperial rule?[16]

Professor Low has argued that in Buganda on two occasions, in 1900 with the Treaty and again in the late 1920s, British rule had taken the risky option, supporting the rising young men against the established elders, and that Buganda and the British had profited thereby. But Buganda was an exception to the norm and it is surely significant that Professor Low acknowledges that, when the third generational crisis under British rule

16. For a favourable view of Creech Jones and Cohen, see R. E. Robinson, 'Sir Andrew Cohen: Proconsul of African Nationalism' in L. H. Gann and P. Duigan ed. *African Proconsuls: European Governors in Africa*, (The Free Press, New York, 1978) pp. 353–363; and 'Andrew Cohen and the transfer of power in Tropical Africa, 1940–51' in ed. W. H. Morris-Jones and G. Fischer, *Decolonisation and after: the British and French experience*, (Frank Cass, London 1980) pp. 50–72. See also R. D. Pearce, *The Turning Point in Africa*, especially pp. 132–205. For a critical view of the new orthodoxy see, J. W. Cell, 'On the eve of decolonisation: the Colonial Office's plans for the transfer of power in Africa, 1947', in *Journal of Imperial and Commonwealth History*, 8, May 1980, no. 3. The view from the grass roots in West Africa has been provided by R. D. Pearce in 'Governors, Nationalists and constitutions in Nigeria, 1935–51', *Journal of Imperial and Commonwealth History*, 9, May 1981, no. 3. Contemporary views of the policy can be found in *The Journal of African Administration*. The following are some of the more interesting; Colonial Office African Studies Branch: 'Local Government reorganisation in the eastern province of Nigeria and Kenya', vol 1, no 1, pp. 18–29; 'The member system in British African territories', vol. 1, no 2, pp. 51–8; 'A survey of the development of local government in the African territories since 1947', supplement to vol. iv, 1952; A. Creech Jones 'The Place of African local administration in colonial policy', vol. 1, no 1, pp. 3–6; and the Earl of Listowel, 'The modern conception of Government in British Africa', vol. 1, no 3, pp. 99–105. Ronald Robinson in his Colonial Office incarnation also contributed to this debate; see 'The Progress of Provincial Councils in the British African Territories', vol. 1, no 2, pp. 59–67, and 'Why Indirect Rule has been replaced by local government in the nomenclature of British Native Administration', vol. 2, no 3, pp. 12–19. Mitchell's view is to be found in his diary for 10 November 1947, where he noted: 'We conferred all day, largely on dry, theoretical ideas of colonial self-government totally divorced from the realities of the present day. The C.O. has got itself into a sort of mystic enchantment and see visions of grateful, independent Utopias beaming at them from all round the world, as if there was—yet—any reason to suppose that any African can be cashier of a village council for three weeks without stealing the cash. It is uphill work; but we bludgeoned them pretty severely from both sides; although the West Africans, other than Milverton, are a silent lot. There is really no understanding whatever of contemporary realities in the CO. Creech blathered a good deal . . .'.

occurred in Buganda in the late 1940s, the colonial authorities backed the establishment rather than their youthful critics.[17]   These problems confronted all the British colonies, and indeed the whole of Africa, in the immediate post-war era.   It can now be seen that colonial governments were presented with a choice between short-term stability with a corollary of longer-term dissatisfaction and mounting political trouble; or short-term instability with the result of longer-run security.   London wanted the latter; colonial governments opted for the former.   The stakes at risk with the short-term instability option were seen as too great.   Colonial rule had existed for too long, become too entrenched, to live dangerously. Safety first was the rule.

Just as in the late 1920s, when the KCA had first stretched its muscles and the Administration had hesitated as to their response (should it be coopted or suppressed?) the late 1940s show a similar process in their attitude to KAU.[18]   Whilst it was moderate and politely functioned within the existing social order in the reserves, it was tolerated, even encouraged, by a few adventurous District Commissioners; but by its nature as a vehicle for educated, self-confident Africans, paradoxically often employed by the government—returning *askaris*, or prosperous peasant farmers and a few traders who had done well out of the high cash crop prices during the war—in fact by its very existence, it posed a challenge to the chiefs.   A few could be absorbed, but the number demanding entry into the colonial governing structure in the reserves were out of all proportion to those who could be peacefully co-opted.   Only the over-turning of the *status quo* could deal with such 'popularity'.   The co-optive capacity of the colonial state, without fundamental restructuring, simply could not cope.   It was these people who were to provide the backbone of KAU in Central Province.[19]

Typical of this group were the ex-*askaris*, most of whom had never been anywhere near the front line.   Their horizons had, however, been immensely broadened and they returned home with more money than most Africans had ever collected before.   Such men were discontented with life in the village, eager to enter trade, build stone houses and better their lot. The trouble was not just that their advance as traders, etc., was hindered by the settler communities, European politicians and Asian traders, but also that they encountered the suspicions of the chiefs and elders and therefore,

17.   D. A. Low, *Buganda in modern history*, (Weidenfeld and Nicholson, 1971) pp. 144–51.
18.   See D. M. Feldman, 'Christians and politics: the origins of the Kikuyu Central Association in northern Murang'a, 1890–1930' (unpublished Cambridge Ph.D. thesis, 1978), pp. 191–202 and pp. 232–238.
19.   See J. M. Lonsdale, 'The growth and transformation of the colonial state in Kenya', pp. 9–12.
    This can clearly be seen in the attempts of the wattle bark traders to gain Government recognition of their association.   Geoffrey Ndegwa to senior Agricultural Officer, Nyeri, 24 July, 1944 in KNA Ag. Dept. 4/220.

automatically, of most District Commissioners. Their ambitions were disappointed. Money was wasted in building stone *dukas* to meet public health regulations, and difficulties were encountered in obtaining the requisite government licences for trading, bus routes, etc. Rather than assisting this new force the government merely watched from the sidelines, if it did not actively oppose.[20]

These men, however, did not become Mau Mau. Even after they had lost all their money in speculative ventures, they were reluctant to contemplate violence, if only because they were only too well aware of the overwhelming forces the colonial state had in its possession to suppress a rebellion. Instead, these people were Kenyatta and Mathu's chief supporters, the constitutionalist wing of KAU. But in the post-war era, if the government could not even succeed in winning over these men by co-option, then the game was all but lost. The 'wild men', the discontented have-nots with nothing to lose, would inevitably adopt more drastic tactics.

As early as 1947, it had already become apparent that Governor Mitchell's policies had failed. The Governor, however, failed to appreciate the seriousness of the situation and the depth of African, and especially Kikuyu, disillusionment with his strategy both in the countryside and the capital. Although the Labour and Agricultural Departments warned that the social engineering campaign in the Reserves was being pushed too far too fast and that a more cautious approach was required unless the Kikuyu were to be completely antagonized and driven into revolt, the Field Administration and the Governor pushed ahead with grim determination not to be deflected by 'political agitators' like Kenyatta.[21] Supported in this resolve by the Kikuyu chiefs, the Governor and his District Commissioners were convinced that they 'knew their Kikuyu' and failed to

20. Fort Hall Annual Reports, 1946 and 1947, and Fort Hall African Merchants' Association AGM, 23 July 1950.
21. Mitchell's attitude towards Kenyatta, and even the constitutionalist African politicians like Eliud Mathu, hardened during 1947. For his report of his first encounter with Kenyatta see CO 533/543/38086/5 (1945–47) 'Kikuyu Memorials and Petitions', Mitchell to Creech Jones 20 January 1947. By 1949 Mitchell was much more hostile, see CO 533/543/38086/38 (1949) 'Petitions: Kikuyu Central Association–Kikuyu Grievances', Mitchell to Creech Jones 28 February 1949. See also CO 533/540/38032 (1949) 'Legislative Council', Mitchell to Creech Jones 11 December 1948, for his suspicions of the linkages between Mathu, Kenyatta and the Communists; and CO 533/549/38232/15 (1946–47) 'European Settlement: Squatters', Mitchell to Creech Jones for a forthright defence of multi-racialism. Mitchell insisted that if Kenya was to 'develop towards British Christian civilisation' British rule must continue for many years. • The alternative was to 'relapse into corruption and barbarism. Just exactly what that means in suffering for the common people can be seen just across our frontier in Abyssinia or in those Central American republics where impatience to secure independence ... has led to the termination of the colonial status before the common people had reached a stage where they had any capacity to protect themselves from the local demagogues who succeeded the Spanish officials. The same collapse of civilisation, justice and economic development could no doubt be produced in Africa by the same processes'. For a more favourable view of Kenyatta see Wyn Harris's humorous account of a meeting to discuss the Kenya African Union's petition to the United Nations in CO 537/3591/38733 (1948): 'Petitions to the United Nations', Wyn Harris'[s] minute of of 15 October 1948.

408   AFRICAN AFFAIRS

respond to warnings from settlers and moderate Africans that the situation
in Central Province and the African locations of Nairobi was out of control.
The Colonial Office, therefore, remained ignorant of the increasing Kikuyu
unrest and unaware that their co-optive strategy was not being followed in
Kenya. In fact the unwillingness of the Kenya authorities to co-opt
Kenyatta and the moderates strengthened the position of the militants,
until the Government was no longer able to control the countryside or
African Nairobi. In 1952 the state collapsed in Kikuyuland under Mau
Mau pressure, finally revealing the bankruptcy of Mitchell's post-war
policies. Let us analyse these in turn.

The Kikuyu Reserve

In the Reserves the communalist prescriptions of the Field Administration proved to be bankrupt remnants from the era of Indirect Rule. The
traditional land authorities among the Kikuyu and the Meru,
the *Muhiriga*[22] and the *Njuri Ncheke*,[23] were no longer able to restrain the
development of capitalist relations in the reserves. Indeed many of the
chiefs and elders—the established elite of Kikuyu society—were in the
vanguard of capital accumulation, land expropriation and the whole
process of increasing social differentiation. The administration had
identified the wrong enemy. Their ideological commitment to 'Merrie
Africa' prevented them from recognizing that their allies the chiefs were as
involved in trade and commercial farming, dubious land deals and the
bribing of Native Tribunals, as their rivals in the Kenya African Union and
the Kikuyu Central Association.[24] The whole post-war agricultural cam-

22. The *mihiriga* were the nine main clans among the Kikuyu, which the Administration
believed had allocated land and supervised cultivation in pre-colonial times. In fact real
power was held by the leaders of the sub-clans, the *mbari*, or even smaller *nyumba* 'household'
groupings, under the loose supervision of a *murumati* or trustee. For the attitudes of the
Field Administration towards indigenous institutions see CO 852.662/19936/2 (1945–46),
'Soil Erosion Kenya'; N. Humphrey, 'Thoughts on the Foundations of Future Prosperity in
the Kikuyu Lands', pp. 56–57; and H. E. Lambert and P. Wyn Harris' memorandum on
'Policy in Regard to Land Tenure in the Native Lands of Kenya'. See also L. S. B. Leakey,
The Southern Kikuyu before 1903, (Academic Press, New York, 1977) vol. i, pp. 7–8 and
109–113; and G. Muriuki, *History of the Kikuyu*, (Oxford University Press, Nairobi, 1974) pp.
112–116.
23. 'A Survey of the Development of Local Government in the African Territories since
1947', *Supplement to the Journal of African Administration* vol. iv, no. 3, July 1952, pp. 33–41;
R. O. Hennings, 'Some Trends and Problems of African Land Tenure in Kenya', *Journal of
African Administration*, vol. iv, no. 4, October 1952, pp. 122–134 and KNA DC/MRU 1.4
'Meru Annual Report 1939', Appendix A.
24. A. Thurston's draft manuscript, 'The Intensification of Smallholder Agriculture in
Kenya: The Genesis and Implementation of the Swynnerton Plan', pp. 75–78; KNA MAA
7/320 'Chiefs Engaged in Commerce, 1948', C. H. Hartwell to all Provincial and District
Commissioners 13 August 1948; and MAA 7/456 'Policy Native Administration Central
Province—Ndeiya, 1946–52', A. C. M. Mullins to Provincial Commissioner, Central Pro-
vince, 5 June 1946. For press attacks on chiefs see MAA 8/102 'Intelligence: Miscellaneous
Press Cuttings, 1948–50', *Mucemanio* 3 July 1948; MAA 8/106 'Intelligence: Mumenyerere,
1947–50', *Mumenyereri* 29 September 1947 and 5 April 1948; and MAA 8/108 'Intelligence:
Daily Chronicle', *Daily Chronicle* 30 April 1948.

paign as originally conceived, therefore, was doomed to failure, since it completely failed to take account of the changes in African society. District Commissioners were attempting to behave like King Canute in the face of the advancing tide of African individualism, and had as little effect. The particular beliefs of the Administration, had a profound impact on the limited imagination of the men on the ground, and helped to ensure that they played into the hands of the settlers and the chiefs.[25] These sub-conscious prejudices enabled the settlers and chiefs to hijack Whitehall's plans for a second colonial occupation, and to use them to suppress their rivals, the African protocapitalists.

The agricultural campaign had been formulated in the Secretariat during the last years of the war when a series of settler-dominated specialist committees had investigated the problems confronting Kenya.[26] Once the Second Colonial Occupation got under way, however, it soon diverged from Whitehall's strategy and all central co-ordination quickly disappeared. The programme was implemented not by the Secretariat or the headquarters of the technical departments in Nairobi, but by District Commissioners and Agricultural Officers in the Reserves. Although the Colonial Office, the Secretariat, and the district *boma* may have believed that they were implementing the same policies, the structure of the colonial state ensured that a metamorphosis took place as instructions passed down the line of command. Thus District Commissioners were able to imprint their own prejudices upon the campaign in their locations, and could ignore those proposals with which they disagreed.[27] They could, therefore, extol the peasant as the backbone of society and propagate the myth of Africa's egalitarian, communalist past, as a useful weapon in their attack upon their African critics in the Kenya African Union.

The emerging African elite posed a double challenge to the political economy of post-war Kenya. They threatened the settlers' monopoly of influence on the Legislative and Executive Councils and their autonomous domain in the White Highlands, while in the Reserves they challenged the political authority of the chiefs and traditional elders and their allies in the

25. B. Moore, *Social Origins of Dictatorship and Democracy*, (Boston, 1966) pp. 491–496; and B. J. Berman's unpublished Yale Ph.D. thesis, 'Administration and Politics in Colonial Kenya', pp. 105–139.

26. KNA Secretariat 1/1/5 'Department of Agriculture Development Plans, 1944'; Secretariat 1/1/12 'Report of the Joint Agricultural and Veterinary Services Sub-committee of the Development Committee'; Secretariat 1/4/12 Report of the Sub-committee on Industrial Development including Electric Power, 1945'; Secretariat 1/7/16 and 1/7/17 'Sub-committee on Social Welfare, Mass Education and Information'; Secretariat 1/18/11 'Memorandum on the Post-war Development of the Medical Services in Kenya, 1944'; Secretariat 1/24/4 'Report of the Sub-committee on Water Development, 1944'; DC/NYI 2/1/20 'Mr Humphrey's Report on South Nyeri, 1944–47'; and DC.NYI 2/1/16 'Development and Welfare Planning, 1944–48'.

27. M. P. K. Sorrenson, *Land Reform in the Kikuyu Country*, (Oxford University Press, Nairobi, 1967) pp. 52–71; and B. J. Berman's unpublished paper 'Provincial Administration and the Contradictions of Colonialism' (1976), pp. 5–20.

Administration. These African accumulators, with access to sources of investment outside the Reserves from employment in comparatively well paid jobs in Nairobi, had been able to transform the peasant option into an alternative to settler commodity production. During the Depression Kikuyu entrepreneurs had momentarily seemed about to undermine the economic base of settler life—the European-owned commercial farms in the White Highlands. Kennedy and Mosley have shown that while the settlers in Southern Rhodesia, with their complete control over the state, had been able to divert resources to sustain European agriculture during the 1930s, in Kenya the tighter reins of the Colonial Office had ensured that the settlers did not always get their way. The Duke of Devonshire's 1923 declaration of African paramountcy effectively precluded settler domination and acted as the moral conscience of the colonial state in Kenya. Settler hegemony, in so far as it existed, had to be conditional; restrained by an unholy alliance between the Colonial Office, the British left and the missionaries.[28]

Kenya had been set on the road to Mau Mau in the 1930s, just when the African challenge to the settlers' vision of Kenya as a 'White Man's Country' had been strongest. Why was this? It looks as though the peripheral British official mind had hedged its bets, unwilling to decide between the settlers and the emerging African capitalists. The Kenya Government had attempted to revive settler agriculture through easy loans from the Land Bank, while also promoting African production in order to preserve its fiscal resources.[29] The Government had lacked the courage to ditch the settlers or to cement an alliance with the emerging African traders and commercial farmers. To abandon settler farming and to rely upon the peasant option, as Harold Macmillan was to suggest in 1942, had appeared to be too big a risk.[30] Thus the conflict was set. The Mitchell Government after the war, however, failed to recognize that both settlers and Africans had prospered since the late 1930s with increased commodity prices. The conflict, therefore, was continued at a higher level after 1945, when both sides were stronger. Because of the Government's failure to decide in the 1930s which side it was going to support, settler and Kikuyu accumulators were on a collision course during the 1940s.

As the war ended the Administration reversed its agricultural policy of the previous fifteen years. African commercial cultivators and traders

28.   CO 533/537/38608 (1944–46) 'Land Policy: Memorandum by the Anti-Slavery Society'; CO 533/556/38664/2 (1947) 'Land Policy: Memorandum by the Labour Party'; and CO 533/558/38690 (1947) 'Fabian Society'; and R. E. Robinson, 'The Moral Disarmament of African Empire, 1919–1947', *Journal of Imperial and Commonwealth History*, 3, October 1979, pp. 93–102.
29.   P. Mosley's Cambridge University thesis (1980), 'The Settler Economies: Studies of the Economic History of Kenya and Southern Rhodesia, 1900–1963', pp. 184–193.
30.   CO 967 57/46709 (1942): 'Sir Arthur Dawe's Memorandum on a Federal Solution for East Africa and Mr Harold Macmillan's Counter-Proposals'.

THE ORIGINS OF MAU MAU   411

were no longer encouraged.   Instead they were identified as a major source of social discontent in the Reserves.   Throughout the first four years of Mitchell's Governorship the Administration and the Agricultural Department attempted to protect the ordinary African—the poor and middle peasants with less than eight acres—from the depredations of their prosperous neighbours.   But, the reality was rather different.   The chiefs increasingly usurped the nominal powers of the *Muhiriga* elders and soon dominated the agricultural campaign, which they used to benefit themselves and their supporters.   Compulsory labour gangs were used to terrace their *shambas* and to extend their cultivation onto commercial grazing land and into the bracken zone.   Despite the miles of terracing which had been dug by July 1947, the ordinary peasant could see little return for his exhausting work.[31]

These tensions between the chiefs and their people were particularly bitter in the locations of the new generation of energetic, young chiefs, who had been appointed after the war, specifically to ensure the success of the campaign.   Unlike their older colleagues they do not appear to have accumulated reserves of support which could be called upon to legitimize their interference in peasant life.[32]   The effects of 'the Second Colonial Occupation' by mid-1947, had already had a profound impact upon the development of the Reserves, and had helped undermine the communal values which the Administration claimed to be defending.   The people had become disillusioned.   The returned *askari*, for example, had seen their ambitions thwarted, their new business enterprises fail, and their savings vanish, it seemed to them because of obstruction by the chiefs and the District Administration.[33]

Meanwhile the banned Kikuyu Central Association functioned underground, becoming increasingly active after its leaders were released from their wartime detention at Kapenguria.   On their return they singled out terracing and the chiefs as their main targets and made strenuous attempts to win the support of the ex-soldiers, who were an important new element in rural life.   Their money and contacts outside the locality were valuable

31.   KNA Ag 4/392 'Central Province District Agricultural Reports, 1948', especially the Soil Conservation Reports from Kiambu, Murang'a and Embu; and Ag 4/451 'Fort Hall Safari Diaries, 1948–51'.
32.   KNA DC/FH 1/26 'Fort Hall Annual Report, 1946', pp. 19–22; DC/FH 1/27 'Fort Hall Annual Report, 1947', pp. 5–6; DC/FH 2/1(b) 'Fort Hall Handing Over Reports, 1926–60', P. S. Osborne to D. O'Hagan, April 1945; and DC/FH 4/6 'Chiefs and Headmen, 1937–1954'.
33.   KNA DC/FH 1/25 'Fort Hall Annual Report, 1945', p. 7; MAA 7/2 'Nyeri Ex-Soldiers Association, 1945–47'; Secretariat 1/12/1 'Man-power and Civil Reabsorption, 1946', pp. 18; and Defence 10/4 'Training: African D Centres', P. C. Central to Civil Reabsorption Officer 31 December 1945.   See also MAA 7/4 'Fort Hall African Merchants' Association, 1950', Resolution of Annual General Meeting 23 July 1950 for protests against the treatment of African traders; and contrast with the Government's attempts to help African shopkeepers in C&I 6/787 'Trading by Africans: Propaganda and Publications, 1945–47' and C&I 6/782 'Trading by Africans, 1946–50'.   See also CS 2/1/126 'Visit Mr Rees-Williams', Kenyatta to Rees-Williams, 6 April 1948.

412   AFRICAN AFFAIRS

new political assets for the older generation of Kikuyu Central Association
stalwarts.[34]

The Plight of the Kikuyu Squatters

It was not, however, in Central Province itself that resistance first raised
its head in 1945 or 1946.   There the Kenya African Union was still trying
to gain admittance to the rewards of the colonial regime.   Almost to the
end, Central Province remained comparatively quiet.   It was in the Rift
Valley that trouble first emerged.   Indeed, this analysis of the growing
economic and political rivalry between the settler powers that be, and
African traders and cultivators, who relied upon the Kenya African Union
to force open the rewards of the colonial state, applied not only in the
Reserves, but even more in the White Highlands, where settler and African
accumulators stood face to face.[35]

The Resident Native Labour Ordinance of 1937, which became operative in 1940, was one of the concessions made by the Administration to the
settlers because of the wartime manpower shortage.   After debating the
issue for three years the Colonial Office had finally agreed to the transfer of
control over the squatter community to the settler District Councils.[36]
The Councils, however, did not really begin to use their power until near
the end of the war.   Until European farmers who had been away in the
armed forces returned home, and the wartime high crop prices had
increased their capital resources, the settler community was not in a
position to utilize any extra land which could be gained by reducing
squatter cultivation and stock rights.   All that changed in 1945.
Immediately the District Councils passed measures reducing squatter
cultivation to one or two acres per family and restricting the size of squatter
herds to ten sheep or goats with no cattle.[37]   Squatter cattle were
unpopular amongst the settlers as one of the strategies adopted by the now
more heavily capitalized European farmers was to diversify from maize
monoculture, which had been their unprofitable lot for most of the inter-
war period, into mixed farming with small dairy herds.   If the veterinary

34.   C. G. Rosberg and J. Nottingham, *The Myth of Mau Mau*, (F. A. Praeger, New York,
1966) pp. 192–195; and O. J. E. Shiroya's unpublished paper 'Kenya Askari in World War II:
their Impact on Political Development in Kenya', pp. 5–14.
35.   See especially KNA Lab 9, files 304 to 340 for detailed information on the formulation
and implementation of squatter policies in the various settler controlled District Councils, and
T. M. J. Kanogo, 'The History of Kikuyu Movement into the Rift Valley, 1900–63; the case
study of Nakuru District' (Nairobi, unpublished Ph.D. thesis, 1979).
36.   KNA Lab 9/594 'Resident Native Labour Ordinance: Operation and Application of
Ordinance 1940–48', memo to Executive Council, 30 July 1940.
37.   See KNA Lab 9/319, 23 March 1945, for details of the Aberdares' new squatter rules;
Lab 9/598 PC, Rift Valley to Chief Native Commissioner 2 March 1945 on the Trans Nzoia
Order; Lab 9/304, Wyn Harris to Chief Secretary 12 April, 1945 for the Labour Commissioner's general reaction to the new orders; and *ibid.* 21 June 1945, for details of the Naivasha
District Council's Resident Labour Ordinance.

THE ORIGINS OF MAU MAU   413

KENYA

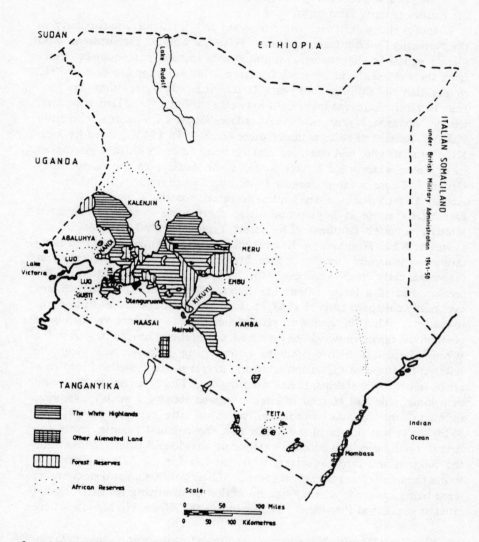

frontier between the reserves and the White Highlands was to mean anything, and since the late 1920s control over bovine pleuropneumonia and
rinderpest had been secured by inoculation on the European side of the
boundary, then it was imperative that disease-infested squatter stock
should be removed as a source of infection for European-owned herds. It
is interesting to note that in the one area where sheep farming was the

mainstay of the settler economy, Molo, it was not squatter stock that were forbidden but, instead, sheep and goats, which they were allowed to keep in the European dairy farming areas.[38]

Within a short period squatter incomes fell drastically, particularly in the Naivasha District Council Area. Here the Labour Department, who looked aghast at the process, estimated that income per squatter family from their *shambas* and livestock fell from 1,400 shillings per year in 1942 to less than 300 shillings four years' later, while wages per thirty-day contract had only increased from eight to twelve shillings.[39] Many squatters, who in Naivasha, Nakuru and the Aberdares District Councils were mainly Kikuyu, refused to reattest under these terms. In 1946, guided by local KCA officials who had operated underground since 1940, they attempted to organize widespread strikes to force the settlers to reconsider their Orders. These began in August 1946, timed to coincide with the visit of Arthur Creech Jones, then Under-Secretary for the Colonies, to Lord Delamere's estate at Soysambu, where there were over three hundred Kikuyu squatter families. The strike rapidly spread throughout the southern White Highlands of Kenya, culminating in a meeting of representatives of squatters from over four hundred farms and Olenguruone at Naivasha early in November 1946. Although the strike alarmed the settlers and to a lesser extent the Labour Department, the movement eventually collapsed early in 1947, because the squatters had no option but to reattest. Many of them were second generation squatters who had been born on the farms on which they worked, their fathers having moved to the White Highlands before 1920 as enterprising Kikuyu, following the Kikuyu tradition of expansion from the overcrowded heartland into new areas, in order to establish their own *githaka*. The first twenty-five years of colonial rule had seemed to offer increased scope for such movement, following the Maasai withdrawal south of the railway in 1911 to 1913.[40] It was not until the 1920s that the colonial regime 'froze' the 'tribal' boundaries and adopted a policy of 'divide and rule'. Meanwhile the Kikuyu and other squatters who had left for the White Highlands found themselves increasingly trapped. Their cultivation and stock rights were being reduced, yet they had no option of returning to their original *githaka* in Central Province. By moving to the White Highlands, where

---

38. KNA Lab 9 331 details the problems of the Nyanza District Council's attempts to control squatters. In Nyanza the conflicting interests of cattle and cereal farmers, also the plantation interests, resulted in a plethora of local options. See especially 'Resume of the Present Resident Labour Position in the Nyanza Province', 30 September, 1948. For more details of Molo and other local options see Lab 9/304 'Resident Labourers General Correspondence'.
39. CO 533 549/38232/15: Wyn Harris's 'A discussion of the problem of the squatter: economic survey of resident labour in Kenya' of 24 February 1947.
40. See V. Harlow and E. M. Chilver (eds.) *History of East Africa*, vol. 2, (Oxford University Press, 1965) pp. 284–5 and R. L. Tignor, *The Colonial Transformation of Kenya: Kamba, Kikuyu and Maasai from 1900 to 1939*, (Princeton, 1976), *passim*.

THE ORIGINS OF MAU MAU   415

they had been comparatively prosperous until the mid-1920s, they had virtually renounced any claim they had in Central Province, where, because of ever-growing population, the pressure on the land was becoming acute.[41]   The squatters in 1946, therefore, had no choice but to stay put, unless they were to become landless urban workers, a prospect which few would voluntarily choose since it would cut them off from the traditional African way of life and provide no security for old age.   The towns also suffered from the added disadvantages of low wages and high prices.

The choice, however, did not always lie in their hands.   Increasingly, the District Councils limited the number of squatters per farm and many farmers were only too willing to turn them off, now that they had sufficient capital to farm more intensively themselves.   A gradual stream of squatters began to flow back to Central Province and into the townships of the Rift Valley.   Militancy increased and violence grew.   Cattle maiming had been part of the 1946 struggle but after their initial defeat this declined: but following the eviction of 4,000 Kikuyu from the Olenguruone Settlement in 1949 and 1950, however, it became widespread once more throughout the Rift Valley.   As a concomitant to this squatter, largely Kikuyu, resistance, oathing grew to ensure solidarity against the enemy.[42]   By 1952 most of the Kikuyu in the White Highlands had taken the Mau Mau oath of unity.

Olenguruone

Olenguruone played a crucial role in encouraging the spread of militancy in the Rift, especially in the Njoro-Molo area, which became an alternative focus of discontent to the Naivasha-Soysambu region.[43]   It was at Olenguruone in 1944 that a new oath was introduced to ensure Kikuyu unity, which was applied not only to men, like the traditional oath, but to the women and children as well.   This oath of unity, a development from the KCA oath, was the foundation of the early Mau Mau oaths.   The long drawn-out struggle at Olenguruone between 1941 and 1950 provided inspiration for the Kikuyu communities, both in the Rift and in Central Provinces.   Close ties already existed between Samuel Koina Gitebi, the Olenguruone leader, and the squatters at Soysambu where he had organized a KISA school in the mid-1930s.   Gitebi also had contacts with the KCA leaders in Limuru, an area which had been the original home for

41. This process is discussed in S. Stichter, *Migrant Labour in Kenya: Capitalism and African Response 1895–1975*, (Longman, 1982) pp. 98–109 and G. Kitching *Class and economic change*, pp. 282–297.
42. T. M. J. Kanogo, 'Rift Valley Squatters and Mau Mau', pp. 243–252; *Kenya Historical Review*, 5, 2 (1977) and F. Furedi 'Olenguruone in Mau Mau Historiography' (unpublished paper, Institute of Commonwealth Studies, London, March 1974).
43. *ibid.* and KNA Lab 9/317 'Resident Labour, Nakuru, 1945–53', Hyde-Clarke to Dempster, 26 June 1946, and Labour Commissioner to Chief Secretary August, 1946; and CO 533/549/38232. 15 for squatter petition to Mitchell, 19 October, 1946.

416   AFRICAN AFFAIRS

many of the people at Olenguruone. He himself had joined the Limuru branch of KCA in 1928, and both Soysambu and Limuru acted as staging-posts for the Olenguruone messengers on their way to Nairobi or Gatundu to see KAU leaders and Kenyatta.[44]

The Kenya government and the Colonial Office were both well aware that Olenguruone was crucial to the future of their policy, but they badly misread the situation. In particular Andrew Cohen in the Colonial Office took a very hard line.[45] If the Kikuyu were allowed to disregard the cultivation rules imposed by the government, then not only would the Olenguruone settlement scheme fail but, as the prototype for the much larger settlements planned after the war, in particular at Makueni, the failure of the government to enforce its will on the Olenguruone mal-contents would endanger the viability of all the other planned areas.[46] Olenguruone, Whitehall and Nairobi agreed, had to be made to work, or, if this was impossible, which by late 1946 it already seemed to be, then Draconian measures would have to be taken and an example made of the trouble causers. This, however, badly backfired. By throwing out the Olenguruone Kikuyu, who claimed to have been given *githaka* land rights in 1941, the word of the government appeared to be untrustworthy. By finally expelling them in 1949 and 1950 with nowhere to go, the govern-ment spread the seeds of militancy throughout the fertile soils of Central Province and the White Highlands.[47] Martyrs were created. These Kikuyu did not passively acquiesce in their fate. The various Mau Mau *Nyimbo* dealing with Olenguruone testify to the effect their opposition had amongst the discontented elements of Kikuyu society.[48]

The expulsions from Olenguruone coincided with the further tightening of the controls on resident labourers. The post-war era, in the eyes of most squatters, showed all too clearly the dominant position of the settlers in Kenya. Compared to the settler politicians KAU was evidently incapable of protecting the interests of its people. The constitutionalists had failed; the militants, the men of violence, could fare no worse.

The Growth of Militancy in Nairobi

This increasing disillusionment with constitutional progress and KAU

44. KNA Lab 9/601 no 78c and C. Rosberg and J. Nottingham, *The Myth of Mau Mau,* pp. 254–5 and Lab 3/41. See also DC/NKU 1/5 Annual Report 1946 for Nakuru–Naivasha–Ravine District pp. 2–3 and p. 6.
45. CO 533/557/38678/1 Cohen minute 14 July 1947.
46. *ibid.* J. Robertson 11 July, 1947. KNA Lab 3/41 D. L. Morgan to Chief Secretary 20 December 1946 and DC/NKU/4/1, memorandum on Olenguruone Settlement by D. O'Hagan to Executive Council and Chief Native Commissioner, 2 March 1950.
47. When the van carrying some of the convicted Olenguruone squatters broke down at Karatina, it was immediately surrounded by inquisitive crowds. After this incident the route to Yatta was changed to avoid Kikuyu areas. DC/NKU/6/2 21 January 1950.
48. *Thunder from the mountain; Mau Mau patriotic songs,* ed. Maina wa Kinyatti (Zed Press, 1980), especially pp. 53–56.

THE ORIGINS OF MAU MAU   417

was also becoming evident in Nairobi and Central Province. Nairobi Africans lived in appalling conditions in the African areas of Pumwani, Kariakor and Shauri Moyo. In 1947 the Nairobi Municipal African Affairs Officer acknowledged that over 16,000 Africans in the city had nowhere to live and were sleeping on verandahs and in buses. Wartime inflation was also particularly severe in Nairobi, which by 1948 had overtaken Mombasa as the area with the highest African cost of living in Kenya; and it was in the capital that Africans most frequently encountered the glaring social and economic gap between their own poverty-stricken position, which in many respects appeared to be deteriorating, and the Europeans' prosperity.[49]

The capital naturally provided the most sophisticated analysis of African politics, militant as well as constitutionalist. Francis Khamisi, Jimmy Jeremiah, Tom Mbotela were the most prominent members of the Nairobi Advisory Council and the Municipal Council, but their hold over the mass of the population was slight. Amongst poor Africans, earning fifty shillings a month or less, these prosperous government servants, clerks and traders were increasingly seen as belonging to a different world with different interests.[50]

The Government's policies also failed in Nairobi. At the end of the war under pressure from the constitutionalist leaders of the Nairobi branch of the Kenya African Union—Khamisi and Awori—the Administration had attempted to increase African participation in local affairs. This 'local government', of course, was purely advisory since the real power remained with the settler controlled Nairobi Municipal Council. But by turning to the African elite, the Administration weakened its ties with the 'old fashioned' tribal associations, through which it had controlled the African locations in the past. Misled by their own mythology of 'de-tribalized' urban Africans, the Administration came to view Nairobi Africans as being fundamentally different from those in the Reserves. Ironically the African elite also failed to recognize that the only way to preserve control over locations like Pumwani and Shauri Moyo, was through a modified system of Indirect Rule, based on the tribal associations.[51]

49. For the standard account of the Kenya economy after 1945 see M. McWilliam, 'The managed economy: agricultural change, development and finance in Kenya', D. A. Low and A. Smith (eds) *History of East Africa* vol. 3, (Oxford University Press, 1977) pp. 251–289. For conditions in Mombasa see KNA Lab 9/1817, 1835 and 1836, and for meetings of the Nairobi African Advisory Council see MAA 2/5/223 and MAA 8/22 'City African Affairs Officer: Correspondence 1947–50'. See also MAA 8/102 and *Hindi ya Muafrika* 6 May 1948; MAA 8/106 and *Mumenyereri* 12 April, 1948 and MAA 7/491 on 'Administrative Policy; Urban Areas Nairobi, 1945–7'.
50. John Spencer, 'The Kenya African Union 1944–53: A Party in Search of a Constituency' (unpublished Columbia University Ph.D.), pp. 178–80, 216–17 and 225–30; and D. Mukaru-Ng'ang'a (unpublished Nairobi MA, 1978), 'A Political History of Murang'a District, 1900–1970: A study of society and politics', pp. 67–70.
51. KNA MAA 7/491 'Administrative Policy: Urban Areas Nairobi, 1945–57', T. G. Askwith to C. Tomkinson, 22 August 1945 and 14 September 1945.

418   AFRICAN AFFAIRS

New arrivals to the city did not transcend their 'political' past, but sought out friends and relations to guide them in the alien environment. Men from neighbouring locations and districts, who spoke the same language, clung together in the new hostile world. Tribal solidarities were of crucial importance in Nairobi. Those already in employment housed and fed their associates, helped them find jobs and establish themselves. Thus the city's refuse disposal gangs were dominated by Meru tribesmen, while the Kiambu Kikuyu provided a high proportion of street hawkers and kiosk owners. When a Nairobi African became unemployed, fell ill or died, he was looked after by friends from his location or district. Whatever the Administration or the African elite believed, for most Africans, the ties of kinship and locality were as important in the alien world of Nairobi as they were in the Reserves.[52]

Tom Askwith, the Nairobi African Affairs' Officer, therefore, had been correct to conclude that a modified network of chiefs and village headmen offered the only real way to preserve control over African Nairobi. Yet despite its suspicion of 'detribalised' Africans the government overruled Askwith and introduced a more democratic system. Although twelve members were originally nominated, and after 1946, elected by the tribal associations, these formed only forty per cent of the Advisory Council. One-third of the members were chosen from specific interest groups, transcending tribal divisions, such as traders' or craftsmen's groups or from minorities, such as the Moslems or women, who formed only thirteen per cent of Nairobi's African population. Another eight members, over one-quarter of the council, were elected by the various African estates or locations, in a fully democratic ward system. Gradually the government planned to increase their members at the expense of the tribal associations' representatives.[53]

This system had been forced on a reluctant Askwith by the liberals in the Secretariat and the Kenya African Union elite, led by Khamisi, Mbotela and Awori.[54] By 1947 it had resulted in a serious weakening of the Field Administration's knowledge of African opinion in the locations. Instead

52. *ibid.* F. Khamisi to Municipal African Affairs Officer, 10 September 1945, for the view of the African elite. See also F. Furedi, 'The African Crowd in Nairobi', pp. 275–289 for one study of political activity in Nairobi during the Mitchell era. T. Hodgkin, *Nationalism in Colonial Africa*, (F. Muller 1956), pp. 63–93, remains the most illuminating brief account of the linkages between urban life and politics. See also D. Parkin, *The Cultural Definition of Political Response: Lineal Destiny among the Luo*, (Academic Press, 1978) pp. 36–44 for an account of tribal divisions in independent Nairobi.
53. KNA MAA 7/491 'Administration Policy: Urban Areas Nairobi, 1945–47', T. G. Askwith's memorandum, 14 September 1945; and MAA 2/5/223 'Nairobi Advisory Council, 1946–49' T. G. Askwith's memorandum on African Advisory Council, 1 September, 1948.
54. *ibid.* MAA 7/491, F. Khamisi to Askwith 10th September, 1945; Notes on Meeting in Secretariat 28 November 1945; and K. G. Lindsey to Chief Native Commissioner 8 December 1945. See also KNA MAA 8/22 'City African Affairs Officer: Correspondence, 1947–50', T. G. Askwith to the Mayor, 1 September, 1948, enclosing report on the Nairobi African Advisory Council.

of directly receiving complaints, their perception of African life was distorted by the prism of the elite-dominated Advisory Council. With only one policeman to every thousand inhabitants and no patronage network under the control of government nominees, the Administration's authority in the locations was minimal.[55] The situation was particularly bad in Shauri Moyo, Kariakor and Pumwani, the three most overcrowded and badly constructed slums, where well over half Nairobi's Africans lived. In these areas the African Workers' Federation and their *Offisi ya Masikini*—the Office of the Poor—exerted considerable influence, while the 'street corner boys' of the Forty Group and the other semi-criminal gangs, made up of the city's unemployed, ensured that during the long hours of darkness Nairobi's African locations were a 'no go' area for the police.[56]

The arrest of Chege Kibachia, the leader of the African Workers' Federation, in August, 1947, and the shooting by the police of the strikers at Uplands a fortnight later, brought Nairobi to the verge of a general strike.[57] Both Tom Mbotela, the constitutionalist Kenya African Union leader, then the Assistant Superintendent of African Locations, and the Municipal African Affairs Officer, warned the Secretariat in October 1947, that the government had virtually lost control over African Nairobi, which was firmly under the domination of Kikuyu street gangs.[58] Despite the Administration's strenuous efforts in 1948 and 1949 to reassert control, under pressure from the settler controlled Municipal Council, this situation continued.[59] Although municipal bye-law 212 enabled the police to arrest and deport to the Reserves hundreds of unemployed vagrants, they soon drifted back, and the city's crime rate continued to rise.[60]

The Forty Group and various small district groupings of Kikuyu youths articulated this disenchantment with the constitutionalists. By October 1947 Mwangi Macharia from Murang'a, an activist in the Forty Group,

55. KNA MAA 8/22 'City African Affairs Officer: Correspondence, 1947–50', especially T. G. Askwith to Superintendent of C.I.D. Nairobi, 29 October 1947; and MAA 7/491 'Administration Policy: Urban Areas Nairobi, 1945–47', Notes on Meeting in Secretariat 28 November 1945.
56. KNA 8/22 'City African Affairs Officer: Correspondence 1947–50', Superintendent African Locations to Superintendent C.I.D. Nairobi 28 October 1947, and T. G. Askwith to Superintendent C.I.D. Nairobi, 29 October 1947.
57. KNA Secretariat 1/12/10 'Labour Unrest: Kenya Colony Emergency Scheme', plans dated 28 March 1947; Secretariat 1/12/8 'Labour Unrest: Intelligence Reports Central Province, 1947', especially reports by Director of Intelligence, 25 September, 1947, and 10 October 1947.
58. KNA MAA 8/22 'Municipal African Affairs Officer: Correspondence, 1947–50', Superintendent African Locations to Superintendent C.I.D. Nairobi, 28 October 1947, and T. G. Askwith to Superintendent C.I.D. Nairobi, 29 October 1947.
59. KNA MAA 7/377 'Legislation: Urban Pass Laws, 1946'; and MAA 8/22 'Municipal African Affairs Officer: Correspondence, 1947–50', meeting on by-laws 211 and 212, 12 October 1948 and 11 November 1949.
60. KNA MAA 8/22 'Municipal African Affairs Officer: Correspondence, 1947–50', G. R. B. Brown to the Mayor 23 May 1950 for his 'Observations on the Nairobi Strike'.

was already declaring at meetings of the Nairobi branch of the African Workers Federation that men like Kenyatta and Mathu, who had been educated in Europe, should not be trusted by workers.[61]   Their interests were entirely different and they would not hesitate 'to sell the workers down the river'.   What was needed, he asserted, were real workers' leaders, men who sprang from the same class and who would really serve them.   This was part of Macharia's campaign to ensure that W. W. W. Awori was not appointed president of the African Workers Federation in succession to the detained Chege Kibachia, but it reflected the growing disillusionment of the African masses with the failures of KAU and the constitutionalist path.

The dissatisfaction received an ideological backbone with the return from India of Makhan Singh.   Singh attempted to instil Marxist class politics into the growing Kenya trade union movement.   The moderate leaders of the East African Indian National Congress, such as Patel and Rana, were mocked, as were their African associates Mathu, Khamisi and Mbotela.[62]   It was from Singh that Kaggia, Kungu Karumba, Macharia, Fred Kubai and Paul Ngei took their lead, mobilizing the trade union movement to seize control over the Nairobi branch of KAU, from where they undermined the position of the constitutionalists.   As early as 1950 their triumph in Nairobi was complete and Kenyatta's leadership was coming under attack.[63]

The militants' control over the capital's slums was demonstrated during the General Strike of May 1950.[64]   Large mobs had attacked the police sent to arrest the strike leaders and armoured cars had to be used to suppress resistance.   Under the direction of Fred Kubai and Bildad Kaggia, who were both members of the Mau Mau Central Committee, the *Muhimu*, as well as trades union leaders, Nairobi became a centre of oathing and Mau Mau activity.[65]   It was from the capital that the campaign in Kikuyuland and the Rift Valley was controlled.   The radicals with their supporters in the trades union also captured control over the moribund Nairobi branch of the Kenya African Union in June 1951, which they used to launch an attack upon the remaining moderates in the leadership at the National Congress in November that year.[66]   The capital, therefore, provided the militants with a secure power base among the urban poor from which to

61.   James Ombwayo and subsequent speeches at the Nairobi branch meeting of the African Workers' Federation, reported by Special Branch to Director of Intelligence, MAA 8/109, 16 December, 1947, for attacks on Kenyatta and Mathu.
62.   M. Singh, *A History of Kenya's Trade Union Movement to 1952*, (East African Publishing House, Nairobi, 1969), pp. 260–2.
63.   *ibid.*   chapter 18; J. Spencer, chapter vi; and B. Kaggia, *Roots of Freedom* (East African Publishing House, Nairobi, 1973) pp. 79–83, 94–8 and 107–115.
64.   KNA Lab 9/87, 'Labour Troubles Nairobi, 1950', for a detailed account.
65.   B. Kaggia, *The Roots of Freedom*, pp. 108–114.
66.   *ibid.*   pp. 79–82; and J. Spencer's unpublished Columbia University Ph.D. thesis, 'The Kenya African Union, 1944–53', pp. 261–271.

THE ORIGINS OF MAU MAU   421

harry the advocates of constitutional politics.   They used Nairobi's central position in the colony's transport network to establish firm linkages between the urban militants and the leaders of radical opposition to the chiefs and the Administration throughout Kikuyuland.[67]

This spate of militant activity, however, alienated the non-Kikuyu elements in the Nairobi African population, as well as the Kikuyu moderates.   Often exploited by Kikuyu landlords, who owned most of the accommodation in the African locations, and subject to the tyranny of the Kikuyu street gangs, the Abaluhya, Luo and migrant workers from the coast became disillusioned with the actions of the Kikuyu militants.   By 1952 the Kikuyu had made themselves almost as unpopular as the Administration with the non-Kikuyu elements in the population, so that when the fight to the death between the Kikuyu and the settlers began in October 1952, they remained neutral observers, waiting on the sidelines to see who would win before they decided to join the contest.   This was one of the reasons that Mau Mau failed to become a truly nationalist movement.

Politics in Central Province and the Growth of Opposition to Terracing

Central Province itself remained moderate.   Although James Beauttah, one of the few of the KCA old guard to support the younger generation of militants, was the provincial vice-president of KAU, outside Murang'a he had little influence.   Central Province KAU was much more under the control of Kenyatta, Mathu and Gichuru than it ever was of Beauttah.[68] But by early 1950 their grip over the local organizations was beginning to slip.   This decline stemmed partly from Kenyatta's failure as a leader.   He had proved himself incapable of delivering the goods to those Kikuyu who wanted to be incorporated into the colonial political and economic order.   Asian traders still controlled the economy, whilst the Second Colonial Occupation subjected all Africans to increased governmental control and the Local Native Councils and chiefs seemed to be mere puppets of the Europeans.   This discontent stemmed from various tensions inside the province, often of a parochial nature.   While it is possible in the Rift Valley and Nairobi to perceive one major cause for increased militancy, the political structure of Central Provence was far more complex.   Although the underlying problem was the impact of the 'Second Colonial Occupation'[69] and enforced 'modernization' on Kikuyu

67.   *ibid.*
68.   See John Spencer, 'James Beauttah: Kenya patriot' (unpublished staff seminar paper, History Department, University of Nairobi) for details of Beauttah's career; and KNA DC/FH 1/24, pp. 4–5; and DC/FH 1/26 pp. 2–4; and DC/FH 1/30, pp. 1–2 for the District Commissioner's comments on his political activities.
69.   By 1952 Agricultural Department staff in Central Province numbered 44 Europeans and 3,506 Africans.   See KNA Ag 4/310, L. H. Brown, Provincial Agricultural Officer.   For an insight into how the second colonial occupation affected African peasants see Ag 4/451 'Fort Hall Safari Diaries, 1948–51'.

traditional society, this took several forms, varying not only from district to district but from location to location. Part of this diversity was a reflection of the continuation of 'the white man's madness': that traditional African explanation for the constantly changing emphases of development dependent upon the whims of the District Commissioners. But, although Africans in Murang'a therefore were primarily concerned with soil conservation and terracing, whilst in Nyeri the issue was more that of cattle dipping, the sheer scale and comprehensive nature of the post-war modernization schemes ensured that it was less simple than that, and that at key moments dipping became an issue in Murang'a and opposition to terracing mounted in Nyeri.[70] Throughout all this Kiambu maintained an ambivalent attitude, preserving modest progress rather than undulating from 'triumphant advance' to the depths of complete crisis.[71]

The essential ingredient in these variations was not the role of the District Commissioner and his district team but that of the chief. Chief Ignatio of location eight in Murang'a provides an outstanding example.[72] From 1945 to mid-1947, when Desmond O'Hagan was the District Commissioner, Murang'a was in the government's opinion the most outstanding district in Kenya, and in Murang'a the great success story was Ignatio's location. Vast acreages were terraced under the traditional *ngwatio* system of communal labour, controlled by over two hundred African agricultural instructors and assistant instructors. But the very intensity of the soil conservation campaign undermined the stability of Ignatio's control over his people.[73] The peasants who actually did the physical labour soon perceived a tremendous weakness in the Agricultural Department's reliance, obsession is perhaps the more appropriate word, on terracing slopes. The issue first came to the fore as a topic for discontent in Murang'a not only because of the intensity of its campaign but also because of the geographical nature of the district, where over ninety per cent of the land was on slopes of over fourteen per cent. The problem was that the Agricultural Department relied on short-based interval terracing. This was adopted because the initial construction of the terraces required far less labour than the building of the more sophisticated broad-based interval terraces. But in Murang'a short-based interval terracing proved largely

70. KNA Ag 4/512 'Provincial Agricultural Officer, 'Fort Hall's monthly reports 1940–49; Ag 4/451 'Safari Diaries, Fort Hall, 1948–51; Ag 4/392 'District Annual Agricultural Reports 1948'; and Ag 4/107 'Annual Reports Veterinary Department, 1942–53'; and Ag 4/113, 'South Nyeri Monthly Agricultural Reports, 1938–49'.
71. KNA DC/KBU 1/36 'Kiambu Annual Report 1945'; pp. 4 and 15; and Ag 4/410.
72. KNA DC/FH 1/26, pp. 1–6; and MAA 8/108 and 'Daily Chronicle' 16 October 1947. See also CO 537/3588/38696, minute by Wyn Harris, January, 1948.
73. Ignatio's location 8 until July, 1947, headed the Murang'a soil conservation league. See KNA DC/FH 4/6 'Chiefs and Headmen, 1937–54'; and Ag 4/451 'Murang'a Safari Diaries, 1948–51', especially entries 2–6 March 1948, and 6–10 July 1948, which should be compared, as by July Ignatio was beginning to reassert control.

THE ORIGINS OF MAU MAU 423

ineffective. By 1947 the peasants had perceived that they had become enmeshed in a vicious circle. Each rainy season a large proportion of the newly-dug terraces were destroyed, and by 1947 more labour was being required to preserve the terraces already built than was being used to construct new terraces. Although half the district was now terraced, even when the whole area had been protected, the demands on African labour two mornings a week would hardly diminish. Their task appeared never-ending.[74]

In the Taita Hills, where the slopes were even steeper than in Murang'a the Agricultural Department and the Administration had perceived from the onset of the campaign that the demands posed on the peasantry to maintain short-based interval terracing would be excessive and they had pressed instead for the construction of broad-based terraces. Although these initially required far more labour, and therefore progress in protecting large acreages was considerably slower, they were able to withstand the run-off following heavy downpours and survived the rainy seasons intact. Labour intensive though they were in the short run, over the longer term they were more effective and did not require the same continual exactions from the African community.[75]

Most Murang'a Africans did not perceive in 1947 the advantages of broad-based terracing, although a few who had worked in the White Highlands and had witnessed the mechanical terracing on European farms by the soil conservation unit favoured this technique.[76] Most, however, became completely disillusioned with the colonial government's campaign. There seemed to be no point whatsoever to all their hard labour. Their dissatisfaction with the government varied directly with the commitment of their chief to the campaign. It was therefore in location eight that tension mounted. By his all-out exertions in favour of terracing, Ignatio largely destroyed his bonds with his own people. Instead of acting as their intermediary with the Administration, he appeared simply to be the enforcer of European wishes and therefore became discredited in their eyes. It was into this scene of potential conflict that Kenyatta stumbled in July 1947.

74. KNA MAA 8/105, especially editorial from *Radio Posta* on 10 and 16 October 1947; and MAA 8/106, letter complaining that chiefs' wives did not have to terrace the land, in *Mumenyereri*, 29 September 1947. See also report of meeting in location 13, Murang'a, which praised Chief Parmenas for caring about the well-being of his people, unlike other chiefs in the same issue.
75. This was pointed out by Benjamin Mang'uru, the secretary of the Githunguri branch of Kenya African Union in *Mumenyereri*, 3 November 1947. See KNA DO Taveta 1/102 Agr 11/1 for K. M. Cowley's memorandum on agricultural productivity in the Taita District, November 1948. Cowley emphasized that 'nothing short of a complete revolution is required'. In Taita the Agricultural Department reached the conclusion that broad-based terracing and the incentive of high priced cash crops were essential to gain African cooperation at least two or three years before their colleagues in Kikuyuland.
76. KNA MAA 8/106, B. Mang'uru's letter in *Mumenyereri*, 3 November 1947.

O'Hagan, the previous District Commissioner, had refused by administrative fiat, to allow Kenyatta to enter Murang'a. Any such visit, he believed, would merely stir up trouble; a quantity of which the local Kenya African Union leaders, James Beauttah and Andrew Ng'ang'a, were quite capable of generating on their own without any outside assistance. Walter Coutts, the new District Commissioner, however, had a more liberal conception of the role of British rule.[77] Whereas O'Hagan was a safety first man, who believed in crushing any incipient opposition with a hard hand as soon as it raised its head and in unwavering support of the chiefs, Coutts wanted to co-opt the economically ambitious supporters of the Kenya African Union, and to replace the chiefs gradually with elected Local Native Councils of progressive Africans. He was in fact a convinced disciple of the new doctrine of controlled political education through local government. He therefore decided to remove the ban on Kenyatta, who thereupon seized the chance to address a mass meeting in Murang'a township, with disastrous consequences for all concerned.

The meeting, on Sunday 21 July 1947, exemplified the problems Kenyatta had to deal with, and the reports of the meeting provide a fascinating study of how his words were interpreted by the Administration and the militants to suit their own presuppositions.[78] One aspect of the terracing campaign was already giving rise to discontent and therefore government concern. This was the use of women to dig terraces. Discussions had already been held in the Secretariat to consider whether female labour should be banned, and a circular letter to all District Commissioners was being drafted. The overwhelming problem, however, was that over seventy per cent of terracing was actually done by Kikuyu women. To exempt them from *ngwatio* service would therefore destroy the foundation of the soil conservation campaign. The circular letter had not therefore been issued, pending further discussions between the Secretariat and the Field Administration, although Britain's commitment to International Labour Regulations, in the opinion of the Secretariat, was an irrefutable argument which would soon require compulsory female labour to be ended.[79]

Kenyatta began by enthusiastically praising the terracing campaign and the progress which had been made in Murang'a. Such work was essential,

77. Contrast KNA DC/FH 1/25 and DC.FH 1/26 with DC.FH 1/27 for the effects of Kenyatta's visit. This idea was suggested to me by Mr O'Hagan in the course of three interviews in Nairobi in April and June 1981.
78. For the Administration's view see KNA DC/FH 1/26 and F. D. Corfield, *The Origins and Growth of Mau Mau: An Historical Survey*, Sessional Paper no 5, of 1959–60 (Government Printer, Nairobi, 1960), p. 67. The militants' view of the meeting is to be found in *Baraza*, 26 July 1947. See also J. Spencer's unpublished Columbia Ph.D. thesis, pp. 210–211.
79. CO 852/19936/2.

he declared, if the fertility of Kikuyuland was to be preserved.[80] This initial statement in praise of soil conservation was subsequently ignored by the Administration, although the militants were to use it to attack Kenyatta.[81] The real problem sprang from what Kenyatta said next, which was to urge that women should not be forced to undertake terracing —the very issue which was preoccupying the Secretariat! The next day soil terracing in Murang'a, until then the outstanding success of post-war development, around which important visitors to the colony, such as Creech Jones, were always taken, ground to a halt. Within twenty-four hours Murang'a passed from being the centre of success to the major problem area of the Administration. Terracing figures fell overnight to less than one-tenth of their previous levels. Kenyatta, of course, got all the blame, and Coutts for one never forgave him.

The Kikuyu militants, however, interpreted the speech in a completely different manner, emphasizing Kenyatta's praise for terracing and ignoring his attack on female labour.[82] For them, Kenyatta was simply too moderate, a supporter of government policy just like the chiefs, whereas they wished to seize the issue to stir up real trouble and encourage direct attacks on the chiefs. This they soon succeeded in doing. Ignatio went in fear of his life, and several attempts were made to kill him. He lost all control over his district, remaining isolated for the next few months in his *boma*, fearing to venture out amongst his people. Although he subsequently reasserted control and outwardly location eight became a centre of 'progress' once more, his hold was never as secure again, and with the outbreak of Mau Mau the location become one of their strongholds in Murang'a.

Ignatio was too much of a government man, with too tight a grip over his people, to be able to act as a neutral intermediary between them and the government, a function which the chief was increasingly required to perform after 1945. The trouble was not simply that he was a government stooge, a 'collaborator', but, even worse, that he firmly believed in what he was doing, an apostle of modernization who set about improving his own smallholding, applying manure, enclosing his land, dipping his cattle, and building terraces. It was in such areas, where the Second Colonial Occupation was most strongly felt, that Mau Mau won its main support as well as its fiercest enemies.[83]

80. Kenyatta in *Baraza*, 26 July 1947.
81. MAA 8/109, 'Intelligence and Security: African Workers' Federation, 1947–8', especially report of 16 December, 1947, and a speech by the representative of the Stain Polishers' Association. See also *Baraza*, 26 February 1948, for signs of the growing African disillusionment with Kenyatta and his failure to attend meetings.
82. *ibid.* and see *Radio Posta*, 16 October 1947.
83. Mau Mau in Nyeri, for example, was strongest in North and South Tetu and Othaya, where superficially the Government's terracing and veterinary policies had been most successful. Ironically even Dedan Kimathi, the Mau Mau leader, had once worked for the Tetu Dairyman's Cooperative, which, epitomized the Government's post-1948 betterment strategy, until he absconded with the funds.

In these areas Mau Mau was indeed a Kikuyu civil war—a civil war based to a considerable extent on social class and differing perceptions of colonial rule. Effective chiefs, because of their commitment to the modernization campaign and their position in the colonial order, were necessarily on one side, supported by the Elders and the staunch Christians; whereas those knocking on the doors of the colonial state, often mission educated clerks and ex-*askaris*, along with the poor, incapable of supporting their families on minute, fragmented *shambas*, went into opposition—although they themselves were divided into constitutionalists and militants, largely along social lines. This division after 1952 merged into that between the passive wing and the forest fighters.[84]

The conflict was reduced in certain locations by the ambivalent behaviour of the chiefs. In Murang'a, the outstanding example of a chief who united his people behind him rather than dividing them against him was Parmenas Githendu of location thirteen.[85] Parmenas had been a prominent figure at Church Missionary Society Kahuhia in the 1920s, a hotbed of the early KCA, and in 1931 he had been selected as the Murang'a man to accompany Kenyatta, the outsider from Kiambu who was not entirely trusted by the KCA heartland of Murang'a, to give evidence to the Joint Select Committee in London. Befriended by Margery Perham, like Kenyatta, he was far more sophisticated and educated than most chiefs. Unlike Ignatio, for example, he spoke English and had contributed a brief autobiography to Perham's book, *Ten Africans*. As a chief, he preserved close relations with the KCA and the independent schools movement in his location. But by 1947, the local administration dismissed him as a lazy drunkard who had failed abysmally to encourage soil conservation in his location, and who had encouraged the independent schools in their campaign against Capon and the Church Missionary Society.[86]

To the Administration Ignatio appeared as outstanding, whereas Parmenas was a complete failure, totally discredited, and in 1948 he was dismissed. But as events were to prove, when the crisis occurred Parmenas, by conciliating rather than alienating the constitutionalist wing

84. For another attack on Chief Ignatio see KNA MAA 8/105, *Radio Posta*, 31 October 1947; and 22 November 1947, for allegations against Chief Muhindi of Nyeri. Other cases of chiefs under attack are MAA 8/132, Chief Native Commissioner to Attorney General, 25 November 1947, for Chief Makimei of Uplands; MAA 8/68 for Chief Waruhiu; and MAA 8/106, *Mumenyereri*, 9 October 1947, and 1 December 1947, for denunciations against several Murang'a chiefs. See also MAA 8/68, Wyn Harris to Mitchell, August 1948, for the Chief Native Commissioner's views on the campaign. For the Christian response see KNA (Murumbi Archive, Muthaiga) KEN/33/1, Rev Martin Capon, the Rural Dean of Mount Kenya, who supplied the Elector's Union with much of their information about Kenyatta's 'subversive activities'.
85. A brief autobiographical account of Parmenas is to be found in M. Perham ed. *Ten Africans* (Faber, 1936). For the Administration's view see DC/FH 4/6 'Chiefs and Headmen, 1937–54'; DC/FH 1/27 pp. 5 and 17; DC/FH 1/28, pp. 22–3; and DC/FH 1/29, pp. 18–9.
86. *ibid.*

of KAU and the local independent schools and churches, ensured that the militants made far less progress in location thirteen than in location eight where Ignatio's zealous commitment to administration policy provided fertile ground for opposition.

Political Passivity in Embu, Meru and Ukambani

The politics of Central Province needs to be analysed on such a locational level, since the role of the chief in interpreting and implementing policy was of crucial importance to the formation of dissent. Unlike Nairobi and the Rift Valley, where the broad outlines of African discontent, especially amongst the Kikuyu, can be discerned, Central Province provides a series of locational peculiarities where the response of the people differed according to their perceptions of the government's programme.

This differing perception perhaps provides an explanation for the lack of involvement of the Meru, Embu and Kamba peoples in Mau Mau. In the first two districts the colonial regime had experimented with African peasant coffee production since 1937. Although during the first decade little was actually achieved, it did provide the bedrock for economic diversification in the late 1940s and early 1950s. After 1946 the Agricultural Department in Meru and Embu encouraged African coffee production on a much wider scale.[87] Broad-based interval terraces were dug instead of the short-based terraces elsewhere in Central Province, as these were a prerequisite for being allowed to grow coffee—a high value cash crop. This not only entailed far less labour on preserving the terraces once they had been built but enabled a tangible reward to be secured for undertaking soil conservation work. By 1952 forty per cent of Meru households and twenty-five per cent in Embu were cultivating coffee or other cash crops, adding considerably to their income.[88] Coffee cultivation, however, was not introduced in Kikuyuland until much later. From 1950 onwards, broad-based terracing was introduced and quickly became more popular than short-based terracing as the peasantry soon perceived that in the long-term it involved far less labour, but the concomitant introduction of high value cash crop production as a reward for terracing by 1952 still lagged far behind the levels in Embu and Meru. In South Nyeri, for example, less than two per cent of households were cultivating

87. KNA Ag 4/9 'Coffee: African in Meru District'; Ag 4/410 'Embu and Meru District Agricultural Annual Reports'; and Ag 4/419 'Agricultural Development in Central Province and the maintenance of soil fertility: the growing of high priced cash crops, 1933–51', especially Director of Agriculture to Senior Agricultural Officer, Nyeri, 13 February 1948.
88. *ibid.* and KNA Ag 4/328 'Annual Reports Agriculture Central Province, 1951'. Chogoria, Meru and Chuka locations had some 2,600 households growing Arabica coffee by 1951, and 3,700 by 1952. By the end of 1952 there were some one million coffee trees in Embu District. See Ag 4/410, especially Embu Agricultural Annual Report, 1952, Appendix II; The annual report of the Coffee Officer, Embu, 1952.

coffee and in Murang'a the proportion was only half a per cent.[89] As a consequence the Kikuyu, unlike their neighbours, could see no reason for the white man's madness and his insistence on terracing, which often destroyed their most valuable crop, wattle, which provided the wealth of many political activists.[90]

The reasons for Kamba non-involvement were different again, and stemmed from the failure of the Administration to mobilize them into soil conservation and destocking after 1945. The real force of the post-war development policies was not felt in Machakos until after 1950, by which time their impact on the Kikuyu was already considerable. As a consequence discontent in Machakos did not begin to reach dangerous proportions until 1954, and in Kitui, where the modernization campaign never got off the ground, conditions remained tranquil. By 1954, however, Machakos was nearly boiling over and the Administration came very close to losing control, just as they had two years earlier amongst the Kikuyu.[91]

According to this interpretation, the Kikuyu cause was not the unusual atavistic response of one tribe to progress but a typical response in specific circumstances. The 'Second Colonial Occupation' was accepted in Meru and Embu, and rejected in Kikuyuland; as African peasants in the former, over quite a broad cross-section of society, could see clear financial gains from their labours. Unfortunately, the carrot did not play such a major role among the Kikuyu, and the only motivating force there was the stick. But, paradoxically, the impact of post-war development was strongest amongst them. The Kikuyu reaction to this forced modernization therefore took place before the programme had really been applied to Ukambani, and their defeat provided a deterrent to Kamba militancy a few years later.

The Kiambu Paradox

The quiescence of Kiambu compared to Murang'a and Nyeri during Mau Mau can also be explained in these terms. There, the high value cash crop was not coffee but the pineapple, which by 1952 was being produced in large quantities for the Nairobi market and for Kenya Canners at Thika.[92] The effect of this very high value cash crop, much more profitable than coffee, was more limited in its pacifying effects because European settlement had produced a far greater disruption of Kiambu society than in

89.   KNA Ag 4/410, 'Nyeri District Agricultural Annual Report, 1952'.
90.   See G. Kitching *Class and Economic Change in Kenya*, pp. 110–116; D. M. Feldman, 'Christians and Politics: The Origins of the KCA in northern Murang'a, 1890–1930', pp. 267–272 and 296–7. For a detailed study of Kikuyu wattle production see M. Cowen, 'Capital and Household Production: The Case of Wattle in Kenya's Central Province, 1908–1964' (unpublished Cambridge Ph.D. thesis).
91.   Machakos District Annual Reports and oral testimony of D. O'Hagan, Provincial Commissioner, Central, and Dr Richard Waller and KNA DC/MKS 1/1/30, 'Machakos Annual Reports, 1951 and 1952', *passim*.
92.   KNA 4/310 Kiambu Agricultural Annual Report, 1952.

Meru and Embu, where virtually no land had been alienated. Indeed, of all the districts of Central Province far more land had been lost in Kiambu than anywhere else. The effects of this, and the return in the early 1950s of squatters, many of whom had come from Kiambu originally, counteracted the prosperity generated by cash crop production. For example, the Olenguruone malcontents had originally come from Limuru, where their *githakas* had been alienated to European settlers.[93] Such people had nothing to lose in a full-scale revolt.

Kiambu society can be divided into three groups, the respective strengths of which are difficult to assess because they varied over time. There were the loyalists headed by Chiefs Waruhiu and Magugu and the committed members of the Presbyterian Church. But Kiambu was also the stronghold of the KAU constitutionalists, whose main leaders—Kenyatta, Mathu, Gichuru—were all Kiambu men. These two groups were the ones who benefitted most from Kiambu's proximity to Nairobi and its transformation into a lucrative market garden area for the city, with a fall-back in years of over-production and the threat of lower prices in the fruit and vegetable canning factory at Thika.[94] The conflict between these two groups was not between 'haves' and 'have nots' but between two factions who wished to maximize their access to the European economy and state apparatus. The chiefs and their supporters, by definition, were entrenched; KAU supporters were demanding equal access and co-option.

Until the 1950s the militants, the have-nots, were weaker in Kiambu than elsewhere in Kikuyuland. It was not until the mass exodus of squatters from the Rift from 1950 onwards that militancy grew. Part of the explanation for this acquiescence was that Kiambu, unlike Murang'a and South Nyeri, exported its *ahoi*, the landless have-nots of Kikuyu society, outside the district to Nairobi, where the militants captured control over the local KAU machine in 1951. As a result the tenor of political dispute in Kiambu was more restrained during the 1940s at least, limited to constitutionalist paths.

Kenyatta's Political Decline

Kenyatta's leadership, however, even here, was largely discredited by 1949. On his return from Britain, Kenyatta had initially appeared to be capable of uniting the constitutionalist and militant wings of KAU. He

93. KNA PC/RVP 6A/1/17/2 'Olenguruone 1948–50', Officer-in-charge Mau Mara Settlement to PC, Central, 9 August 1940, list of squatters provisionally accepted on the recommendation of the District Commissioner, Kiambu and Kiambu LNC sub-committee at Chura on 5 August, 1940. See my forthcoming article 'Olenguruone 1940–1950' in *Kenya in the Twentieth Century* ed. B. A. Ogot (Nairobi).
94. KNA Ag 4/410 Kiambu Agricultural Annual Report, 1952; and Commerce and Industry 6/418, 'Kenya Canners Ltd, 1948–51' for their detailed negotiations with the government.

430   AFRICAN AFFAIRS

was the undisputed leader: the man who knew the ways of the European even better than Mathu. Moreover he had quickly recemented his links with Kikuyu society. His marriages to the daughters of Chief Koinange and Chief Muhoho consolidated his position in the Kiambu establishment.

With his power base secured in mid-1947 Kenyatta launched a widespread campaign to secure funds for Githunguri Teachers Training College, and for the next year, until mid–1948, monthly meetings were held at Githunguri where representatives of all Kikuyu *riika* reported how much they had collected from their age mates in the previous four weeks.[95] These monthly gatherings often raised £2,000, but little progress was made in rebuilding the school. Gradually discontent grew; the Githunguri teachers threatened to go on strike as they had not been paid for nearly six months, and the government waited with glee for Kenyatta and the Kenya African Union to be totally discredited.[96]

This did not happen because Gichuru and Mbiyu Koinange intervened. In June 1948, Kenyatta was summoned to a gathering of thirty prominent Kikuyu at a secret meeting at James Gichuru's house, where his administration of the school was strongly criticized.[97] After this Kenyatta was a spent force, a mere figurehead amongst the moderates, whilst the militants openly attacked him. Kenyatta realized that his position was slipping badly and that his attempts to reassert his influence were failing. In consequence he took to excessive drinking as solace for his lost political opportunity.[98]

By 1949, he was a completely discredited force, discarded in all practical respects by his supporters, but clinging to his position as President of the Kenya African Union because any attempt to oust him by the moderates would damage KAU's already waning support, whilst playing into the hands of the militants by enabling them to rally round as supporters of Kenyatta and to use his residual mystique, which remained amongst the masses, even though his practical influence was slight. Equally, the militants could not ditch Kenyatta as to do so would remove the protective smoke-screen which he provided, and expose them to the full wrath of Mathu and the Gichuru faction. Neither side, therefore, could afford to get rid of him, much as they would both have liked to do so.[99]

95.   KNA MAA 8/106 and *Mumenyereri* 17 November, 1947; 19 January, 1948; and 16 February, 1948.
96.   CO 537/3591/38733, Mitchell to Cohen 18 October, 1948; KNA MAA 8/106, *Mumenyereri*, 5 April and 26 April, 1948; and MAA, *Radio Posta*, 27 January 1948.
97.   KNA MAA 8/102, Director of Intelligence to Chief Native Commissioner, 16 June 1948.
98.   See P. Abrahams, 'The Blacks', p. 59.
99.   For a temperate statement of the radicals' opinions of Kenyatta, see B. Kaggia *Roots of Freedom*, pp. 79–82. W. W. W. Awori's view is to be found in KNA MAA 8/109, in a report of the Director of Intelligence to Wyn Harris, 21 October 1947. Following Chege Kibachia's detention, Awori and H. S. Gathigira tried to take over the AWF as a rival political movement to Kenyatta's KAU. Awori had been the vice-president of KAU until Kenyatta and his KCA cronies ousted him.

THE ORIGINS OF MAU MAU 431

Given this assessment, the question arises as to how far the Administration understood this power struggle inside KAU and Kenyatta's position. At least two possible explanations exist for his arrest on 20 October 1952, as the organizer of Mau Mau. The first, and machiavellian, interpretation—which I do not believe but for which there is a surprising amount of evidence—is that the Administration knew exactly what they were doing when they arrested Kenyatta. They knew that they were creating a martyr, one more prison graduate, and that was exactly what they wanted to do. The Special Branch for the last five years had been providing sophisticated analyses of KAU political divisions.[100] They saw Kenyatta as essentially a moderate man, not fanatically anti-European; a man who could perhaps later bind together the wounds of a divided country: but a man who, because of his moderation, had lost control over the movement. If this interpretation, which the Special Branch was constantly providing to the Chief Native Commissioner, had been accepted, it is possible that the Mau Mau Emergency should be seen not only as a pre-emptive strike to remove from circulation the militant threat to colonial rule but also as a device to rehabilitate him in the eyes of politically conscious Africans and to create a martyr to the cause of Kenya's freedom who would subsequently prove as moderate and susceptible to 'reason' as Nehru had in India.

This interpretation is supported not only by certain evidence from the Special Branch but also of a few settler leaders who were furious with the Administration for arresting Kenyatta. What they said in public to their settler audiences about him as the evil genius behind Mau Mau bore little resemblance to their view of him as a moderating influence, which they expressed in private. Ewart Grogan, for one, saw the arrest as a tremendous error of judgement.[101] The question is: Did the colonial Kenya government agree with this interpretation of Kenyatta's position and were they playing a double bluff? Alas, despite the charms of such a move by the British, one must confess that it appears to be too far-fetched and the more probable explanation for Kenyatta's arrest was rather more prosaic.

Despite what the Special Branch was telling them in private, the Secretariat refused to believe that Kenyatta was not responsible for Mau Mau. Because of the structure of the colonial state, the Secretariat relied overwhelmingly on the reports provided by the provincial administration:

100. This can be discerned from KNA MAA 8/8 'Intelligence Reports–Confidential, 1946–7'; MAA 8/32 'African Press 1951–2'; MAA 8/71 'Communism'; MAA 8/102 'Intelligence and Security'; MAA 8/103 'Intelligence and security—letters to East African Standard'; MAA 8/105 Radio Posta; MAA 8/106 *Mumenyereri*; MAA 8/108 *Daily Chronicle*; MAA 8/109 'African Workers' Federation'; MAA 8/110 *Colonial Times*; and ARC/MAA/2/5/146, 'KAU 1948–52'.
101. Interviews with Mervyn Cowie and Clive Salter, July 1981, and Special Branch reports.

members, like themselves, of the elite administrative cadre.[102]   These
reports blamed Kenyatta and KAU as the cause of all discontent in the
reserves.   Compared to the sophisticated understanding of KAU factionalism provided in the Special Branch reports, their assessment was very
simplistic.   Little knowledge was shown as to the deep divisions within
KAU, which was viewed as a purely monolithic movement, united behind
Kenyatta's all-encompassing evil leadership.[103]   The source of this information was often simply the prejudice of the District Commissioners
against African politicians, or went one stage further back to the chiefs,
who saw them as a threat to their positions.[104]

The prejudices of the Secretariat in favour of the all-knowing District
Commissioner, the man who knew 'his' people, plus the fact that the interpretation offered coincided with the Secretariat's and Mitchell's personal
dislike for the emerging class of African politicians,[105] ensured that this
view of Kenyatta was favoured and the Special Branch's was ignored.
Consequently they rehabilitated Kenyatta by making him a martyr by
chance rather than by design.   Fortunately for British interests, the
rehabilitated Kenyatta was to prove himself as confirmed a moderate as the
Special Branch had always suggested he was.

Only those two wily politicians Kenyatta and Macmillan recognized in
the 1940s that until the British selected and supported a Kenya Governor
who had the courage to sacrifice the settlers and to incorporate the emerging African elite around Kenyatta and his faction inside KAU, long-term
political stability was impossible.   Mitchell, despite his vast experience of
East Africa, had not even begun to understand the problem.   In 1942,
however, Harold Macmillan when he served briefly as Under-Secretary for
the Colonies had been willing to grapple with settler hegemony.   After
only a few months at the Colonial Office, and unencumbered by any
prevous knowledge of Africa, he had reached from impeccably conservative
premises the radical conclusion that settler farming was inefficient and
uneconomic and proposed that the European farmers in the White Highlands must be bought out and the Kikuyu allowed to settle on collective
farms in the Rift Valley if a peasants' revolt within ten years was to be

102.   B. J. Berman, 'Administration and Politics in Colonial Kenya', (unpublished Yale
Ph.D., 1973), especially pp. 391–404 and 424–432.   Berman's 'Bureaucracy and Incumbent
Violence: Colonial administration and the origins of the Mau Mau Emergency in Kenya',
British Journal of Political Science 6, pp. 143–175 is also interesting, although fundamentally
wrong.
103.   This was still the version offered by F. D. Corfield in *The Origins and Growth of Mau
Mau*.   See CO 533/543/38086/38, for Mitchell's explanation to Creech Jones, 28 February
1949.
104.   See my unpublished Cambridge (1983) thesis, 'The Governorship of Sir Philip
Mitchell in Kenya, 1944–1952', pp. 212–261.
105.   Mitchell's dislike of 'political agitators' was intense and often vented.   See CO
533/540/38032, Mitchell to Creech Jones, 11 December 1948; and CO 533/549/38232/15,
letter of 14 April 1947.

averted.[106]   This went too far for the Whitehall establishment.   The cautious Colonial Office chose instead to 'sand-bag' the settlers from behind and to sap their strength by using their overweening ambitions to pull them down.   The settlers, however, captured Mitchell and multi-racialism failed.   It was the Mau Mau rebellion which foreclosed the settler option once and for all, and enabled Macmillan and Kenyatta in the early 1960s, with the help of Macleod, Blundell, Mboya and MacDonald, to reach an arrangement which satisfied the Kikuyu elites (both loyalist and Kenyatta-ite) and the British.[107]   Ironically this solution bore an uncanny resemblance to Macmillan's 1942 plan.   As Prime Minister and prison martyr in the early 1960s, Macmillan and Kenyatta were able to secure a political solution very similar to the one they had both advocated, from their different sides of the colonial fence, in the 1940s, and to ditch their intransigent allies.

106.   See CO 967/57/46709 (1942): 'Sir Arthur Dawe's Memorandum on a Federal Solution for East Africa and Mr Harold Macmillan's Counter-Proposals', H. Macmillan to Sir George Gater, 15 August 1942.
107.   D. Goldsworthy, *Tom Mboya*, (Heinemann, 1982) pp. 93–146 and 166–193; G. Wasserman, *Politics of Decolonization* (Cambridge University Press, 1976) *passim;* Sir Michael Blundell, *So Rough a Wind* (Weidenfeld and Nicholson 1946), pp. 261–318; D. F. Gordon, 'Mau Mau and Decolonization', *Kenya Historical Review*, 7, 2, pp. 329–345; and B. E. Kipkorir, 'Mau Mau and the Politics of the Transfer of Power in Kenya', in the same volume, pp. 314–326.

[10]

The Mau Mau Rebellion, Kikuyu Women, and Social Change

Cora Ann Presley

Résumé

Remarquablement absents dans la littérature historique sur la révolte Mau Mau et le nationalisme kényan, sont à la fois l'affirmation de la participation féminine et des renseignments sur cette participation. De représenter la révolte comme une lutte entre hommes africains et européens, ignore l'initiative des femmes et leur souci de changement, en dissimulant les effets néfastes du colonialisme sur les femmes, les changements dans leur statut et leurs protestations contre les changements économiques et culturels. En outre, d'ignorer l'activisme politique féminin obscurcit le processus qui a élargi la participation politique pour permettre l'inclusion de politiciennes dans le Kenya moderne. Cette article critique les études actuelles sur le nationalisme Kikuyu, en révélant la force cachée mais puissante du nationalisme féminin indépendant et parallèle. Il examine l'importance du rôle des femmes dans le nationalisme militant et suggère que ces activités ont donné lieu à une lutte pour un leadership féminin dans le Kenya post Mau-Mau.

Introduction

In his 1982 work, *Essays on Mau Mau: Contributions to Mau Mau Historiography*, Robert Buijenthuis surveys the state of scholarship on the Mau Mau rebellion in Kenya from the 1950s to the 1980s. Buijenthuis, an early scholar of the Mau Mau rebellion and Kenyan nationalism, ably assesses the questions that researchers and participants in Mau Mau have addressed. Some of the fundamental questions explored are: What were the origins of Mau Mau? What were its patterns of recruitment and definition of membership? A second level of questions attempts to delineate the political, ideological, and personal connections of Mau Mau to nationalist associations in the pre-1948 period. Third, the historiography has focused on the different phases of the Mau Mau rebellion. A fourth concern has been how the colonial state and the British government marshalled their forces to counter and defeat Mau Mau. These questions were widely explored from the 1950s to the 1970s. Beginning in the 1970s, questions of class and local level analysis came into vogue. Typical questions were: Which of the Kikuyu districts in the Central Province contributed members to the rank and file as opposed to

503   Presley: The Mau Mau Rebellion

the Mau Mau leadership? Was Mau Mau a conflict or civil war between rural / urban populations and elite mass / sectors of society? Or was it best understood as labor conflict which evolved between the lumpenproletariat and the skilled workers in the trade unions?

All of these questions have deepened our understanding of the multifaceted nature of Mau Mau and have revealed cleavages in Kikuyu society. Some cleavages began in the pre-colonial period. Others were introduced under the colonial regime. While debate rages over some of these issues, in particular over local level and class differences in Mau Mau participation, scholars still exclude from consideration women's contribution to the rebellion and to Kenyan nationalism in general. The earlier Mau Mau studies did not examine women's participation. (See Rosberg and Nottingham 1966; Tignor 1976; Kilson 1955; Buijenthuis 1973, 1982; Kanogo 1987; Barnett and Njama 1966; Clayton and Savage 1975; Furedi 1973; Furedi 1974; Kanogo 1977; Tamarkin 1978; Coray 1978; Newsinger 1981; Stichter 1975; Tamarkin 1976; Leakey 1952, 1954; Majdalany 1963; Ogot 1972; Sorrenson 1967). With the exception of a few works, such as Tabitha Kanago's recent book on Mau Mau and squatters in the Rift Valley, 1980s scholarship accords women only token acknowledgement as participants in the "passive wing" of Mau Mau (Kanogo 1987). By not questioning women's contribution to Kenyan nationalism and Mau Mau, analyses continue to project a view that Mau Mau was a conflict among males. The following dyads were created:

Africans *versus* Europeans

nationalists *versus* loyalists

mass *versus* élites

rural *versus* urban

lumpenproletariat *versus* trade union members

Research has ignored an important aspect of Kenyan nationalism: the development of nationalist sentiment and activity among women since the 1920s; and the colonial state's response to women's nationalism.

The Government's response was to alter social policy. The center-piece of this was the development of a department whose policies and programs were directed specifically to wean women away from Mau Mau. These policies were developed in response to two needs. The first was to isolate the military force of Mau Mau and to defeat it by attacking and cutting off its popular support, which the British called the "passive wing," composed largely of women. Their function was to supply information, to smuggle arms, food, clothing, and medicine to the guerilla army, and to maintain the lines of transit for recruits travelling from the urban and rural sectors of the Central Province to join the military forces in the forest.[1] The phrase "passive wing" hides the importance of this type of activity. The women and men who were the support troops of Mau Mau should more aptly be termed the non-combatant forces. They were treated as a serious force by the British.

The second part of the Government's policy was a program aimed at capturing the loyalty of the Kikuyu. This involved villagization and a fullblown propaganda program whose major purpose was to detach women from Mau Mau. The Government paid special attention to women's activism since key officials believed that women were "far more rabid and fanatical than the males" and more violent in their support of Mau Mau.[2] In response to women's "fanaticism" institutions designed to address such unmet needs as education, health care, access to a clean and reliable water supply, and child-care were created. The policy acknowledged, perhaps for the first time, that the colonial government had a primary responsibility for the welfare of rural populations. The Community Development Department, which was created in 1954, addressed these problems. It was given a large annual budget of £250 000 and a staff which included Africans as well as Europeans (Great Britain 1954, 80).[3]

This Department was part of the British struggle to control women. Before the 1920s, the contest over who would control women, African or European males, revolved around jural issues: chiefly the marriage laws. The colonial state, of course, won the contest (Presley 1986, 149-200).[4] Other conflicts of this nature revolved around female circumcision and women's wage labor.[5] Women's massive participation in Mau Mau contributed to the rebellion's initial psychological, if not military successes. A total of 34 147 women were sentenced to prison for violation of the Emergency Regulations from 1952 to 1958 (see Table 1). Thousands of these women were repeat violators of the regulations, which included taking oaths and aiding the forest fighters through supplying food, guns and information. Thus, from the standpoint of both the British and the nationalists, wooing women's loyalty was an essential ingredient in winning the war.

The Image of Women Nationalists

When women's activities are described in the pro-colonial histories, two pictures of women emerge. Women are seen either as victims of Mau Mau or as prostitutes who, through personal contact with male nationalists, were drawn to Mau Mau while resident in Nairobi. The view of women as victims of Mau Mau originates from the colonial record. Women are presented by officials as the physical and psychological victims of atavism. The first type of victimization characterizes women as being forcibly compelled to take the oath of allegiance to Mau Mau. A 1952 Special Branch report on intimidation in oathing recounted the forced oathing of a Catholic Kikuyu woman. She was stripped naked, severely beaten to the point of unconsciousness, and upon her revival compelled to "drink blood from a bottle, and perform the other disgusting rites constituting the Mau Mau ceremony" (Corfield 1960, 155-156.) Another 1952 incident contributed to the view of women as victims. In Nyeri, the District Commissioner reported that forcible oathings of women and children were widespread (Corfield 1960, 134). Further fuel was added to this image of women by writers who were openly antagonistic to Mau Mau. In *State of Emergency*, F. Majadalany portrayed women's attraction to Mau Mau as being caused by a misdirected hero-worship of nationalists, described as "young thugs and criminals." According to Majadalany, however: "When the fighting gangs were formed each included its quota of women, and though their first function was to act as pack transport (with some concubinage on the side) many of them became ferocious and implacable fighters too" (1963, 60).

Both F. D. Corfield and Majadalany ascribe irrationality and bestiality to Mau Mau. One measure of its supposed fanaticism was the repeated attacks on Loyalist women (Corfield 1960, 101). In the Lari Massacre (26 March 1953) eighty-four Loyalists were killed, two-thirds of the victims women. During 1952 Mau Mau military actions killed twenty-three loyalists of whom two were women and three were children (Corfield 1960, 157; Majadalany 1963, 137-147). While the rebellion was in progress, a popular British tactic was to portray women as Mau Mau's principal victims. However, only ninety eight of the 1 024 Kikuyu killed by Mau Mau were women (Buijenthuis 1982, 184). This figure represents actual deaths and does not include threats, beatings, and other intimidation.

The image of women nationalists as prostitutes originates from district and provincial reports. Women nationalists began to be described as prostitutes when the Kenya African Union (KAU) successfully staged mass rallies. For example, a rally in Nyeri on 26 July 1952 was described by the District Commissioner: "Over 20 000 men, women and children attended. KAU insinuated over 40 bus loads of Nairobi thugs and prostitutes, who were clearly under instructions to excite the crowd" (Corfield 1960, 136-137). In describing the participation of the Meru in Mau Mau, J.T. Kamunchulah repeats the theme of a connection between prostitution and women's activism. He attributes the success of the Mau Mau in acquiring arms from government soldiers from 1950 to 1952 to "a network of communication with prostitutes, who lay 'tender traps' for African askaris, of ambushing the African askaris in dark streets and abducting and later suffocating them to death" (Kamunchulah 1975, 193).

Women, Nationalism, and the Colonial Infrastructure

These views suggest that women were attracted to Mau Mau for other than political reasons and that, moreover, only those women who were pariahs in European and African society were likely to be seduced by Mau Mau nationalism. These images of detribalized women as the initial female contingent of Mau Mau are counter-factual. In the first year of the Emergency, local level British officials noticed that large numbers of women were actively involved in Mau Mau. The accepted explanation for women's attraction to Mau Mau was that they had had less exposure to British institutions such as the missionary schools, fewer opportunities for employment in the settler economy, and were more "primitive" than males who had become westernized.[6] Indeed, Kikuyu women were not as tied to the day to day structures of colonial rule as were their men. Nonetheless, they were affected by colonialism. In the pre-colonial period women farmed land which was later alienated by the Crown Lands Act (1902). Loss of land produced scarcity. Consequently, women as well as men were affected by overpopulation and land pressures which the introduction of the settler economy and state had induced. In the areas dominated by the settler economy, women were an important part of the labor economy, used extensively as seasonal laborers in the production of coffee, the country's leading export. During the harvest season, female and juvenile labor made up sixty percent of the labor force (Presley 1986, 108-119).[7] Missionaries intensively recruited women. They viewed themselves as champions of the alleviation of women's misery through stamping out customs they perceived as devaluing and harmful. From the European standpoint, these included the payment of bridewealth, prohibitions on remarriage of widows, and female circumcision. Though mission efforts at educating girls always received a lower priority than those directed toward boys, the rural schools and churches focused on persuading women to accept western mores, customs, and values (Temu 1972, 106-107; Presley 1986, 149-164).

Colonial laws also were directed toward women. The effect of land alienation has already been mentioned. Other colonial laws such as communal labor (1908) and the hut and poll taxes (1910 and 1934) were also assessed against women. These laws caused resentment, and combined with the issues of female circumcision, unfair labor practices, taxation, lack of adequate education, and exclusion from politics, they drew women to the nationalists' ideology.

Affected by colonial laws, women, long before Mau Mau, had registered their protest against these laws. Colonial officials did not, however, treat women's resistance as an integral part of the rising tide of protest dating to the 1920s. Several indicators of women's activism were dismissed as being instigated by others. Women had organized labor strikes over the conditions on the coffee estates. These strikes, notably one in 1947, were dismissed as being caused by male agitators (Presley 1986a, 129-148).[8] Another major incident occurred in 1947 and 1948, when women of Fort Hall District participated in what was termed "The Revolt of the Women." This was a protest against a scheme to compel women to dig terraces in their fields for the purpose of soil conservation. According to the Corfield report, this protest was initiated by the Kenya African Union. At a large meeting, an agreement was reached that women would not participate in the government scheme. The women's unanimous support for this agreement meant that none of them showed up for the communal labor, and "by the end of August all communal labour was virtually at a standstill" (Corfield 1960, 67). The Corfield Report consistently interpreted women's agitation as aberrant:

> During the earlier part of the year [1948] agitation against soil conservation continued in Fort Hall district and led to a minor political upheaval known as "The Revolt of the Women" in two locations of that district. Disruptive elements outside the district continued to agitate against the co-operation of women in soil conservation work, and this later led to a full-scale descent of the women themselves to district headquarters. This as the District Commissioner commented, marked a growing tendency which was entirely alien to normal Kikuyu custom, indicating that agitators had been at work (1960, 77).

Women in the Mau Mau Rebellion

Women's participation in public arena politics was indeed alien to Kikuyu custom. Colonialism changed women's political roles. This change did not originate in the decade before the State of Emergency was declared but predated Mau Mau by twenty years.[9] Small groups of women became nationalists in the 1930s. Over the next twenty years, they recruited thousands of other women to the nationalists' cause.[10] Women gained recognition from the major nationalist associations, the Kikuyu Central Association (KCA) and the Kenya African Union (KAU) before these organizations were proscribed by the government.[11] Their roles in the Mau Mau rebellion were as multifaceted as the revolt itself. Women had primary responsibility for the organization and maintenance of the supply lines which directed food, supplies, medicine, guns, and information to the forest forces. They also recruited for Mau Mau. They officiated at and participated in oathing ceremonies (Corfield 1960, 84). In 1950 the Kiambu District Commissioner reported to his superiors that men were no longer administering oaths of loyalty to Mau Mau:

> Women, however, were proceeding with the work of oath-giving.... For a woman to administer a Muma oath would be utterly contrary to Kikuyu custom, although it must be admitted that until the Dedan oaths were started it was also unknown for a woman to have a Muma oath (Corfield 1960, 90).

A break with custom in giving and taking oaths was one of the many changes in gender roles nationalism introduced for women.[12] They also joined the forest forces and served as combat troops. They were so important to the movement that the British rounded them up in the military sweeps, aimed at arresting the leaders and the more active Mau Mau adherents who were not in the forests. Their high visibility in the movement is indicated by their mention in colonial records. In 1953 women's activism caused the District Commissioner of Kiambu to pass on this observation to his superiors:

> In September, the Chura location appeared to become a centre of the Mau Mau central committee, and every Itura had its own sub-committee, nor did they lack a women's section. the latter throughout may well be described as the "eyes and ears of Mau Mau."[13]

The 1953 *African Affairs Report* notes:

> The part played by women to aid the terrorists was considerable. They not only fed them but carried food to gangs in the forest, and some were caught dressed as Mau Mau "askari" [soldiers]. The attitude of the women of the tribe towards the Emergency was, in general, particularly distressing ... the primitive and indigenous cult of Mau Mau has had for many a powerful appeal. There have been instances of female relatives being privy to the murder of their loyal menfolk.[14]

Kikuyu women joined the nationalist associations to improve their economic status, to gain access to the political process, to further their education, and to abet the return of alienated land. Muthoni wa Gachie was a member of KCA and KAU in the 1940s. She recounted women's motives as being political in origin:

Q: When did you join?
A: I joined in April of 1945.
Q: Why did you become a member?
A: So that I could be a politician of the country.
Q: Were there other women who were members?
A: Yes. there was a group of us.
Q: How many?
A: The whole of Central Province.
Q: Were women already members when you joined?
A: Yes, very many were already members.
Q: What did KCA want?
A: We wanted only to make the Europeans to go from the country.
Q: What were your responsibilities as a member?
A: I was cooking for visitors and I contributed for Mzee [Kenyatta] to go to Europe. We were fighting so we would know how to become independent....

Q: Were you a leader?

A: Yes, even I was taken to prison. When the war started we thought of some people going to the forest. We were cooking food and taking it to the forest. We were carrying guns, if we would give it to her and she would take it to the forest. We went during the night. During the day the Homeguards came to collect us. We were brought here to dig the ground with our hands. Some were killed. Others were jailed for some years. Then from there the war slowly came to an end.

Q: How long did you spend in jail?

A: In one year I was jailed three times. This was in 1958. Then I was detained in 1959 for one year. I was detained at Athii River, then I was taken to Embu.[15]

Wagara Wainana also described herself as a leader of Mau Mau. Unlike Muthoni wa Gachie, she was able to avoid being placed in detention.

Q: When did you take your first oath?

A: About 1948.

Q: How many did you take?

A: Only two.

Q: Were you a member of the Mau Mau committee?

A: I was a committee member of KAU and of Mau Mau.

Q: Which area did you represent?

A: I represented Karura (Muthurura) Kiambaa.

Q: Was your husband involved in politics?

A: Yes.

Q: How was it that you were not put in prison?

A: I was not detained because my husband was beaten. My co-wife's son was also detained. The co-wife was sick so that there was no one left so that the Europeans left me to care for the sick.

Q: Did they know that you were an active Mau Mau?

A: They knew [there were Mau Mau in the area] but not who the actual person was unless the other Kikuyu told them.

Q: Did you get put into the villagization program?

A: Yes, we built the villages.

Q: Did you carry on the work of Mau Mau from the villages?

A: Yes, we continued after that. We women were taken to a place and forced to do work for nothing. This place was called Kianjogu.... We did digging and we didn't know the reason we were doing this digging. We dug all around the camp, sweeping and clearing the camp. Then we were taken to another camp. We stayed in Kianjogu for seven months. Then we were taken to a village for four years and then I went to my farm. This was in 1955. We were only fighting and in the end we were helped by God. In the 1930s the women started the Mumbi Central Association and when Kenyatta came back from England he called us all together and organized us. I took food to the Mau Mau. We also took guns. When I was taking food, I was hiding from the Europeans when another one of us saw the police, she started screaming and ran down to the river. I grabbed her by the throat so that we could not be heard. When the soldiers came near, I ran away and the other one was screaming again. Then the other one was caught and put into detention.[16]

Wangui wa Gikuhiu joined KCA when it was first organized. Though an active supporter of Mau Mau, she described herself as "only a member." Women leaders "did the work of talking about how to get the land."[17] Priscilla Wambaki, a leader before Mau Mau and a KANU (Kenya Africa National Union, the ruling party) leader in her division in the independence period, recalled the beginning of women in politics:

Q: Were you a member of a political party?
A: Yes, I was a member of KAU.
Q: Did you belong to KCA?
A: KCA was the one before KAU, but I was only a member of KAU.
Q: Did you ever hear of an organization called Mumbi Central Association?
A: I was a member of Mumbi Central Association. I was also a member of KAU.
Q: When did you join Mumbi Central Association?
A: I can't remember the year but I joined it with Wambui Wangaram and I worked with Rebecca Njeri....
Q: What did Mumbi Central Association want to accomplish?
A: Kiama kia Mumbi had the aim to preserve the customs, to not allow them to dissolve. But before we went further the war started.... First women were not invited to join Kikuyu Central Association. We met together and decided we didn't like this so we asked the pastor of the church to help us. He did and we raised money and started Mumbi Central Association. We would have dances to raise money and the men could not matter. It was only Mbiyu Koinange who was allowed. After a while we joined the men again.
Q: How much money did you raise for Kiriri?[18]
A: I don't know since the books were destroyed, but it was much more than 100 000 shillings.
Q: How many oaths did you take?
A: ... Only children did not take the oath. I won't talk about that. I want to tell how Mbiyu helped to build the dormitories so that you can understand the role women played when Mzee [Kenyatta] came from Europe. We met with him. We had not completed the dormitories. We had no windows. He helped us, he was on our side. From that time on he was on our side. If there were no women, then the war would not have been carried on. And the women were mostly girls, because if the men were beaten, they would tell the secrets and the girls would not. Even Mzee knew that the girls played a great part and that is why he gave us Madaraka....[19]

511   Presley: The Mau Mau Rebellion

TABLE 1

Women Admitted to Prisons, 1952–1958

Year	Number	Number Sentenced	Recidivists	First Offenders
1952	347	n / a	n / a	n / a
1953	4 415	3 132	55	3 077
1954	9 609	8 494	290	3 204
1955	13 265	11 467	1 506	9 961
1956	8 900	7 906	1 627	6 279
1957	8 854	7 472	2 068	5 404
1958	7 295	5 976	1 873	4 103

SOURCE: Kenya Colony and Protectorate, Kenya Prisons. *Annual Report.* 1953, 8;
Kenya Prisons, *Annual Report.* 1956, 8-9; Kenya Prisons, *Annual Report.* 1958,
10.

TABLE 2

All Africans Admitted to Detention Camps,
1948–1957

Year	Number
1948	16 369
1949	16 637
1950	18 037
1951	18 257
1952	23 201
1953	32 862
1954	25 979
1955	30 247
1956	41 441
1957	53 080

SOURCE: Kenya Colony and Protectorate, *Annual Report on the Treatment of
Offenders.* 1957, 2.

Women's activism sparked a response from the Government. They were arrested, detained, and interrogated in large numbers. When the Emergency officially ended in 1956, of the 27 841 Kikuyu who were still in the detention camps, 3 103 were women (*Daily Chronicle* 7 September 1956). Tables I and 2 reveal the number of women imprisoned during the Mau Mau period compared to the total number of Africans detained in the camps. Of the 13 265 females admitted to prison in 1955, 1 714 were discharged from prison custody, 11 467 were sentenced to imprisonment (9 961 of these were first offenders, the balance were repeat offenders).[20] Virtually all women imprisoned were suspected of Mau Mau involvement.

Before the Emergency, there was so little female crime that no particular prison facilities had been built. To the surprise of the colonial government, when Mau Mau activities became pronounced, women's participation was on such a large scale that a facility had to be built to house them. The Kamiti prison was extended to accommodate the upsurge in women prisoners and detainees; the camp included 1 335 women prisoners and 1 010 women detainees by the end of 1954.[21] Women were also detained in other facilities. The Athii River detention camp which was built in 1953 to contain violaters of the Emergency Regulations had ten compounds containing 1 429 detainees. One of the compounds was reserved for twenty-seven female detainees.[22] Most women prisoners were sentenced for violations of the Emergency regulations.[23] A large proportion of the women sentenced were first time offenders. Sentences ranged from short terms of one or two months to the full duration of the Emergency, with a majority sentenced to terms of six months or less – twenty percent (1952) and twenty-seven percent (1953) were sentenced to six months to two years. As Mau Mau became more threatening, the length of sentences increased.

The camps were not merely holding facilities. Prisoners were required to work and also to go through a re-socialization process whose goal was to get them to renounce Mau Mau and be "cleansed."[24] The Community Development organization was involved in rehabilitating prisoners.[25] At Kamiti, the Department was given some control over the detainees' "leisure time."[26] Nearly three hundred female detainees attended classes. They received instruction in animal husbandry, hygiene, health, agriculture, and local government.[27] However, these classes were not the most important aspect of the organization's work in the struggle to defeat Mau Mau. The Department also ran child-care facilities.[28]

Most of the apparent success the Government achieved in converting Mau Mau detainees in 1955 and 1956 was among female prisoners in Kamiti prison. Several facilities for women were maintained around the colony, but Kamiti was for the "hardcore" Mau Mau women.[29] The number of women released from the Kamiti facility in 1956 was 1 194 leaving 1 384 women in

the camp. In 1957 4 220 women were released and 174 remained in detention. Many "hardcore" women were not released until 1960. The rehabilitation efforts among women were so "successful" that by 1957 Mau Mau
women detainees were:

> ... processed straight to their homes on release and have not passed through the
> pipe line camps in their own areas as is the case with men. This is a tribute to
> the thorough and successful rehabilitation work undertaken at the camps.[30]

Community Development officers were aided in their work of detaching
women from Mau Mau by the missionaries. The Christian Council of Kenya
sent representatives to the camps to hold Christian services and "cleanse"
women prisoners of their radical beliefs.[31] The Department categorized prisoners according to the strength of their attachment to Mau Mau and
response to rehabilitation. The "Y" category were those who were responding to re-socialization.[32] Kamiti women prisoners were considered to be in
the "Y" category of rebels. Confession was stressed. When word circulated
that those who confessed could gain an early release, the number of peni-
tents rapidly soared (Wipper 1977, 255).

Conditions in the Prisons

Former women prisoners at Kamiti described conditions of terror, physical
punishment, and forced labor. They received inadequate food and clothing.
Conditions for women Mau Mau and / or Mau Mau suspects were similar to
those for males who were arrested and detained. Interviews with former
Mau Mau female prisoners reveal a prison system which meted out harsh
treatment.[33] Women in Kamiti were required to work for the prison system.[34] Light work of raising vegetables and fruit was given as a reward for
co-operating with the rehabilitation program, another impetus to confess.[35]
This co-operation usually took the form of taking a pledge renouncing Mau
Mau and giving information about Mau Mau activity in the prisons and elsewhere. The more intransigent were required to work on road-building and
quarrying stone. The prison commandant reported in 1955 that 199 000 running feet of stone was quarried by Kamiti prisoners.[36] Once the stones were
quarried and dressed, women prisoners transported them on their heads. In
1954 women helped to terrace the thirty-five acre prison farm. The value of
the labor extracted from these women through the cultivation of the
197 305 pounds of vegetables they raised in 1956 was £1 973.[37] Other forms
of punishment included solitary confinement, the withholding of food, and
corporal punishment.[38] Harsh and inhuman treatment was the rule in the
prisons and detention camps according to former Mau Mau prisoners. The
following is from an interview with one of them, Priscilla Wambaki:

Q: Were you detained?

A: Yes.

Q: Where were you taken?

A: I was taken to Kajado in Maasailand.

Q: When was this?

A: It was in 1952. That was the time when Mzee [Kenyatta] was detained with Rebecca Njeri.... [Njeri was the most prominent woman nationalist, detained at the same time as Kenyatta]. I was in detention for one year then I was taken to the Athii River [camp].... At Kajado only the women leaders were detained. Men were there also but the women were kept separate. We were not forced to work but kept locked in our rooms. There we were beaten but not too much. But when we were taken to the Athii River, we were beaten very much. All of the members of KAU, men and women were detained. Women were not many at Athii River, we were about two hundred, but the men were uncountable. Those who were involved in politics or any other movement but not the church were taken to Kamiti. This was in 1954, and only women were there. We were beaten and very many died. During that time people were hanged in great numbers and we buried many there. We were not afraid of the corpses, even if we were doing this job we were still beaten. We could see some corpses with the blood from the beating still on them. During the time of getting food in the prison the young girls would pull the carts, they were tied three by three to the carts in order to pull them to where they were to get the food and then they had to pull the carts back to Kamiti. Even now, I remember what was done when I see a young girl like you.... We would leave the prison to dig the terraces. We took breakfast at 5:00 a.m. We had *uji* [boiled ground maize meal]; the girls would bring it from two miles away; then we took the *jembes* [hoes] and basins to dig the terraces; we were only women.... We got *ugali* [boiled ground maize meal] with boiled beans or boiled cabbage. We worked up to three then we took supper at four. After that we were locked in the house and one could go to wash. We were fed *ugali*, and it was not well cooked. If there were no beans or cabbage, we got only one boiled potato with the *ugali*.

Q: Was there any meat, eggs, milk or tea?

A: No! Even the children couldn't get these things. I am disappointed to hear that many people believe that women did nothing in the war; we buried the bodies. The children of Kamiti were tied with ropes together to be guarded while we women worked. They gradually died off. It was due to hunger. We suffered a lot from hunger.... Kamiti was a hell prison. Some were dying, some were beaten to death, sometimes they died after work. We were happy when someone died because we said "Now she is free!" I was still in Kamiti in 1956.[39]

Muthoni wa Gachie was detained in 1959. Her experiences were consistent with those recounted by other respondents. She talked of torture inflicted by the Homeguards.

515   Presley: The Mau Mau Rebellion

Q: Were you a leader?

A: Yes, even I was taken to prison.... When we were in detention the work was only to be beaten, given hard work and not enough food. We spent one week digging trees with other women.

Q: Why were you detained?

A: Because I was speaking about the Government.

Q: What did you say?

A: I was saying that Europeans should be taken to their homes and our children should be given education.

Q: How did the European know about you?

A: Other people reported me.

Q: Were you married then?

A: Yes.

Q: Did your children go to detention with you?

A: No, they were not in detention with me but they suffered because they lacked food, clothing and education.

Q: Was your husband involved?

A: He was also jailed but not put into detention.

Q: Who took care of the children while you were in jail and detention?

A: Only God. Our homes were burnt, cattle were taken, we were left with no clothing and wore banana leaves. Even that women gave birth on the way. We had nothing to help the child. We removed the headscarf to carry the child. Bottles were put in our private parts as a punishment.

Q: Where were you detained that they did these things?

A: Just here at Githunguri. The Homeguards were doing this.

Q: Were they doing this to make you admit Mau Mau?

A: They were doing this so that the Europeans could give them something.[40]

The fact that women were a significant portion of the prison population and that they were not accorded any special treatment because of gender is little known and rarely mentioned in the historiography of Mau Mau, although these facts were not hidden from public view during the Emergency. Indeed, the treatment of women prisoners caused a minor scandal in 1956 in Kenya and England. Eileen Fletcher, a former member of the Kamiti Prison staff, revealed the poor conditions and abuse by officials at Kamiti in her testimony before members of the House of Commons in London and in statements and interviews with the British press. She recounted that underage girls were wrongfully detained. In the course of several House of Commons debates on the subject, an official inquiry into the prison system was initiated (Presley 1986, 256-264; *Tribune* [London] 16 November 1956; *Daily Chronicle* [Nairobi] 31 May and 7 September 1956]. After the inquiry, annual reports on the conditions in the prisons included detailed information on the treatment of prisoners and the punishment or dismissal of wardens and staff for their mistreatment of prisoners.

Greater administrative attention to reporting on prison conditions was not enough, however, to ensure the end of abuse. The scandal involving the murder of eleven male detainees at the Hola Camp in 1959 finally brought an end to the detention system and the "pipeline" process of gradually releasing detainees from high to ever lower security facilities until finally they were released to their home villages.[41]

The Impact of Social Policy on Women's Nationalism

When the remaining women detainees were released and returned to their villages in 1960, they discovered that the Government had radically altered village life as a part of its war against Mau Mau. The campaign against women was a major part of this. This change was achieved through the villagization program. Initially begun as a punitive measure, the project became a centerpiece of social policy.[42] The turning point in defeating Mau Mau on the home front was achieved when activists or those suspected of being activists were rounded up. The entire Kikuyu population was semi-imprisoned in guarded villages. The importance of the villagization program in the defeat of Mau Mau was recognized in official circles. Addressing the Legislative Assembly in 1955, the Governor, Sir Evelyn Baring stated:

> ... it has been possible in many areas to arrange a system of movement control by which villagers going to work on their *shambas* [farms], or herding their cattle, do so under escort from either the Tribal Police or the Watch and Ward Units. It is the establishment of this system which in many areas has broken the physical contact with the gangs. The individual gangsters must often have hidden in a hole in a sisal hedge and have slipped out for a few minutes to tell a woman working in her field that food must be left at a certain place at a certain time or else there would be trouble. In this way the fear of the terrorist was maintained. Now, there can be no absolute certainty, but it appears probable that the new system has in most areas broken that physical contact and dissipated that fear.... As a result too, the flow of information from the villagers has greatly improved.[43]

The breaking of contact between villagers and Mau Mau fighters meant that women who were not imprisoned during the Emergency had their own intensive encounters with the regime. The object of these encounters was, of course, to defuse nationalism and curtail their Mau Mau activities. Just as in the prisons and detention camps, the main plank of the policy was the withholding and granting of benefits to sway the non-combatant wing away from radical nationalism. One of the consequences of being identified as Mau Mau was loss of land. The Government confiscated the land of Mau Mau members and reallocated it to "deserving Loyalists." The instrument for this policy was the Community Development Department. It was thought to have the potential for creating a true social revolution in the villages, its major goal being:

> ... to teach the women in the new villages a new way of life and to show them
> that the possibilities of community life in a smaller area offer better opportuni-
> ties for improved homes than the old scattered villages – as indeed they do.[44]

The relocation scheme was begun in 1954 and began to be phased out in 1958.[45] It involved the forced relocation of the entire Kikuyu population of the three Kikuyu districts in Central Province. More than eighty thousand Kikuyu households were uprooted in Kiambu District in 1954 and 1955. Also, more than seventeen thousand squatters who were ejected from the Rift Valley by settler farmers joined the Kikuyu who were required to live in the new villages.[46] For Kiambu District, the focus of my research, this involved over 300 000 men, women, and children. They were compelled to build new villages and tear down or abandon their homesteads. They lived under guard behind barbed-wire fences. To farm, women were escorted to their fields by the Homeguard. Everyone had to be back behind the barbed-wire fences by the 4:00 p.m. curfew.[47] In 1955 threats of the confiscation of land and the imposition of a twenty-four hour curfew were used in Kiambu District to break the "passive wing."

Abuse of villagers under the authority of the Homeguard was reported. Milka Ngina who spent the Emergency in the guarded villages recalled:

> A: We were beaten and forced to dig the terraces. They beat us very much and it
> was the Homeguard who did the beating.
> Q: Did you take the oath?
> A: Yes, I took very many, and we were beaten when we took the oath.
> Q: Were you put into detention?
> A: Some women were detained but not all of them.
> Q: Did Kenya become independent because of Mau Mau?
> A: Yes, because they bought the freedom with blood.
> Q: Did others in your family take the oath?
> A: All the Kikuyu took the oath at that time.
> Q: Was there any fighting around your home?
> A: Yes.
> Q: What happened?
> A: We were beaten by the Homeguard because the Mau Mau passed through
> our homes. I myself was almost beaten to death.
> Q: Why did the Homeguard help the British?
> A: We were beaten by the Homeguard because the Mau Mau were not on good
> terms with the Homeguard and those who were giving food were on good terms
> with the Mau Mau.[48]

Catherine Wajiru, who lived in Embu during the Emergency, was also exposed to the civil war between Mau Mau supporters and the Loyalists (Kikuyu seen as loyal to the colonial regime).

Q: Did you help the freedom fighters?

A: Yes.

Q: How did you help?

A: I gave them cooked food.

Q: Does that mean that there were freedom fighters in Embu?

A: Yes, they were there because they were living in the forest near us.

Q: Were you happy to give them food?

A: We gave them food because we had no security and if we refused to give them food, they could beat us.

Q: Were you living near Embu people?

A: Yes, we were mixed. We built the homes in the same place and we worked on the *shambas* with other groups.

Q: Did the Embu give food?

A: Yes, they did. They stopped giving them food when the villages were built but before that the Mau Mau would take goats and even cows by force. Also we were beaten by the colonials if they found that we were giving food. There were spies called Homeguard who would tell when you helped.

Q: Were you beaten?

A: Yes, I was beaten very much and my husband died during that time because of the beating.[49]

Villagization was successful in demoralizing the non-combatant wing. The African Affairs Department recorded:

The withdrawal of the surrender terms on 10 July was combined with local propaganda, so that at the end of June and the beginning of July the volume of confession swelled to such a degree that the teams were unable to cope. A very great deal of Mau Mau funds was handed in as well as guns and ammunition. The threat of confiscation of land, together with the imposition of 24-hour curfews also had a considerable effect in breaking the last efforts of the *Mau Mau* to conceal information. The confession teams in the settled areas ... had an extremely difficult job to begin with ... they subsequently achieved remarkable and effective results in breaking the passive wings on the farms and discovering the main gang bases or food depots.[50]

The major point of contact under these semi-concentration camp conditions was through the Community Development Department. Initially, most of the Department's annual budget of 250 000 pounds was spent on the work of rehabilitation.[51] The Department focused on women:

519   Presley: The Mau Mau Rebellion

In view of the large numbers of women and children to be found in these villages whose husbands are either serving sentences, detained, working in the
home guard, operating in the forests or living in the towns, the accent of rehabilitation must be on women.[52]

The Department's major vehicle for influencing women was through the
Maendeleo ya Wanawake (Progress among Women) clubs. The clubs had
begun in the late 1940s but did not have a significant membership until the
Emergency. Membership in the organization expanded tremendously during
the Emergency years since it could be the crucial difference between survival and starvation under the villagization program. The work of the clubs
included running day nurseries, making and supervising the distribution of
soup, distributing milk to hungry children, and "caring for children whose
parents were missing or dead."[53]

These humanitarian efforts were affected by the Emergency since the
"Work of Maendeleo clubs [was] hampered by subversive propaganda and
additional communal work necessary in the rehabilitation of and fortifying

TABLE 3
Maendeleo ya Wanawake Clubs

District	Clubs	Members
Army Camps	8	400
Kiambu	45	5 050
Fort Hall	35	3 250
Nyeri	100	7 500
Embu	25	1 250
Meru	1	20
Settled Areas	10	300
Naivasha	1	45
Thompson's Falls	1	85
Nairobi	5	400
Machakos	94	10 000
Other Districts	183	8 510
Total	508	36 810

SOURCE: Kenya Colony and Protectorate,
Community Development Department, AR /
1954, 13.

villages." The clubs were only able to meet after the four o'clock curfew.[54] The Department measured its success through the increase in membership. In 1954 the membership totalled 36 810 in 508 clubs (see Table 3). Kiambu women joined forty-five of the clubs with a membership of 5 050.[55] Forty-five percent of the members came from the three Kikuyu districts of Kiambi, Fort Hall and Nyeri, and Nairobi where Mau Mau activities were greatest.

In addition to administering to the needy, the Community Development programs were "responsible for internal broadcasting, libraries, the distribution of papers, classes, *barazas* [public gatherings], recreation and instruction in various forms."[56] The purpose of the education component of the program was to counteract Mau Mau by providing a course of "general knowledge."[57] Typically, this included bringing books, pamphlets, and a film truck to villages. This information stressed the positive benefits of colonialism and the evils of Mau Mau.[58] The Government viewed the clubs as "an effective instrument against subversive elements."[59]

In the guarded villages, the clubs were used to aid the security forces. Club members gathered information about Mau Mau activities and tried to persuade Mau Mau adherents to abandon the movement.[60] Women were told that they had to become allied with the Government rather than with Mau Mau. If they chose to remain publicly sympathetic to Mau Mau, they lost access to the services which the clubs offered.[61]

> In most areas where the backbone of Maendeleo clubs had been in existence since 1951-53, the club members have in many cases been of value to the Security forces giving information freely and persuading others to give up *Mau Mau*. In at least one case they played an important part in the capture of a *Mau Mau* general. The women realized that the ideals of *Maendeleo* and *Mau Mau* were incompatible and they would have to choose between them. It is very encouraging to note that the numbers of clubs and members in these areas are on the increase as more and more realize that *Mau Mau* has brought nothing but distress and sorrow.[62]

This persuasive message resulted in a tremendous growth in membership. By 1955 the number of clubs increased to 596 with a membership of 43 000.[63] The benefits of belonging or simply being associated with the clubs were particularly crucial in 1955 and 1956 when famine struck Kiambu District.[64] A scarcity of food was induced by the curfew, for women had fewer hours available to them in which to fetch water and fuel and to cultivate their fields.[65] During the famine, the 107 clubs in Kiambu District operated soup kitchens and increased their milk allotments.[66] In 1956 there were 34 500 fully paid members, in addition to 11 500 women who benefitted from the club services but were unable to pay the membership fees.[67] By the end of 1957, the number of clubs had grown to 986, but fully paid membership had declined to 33 613.[68]

One of the goals of the Community Development Department was to train Africans to be good citizens according to British standards. A byproduct of this was women's representation on the village and district councils. By 1955 "Maendeleo members [were] coming forward to take their place on locational and District Councils in greater numbers, so that in future there is hope that the voice of the women will be heard more and more."[69]

Conclusion

Viewing Mau Mau from the female perspective adds several important aspects to the understanding of the rebellion. It illuminates an often repeated statement that landless and less affluent Kikuyu were more likely to take part in Mau Mau whereas the better off Kikuyu publicly took sides with the British and joined the loyalist forces as Homeguards. In some families, women were deeply involved in Mau Mau while males publicly disassociated themselves from it. There are two possible explanations for this phenomenon. First, women's involvement with Mau Mau cut across "class" lines. Wives of prominent Kikuyu were jailed. At least one woman organizer was the wife of a chief. Second, women's involvement in radical nationalism expresses the ambiguity of prominent families' identification with Mau Mau. Males of such families might have silently supported Mau Mau while maintaining a public face as Loyalists. If men openly supported the rebellion, the consequence was loss of more land and privileges. This may have led to a perception that it was marginally safer for women to carry out the family's commitment to Mau Mau. The entire family need not then be impoverished by supporting it. A nationalist female, if arrested and detained, could be easily discredited and disowned. Whether this was deliberate family policy among a number of families is of course unknown. It may, however, explain some of the curious features of Mau Mau reported by the Government and uncovered in oral interviews. Specifically, it may explain the Government's contention that women were more rabid and fanatical, that men had stopped giving oaths, and that women were assuming these responsibilities. It may also explain the Government assertion that women of loyalist families were involved with Mau Mau. Mau Mau women reported to the author that their husbands, though considered loyal to the Government, knew of the aid they gave to the Mau Mau rebels and did not report them.

Women's participation in the violent Mau Mau revolt focused Government attention on the need to use some of its resources to develop programs to serve women and their needs. In order to defeat Mau Mau militarily, it was crucial for the British to isolate the guerilla fighters from their supplies. Mere isolation, however, was not sufficient. The non-combatant force, led and organized to a large degree by women, had to be engaged with force and persuasion. Thus, women were jailed in increasing numbers from 1954 to 1957. The increase occurred at the same time that the British victory over Mau Mau was assured. It is my contention that this was not mere coincidence, but that success in the war against women was a necessary ingredient in the war against Mau Mau. The campaign of propaganda and education was designed to convince women not already Mau Mau activists that disassociation from Mau Mau held positive rewards. First, the entire Kikuyu population was relocated to villages which were closely supervised by the Security Forces, the Homeguard, and the new Community Development Department. Within three years of this policy, a drop in Mau Mau activities occurred. The British government started a social revolution by providing an extensive social services program. Women were the first to be experimented upon since the Government recognized that they had to be detached from Mau Mau for final victory to occur. This had consequences for post-Mau Mau Kenya. The creation of the Community Development Department was the precursor of the Community Development Program in independent Kenya and, much later, the Women's Bureau. The contemporary Maendeleo ya Wanawake clubs also owe their origin to women's vigorous nationalism during Mau Mau. In the 1980s the Maendeleo clubs number over six thousand. Maendeleo is Kenya's largest women's organization (Ndumbu 1985, 86; Wipper 1975; Wipper 1975-76).

One reason for the lack of research on women's nationalism is that scholars followed the line taken by the colonial government. Until thousands of women were imprisoned for Mau Mau offenses, colonial administrators dismissed incidents which indicated that women were actively involved in resisting colonialism. In the case of labor stoppages and protests against terracing, district officers maintained that women's activism was caused by male agitators. Therefore, psychologically, the administrators were unprepared for women's protest. It seemed to them to be sudden, fanatical and unexpected.

Historians of Mau Mau have also treated women's nationalism as incidental to the main currents of nationalism. Their sources of data for the study of Mau Mau have been almost exclusively male, whether they were Europeans or Africans. The use of this data source and perspective has created the false paradigm that politics was mainly a male concern. Consequently, the questions posed to male respondents and the official records focus on the actions of men. When men did comment on women's involvement, it did not seem to be a major thread of the rebellion. In searching for answers to a political dilemma, scholars have naturally looked to those departments which had responsibility for political and economic issues. The full story of the colonial battle against women's nationalism is not revealed by political records, though important indicators occur there. In the social services area, even more revealing data surface. Since the colonial officials were trapped in their 1950s perceptions of women, they relegated policies dealing with women to community development. As the Community Development report noted, the voice of women began to be heard during the Mau Mau rebellion, although women had spoken out through their protest, be it on economic, political, or social issues, for over twenty years in colonial Kenya. When they took up arms and supported violent rebellion, their voices began to be heard. The legacy for contemporary Kenyans is to acknowledge women as equal partners in politics.

Notes

1. For a more extensive treatment of women's roles and contributions to the rebellion see Presley 1986c.

2. Kenya National Archives (KNA), Native Affairs Department (NAD), *Annual Report (AR) 1953*, 25; Kenya Colony and Protectorate (KCP), Community Development Department (CDD),*AR 1956*, 4.

3. The original Community Development staff included twenty-four European Rehabilitation Officers and thirty-seven African Rehabilitation Officers.

4. KNA. *Political Record Book, Kiambu District 1912*, KBU / 109 / Part II(K), 10; KNA. *Political Record Book, Kiambu District 1908-1912*, KBU / 76, 85-87).

5. For female circumcision see: KNA. NAD. *AR 1929*, 11-12; Rosberg 1966, 106-125; Murray 1974; Presley 1986a. For women's wage labor see Presley 1986b.

6. KNA, NAD, *AR 1953*, 25; KCP, African Affairs Department (AAD), Central Province (CP), *AR 1953*, 27.

7. KNA, NAD, *AR 1926*, 79, 87; KNA, NAD, *AR 1925*, 64.

8. KNA, *AR 1946*, KBU / 38, 1-2.

9. There is well documented evidence that Kikuyu women's public political activity predated Mau Mau by at least thirty years going back to the Harry Thuku Riot in 1922 (see Wipper 1988).

10. Interviews with former women nationalists conducted in 1978. The main women who described the organization of the women's network are: Wambui Wagarama, Nduta wa Kore, Phillis Wanjiko (Margo) wa Mimi, Priscilla Wambaki and Mary Wanjiko. See Presley 1986, 222-227.

11. I interviewed Kikuyu women nationalists in 1978. They told me of the development of women's nationalism. In 1930 women of Kiambu district formed their own nationalist association because they were excluded from formal participation in the KCA. After three years of organizing other women, they approached the Kiambaa branch of KCA and were able to persuade the leaders that women's organizational talents were indispensable to it. From then onwards, each location had a women's wing. See Presley 1986c.

12. Oath-taking by Kikuyu women appears to have occurred in the Harry Thuku movement in the early 1920s (see Wipper 1988).

13. KNA. *Political Record Book, Kiambu District 1953*, KBU / 44, 1.

14. KNA. AAD. CP. *AR 1953*, 27.

15. Interview on 10 January 1979 in Githunguiri, Kiambu District.

16. Interview on 29 April 1978 in Kiambu.

17. Interview on 13 May 1979 in Ruiru, Kiambu.

18. Kiriri was the women's dormitory at the Githunguri Independent School which was established by nationalists after the break with church and government controlled education which resulted from the circumcision controversy. Mbiyu Koinange and his father Sr. Chief Koinange were the driving forces behind changing the Githunguri School into the Kenya African Teachers College, an institution for the higher education of all Africans in Kenya. When it formally opened in 1939, there was a feeling among nationalistic Kikuyu that education was the key to political power (Rosberg and Nottingham 1966, 179-180).

19. Interview on 23 May 1979 in Juja, Kiambu. Madaraka Day marks the granting of internal self-government in 1963, about half a year before independence.

20. KCP. *Treatment of Offenders Annual Report 1957*, 10.

21. KCP. "Report on the General Administration of Prisons and Detention Camps in Kenya," by G. H. Heaton 1953, 3; KCP. *Report on the Treatment of Offenders for the year 1953*. 4; KCP. *Report on the Treatment of Offenders for the Year 1954*. 4.

22. KCP. *Report on the Treatment of Offenders for the year 1953*, 16-17.

23. KCP. *Treatment of Offenders Annual Report 1956*, 8-9.

24. KCP. CDD. *AR 1954*, 21-24; KCP. CDD. *AR 1955*, 22-26.

25. KCP. *Treatment of Offenders Annual Report 1955*, 2.

26. KCP. *Treatment of Offenders Annual Report 1955*, 2.

27. KCP. *Treatment of Offenders Annual Report 1956*, 2.

28. KCP. CDD. *AR 1956*, 6.

29. KCP. CDD. *AR 1954*, 30.

30. KCP. CDD. *AR 1956*, 4.

31. KCP. CDD. *AR 1955*, 22-23.

32. There were four categories: (1) Z1 – Mau Mau leaders who refused to respond to the rehabilitation program; (2) Z2 – rank and file who refused to renounce Mau Mau; (3) Y – those who responded to rehabilitation; and (4) X – those who were rehabilitated and placed on parole. See KCP. CDD. *AR 1956*, 3-6.

33. Oral interviews: Tabitha Mumbi, Thika, 24 May 1979; Elizabeth Gachika, Kiambu Town, 7 January 1979; Nduta wa Kore, Tingang'a, 13 January 1979; Wambui Wangarama, Kabete, 29 April 1979. See Presley 1986c for extensive oral interviews with Mau Mau women.

34. KCP. *Report on the Treatment of Offenders for the year 1953*. 4-5; KCP. *Treatment of Offenders Annual Report 1955*, 16, 18.

35. Convict labor was an important source of both income and supplies for the Department of Prisons. In 1953 the value of the agricultural produce raised by prisoners totalled £10 220. The amount of revenue received from prison industries amounted to £150 595, and £15 897 was given to the system as payment for using convict labor on the East African Railway, Harbour Administration, and other authorities. See KCP. *Report on the Treatment of Prisoners for the year 1953*, 14-15. In Kamiti, the value of vegetables raised by female prisoners was £1 973 in 1956. See KCP. *Treatment of Offenders Annual Report 1956*. 14-15.

36. KCP. *Treatment of Offenders Annual Report 1955*, 15.

37. KCP. *Treatment of Offenders Annual Report 1956*, 14.

38. KCP. *Report on the Treatment of Offenders. Kenya Prisons for the year 1954*, 11.

39. Interview 23 May 1979 at Juja, Kiambu.

525   Presley: The Mau Mau Rebellion

40. Interview 10 January, 1979, Githunguri, Kiambu.
41. KNA. *Records of Proceedings and Evidence into the Deaths of Eleven Mau Mau Detainees at Hola Camp in Kenya*, 1959; Rosberg and Nottingham 1966, 335-344.
42. KCP. AAD. CP. *AR 1954*, 33.
43. KCP. *Legislative Council Debates* 18 October 1955, 4.
44. KCP. CDD. *AR 1954*, 31.
45. KCP. CDD. *AR 1958*, 7.
46. KCP. AAD. CP. *AR 1955*, 35, 51.
47. KNA. CDD. *AR 1957*, 33; KNA. AAD. *AR 1954*. 33.
48. Interview 11 May, 1979, Kiambu town.
49. Interview with Catherine Wajiru, Kitambaya, Kiambu, 11 May 1979.
50. KCP. AAD. *AR 1955*, 37.
51. KCP. CDD. *AR 1955*, 1.
52. KCP. CDD. *AR 1954*, 31.
53. KCP. CDD. *AR 1955*, 7.
54. KCP. CDD. *AR 1955*, 7.
55. KCP. CDD. *AR 1954*, 13.
56. KCP. CDD. *AR 1955*, 25.
57. KCP. CDD. *AR 1955*, 25.
58. KCP. CDD. *AR 1952*, 9; KCP. CDD. *AR 1956*. 1-10.
59. KCP. CDD. *AR 1954*, 12-13.
60. KCP. CDD. *AR 1955*, 7. These activities caused the Maendeleo movement to be severely stigmatized among the Kikuyu in the early period of independence. (See Wipper 1975-76, 199-204.)
61. KCP. CDD. *AR 1955*, 7.
62. KCP. CDD. *AR 1955*, 7.
63. KCP. CDD. *AR 1955*, 12.
64. KCP. AAD. CP. *AR 1955*, 48.
65. The connection to the Emergency conditions and the famine in the district is clear. No mention is made in the colonial records of famine in other parts of Kenya in 1956.
66. KCP. CDD. *AR 1956*, 13-14.
67. KCP. CDD. *AR 1956*. 10.
68. KCP. CDD. *AR 1957*, 8.
69. KCP. CDD. *AR 1955*. 6.

Bibliography

Barnett, Donald and K. Njama. 1966. *Mau Mau From Within: Autobiography and Analysis of Kenya's Peasant Revolt*. New York and London: Monthly Review Press.

Buijenthuis, Robert. 1982. *Essays on Mau Mau: Contributions to Mau Mau Historiography*. Leiden: African Studies Centre No. 17.

————. 1973. *Mau Mau Twenty Years After: The Myth of the Survivors*. The Hague-Paris: Mouton.

Clayton, Anthony. 1976. *Counter-Insurgency in Kenya. 1952-60*. Nairobi: TransAfrica Publishers.

Clayton, Anthony and Donald Savage. 1974. *Government and Labour in Kenya. 1895-1963*. London: Frank Cass.

Coray, Michael. 1978. "The Kenya Land Commission and the Kikuyu of Kiambu."
    Agricultural History 52, no. 1: 179-193.
Corfield, F.D. 1960. *Historical Survey of the Origins and Growth of Mau Mau*. Lon-
    don: HMSO (Cmnd 1030).
Furedi, Frank. 1974. "The Social Composition of the Mau Mau Movement in the
    White Highlands." *Journal of Peasant Studies* 1, no. 4: 486-505.
————. 1975. "The Kikuyu Squatters in the Rift Valley, 1918-1929." *Hadith* 5: 177-
    194.
Furley, Q.W. 1972. "The Historiography of Mau Mau," *Hadith* 4: 105-133.
Great Britain. 1954. *Colonial Office Report on the Colony and Protectorate of Kenya*.
    London: HMSO.
Kamunchulah, J.T. 1975. "The Meru Participation in Mau Mau." *Kenya Historical
    Review* 3, no. 2: 193-216.
Kanogo, Tabitha. 1987. *Squatters and the Roots of Mau-Mau 1905-1963*. Columbus:
    Ohio University Press.
Kilson, Martin. 1955. "Land and the Kikuyu: A Study of the Relationship Between
    Land and Kikuyu Political Movements." *Journal of Negro History* 40: 103-153.
Leakey, L.S.B. 1952. *Mau Mau and the Kikuyu*. London: Methuen & Company.
————.1954. *Defeating Mau Mau*. London: Methuen and Company.
Majdalany, F. 1963. *State of Emergency: The Full Story of Mau Mau*. Boston: Hough-
    ton Mifflin Company.
Mungai, Evelyn and Joy Awori. 1983. *Kenya Women Reflections*. Nairobi: Lear Pub-
    lishing Co.
Murray, Jocelyn. 1974. "The Kikuyu Female Circumcision Controversy with Special
    Reference to the Church Missionary Society's 'Sphere of Influence.'" Ph.D. thesis,
    University of California, Los Angeles.
Ndumbu, Abel. 1985. *Out of My Rib: A View of Women in Development*. Nairobi:
    Development Horizons.
Newsinger, John. 1981. "Revolt and Repression in Kenya: The 'Mau Mau' Rebellion,
    1952-1960." *Science and Society* 45, no. 2: 159-185.
Ogot, B. A. 1972. *Politics and Nationalism in Colonial Kenya*. Nairobi: East African
    Publishing House.
Presley, Cora. 1986a. "The Transformation of Kikuyu Women and their National-
    ism." Ph.D. thesis, Stanford University, Stanford, California.
————. 1986b. "Labor Protest Among Kikuyu Women, 1912-1947." In *Women, Race
    and Class in Africa*, edited by Claire Robertson and Iris Berger. New York: Holmes
    and Meier Press.
————. 1986c. "Women in the Mau Mau Rebellion." In *In Resistance: Studies in Afri-
    can, Afro-American and Caribbean Resistance*, edited by Gary Okihiro. Amherst:
    University of Massachusetts Press.
Rosberg, Carl and John Nottingham. 1966. *The Myth of Mau Mau: Nationalism in
    Kenya*. New York-Washington: Frederick A. Praeger.
Sorrenson, M.P.K. 1967. *Land Reform in the Kikuyu Country*. London: Oxford Uni-
    versity Press.
Spencer, John. 1974. "The Kikuyu Central Association and the Genesis of Kenya Afri-
    can Union." *Kenya Historical Review* 2, no. 1: 67-79.
————. 1985. *The Kenya African Union*. London: KPI Limited.
Stichter, Sharon. 1975. "Workers, Trade Unions and the Mau Mau Rebellion." *Cana-
    dian Journal of African Studies* 9, no. 2: 259-275.

527   Presley: The Mau Mau Rebellion

Tamarkin, M. 1976. "Mau Mau in Nakuru." *Journal of African History* 17, no. 1: 119-134.

———. 1978. "Loyalists in Nakuru During the Mau Mau Revolt and its Aftermath." *Asian and African Studies* 12, no. 2: 247-261.

Temu, A.J. 1972. *British Protestant Missions.* London: Longman Group.

Tignor, Robert. 1976. *The Colonial Transformation of Kenya: The Kamba, Kikuyu and Maasai from 1900 to 1939.* Princeton: Princeton University Press.

Wipper, Audrey. 1975. "The Maendeleo ya Wanawake Organization – The Co-optation of Leadership." *African Studies Review* 18, no. 3: 329-355.

———. 1975-76. "The Maendeleo ya Wanawake Movement in the Colonial Period: The Canadian Connection, Mau Mau, Embroidery and Agriculture." *Rural Africana*: 195-214.

———. 1988. "Kikuyu Women and the Harry Thuku Disturbance: Some Uniformities of Female Militancy." *Africa* 59, no. 3: forthcoming.

Zimbabwe

[11]

THE EFFECTS OF THE WAR
ON THE RURAL POPULATION
OF ZIMBABWE

by T.J.B. Jokonya

The guerrilla war in Rhodesia had been raging since 1966. In the last few years it had intensified with every increasing ferocity with the result that hundreds and thousands of victims have streamed from war zones, which cover more than 80 percent of the country. These peasants had left their homes to trek across the borders of neighboring countries either voluntarily to sign up in nationalist revolutionary movements or simply to escape from certain death. Others had fled into Rhodesian towns and cities after their homes had been destroyed and here they arrive

> with the clothes they wear, clutching the few odds and ends they have
> managed to salvage from the devastation they have left behind.[1]

The inhumanity that had resulted from the bitter struggle between the liberation forces and the White racist regime had reached an alarming proportion. The extent of the atrocities in the Rhodesian conflict prompted the International Committee of the Red Cross (ICRC) to issue a press statement through A. Hay, its President, on Tuesday, March 20, 1979 in which he appealed to all the parties to the conflict to respect and observe fundamental humanitarian principles. In particular the ICRC requested the

> Transitional Government in Salisbury to put an end to the executions of
> captured members of the nationalist forces and of persons sentenced to
> death for offences of a political character: to allow the ICRC delegates
> to visit, in their places of detention, all captured members of the
> nationalist forces, political detainees, persons detained under marshal
> law, and civilians forcibly removed from their homes in the war affected
> areas and temporarily detained in camps . . .[2]

The suffering, whether in the form of murders, massacres, maimings, and deprivation is likely to have, indeed is already having long term effects which have transformed a whole way of life of the peasant population within the lifetime of an individual. These changes, their causes and ramifications that have occurred throughout the core of rural Zimbabwe have left a permanent mark on the history of this country. It is this change that we have termed "the proletarianisation of the peasants." The title is a poor translation of a famous Zimbabwean artist T. Mapfumo's famous song, *Chirizevha Chapera* (which translated literally means: The End Of The Tribal Trust Lands).[3]

In examining the effects of the war on the rural peasants we are aware that such an emotive current topic may not be ideal for an academic international seminar more so because it is extremely difficult to get objective oral evidence and concrete written source material. Be this as it may the exercise is a useful historical undertaking.

Before looking at the causes and ramifications of this tragic conflict it may be useful to state the implication of proletarianisation of the peasant in the context of the Zimbabwe conflict. The term proletariate in its Marxist sense is defined in several ways depending on the orientation of individual authors. For the purposes of this paper we shall accept S. Stichter's definition of proletariate or working class — where he sees the notion of class structurally referring to a social category defined by its relation to the various means of production or of administration. He also sees class concept in a social sense, referring to "class-related consciousness and action, especially political-economic action on the individual and collective levels." Structurally then Stichter defines the working class as "those who have no access to, or do not make use of their access to, productive means, but who instead sell their labor-power for a wage on the market."[4] This definition is very similar to Engel's own definition which refers to the proletariat's "Weal and Woe," life and death, and whole existence being dependent upon the demand for labor.[5] It is on this concept of proletariat that Marx developed his belief that the working class constituted the vanguard of the revolution. The definition quite clearly excludes the Zimbabwe peasants although in its revolutionary context it was modified by such Marxists as Lenin and Mao who saw the peasants as having an important revolutionary role as allies of the working class. Indeed Fanon goes as far as reversing the revolutionary roles of these two classes in developing countries. As far as he is concerned it is the poor peasants, not the workers, who are the wretched of the earth. The native proletariat enjoying a privileged and comparatively well-remunerated position have everything to lose in a war of national liberation.[6] Fanon's view is a subject of controversy among Marxists but in terms of the objective conditions in the Zimbabwe struggle there can be no doubt that it is the peasants who are the revolutionary class.

Coming back to our problem of the war refugees it would appear that they fall within some of Stichter's criteria on the definition of a proletariat insofar as they have been deprived of access to productive means. We shall return to this much

Effects of the War on the Rural Population of Zimbabwe 135

later in this paper. A more embracing concept of the proletariat which would include the peasants who have been displaced by the war may be that put forward by W. Elkan in *Migrants and Proletarians*. Elkan sees migrant proletarians as short term migrant workers who constitute the bulk of the unskilled urban workers, those who perpetually revolve between country and urban centers, permanent town dwellers and, finally, those who have made town their home. The last group, Elkan suggests,

> are to all intents and purposes proletarians, but who yet retire eventually to the countryside and much of whose urban life is given up to laying plans for this eventuality.[7]

Looking at these categories it would seem that Zimbabwe war refugees fall into at least two of them and are therefore proletarians. But before we can finally classify these war victims it is necessary to examine the causes and effects of this exodus from the country to urban centers.

At the beginning of this paper we suggested that the war of liberation which had been raging since 1966 had led to misery and complete transformation in the lives of rural population. One of the common features of man is the process of adaptation to changed circumstances. Guevara in his *Reminiscences* made this point succinctly when he said that in a state of war,

> the individual must undergo an adaptation to enable him to resist the bitter experience that threatens his tranquility.[8]

In Zimbabwe the migration to neighboring states and to urban centers constituted this process. A close examination of the activities of the combatants will show why they had to flee or perish.

The launching of the war of liberation by nationalist movements in 1966 marked the beginning of an era in Zimbabwe. We shall not go into the root causes of the conflict here. What is important is that from the very first time that the war of liberation was launched the rural population almost everywhere recognized what the exponents of the regime called "Terrs" (short for Terrorists) as comrades in misfortune if not in the struggle. The use of the endearing word (vanaMukoma, "the Brothers") to describe forces of liberation clearly shows the comradship between the peasants and the revolutionaries. The regime's security forces responded with ruthlessness and brutality which has alarmed even its admirers. Terror was unleashed on the peasants beyond the normal requirements of the enforcement of law and order. The story of counterinsurgency by Rhodesian security forces is a catalogue of the most unscrupulous brutality. We shall examine a few of these to make our point, i.e., the Makoni, the Gutu, the Nyamaropa, and Domboshawa incidents.

In the Makoni Tribal Trust Land there was a *kurovaguva* (a Shona rite performed sometimes after burial) gathering. While people were gathered, helicopters appeared, shots were fired, and explosives thrown at them. One of the people inside the house came out with his hands up and called the others to do the same. The majority of the people came out with their hands raised and stood around the body of their relation who had been killed, but a few ran into a maize field nearby. Shots were fired from the helicopter into the maize field and a number of security forces who had apparently been dropped from the helicopters approached the village. The villagers shouted at them to stop shooting, pointing out that they were merely performing formal rites. The security forces ordered some men into the maize field to bring out the bodies of those who had been killed. All in all seven people had been killed. When a priest who performed funeral services asked the security forces why they had killed people the authorities simply said, that it was "an unfortunate incident."

On the evening of May 14, 1979, the now infamous "Gutu massacre" took place. On this evening people of Gutu Tribal Trust Land (TTL) and Devure Purchase Area were called to a meeting by some eight to 10 freedom fighters. From evidence solicited from the survivors it is not clear whether people came willingly or they were forced. What is important is that the guerrillas were armed and when peasants are summoned by armed men whether they are guerrillas, security forces, or auxilliaries, only the fool would refuse to attend. Although there were about eight guerrillas in the village only one addressed the crowd, estimated between 160 and 200 people. The rest of the guerrillas were apparently guarding the place from a distance. Security forces eventually came to the scene and one shot is reported to have been fired by the guerrilla who also called out to people to lie down. There was a pause and then an eye witness heard the order "Fire!" and a burst of heavy firing ensued. The shooting appeared to be directed at the prostrate crowd. A hand grenade or "something that gave out a bright light" was thrown at the crowd by the security forces. Survivors say there were no guerrillas present in the crowd save the one who had been addressing the crowd. The security forces were said to be shooting at such close range they must have seen there was only one guerrilla and that they were shooting at unarmed civilians. The survivor who gave us this version says he owed his life to the fact that the two dead people lay on top of him.[9]

As in many such incidences that have occurred in the Zimbabwe conflict it is difficult to get an exact picture of what happened. The number of people killed at Devure is given as 50 by the security forces and eye witnesses quote figures of 74, 120, and sometimes as high as 150. The Annual Report of the Gwelo Diocese who were involved in relief work after the event implied that many more people died than were reported. It states that

> The number reported from Gutu includes children and juveniles whereas the other 67 victims are mostly adults who were reported because help was needed for the dependents. This implies that the number of people killed is much greater.[10]

There does not seem to be any doubt that at least 67 people were killed and, if as the report from the Diocese of Gwelo suggest 67 of these were adults the figure of well over 100 would appear to be correct. The Government Press statement read as follows:

Effects of the War on the Rural Population of Zimbabwe 137

> In the resulting fire-fight 50 curfew breakers were killed, and another 24 wounded.[11]

There are facts about this incident which are indisputable. It is certain that despite the claim by the authorities there were no curfew breakers since the meeting was held in the village between houses. None of the dead people were killed in crossfire as the guerrillas did not direct the fire at the security forces and as has now since been proved only one and not more than two or three shots were fired by the guerrillas and these injured no one. It is indisputable that as a result of the orders given by the security forces at least over 60 people were killed. People who were seriously wounded were left unattended until long after the event. It is significant that the black parties in the Transitional Government all condemned the action of the security forces and demanded an independent inquiry to no avail.

The Domboshawa incident was not very different from that of Devure. On June 10, 1978, security forces attacked a guerrilla position on a hill near Domboshawa in Chinamhora Tribal Trust Land. One guerrilla ran into a village and security forces mounted a ground to air attack killing 22 people — 19 of them were women and children — and of these, nine were burned to death inside a hut and 11 were shot inside a kitchen. Once again there was no question of curfew breaking or people being caught in crossfire.[12] On August 9, 1978, yet another incident took place at Nyamaropa Village where people had gathered at the funeral of a well known teacher. On the instructions of the local people a red flag was flying to indicate the nature of the gathering. Despite this security forces came and attacked the villagers in a ground and air operation. At least 10 people died instantly and many others were wounded. The ground forces then ordered people to bury the dead in communal graves. Many of the injured were taken to a hospital where about 10 people died bringing the total death toll to 20. This incident was not reported in any military communique nor was it reported in the local press.[13] The disregard for human rights on the part of the security forces here extended to the disposal of the dead.

There can be no doubt that brutality of the security forces were calculated to instill fear in the hearts of the peasants in order to stop them from supporting the guerrillas. Even the regime's ministers fully approved the indiscriminate operations against the rural population. P. van der Byl, Minister of defense, in 1976 demonstrated this when he said,

> If the villagers harbor terrorists and terrorists are found running about in villages, naturally they will be bombed and destroyed in any manner which the commander on the spot considers to be desirable in the suitable prosecution of a successful campaign . . . Where the civilian population involves itself with terrorism, then somebody is bound to get hurt and one can have little sympathy for those who are mixed up with the terrorists when finally they receive the wrath of the security forces.[15]

This kind of attitude from a Minister of Defense shows that in the prosecution of the war the normal respect for human beings as laid down under the Geneva

Convention did not apply. The failure to respect customary law that we saw in the Nyamaropa incident was extended in other areas. Often bodies of Africans killed by security forces were displayed to villagers as a warning to others. There have been several cases of this inhumane treatment of the dead. Hodges, for example, cites a case in Belingwe TTL where five bodies were displayed in Chief Mapirawana's Kraal.[16] Again the Minister appears to have supported these barbaric acts. On July 31, 1975, speaking in Parliament the Minister of Defense told MPs:

> As far as I am concerned, the more curfew-breakers that are shot the
> better, and the sooner it is realized everywhere the better.[17]

The reaction of the security forces must be seen in the light of the activities and successes of the guerrillas to disrupt civil administration in the TTLs. White District Officers and maintenance personnel have found their normal life impossible. In many cases they have lost their lives. Looking at the civil administration it is significant that by mid-1978 no less than 3,000 "non combatants" had lost their lives in the war. These figures included some 114 personnel of the Department of Internal Affairs killed on duty, 25 missing or abducted, and 243 wounded.[18] The campaign of the guerrillas to disrupt civil administration has been the most successful aspect of their struggle against the Smith Regime. Wilkinson commenting on this aspect of the war stated that in the early stages the administration

> appeared to have been thrown off its balance by the suddenness of
> attacks and the significant degree of support the guerrillas had secured
> among the local population.[19]

The efforts of the administration to cope with the war were not confined to military operations and the "shoot on sight" policy towards curfew-breakers that we have examined. Administrative arrangements were devised which were equally vicious and disruptive to normal life. In particular the laws which had been introduced in the name of "the preservation of law and order" in the 1960s were amended in order to cope with the new situation. The Emergency Powers Act and the Law and Order Maintenance Act constituted the lynch-pin of the legal precautions. The former was amended no less than 32 times and the later 12 times since 1965.[20] These amendments brought about such penalties as death or life imprisonment for acts of terrorism, failure to report the presence of the guerrillas, and supplying them with food. Other measures added to strengthen the draconian laws were the granting of powers to Provincial Commissioners to impose collective fines on communities in which contact with guerrillas were suspected. These punishments and fines have taken a different form in different TTLs. In Chiweshe and Masembura, for example, cattle were confiscated and in many cases entire villages were burned down by the security forces and the residents were subjected to brutal treatment. Reports of rape and burning of granary have been received from different parts of the country.[21] District Commissioners have also been empowered, since 1974, to recruit local residents in so-called "Border Zones" for

Effects of the War on the Rural Population of Zimbabwe   139

forced labor to build roads, bridges, fences, and as if this was not enough, District Commissioners have been given power to

> inflict corporal punishment on anyone who behaves in a contemptuous [sic] manner towards the District Commissioner and his staff.[22]

Another administrative device of the regime that disrupted rural life and caused tremendous hardships socially and economically was the "Resettlement Program." The idea started before U.D.I. during the federation days when 113,000 Africans were removed from TTLs to make way for White Settlers. The Tangwena case which received much international publicity was one of the programs. Other cases such as the removal of 8,000 peasants from Victoria Province to Gokwe in the late 1960s were equally significant albeit less publicized.[23] The resettlement program was however not as comprehensive as the creation of Protected Villages (PVs) or "Strategic Hamlets" which constituted the regime's most oppressive measure against the peasant population. The PVs, which Africans call Keeps, were set up from 1973 to 1977 in response to fairly successful operations by the Zimbabwe African National Liberation Army (ZANLA) in the North East, East, Southern, and lately Central Mashonaland. During this period no less than 203 protected villages were set up and well over half a million people were crowded into these neo-concentration camps. The areas mostly affected were the TTLs in the operational area. The table below gives a synopsis of this program. The total number of PVs is believed to have reached the 220 mark by the middle of 1978 occupying an area extending from the North East, East, Southern to Central Mashonaland, and Western operational zone.[24]

The creation of the PVs was seen by the authority as an evil necessity which would facilitate military operations. The British had used this method in Malaya in suppressing the post-World War II Malayan disturbances and later in Kenya against the Mau Mau Movement. In Mozambique the Portuguese had unsuccessfully used the Aldeamentos against Frelimo. The Rhodesian regime stated that the aim of the PVs was to protect peasants from guerrillas and to isolate the latter from their source of food, shelter, information, and recruits. While the last reason was genuine, the question of protecting peasants from guerrillas was a piece of propaganda. It is doubtful that the regime was at any time seriously concerned about the security of the Villagers whom they indiscriminately bombed and oppressed. Weinrich ridiculed this whole idea of protection when she said that

> protected villages are built in such a way that the only persons really protected are the European administrators and the African attendants.[26]

The so-called protected villages are nothing short of death traps for the poor Africans. In *From Rhodesia to Zimbabwe* Bratton gives a vivid description of the PVs. According to him the size of a plot alloted to each family is 15 square yards and here the peasants were to build a house and a latrine and to keep poultry. He goes on to say,

> sanitary facilities are primitive; typhoid and diarrhoea are not
> uncommon. The movement of the rural population in and out of
> protected villages, is closely monitored by means of regular
> identification checks and by a dusk-to-dawn curfew. Food may not
> leave or keep.[27]

This neo concentration camp then is the regime's idea of protecting the peasants.
The rural people have never hidden their dislike for the PVs. Our discussion with
ex-PV residents clearly revealed a near pathological hatred for this so-called
protection.[28] Only paid officials of the regime have piously expressed gratitude for
the so-called protection. A government spokesman revealed this hatred in April
1977 when he said that the peasants refuse to budge,

> But we have been forced to press-gang them. We take a truck to them
> and say: Get your sewing machine on the back of that truck. You are
> moving whether you like it or not.[29]

The result of the regime's policy will probably never be fully realized for some
time to come. While international agencies like the ICRC, Christian Care, Catholic
Social Service Department (CSSD), and others have consistently pointed to the
inhumanity in the PV program the regime continues to pursue it ferociously. The
draconian laws, the resettlement program, and the PVs have been buttressed by a
scorched earth policy. Bratton says of this policy that

> at the time of resettlement, existing villages and crops have been put to
> the torch or poisoned. Cattle have been summararily sold. The money is
> retained by the state, in part to purchase food for residents of the Keeps,
> in yet another manifestation of the perverse Rhodesian interpretation of
> self-help.[30]

Needless to say that the scorched earth policy has led to the destruction of the
peasant mode of production. In addition the imposition of curfew in operational
areas and marshall law in 90 percent of the country has made normal economic
activity impossible in rural areas. It has also cut the rural population from its other
supplementary source, the supply from urban centers where relatives used to bring
money and additional food. This very carefully planned program of repression has
made rural areas uninhabitable. T. Mapfumo, the Shona artist graphically
depicted this in his famous song "Chirizevha Chapera"* for which he was rewarded
by a term of imprisonment. Weinrich in her "Strategic Resettlement in Rhodesia"
has shown that in such areas as Chiweshe TTL agricultural production has
collapsed as a result of government policy.[31]

The exodus of people from the rural areas which we have called the
proletarianisation of the peasants is a direct product of the policy of the regime and
of the war situation as a whole. Harrassed by the forces of "law and order"
thousands of people have simply left their homes to seek shelter either in urban
centers or in neighboring countries. The fear that government policy engendered in
the hearts of the rural population was revealed in a series of interviews that the
Rhodesia Herald had with war refugees from different parts of the country. For

Effects of the War on the Rural Population of Zimbabwe 141

example, on February 12, 1979, a woman from Siyoka TTL in Beitbridge alleged that she and her children had left home four months ago, "our homes were burned down and we were beaten up." When asked when she thought she would go back she said "I am not going back home again. I would rather starve in town than go back."[32] A 35-year-old woman from Kezi came to Bulawayo with seven children because they could not plow in their fields. "Because of the fear when you hear a knock in the night and you do not know who is knocking." A Wankie man said he had a lot of cattle at home, "But I find I cannot even pay school fees for my children." A 62-year-old man summed up the whole problem when he said, "There is war at home. If the sun sets while you are in the bush, you climb up a tree and sleep there. You won't fall asleep easily because you are afraid you might fall off, but it is better to lose sleep than die."[33]

One could go on reciting the experience of individuals in the war torn rural areas. What is clear from all these accounts is that although the general state of the war as well as the action of guerrillas in some areas caused a revolution in rural areas the policy of the regime must take pride of place in the exodus of people. The difference between government policy and the action of guerrillas is that the latter's strategy, particularly in ZANLA operational areas, was aimed at stiffing the scorched earth policy of the regime. The stated policy of the liberation forces was to subvert the extension of the regime's state apparatus into rural areas. They did this by opposing civil administration, carrying out political education at the "Pungwes" (political meetings usually held at night) where people were advised to refuse payment of council tax, school fees, cattle tax, and forced labor. Hodges says by 1977 this policy had affected no less than 36,000 children and 494 teachers in Manicaland alone.[34] Cattle-dipping programs had collapsed and government-owned bottle stores and beer halls had been burned to the ground. On May 23, 1977, Peter Parsons admitted that African councils had been put under judicial management of local district commissioners because, "councillors' lives have been threatened and all the councils have been on the verge of collapse."[34] The opposition to civil administration has been intensified and now covers the entire rural area of Rhodesia. In August 1978 the *Rhodesia Herald* reported that 947 African schools with a population of 231,550 had closed.[35] We should point out here that in some selected areas the government itself ordered closure of schools, hospitals, stores, and other institutions "in order for the police and soldiers to be able to do their work properly."[36] Whatever the intentions of the combatants in the Rhodesian conflict has each side intensified its policy so did the suffering of the people increase. The movement of people into urban centers was in relation to the degree of this suffering.

As we stated earlier the number of people who fled to urban centers or neighboring countries is difficult to estimate. Because the government has not considered the whole issue a national problem it has not used its resources to assess the nature and magnitude of the problem. Indeed the whole war refugee problem has been left to voluntary agencies. The other reason why accurate figures cannot be obtained is that the movement is a continuous process. The rough estimates made by voluntary agencies clearly show that Umtali as a frontier city has relatively more war refugees than any other town. In 1978 the community services department estimated that Umtali probably had 30,000 war refugees living in the townships of Sakubva and Dangamvura.[37] Bulawayo, the second city, was not as badly affected as Umtali. R. Mtombeni, field officer of ICRC, said the number of refugees under their relief program had risen to 2,000 by February 1979. This represents a fairly small fraction of the actual total as Mtombeni himself pointed out when he said "This is only the tip of the iceberg, as our statistics take into account only those who have registered for aid with us."[38] Gwelo and the Midland Townships have even more acute problems than Bulawayo. The Catholic Diocese of Gwelo in its Annual Report pointed out that

> The refugees' problem in Gwelo is continuously growing and we have
> brought this to the attention of the ICRC . . .[39]

In January 1979 the Gwelo City Council was alarmed by the growing war refugee problem. A. Smart, the town clerk, called for a national policy in dealing with this serious problem. He pointed out that the whole issue was particularly acute in towns like Redcliff, Rutendo, and Torwood because of their proximity to operational TTLs.[40]

Salisbury probably comes a close second to Umtali in hosting war refugees. Like in other urban centers no accurate figures exist. In July 1978 the *Rhodesia Herald* reported that the capital had a daily inflax of 400 war refugees. In March of the same year the recorded number of war squatters in Harare alone was 1,190 and by June that figure had gone up to 4,000.[41] This figure represents a small fraction of war refugees in Harare. As far back as 1977 the government had a cleared area in the Old Bricks area of 9,800 families.[42] If we take the average size of the family as five, which is a conservative figure, then the number of refugees in the Old Bricks area alone would be no less than 49,000. The attempt to forcibly move people from Harare meant that many became what Ben Maclean called the "Invisible" community of squatters.[43] W. Chinuku, Coordinating Officer of ICRC in Salisbury believes that the war refugees in Salisbury alone number between 25,000 and 30,000, a figure which he says excludes refugees in Chitungwiza[44] which are probably a lot more than this figure. The picture that emerges then from this survey of the war refugee problem is that even without accurate statistical facts there are no less than at least 100,000 rural peasants in Rhodesian urban centers who are victims of the war.

The number of war refugees is much greater than this nationally. There are many more rural people in neighboring African countries than are found in the country's towns and cities. Again as with the exodus into towns and cities the actual number of Rhodesian refugees in Zambia, Botswana, and Mozambique is not known. The Trustees of the African Fund in a leaflet entitled *Zimbabwe Refugees From Injustice* estimated the number of Rhodesian refugees as 70,000.[45] On February 10,

Effects of the War on the Rural Population of Zimbabwe 143

1979, the *Herald* reported that some 400 refugees were being airlifted daily into Zambia from Botswana. "Most of them able-bodied young men of military age."[46] These were part of a contingent of 10,000 who were living in a transit camp. The United Nations High Commission for refugees announced in Gaborones in May 1979 that, "By the end of April there were 19,800 Rhodesian refugees in Botswana."[47] The latest estimate of refugees from Rhodesia given by the Catholic Institute for International Research who, through its sister organization the Zimbabwe Project, gives aid to refugees from Rhodesia is 45,000 in Zambia, 80,000 in Mozambique, and 28,000 in Botswana, making a total of 153,000.[48] The figure is almost certainly higher than this since the inflax into these countries is continuous. In any case the registered number does not take into account many refugees who do not declare themselves. These usually enter the country and attach themselves to relatives who are working in Zambia. This international dimension of the effects of the war on the rural population also excludes the number of men who have voluntarily left their homes to enlist in the national liberation struggle which is easily within the region of 35,000 ZANLA and 20,000 Zimbabwe African Peoples Revolutionary Army (ZIPRA). The Rhodesian conflict thus means that no less than 333,000 people have moved from the rural areas into towns and cities or neighboring countries. This represents a substantial part of the country's population and if, as this paper assumes the majority of them will not return to the rural areas after the war then the process of proletarianisation is indeed revolutionary.

Before we return to this question it may be useful to note that the sufferings that the rural population has endured at the hands of the security forces either as a result of the "scorched earth policy," the PV program, or the reprisals metted out to so-called "curfew breakers" or non observance of marshall law regulations has not been miligated by their migration to urban centers. The government which claimed to have the interests of the people in the PV program did not worry about these war victims when they came into town. The press, voluntary agencies, and black members of parliament unsuccessfully urged the government to stop being "complacent and callous" toward refugees.[49] The state of the refugees at Musika near the city's largest bus terminal in particular became the symbol of the suffering of these displaced people. The *Rhodesia Herald* describing their state graphically exposed their misery when it stated

> at night they put up flimsy plastic shelters which are their sole protection from cold. In the pathetic shelters families huddle together — father, mother, and children in an area hardly bigger than a simple bed blanket would cover.[50]

These shelters for which the unfortunate people are charged $1 by the local authority are pulled down every morning. At the time of writing the *Herald* note that there were two exceptions to this daily routine and they owed

> their reprieve to two babies whom they protect under their tottering

roofs. In one is a baby born only a week ago, and in another is a month old baby.[51]

The only form of help that these people had whether in Salisbury or in any other part of the country came from voluntary relief agencies. In particular the ICRC, Christian Care, and CSSD. Christian Care's Salisbury Office, for example, helped 2,577 people during March 1979 and by April that figure had gone up to 3,550.[52] In both cases the figure excluded those who were helped by other agencies. The ICRC's program involved helping 50,383 people in Rhodesia in 1979: 6,439 in Victoria Province; 15,739 in Matebeleland; 13,603 in Mashonaland; and, 14,602 in Manicaland. In addition, 295 tons of food staffs, 4,175 blankets, 5,818 articles of clothing, and over five tons of soap were distributed. This represented an expenditure of 275,000 Swiss Francs. Another 200,000 Swiss Francs went into providing medical care and houses.[53] The CSSD's expenditure on relief to war refugees is given in their annual report as $93,370,30.[54] This is only part of the sum spent by this organization. S. Matindike informed us that in addition to this national organization there are Diocesan Organization and Parish relief agencies which have their own relief funds.[55] The scale of operation of these agencies though impressive does not in any way go far enough to alleviate the sufferings of these proletarians in the making. It is symptomatic of the nature of the regime in this country that such a catastrophic event like the displacement of nearly a million people has not received official recognition.

It is difficult within the scope of this paper to state categorically that these displaced people who fled from their homes either to swell the ranks of the liberation forces or the escape from the attrocities of the security forces are proletarians in the making. It is conceivable that if and when there is an end to hostilities some of the war refugees will return to their homes to reengage in a subsistence economy. On the other hand it is more likely than not that many of the people who have fled from the rural areas will become permanent urban dwellers. If only half of these people remain in urban centers, which is not unlikely, then the war like the agricultural revolution in England will have turned a very large part of the rural population into urban proletarians within the life span of an individual. In other words, they will have been deprived of access to, or will not as a result of the war, make use of their access to productive means and will depend on the sell of the labor-power for a wage on the market. The Zimbabwe war refugee may not meet all the criteria of working class but if we accept Alkan's definition of a proletariat or that of Stichter then the war has proletarianized the rural population of Zimbabwe. In more ways than one war victims may be regarded as more proletarian than the bulk of the present urban proletariat or urban labor force in Zimbabwe Rhodesia. This is because, as Elkan observed in "The Migrant Proletarians" the majority of employees who seek and obtain work in urban centers do so only as part of families. In the majority of the cases the rest of the family continues to live and work in the Tribal Trust Lands supplementing their earnings by raising a few crops and livestock. In the case of war refugees the process of deprivation of access to

Effects of the War on the Rural Population of Zimbabwe   145

productive means is complete. Entire families have been uprooted from their homes into urban centers and neighboring countries.

The question, of course, may be asked whether this is not an ephemeral phenomenon. After all, permanency in a social situation is partly a distinguishing feature of a proletarian. We have already said that given the end of the war some people who are now either in neighboring countries or urban centers will return home but as has already been seen that a significant number of these will not return. Our interview with refugees at Musika and in Chirambahuyo has shown that many people who were forced out of their homes would never go back again even if conditions returned to normal. In our interviews it was clear that urban life has become a permanent reality to these people. Only very few people expressed desire to go back to the rural areas. Mrs. Dorica Kazingizi from Mtoko, who was quoted by the *Herald* as saying, "It is a hard life, but we are doing the best we can. There is nothing for us here, but neither is there anything for us where we came from besides the possibility of death as a result of the war."[56] The women from Beitbridge whom we have already quoted previously represent a wide cross section of the view of war refugees. It is clear that given the devastating nature of the repression in the operational areas many rural people will not return to their homes. All that they worked and lived for and many people that were dear to their families and friends have been destroyed. They have nothing but dark memories of what used to be home sweet home. They have now began a new way of life, a hard new way of life as Mrs. Kazingizi said. They will stay now and swell the urban proletariat. The following extract from the Christian Care Coordinator's report in April 1979 gives a picture of the state of affairs of these people which cannot be reversed. These reports speak for themselves and it is not far fetched to conclude that the majority of these people will probably never go back again to the Tribal Trust Lands.

Looking back then at our concept of Proletarian there appears to be a justification in calling the displacement of the people from rural to urban centers proletarianization. It may be that from a Marxist point of view these displaced peasants do not quite fit the definition since they are neither wage earners nor have they a related class consciousness. But inasmuch as these people have been vanguard of the struggle against colonial oppression then they have constituted to the revolutionary role that Marx said belonged to the proletariat. If we accept Fanon's view of who constitutes the wretched of the earth in colonial situations then we can with justification say that it is the peasant who "having nothing to lose but their impoverishment" and retaining pride in the face of all farms of indignity have represented the revolutionary force. In responding to the forces of reaction they have been mobilized and risen to the challenge of the war and like the peasants of Eighteenth Century England have moved into the urban areas to swell the ranks of the proletariate. The size of this migration from rural areas is significant; the nature of repression which has deprived people of their livelihood is likely to make their migration permanent. While encamped in the urban centers the former rural peasants have begun to develop a consciousness that is bound to distinguish them from their fellow peasants who did not flee from the effects of the war. The process of adaptation which have enabled the peasants to resist possible extermination is already beginning to enable these rural people to find new ways of making a living. A few of them have managed to get employment in the tight labor market while others have become self employed. They earn precarious living by selling anything that they collect from the municipal dump or other sources.

FOOTNOTES

1. Extract from the Report of St. Peter's Parish Relief Work, 1979, p. 1.

2. International Committee of the Red Cross Bulletin, N. 39, 4 4 79, p. 1.

3. T. Mapfumo, *Chirizevha Chapera*, by Chris Matema, June 30, 1978.

4. S. Stichter, "The Formation of a Working Class in Kenya," in *The Development of an African Working Class*, edited by R. Sanbrook and R. Cohen (Longman, 1979), p. 22.

5. F. Engels, *Principles of Communism*, in "The Communist Manifesto," edited by D.R. Ryzanoff (Martin Lawrence, 1930), p. 319.

6. F. Fanon, *The Wretched of the Earth* (Penguin 1963), p. 86.

7. W. Elkan, *Migrants and Proletarians: Urban Labor in the Economic Development of Uganda* (OUP), p. 6.

8. Che Guevara, *Reminiscences of the Cuban Revolutionary War* (Penguin 1968), p. 181.

9. CCJPR Report on the Makoni incidents.

10. CCJPR Report on the Gutu Massacre compiled from Eye Witness reports, submissions from local missions that were involved in relief, and also author's interview with two survivors.

11. Fr. W. Kaufmann, Mutero Mission, Gutu. Report submitted on 1 8 78 entitled, "Further Situation Report on the 'Gutu Incident.'"

12. CCJPR Report on Domboshawa incident.

13. CCJPR, Position Paper on the Domboshawa killings and author's interview with one eye witness.

14. CCJPR, Nyamaropa Report, "A Collection of Evidence on the Killings at Nyamaropa."

15. T. Hodges, *Counterinsurgency and the Fate of Rural Blacks*, Africa Report, September-October 1977, p. 15.

16. *Ibid.*, p. 19.

17. *Ibid.*

18. N. Bratton, *From Rhodesia to Zimbabwe: Beyond Community Development* in CCJPR, Rhodesia: The Propaganda War (London CIIR, 1977), p. 12.

19. A. Wilkinson, "From Rhodesia to Zimbabwe" in B. Davidson, J. Slovo, and A. Wilkinson, *Southern Africa: The New Politics of Revolution*. Harmondsworth, Middlesex, Penguin, 1976, p. 262.

20. Bratton, *op. cit.*, p. 37.

Effects of the War on the Rural Population of Zimbabwe   147

21. Interview with Harare refugee residents 6 5 79.

22. Wilkinson. *op. cit.*. p. 286.

23. A.K.H. Weinrich. *Chiefs and Councils in Rhodesia* (Heinemann 1971). p. 18.

24. G. Matatu. "Zimbabwe: Inside Story." Africa 81. May 1978. p. 13.

25. CCJPR. Rhodesia. p. 15.

26. A.K.H. Weinrich. "Strategic Resettlement in Rhodesia." *Journal of Southern African Studies.* 3. 2. 1977. p. 217.

27. Bratton. *op. cit.*. p. 41.

28. Interview with family X at Harare refugee camp. 3 5 79.

29. Hodges. *op. cit.*. p. 18.

30. Bratton. *op. cit.*. p. 41.

31. Weinrich. *op. cit.*. p. 217.

32. *The Herald.* February 12. 1979.

33. *Ibid.*

34. Hodges. *op. cit.*. p. 17.

35. *Rhodesia Herald.* August 25. 1978.

36. Government of S. Rhodesia Notice to Residents of Mososo TTL in CCJPR. Civil War In Rhodesia: A selection of press-cuttings (London CIIR 1976).

37. *The Rhodesia Herald.* August 5. 1978.

38. *The Herald.* February 12. 1979.

39. Annual Report — Gwelo Diocese Emergency Relief. January 1978-November 30. 1978.

40. *The Herald.* January 30. 1979.

Part III
South Africa:
States, Terrorism, and Resistance

Part III
South Africa
States, Terrorism, and Resistance

General

[12]

TERRORISM AND INSURGENCY IN SOUTH AFRICA

By F. McA. Clifford-Vaughan

The Use of Violence

Studies of terrorism commence with difficulties over nomenclature. This is especially true of the activities of those groups in Southern Africa whose proclaimed aims are 'national liberation,' 'freedom' and 'justice' — and whose opponents are thus presumed to resist these desirable states. Such terms as 'freedom fighters' (with or without inverted commas), 'guerrillas,' 'liberation forces' and 'democratic, progressive, peace-loving movements,' would seem to preclude any discussion of their aims. However, at least as far as this paper is concerned, any debate as to what to call the perpetrators of bomb and other outrages in South Africa may perhaps best be settled by using their methods rather than their stated aims as the criterion. The placing of landmines on public roads, the setting of limpet mines in shopping centers, the murder of local government officials and the destruction of their homes are all elements in a series of terror tactics and part of a larger strategy of revolutionary war.

The South African government judges the 'active propaganda' methods of Lenin to be terrorism. Terrorists are considered to be criminals, who are arrested and tried in the courts when possible. To this end, the government uses the complicated provisions of the Internal Security Act and other legal rules to prosecute individuals arrested by the South African Police.(1)

It should be mentioned that the South African police force is a para-military gendarmerie which is legally the 'first line of defence' in the security of the Republic. From time to time, the South African Defence Force (SADF) — mainly the Army — assists the police in this task but the SAP is the force primarily responsible for combatting terrorism.

A point worth making at this juncture concerns the attitude towards acts of political violence in sub-Saharan Africa, especially when compared to Western European norms of civil behavior.(2) Violence is endemic in African political life and there are many examples of this in existing political regimes throughout the continent.(3) A tolerance of violence is also characteristic of a frontier or settler society, which means that all communities are affected. What would be considered by governments and electorates in Europe to be unacceptable force is commonplace in Africa.(4)

Violence is thus, unfortunately, a fact of life in black Africa, and the use of terror is part of the apparent norm of political action. The possibility that, under certain conditions, the aim may become lost and violence (hence terror) unleashed, is not confined to any race group or community within the Republic.

Terrorism, as part of the overall attack on the existing government and social system, may also be seen as an outcome of a lack of inhibitions regarding the use of violence and of the established tactics now known as revolutionary warfare. This latter, based on the theories of Mao Tse-tung, Lenin and Clausewitz concerning the political dimension of war, is perceived as a threat to the security of the state and is the principle security preoccupation in South Africa.

Terrorism is included among the tactics being used in an attempt to force the surrender of the present government and the installation of a 'progressive' or revolutionary regime. One's perception of its aim — 'libertion' and/or 'capitulation' — is not necessarily based on one's racial origins(5) but depends on many factors, including one's terrorism toleration quotient.

The terror campaign in South Africa is conducted by their own admission, by the African National Congress (ANC), through its military wing, Umkhonto we Sizwe (MK) — 'Spear of the Nation.' Its stated strategy is to destroy the existing political, economic and social structure of South Africa by means of (i) political subversion and propaganda; and (ii) sabotage and terrorism.(6) Such tactics, in effect, amount to a revolutionary-war strategy, as will be demonstrated in this presentation.

The term 'revolutionary war' has been widely interpreted as the forcible attempt by politically organized groups to gain control of a country's decision-making structure through unconventional warfare and terrorism, which is integrated with political and social mobilization on the premise that 'the people are both the targets and actors.'(7)

Armed Action

The so-called 'Second Umkhonto Campaign' of the ANC's program of incursion and terrorist action can be said to have

TERRORISM & INSURGENCY IN SOUTH AFRICA 261

commenced in 1976.(8) Mozambican territory had become available for terrorists, due to the seizure of power in that country by a Marxist regime. Furthermore, Mozambique's border with Swaziland provided a channel for infiltration into the Republic. Although it has been suggested that direct crossing of the Mozambique/Natal border also took place, in fact it seems that such frontier crossings were made mainly by peasants from Mozambique looking for work and food in South Africa. The main terrorist infiltration took place through Swaziland to the railhead at Golela on the South African/Swazi border. Some (later-captured) terrorists took the train to Durban, while buses and private cars were also used to transport groups and their weapons to safe houses in the black townships surrounding the large urban areas.

In the years that followed, unrest already existing in large towns like Soweto caused many young blacks to become radicalized and flee the country. Some joined the ANC. Towards the end of 1978, according to security forces calculations, about 4,000 fugitives were receiving indoctrination and insurgency training in Tanzania, Angola and Libya. Many of these formed the cadres that returned clandestinely to South Africa in the manner described.

In 1978-9, the border area of the Transvaal and Natal was made an operational area by the Ministry of Defence, following increased activity by terrorist gangs. An attack on a store at Palindaba in Northern Natal by a group using rocket launchers had placed the whole area in a state of readiness, as had the arrest in that area, in late 1977/early 1978, of persons ferrying Soviet military equipment such as rifles, ammunition and landmines. Arms caches were also discovered and the South African Police successfully broke up plans to establish further caches in the tribal areas of Kwa Zulu.

Groups based in Mozambique used the relatively easy route via Swaziland into South Africa, with the intention of setting up an insurgency network in that northern area. Although at first sight this might appear to be classical guerrilla territory, it is in fact a fairly populous area and is not suitable for guerrilla bases since it is fairly well covered by both the SADF and the Police, as well as by a developed intelligence network. The various successful security force actions there, with regard to arrests of suspects and discoveries of arms caches, is due to these activities and to increased ground and air coverage of the

whole area. Counter-insurgency civic action, with the cooperation of the local population, also contributed to the success
of this operation.

The growing number of incidents attributable to ANC
action between 1977 and 1983 has been documented by several
civilian observers,(9) researchers in the field of terrorism,(10)
as well as official statistical studies. As a result, more than 200
incidents in this period can be classified according to targets
aimed at and methods used.(11)

Over the period January 1977 to April 1986 there were 454
acts of terrorism,(12) of which several sabotage attacks could
be said to have succeeded in their aim of gaining attention. For
example, oil storage tanks at Sasolburg were fired; RPG missiles
were launched at the Voortrekkerhoogte military base, just outside Pretoria; and the Koeberg nuclear power station in the
Cape was limpet-mined. There were also increased incidents
of terrorism against people, as opposed to installations, such
attacks being augmented by about 40 percent from April
1985.

Soft Targets

A successful terrorist act of armed propaganda took place in
Pretoria on 20 May 1983, when a car bomb was detonated in
a busy street, killing 19 people and injuring more than 200. This
was claimed as a military victory, since it was outside an office
block containing, amongst other tenants, SA Air Force personnel.

This incident seems to have been a turning point in the
tactics of the ANC and to have ended the myth propagated by
them and their supporters that their bombs were somehow
selective. Since the Pretoria car bomb was a deliberate terrorist
act in the center of the capital city, in a crowded area during
the afternoon rush hour, it could hardly have been likely not
to cause casualties. Thus, the previously oft-heard view that
casualties resulting from ANC bombs were accidents was firmly
laid to rest.

The indiscriminate bombings that followed(13) were proof
that a new line was being adopted — an escalation from 'harmless sabotage' to the 'murder of innocents.' The 'soft target'
tactic had come into being.

More recently, the adverse reaction of all race groups to the casualties resulting from bomb attacks in urban centers such as Johannesburg, Durban, Cape Town and Queenstown, has caused the ANC to change its policy of claiming responsibility for these acts.(14) The landmine explosions in the Transvaal rural areas have also caused what the ANC called 'problems and complications on questions of policy.'

An unfavorable international response is no doubt feared by the group and the 'not us' policy may also be a sign that factions within the ANC wish to dissociate themselves from the 'soft target' tactics of the MK wing. Some justification for their fear of losing support in the USA is perhaps borne out by a statement from the White House that Americans are shocked by the violence of the terrorist campaign: 'We are not going to help the bomb throwers, we are not going to aid them in an armed struggle.'(15)

So far as can be judged, this reaction has had no effect on the MK's actions and it is possible that they believe that the recently imposed sanctions against South Africa are a sign that the international community, so supportive in the past, will be so again, overlooking — in the best liberal *realpolitik* tradition — any terrorism committed in the name of 'wars of liberation.'

These increasing acts of terror, combined with certain changes within the structure of the ANC,(17) have been designed to advance 'the struggle' from the 'armed propaganda' phase to an intensification of 'the people's war.'(18)

Overt Terrorism

That the ANC has changed its overall tactics is clear from rhetorical statements emanating from the external wing, which now stresses the People's War strategy rather than Armed Propaganda. Joe Modise said:

"Armed propaganda" is simply using various forms of force to emphasise your point. The sabotage actions that heralded the birth of MK in 1961 were classical examples of armed propaganda.(19)

The change of tactics has been forced by their failure to 'provide a detonation for a popular resolution, and the resilience of the South African government'(20) — a fact that is not often the subject of rhetorical declamation.

The terror tactics now adopted fit more closely into the pattern which is recognizable from other insurgency areas.

This includes bombs in urban areas, landmines planted on country roads and the murder of black community leaders. The use of the particularly horrifying 'necklace' is a form of atrocity which, strangely, seems to escape unanimous condemnation (a rubber tire is placed over the victim's previously broken or severed arms, before he is doused with petrol and set alight). This process of eliminating 'stooges and puppets' was described by Theba Mbeki (ANC member of the South African Communist Party and Director of Information and Publicity) as 'cleansing the water in which the fish (guerrillas) must swim.' In other words, he used Mao Tse-tung's famous analogy to indicate that the aim is to make the area safe for terrorists.

In Rural Areas

The Second Consultative Conference of the ANC/SACP at Kabwe, Zambia, in June 1985, confirmed the policy of indiscriminate terror and political violence. At this meeting, Oliver Tambo stated that 'the distinction between "soft" and "hard" targets is going to disappear in an intensified confrontation, in an escalating conflict.' Translated into action, this meant that Soviet-supplied landmines were planted on farm roads in the Northern Transvaal agricultural area, resulting in the death and maiming of civilians, both black and white.

This policy decision is, in fact, in line with the stated views of the SACP, who consider that armed struggle should originate in rural areas and then be coordinated with armed effort in the townships, the whole operation to be orchestrated by trained cadres whose objective is to politicize the masses.(21)

Despite denials, the black African territories adjacent to South Africa have harbored terrorist gangs, with — or more unlikely, without — governmental knowledge. Subsequently, a diplomatic demarche and military counter-insurgency actions have been directed by South Africa against Zimbabwe, Botswana and Zambia.

The Kkomati Agreement between South Africa and Mozambique has impeded the transit and harboring of terrorists in the latter territory. This has been recognized by the ANC, who nevertheless declare that the 'armed struggle will intensify,' no doubt basing this assumption on a notion of internal, rather than external, recruitment to the ranks of terrorists. In a British newspaper, Joe Slovo claimed that the military strategy

TERRORISM & INSURGENCY IN SOUTH AFRICA 265

did not depend on cross-frontier bases such as other African 'liberation movements' had enjoyed. Rather, he claimed, "we have got the capacity to intensify the armed struggle in South Africa.'(23)

This kind of rhetoric does not take into account (or ignores, which is more likely) the facts of counter-insurgency and rural awareness. The climate of revolutionary fervor is low among those who live in rural areas, both white and black.

In the Towns and Cities

A campaign which has borne much more fruit from the point of view of propaganda is the calculated placing of terror bombs in certain South African towns and cities. Together with civil disobedience, strikes and boycotts, a serious threat to law and order has been posed. Whether the political aim achieved has been worth the death and destruction has not yet been assessed. Certainly, the state has not collapsed, nor has the government faltered in its task of restoring order, in spite of some mistakes and continuing severe criticism worldwide.

The severe reaction of the government in imposing a State of Emergency, first in selected magisterial districts and then in the whole Republic, has caused disruption to the carrying out of successful urban bomb attacks. Although there have been deliberate attempts to cause loss of life and presumably terrorize spectators, such efforts have been either counter-productive or have resulted in arrests and subsequent trials, and in one case execution of the bomb planters.

Between August and December 1985, there were 42 bombing incidents in the Republic. Those in Pretoria, Bloemfontein and Durban caused casualties to civilians, mainly women and children since the targets in most cases were shopping centers, supermarkets, busy streets, cafes and such like "soft targets."

On 23 December 1985, a limpet mine of Soviet origin exploded in a shopping center at Amanzimtoti, a resort near Durban. The target itself and the timing of 1045 A.M., when the area was likely to be thronged with pre-Christmas shoppers, were clearly designed to cause maximum casualties and panic.(24) The intention to kill and maim civilian women and children was thus amply demonstrated.

ANC disclaimers for some of these actions are not borne out by their subsequent statements, nor by their obvious lack of interest in any casualties caused. Indeed, some observers with special knowledge(25) have confirmed that such attacks result from a 'change of strategy' and that they are intended to 'have an impact on all sections of the community.'

The use of car bombs in urban areas has also formed part of the 'new' policy of terror. In 1985, two car bombs exploded at rush-hour in Durban. One was detonated 'prematurely' and killed five passers-by. As part of the ANC's intention to 'raise the political consciousness of the masses,' such acts certainly succeed in causing death to innocent people of all races.

Mobilization of the Masses

The 'mobilization of the masses' in South Africa has been a major function of front organizations for the banned African National Congress/South African Communist Party, at least since 1970, when the explosive power of youth groups was realized.(26) This has developed into the politicization of black and colored schools, and other educational centers. A direct result is school boycotts, also burning of classrooms, books and the occasional teacher. Throwing of stones at motorcars on the highway has increased, too.

In the process, 'Black Consciousness' has been fostered and groups adopting this philosophy or psychological attitude,(27) especially students at tertiary establishments, are playing a large part in attempting to politicize the majority group of the population.

It should be noted that the establishment of the South African Student Organisation (SASO) in 1969 was a conscious effort by Steve Biko and others at the University of the North, Turfloop, to break away from the all-white leadership of the National Union of South African Students (NUSAS). Most of the followers of SASO were supporters of the Pan African Congress. Indians and coloreds were also admitted to membership of SACP, giving a new dimension to the concept 'Black Africa.' After 1975, Biko adopted the view that the ANC was the primary revolutionary movement and that the Black Consciousness Movement should amalgamate with the ANC. Other groupings with Black Consciousness principles and ANC leanings include the Azanian Peoples Organisation and the Azanian Student Organisation, to name but two.(28) All are actively engaged in mobilization and politicization, if not in 'active measures.'

In addition, the admission of black students to English-medium white universities has now brought black activism to areas that were formerly affected only by white radical activism.

In a directive issued by the Politburo of the SACP in May 1986, a series of points was raised in order to 'promote uniformity throughout their ranks and to encourage a similar approach within the ANC.' This approach stresses that 'our broad strategy for achieving people's power is to mobilize the masses for a seizure of power through a combination of political action and armed struggle in which partial and general uprisings will play a vital role in the developing stages of People's War.'(29)

The drawing of 'politicized' individuals into the ranks of the ANC/SACP and the use of front organizations such as the United Democratic Front and the trade union movement come as no surprise, given the doctrinal requirements of revolutionary war techniques:

> A massive disinformation program has been launched to sell the idea that detained communists are actually oppressed nationalists. A poll held recently in Soweto revealed that 90 percent of high school students in the town thought Mandela had been convicted for supporting the rights of blacks; none knew of his membership of the SACP and only 2 percent had heard of Rivonia, subsequent to which Mandela was tried and convicted on charges of attempting to overthrow the state by force.(30)

Township Unrest

Using the dialectical combination of mobilization and terrorism, the black townships have been an important target of ANC/SACP cadres, from the point of view of both politicization and terrorist activities.

The objective, clearly stated by Tambo, of 'making the townships ungovernable' is 'to bring about the kind of society that is visualized in the Freedom Charter.' 'We have to break down and destroy the old order. We have to make . . . our country ungovernable . . . for power to pass into the hands of the people as a whole.' He also makes reference to the recent concessions made by the government with the object of dismantling *apartheid* and its efforts to raise the material conditions of black people as 'inconsequential games presented as an effort to reform . . . there is no middle road.'(31)

This intransigent attitude is reflected in the stance of the UDF and other front organizations regarding the real changes made in the laws affecting black people's socio-economic position. No possible changes, save complete destruction of the present governmental system, would appear to be acceptable to them. With such inspiration and the social conditions prevailing in some townships, a fertile 'revolutionary seedbed'(32) has been developed and put into action. The result has been 'a hellsbroth' of intimidation, arson, murder by most brutal means, including the infamous 'necklace,' stonings, bombings, hand grenades, petrol bombs, limpet mines, shootings, stabbings, rapes, robbery and the burning of homes — often with the victims being burned alive or killed as they try to escape the flames.

Targets have been mainly local government officials and policemen, and their families, including any blacks not identified as favorable towards the objectives of the ANC — that is, revolution.

The ultimate aim of creating 'liberated zones' and 'parallel hierarchies' has been moderately successful in some limited township areas, but not to the extent that a successful revolutionary war situation can be assumed.

Meantime, the targets outlined by Tambo and the ANC/ SACP alliance are: destruction of local government structures, elimination of local government officials, indoctrination (politicization) of all youth groups, creation of front organizations and the take-over of existing groups, elimination of moderate black influences through murder and intimidation, and the creation of an alternative parallel structure of government. All are known characteristics of revolutionary war techniques, well documented from historical precedents such as Indo-China/Vietnam, Malaya, Nicaragua, Laos, and China, to name but a few.(33)

The Standing of the ANC

There is considerable ignorance and misunderstanding about the real objectives of the ANC, both inside and outside South Africa.

TERRORISM & INSURGENCY IN SOUTH AFRICA 269

Internally

Within the Republic, the public dissemination of information has been controlled by governmental regulations to prevent the distribution of misinformation and to reduce public anxiety. This has considerably limited what can be reported for public consumption. Within this situation, the English-language media is accused of left-wing bias, the Afrikaans press of complicity with the government, while the black and Indian press is blamed for misinformation and speculation regarding the origins and motives of terrorist acts — a situation which is exploited, quite naturally, by cadres of ANC/SACP and by UDF, AZAPO and other front organizations engaged in subversion. Most of the sources quoted in this paper — and certainly *Sechaba*, Tambo and Slovo — are legally prohibited from being quoted in the Republic. This creates uncertainty among the literate population as to the intentions and objectives of the insurgents. Businessmen and students naively clamor to have meetings with the ANC, in Zambia or Zimbabwe, 'to find out their aims!'

Universities are allowed to possess banned material for research purposes but its reading is again controlled by government regulation. Academics with access to such information who condemn the methods and aims of the ANC/SACP and their front/support organs, are not permitted to quote from what they have read and are consequently accused by the ill-informed student body of being 'reactionary fascists.' As a result of such ignorance, the gutting by firebombs of the departments of Political Science and Social Studies at the University of Natal, on 21 March 1986, caused an outburst of speculation as to the perpetrators. Opinions ranged widely from 'police agents' to 'unknown left-wingers.' The obvious conclusion would have been the ANC, since such action is in keeping with their past trackrecords and the intimidation of selected academics is known to be on their agenda.

The tactics used seem to be those of Marighella rather than Mao, but someone has obviously also read his Sun Tzu on the subject of winning without actually fighting!

The state's response, one feels, should be to make all this information freely available (34) or, at least, not to impede its propagation. Since the general view seems to be that the ANC, even after 10-odd years of activity, is really no nearer to gaining final victory, it might be a good notion also to allow this fact to be widely disseminated by those who wish to do it. After all, propaganda and information, based on reliable intelligence are important factors in combatting insurgency operations.

Internationally

Outside South Africa, the ANC seems to be regarded in many quarters as worthy of assistance in its noble fight against the evils of apartheid. In reality, its methods and objectives go considerably further than is generally appreciated. It is as well to point out that examples abound of mistaken perceptions by outsiders as to the intentions of African 'liberation' movements.(35) Such examples are quite prevalent elsewhere, too. The ANC/SACP alliance, by its own claim, is aiming for a revolutionary seizure of power and the subsequent transformation of South Africa's economic and social system to a Marxist or Marxist-Leninist model. The significance of this for the West is obvious.

ANC/SACO Tactical Problems — An Appreciation

The aim of the ANC/SACP combination is clearly the seizure of state power and the overthrow of the present governmental system, as well as the restructuring of all means of production, distribution and ownership. This ambition has taken the form of an attenuated type of revolutionary war, using the techniques of terrorism and mass mobilization. However, in spite of changing tactics over the past twenty years, the state of revolutionary activity in the Republic is still at a relatively low level.

For twenty years the population has been subverted and indoctrinated as part of the mobilization strategy. But more than that is required for the successful completion of a two-stage revolutionary seizure of power. The survival of the ANC/SACP also depends on the outcome of armed violence, which latter is perceived as vital to success.

Previous experience during the sixties, which saw the breaking up of the sabotage campaigns of Umkhonto and the unsuccessful Operation Mayibuye,(36) through the security forces' counter-insurgency operations, showed that the South African government had the will to make such attempts highly unprofitable. Failure, because of good COIN techniques, to

TERRORISM & INSURGENCY IN SOUTH AFRICA 271

establish viable bases and 'liberation zones' within the borders of South Africa, also demonstrated the preponderance of power of the state in its pursuance of a policy of applied total strategy. The security forces dominate the areas in which they operate and guerrilla warfare on a scale large enough to topple the government of the day is unlikely. The idea of 'liberated zones' is very far from being achieved, with subsequent telling implications for the development of full-scale insurgency.

Without safe havens, bases and training areas, the necessary organized networks and structures cannot be constructed, and without these, a guerrilla army of the type foreseen by the ANC/SACP cannot be created. As a consequence, the ANC/SACP's external policy has been developed as the only feasible way to ensure bases for the prosecution of a revolutionary war. However, with some of these bases closed and with others pinpointed or the object of surgical raids by the South African Defence Force, the ANC now has organizational problems which it is unable to solve practically.

The 'frontlines states' and 'progressive' socialist countries all give aid to the revolutionary activities of the ANC in South Africa — bases for training and indoctrination are in operation in Libya, Zambia, Tanzania, even the Soviet Union and East Germany(37) — but the attrition rate amongst the products of these bases, due to security force action and natural wastage, plus the fact that most of these trained insurgents are outside South Africa's borders, is high enough to cause problems for the ANC/SACP hierarchy.

The acquisition of weapons seems to be less of a problem. The donor states seem happy to provide limpet mines, land mines, AK 47 assault rifles and RPG rocket launchers in large numbers to the ANC, which in effect acts as their agents. Local supplies of weapons are unobtainable, except from the odd theft. Hardware of a conventional-warfare nature is nonexistent, being inappropriate except in Angola. These weapons are almost entirely Soviet and East European in origin.

Conclusion

That change is taking place is undeniable, throughout the whole spectrum of South Africa's internal policies, its social, economic and political life. This process, once started, cannot be stopped, except by a major cataclysmic revolutionary

272   JOURNAL OF SOCIAL, POLITICAL AND ECONOMIC STUDIES

uprising. Whether its results will be viewed as beneficial, or otherwise, to the people of South Africa depends on the ideological framework within which one is operating.

In examining the 'alternative solution' offered by the ANC, any question as to whether that organization's leaders are members of the SACP seems immaterial, since their ideas, tactics, rhetoric and inspiration are Leninist, if not altogether Marxist, and as such are unacceptable to non-Marxists who are aware of what is at stake.

The successful continuation of terrorism of the type now occurring in South Africa, under the aegis of the ANC, will lead to disaster for all; blacks, whites, the economy and the progress of future development. For this, if for no other reason, the international community should cease its aid to terrorist-oriented groups, no matter how noble their stated aims may appear. The kind of change envisaged by its perpetrators cannot result in anything other than total chaos . . . a chaos that would be exploited by those who seek to use such conditions for their own political and ideological purposes.

ACKNOWLEDGEMENTS

This article is based on a presentation to the International Academic Conference on Research in Terrorism, held at the University of Aberdeen in April 1986.

FOOTNOTES

(1)   Terrorism is defined in the Internal Security Act.
The narrow legalistic view of terrorism is not shared by all Security Forces engaged in counter-insurgency operations (COIN OPS). The Army, for example, pays great attention in its training program and operations to the political aspects of terroristic acts. Troops are taught the elements of revolutionary warfare techniques and the aims of the 'terrs' — an expression used generally by SF officers when referring to ANC/SACP cadres. Civil Action and other socio-economic programs are also carried out by Security Force personnel as part of COIN OPS.
(2)   Western European studies of the phenomenon of political terrorism are extensive and are probably based upon a view that 'le terrorism est un moyen politi-

TERRORISM & INSURGENCY IN SOUTH AFRICA 273

que, une manifestation de violence collective, une force' Bonthoul G. and Carrere R.: *Le Defi de la Guerre, 1740-1974,* (PUF, 1976). Wardlaw G.: *Political Terrorism,* Cambridge, 1982; Wilkinson P.: *Political Terrorism,* Macmillan, 1974; and Laquer W.: 'The Anatomy of Terrorism' in *Ten Years of Terrorism,* London, RUSI, 1970; offer explanations for terror based on political culture and democratic permissiveness, as well as national character.

(3)   Cf., eg. Kunert D.T.: *Africa: Soviet Strategy and Western Counter-Strategy.* Occasional Paper No. 1, SA Forum, 1981, pp. 6 *et seq.*

(4)   Cf. Walter, E.V.: *Terrorism and Resistance: A Study of Political Violence,* OUP, 1969, p. 12 *et passim.*

(5)   The terms 'white,' 'black,' 'Indian' and 'colored' (mixed race), as used in this paper, are widely used in South Africa as a means of differentiation throughout South African society. For example, institutions like the Black Students Society identify themselves as such. Tribal names are also used as a means of identification — for example, Inkatha is described (by its own members) as a Zulu cultural movement. The ANC appears to consist mainly of people of Xhosa origin.

(6)   'ANC Strategy and Tactics, 1969' in *Sechaba,* 1970.

(7)   Cf. Taber R.: *War of the Flea,* 1974. Wilkinson P.: *Terrorism and the Liberal State,* London, 1977; and Wardlaw G.: *op. cit.,* pp. 3-17, *et seq.,* have similar definitions. See also Kunert D.: *The Kremlin, the world revolutionary process and African 'national liberation movements.'* SA Institute of International Affairs, Occasional Paper, 1977.

(8)   Lodge, T.: 'The African National Congress, 1982,' in *South Africa Review,* No. 1, 1983, p. 50. (Published by Ravan Press, Johannesburg.) Lodge is seen in some quarters as an apologist for the ANC. Cf., for example, *APN,* No. 71, December 1985 (*Aida Parker Newsletter,* Johannesburg).

(9)   Among them, Professor M. Hough, Director, Institute for Strategic Studies, University of Pretoria.

(10)   Cf., for example, Morris M.: *Aspects of Unrest and Terrorism in RSA, 1986. 'No Confidence Debate: Special Review',* p. 23. Morris says, *inter alia:* 'In the nine years between January 1977 and January 1986 there were 398 terrorism or sabotage incidents and an attrition of 201 terrorists arrested, 79 terrorists and 85 civilians killed.'

(11)   Targets included police stations, administrative offices, court buildings, the homes of MPs and offices of private firms, especially those having labor troubles. These targets were chosen with the aim of establishing an ANC following amongst blacks in the urban areas. The attacks on police stations were clearly aimed at producing propaganda since there was no attempt to capture any weapons. Indeed, most of the attacks failed to achieve anything except the deaths of the participants.

(12)   Cf. Morris M.: op. cit.

(13)   4 April 1984: a car bomb in Durban killed 3, injured 22. 14 June 1985: a car bomb exploded in area of Durban beachfront frequented by young people, killing 3 women and injuring 60. Details and figures from the press are collated in *SA Digest,* published by the Bureau for Information, Pretoria.

(14)   Kumalo, S., in *Sunday Times* (Johannesburg), 10 August 1986.

(15)   U.S. White House official, quoted by Neil Lurssen, *Sunday Tribune* (Durban), 10 August 1986.

(16)   Cf. Morris M.: *RSA Law and Order 1986. Key Issues in Parliament. Special Review,* p. 5 et seq. See p. 23: Between 1 September 1984 and 24 January 1986, 327 fatalities and 1,429 non-fatalities were inflicted by mob elements.

(17)   A Revolutionary Council, responsible from 1969 for military planning and consisting of ANC and SA Communist Party members, was abolished. It was replaced by a Military Committee under Joe Modise (Umkhonto leader), a Political Committee under John Nkadimeny and a Coordinating Joint Committee. The latter played a leading role in the SA Congress of Trade Unions. The goal of more effective

political and armed insurgency activity was clearly the object of this joint organization. Cf. Lodge T.: 'The African National Congress, 1983' in *SA Review*, No. 2, 1984, p. 24 (Johannesburg).

(18)   Cf. Lodge, T.: op. cit. He cites 'South Africa: People's War Now,' in *Africa Now*, August 1983, p. 21.

(19)   Quoted by P. Powell, in *The African National Congress/South African Communist Party and People's War: an overview*. Unpublished paper read at University of the Orange Free State, 18 August 1986.

(20)   Powell, P.: op cit.

(21)   Cf., Gann, L. H. and Duignan, P.: *Why South Africa Will Survive*, Cape Town, 1981, p. 198.

(22)   In November 1985, six landmines killed one civilian and injured one civilian and four soldiers. In December, another mine killed six and injured five. In January 1986, in the Ellisras area, two civilians were killed by a further landmine.

(23)   *Sechaba*, November 1984, pp. 28-29.

(24)   Five were killed and 61 seriously injured. The perpetrator was caught, tried and executed. Part of his defense was that he did not want to kill people. After his defense failed, he claimed that he was an ANC member and was glad to have set the limpet mine.

(25)   Cf. Lodge T.: 'Mayihlome — Let Us Go To War — From Nkomati to Kabwe — The African National Congress, January 1984 — June 1985,' in *SA Review*, No. 3, 1986, pp. 228-9 (Johannesburg).

(26)   'Primary objectives for infiltration during the 1970's were black youth organisations, black trades unions and certain specifically created 'front organisations,' as well as the 'liberal, white, English-speaking universities.' *Interview with a security force officer, 1986.*

(27)   Clifford-Vaughan, F. McA.: *Black Consciousness*, unpublished paper 1985.

(28)   Cf. van Jaarsveld, J. J. H.: *Rol van die Bevolking in Insurgensie met Spesifieke Verwysing na Revolusionere Organisasies in die Republiek van Suid-Afrika.* M.A. Thesis, U.N.I.S.A. 1984 (unpublished). The author lists 19 black and nine white 'revolution-supporting' organizations, including the now-banned Congress of South African Students (COSAS). There are also front organizations, such as the United Democratic Front (UDF), which are multiracial.

(29)   Politburo (SACP) Central Committee meeting, March 1986. *SACP Directive/Discussion Document*, 17 pp.

(30)   Conversation with security force officer, 1986.

(31)   Oliver Tambo in a broadcast on *Addis Ababa Radio Freedom*, at 17:30 P.M., 6 August 1985.

(32)   Both govermental and academic, research have identified grievances and perceived political and socio-economic inequalities. The complexity of the matter is stressed by Professor L. Schlemmer in several works appearing in *Indicator SA*, published by the University of Natal. A government *White Paper on Urbanisation*, amongst other reports, recognizes that legitimate areas of discontent do exist and that problems of management and the implementation of development plans are not easily solved. The need for participation by the private sector is emphasized.

(33)   The literature on revolutionary war and its tactics and techniques is extensive amongst the better known commentators, e.g.: Taber R., *War of the Flea*; Kitson F., *Low Intensity Operations*; Cilliers, S., *Counter-Insurgency in Rhodesia*; Elliott-bateman, M., *The Fourth Dimension of War*; Laquer, W., *Guerilla*; Thompson, Sir Robert, *Defeating Communist Insurgency*; Wilkinson, P., *Terrorism — International Dimensions*. The proponents of this form of warfare, using terrorism, mass-mobilization, etc., are also well known: Mao Tse-tung, Marighella, Lenin, and their imitators, Slovo, Tambo, Mandela.

(34)   The Bureau of Information has lately issued a series of booklets, including

TERRORISM & INSURGENCY IN SOUTH AFRICA 275

Talking with the ANC, January 1986, which gives selected facts and statements from ANC/SACP sources. *The Argus* (Cape Town) was quick to point out, 4 June 1986, that this booklet breaks the law of the *Prisons Act* and the *International Security Act* by quoting Tambo and other banned persons and by publishing a photograph of Mandela.

(35)   Friedland, E.: *A Comparative Study of the Development of Revolutionary Movements in Africa*. Ph.D. Thesis, University of Michigan, 1980. Especially that part entitled 'Radical Nationalism and Armed Struggle,' p. 384 et seq. The literature cited therein is also noteworthy.

See also Suttner R. and Cronin, J.: *Thirty Years of the Freedom Charter*, Ravan Press, Johannesburg, 1986 (banned in South Africa); and Hudson, P.A.: 'The Freedom Charter and Socialist Strategy in South Africa,' in *Politikon*, Vol. 13, No. 1, June 1986, pp. 75-90. All these give Marxist orienated views. The Report of the Study Commission on United States' Policy toward Southern Africa, *South Africa: Time Running Out*, University of California, 1981, gives a wider view of the 'liberation struggle.'

(36)   This was a full-scale plan for the violent seizure of power in South Africa, involving armed uprising, seaborne invasion of trained guerrilla forces and the complete destruction of the Republic. Mandela, amongst others, was tried and convicted of this and has refused to abjure violence as a condition of release.

(37)   Captured ANC terrorists state that the campaign depends on external base facilities. Arms and ammunition were smuggled in most of these cases from Lesotho, Mozambique (using Swaziland as a condui), Botswana and, to a lesser degree, Zimbabwe. Training in Angola, Tanzania, Mozambique, East Germany and the USSR is well established. Attempts at setting up safe houses in the Republic were not usually successful and most groups attempted to exfiltrate to neighboring states after their missions.

ERRATA

Journal of Social, Political and Economic Studies
Vol 12 No 3 Fall 1987

Article TERRORISM AND INSURGENCY IN SOUTH AFRICA
By Professor F. McA. Clifford-Vaughan

Page 263   4th line from bottom of page
       popular resolution should read popular revolution

Page 263   End of second paragraph.
   After 'wars of liberation.' ADD:
   In any event, attacks on civilian targets continue.(16)

Page 264

After third paragraph ending ,politicize the masses.(21)   ADD NEW PARAGRAPH:

The incidents at Ellisruls and in the Messina area (22) seem to
have been the work of infiltrated terrorists from Botswana and
Zimbabwe, which would tend to prove the well known insurgency
requirement   that external bases are necessary when operating in hostile
territory, which the South African rural areas must be seen to be for terrorists.

Page 264

Beginning of last paragraph:

For 'KKomati' read Nkomati

Page 267

Paragraph three, beginning "A massive disinformation program" should not
be indented, but is part of the main text.

The errors are regretted, and occurred due the long postal delays in
communications with the author in South Africa.

[13]

COMMUNISM, TERRORISM, AND
THE AFRICAN NATIONAL CONGRESS

By Samuel T. Francis

The escalation of internal political violence, including riots and organized terrorism, in the Republic of South Africa since the summer of 1984 has produced a pronounced hostile reaction to South Africa on the part of Western governments and public opinion. Despite the presence of comparatively moderate opponents of apartheid, such as Chief Buthelezi, in South Africa, fashionable entertainment figures, opinion makers, and many political leaders in the West have sought to glamorize the most violent and extreme forces in that country, the African National Congress (ANC) and its convicted leader Nelson Mandela. The glamorization is not confined to persons like singer Little Stevie Wonder, but extends also to important governmental leaders in the Reagan Administration and even to the South African business establishment. On March 13, 1986, Assistant Secretary of State for African Affairs Chester A. Crocker described the ANC in Congressional testimony as "freedom fighters," thus placing this organization and its terrorist cadres in the same category as the Contras of Nicaragua, UNITA of Angola, and similar anti-Communist guerrillas in Afghanistan and Indochina. On September 13, 1985, a delegation of seven South African businessmen, led by Gavin Relly of the conglomerate Anglo-American Corporation, met with ANC leaders in Lusaka, Zambia in an effort to find some common ground between the two groups. To date, this effort does not appear to have been successful.

The ANC, in fact, has been under the effective control of the South African Communist Party (SACP) since the late 1940s. Although not all of its leaders are Communists, enough of them are members of the Party to exert a controlling influence in the organization and hence render the ANC in effect a Soviet controlled satellite that promotes the Soviet goals of "national liberation" in the Republic of South Africa and in southern Africa generally. Moreover, the ANC has embarked on a course of "armed struggle" as a tactic of proletarian revolution in South Africa with the consent and encouragement of the

SACP. While making use of terrorism — for which the term "armed struggle" is a Leninist euphemism — the ANC has also in recent years sought to gain political power through legal organizations such as the United Democratic Front and through clever manipulation of public opinion in South Africa as well as outside it.

The African National Congress was founded on January 8, 1912 in Bloemfontein in the Union of South Africa. Often described as the oldest African nationalist organization, the ANC for many years was indeed nationalist in its goals, seeking to unify the tribes of South Africa as a single people. By the 1940s, however, the ANC and the SACP, founded in 1921, began collaborating against the institutions of white supremacy. In 1947 the two organizations worked together in a campaign against the "pass laws," and in 1945 the ANC, SACP, and South African labor unions jointly staged the largest public gathering in the history of Johannesburg in observation of the Allied victory over Germany. In 1950 the ANC and SACP and other organizations sponsored mass rallies in opposition to the recently adopted policy of apartheid.

One source for the increasing closeness between the ANC and the Communists was a militant faction within the ANC Youth League which came under the influence of the Communist leader Yussuf Dadoo. The Youth League argued for a far more confrontational policy than the parent body was willing to endorse. Several leaders of the Youth League undertook visits to Soviet Bloc states without the knowledge of ANC leader Albert Luthuli, and the arrest and trial of these persons after their return served to discredit and embarrass Luthuli. By 1958 the Communist influence in the ANC had reached such an extent that the nationalists in the organization broke off and founded the Pan African Congress (PAC).

The SACP was outlawed in 1950 under the Internal Security Act of that year, and the Party in fact became a clandestine organization. The ANC remained a legal organization until, in the wake of the "Sharpeville massacre" of March 21, 1960 and the calling of a general strike by the ANC on March 26, the government banned the ANC and the PAC under the Unlawful Organisations Act. The ANC has remained an illegal and clandestine organization in South Africa since that time.(1)

Public confirmation of the powerful Communist influence in the ANC in recent years was provided by Bartholomew

THE AFRICAN NATIONAL CONGRESS   57

Hlapane, a former member of the National Executive Committee (NEC) of the ANC and of the Central Committee of the SACP, in testimony before the Subcommittee on Security and Terrorism of the Senate Judiciary Committee on March 25, 1982. Mr. Hlapane was able to identify seven of the 22 members of the NEC as members of the SACP. South African intelligence sources confirmed the identification of six of these persons as Communists as well as of five other members of the NEC. The eleven members of the NEC who were at that time known to be members of the Communist Party were: Yussuf Dadoo, Vice President of the NAC; Alfred Nzo, Secretary General; Dan Tloome, Deputy Secretary General; Joe Slovo, Deputy Chief of *Umkhonto we Sizwe,* the "military arm" of the ANC; Josiah Dele, Director of International Affairs; Mziwandele Piliso, chief of personnel and security; and Reginald September, Moses Mabhida, Stephen Dlamini, Hector Nkula, and John Nkadimeng, members of the NEC. Hlapane also identified Thabo Mbeki, chief of the political department of the ANC, as a member of the SACP, as did witness Delphine Kava. Thus, a majority (12 out of 22) of the members of the National Executive Committee of the ANC were identified members of the Communist Party. Neither Hlapane nor other witnesses nor South African intelligence sources were able to identify Oliver Tambo, President of the ANC, as a Communist, and Hlapane testified that to his knowledge Tambo was not a Communist. Tambo, Afred Nzo, and Yussuf Dadoo until his death in 1983 were members of the Presidential Committee of the World Peace Council, widely recognized as a Soviet controlled front organization, and Dadoo·was also Chairman of the South African Communist Party. Joe Slovo himself is reputed to hold the rank of colonel in the Soviet KGB, although he has reportedly denied this.(2)

The closeness of the ANC leadership to the Soviet Union and the SACP is evident also in many public statements of both ANC and Communist leaders. In January, 1984, a writer in *Sechaba,* the official organ of the ANC which is printed in East Germany, wrote "The ANC has been a consistent champion of the cause of world peace, and 'voices its full support for recent Soviet peace initiatives which are aimed at making this planet a secure place.' (Alfred Nzo, 1983)." In May, 1984, Alfred Nzo stated in an interview, "We recognise instead that the Soviet Union and other Socialist countries are our dependable allies, from whom no force is going to succeed in separating us."(3) An editorial in *The African Communist*, official organ of the SACP, speaking of Chester Crocker and "his racist friends in the apartheid regime," noted in 1984, "They would like to separate the ANC from its natural allies, the independent African counties and the socialist countries. They would like the ANC to separate itself from its ally, the South African Communist Party."(4) In a message to the second Consultative Conference of the NAC, held in Lusaka, Zambia, on June 16-23, 1985, the SACP stated "The South African Communist Party has a long history of association with the ANC — an association which has now developed into a brotherly alliance . . . . From the earliest days communists have worked unstintingly to strengthen the ANC."(5) In a Presidential Statement to the NAC by Oliver Tambo in 1984, Tambo noted, "The Socialist countries remain a solid pillar of support to our national liberation struggle. We are assured of their continued internationalist solidarity till the triumph of our revolutionary struggle."(6) On April 11-16, 1983, Alfred Nzo participated in an international conference to commemorate the death of Karl Marx hosted by the Central Committee of the East German Socialist Unity Party (SED), held in East Berlin. Aside from his praise for the founder of Communism, Nzo noted that the "fascist regime" of South Africa, "with its allies in Washington," "hopes that it can persuade the masses of our people and those of our region as a whole to turn their backs on the national liberation movement and the national liberation forces to turn against their natural alliance with the GDR, the Soviet Union and the world socialist system as a whole."(7) Oliver Tambo has noted that "It is a matter of record that for much of its history, the South African Communist Party has been an integral part of the struggle of the African people against oppression and exploitation in South Africa ... Today the ANC and the SACP have common objectives in the eradication of the oppressive and exploitative system that prevails in our country: the seizure of power and the exercise of their right to self-determination by all the people of South Africa." Moses Mabhida, who is the General Secretary of the SACP, stated in response to Tambo's remarks that the SACP "fully supports the same programme of liberation as the African National Congress, for the seizure of power and majority rule ... Our Party's relationship with the African National Congress is based

THE AFRICAN NATIONAL CONGRESS

on mutual trust, reciprocity, comradeship in battle and a common struggle for national liberation. Our unity of aims and methods of struggle are a rare instance of positive alignment between the forces of class struggle and national liberation."(8) Such statements, of which those presented here are only a sample, suggest the closeness of the ANC to the SACP, the Soviet Union, and the World Communist movement.

Nelson Mandela has never been a member of the Communist Party, although he has acknowledged the influence of Marxism on his thinking and political activities, and he played an important role in the transition of the ANC from a non-violent to a violent organization. In 1961, according to Mandela's statement during his trial in 1964, Mandela and others in the ANC leadership formed the "military arm" of the ANC, *Umkhonto we Sizwe*, "Spear of the Nation," or MK. The occasion for its formation was the shootings at Sharpeville and the subsequent outlawing of the ANC. Although the Sharpeville shootings were the response of police defending themselves against mob violence, the incident was used by Mandela to argue that "Violence by the African people had become inevitable."(9) On December 16, 1961, MK carried out its first attacks on government buildings in Johannesburg, Durban and Port Elizabeth. Mandela was arrested in August, 1962, and on July 11, 1963, South African police raided a farm at Lilliesleaf, near Rivonia, and arrested a number of ANC and SACP members. The police also seized documents and materials at the farm that revealed the MK plan for nation-wide sabotage and terrorism. This plan, called "Operation Mayibuye," involved eventual invasion of South Africa by foreign powers, and persons implicated in the terrorist conspiracy had developed contacts with the Soviet Union, Cuba, and Communist China, as well as with pro-Soviet African states. In 1966, Abram Fischer, a leader of the SACP, testified at his trial that the leaders of MK had given assurances to the Party that no terrorist action would be carried out without the prior approval of the Party.(10) In 1982 Bartholomew Hlapane, who had held leadership positions in both the SACP and the ANC in the early 1960s, confirmed Fischer's statement in testifying that "No major decision could be taken by the ANC without the concurrence and approval of the Central Committee of the South African Communist Party. Most major developments were in fact initiated by the Central Committee," and Hlapane also stated that "The Military Wing of the ANC . . .

was the brainchild of the SACP, and after the decision to create it had been taken, Joe Slovo and J.B. Marks [also a member of the SACP] were sent by the Central Committee of the SACP to Moscow to organise arms and ammunition and to raise funds for Umkonto We Sizwe."(11)

The arrest of the ANC leaders and their subsequent conviction and imprisonment seriously impaired the capacities of the ANC and the SACP for sustaining a terrorist campaign in South Africa. Nevertheless, the SACP itself, in its program adopted at its Fifth National Conference in 1962, concluded that:

> The Communist Party considers that the slogan of "nonviolence" is harmful to the cause of the democratic national revolution in the new phase of the struggle, disarming the people in the face of the savage assaults of the oppressor, dampening their militancy, undermining their confidence in their leaders. At the same time, the Party opposes undisciplined acts of individual terror. It rejects theories that all nonviolent methods of struggle are useless or impossible, and will continue to advocate and work for the use of all forms of struggle by the people, including noncollaboration, strikes, boycotts, and demonstrations.(12)

The SACP rejection of reliance on non-violence was in fact a condemnation of the old non-violent policies of the NAC and a successful effort to push the ANC into dependence on illegal, revolutionary and violent strategies.

The Communist statement endorsing violence but rejecting individual terrorism and refusing to reject non-violent forms of struggle is also perfectly consistent with the classical Leninist theory of revolutionary strategy. Communist revolutionary doctrine does not ordinarily rely exclusively on terrorism as a tactic of revolution, and indeed the term "terrorism" had had negative connotations in Leninist terminology due to Bolshevik rivalry with the "Terrorist" faction of the Social Revolutionaries in early twentieth century Russia. Nevertheless, Leninism allows for, and under some conditions demands, the use of terrorism under the euphemisms "armed struggle" or "guerrilla warfare," as a means of bringing about a revolutionary situation or the revolution itself. Lenin authorized the use of terrorism by the Bolsheviks in the form of bank robberies or "expropriations" in Czarist Russia, and his writings specifically endorse

THE AFRICAN NATIONAL CONGRESS   61

the equivalent of terrorism under other names. The only stipulations in Leninist strategy on the use of terrorism are that it
remain under the political control of the Party and that it
advance Communist goals. In the 1960s, Marxists such as Che
Guevara and Regis Debray sought to formulate a new theory of
revolution that was almost entirely dependent on "armed
struggle" or "guerrilla warfare," carried out by small independent *"focos"* with little contact with or control by a Communist Party. Among African revolutionaries — and Guevara
himself fought in the Congo in 1965 — this theory challenged
the political control of the Communists over revolutionary
movements.(13)

ANC use of terrorism was limited between the exposure of
Operation Mayibuye and the late 1970s, mainly because the
ANC lacked the capacity and the infrastructure to sustain a
terrorist or guerrilla movement. Nevertheless, a conference of
the ANC at Morogoro, Tanzania, from April 25 to May 1, 1969
endorsed the use of armed struggle as an instrument useful to a
revolutionary seizure of power, though it strongly rejected the
Guevarist reliance on armed struggle.(14) Although terrorist
and sabotage incidents occurred in South Africa in the late
1960s and early 1970s, they were comparatively minor and
sporadic.

The event that resuscitated revolutionary activities in general
and terrorism in particular in South Africa was the Soweto
riots of 1976. These disturbances, which revealed widespread
discontent in South African black townships, apparently
caught the ANC and the SACP off guard. Nevertheless, they
rushed to take advantage of them. In addition, the consolidation of pro-Soviet Marxist regimes in the former Portuguese
colonies of Mozambique and Angola in 1975 established bases
from which South African revolutionaries could gain access to
South Africa. Between October 24, 1976 and November 20,
1980, the ANC was responsible for 28 known acts or attempted
acts of sabotage or violence in South Africa in which at least 13
persons were killed. These statistics probably underestimate
the amount of violence for which the ANC was responsible,
since during the same period at least 55 other incidents of
violence occurred for which responsibility is uncertain. In
September, 1981, *Sechaba* claimed responsibility for 20 acts of
violence between January 26 and August 11, 1981, and stated

that these were "some of the actions reported during 1981."

Major acts of terrorism carried out by the ANC in 1980 included the sabotage of Sasol near Pretoria and the attempted robbery of a bank in Pretoria. The latter incident occurred on January 25, 1980, when three ANC members, armed with Soviet AK-47 assault rifles and hand grenades, raided a suburban bank in Pretoria and took 25 persons hostage. The terrorists demanded the release of Mandela, the revolutionary white poet Breyten Breytenbach, and ANC leader James Manze, imprisoned for smuggling Soviet weapons from Mozambique into South Africa in 1979. The terrorists murdered one of their hostages, a nineteen year old female teller, and were themselves killed after South African Police stormed the bank. Before they died the terrorists detonated hand grenades among the hostages, killing another woman and wounding 11 others.

The attack on Sasol, the South African Coal, Gas, and Oil Conversion Corporation, occurred on June 1, 1980 and caused $7 million in damages due to bombs placed by the ANC. A security guard was wounded by the saboteurs. The ANC at the same time placed three plastic explosive devices at the headquarters of the U.S. owned Fluor Corporation, but these bombs were discovered before they were detonated. The bombs placed at Sasol were of Soviet origin.

The increase in terrorism by the ANC in the late 1970s and early 1980s reflected a new tactical line on the part of the ANC and the SACP. In 1977 the Central Committee of the SACP concluded that "SOWETO has closed the debate about the legitimacy of resorting to armed struggle," and in 1970, writing in *The African Communist*, an ANC leader under the pseudonym "Comrade Mzala" stated that "in this period of struggle the urgent task of our movement is to inject into the masses of our people a feeling of confidence in their own potential to overthrow the racists, by means of vigorous revolutionary action, the main content of which must be effective, and sustained guerrilla operations including a nation-wide sabotage campaign reminiscent of the early sixties, and thus continue from where Rivonia left off."(15) Mzala was careful to advocate a campaign of terrorism consistent with Marxist-Leninist strategy, but he concluded that:

> Experience of other countries like Algeria, Cuba, Angola, on the contrary, shows that guerrilla struggle can bring about a revolutionary situation. Nowadays, this is

THE AFRICAN NATIONAL CONGRESS 63

more so because the liberation forces have at their disposal an advantage (which the Russian revolutionaries
never had), that is, the existence of a socialist community
which is committed to the principles of proletarian inter-
nationalism. (16)

As a result of the decision to embark more fully on the
"armed struggle" tactic, terrorist incidents in South Africa in
the early 1980s were the bloodiest in the history of the nation.
Thus, on May 20, 1983, a car bomb exploded outside the
headquarters of the South African Air Force in Pretoria at rush
hour, killing 17 persons and seriously injuring nearly 200. This
incident, the most lethal terrorist act in South African history,
was followed by similar bombings with lethal purposes. On
April 3, 1984 two bombs exploded in Durban, again during the
rush hour, killing three and wounding 22. On July 12, 1984,
another ANC bomb in Durban killed five and wounded 27
persons. Between 1977 and 1984, 64 persons, including 19
blacks, were killed by ANC acts of terrorism, in addition to
12 South African police officers and witnesses murdered by
the ANC from 1976 to 1982. The witnesses killed by the
ANC included Bartholomew Hlapane, whose testimony revealed
the extent of Communist control of the ANC before the U.S.
Senate. He and his wife were murdered by ANC gunmen in their
home in December, 1982, a few months after his testimony,
Their fourteen year old daughter Brenda Hlapane was seriously
wounded and today remains confined to a wheelchair.

Throughout the period of terrorist escalation in South
Africa, the Soviet Union and its satellites provided strong
material and moral support to the ANC. At the height of the
ANC terrorist campaign, Oliver Tambo stated in East Berlin on
August 28, 1984, "If our struggle today is strong, then this is
thanks to the steady support of the GDR, the Soviet Union, and
other socialist states."(17) Soviet support for revolutionary and
terrorist activities in southern Africa is part of its general
support for "national liberation movements" and the "anti-
imperialist struggle," which is part of the Soviet Constitution
of 1977 (Article 28) and has been an important theme of
Soviet foreign policy since the 1960s. According to Dr. Igor
Glagolev, who before his defection to the West in 1976 was an
advisor and consultant to the Central Committee and the
Politiburo of the CPSU:

The decision to begin an offensive for the conquest of

southern Africa was taken by the Politiburo of the Com-
munist Party of the Soviet Union near the end of the
1960's . . . . The Soviet leadership controls through him
[Yussuf Dadoo] not only the South African Communist
Party but the African National Congress and the South
African Indian Congress as well.(18)

Several witnesses before the Subcommittee on Security and
Terrorism in March, 1982 testified to their training by Soviets
and Cubans in the Soviet Union and Africa. Nokonno Delphine
Kava of the ANC testified on March 1924 and related how she
had spent the period from September, 1978 to February,
1979 in the Soviet Union. While there she was made to study
Marxism but was subjected to abuse, sexual harassment, and
psychiatric "re-education" for recalcitrance to absorb Marxist
indoctrination. Jeffrey Bosigo, also formerly with the ANC,
testified to his training in Angola on Soviet weapons by Cuban
and African instructors and of further weapons and ideological
training for six months in 1977 and 1978. Ephraim Mfalapitsa,
testifying on March 25, related the story of his training in East
Germany in 1977 while a member of the ANC. On July 3,
1984, the author interviewed a former member of the ANC,
"Peter," from Germanstown near Johannesburg, then in the
custody of the South African Police. Peter, a 33 year old Zulu,
joined the ANC after the Soweto riots of 1976 and received
military and ideological training in the Ukraine from September, 1976 to March, 1977. After his return to Africa he was
conscripted into the Angolian army to fight against UNITA,
and this experience initiated his disillusionment with the ANC.
His principal goal was to operate in South Africa, and he cared
little for Angolan problems. Later, Peter became part of a
Special Operations unit of the ANC directed by Joe Slovo, and
in 1984 he was sent on a mission into South Africa with orders
to construct a car bomb from materials secretly cached in
Swaziland and to place the bomb near the headquarters of the
South African Defence Force in Pretoria. He was supplied with
a radio transmitter to detonate the bomb, and according to
South African Police officials, the transmitter was manufactured by the Irish Republican Army. Peter was intercepted by
authorities as he entered Swaziland and, because of his growing
disillusionment with the ANC, readily confessed his activities
and began collaboration with the authorities.

Soviet support for terrorism in South Africa is apparently

THE AFRICAN NATIONAL CONGRESS 65

not confined to material support for rank and file terrorists but is formulated at the highest levels of the Soviet government. The Soviet ambassador to Zambia from 1979 to 1981 was Vasily Solodovnikov, the former head of the African Institution of the USSR Academy of Sciences. He served as "spokesman" for Soviet policy in southern Africa during his tenure as ambassador, and, according to South African Minister of Police Louis de Grange, he played an important role in the planning of ANC and Communist strategy in South Africa.(19) After Solodovnikov's recall in 1981, the Soviet ambassador to Botswana, Mikhail Petrov, is reported to have assumed his function of establishing an ANC infrastructure in Botswana, from which ANC terrorists could infiltrate South Africa. Petrov is reported by South African intelligence sources to hold the rank of general in the KGB.(20)

The Soviets have provided large amounts of weapons and military equipment to the ANC for terrorist purposes. Oliver Tambo has been quite frank about his acceptance of such weapons. Interviewed in *Newsweek* (September 16, 1985) Tambo responded to the question, "Where do you get your weaponry?"

We get them from the socialist countries, principally the Soviet Union, from the Organization of African States [?] and from individual African countries. The West does not give us any, but we would take them if they did. We would like to get Western weapons as a gesture of support from the West.

This response — that "liberation movements" must obtain weapons from the Soviet Bloc because Western states will not provide them — is a common argument among Marxist terrorist groups. Most Western states, of course, do not provide weapons and support to anti-Western Marxists and terrorists because these states reject both the ends and methods of the "liberation" movements, although Norway and Sweden are reported to have provided large sums of money to the ANC specifically for non-military purposes.(21) Anatoliy Gromyko, the current director of the African Institute of the USSR Academy of Sciences, affirmed Soviet material support for the ANC in a broadcast over Radio Moscow on January 8, 1986.

The people of the Soviet Union . . . actively support the struggle of the ANC of South Africa . . . . The Soviet Union, through its government and organizations, collects donations that are entrusted to the Soviet Committee for the Defense of Peace and a part of these funds is used to support those in the struggle in South Africa.(22)

Yet the resurgence of terrorism of a particularly lethal and spectacular kind by the ANC in the early 1980s was in one respect a sign of weakness. The ANC was unable to create a widespread guerrilla war, and its terrorism was limited largely to civilian targets or isolated police and military positions. The Nkomati Accords between South Africa and Mozambique of March 16, 1984 undercut the ability of the ANC to use Mozambique as a base of infiltration into South Africa or to sustain an infrastructure within South Africa. ANC tactics from 1983 began to emphasize "forms of struggle" other than terrorism and guerrilla war. In remarks in a Presidential address on the occasion of the 71st anniversary of the ANC on January 8, 1983, Oliver Tambo emphasized the need for "strengthening the offensive power" of the ANC in political action:

To increase our offensive power:

* we must organise the people into strong mass democratic organisations;

* we must organise all revolutionaries into underground units of the ANC;

* we must organise all combatants into units of *Umkhonto we Sizwe*;

* we must organise all democratic forces into one front for national liberation.(23)

Tambo also emphasized the lack of political organization of revolutionary forces in South Africa and the need to work with trade unions, youth and student groups, "among the women, among the cultural and sports workers, the religious community and at the civic level." This emphasis on political agitation did not displace terrorist tactics, however, for the ANC, Tambo re-asserted, "upholds a strategy which combines revolutionary mass political action with revolutionary armed struggle."(24)

Exactly one year later, Tambo re-asserted this tactical line: "To march forward must mean that we advance against the regime's organs of state-power, creating conditions in which the country becomes increasingly ungovernable," and he repeated the need to expand "organisational and educational work." He also took the opportunity to praise the United Democratic Front:

At this juncture allow me to single out the creation of

THE AFRICAN NATIONAL CONGRESS   67

the UDF as a historic achievement in our people's efforts
to unite in the broadest possible front for the struggle
against the inhuman apartheid system. The formation of
the United Democratic Front was a product of our people's determination to be their own liberators.(25)

And Tambo repeated that "We shall achieve victory through a
combination of mass political action and organised revolutionary violence."

The outbreak of riots and terrorist attacks in several black
townships in the summer of 1984 reflected in part the new
tactics of the ANC as well as of other militant organizations
such as AZAPO, which agitate within schools and social groups
to instigate mob action within the townships to make the country ungovernable. Thus, ANC's Radio Freedom re-iterated Tambo's call for "going on the offensive":

We have pointed out that the houses of lackeys have
been petro-bombed . . . . The houses of politicians have
also come under fire . . . . We attack only those we can
capture or destroy. Remember: at all times, surprise is the
best form of attack. When we ambush these patrols they
should not be given time to even think or consider their
next move.(26)

Tambo's remarks in his address of 1984 were the subject of
extensive analysis and commentary by L. Mzansi in *The African
Communist* later in the year. Mzansi sought to analyze Tambo's
call for "united mass action of the people," in distinction to the
armed struggle, in light of the ideas of the "theoretical founder"
of the 1930s organization, the Popular Front against Fascism
and War, Georgi Dimitrov. "The basic strategy worked out by
Dimitrov and adopted by the CI [Communist International],"
wrote Mzansi, "was to form the broadest possible front of
democratic classes and strata as the basis of the defense of
democratic rights against fascism and war."(27) Mzansi applied
the concepts developed by Dimitrov to the UDF role in "united
mass action."

The "political action" envisioned by Tambo and Mzansi, it
must be emphasized, is not peaceful or democratic in any
Western sense but is oriented to the further expansion of armed
struggle beyond the confines of MK to the broader black population. "Comrade Mzala" emphasised this point in an article in
Sechaba in January, 1985:

Our task in this regard is to continue as we are already

doing to form the nuclei of armed guerrilla units, operating both in the towns and countryside, which should exist not merely to fight to destroy the enemy's military strength, but also to shoulder such important tasks as mobilising the masses, organising them, arming them, and helping them to form revolutionary organs of self-government . . . . At the grass-roots level, armed struggle must be demystified, workers and peasants should be capable of imagining that they themselves are capable of carrying out combat operations.(28)

In his anniversary message for 1985, Tambo praised the combination of political and armed struggle for its accomplishments in furthering the revolutionary processes, and he singled out for commendation the militant trade unions, the students and working youth, and women, and called for further "organisation and mobilisation of our rural masses." "As we stated last year," said Tambo,

> . . . our struggle consists of four interlinked and mutually reinforcing elements. These are, first, the vanguard role of the underground structures of the ANC; second, the united mass political action of the people; third, the armed offensive spearheaded by *Umkhonto we Sizwe*; and fourth, the international campaign to isolate the apartheid regime while winning world-wide moral, political and material support for the struggle. With regard to the second of these elements, there can be no doubt that we have registered great successes in raising the united mass action of the people to higher levels.(29)

It would seem that Tambo's self-congratulation is at least partially justified. While the ANC is not solely responsible for the continued violence in the townships and the level of terrorism in South Africa, its propaganda and political and terrorist activities certainly have encouraged and contributed substantially, and while South Africa is far from becoming ungovernable, there remain continuing problems of law enforcement and public administration in the townships where political violence has been sustained. As Tambo acknowledged, the purpose of the ANC's revolutionary violence is not so much the overthrow of the government as the establishment of an "alternative power" that will replace the existing structures of the government.

Our mass democratic and revolutionary movement

THE AFRICAN NATIONAL CONGRESS 69

> should emerge even more forcefully as the alternative power in our country . . . . One of our central tasks in the coming period is to transform the potential we have created into the reality of people's war.(30)

Thabo Mbeki, "publicity director" of the ANC, has also emphasized that the ANC political contacts, including international and domestic "establishment" contacts, would parallel and re-inforce the intensification of armed struggle, mass strikes, and boycotts. "We are moving close to our objective of waging a people's war of liberation," as Mbeki told the *Washington Post* in March, 1986. As the *Post* itself expressed the goals and methods of the ANC,

> It is clearly a two-track strategy — intensifying the physical pressure on the white power structure to increase its inner doubts and divisions, while trying to take advantage of these divisions to build an alliance broad enough to pressure the administration into opening the door to negotiations.(31)

Despite variations within the tactical line of the ANC over the years, there has been a persistent unity, which is reflected in similar or parallel pronouncements by the leaders of the SACP. This unity consists in a commitment to violence and organized terrorism as proper instruments of revolutionary strategy, but it is important not to over-simplify this commitment. While the ANC and its Communist allies emphasize the use of political violence, they also, in the best tradition of Leninism, emphasize the control and coordination of violence by political organizations and for political ends. War, as Clausewitz had taught and as Lenin never tired of repeating, is an extension of politics by other means and must be subordinated to political ends. The end that the ANC and SACP pursue in South Africa is the "seizure of power," and terrorism, guerrilla warfare, armed struggle, mob violence, or any other form of violence or struggle is useful only in so far as it contributes to that end. The political organization and agitation that the ANC sponsors is also subordinate to this end and intended to encourage the delegitimization and destabilization of the South African regime, to interact with armed struggle to "make the country ungovernable," to make possible the "waging of people's war," and eventually to create an "alternative government" that will replace existing political and administrative structures. Whatever faults and failures may be found in South

70   JOURNAL OF SOCIAL, POLITICAL AND ECONOMIC STUDIES

African government and society, the glamorization by Western
opinion leaders of the ANC and of Nelson Mandela, a principal
architect of its revolutionary strategy, does little to contribute
to an understanding or a resolution of South African problems
and does much to obscure the brutalities for which the ANC
and SACP are responsible and which their ideology and strategy
fully endorse.

FOOTNOTES

(1)   *Soviet, East German and Cuban Involvement in Fomenting Terrorism in
Southern Africa,* Report of the Chairman of the Subcommittee on Security and
Terrorism to the Committee on the Judiciary, U.S. Senate, 97th Congress, 2nd
Session, November, 1982, pp. 4-7 (hereinafter cited as *Report*).

(2)   *Washington Post,* February 1, 1985, p. A24.

(3)   *Sechaba* (August, 1984), p. 7.

(4)   *African Communist,* no. 99, 4th Quarter, 1984, p. 8.

(5)   *Documents of the Second National Consultative Conference of the African
National Congress, Zambia, 16-23 June, 1985* (Lusaka, Zambia: African National
Congress, 1985), p. 58.

(6)   *Sechaba* (March, 1984), p. 13.

(7)   "ANC Honours Karl Marx," *Sechaba* (June, 1983), p. 8.

(8)   *Umzebenzi,* no. 1 (1985).

(9)   Nelson Mandela, "Statement during Trial," in John Gerassi, ed., *The
Coming of the New International* (New York and Cleveland: World Publishing
Company, 1971), p. 331.

(10)   *Terrorism,* A Staff Study prepared by the Committee on Internal Security,
U.S. House of Representatives, 93rd Congress, 2nd Session, 1974, pp. 60-63.

(11)   *Report,* p. 21.

(12)   Gerassi, ed., *New International,* p. 350.

(13)   See Samuel T. Francis, *The Soviet Strategy of Terror* (rev. ed.; Washington:
Heritage Foundation, 1985), chaps. 3 and 4, for more discussion of these matters.

(14)   See Gerassi, ed., *New International,* pp. 350-56.

(15)   "Comrade Mzala," [pseud.], "The Immediate Task of Our Movement,"
The African Communist, 3rd Quarter, 1980, p. 65.

(16)   Ibid., pp. 68-69.

(17)   *Foreign Broadcast Information Service/Middle East and Africa,* August
30, 1984, p. U6.

(18)   *Congressional Record,* December 12, 1979, p. E6099.

(19)   Testimony of Dr. Peter Vanneman, *The Role of the Soviet Union, Cuba,
and East Germany in Fomenting Terrorism in Southern Africa,* Hearing before the
Subcommittee on Security and Terrorism of the Committee on the Judiciary, U.S.
Senate, 97th Congress, 2nd Session, I, 42.; *To The Point,* 13, June 1980, p. 12.

(20)   *Foreign Broadcast Information Service/Middle East and Africa,* June 19,
1985, p. U8.

(21)   *Newsweek,* September 16, 1985, p. 26.

(22)   *Foreign Broadcast Information Service/Middle East and Africa,* January
18, 1986, p. J1.

(23)   *Sechaba* (March, 1983), p. 5.

(24)   Ibid., pp. 5 and 6.

THE AFRICAN NATIONAL CONGRESS   71

(25)   *Sechaba* (March, 1984), pp. 4 and 8.
(26)   *Foreign Broadcast Information Service/Middle East and Africa*, October 24, 1984, p. U10.
(27)   *African Communist*, no. 99, 4th Quarter, 1984, p. 20.
(28)   *Sechaba* (Janaury, 1985), p. 27.
(29)   Ibid., (March, 1985), p. 9.
(30)   Ibid., p. 12.
(31)   *Washington Post*, March 7, 1986, p. A29.

[14]

SHOULD SOUTH AFRICA BE NAMED A TERRORIST STATE?

I. INTRODUCTION

The United States Democratic Party has adopted the position that South Africa should be named a terrorist state.[1] This suggested action is to be taken in conjunction with the imposition of comprehensive sanctions against South Africa and the mandatory withdrawal of American corporations from that country.[2] The Reverend Jesse Jackson, who urged the adoption of this position, did so on the basis of South Africa's "actions toward its neighbors and its black majority."[3] One policy analyst has stated that the position is "part of the campaign to increase international pressure on South Africa to change its system."[4] This statement illustrates a widespread sentiment that the South African Government must be forced to dismantle its present political system; that system is apartheid.

Apartheid is defined as "[a] system of institutionalized racial discrimination and exploitation in South Africa."[5] Apartheid exploits eighty-five percent of the South African population for the benefit of the fifteen percent white minority.[6] In order to maintain its system of white supremacy, the South African Government has resorted to repressive measures.[7] The government

---

1. THE 1988 DEMOCRATIC NATIONAL PLATFORM 7 (available at the *Brooklyn Journal of International Law* library) [hereinafter THE DEMOCRATIC NATIONAL PLATFORM]; telephone interview with Ginny Terzano, Press Secretary, Office of the Democratic National Committee (Aug. 11, 1989). The platform uses the term "terrorist state." *Id.* This term is shortened from language contained in the Export Administration Amendments Act of 1985 (EAAA), 50 U.S.C. § 2405(j) (Supp. IV 1986). This legislation authorizes the Secretary of State to maintain a list of countries that have "repeatedly provided support for international terrorism." *Id.* This Note uses the term "terrorist state" in place of "sponsor of international terrorism" as defined by the United States Code.

2. THE DEMOCRATIC NATIONAL PLATFORM, *supra* note 1, at 7.

3. Bernstein, *Naming Pretoria a Terrorist State Is No Simple Job*, 4 INSIGHT 30 (June 27, 1988) [hereinafter Bernstein] (statement of Stephen Coats, policy analyst for the Jackson campaign).

4. Bernstein, *supra* note 3.

5. 12 S. AFR. Y.B. INT'L L. 270 (1986-87) (statement of Mr. H.J. Coetsee, Minister of Justice of South Africa during Debates of the House of Assembly, Feb. 6, 1986, at cols. 329-34).

6. 134 CONG. REC. H6920 (daily ed. Aug. 11, 1988) (statement of Rep. Brown).

7. The press blackout since 1986 imposed under the state of emergency limits information regarding government brutality. There are, however, several recently reported incidents of violence resulting from the repression. The most recent violence erupted during the black protest of the September 6, 1989 national elections from which black

uses the legal system to inhibit protest against racial inequality. For example, two years of civil unrest caused by black resistance to apartheid laws prompted a state of emergency that was declared in June of 1986.[8] On June 9, 1988, former South African

votes were excluded. Two Black leaders, Archbishop Desmond Tutu and Reverend Allan Boesak, claimed that police instigated election-day violence that led to 29 deaths. A police officer substantiated this claim. Lieutenant Gregory Rockman risked his 12-year career to report his account that police stormed an unarmed crowd of 30 peaceful student protestors on election day. Rockman stated that the police stormed the students like wild dogs and beat them with rubber whips. Wren, *Pretoria Officer Tells of Abuses*, N.Y. Times, Sept. 9, 1989, at A5, col. 1.

Some of the reported violence erupts between police and workers striking over poor conditions. An example of such violence occurred on April 22, 1987, when police shot six striking railway workers. 28 died in general strike violence in 1987. Burdzik, *South African Events of International Significance — 1987*, 13 S. AFR. Y.B. INT'L L. 315, 317-20 (1987-88) [hereinafter Burdzik, *South African Events — 1987*].

Other reports include unrest resulting from the forced removal of blacks from their communities under antisquatter legislation and the Group Areas Act, which are instruments used to enforce racial segregation. Group Areas Act, No. 36 (S. Afr. 1966) (as amended 1986); Prevention of Illegal Squatting Act, No. 52 (S. Afr. 1951) (as amended 1986). On January 1, 1986, 21 people were killed during fighting over the transfer of 120,000 residents of Lebowa to Kwandebele. On May 27, 1986, authorities sent bulldozers to the Crossroads squatter camp to raze a 60-acre area of land. Burdzik, *Southern African Events of International Significance — 1986*, 12 S. AFR. Y.B. INT'L L. 275, 275-80 (1986-87) [hereinafter Burdzik, *Southern African Events — 1986*]. In June of 1986 security forces were seen directing white vigilante groups that attacked residents at the Crossroads squatter camps. *South Africa*, in AMNESTY INT'L REP. 104 (1987).

Links between security forces and white vigilante groups were also reported in connection with attacks on black community leaders. It is suspected that such groups, which were aided by security forces, were responsible for the January 1986 killing of Chief Ampie Maysia and the December 1986 killings of apartheid opponents Dr. Fabian Ribeiro and his wife. *Id.* at 103-04.

The security forces have prevented blacks from holding public meetings. On March 26, 1986, 11 people were killed by police at a mass meeting in Bophuthatswana. On June 15 and 16 of that year, entire church congregations were arrested for attending services to commemorate the killings of student protestors in 1976, and certain people were not released for several months. Some children were released only after being sent to "rehabilitation camps" run by the security forces. *Id.* at 99-101.

8. The President, P.W. Botha, in his declaration of a state of emergency, stated:

Whereas in my opinion it appears that circumstances have arisen in the [r]epublic [that] seriously threaten the safety of the public and the maintenance of public order, and that the ordinary law of the land is inadequate to enable the [g]overnment to ensure the safety of the public and to maintain public order,

I therefore, in terms of section 2(1) of the Public Safety Act, 1953 (Act 3 of 1953), hereby declare that a state of emergency exists within the [r]epublic as from 12 June 1986.

Botha, *Proclamation by the State President of the Republic of South Africa: Declaration of a State of Emergency*, No. R. 108 (1986), *reprinted in* 252 GOV'T GAZETTE 10279-1 (No. 3963, June 12, 1986).

President P.W. Botha renewed the state of emergency;[9] it is still in effect.[10] More than two thousand people have died since the beginning of the unrest in 1984.[11] Approximately 30,000 people have been detained without charge under the emergency laws,[12] and nearly 10,000 children number among the detainees.[13]

As a result of frustrated attempts to negotiate peacefully with the South African Government, some opposition groups have resorted to violence. There are two such groups, the African National Congress (ANC)[14] and the South West Africa People's Organization (SWAPO).[15] Founded in 1912, the ANC is a South African antiapartheid organization that has engaged in a limited armed struggle against the South African Government since it declared the organization illegal in 1960.[16] SWAPO is an

---

9. Battersby, *Pretoria Extends Emergency Rule for a Year*, N.Y. Times, June 10, 1988, at A5, col. 1 [hereinafter Battersby, *Pretoria Extends Emergency Rule*].

10. Wren, *DeKlerk Puts Limits on New Campaign of Protest*, N.Y. Times, Aug. 27, 1989, at A5, col. 1.

11. Battersby, *Pretoria Extends Emergency Rule*, supra note 9. Deaths have also occurred at the hands of fellow blacks. Such attacks occur against the backdrop of political factionalism. Recent violence in the Natal Province has been characterized as a struggle between two antiapartheid movements, the United Democratic Front ("the [nationwide antiapartheid] umbrella organization") and Inkatha (a militant Zulu movement). *Id.* "[T]he violence has degenerated into killing, burning, and looting for baser motives: territorial supremacy, criminal greed, grudges, and revenge under a veneer of political justification." Wren, *Blacks Battle Fellow Blacks in Natal*, N.Y. Times, Jan. 29, 1989, at A12, col. 1.

12. Battersby, *Pretoria Extends Emergency Rule*, supra note 9; *see also* 134 Cong. Rec. H6919 (daily ed. Aug. 11, 1988) (remarks of Rep. Brown).

13. 134 Cong. Rec. H6919 (daily ed. Aug. 11, 1988) (remarks of Rep. Brown).

14. The African National Congress (ANC) is the leading South African antiapartheid organization. It has both a political and a military wing. The political wing is led by Oliver Tambo in the absence of Nelson Mandela, who had been imprisoned for 25 years. The chief of staff and deputy commander is Martin Thembisile Hani. Battersby, *South Africa's Curbs Harden Rebels*, N.Y. Times, June 7, 1988, at A8, col. 1 [hereinafter Battersby, *Harden Rebels*].

15. South West Africa People's Organization (SWAPO) guerrillas have been fighting for Namibian independence from South Africa for more than 20 years. Pear, *Southern Africa Pact Set, Too*, N.Y. Times, Aug. 9, 1988, at A1, col. 4 [hereinafter Pear, *Pact Set*]. In 1976 the United Nations recognized SWAPO as the only true representative of the Namibian people and granted it observer status. G.A. Res. 31/152, 31(I) U.N. GAOR Supp. (No. 39) at 130, para. 2, U.N. Doc. A/31/437 (1976). That same year the United Nations Security Council adopted Resolution 385, which called for South Africa to withdraw from Namibia. S.C. Res. 385, 31 U.N. SCOR (1885th mtg.) at 8, U.N. Doc. S/INF/ 32 (1976). There have been recent breakthroughs in negotiations for peaceful change. South African withdrawal from Namibia, however, is linked to the withdrawal of Cuban troops from Angola. Pear, *4 Nations Agree on Cuban Pullout From Angola War*, N.Y. Times, Oct. 10, 1988, at A1, col. 2 [hereinafter Pear, *Pullout From Angola*]; Pear, *Pact Set, supra*.

16. Battersby, *Harden Rebels, supra* note 14.

organization fighting for Namibian independence from South
Africa, which has governed the territory since 1915.[17] In attempts to suppress these opposition groups, the South African
Government has conducted raids into neighboring states.[18] The
South Africans claim that such groups are responsible for terrorist activities against South African civilians.[19] The victimized
states, however, argue that the raids are part of a South African
campaign to destabilize its black-ruled neighbors so that they
will remain dependent on South Africa for their economic viability.[20] South Africa is interested in maintaining the dependency
of these neighboring states so that they will be unable to significantly assist the ANC or SWAPO in their armed struggles.[21] If
these raids are conducted for the purpose of destabilizing regional governments rather than for the legitimate purpose of re-
taliating against armed rebels, then South Africa could be characterized as a terrorist state.[22] Black leaders in the southern
African region, however, urge that merely naming South Africa a
terrorist state is not enough. Instead, black leaders believe that
"the real solution to our problems is the end of apartheid."[23]

17. Partington, *Walvis Bay: South Africa's Claims to Sovereignty*, 16 DEN. J. INT'L
L. & POL'Y 247 (1988). In 1920 the League of Nations issued the Mandate for the Administration of South West Africa (Namibia), giving South Africa full power of administration and legislation over the territory. Dore, *Self-determination of Namibia and the
United Nations: Paradigm of a Paradox*, 27 HARVARD INT'L L.J. 159, 161 n.11 (1986).

18. In 1987 the South African Government conducted raids against alleged ANC
bases in Mozambique, Zambia, and Botswana. Three people were killed in the
Mozambique raid and four people were killed in the Zambia raid. U.S. DEP'T OF STATE,
PATTERNS OF GLOBAL TERRORISM: 1987, at 33 (Aug. 1988) [hereinafter PATTERNS OF
GLOBAL TERRORISM]. Four people were killed in the July raid in Botswana. 134 CONG.
REC. H6922 (daily ed. Aug. 11, 1988) (statement of Rep. Miller).

19. The South Africans claim that ANC bombings inside the country have increased
fourfold since 1985. During the period of early April to early June of 1988 a rash of
bombings in Johannesburg, Pretoria, and Soweto killed at least four civilians and
wounded 25 more. Battersby, *South African Rebel Commander: A Portrait in Erudition
and Ruthlessness*, N.Y. Times, June 12, 1988, at A16, col. 1.

20. The dependence of these states limits their ability to apply economic sanctions
or to provide assistance to South African opposition groups for fear of economic retaliation by the South African Government. Schmemann, *For Black Ruled Countries, South
Africa Is Both Lifeline and Mortal Threat*, N.Y. Times, Mar. 6, 1987, at A6, col. 1 [here-
inafter Schmemann, *Black Ruled Countries*].

21. Schmemann, *Black Ruled Countries*, *supra* note 20. An additional incentive for
ensuring weak economies in the neighboring states is the maintenance of a market for
South Africa's trade surplus. *Id.*

22. For the definition of international terrorism, see *infra* note 36.

23. *See* Schmemann, *Black Ruled Countries*, *supra* note 20. *See also* 41 U.N. SCOR
(2686th mtg.) at 58, U.N. Doc. S/PV.2686 (1986) (statement of U.N. Rep. Legwaila of
Botswana).

According to the United States Department of State (State Department), apartheid is the primary cause of instability in Southern Africa.[24] Former Secretary of State George Schultz stated that "[a]ttacks on apartheid, and defense of it, account for almost all the cross-border violence in the region."[25] Although the United States Government agrees apartheid must be dismantled, disputes arise over the methods to be employed to achieve this goal.[26] Generally, the Republican Party argues that economic sanctions against South Africa will only hurt poor blacks while proving ineffective as a punitive measure against the ruling whites.[27] Contrastingly, the Democratic Party argues that economic sanctions are necessary to increase pressure on a truculent government that has refused to hear the entreaties conveyed through a quieter diplomacy.[28]

The root cause of all this, is, of course, the existence of *apartheid*. The central issue that the [c]ouncil should therefore address is the elimination of *apartheid* for, if *apartheid* were completely eliminated, peace would return to the region . . . . If we still want peaceful change in South Africa, we still have one last peaceful option: the imposition of mandatory and comprehensive economic sanctions against South Africa.

41 U.N. SCOR (2686th mtg.) at 58, U.N. Doc. S/PV.2686, at 18 (1986) (statement of U.N. Rep. Ngo of Zambia).

"[I]n order to guarantee peace and security in the region, the international community should take immediate steps to isolate the South African regime by imposing comprehensive mandatory economic sanctions." 41 U.N. SCOR (2686th mtg.) at 58, U.N. Doc. S/PV.2686, at 83-85 (1986) (statement of U.N. Rep. Mudenge of Zimbabwe).

24. *The Democratic Future of South Africa*, 87 Dep't St. Bull. 9 (Nov. 1987) (Secretary of State George Schultz's address before the Business Council for International Understanding in New York City on Sept. 29, 1987).

25. *Id.*

26. Secretary Schultz stated: "[W]e are united in our opposition to apartheid. It must be eliminated, and it will be eliminated. On that, all Americans, Republicans, or Democrats, liberal or conservative, agree." *Id.*

27. According to President George Bush:

Unfortunately, the political and economic effects of the sanctions have been marginal to negative: we believe the South African [G]overnment has made little progress in dismantling apartheid and black South Africans have been set back economically . . . . The debate over sanctions is about means, not ends. But sanctions are not a policy in and of themselves. Under present circumstances, I will not recommend further sanctions. Rather, we must continue to use diplomacy and negotiations for constructive change.

Vice President George Bush On the Issues 4 (1988) (available at the *Brooklyn Journal of International Law* library).

28. The Democratic Party espouses that:

We believe that the time has come to end all vestiges of the failed policy of constructive engagement, to declare South Africa a terrorist state, to impose comprehensive sanctions upon its economy, to lead the international community in participation in these actions, and to determine a date certain by which United States corporations must leave South Africa.

Existing economic sanctions against South Africa are contained in the United States Comprehensive Anti-Apartheid Act of 1986 (CAAA).[29] In 1988 the House of Representatives proposed the Anti-Apartheid Act Amendments[30] (1988 AAA) to amend the CAAA. If passed, the 1988 AAA would have imposed new sanctions and strengthened existing ones by requiring a total trade embargo against, and mandatory withdrawal of, American corporations from South Africa and a prohibition on military and intelligence cooperation between the United States and South Africa.[31] The Senate has taken no action regarding the 1988 AAA.[32] A new proposal, the Anti-Apartheid Amendments Act of 1989 (1989 AAA), modifies these sanctions.[33] In addition

---

THE DEMOCRATIC NATIONAL PLATFORM, *supra* note 1, at 7.

29. Comprehensive Anti-Apartheid Act of 1986, 22 U.S.C. §§ 5001-5116 (Supp. IV 1986). The Comprehensive Anti-Apartheid Act of 1986 (CAAA) codified an existing arms embargo, prohibited exportation of computers to the South African Government, and instituted limited economic sanctions against South Africa. Some of these sanctions are: prohibition on the importation of krugerrands (section 301); prohibition on new loans to the government of South Africa (section 305); prohibition on importation of uranium and coal (section 309); prohibition on new investment in South Africa (section 310); prohibition on importation of agricultural products and food (section 319); prohibition on importation of iron and steel (section 320); prohibition on exports of crude oil and petroleum products (section 321); prohibition on sugar imports (section 323). *Id.*

30. COMM. ON FOREIGN AFFAIRS, THE ANTI-APARTHEID ACT AMENDMENTS OF 1988: REPORT ON 1580, H.R. Rep No. 642, 100th Cong., 2d Sess., pt. 1, at 1-9 (1988) [hereinafter REPORT ON H.R. 1580].

31. For a section-by-section analysis of H.R. 1580, see REPORT ON H.R. 1580, *supra* note 30, at 18-23. The proposed 1988 amendments to the CAAA required all United States corporations to withdraw from South Africa and imposed a total trade embargo against that country. Section 301 prohibited any United States citizen from investing in South Africa. This provision could be waived by the President up to 180 days after the provision would have taken effect with a showing of good cause. The President, however, would be unable to waive the existing restrictions on investment from the 1986 act. Section 302 prohibited the importation of any article "grown, produced, extracted, or manufactured in South Africa." Section 303 prohibited any export goods and technology from the United States to South Africa. The only exceptions to the economic sanctions were: section 302(b)(1) (certain strategic minerals not available from alternative, reliable suppliers — the prohibition included uranium hexaflouride that has been manufactured from South African uranium, closing a loophole in the CAAA of 1986, which only prohibited the importation of uranium ore or uranium oxide in its unprocessed form); sections 302(b)(2) and 303(b)(1) (the importation and exportation publications); section 302(c) (imports from South African enterprises wholly owned by blacks); section 303(b)(3) (commercial sales of agricultural products); and sections 303(b)(2) and 303(d) (charitable donations). Political sanctions in section 309 included a prohibition on military and intelligence gathering cooperation between the United States and South Africa. REPORT ON H.R. 1580, *supra* note 30, at 18-23.

32. Telephone interview with Staff Member, Senate Foreign Relations Committee (Dec. 12, 1989).

33. H.R. 21, 101st Cong., 1st Sess. §§ 301, 303-04, 315, 603(b), 401(b)-402 (1989).

to stiffen economic sanctions like those contained in the 1988 and 1989 AAAs, the Democratic Party wants South Africa to be named a terrorist state.[34]

Increased economic or political pressure may be the only method available to force the South African Government to dismantle apartheid and end cross-border violence.[35] Naming South Africa a terrorist state, however, may not be the best method to achieve this goal. This Note first discusses the South African system of apartheid and the United States policy regarding that system to date. It then analyzes the United States definition of international terrorism. An examination of South Africa's acts against other nations is then compared with the State Department's definition of terrorism.[36] This Note explores the possible effects that naming South Africa a terrorist state may have on United States policy towards South Africa and on American foreign policy in general; it considers the practical re-

---

The new bill adds: section 301 (an exemption for the prohibition on investment in South Africa regarding emigrant nonresident South African assets that are subject to transfer and disposition restrictions under South African law); section 303 (an exemption for the prohibition on exports from the United States to South Africa regarding goods and technology for use by news media organizations subject to United States jurisdiction that provide assurances that such goods or technology will not be used by or transferred to any South African entity); section 315 (a one time waiver of the prohibition on issuance of oil and mineral leases for persons found to export oil to South Africa or maintain investment there); section 603(b) (a broader range of penalties for violations of the act); sections 401(b) to 402 (a requirement that the President submit a report to Congress evaluating the success of attempts to achieve multilateral measures to dismantle apartheid and if that evaluation is positive, then the President may impose penalties on a foreign entity for violations); section 402 (a waiver to the application of penalties against a foreign entity if from an industrialized democracy under an agreement with the United States on multilateral measures to dismantle apartheid); section 304 (an exception to the prohibition against intelligence-gathering cooperation between the United States and South Africa for intelligence obtained indirectly through a third country and intelligence and diplomatic activities concerning Cuban military forces and other Communist countries acting in concert with Cuban forces). H.R. 21, 101st Cong., 1st Sess. §§ 301, 303-04, 315, 603(b), 401(b)-402 (1989).

34. THE DEMOCRATIC NATIONAL PLATFORM, *supra* note 1, at 7.

35. Cross-border violence is violence that occurs when guerrillas based in neighboring countries cross over the border into South Africa to attack; it also occurs when the South African forces cross the borders into the neighboring countries to attack alleged guerrilla bases or to retaliate against a neighboring country for harboring guerrillas. *See* Kwakwa, *South Africa's May 1986 Incursions Into Neighboring African States*, 12 YALE J. INT'L L. 421, 440 (1987) [hereinafter Kwakwa, *Incursions*].

36. The State Department defines "terrorism" as: "[P]remeditated, politically motivated violence perpetrated against noncombatant targets by subnational groups or clandestine state agents, usually intended to influence an audience. 'International terrorism' is terrorism involving the citizens or territory of more than one country." PATTERNS OF GLOBAL TERRORISM, *supra* note 18, at V.

sults of naming South Africa a terrorist state regarding the increased pressure for change in that region. This Note argues that naming South Africa a terrorist state would be an indirect and ineffective method of increasing pressure on South Africa to dismantle apartheid or end cross-border violence. It also argues that since apartheid is recognized as the underlying cause of cross-border violence in the region,[37] attention would be better focused on dismantling apartheid. While naming South Africa a terrorist state may further isolate it in the international community, such an act could prove damaging to United States foreign policy. Naming South Africa a terrorist state for actions similar to those taken by the United States[38] could damage the integrity of American foreign policy. In order to influence change in South Africa, which is an area of strategic importance because of its vast mineral wealth, the United States must maintain consistency in its foreign policy.[39] Consideration of the fact that evidence of South African involvement in international terrorism is scant compared with that of the internal terror of apartheid[40] strengthens this conclusion. Further, such limited evidence is contrary to the State Department's principle that to be added to the list of state sponsors of international terrorism, a state must repeatedly provide support for acts of international terrorism.[41]

---

37. *See supra* note 24 and accompanying text.

38. South African support for the right wing Mozambican guerrilla group Renamo is similar to United States support for the Nicaraguan *contras*, a right wing guerrilla group. Both groups have been accused of committing human rights violations against civilians. *See* R. Gersony, Summary of Mozambican Refugee Accounts of Principally Conflict-Related Experience in Mozambique (Apr. 1988) (available in the *Brooklyn Journal of International Law* library) [hereinafter R. Gersony]; *see also* AMERICAS WATCH COMMITTEE, HUMAN RIGHTS IN NICARAGUA (Aug. 1987-Aug. 1988) [hereinafter AMERICAS WATCH REPORT]. South Africa's preemptive strikes against alleged ANC bases can be compared with the United States preemptive strike against alleged terrorist bases in Libya. For a discussion of these strikes, see Kwakwa, *Incursions, supra* note 35, at 421.

39. "Every nation's foreign policy depends substantially on its 'credit'-on maintaining the expectation that it will live up to international mores and obligations." L. HENKIN, HOW NATIONS BEHAVE: LAW AND FOREIGN POLICY 52 (2d ed. 1979) [hereinafter L. HENKIN]. Some scholars take the position that immediate national interest should be considered a priority over maintaining an image of integrity by obeying international law. For a discussion of these opposing views, see *id.* at 331-39.

40. In 1987 the total acts of international terrorism in the entire Sub-Saharan region was the lowest in the world, accounting for less than four percent of the attacks worldwide. These attacks occurred in 14 countries. PATTERNS OF GLOBAL TERRORISM, *supra* note 18, at 30.

41. The Secretary of State makes such a determination in order to institute export controls under the Export Administration Act of 1979 (EAA), as amended by the EAAA:
    (1) The Secretary [of Commerce] and the Secretary of State shall notify

This Note suggests that the best method of increasing pressure on the South African Government to dismantle apartheid is to impose comprehensive economic and political sanctions against it, while supporting, as much as possible, the economies of the neighboring black-ruled states and the blacks within South Africa. Any new sanctions that would result from naming South Africa a terrorist state would be limited to items of potential military use,[42] as opposed to the total trade embargo provided by the 1988 AAA.[43]

II. BACKGROUND

A. Apartheid

The term apartheid was first coined in 1948 by the South African Nationalist Party.[44] Formal separation of the races in South Africa, however, existed at the formation of the Union[45]

---

the Committee on Foreign Affairs of the House of Representatives and the Committee on Banking, Housing, and Urban Affairs and the Committee on Foreign Relations of the Senate at least 30 days before any license is approved for the export of goods or technology valued at more than $1,000,000 to any country concerning which the Secretary of State has made the following determinations:

(A) Such country has repeatedly provided support for acts of international terrorism.

(B) Such exports would make a significant contribution to the military potential of such country, including its military logistics capability, or would enhance the ability of such country to support acts of international terrorism.

(2) Any determination which has been made with respect to a country under paragraph (1) of this subsection may not be rescinded unless [at least 30 days before the proposed rescission the President certifies that] —

(A) the country concerned has not provided support for international terrorism, including support or sanctuary for any major terrorist or terrorist group in its territory, during the preceding 6-month period; and

(B) the country concerned has provided assurances that it will not support acts of international terrorism in the future.

Export Administration Act of 1979, 50 U.S.C. § 2405(j) (1982 & Supp. IV 1986).

42. *See* Export Administration Act of 1979, 50 U.S.C. § 2405(j)(1)(B) (1982 & Supp. IV 1986); Arms Export Control Act of 1976, 22 U.S.C. § 2780(a) (1982 & Supp. IV 1986).

43. REPORT ON H.R. 1580, *supra* note 30, at 9-11.

44. A. BLAUSTEIN & G. FLAZ, CONSTITUTIONS OF THE COUNTRIES OF THE WORLD 6 (1988) [hereinafter A. BLAUSTEIN & G. FLAZ]. The Nationalist Party is led by the white Afrikaaners who are of Dutch and French extraction. Their ancestors were farmers who began cultivating South African land 300 years ago. *United States Relations in South Africa*, 76 DEP'T ST. BULL. 464, 467 (May 9, 1977) (statement of William E. Schaukle, Jr., Assistant Secretary for African Affairs).

45. South Africa was formally known as the Union of South Africa from 1909 until

in 1909.[46] Several early laws facilitated this separation. The
Black Labour Regulation Act, which restricted the ability of
blacks to obtain skilled work, was passed in 1911.[47] In 1913 The
Natives[48] Land Act allowed freehold ownership of land only by
whites.[49]

One of the bulwarks of modern day apartheid is the Group
Areas Act of 1966 (Group Areas Act).[50] The Group Areas Act
established separate living areas for blacks and whites.[51] Blacks
found living in white areas or whites who rent to blacks in white
areas can be fined up to 400 rand and imprisoned for up to two
years.[52] The convicting court can also bring an action for ejectment against the violator.[53] Enforcement of this act has reportedly relaxed over the past five years, leading to the development
of racially mixed or "grey areas."[54] On July 1, 1988, however, the
South African Government proposed amendments to the Group
Areas Act, which provided for much stricter enforcement.[55] Nev-

---

1961 when its name was changed to the Republic of South Africa. A. BLAUSTEIN & G.
FLAZ, *supra* note 44, at 1.

46. A. BLAUSTEIN & G. FLAZ, *supra* note 44. Under the 1909 Constitution (as before
in the Orange Free State, the Transvaal, and Natal), the franchise (the right to vote) was
limited to whites. Nonwhites could not be members of either house of the legislature. *Id.*

47. Black Labour Regulation Act, No. 15 (S. Afr. 1911).

48. The word "native" is a term white South Africans previously used to refer to
black South Africans. Tutu, *The United States and South Africa: Human Rights and
American Policy*, 17 COLUM. HUMAN RTS. L. REV. 1, 5 (1985) [hereinafter Tutu].

49. Bantu Natives Land Act, No. 27 (S. Afr. 1913).

50. Group Areas Act, No. 36 (S. Afr. 1966) (as amended 1986).

51. Section 17(1) of the Group Areas Act states:

As from the specified date, no person who is a member of any group shall
occupy and no person shall allow any such person to occupy any land or premises in a specified area [that] was not lawfully occupied and is not under section 18 deemed to have been occupied at the said date by a person who is a
member of the same group, except under the authority of a permit.

Group Areas Act, No. 36, § 17(1) (S. Afr. 1966) (as amended 1986).

52. As of Monday, September 11, 1989, one rand is the equivalent of .3456 dollars.
N.Y. Times, Sept. 12, 1989, at D18, col. 2.

53. *See* Group Areas Act, No. 36 (S. Afr. 1966) (as amended 1986).

54. "Grey areas" are multiracial areas in some of the major cities that are designated for whites. Battersby, *Pretoria Presents Plan to Buttress Segregation Law*, N.Y.
Times, July 2, 1988, at A1, col. 3 [hereinafter Battersby, *Pretoria Presents Plan to Buttress Segregation Law*]. The relaxation of enforcement of the Group Areas Act may have
been the result of President Botha's effort to reform the apartheid system. *Id.*

55. The proposed amendments to the Group Areas Act provided for several multiracial residential areas. At first glance this provision appeared to be a relaxation of strict
residential segregation. Most of the areas that were to become multiracial, however, are
already integrated because of the eased enforcement of the present act. Wren, *Residential Apartheid Arouses Anger*, N.Y. Times, Oct. 4, 1988, at A12, col. 1.

The Group Areas Act prohibits the eviction of those who have breached the act

ertheless, former President Botha rejected the amendments that conservatives urged him to pass.[56]

Another set of laws that significantly restricted the movements of blacks within South Africa were those known as the pass laws.[57] Until recently, a black person was required to carry a pass in order to work in, or even enter, a white area.[58] Under the pass laws it was a punishable offense for a black to be found

---

without providing alternative housing. *See* Group Areas Act, No. 36 (S. Afr. 1966) (as amended 1986). The 1988 amendments would have eliminated this safeguard and stiffened penalties. Landlords who rented to tenants of another race faced the forced sale of their properties. Battersby, *Pretoria Presents Plan to Buttress Segregation Law, supra* note 54.

56. *Tighter Race Law is Rejected in South Africa*, N.Y. Times, Nov. 30, 1988, at A5, col. 1. President Botha resisted pressure from conservative whites to pass the strict legislation in favor of bolstering his conciliatory image abroad as part of an attempt to ease South Africa's isolation in the international community. Wren, *Pretoria Retreats on Measure to Enforce Segregation Law*, N.Y. Times, Oct. 21, 1988, at A1, col. 7 [hereinafter Wren, *Pretoria Retreats*].

57. "Pass laws" is a common usage name for all legislation requiring blacks to carry passbook identification. LAWYERS COMMITTEE FOR HUMAN RIGHTS, CRISIS IN CROSSROADS: A REPORT ON HUMAN RIGHTS IN SOUTH AFRICA 5 (Jan. 1988). "The central pieces of legislation in the influx control system were the Black (Urban Areas) Consolidation Act of 1945 and the Native (Abolition of Passes and Coordination of Documents) Act of 1952." *Id.* at 5 n.16.

58. The two central pieces of legislation that required blacks to carry passes were the Black (Abolition of Passes and Co-ordination of Documents) Act of 1952 and the Black (Urban Areas) Consolidation Act of 1945. Black (Abolition of Passes and Coordination of Documents) Act, No. 67 (S. Afr. 1952); Black (Urban Areas) Consolidation Act, No. 25 (S. Afr. 1945). In 1975 section 10(1) of the Black (Urban Areas) Consolidation Act stated:

No Bantu [black] shall remain for more than [72] hours in a prescribed area unless he produces proof in the manner prescribed that —

(a) he has, since birth, resided continuously in such area; or

(b) he has worked continuously in such area for one employer for a period not less than [10] years or has lawfully resided continuously in such area for a period of not less than [15] years, and has thereafter continued to reside in such area and is not employed outside such area and has not during either period or thereafter been sentenced to a fine exceeding 100 rand or to imprisonment for a period exceeding six months; or

(c) such Bantu is the wife, unmarried daughter, or son under the age at which he would become liable for payment of general tax . . . of any Bantu mentioned in paragraph (a) or (b) of this sub-section and after lawful entry into such prescribed area, ordinarily resides with that Bantu in such area; or

(d) in the case of any other Bantu, permission so to remain has been granted by an officer appointed to manage a labour bureau in terms of the provisions of paragraph (a) of sub-section (6) of section 21 of the Bantu Labour Regulation Act, 1911 (Act No. 15 1911), due regard being had to the availability of accommodation in a Bantu residential area.

Black (Urban Areas) Consolidation Act, No. 25, § 10(1) (S. Afr. 1945) (as amended 1975).

in a white area without this identification.[59] As many as 250,000 blacks have been arrested annually for violations of these laws.[60]

The pass laws were abolished by President Botha on July 1, 1986.[61] Despite this reform, change has been slight; authorities still control the movement of blacks in urban areas through antisquatter legislation.[62] These laws operate as antiloitering or antivagrancy statutes that prevent blacks from remaining in white

---

59. The burden was on the accused to prove a valid reason for remaining in the restricted area. Black (Urban Areas) Consolidation Act, No. 25, §§ 3A(5)(d), 13(2) (S. Afr. 1945) (as amended 1975). Section 14(1A) provided that a person convicted of a violation was to be removed:

> to a rural village, settlement, rehabilitation scheme, institution, or other place indicated by the Secretary [and] shall be detained thereat for such period and perform thereat such labour as may be prescribed by the law in terms of which such rural village, settlement, rehabilitation scheme, institution, or place was established.

Black (Urban Areas) Consolidation Act, No. 25, § 14(1A) (S. Afr. 1945) (as amended 1975). Section 14(2) provides that the person convicted may be detained in prison until the warrant is issued for removal. *Id.* at § 14(2).

60. *South Africa*, in AMNESTY INT'L REP. 99 (1987).

61. *Id.* The pass laws were repealed by the Abolition of Influx Control Act, No. 68 (S. Afr. 1986). *South Africa*, in AMNESTY INT'L REP. 100 (1987).

62. Battersby, *Pretoria Presents Plan to Buttress Segregation Law*, *supra* note 54, at A4, col. 3. The Prevention of Illegal Squatting Act, No. 52 of 1951, states in part:

> 1. Prohibition of Illegal Squatting. Save under the authority of any law, or in the course of his duty as an employee of the government or any local authority, no person —
>> (a) shall enter upon or into without lawful reason, or remain on or in any land or building without the permission of the owner or the lawful occupier of such land or building whether such land is enclosed or not;
>
> 2. Penalties — (1) Any person contravening the provisions of section 1 shall be guilty of an offence and liable to a fine not exceeding R1000 or to imprisonment for a period not exceeding six months, or to both such fine and such imprisonment.
>
> 3. Orders for ejectment, removal of trespassers, demolition of structures, etc. —
>
> (1) The [c]ourt [that] convicts any person under section 2 of a contravention of section 1, may —
>> (a) in addition to any other penalty inflicted, make an order for the summary ejectment of such person from the land or building, concerned;
>> (b) issue such further orders, give such instructions, and confer such authority as may be reasonably necessary —
>>> (i) to give effect to said order for ejectment;
>>> (ii) to effect the transfer of such person and his family and dependents to such other place, whether within or without the jurisdiction of the said [c]ourt, as it may indicate . . . ;
>>> (iii) to ensure the demolition and removal from the said land of all buildings, or structures which may have been erected thereon by any such person or on his behalf.

Prevention of Illegal Squatting Act, No. 52 (S. Afr. 1951) (as amended 1986).

areas after the work day has ended.[63] These laws also permit the demolishment of the makeshift black settlements on the edges of white areas, which had been built to reduce the black workers' travel time from their jobs in the white areas.[64] In June of 1988 the South African Government proposed stricter anti-squatter legislation.[65] This stricter legislation was proposed to close gaps in the government control of movement by blacks that presumably occurred when the pass laws were abolished.[66] Despite pressure from conservative whites, President Botha rejected this legislation at the same time that he refused to pass the Group Areas Act Amendments.[67]

South Africa's Bantustan (homelands) policy lays the framework for the ultimate separation of the races.[68] The goal of this policy is to have each ethnic group live in its own tribal area; these areas would eventually become completely independent.[69] In practice, however, the policy only applies to blacks.[70] The result of this policy has been the denial of civil rights to the black urban work force of South Africa. The black workers are stripped of citizenship rights and forced to take on the citizenship of a "homeland" they may have never seen.[71] If these blacks

---

63. *See* Prevention of Illegal Squatting Act, No. 52, § 1 (S. Afr. 1951) (as amended 1986). *See* INTERNATIONAL LABOUR OFFICE, SPECIAL REPORT OF THE DIRECTOR-GENERAL ON THE APPLICATION OF THE DECLARATION CONCERNING THE POLICY OF APARTHEID IN SOUTH AFRICA 59-61 (Int'l Labour Conference, 75th Sess., 1988) [hereinafter SPECIAL REPORT OF THE DIRECTOR-GENERAL].

64. Black (Urban Areas) Consolidation Act, No. 25, § 3A (S. Afr. 1945) (as amended 1975); SPECIAL REPORT OF THE DIRECTOR-GENERAL, *supra* note 63.

65. *See* Battersby, *Pretoria Presents Plan to Buttress Segregation Law*, *supra* note 54.

66. *See* Battersby, *Pretoria Presents Plan to Buttress Segregation Law*, *supra* note 54.

67. The conservative whites forced Botha to choose between courting internal political support or improving South Africa's image internationally. Wren, *Pretoria Retreats*, *supra* note 56.

68. Under the homelands policy the white South Africans can legitimize denial to blacks of a share in South Africa's riches and denial of political rights because, once they are moved to a homeland [that] is declared independent, they are no longer citizens of South Africa. SPECIAL REPORT OF THE DIRECTOR-GENERAL, *supra* note 63, at 59-69.

69. Ferguson & Cotter, *South Africa: What Is To Be Done*, FOREIGN AFF. 253, 256 (Jan. 1978) [hereinafter Ferguson & Cotter].

70. SPECIAL REPORT OF THE DIRECTOR-GENERAL, *supra* note 63. A homelands policy is not considered feasible for the coloureds because these population groups are scattered throughout the white population. A. BLAUSTEIN & G. FLAZ, *supra* note 44, at 6. A coloured person means any person other than a European, Asian, or black. Coloured Persons Settlement Act, No. 7 (S. Afr. 1946).

71. *United States Relations in South Africa*, 76 DEP'T ST. BULL. 464, 469 (May 9, 1977). The "homelands" consist of remnants of arid tribal lands that constitute 13% of

wish to work in the mainstream economy they must first register for alien work permits.[72]

In 1986 President Botha promised to reform the Bantustan policy by restoring South African citizenship to blacks who were denaturalized when four of the homelands were declared independent.[73] He passed the Restoration of South African Citizenship Act of 1986 to implement this reform.[74] President Botha's plan, however, only applies to blacks considered permanent residents of the Republic of South Africa: that is, only those people who reside in urban areas.[75] Only 1.75 million out of nine million black South Africans are eligible for citizenship under the restoration plan.[76]

In an effort to quell the unrest caused by systemic denial of civil rights,[77] the South African Government has passed a series of repressive legislation.[78] The General Law Amendment Act of 1963 provided that South Africans could be detained for ninety days without being formally charged with a crime.[79] Similarly, the Criminal Procedure Amendment Act of 1965 provided for an

---

South African land. Ferguson & Cotter, *supra* note 69; SPECIAL REPORT OF THE DIRECTOR-GENERAL, *supra* note 63. These black tribal areas contain virtually none of the rich resources that white South Africa possesses. Such a limited basis for economic viability severely diminishes the possibility of true independence from white South Africa. For a description of the homelands policy, see Tutu, *supra* note 48, at 4. For a discussion of the economic problems facing the homelands, see SPECIAL REPORT OF THE DIRECTOR-GENERAL, *supra* note 63, at 66.

72. SPECIAL REPORT OF THE DIRECTOR-GENERAL, *supra* note 63, at 63.

73. SPECIAL REPORT OF THE DIRECTOR-GENERAL, *supra* note 63, at 59; St. Jorre, *South Africa Embattled*, FOREIGN AFF. 538, 541 (1987) [hereinafter St. Jorre]. "The 1987 Special Report referred in some detail to the introduction of three [a]cts [that] the [g]overnment stated had been introduced to 'dismantle apartheid.' These were the Identification Act, the Restoration of South African Citizenship Act, and the Abolition of Influx Control Act." SPECIAL REPORT OF THE DIRECTOR-GENERAL, *supra* note 63, at 59. *See* Identification Act, No. 72 (S. Afr. 1986); Restoration of South Africa Citizenship Act, No. 73 (S. Afr. 1986); Abolition of Influx Control Act, No. 68 (S. Afr. 1986).

74. Restoration of South African Citizenship Act, No. 73 (S. Afr. 1986).

75. St. Jorre, *supra* note 73, at 543.

76. St. Jorre, *supra* note 73, at 543.

77. Such denials of civil rights include exclusion from the right to vote for the central government, exclusion from representation in the legislature, restriction of freedom of movement, and restriction on the ability to earn a living. *See, e.g.,* Group Areas Act, No. 36 (S. Afr. 1966) (as amended 1986); Prevention of Illegal Squatting Act, No. 52 (S. Afr. 1951) (as amended 1986); Black (Urban Areas) Consolidation Act, No. 25 (S. Afr. 1945) (as amended 1975).

78. The bulk of this legislation was passed after the Sharpville uprising of March 1, 1960. Ferguson & Cotter, *supra* note 69, at 256.

79. General Law Amendment Act, No. 37 (S. Afr. 1963).

180 day detention without charge.[80] In 1967 the Terrorism Act was passed.[81] This act contained a very broad definition of terrorism allowing for mass arrests for suspected "terrorist" activities.[82] The minimum penalty for violation under the Terrorism Act was five years imprisonment; the maximum penalty was death.[83] This act was later consolidated into the Internal Security Act of 1982, which like the Criminal Procedure Amendment Act of 1965, provides for a 180 day detention without charge.[84]

---

80. Criminal Procedure Amendment Act, No. 98 (S. Afr. 1965).

81. Terrorism Act, No. 83 (S. Afr. 1967).

82. *Id.* Section 2 of this act includes as a violation any act committed anywhere in the world with the intention of endangering the maintenance of law and order in the Republic of South Africa. The accused has the burden of proof that he or she did not commit an act and did not intend to commit an act that would have one of 12 broadly defined results including:

    (b) to promote, by intimidation, the achievement of any object;

    (c) to cause or promote general dislocation, disturbance or disorder;

    (d) to cripple or prejudice any industry or undertaking or industries or undertakings generally or the production or distribution of commodities or foodstuffs at any place;

    . . .

    (f) to further or encourage the achievement of any political aim, including the bringing about of any social or economic change . . . under the guidance of or cooperation with or with the assistance of any foreign government or any foreign or international body or institution [for example, cooperation with the World Health Organization to end malnutrition is an act of terrorism. *See* Landis, *Security Legislation in Namibia: Memorandum of the South West Africa (Namibian) Council,* 11 YALE J. INT'L L. 48, 60 n.76 (1985) [hereinafter Landis]];

    . . .

    (h) to cause substantial financial loss to anyone in the [s]tate;

    (i) to cause, encourage, or further feelings of hostility between the [w]hite and other inhabitants of the [r]epublic;

    . . .

    (k) to obstruct or endanger the free movement of any traffic on land, at sea, or in the air;

    (l) to embarrass the administration of the affairs of the [s]tate. Terrorism Act, No. 83, § 2(z) (S. Afr. 1967).

83. Terrorism Act, No. 83, § 2 (S. Afr. 1967). In November of 1988 the *New York Times* reported that 274 people were awaiting execution, 30% of whom were convicted of politically-motivated crimes. From January to November 1988 115 people were executed for various capital crimes. Battersby, *Pretoria Won't Return Mandela to Jail,* N.Y. Times, Nov. 25, 1988, at A3, col. 4. In 1986 128 people were hanged in South Africa. Murray & Mangan, *Hangings in Southern Africa: The Last Ten Years,* 3 S. AFR. J. HUM. RTS. 387 (1987).

84. Internal Security Act, No. 74, § 50A (S. Afr. 1982) (as amended by the Internal Security Amendment Act, No. 66 (S. Afr. 1986)). This act delineates when "temporarily operative powers of detention" become operative:

    (1) If a police officer of or above the rank of warrant officer is of the opinion that the detention of a particular person will contribute to the termination, combating, or prevention of public disturbance, disorder, riot, or public vio-

The broad scope of this act makes it a powerful tool for suppressing peaceful as well as violent protest.[85]

Enforcement of these repressive laws has frequently caused
eruptions of violence.[86] Several confrontations between the
South African police and black protesters, which have triggered
the implementation of sanctions by the United States,[87] illustrate a pattern of unrest in South Africa.

The first of these uprisings was the Sharpville uprising of
March 21, 1960.[88] This incident began as a peaceful protest
against the pass laws[89] and ended with the death of sixty-nine
people.[90] In 1976[91] another surge of unrest erupted in South Af-

---

lence at any place within the [r]epublic, he may without warrant arrest that
person or cause him to be arrested and cause him to be detained without a
warrant of detention for a period not exceeding 48 hours in a prison referred to
in section 20(1) of the Prisons Act, 1959 (Act No. 8 of 1959), including a police
cell or lock-up.

(2) If a commissioned officer as defined in section 1 of the Police Act, 1958
(Act No. 7 of 1958) of or above the rank of lieutenant-colonel is of the opinion
that the further detention of a person referred to in subsection (1) will contribute to the termination, combating, or preventing of public disturbance, disorder, riot, or public violence at any place within the [r]epublic, such officer may,
under written order signed by him, have such person so detained for the further period ordered in the written order or until that person's earlier release is
ordered by such officer: Provided that no such person shall, on any particular
occasion when he is detained in terms of the provisions of this section, be so
detained for a period exceeding 180 days as from the date of his arrest.

Id.

85. *See supra* note 84.

86. *South Africa,* in AMNESTY INT'L REP. 104 (1987).

87. Major United States responses to South African repression have occurred after
significant periods of unrest. For further discussion of these responses, see *infra* notes
111-31 and accompanying text.

88. Nicholson, *Nothing Really Gets Better: Reflections on the Twenty-Five Years
Between Sharpville and Uitenhage,* 8 HUM. RTS. Q. 511, 511-12 (1987) [hereinafter
Nicholson].

89. Nicholson, *supra* note 88, at 512. "The campaign was designed to highlight the
injustices of the pass laws." *Id.* at 513.

90. Nicholson, *supra* note 88, at 513. Thousands of blacks gathered at a police station to present themselves to be arrested for failing to carry their passes. The police
threw tear gas and arrested the leader of the group. The crowd responded by throwing
stones. Two shots were heard and the crowd surged forward toward the police station.
Two officers then shot at the crowd without orders; 50 more followed suit. The crowd
dispersed, leaving 69 dead and 178 wounded. On March 27, 1960, the national police
commissioner suspended the pass laws. On April 9, 1960, Prime Minister Dr. Hendrik F.
Verwoerd was shot in the head. Pear, *Pretoria's National Party: Vehicle for Africaner
Party,* N.Y. Times, Sept. 7, 1989, at A1, col. 5. During his recovery he said that recent
events were no reason to change policy, and he restored the pass laws. Nicholson, *supra*
note 88, at 512.

91. Because of the police crackdown after the Sharpville massacre, when an entire
generation of black political and trade union leaders were imprisoned, and as a result of

rica.[92] Black students boycotted classes in the township of Soweto to protest inequality in education,[93] and rioting occurred on a large scale.[94] In efforts to suppress the protests, the police shot 400 people.[95] In September of 1977 Stephen Biko, student leader of the Black Consciousness Movement, died while in detention.[96] One month after this incident, the South African Government employed sweeping measures to quiet the opposition voices.[97] In one day, October 19, 1977, the South African Government placed nearly fifty black leaders in preventive detention, shut down black-run newspapers, banned eighteen antiapartheid organizations, and banished six white lay and church leaders for five years because they had spoken out for black rights.[98]

In 1984 unrest developed in Langa Township (the city, township) Uitenhage[99] when police prevented meetings between

---

the homelands policy that broke down political networks by removing blacks to their respective "homelands," the apartheid system stabilized by quelling protest. The policy of sending black students to all black universities, however, facilitated the development of a protest movement from a new generation. Black universities were the breeding grounds for the Black Consciousness Movement. Repression of protest from these students led to violence in 1976. B. LAPPING, APARTHEID: A HISTORY (1986) [hereinafter B. LAPPING].

92. *See* B. LAPPING, *supra* note 91.

93. Ferguson & Cotter, *supra* note 69, at 261.

94. *See generally* B. LAPPING, *supra* note 91.

95. Nicholson, *supra* note 88, at 515.

96. *Concern Expressed on Recent Events in South Africa*, 77 DEP'T ST. BULL. 897 (Dec. 19, 1977) (statement by Richard M. Moose, Assistant Secretary for Africa of House Committee on International Relations). Stephen Biko, a medical student, was the leading writer and thinker of the Black Consciousness Movement. The Black Consciousness Movement was not an organization but rather a set of ideas contained in writings and speeches that expressed the opinions of the youth of black South Africa. Biko, who limited his work to philosophical speeches and social work to avoid arrest under the Terrorism Act, *see* Terrorism Act, No. 83 (S. Afr. 1967), was arrested under that act's provisions on August 18, 1977. Biko was kept naked and manacled for 20 days, he was heavily beaten during interrogation, and he subsequently died from brain damage. The official cause of Stephen Biko's death was suicide. B. LAPPING, *supra* note 91, at 157-61. A motion picture, *Cry Freedom*, was made about the death of Steven Biko. *Cry Freedom* (Universal City Studios, Inc. 1987).

97. *Concern Expressed on Recent Events in South Africa*, 77 DEP'T ST. BULL. 897, 897-98 (Dec. 19, 1977) ("blatant suppression of legitimate expression of political thought and violation of the rights of the individual").

98. *Id.* at 897.

99. Langa Township is located on the outskirts of Uitenhage, a city on the Eastern Cape of South Africa. *The Langa Shootings: Editor's Introduction*, in Majodina, *A Short Background to the Shooting Incident in Langa Township, Uitenhage*, 8 HUM. RTS. Q. 488 (1987) [hereinafter Majodina].

boycotting black students and concerned parents.[100] The unrest continued throughout 1985 with shootings reportedly occurring almost daily.[101] The police rescheduled a joint funeral for three of the shooting victims one day before it was to be held because they realized that a funeral held on a weekday would set the stage for masses of workers to stay away from work in order to attend.[102] The following day, however, a procession of 5,000 people marched toward KwaNobuhle where the funeral was to be held.[103] The procession met with police who were patrolling the area in armored tanks.[104] After the police opened fire, twenty marchers were killed and twenty-seven more were injured.[105] Subsequently, 239 people were arrested for protesting the Uitenhage killings.[106]

In an effort to end the sustained unrest, the South African Government imposed a state of emergency in thirty-six districts on July 20, 1985.[107] President Botha briefly lifted the state of emergency on March 7, 1986.[108] Four months later, however, he announced a nationwide state of emergency,[109] which remains in effect today.[110] This continued unrest in South Africa requires a

---

100. Majodina, *supra* note 99, at 489.

101. Majodina, *supra* note 99, at 491.

102. Majodina, *supra* note 99, at 492. "It is known that they tend to prevail on the authorities concerned not [to] ban weekend funerals." *Id.* at 493. Weekend funerals were banned by section 46 of the Internal Security Act; however, employees and the authorities knew that a weekday funeral would keep large numbers of blacks away from work. Haysom, *Langa Shootings and the Kannemeyer Commission of Inquiry*, 8 HUM. RTS. Q. 495, 498 (1987) [hereinafter Haysom].

103. *See* Majodina, *supra* note 99, at 493.

104. Haysom, *supra* note 102, at 500; Nicholson, *supra* note 88, at 513. The police claimed that the crowd threw stones at the tanks; the community stated that it slowly continued its procession when the police opened fire. The commission appointed to investigate the incident found no evidence of a stoning, but declared that there must have been one because stonings had occurred in the past. Haysom, *supra* note 102, at 501-05.

105. Nicholson, *supra* note 88, at 513. The South African Yearbook reports the death toll at 19. Burdzik, *Southern African Events of International Significance — 1985*, 11 S. AFR. Y.B. INT'L L. 267 (1985-86) [hereinafter Burdzik, *Southern African Events —1985*].

106. Burdzik, *Southern African Events — 1985, supra* note 105, at 267.

107. Burdzik, *Southern African Events — 1985, supra* note 105, at 268.

108. Burdzik, *Southern African Events — 1985, supra* note 105, at 276.

109. Burdzik, *Southern African Events — 1985, supra* note 105, at 277.

110. The new leadership of President F.W. de Klerk stirs hopes in Congress and the Bush Administration that a political settlement will end apartheid. The Bush Administration wants to give de Klerk a chance to implement his policies. Democrats in Congress are willing to wait until Spring of 1990 for signals of change, such as release of political prisoners, lifting the ban on antiapartheid organizations, negotiations with black leaders, and lifting the state of emergency. Democratic Congresspeople would like to work out an

strong American response.

B. *The American Response*

The United States Government has implemented sanctions against the South African Government during times of significant South African unrest. In 1963 after the Sharpville massacre,[111] the United States supported United Nations Security Council Resolution 181,[112] which called for all countries to participate in a voluntary arms embargo against South Africa.

In the wake of the Soweto killings, the death of Stephen

---

agreement with President Bush to implement additional sanctions if these signals fail to appear by spring. Pear, *De Klerk Stirring Washington Hopes*, N.Y. Times, Sept. 6, 1989, at A3, col. 1. One incident that may indicate de Klerk's flexibility occurred September 13, 1989. De Klerk gave the first authorization in memory for a political protest march. Archbishop Desmond Tutu and Reverend Allan Boesak led the march in Capetown. Capetown's white mayor, Gordon Oliver, and some of the city council joined in the march that protested police brutality inflicted on protestors of the recent national elections, which excluded black participation. Wren, *Thousands of Marchers Conduct Multiracial Protest in Capetown*, N.Y. Times, Sept. 14, 1989, at A1, col. 1.

111. Prior to the Sharpville uprising of 1960 "the United States never agreed to wording in the United Nations resolutions 'condemning' apartheid." G. HOUSER, RELATIONS BETWEEN THE UNITED STATES OF AMERICA AND SOUTH AFRICA, NORTH AMERICAN REGIONAL CONFERENCE FOR ACTION AGAINST APARTHEID 2 (June 18-21, 1984). During the 1950s the United States agreed with the South African position that a government's treatment of its own nationals was a domestic affair, which allowed no interference by another state or organization. Ferguson & Cotter, *supra* note 69, at 259.

112. Security Council Resolution 181 of August 7, 1963 states:
"The Security Council, . . .
1. *Strongly deprecates* the policies of South Africa in its perpetuation of racial discrimination as being inconsistent with the principles contained in the Charter of the United Nations and contrary to the obligations as a [m]ember of the United Nations;
2. *Calls upon* the [g]overnment of South Africa to abandon the policies of *apartheid* and discrimination, as called for in Security Council Resolution 134 (1960), and to liberate all persons imprisoned, interned, or subjected to other restrictions for having opposed the policy of apartheid;
3. *Solemnly calls upon* all [s]tates to cease forthwith the sale and shipment of arms, ammunition of all types, and military vehicles to South Africa;
4. *Requests* the Secretary-General to keep the situation in South Africa under observation and to report to the Security Council by 30 October 1963.
S.C. Res. 181, 18 U.N. SCOR (1056th mtg.) at 7, U.N. Doc. S/5386 (1963).

In 1964 the United States ended direct loans to South Africa through the Export-Import Bank — an independent federal agency that aids in financing exports and imports by underwriting commercial and political risks. L. HENKIN, R. PUGH, O. SCHACHTER & H. SMIT, INTERNATIONAL LAW 1210 (2d ed. 1987) [hereinafter L. HENKIN, R. PUGH, O. SCHACHTER & H. SMIT]. This sanction was ineffective in practice. Although direct loans through the Export-Import Bank were prohibited, the bank could guarantee privately-financed loans until 1978. *United States Relations in South Africa*, 76 DEP'T ST. BULL. 464, 470 (May 9, 1977); K. OYE, EAGLE DEFIANT 344 (1981) [hereinafter K. OYE].

Biko, and the government crackdown on antiapartheid organizations, the United States was one of many nations that voted for Security Council Resolution 418 (Resolution 418).[113] Resolution 418 established a mandatory arms embargo,[114] similar to the voluntary arms embargo of 1963.[115]

During the unrest precipitated by the Uitenhage killings,[116] former United States President Ronald Reagan imposed mild sanctions against South Africa.[117] These included prohibitions against: making or approving loans to the South African Government or any entities owned or controlled by that government; exports of computers, software, and related technology to South African military or apartheid-enforcing entities; the export of nuclear materials to South Africa; importation of arms, ammunition, or military vehicles from South Africa; and a ban on the importation of krugerrands.[118] By implementing his sanctions

---

113. Security Council Resolution 418 of November 4, 1977 states in part:

Convinced that a mandatory arms embargo needs to be universally applied against South Africa in the first instance,

Acting therefore under [c]hapter VII of the Charter of the United Nations,

1. *Determines,* having regard to the policies and acts of the South African Government, that the acquisition by South Africa of arms and related *matériel* constitutes a threat to the maintenance of international peace and security;

2. *Decides* that all [s]tates shall cease forthwith any provision to South Africa of arms and related *matériel* of all types, including the sale or transfer of weapons and ammunition, military vehicles and equipment, paramilitary police equipment, and spare parts for the aforementioned, and shall cease as well the provision of all types of equipment and supplies and grants of licensing arrangements for the manufacture or maintenance of the aforementioned;

3. *Calls upon* all [s]tates to review, having regard to the objectives of the present resolution, all existing contractual arrangements with and licenses granted to South Africa relating to the manufacture and maintenance of arms, ammunition of all types, and military equipment and vehicles, with a view to terminating them;

4. *Further decides* that all [s]tates shall refrain from any [cooperation] with South Africa in the manufacture and development of nuclear weapons;

5. *Calls upon* all [s]tates, including [s]tates nonmembers of the United Nations, to act strictly in accordance with the provisions of the present resolution.

S.C. Res. 418, 32 U.N. SCOR (2046th mtg.) at 5-6, U.N. Doc. S/12436 (1977).

114. *Id.*

115. *See* S.C. Res. 181, 18 U.N. SCOR (1056th mtg.) at 7, U.N. Doc. S/5386 (1977). Additionally, in 1978 procedures on the sale of civilian aircraft were tightened in order to control their use for paramilitary purposes, and further restrictions were imposed on the Export-Import Bank of Washington to guarantee loans only to firms that follow fair employment practices. *United States Relations in South Africa,* 76 Dep't St. Bull. 464, 470 (May 9, 1977); *see* K. Oye, *supra* note 112.

116. *See supra* notes 99-106 and accompanying text.

117. Exec. Order No. 12532, 50 Fed. Reg. 36,861 (1985).

118. *Id.*

through an Executive order, President Reagan was able to pre-empt the possible imposition of stronger sanctions by Congress.[119] The President opposed the employment of stronger sanctions because he felt that they would hurt poor blacks more than the white South African Government and would not aid peaceful change.[120]

On September 12, 1986, Congress passed the Comprehensive Anti-Apartheid Act (CAAA).[121] President Reagan vetoed the CAAA because he opposed the employment of sanctions as a solution to the apartheid issue.[122] Congress subsequently overrode the veto.[123] In addition to the sanctions implemented by President Reagan, the CAAA includes prohibitions against: the importation of products produced by companies owned or controlled by the South African Government; air transportation between the United States and South Africa; the importation of uranium and coal from South Africa; new investment in South Africa; the importation of agricultural products from South Africa; the importation of iron and steel from South Africa; and the exportation of crude oil and petroleum products to South Africa.[124] There are loopholes, however, within the CAAA that impede full enforcement of these sanctions.[125]

---

119. St. Jorre, *supra* note 73, at 557.

120. President Reagan's policy towards South Africa was one of "constructive engagement." This policy was formulated by Chester Crocker, the Administration's Director of African Affairs, who first used the term "constructive engagement" in an Article published in *Foreign Affairs* in 1980. In that Article Crocker outlined a policy that called for continued United States economic involvement in South Africa. According to Crocker, blacks would not be able to obtain political rights until they achieved an economic base that would enable them to demand a larger share of political power. Accordingly, United States corporations can help benefit blacks economically and set an example of fair employment practices. It is essential to this policy that the channels of communication remain open between the two governments and that positive change is publicly supported. Therefore, sanctions, which are used to condemn, do not fit into this scheme. For further detail on the policy of "constructive engagement," see Crocker, *South Africa: Strategy For Change*, in FOREIGN AFF. 321 (1980).

121. Comprehensive Anti-Apartheid Act of 1986, 22 U.S.C. §§ 5001-5116 (Supp. IV 1986). *See* Burdzik, *Southern African Events — 1986, supra* note 7, at 279.

122. Reagan vetoed the CAAA on September 26, 1986. Burdzik, *Southern African Events — 1986, supra* note 7, at 279.

123. The congressional override occurred on October 2, 1986. Burdzik, *Southern African Events — 1986, supra* note 7, at 279.

124. Comprehensive Anti-Apartheid Act of 1986, 22 U.S.C. §§ 5051-5073 (5053, 5056, 5059, 5060, 5069, 5070, 5071) (Supp. IV 1986).

125. For example, the CAAA maintained the commercial end-use exception of Resolution 418. *See* S.C. Res. 418, 32 U.N. SCOR (2046th mtg.) at 5-6, U.N. Doc. S/12436 (1977). If commodities with a dual use (both military and civilian) are destined for a nongovernment user, they can be legally exported. After the commodities have been ex-

In August of 1988 the United States House of Representatives passed amendments to the CAAA, which called for a total trade embargo against South Africa, mandatory withdrawal of American corporations from that country, and a prohibition on military and intelligence cooperation between the United States and South Africa.[126] These amendments, however, have not been acted on by the Senate.[127] A modification of the amendments has recently been proposed.[128] Additionally, the Democratic Party suggests that the State Department should name South Africa a sponsor of international terrorism.[129] It is likely that the Bush Administration will resist both the implementation of new economic sanctions and the naming of South Africa as a sponsor of international terrorism since the President's views on these issues echo the policies of his predecessor.[130] Nevertheless, the Bush Administration seems committed to expanding economic aid to black groups in South Africa and the black-ruled frontline states.[131]

III. INTERNATIONAL TERRORISM

A. *The United States Definition*

In order to determine the merits of a decision to name

---

ported, it is difficult to monitor possible rerouting to government agencies. Comprehensive Anti-Apartheid Act of 1986, 22 U.S.C. § 5067(b) (Supp. IV 1986). Another example is the prohibition on importation of uranium from South Africa. The CAAA prohibits importation of uranium ore and uranium oxide. *Id.* at § 5059(a). United States companies, however, are still able to import partially processed uranium from South Africa. Sanger, *Utilities in Japan to Shun Uranium from South Africa*, N.Y. Times, Nov. 2, 1988, at A1, col. 3.

126. The 1988 amendments to the CAAA are contained in H.R. 1580, which passed the House of Representatives on August 11, 1988. 134 CONG. REC. H6960 (daily ed. Aug. 11, 1988). The major exception to a complete trade embargo is the allowance for the importation of strategic minerals from South Africa that are necessary for the economy or defense of the United States. REPORT ON H.R. 1580, *supra* note 30, at 2. In addition to these measures, the United States must cease any cooperation with the South African Government regarding the gathering of intelligence. *Id.* at 5. The amendments also include a provision requiring the State Department to compile a report on any involvement by the South African Government in acts of international terrorism. *Id.* at 8.

127. *See supra* note 32.

128. H.R. 21, 101st Cong., 1st Sess. (1989).

129. THE DEMOCRATIC NATIONAL PLATFORM, *supra* note 1, at 7.

130. *See supra* note 27. The Bush Administration acknowledges that economic sanctions stimulated South African whites to think about a political settlement, but also notes that the sanctions failed to produce such a settlement. Friedman, *White House Seeks a Pretoria Stance*, N.Y. Times, June 28, 1989, at A5, col. 1.

131. Friedman, *White House Seeks a Pretoria Stance*, N.Y. Times, June 28, 1989, at A5, col. 1.

South Africa a terrorist state, one must begin with an understanding of the meaning of international terrorism. "Terrorist state" is the shortened reference to the term "sponsor of international terrorism."[132] There has been some disagreement over the definition of international terrorism.[133] The dissension stems from arguments as to the differences between legitimate insurgencies and terrorist groups and whether internal repression by a colonial or racist regime may in fact be considered terrorist activity.[134] If internal repression is considered a component of the definition of international terrorism, South Africa's actions against its own citizens, which are carried out within its own borders, may be defined as international terrorism. Further, if guerilla groups supported by the South African Government are considered terrorists rather than legitimate insurgents, then South Africa becomes a sponsor of international terrorism. Conversely, if the ANC is considered a terrorist organization, South Africa's actions against it through guerrilla-like activities would be characterized instead as legitimate defensive measures.

The Export Administration Act of 1979 authorized the United States Secretary of State to determine which nations are sponsors of international terrorism.[135] The State Department defines terrorism as: "Premeditated, politically motivated violence perpetrated against noncombatant targets by subnational groups or clandestine state agents, usually intended to influence an audience."[136] Thus, according to the State Department, legitimate insurgents do not deliberately attack civilians. International ter-

---

132. *See supra* note 1.

133. The nonaligned members of the United Nations include acts of colonial and racist regimes in their definition of international terrorism:

Acts of violence and other repressive acts by colonial, racist, and alien regimes against peoples struggling for their liberation . . . ;

Tolerating or assisting by a [s]tate the organizations of the remnants of fascist or mercenary groups whose terrorist activity is directed against other sovereign countries.

Ad Hoc Committee Proposal on the Definition of International Terrorism. 28 U.N. GAOR Supp. (No. 28) at 21, U.N. Doc. A/9028 (1973).

134. *Id.*

135. Export Administration Act of 1979, 50 U.S.C. §§ 2401-2420 (1982 & Supp. IV 1986). This act amends the EAA of 1979, which originally authorized the Secretary of State to determine those states that have "repeatedly sponsored international terrorism." *See id.* at § 2405(j). The Arms Export Control Act of 1976, as amended by the Omnibus Diplomatic Security and Anti-Terrorism Act of 1986, also authorizes this determination. Arms Export Control Act of 1976, 22 U.S.C. § 2780 (1982 & Supp. IV 1986).

136. PATTERNS OF GLOBAL TERRORISM, *supra* note 18, at v. The report stressed that the definition is not a legal one and as such, not universally accepted. *Id.* at iv.

rorism is defined by the State Department as: "terrorism involving the citizens or territory of more than one country."[137] Therefore, internal repression would be excluded from the United States definition of international terrorism. When discussing state-sponsored international terrorism as defined by the Jonathon Institute,[138] one commentator has stated:

> When we see, therefore, an enduring campaign of terrorism in a country, it is not too far-fetched to suspect state involvement. I do not refer, of course, to internal state terror, a practice made infinitely more horrible in this century by the Russian and Chinese revolutions, and by Nazism. I mean the involvement of foreign governments in assisting terrorist groups to subvert or topple the home regime. Again, that is the distinguishing feature of terrorism in our time.[139]

Since apartheid by its definition[140] is practiced within South Africa's borders against its own citizens, it is a form of internal terrorism and therefore excluded from the State Department's definition of international terrorism.

B. South Africa as a Sponsor of International Terrorism

When considering naming South Africa a terrorist state, and

---

137. PATTERNS OF GLOBAL TERRORISM, *supra* note 18, at v. In a 1985 interview United States Secretary of State George Schultz drew a distinction between terrorism that purposefully targets civilians and legitimate insurgencies that focus on military or paramilitary targets: "[Terrorism's] targets are civilians, noncombatants, bystanders, or symbolic persons or places. An insurgent is in revolt against an established government. His objective is political power. His methods are military or paramilitary. He actively seeks support usually within one country." 132 CONG. REC. S9162 (July 16, 1986) (Remarks of Sen. Helms, quoting Secretary of State Schultz).

Former Attorney General Edwin Meese drew the same distinction in his address to the Jonathon Institute, *see infra* note 138, in May of 1985:

> I think Benjamin Netanyahu summed it up very well when he said: 'Terrorism is the deliberate and systematic murder, maiming, and menacing of the innocent to inspire fear for political ends.' Now I suggest that that definition is vitally important . . . [i]t provides a clear distinction [that] separates terrorism from ordinary warfare, or legitimate military activity, because . . . the targets . . . are innocent civilians, rather than combattant forces.

Id.

138. The institute was named after Jonathon Netanyahu, the sole casualty of the Entebbe rescue. The institute is devoted in part to the study of terrorism and ways to combat it. B. NETANYAHU, TERRORISM HOW THE WEST CAN WIN, ix (1986) [hereinafter B. NETANYAHU] (Benjamin Netanyahu is Israel's permanent Representative to the United Nations and editor of *Terrorism: How the West Can Win,* a collection of essays based on the Jonathon Institute proceedings of 1986).

139. B. NETANYAHU, *supra* note 138, at 14.

140. *See supra* note 5.

therefore a sponsor[141] of international terrorism, the system of apartheid that utilizes internal repression to maintain white supremacy cannot be included in this consideration because of the State Department's narrow definition of international terrorism. To consider South Africa a sponsor of international terrorism, one must examine actions taken by the South African Government against other nations or citizens of other nations.[142]

Two substantial claims against South Africa that support naming it a terrorist state include: South African support for the brutal guerrilla group, the Mozambique National Resistance Movement (Renamo),[143] in its campaign to overthrow the Marxist government of the Front for the Liberation of Mozambique (Frelimo);[144] and South African retaliatory raids and preemptive

---

141. The State Department's report on terrorism enumerates various forms of state-sponsored terrorism that include provisions of sanctuary, training, financial support, weapons and explosives, and diplomatic encouragement and assistance. *See* PATTERNS OF GLOBAL TERRORISM, *supra* note 18, at 33.

142. PATTERNS OF GLOBAL TERRORISM, *supra* note 18, at 33.

143. Refugee accounts of atrocities attributed to Renamo, which include forced labor, rape, mutilation, and arbitrary execution, are recounted in a State Department report issued in April 1988. R. Gersony, *supra* note 38.

144. Bernstein, *supra* note 3, at 31. South Africa could be supporting Renamo in order to destabilize the Frelimo government because it is a Communist government that borders noncommunist South Africa and because it has allowed the ANC to maintain bases inside its territory. These are the same reasons given for South African support of the National Union for Total Independence of Angola (UNITA) rebel group in Angola.

I have warned our neighboring [s]tates, and now I am again asking them, to gain territorial control of their own areas. If they are not prepared to keep the ANC and SWAPO out of their territories, I have offered them the services of the [South African] Defence Force [that] will be prepared to assist them. If that is not done, the [Republic of South Africa] will be compelled to take action, outside our territorial boundaries, against these terrorist organisations, because we cannot freely permit the ANC and SWAPO to enter the country . . . . As I have promised, I now come to the external, but certainly Moscow-inspired, threat to our country. It is, of course the continual responsibility of the Defence Force and of Armscor to keep themselves abreast of the developments taking place in our neighboring states and in other states on the subcontinent of Africa. By monitoring and properly evaluating the arms built-up in our neighboring states, the kindred defence forces are able to get themselves into a state of preparedness so that the territorial integrity of our country can be properly protected and maintained . . . . It is not only my personal opinion, but also that of all information and intelligence organisations in the Western world, that this arms build-up is part of Russia's indirect strategy with which to our detriment it wants to disturb the balance of power on our subcontinent. With a view to building up strategic mobility against our region, the Russians are trying to safeguard themselves by granting support to SWAPO and ANC base areas. Angola is where it has its firmest stronghold. *Remarks of General de Malan, Minister of Defence, Debates of the House of Assembly,* May 14, 1986, cols. 5588-90, in 12 S. AFR. Y.B. INT'L L. 217-18 (1986-87).

strikes against alleged ANC and SWAPO[145] bases in neighboring countries that have resulted in civilian deaths.[146] An analysis of these two claims must include an evaluation of substantiating evidence supporting the claims, South African defenses, and the likelihood of a State Department characterization of such acts as sponsorship of international terrorism.

Renamo's recent fighting against Frelimo has been carefully studied by the State Department.[147] The State Department released a report in April of 1988 which conservatively estimates that Renamo was responsible for the murder of 100,000 civilians and caused approximately 870,000 people to flee the country.[148] In 1987 the number of refugees fleeing Mozambique increased by 300 percent.[149]

According to their report, Renamo qualifies as a terrorist group under the State Department definition of terrorism because it deliberately tortures civilians.[150] The Renamo guerillas reportedly shoot indiscriminately at civilian targets and abduct prisoners to be used as porters.[151] Those caught attempting to

---

145. *See supra* notes 15, 16. An additional argument could be made that South Africa is involved in international terrorism because of its application of its own repressive laws to Namibia, which it occupies in violation of Security Council Resolutions 385 and 435. *See* Landis, *supra* note 82, at 52-62. South Africa, however, has recently agreed to work out a timetable for withdrawal from Namibia. The agreement is tied to the withdrawal of Cuban troops from Angola. *See* Pear, *Pullout from Angola, supra* note 15.

South Africa's support of the Angolan rebel group, UNITA, against which human rights violations have been attributed, is another possible reason to name South Africa a terrorist state. *See Angola*, in AMNESTY INT'L REP. (1987). The United States, however, joins South Africa in supporting this anti-Marxist guerrilla group. The United States plans to continue this support in spite of the recent negotiations. Former Assistant Secretary of State for African Affairs, Chester Crocker, stated: "The Soviets themselves have not offered to act with restraint . . . we are not going to unilaterally disengage." Pear, *Panel to Monitor Truces in Africa*, N.Y. Times, Aug. 10, 1988, at A6, col. 1.

146. Battersby, *Harden Rebels, supra* note 14, at A8, col. 1. Other allegations include South African responsibility for the murder of Dulcie September, an ANC member, which occurred in Paris in April 1988; and responsibility for an April 1988 car bomb explosion in Maputo, Mozambique, which resulted in the loss of an arm for lawyer, Albie Sachs, a member of the ANC. Bernstein, *supra* note 3, at 31. The victims of these acts were members of an opposition group that conducts a limited guerrilla warfare against some civilian targets. Therefore, even if South Africa was found responsible, it would argue that these people could not be truly considered noncombatants. Another allegation is that South Africa was responsible for the death of Mozambican President Samora Machel who died in a plane crash inside South African territory on October 19, 1986.

147. Battersby, *Pariahs Abroad, Mozambique Rebels Fight On*, N.Y. Times, July 31, 1988, at A1, col. 1 [hereinafter Battersby, *Pariahs Abroad*].

148. R. Gersony, *supra* note 38, at 1.

149. R. Gersony, *supra* note 38, at 1.

150. *See* R. Gersony, *supra* note 38.

151. R. Gersony, *supra* note 38, at 31-34. Men are often used as porters, forced to

flee an area of Renamo control are publicly executed.[152] Towns that are not under Renamo control are subject to attack by the guerillas.[153] Children, who could not be found when their parents fled from a Renamo attack, have allegedly been mutilated.[154] There have also been several reports of mutilation of adults, involving severed ears, limbs, noses, and lips.[155]

In 1984 South Africa and Mozambique signed the Nkomati Accord, in which each country agreed to withdraw support of cross-border opposition groups.[156] South Africa admitted breaking the accord in September of 1985.[157] It characterized the breach as "technical," claiming that clandestine flights over Renamo bases were made to deliver humanitarian aid.[158] A captured rebel official's diary, however, was said to have recorded the receipt of twenty-six tons of munitions from South Africa.[159] The South Africans countercharged that the Mozambican Government also broke the agreement by allowing the operation of ANC bases on its territory.[160]

The South Africans are reportedly making efforts to reinstate the lapsed Nkomati Accord.[161] Further, the government contributed military equipment to the Mozambican Government

---

march long distances without food or water carrying Renamo's supplies because of a lack of mechanized transport; many die along the route. *Id.* at 16-28.

152. R. Gersony, *supra* note 38, at 25.

153. R. Gersony, *supra* note 38, at 29.

154. R. Gersony, *supra* note 38, at 34.

155. R. Gersony, *supra* note 38, at 34.

156. Article 3 (1) of the Nkomati Accord states:

The High Contracting Parties shall not allow their respective territories, territorial waters, or air space to be used as a base, thoroughfare, or in any other way by another state, government, foreign military forces, organisations, or individuals [that] plan or prepare to commit acts of violence, terrorism, or aggression against the territorial integrity or political independence of the other, or may threaten the security of its inhabitants.

Agreement on Non-Aggression and Good Neighbourliness Between the Government of the Republic of South Africa and the Government of the People's Republic of Mozambique, Mar. 16, 1984, Mozambique-South Africa, *reprinted in* 23 I.L.M. 282 (1984).

157. Cowell, *South Africa Admits Breaking Mozambique Pact*, N.Y. Times, Sept. 20, 1985, at A7, col. 1 [hereinafter Cowell].

158. Cowell, *supra* note 157.

159. Battersby, *Pretoria and Mozambique in Pact*, N.Y. Times, May 26, 1988, at A10, col. 2 [hereinafter Battersby, *Pretoria and Mozambique in Pact*]; Cowell, *supra* note 157.

160. Battersby, *Pretoria and Mozambique in Pact*, *supra* note 159, at A10, col. 2.

161. Wren, *Pretoria Aids Mozambique's Military*, N.Y. Times, Nov. 30, 1988, at A3, col. 15; Battersby, *Pariahs Abroad*, *supra* note 147; Battersby, *Pretoria and Mozambique in Pact*, *supra* note 159.

to help protect Cabora Bassa, a hydro-electric plant in Mozambique that has been inoperative as a result of Renamo interference.[162] Cabora Bassa has the potential to provide all of Mozambique's energy needs as well as eight percent of South Africa's needs.[163]

South Africa claims that it no longer provides any support for Renamo.[164] Nevertheless, in *Patterns of Global Terrorism: 1987*, the State Department reported that South Africa still provides Renamo with various measures of assistance.[165] Even if it is true that South Africa has given support to Renamo since the 1985 breach, it remains impractical for the United States to name it a terrorist state for this reason alone.

Naming South Africa a terrorist state could raise questions about United States support for guerilla groups that have reportedly violated human rights, including the Nicaraguan *contras*. Questions have been raised in Congress regarding the *contra* movement,[166] and several members of Congress have stated that the *contras* should be considered terrorists.[167]

---

162. Battersby, *Pariahs Abroad, supra* note 147.

163. Battersby, *Pariahs Abroad, supra* note 147.

164. Bernstein, *supra* note 3. Horace Van Rensberg, counselor at the South African Embassy in Washington stated: "We did give them some training and we did supply them with some weapons and ammunition and logistical support . . . [b]ut that stopped and has not been resumed at any time since 1984." *Id. Remarks of R.F. Botha, Minister of Foreign Affairs, Debates of the House of Assembly,* May 5, 1986, cols. 4961-63 ("[w]e are not assisting Renamo. We have no contact with Renamo. It would be a violation of the Nkomati Accord to assist them"). 12 S. Afr. Y.B. Int'l L. 236 (1986-87).

165. Patterns of Global Terrorism, *supra* note 18, at 32-33.

166. The Reagan Administration supported the *contras*, an anti-Marxist rebel group that has been fighting to overthrow the Sandinistas in Nicaragua. Pear, *Wright Disclosure Termed Accurate,* N.Y. Times, Sept. 25, 1988, at A15, col. 1. Human rights violations against civilians have been attributed to the *contras,* including the destruction of farming cooperatives, forced labor, arbitrary executions, and deliberate killings of women and children. *See* Americas Watch Report, *supra* note 38, at 103-24. The United States, as well as the South Africa Government, supports UNITA, which has reportedly committed human rights violations against civilians. *See supra* note 123.

167. Representative Studds, for example, stated:

We do not have to support terrorism to contain the foreign policy excesses of the [g]overnment of Nicaragua. . .[t]he United States maintains a list of countries who support international terrorism. Libya is on that list. So is the Soviet Union. No one ought to be able to argue that the United States belongs on it as well . . . we have feared terrorist action against the Strait of Hormus or the Persian Gulf . . . [t]his month we attacked the far more fragile oil lifeline of Nicaragua, a tiny, wretchedly poor country . . . we set an example for terrorists everywhere; we invited them to learn from us, and to imitate our lack of respect for human decency and international law.

133 Cong. Rec. H4740 (daily ed. June 15, 1987) (statement of Rep. Studds).

I refer again to the definition of terrorism. Terrorism, according to the diction-

To name South Africa a terrorist state because of support for an anti-Marxist guerilla group with a history of human rights violations would be hypocritical when the United States is supporting a similar organization in Nicaragua. In addition, this action could increase criticism for the United States in its support of anti-Marxist insurgencies.[168]

Other actions analyzed in the consideration of naming South Africa a terrorist state are its military incursions into neighboring states.[169] In May of 1986 South Africa conducted three simultaneous raids against alleged ANC bases in Zambia, Zimbabwe, and Botswana.[170] South Africa claimed that the raids

---

ary, is the use of terror, violence, and intimidation to achieve an end. And any other definition of terrorism that one can find, including that in the statutes, would fit exactly what the [*contras*] are doing today.

132 CONG. REC. S11,475 (daily ed. Aug. 13, 1986) (statement of Sen. Pell). "These acts are not an aberration. They are part of a deliberate campaign of terrorism against civilians — destroying health clinics, blowing up buses full of peasants. That is how the [*contras*] have been prosecuting the war." 133 CONG. REC. S3081 (daily ed. Mar. 12, 1987) (statement of Sen. Cranston).

168. *See* L. HENKIN, *supra* note 39. Some conservatives in Congress have criticized the Reagan Administration for inconsistency in its policy of supporting anti-Marxist insurgencies because of its refusal to support Renamo. American leaders who have argued for Renamo support include Senators Jesse Helms, Dan Burton, and Malcolm Wallop. The initiative faltered because of the Iran-*contra* affair and the retirement of CIA Director William Casey, who was the most forceful advocate for the rebels within the Reagan Administration. Pear & Brooke, *Rightists in U.S. Aid Mozambique Rebels*, N.Y. Times, May 22, 1988, at A1, col. 4 [hereinafter Pear & Brooke]; Lewis, *Bid to Have U.S. Back Mozambique Rebels Halted*, N.Y. Times, Mar. 16, 1987, at A9, col. 1; Lewis, *Reagan Tells Mozambican of Distress That Pretoria Violated Pact*, N.Y. Times, Sept. 20, 1985, at A7, col. 2 [hereinafter Lewis, *Reagan Tells Mozambican of Distress*].

The Reagan Administration was encouraged by the Frelimo government's overtures to the United States. The Administration appeared to view this as a setback for Soviet influence in southern Africa. Lewis, *Reagan Tells Mozambican of Distress*, *supra*.

Some private conservative organizations in the United States have supported Renamo. Louisiana businessman, James U. Blanchard, III, has contributed between $50,000 to $75,000 since 1986 for the purchase of medical supplies and radios. The conservative American group, Freedom, Inc., has contributed knives, walkie-talkies, and other supplies, as well as $15,000 to a Renamo lobbying group in 1987. Free the Eagle, another conservative lobbying organization, has contributed office space, telephones, and traveling expenses for the Renamo lobbying group. Pear & Brooke, *supra*.

169. *See* PATTERNS OF GLOBAL TERRORISM, *supra* note 18, at 33.

170. The Botswana attack resulted in one Botswanan death. The Zambian raid resulted in one death and the wounding of 10 other people including two Angolan refugee children. Kwakwa, *Incursions*, *supra* note 35, at 425. Further raids include an incursion into Zambia and alleged attacks in Mozambique during 1987. On April 25, 1987, South African defense forces raided Livingstone, Zambia. The South Africans claim that five ANC "terrorists" were killed, while Zambia reported that four Zambian citizens were killed, and one was injured. On May 29, 1987, Mozambican authorities accused South Africa of conducting four separate attacks on Maputo targets resulting in three deaths. Burdzik, *South African Events — 1987*, *supra* note 7, at 318.

were conducted in legitimate self-defense against ANC "terrorists."[171]

South Africa further defended its actions by citing to international law[172] and Western countries' approaches to combating international terrorism.[173] The day after South Africa conducted the raids President P.W. Botha said:

> It is a particularly serious transgression of international law for states to provide sanctuary to elements [that] plan, instigate, and execute acts of terror against other states, as is happening in Southern Africa. It is an established principle of international law that when this occurs, the state against which such acts are perpetrated has the right to resort to acts of self-defence and to carry out [preemptive] strikes. Israel attacked the

---

171. South Africa's permanent representative at the United Nations stated that: South Africa will not tolerate activities endangering our security. Although it is committed to resolve its differences with its neighbors by peaceful means, South Africa will not hesitate to take whatever action may be appropriate for the defence and security of our people and for the elimination of terrorist elements [that] are intent on sowing death and destruction in our country and in our region. We will not allow ourselves to be attacked with impunity. We shall take whatever steps are appropriate to defend ourselves.
Statement of Mr. K. von Schirnding, South Africa's Permanent Representative at the United Nations, in an Address to the Security Council, May 19, 1986, in 12 S. AFR. Y.B. INT'L L. 220 (1986-87).

172. The principles cited are interpreted from article 2(4) of the United Nations Charter (Charter): "All [m]embers shall refrain in their international relations from the threat or use of force against the territorial integrity or political independence of any [s]tate, or in any other manner inconsistent with the [p]urposes of the United Nations;" and from article 51: "Nothing in the present Charter shall impair the inherent right of individual or collective self-defence if an armed attack occurs against a [m]ember of the United Nations . . . ." I. BROWNLIE, BASIC DOCUMENTS IN INTERNATIONAL LAW 15, 17 (3d ed. 1972) [hereinafter I. BROWNLIE].

The 1970 Declaration on Principles of International Law Concerning Friendly Relations and Co-operation Among States in Accordance with the Charter of the United Nations, G.A. Res. 2625, 29 U.N. GAOR Supp. (No. 28) at 123, U.N. Doc. A/8028 (1970), states that: "Every [s]tate has the duty to refrain from organizing or encouraging the organization of irregular forces or armed bands, including mercenaries, for incursion into the territory of another [s]tate." *Id.* For a discussion of the application of these principles to the three raids, see C. BOTHA, *Anticipatory Self-defence and Reprisals Re-examined. South African Attacks on ANC Bases in Neighboring States: The 'Guns of Gabarone' or 'RAIDs Disease'?,* 11 S. AFR. Y.B. INT'L L. 142-51 (1985-86).

173. President Botha stated:
The ANC is responsible for the perpetration of no fewer than 193 serious acts of terrorism in South Africa since April of last year. South Africans cannot tolerate this without taking notice and action. We will fight international terrorism in precisely the same way as the Western countries, despite the sanctimonious protests of the guardian of international terrorist movements, the United Nations.
12 S. AFR. Y.B. INT'L L. 222 (1986-87).

PLO headquarters in Tunisia and America attacked Libyan installations. These are cases in point.[174]

The states that were subjected to the raids contradicted the South African claims. Botswana countered South Africa's claim that the housing project it bombed contained ANC boarders by stating that the claim was false and that Botswana had in fact never housed ANC members within its borders.[175] The building bombed in Zambia was actually a United Nations center for Southern African refugees.[176]

Zimbabwe was the only country that admitted the target hit by South Africa was an ANC base.[177] Zimbabwe defended itself by claiming that the ANC is a national liberation movement recognized by the United Nations and the Organization of African Unity (OAU),[178] and as a member of these two organizations, it has a duty to allow the ANC to use its territory to assist in the fight against the South African's racist regime.[179] All three countries also claimed that the motive for the raids was not self-defense but part of South African efforts to destabilize neighboring independent states.[180]

---

174. *Id.* at 221.

175. 41 U.N. SCOR (2686th mtg.) at 52, U.N. Doc. S/PV.2686, at 52 (1986).

176. *Id.*

177. 41 U.N. SCOR (2686th mtg.) at 86-87, U.N. Doc. S/PV.2686 (1986) (statement of U.N. Rep. Mudenge of Zimbabwe).

178. The Organization of African Unity (OAU) is a regional organization with 32 charter members. Its charter's stated purposes are the promotion of unity between African states and the defense of sovereignty, territorial integrity, and independence of its member states. L. HENKIN, R. PUGH, O. SCHACHTER & H. SMIT, *supra* note 112, at 795. Such regional organizations are permitted under Article 52(1) of the Charter:

> Nothing in this Charter precludes the existence of regional arrangements or agencies for dealing with such matters relating to the maintenance of international peace and security as are appropriate for regional action, provided that such arrangements or agencies and their activities are consistent with the [p]urposes and [p]rinciples of the United Nations.

U.N. CHARTER art. 52(1); *see* I. BROWNLIE, *supra* note 172, at 17.

179. 41 U.N. SCOR (2686th mtg.) at 86-87, U.N. Doc. S/PV.2686 (1986) (statement of U.N. Rep. Mudenge of Zimbabwe).

180. United Nations representative, Mr. Mudenge from Zimbabwe, stated:

> Pretoria has been systematically implementing its own policy of sanctions against its neighbors. The policy involves the use of economic, military, and political sanctions against each one of us . . . . South Africa is also known to have brought about the death of at least 100,000 people in neighboring [s]tates through its destabilization activities.

41 U.N. SCOR (2686th mtg.) at 91-95, U.N. Doc. S/PV.2686 (1986) (statement of U.N. Rep. Mudenge of Zimbabwe).

The states in the Southern African region are economically dependent on South Africa. South Africa apparently uses economic and military pressure to keep these coun-

The United States, which condemned the South African raids, claimed that the circumstances differed between these raids and its own raid against Libya.[181] The United States representative at the United Nations Security Council stated that Libya had become the principal proponent of state-sponsored terrorism in the world, while Botswana, Zambia, and Zimbabwe have attempted a constructive solution to put an end to the cross-border violence that had been directed against South Africa.[182]

The United States agrees with South Africa in recognizing ANC culpability for acts of terrorism.[183] The ANC has appar-

---

tries weak and unable to give the ANC substantial support. Schmemann, *Black Ruled Countries, supra* note 20.

181. 41 U.N. SCOR (2686th mtg.) at 111, U.N. Doc. S/PV.2686 (1986) (statement of U.N. Rep. Byrne of the United States). Mr. Ngo, the representative from Zambia, condemned the United States raid against Libya as well as the South African raid as acts of terrorism:

> The bombing of Libya by the United States [A]dministration has no doubt encouraged the racist regime of South Africa to step up its acts of aggression. The Pretoria regime has now followed its master's tactics of finding the flimsiest reasons to take innocent lives. Like the United States of America, South Africa has grossly abused its power. We have again witnessed [s]tate terrorism at its worst.

41 U.N. SCOR (2686th mtg.) at 16-17, U.N. Doc. S/PV.2686 (1986) (statement of U.N. Rep. Ngo of Zimbabwe).

182. 41 U.N. SCOR (2686th mtg.) at 111, U.N. Doc. S/PV.2686 (1986) (statement of U.N. Rep. Byrne of the United States). One of their objections was the timing of the raids. The governments of the three raided countries were involved in discussions with South Africa regarding cross-border violence. The raids took place four days before a scheduled meeting with Botswana. *Id.* The South Africans claimed that peaceful efforts to resolve the problem had been exhausted prior to the attack. 41 U.N. SCOR (2686th mtg.) at 23-26, U.N. Doc. S/PV.2686 (1986) (statement of U.N. Rep. von Schirnding (quoting President Botha during an address to the South African Parliament on June 19, 1985)). 12 S. AFR. Y.B. INT'L L. 221 (1986-87).

183. The CAAA stated that:

> a) United States policy toward the [ANC], the Pan African Congress, and their affiliates shall be designed to bring about a suspension of violence that will lead to the start of negotiations designed to bring about a nonracial and genuine democracy in South Africa.

> b) The United States shall work toward this goal by encouraging the [ANC] and the Pan African Congress, and their affiliates, to —

> 1) suspend terrorist activities so that negotiations with the [g]overnment of South Africa and other groups representing black South Africans will be possible; . . .

> 4) reexamine their ties to the South African Communist Party.

Comprehensive Anti-Apartheid Act of 1986, 22 U.S.C. § 5012 (Supp. IV 1986); *see also* PATTERNS OF GLOBAL TERRORISM, *supra* note 18, at 33. In this report the State Department characterized some of the ANC's actions as terrorism. *Id.* The State Department, however, does not characterize the ANC as a terrorist group. The State Department repudiated a recent Pentagon report that listed the ANC as a terrorist group. State De-

ently been responsible for civilian deaths.[184] Former Secretary of State George Schultz indicated that even if an insurgent group was justified in fighting a repressive regime, terrorist acts cannot be tolerated:[185]

> Those who strive for freedom and democracy will always have the sympathy and, when possible, the support of the American people. We will oppose guerilla wars whenever they threaten to spread totalitarian rule or deny the rights of national independence and self-determination. But we will oppose terrorism no matter what banner it may fly. For terrorism in the service of any cause is the enemy of freedom.[186]

The military leader of the ANC, Thembisile Hani, conceded that the ANC has targeted civilians.[187]

If the ANC can be characterized as a terrorist group and South Africa's purpose for raiding Zimbabwe, Zambia, and Botswana was to destroy ANC bases, then it would follow that the raids were legitimate preemptive strikes. Secretary of State George Schultz advocated preemptive strikes as a necessary method to combat international terrorism:[188]

> From a practical standpoint, a purely passive defense does not

---

partment spokesperson, Charles E. Redman, said that the Pentagon report was an information document and was not intended as a policy publication. Pear, *U.S. Report Stirs Furor in South Africa*, N.Y. Times, Jan. 14, 1989, at A3, col. 4.

184. After the raids took place in 1986, several bombings occurred. In Durban a car bomb exploded killing three women and injuring 69 people. A bomb explosion at a bus stop injured six women and two children, one a two-week old baby. Another bomb exploded at a bus stop during peak hours injuring 20 people. 11 S. AFR. Y.B. INT'L L. 155-56 (1985-86).

The July 30, 1988 bombing of a shopping mall killed one and injured 56 the day after the South African Government banned the movie *Cry Freedom. See supra* note 96. That was the fifth bombing in a two-day period. The South African Government blamed the ANC for most of the 90 bombings that had occurred in the 25 months since the state of emergency was imposed. Battersby, *Pariahs Abroad, supra* note 147, at A16, col. 1.

185. Schultz, *The Challenge to Democracies,* in B. NETANYAHU, *supra* note 138, at 20.

186. *Id.*

187. Mr. Hani stated in a *New York Times* interview:

I don't think most whites want to die for apartheid . . . [o]ur intention is to make them see, so that when they are maimed and they are in the hospital, others will visit them and will say: this is the price of apartheid . . . . I know that a few blacks were maimed in a recent land mine blast in eastern Transvaal Province. Their response was, 'I am sorry that I lost a leg but I know that the action was not intended for me'.

Battersby, *South African Rebel Commander: A Portrait in Erudition and Ruthlessness,* N.Y. Times, June 12, 1988, at A16, col. 1.

188. B. NETANYAHU, *supra* note 138, at 23.

provide enough of a deterrent to terrorism and the states that
sponsor it. It is time to think long, hard, and seriously about
more active means of defense — defense through appropriate
preventive or preemptive actions against terrorist groups
before they strike.[189]

Since the South African raids could be construed as legitimate
preemptive strikes and since the entire sub-saharan African region has the lowest percentage of terroristic attacks in the
world,[190] it is unlikely that the State Department will add South
Africa to the list of states that repeatedly sponsor international
terrorism. Moreover, naming South Africa a terrorist state because of preemptive strikes similar to those carried out by the
United States would damage the United States credibility in the
area of foreign affairs by creating a hypocritical image.[191] Applying a double standard could limit American influence in South
Africa, an area that is of strategic importance to the United
States.[192] Furthermore, if the Soviet Union was to obtain control
of South Africa's rich resources, it would possess an economic
leverage against the United States.[193] Thus, the United States
has a significant interest in maintaining non-Communist rule in
South Africa.[194] Naming South Africa a terrorist state because of

---

189. B. NETANYAHU, *supra* note 138, at 23. In an apparent attempt to implement
these principles, President Reagan signed an intelligence order in 1985 that gave CIA
operatives broader legal protection for counterterrorist preemptive strikes. Under the
order actions taken by a CIA operative during such a strike would be deemed lawful if
performed in good faith. The order was designed to protect the operatives from legal
culpability. Engelberg, *U.S. Order on Anti-Terror Strikes Is Disclosed*, N.Y. Times, Oct.
6, 1988, at A13, col. 1.

190. PATTERNS OF GLOBAL TERRORISM, *supra* note 18, at 30.

191. *See* L. HENKIN, *supra* note 39.

192. *U.S. Minerals Supply and South Africa — Issues and Options: Oversight
Hearings Before the Subcomm. on Mining and Natural Resources of the Comm. on Interior and Insular Affairs of the House of Representatives*, 100th Cong., 1st Sess. 153-58
(1987) [hereinafter *Oversight Hearings*]. South Africa contains strategic minerals important to the United States, which are not otherwise available. These minerals include
uranium, platinum, chromium, manganese, and gold. Section 504(b) of the CAAA calls
for development of a program to reduce dependency on South Africa for these minerals.
Comprehensive Anti-Apartheid Act of 1986, 22 U.S.C. §§ 5001-5116 (Supp. IV 1986).
Research is currently underway to find alternative resources and substitutes for South
African chromium and platinum group metals, manganese, and vanadium. *See Oversight
Hearings, supra*, at 100-16.

193. "The problems of the Republic of South Africa are likely to remain a huge
thorn in our sides and an opportunity for Moscow." S. HOFFMAN, PRIMACY OR WORLD
ORDER 82 (1st ed. 1980) [hereinafter S. HOFFMAN].

194. The ANC reportedly has ties with the Soviet Union. *See* Comprehensive Anti-
Apartheid Act of 1986, 22 U.S.C. § 5012 (Supp. IV 1986). South African Ambassador to

its preemptive raids against ANC targets could hamper the United States ability to combat international terrorism by setting a precedent that rejects a military solution to the problem of terrorism.

IV. PRACTICAL RESULTS OF NAMING SOUTH AFRICA A TERRORIST STATE

In order to determine whether naming South Africa a terrorist state would significantly increase pressure on the South African Government to abandon its controversial internal and external policies, one must compare United States treatment of South Africa and the state-sponsors of international terrorism in the area of export control. Export control is the only area regulated by statute concerning United States policy toward sponsors of international terrorism.[195] States currently on the State Department list[196] of sponsors of international terrorism are Cuba, Iran, Libya, Syria, South Yemen (P.D.R.Y.), and North Korea.[197] The purpose of the export controls imposed on the state-sponsors of international terrorism is to prevent the expansion of military capability.[198] The export controls imposed on South Africa, however, are intended instead to persuade the government to end apartheid.[199] Therefore, naming South Africa a terrorist state would not lead to stiffer economic or political sanctions.

---

the United States, Herbert Beukes, claims that the objective of the ANC is to transform South Africa "into a Marxist political and economic totalitarianism." Beukes, *South African Response*, 10 TERRORISM 125 (1987). For the view that black South African nationalists are not communists, see contra S. HOFFMAN, *supra* note 193, at 261. They may be anti-American, however, if United States policy obstructs their goals. Hoffman also states that the practice of dividing a government between moderates and radicals and then siding with the moderates, no matter how flawed, is unsound policy. *Id.*

195. Both the EAAA and the Arms Export Control Act of 1976 (AECA) require the Secretary of State to maintain the list of states that sponsor international terrorism and provide for export controls to be exercised against such states. Export Administration Act of 1985, 50 U.S.C. §§ 2401-2420 (Supp. IV 1986); Arms Export Control Act of 1976, 22 U.S.C. §§ 2751-2794 (1982 & Supp. IV 1986).

196. The list is not permanent. A state can be removed from the list if it has suspended terrorist activities for at least six months and has provided assurances that it will not support future terrorist acts. Export Administration Act of 1985, 50 U.S.C. § 2405(j)(2)(B) (Supp. IV 1986).

197. 22 C.F.R. § 126.1(d) (1988).

198. U.S. DEP'T OF COMMERCE, 1988 ANNUAL FOREIGN POLICY REPORT TO THE CONGRESS 12 (1988-89) [hereinafter 1988 ANNUAL FOREIGN POLICY REPORT].

199. REPORT ON H.R. 1580, *supra* note 30, at 9-11; 1988 ANNUAL FOREIGN POLICY REPORT, *supra* note 198, at 52.

The statutes that govern export controls are the Export Administration Amendments Act of 1985 (EAAA)[200] and the Arms Export Control Act of 1976 (AECA).[201] The AECA regulates the export of military items.[202] Categories of regulated items are contained in the United States Munitions List (Munitions List), which the State Department maintains and periodically updates.[203] The EAAA applies to all nonmilitary controlled commodities that are contained in the Commodity Control List.[204]

Under AECA regulations exports of Munitions List items are restricted for both South Africa and the states sponsoring international terrorism.[205] There is an exception, however, to the regulations with regard to South Africa.[206] If the Assistant Sec-

---

200. Export Administration Act of 1985, 50 U.S.C. §§ 2401-2420 (Supp. IV 1986). This statute was amended in 1986 by the CAAA, which strengthened controls on exports destined for South Africa. Comprehensive Anti-Apartheid Act of 1986, 22 U.S.C. §§ 5001-5116 (Supp. IV 1986).

201. Arms Export Control Act of 1976, 22 U.S.C. §§ 2751-2794 (1982 & Supp. IV 1986). Prior to passage of the CAAA this statute covered arms exports to South Africa because of the United States arms embargo, consistent with Resolution 418. S.C. Res. 418, 32 U.N. SCOR (2046th mtg.) at 5-6, U.N. Doc. S/12436 (1977). The statute was amended by the Omnibus Security and Anti-Terrorism Act of 1986 to include the provision restricting exports to states that sponsor international terrorism. Arms Export Control Act of 1976, 22 U.S.C. §§ 2751-2794 (1982 & Supp. IV 1986).

202. S.C. Res. 418, 32 U.N. SCOR (2046th mtg.) at 5-6, U.N. Doc. S/12436 (1977).

203. The United States Munitions List is part of the International Traffic in Arms Regulations (ITAR), which is the means of implementing the AECA. 22 C.F.R. §§ 120-30 (1988). The regulations are enforced by the State Department's Office of Munitions Control (OMC). Arms exporters must be licensed by the OMC. Overman, *Reauthorization of the Export Administration Act: Balancing Trade Policy with National Security,* 17 LAW & POL'Y INT'L BUS. 327-28 (1985). The Munitions List contains 21 broad categories of military items that are divided into subcategories. 22 C.F.R. § 121.1 (1988).

204. Exporters of controlled commodities or technical data must obtain individual licenses from the Commerce Department's Office of Export Administration (OEA), unless the AECA is the applicable statute. The Commodity Control List contains 10 categories of restricted items. The list is part of the Export Administration Regulations (EAR), through which the EAAA is implemented. 15 C.F.R. § 399.1 (1988).

205. 22 C.F.R. § 126.1 (1988).

206. *Id.* The regulation states:
    South Africa is subject to an arms embargo and thus to the policy specified in paragraph (a) of this section. In accordance with section 317 of the [CAAA], exceptions may be made to this policy only if the Assistant Secretary for Politico-Military Affairs determines that:
    (1) The item is not covered by United Nations Security Council Resolution 418 of November 4, 1977; and
    (2) The item is to be exported solely for commercial purposes and not for use by the armed forces, police, or other security forces of South Africa or for any similar purpose. Such exceptions are subject to the prior congressional notification requirements specified in section 318 of that [a]ct.

retary for Politico-Military Affairs determines that an item is to be exported solely for commercial purposes and not for use by the military or police, the export will be allowed.[207] The notification provisions of the CAAA require the President of the United States to notify Congress of a decision to export a dual-use item to South Africa and to certify that such an item will be used solely for commercial purposes.[208]

Like the AECA, EAAA regulations apply to both South Africa and the states found to sponsor international terrorism.[209] The strength of the controls, however, vary in application to each state, and between the terrorism-sponsoring states.[210] These variations include the type of commodity controlled and the frequency of issuing validating licenses.[211] The regulations that halt exports to South Africa are generally less effective than regulations affecting the state sponsors of international terror-

---

Id.

207. *Id.*

208. Notification of Certain Proposed United States Munitions List Exports

(a) Notification of proposed export; certification of use solely for commercial purposes —

Notwithstanding any other provision of this chapter, the President shall —

(1) notify the Congress of his intent to allow the export to South Africa of any item [that] is on the United States Munitions List and [that] is not covered by [Resolution 418] of November 4, 1977, and

(2) certify that such item shall be used solely for commercial purposes and not exported for use by the armed forces, police, or other security forces of South Africa or for other military use.

(b) Congressional Joint Resolution of disapproval of export;

(1) No item described in subsection (a) of this section may be exported if the Congress, within 30 days of continuous session after a certification is made under subsection (a)(2) of this section, enacts, in accordance with section 5112 of this title a joint resolution disapproving such export.

Arms Export Control Act of 1976, 22 U.S.C. § 5068 (1982 & Supp. IV 1986).

209. 15 C.F.R. §§ 385.1, 385.7, 385.4 (1988).

210. *See* 1988 ANNUAL FOREIGN POLICY REPORT, *supra* note 198, at 8-34, 38-45, 50-57.

211. North Korea and Cuba are subject to the strongest controls: validated licenses, which are documents issued by the OEA under the authority of the EAA and require an individual application, 15 C.F.R. § 370.2 (1988), are required for the exportation of all aircraft including ultralights and gliders to Iran and Syria. Aircraft destined for South Yemen only require a validated license if each aircraft is valued at three million dollars or more. Licenses are required for all helicopters destined for South Yemen. Licenses for aircraft to be exported to South Yemen are generally considered favorably on a case-by-case basis for civilian end use. Validated licenses are required for the exportation of scuba equipment to Iran but not to Syria, South Yemen, or South Africa. *See* 1988 ANNUAL FOREIGN POLICY REPORT, *supra* note 198.

ism because of the commercial end-use exception,[212] although
some of the regulations affecting terrorism-sponsoring states
contain a similar exception.[213] Thus, the variations in the export
controls imposed on the states determined to sponsor international terrorism indicate that South African export controls may
not necessarily be strengthened if it is added to the list as an
international terrorist state. Enforcement problems exist for export controls on all regulated states.[214] The United States Department of Commerce outlined these obstacles in its 1988 Annual Foreign Policy Report to the Congress.[215] The problems
include direct leaks, end-use verification leaks, and reexports of
controlled commodities by third countries.[216] According to the
report, direct leaks occur through American exporters who either
are unaware that certain commodities are regulated or deliber-

---

212. For an explanation of the term "end use" in this context, see 1988 ANNUAL
FOREIGN POLICY REPORT, *supra* note 198. Licenses will be granted on a case-by-case basis
for computers, computer software, and goods or technology to service computers that are
not to be exported to apartheid enforcing entities. Further exceptions on computer exports may be allowed for humanitarian purposes and for foreign computer systems where
the United States content is less than 20%. *Id.* at 51. This exception is a large loophole
in the statute because the most important components of computers make up less than
20% of the system. *See* Paretzky, *The United States Arms Embargo Against South
Africa: An Analysis of the Laws, Regulations and Loopholes,* 12 YALE J. INT'L L. 133-57
(1987) [hereinafter Paretzky]. Licenses will also be validated for exportation of aircraft
to civilians. *See* 1988 ANNUAL FOREIGN POLICY REPORT, *supra* note 198, at 50.

213. Civilian end use is considered in validation of license applications for all exports to South Yemen on a case-by-case basis. 1988 ANNUAL FOREIGN POLICY REPORT,
supra note 198, at 11. License procedures for Iran, Syria, and Libya contain an exception
that allows the export of foreign equipment with less than 20% American-manufactured
components. *Id.* at 9, 10, 25.

214. 1988 ANNUAL FOREIGN POLICY REPORT, *supra* note 198, at 20, 32, 54-55. Those
states listed as terrorist are Cuba, North Korea, Iran, Libya, Syria, and South Yemen.
Other regulated states include Vietnam, Cambodia, the Soviet Union, South Africa, and
Namibia. *Id. See also supra* note 213 and accompanying text.

215. *See* 1988 ANNUAL FOREIGN POLICY REPORT, *supra* note 198.

216. 1988 ANNUAL FOREIGN POLICY REPORT, *supra* note 198, at 3, 20, 32, 54-55. The
report states that leaks, directly and through reexports by third countries, are a special
problem regarding export controls to South Africa, Syria, Iran, and South Yemen on
aircraft and parts, especially nonstrategic aircraft. The difficulties of controlling these
exports are exacerbated by the perception of the exporting community that these items
are not subject to controls and the fact that these exports are not controlled to most
other countries in the region of the controlled states. *Id.* at 20, 55. Difficulties in controlling the export of chemicals are increased by a lack of technical expertise of enforcement
personnel and the fact that some of the controlled chemicals have legitimate end uses
that limit the ability to detect contraband shipments. *Id.* at 32. The report cites the
major problem regarding export controls to South Africa as end-use verification on computer exports. *Id.* at 55.

ately circumvent the export regulations.[217] End-use verification leaks occur when controlled items are sent to civilian end users through the commercial end-use exception to the act and then are rerouted to military agencies.[218] Reexports of controlled commodities occur either through ignorance of the American export regulations or deliberate circumvention of the laws by third countries.[219] Export control violations have been reported on exports to state sponsors of international terrorism as well as exports to South Africa.[220] Since regulations applicable to terrorist states are susceptible to the same enforcement problems as those applicable to South Africa, stricter enforcement of export controls to South Africa cannot be achieved simply by naming it a terrorist state. The solution lies not in naming South Africa a terrorist state but by closing the end-use loopholes and improving the enforcement mechanisms.[221]

---

217. *See* 1988 ANNUAL FOREIGN POLICY REPORT, *supra* note 198.

218. *See* 1988 ANNUAL FOREIGN POLICY REPORT, *supra* note 198.

219. *See* 1988 ANNUAL FOREIGN POLICY REPORT, *supra* note 198.

220. On South Africa, see G. HOUSER, RELATIONS BETWEEN THE UNITED STATES OF AMERICA AND SOUTH AFRICA 8-11 (North American Regional Conference for Action Against *Apartheid*, U.N. Headquarters, N.Y. June 1984) [hereinafter G. HOUSER]; NARMIC, MILITARY EXPORTS TO SOUTH AFRICA-A RESEARCH REPORT ON THE ARMS EMBARGO (Jan. 1984) (available in the *Brooklyn Journal of International Law* library) [hereinafter NARMIC REPORT]; *see* Paretzky, *supra* note 212. On export violations of state sponsors of international terrorism, see *Tower Report*, in REPORTS OF THE PRESIDENT'S SPECIAL REVIEW BOARD (Feb. 26, 1987) [hereinafter *Tower Report*]; Note, *Prohibiting Indirect Assistance to International Terrorists: Closing the Gap in U.S. Law*, 6 FORDHAM INT'L L.J. 530 (1983); Note, *Export Controls and the U.S. Effort to Combat International Terrorism*, 13 LAW & POL'Y INT'L BUS. 521 (1981). One such incident involved an advanced United States computer that was seized in Sweden and was about to be sent to the Soviet Union. Former Secretary of Defense Caspar Weinberger stated that the computer could be used to make "faster, more accurate, and more destructive weapons." NARMIC REPORT, *supra*, at 1. That computer was first exported to South Africa from the United States. *Id.* The most notorious export control violation regarding a state sponsor of international terrorism — the Iran-Contra Affair — involved the illegal export of arms to Iran. The profits of the arms deal were illegally diverted to the Nicaraguan rebel group, the *contras*. *See Tower Report*, *supra*.

221. The 1987 testimony to Congress by William B. Robinson, Director of the OMC, Bureau of Politico-Military Affairs, United States State Department, revealed that the OMC had only seven full-time licensing officers to review 49,000 new applications by companies to export arms a year. In 1986 only 641 applications were rejected although the officials asserted that they returned 10% as unacceptable. *Federal Licensing Procedures for Arms Exports: Hearings Before the Comm. on Government Affairs of the United States Senate*, 100th Cong., 1st Sess. 12-5 (1987) (statement of William B. Robinson). Congress recently passed the Omnibus Trade and Competitiveness Act of 1988 on August 23, 1988, in an attempt to streamline export procedures and the commodity control list, and to enhance enforcement of export controls. Omnibus Trade and Competitiveness Act of 1988, Pub. L. No. 100-418, 102 Stat. 1346 (codified as amended

An alternative means of strengthening pressure against South Africa, which is more extensive in regard to concrete measures,[222] is the passage of comprehensive sanctions such as those that were proposed in the 1988 AAA.[223] The proposed amendments, sponsored by Representative Ron Dellums of California, would have required a near total trade embargo against South Africa and the mandatory withdrawal of American corporations from that country.[224] Additionally, the 1988 AAA would have prohibited military and intelligence cooperation between the United States and South Africa. This trade embargo would close the commercial end-use loophole, while continuing to allow the importation of strategic minerals.

V. CONCLUSION

The United States must exert greater economic and political pressure in order to soften the South African Government's rigid stance on apartheid and thereby end internal and cross-border violence. Attaching the label of a terrorist state to a government that already has the vile distinction of ruling a racist regime adds no practical leverage against it. The United States and the international community have employed symbolic measures time and again to condemn apartheid without result. Naming South Africa a terrorist state is a symbolic measure that carries with it none of the economic and political sanctions of the 1988 or 1989 AAAs.[225]

Not only is this measure ineffective, but it is potentially harmful to United States diplomacy. Naming South Africa a terrorist state would be hypocritical in light of similar actions taken by the United States, such as funding guerrilla groups that violate human rights. An image of hypocrisy can only hinder the United States ability to affect peaceful change in South Africa, which is an area of strategic importance to the United

---

at 15 U.S.C. § 4011 (1988)).

222. The proposed amendments would have had a stronger practical impact on sanctions because they called for comprehensive economic sanctions, whereas naming South Africa a terrorist state probably would not strengthen sanctions even on items pertaining to military capability. REPORT ON H.R. 1580, *supra* note 30, at 9-18; 1988 ANNUAL FOREIGN POLICY REPORT, *supra* note 198, at 52-53.

223. REPORT ON H.R. 1580, *supra* note 30, at 9-18.

224. REPORT ON H.R. 1580, *supra* note 30, at 9-18. This bill was passed in the House of Representatives on August 11, 1988. 134 CONG. REC. H6960 (daily ed. Aug. 11, 1988).

225. REPORT ON H.R. 1580, *supra* note 30; *see also* H.R. 21, 101st Cong., 1st Sess. (1989).

States because of its mineral wealth. Additionally, a hypocritical image could injure the integrity of the United States in the arena of foreign affairs. Furthermore, naming South Africa a terrorist state for attacks against ANC members based in other countries could set an international precedent that rejects a military solution to the problem of international terrorism.

It appears that the very restrictions that maintain the system of apartheid, which subject eighty-five percent of the South African population to the equivalent of modern-day slavery at the hands of a fifteen percent minority, must ultimately bring about apartheid's destruction. Nevertheless, if change is to be brought about peacefully, meaningful measures must be advanced presently. Naming South Africa a terrorist state lacks the strength necessary for the task. Instead, strict economic and political sanctions effected diligently, along with economic support for the bordering black-ruled states may force the hardened government of South Africa to yield.

Elisabeth Love Goot

[15]

South Africa: Terrorism and State Disintegration

HERBERT M. HOWE

Georgetown University

My topic is terrorism in South Africa, especially government-sponsored terrorism.

Government terrorism, by which I mean state-sanctioned physical violence against noncombatants or innocents for political means, forms part of a "treat and beat" scenario. Treat and beat, a carrot-and-stick approach, is the government using physical repression and economic inducements to win a sizable minority of blacks over to its side. The government has pumped money into the black townships in the last several years for such social services as electrification. At the same time the government has tried to preempt the black leadership, especially the United Democratic Front, through various bannings and physical repression.

The government sometimes aids black-on-black violence to justify its position, saying, "We're obviously not perfect but look what happens if we lose control. The blacks, all these different tribes or groups, are really going to go at it." The resulting white fear could then reinforce white unity.

Certainly economic, ideological, or personal differences have existed between the black organizations, notably between Chief Gatsha Buthelei's Inkatha in Natal and the

419

national United Democratic Front. But I argue that the government has oftentimes exacerbated these differences by aiding some of the more pliable black groups, e.g., Inkatha, against other black groups in a divide-and-rule policy. That has happened in Natal, where since mid-1985 Inkatha has killed up to a thousand other blacks while mostly UDF members have killed a smaller number of Inkatha activists. In many cases the victims apparently did not even belong to a political grouping. One way the government has helped this terrorism is not, until recently, to have prosecuted Inkatha very much, not to have the police go after the Inkatha impis but, rather, go after the UDF comrades in that area. It's a policy of hit one, but don't hit the other.

The government has helped other vigilante groups, notably the *witdoeke*, or "whitescarves," in Capetown. These are generally older, more conservative individuals within such townships as Nyanga, Langa, Guguletu, or Crossroads. Within a period of several months in 1986, raids by the conservative blacks against the usually younger and more politically radical blacks left over a hundred thousand people homeless in Capetown. If you've ever seen the Cape townships, you know that to be left homeless is insult on injury. The government has sometimes furnished transportation, weaponry, and intelligence to these vigilantes while pursuing the young militants of the UDF or ANC.

Another form of government-assisted black-on-black violence, after the Inkatha-UDF and Witdoeke-Comrades, is in the homelands. South Africa presently has four "independent" homelands: Transkei, Ciskei, Venda, and Bophuthatswana. These homeland governments are sometimes more repressive than the South African government. The South Africans sometimes give security assistance/guidance to the homelands, which have initiated actions against the Charterist organizations—the ANC and UDF—with special ferocity. During the 1983 bus strike in Ciskei, that government gained special notoriety with its "TV" and "Boeing" interrogation methods.

Whither terrorism in South Africa? A real danger exists of the government gradually losing control of coercion and an African Lebanonization occurring. Some Zulu groups may be dropping their subservience to Chief Buthelezi, especially in the Pietermaritzburg-Edendale area. ANC groups are gradually growing more autonomous of ANC command and structure. The ANC's military wing, Umkhonto We Sizwe (Spear of the Nation), has units within the South African townships exhibiting increased independence of the older, more conservative ANC leadership. More ANC terrorism has occurred this year—1988—e.g., bomb blasts killing innocent people at nonstrategic locations. The Lusaka leadership of the ANC appears divided about physical violence against essentially innocent South Africans.

While more fractionalization is happening among the blacks in South Africa, it is also occurring with whites. In November of 1988 a white man in Pretoria took a submachine gun or machine pistol into the streets and shot specifically at blacks. The toll was six killed and some 20 wounded. He was smiling all the time, the press reports stated. He belonged to a very radical, reactionary white group which the government banned while not banning the much more powerful group called the AWB, which, reportedly, is extensively connected to the South African police and, to a smaller extent, to the South African Defense Force.

Observers feel that the AWB is growing both numerically—in 1986 it doubled its membership—and in the sophistication of its weaponry. Increasingly, with the conservative drift away from the Nationalist party, the Conservative Party is rapidly enlarging. The CP presently has 23 parliamentary seats, but if the elections are held in 1989 the CP could possibly double its holdings.

The opposition forces on the left also enjoy better armaments. In the spring of 1988 a white unit within Umkhonto We Sizwe was caught near a nuclear reactor armed with a SAM-7 missile system.

Again, where does this lead us? The government's "treat and beat," its embourgeoisement policy of lifting some blacks into the middle class while using limited amounts of terrorism, black-on-black or white-on-black, probably won't work. As blacks receive more economic and social standing they'll want increased political standing as a sign of their equality and if the government's not willing to give it, stronger militancy, if not violence, will occur.

Within the ANC this drive toward more violence or terrorism against whites is happening. It's increasingly against "soft" targets; perhaps we'll someday read tragic news of busloads of white children blasted by landmines. This has not yet occurred, but within Umkhonto circles, young militants believe that complacent whites will require successive shocks to jar their complacency.

This quasianarchistic scenario of the government gradually losing sizable control to forces on the left and on the right is a real possibility. I don't think that it is a probability, but it certainly stands as more of a possibility than it was five years ago.

[16]

Political Studies (1984), XXXII, 68–85

Insurgency, Terrorism and the Apartheid System in South Africa

PAUL RICH

University of Aston in Birmingham

This article discusses the development of guerrilla insurgency in South Africa and the government response centred around the concept of 'total strategy'. After distinguishing analytically between the notions of 'terrorism' and 'guerrilla warfare', the insurgent campaign is seen to have a threefold impact in terms of loss of economic confidence, sapping of white morale and a mobilization of black political consciousness. The resulting response of 'total strategy' effectively represents an escalation of previous efforts to entrench a black middle class as a factor to enhance political stability, though political isolation of South Africa from close western support makes it problematical that the South African state can avoid a strategy of full-scale counter-terror to the increased insurgency threat.

Since the 1976 riots in Soweto and other black townships in South Africa, black political protest has taken a variety of different forms. In addition to the township burnings and killings which so successfully captured the international headlines, strikes by black workers have continued from the strike wave initiated in Durban in 1973. Furthermore, since the grenade attack on a police van in the Eastern Transvaal in November 1976 by African National Congress (A.N.C.) guerrillas, there has been an escalating wave of sabotage and bomb attacks, leading most dramatically to the blowing up of the SASOL II plant in the Orange Free State in 1980. Though this type of action has not yet developed to the phase of fully-fledged guerrilla warfare, undoubtedly its effects on South African policy have been significant in a period of growing political uncertainty surrounding the attainment of black majority rule in Zimbabwe under the Presidency of Robert Mugabe.

It might be concluded that this upsurge of 'terrorism' by South African blacks marks the start of a new phase of violent resistance to white power in South Africa after its initial thwarting in the early 1960s. Whilst two decades ago the South African government still had the advantages of the protective geographical barriers afforded by Portuguese colonial power in Mozambique and Angola and by the Rhodesian settlers to the north of the Limpopo river, this protection has now gone, leaving the country increasingly exposed to infiltration. In addition, the bannings of the A.N.C. and Pan-African Congress (P.A.C.) in 1960 following the Sharpeville shootings and the escalating repression of black political movements and leaders have produced a much harder generation of political activists. The original founders of the

0032-3217/84/01/0068-18/$03.00 © 1984 *Political Studies*

A.N.C. underground movement *Umkhonto we Sizwe* ('Spear of the Nation') under the leadership of Nelson Mandela and Walter Sisulu moved only gradually from the dominant A.N.C. strategy of non-violence to one based upon a military strategy of sabotage as part of a political campaign to mobilize black resistance. In the years since Umkhonto's destruction in 1963–4, the predominantly liberal ideology of the A.N.C. of the 1950s, based upon a political ideal of multiracialism and black majority rule through the parliamentary franchise, has given way to an eclectic ideology of Marxism and black consciousness. The new generation of black political activists in the 1970s has been schooled in the Bantu Education system established by Drs Verwoerd and Eiselen in the 1954 Bantu Education Act and the 1959 Extension of University Education Act, which segregated the universities and removed most black students to the 'bush universities' established as part of the Homelands policy. Here the 'black consciousness' philosophy was developed as part of a search for an independent black cultural identity that scorned the precepts of liberal multiracialism. This pursuit of black liberation easily allied itself to a Marxist ideology once a number of black activists fled into exile in the wake of the Soweto riots and allied disturbances in 1976. It is this amalgam which currently informs the present strategy of sabotage and movements towards guerrilla warfare initiated by the A.N.C. and the revived *Umkhonto*.

However, to see this upsurge in sabotage as the simple extension of a 'revolutionary situation' into the very bastion of white settler power[1] may be premature. Previous phases of violent black political upsurge in South African history, from the strike waves that led to bloodshed after both the First and Second World Wars to the wave of state repression after Sharpeville to clamp down on violence in the Eastern Cape and Pondoland,[2] indicate that there is a close and important dyadic relationship between black resistance and white state response in South African politics. As this article argues, the moves by the A.N.C. towards initiating a guerrilla struggle undoubtedly enhance its claims to political legitimacy as a 'National Liberation Movement' in South Africa. But, in a semi-industrial state with considerable military and economic power, the governmental response to this is likely to be both sophisticated and ruthless in its efforts to drive a wedge through African political leadership.

This article seeks therefore to analyse first the nature of this guerrilla challenge to South African state power and then the possible range of governmental responses over the next few years. The premise of this discussion is that there is a basic analytical distinction to be made between the two forms of political violence that pass under the general classification of 'terrorism' and 'guerrilla warfare'. As Paul Wilkinson has pointed out, 'terrorism' is by its very nature indiscriminate, arbitrary and unpredictable and is rooted in a tradition of nihilist political thought that glorifies in the destruction of the structures of governmental power through violence for its own sake.[3] To this extent 'terrorism' is fundamentally amoral in that terrorists exhibit an

---

[1] N. Shamuyarira, 'A Revolutionary Situation in Southern Africa', *The African Review*, 4 (1974), 159–79.

[2] Muriell Horrell, *Action, Reaction and Counteraction* (Johannesburg, S.A.I.R.R., 1971).

[3] Paul Wilkinson, *Political Terrorism* (London, Basingstoke, Macmillan, 1974), pp. 13–16.

70   *Insurgency, Terrorism and the Apartheid System in South Africa*

indifference to all existing moral codes for the sake of their own particular political creed:

> Political terror, if it is waged consciously and deliberately, is implicitly prepared to sacrifice all moral and humanitarian considerations for sake of some political end. Ideologies of terrorism assume that the death and suffering of those who are innocent of any crime are means entirely justified by their political ends.[4]

'Guerrilla warfare', on the other hand, is derived from a tradition of small-scale armed resistance to state power dating back at least to the early nineteenth century. The word 'guerrilla' is Spanish, meaning 'small war' and developed from the period of Spanish resistance to the Napoleonic occupation of Spain between 1808-14. In its assumption that the use of armed force against state power is a logical extension of existing political objectives, guerrilla warfare exhibits a far greater degree of predictability and political morality than terrorism. In the twentieth century, these facets of guerrilla warfare have been accentuated by numbers of Marxist theorists of 'people's war' such as Mao Tse Tung, Ho Chi Minh and General Giap who have employed guerrilla warfare as a means of popular mobilization of peasantries in China and Vietnam against the controllers of state power, whether they be the class of landlords behind Chiang Kai Chek's Kuomintang or the French colonial administration in Indo-China. Guerrilla warfare in this scenario becomes but one phase in a wider strategy of political and military mobilization which frequently ends up in a more conventional phase of military conflict, as in the latter phases of the Chinese civil war in the late 1940s or the run-up to the French defeat at Dien Bien Phu in Vietnam in 1954.

This distinction analytically, however, does not mean that in practice the two modes of political violence do not frequently blur into each other. Political terrorists often have a coherent ideology which prompts action in areas outside that of political violence for its own sake, as in the periodic pursuit of electoral influence by the Provisional IRA in Northern Ireland—a hunger strike campaign in 1981. Likewise, guerrillas frequently resort to more unpredictable and amoral methods of political terror in order to gain control and influence over populations they perceive as actual or potential bases of political support. In the Vietnamese case this took the form of random assassinations of village headmen by the National Liberation Front ('Vietcong') which both eliminated alleged 'class enemies' and instilled a high degree of fear into the rural population. This terrorist dimension of guerrilla warfare is further heightened by the greater uncertainty and lack of clear political support in the urban context. In contrast to the more favourable possibilities for guerrillas among largely rural populations, where underground networks and military base areas can be established, guerrillas suffer the continual problem in the urban context of isolation from the people whose support they are seeking. The operation of secret police infiltration and the control by the state over the mobility of the urban population has led some analysts to conclude that the prospects for urban guerrilla warfare alone

---

[4] Wilkinson, *Political Terrorism*, p. 17.

leading to the overthrow of state power are very poor.[5] Even the classic film *The Battle of Algiers* by the Marxist film director Gillo Pontecorvo, celebrating the F.L.N. (Front Liberation Nationale) victory against French colonial rule in Algeria in the war of 1954–62, showed how the attempt at urban guerrilla activity in Algiers itself, based upon the Kasbah, was eventually crushed by the ruthless military counter-insurgency of General Massu. '. . . [T]he guerrilla group in a city', one scholar has concluded, 'will only be able to act as "the fish out of water" in limited sectors, having to get out of them in order to capture control over various strategic institutions and in so doing, they may encounter a population which is not even normally passive, but actively hostile.'[6] These factors are further accentuated in the South African situation by the virtually complete pattern of territorial segregation in towns, leading to the isolation of the black townships from the heart of the city economy and the necessity for insurgency groups to work in 'white' city areas governed by the operation of the pass law system.

A.N.C. guerrilla strategy in South Africa, therefore, has tended to grow out of a more conventional model of rural insurgency, though this is not to conclude that it does not possess dynamics which may carry it eventually into the urban context on a systematic scale, given the highly urbanized nature of South African society and economy. For the most part, A.N.C. guerrilla activity has tended to reflect hitherto what one analyst has perceived as the 'truncated, disjointed, unrefined, eclectic, nebulous, and situationally specific' nature of African guerrilla warfare theories[7] and relied upon a generally rural base in neighbouring areas, especially Mozambique after the fall of Portuguese colonial rule there in 1974. The pattern of this guerrilla activity over the past few years, however, manifests a certain political rationale which has, as the next section shows, governed the South African state's response.

The Political Potential of the Guerrilla Strategy

The escalation of the present A.N.C. sabotage campaign to one of full scale guerrilla warfare serves at least three important objectives in the A.N.C. struggle to overthrow white power: (1) it can have a serious impact on the South African economy and the confidence of international investors; (2) it can sap white political morale and weaken the ideological underpinnings of the apartheid regime and (3) it can serve as an important catalyst for the mobilization of black political consciousness which can result in other forms of resistance such as strikes, go-slows, mass demonstrations and street protest. It is worth, therefore, discussing these three features in terms of the likely form that political violence may take, especially as much discussion of this issue is

---

[5] Paul Wilkinson, *Terrorism and the Liberal State* (London, Macmillan, 1977), p. 63 and Andrew Mack, 'The Non-Strategy of Urban Guerrilla Warfare' in Johan Niezing (ed.), *Urban Guerrilla* (Rotterdam, Rotterdam University Press, 1974), pp. 22–45. However, Geoffrey Fenirbairn has noted the growth of terrorism in such countries as Uruguay, West Bengal and Northern Ireland as a weapon of revolutionary warfare 'even in societies whose "repressive apparatus" could not possibly be accused of having provoked or necessitated such behaviour', *Revolutionary Guerrilla Warfare* (Harmondsworth, Penguin, 1974), p. 356.

[6] Hakon Wiberg, 'Are Urban Guerrillas possible?' in Niezing, *Urban Guerrilla*, p. 16.

[7] Kenneth W. Grundy, *Guerrilla Struggles in Africa* (New York, Grossman, 1971), p. 72.

pursued in terms of 'terrorism' and the simplistic labelling of all A.N.C. political activity as part of an ideological 'total onslaught' on the South African state.[8]

i. The Economic Impact

Given the dependence of the South African economy upon both continued investment and advanced technology for its restructuring in the direction of a high wage, capital-intensive outpost of western capital, sabotage can be of some economic significance. Though the present campaign initiated around 1976 began with attacks on the police and agents of the state, more recent attacks on such installations as the ESCOM Ermelo and Pretoria Municipal Power Stations and the SASOL II Plant indicate a recognition of the dependence of the economy upon high-cost energy and its extreme sensitivity to disruption in this sphere. As Dr Mike Hough, strategic studies expert of the Pretoria Institute for Strategic Studies, has pointed out, oil, energy and gold are the obvious central targets for such a sabotage campaign as they lead to the diversion of considerable military capacity away from a more mobile offensive capability towards defending fixed targets.[9]

This economic impact is also linked to the importance of Natal as a target for the sabotage attacks. Given the closeness of the Mozambique border, the province has been especially vulnerable to A.N.C. guerrillas, who have also chosen obvious targets like the Natal Coast Railway, where a bomb was planted in June 1981 between Felixton and Mzingwenya, as well as the more sensational case of two car showrooms in Durban being wrecked on 26 July the same year.[10] Such bombings excited international publicity at a time when a reconsideration had begun in western circles, especially Washington, on the need to both continue and, if need be, enhance economic ties with South Africa. Even the mainstream liberal position in the United States, represented by the report of Study Project on U.S. Policy Towards Southern Africa, *South Africa: Time Running Out*, argued for the continuation of existing American investment in South Africa, though strictly abiding to the guidelines of the Sullivan Principles,[11] so the escalation of the sabotage attacks dramatically emphasized the dangerous political implications of this, should the military struggle escalate.

The concentration upon economic targets is made more explicable in terms of the A.N.C.'s long term political objectives. Ever since December 1960, in the wake of Sharpeville, the UN has given a certain legitimacy to campaigns of national liberation in Southern Africa with the General Assembly Resolution

[8] For an analysis of this use of the 'terrorist' term by South African propaganda see Deon Geldenhuys, *Some Foreign Policy Implications of South Africa's 'Total National Strategy', with particular reference to the '12 Point plan'* (Johannesburg, The South African Institute of International Affairs, 1981), *passim*. See also Genl. Magnus Malan, *Die Aanslag Teen Suid-Afrika* (Pretoria, Institute for Strategic Studies, November 1980).

[9] *Rand Daily Mail*, July 22 1981.

[10] *Sunday Express*, August 2 1981.

[11] *South Africa: Time Running Out* (Berkeley and Los Angeles, University of California Press, 1981), pp. 427–30. The Report favoured 'no expansion and no new entry' of American investment, and did not consider that the Sullivan principles should be perceived in a static manner.

1514, known as the Declaration on the Granting of Independence to Colonial countries.[12] The more recent protocol agreement sponsored by the International Red Cross to extend the Geneva Conventions from wars between states to wars of national liberation has led to the A.N.C. signing of them and agreeing to the 'humanitarian conduct of war'.[13] As the first 'liberation movement' to sign the Protocol, the A.N.C. clearly hopes to gain increased international legitimacy as an alternative government for the whole of South Africa, and this clearly involves the minimum amount of assaults on ordinary civilian targets as opposed to those of the state and military machine.

ii. Sapping White Morale

The economic impact of the attacks is linked to a concern to undermine the ideological and political supports of the apartheid system. Attacking military targets *per se* is likely to have only minimal impact on white psychology since already an important political barrier could be said to have been created in white thinking via 'the border' in Namibia and the continued involvement of troops in 'the operational area'.[14] White South African society has experienced considerable militarization over the past decade or so with the compulsory military draft and the excursions into Angola in 1976 and since. In one respect, this military base to white settler power goes far back into history, rooted as it is in historical myths of Trekkers and wars against African tribes. The dissemination of fiction in the genre of John Buchan's *Prester John*, which includes a successful campaign to suppress a black political uprising, indicates the cohesiveness of this ideology of racial separateness and the frontier-type mythology in the continued military superiority of white power over Africans.[15] As David Halberstam has pointed out in a perceptive article, this myth is reduced to the crude racist concept of 'the K (i.e. Kaffir) factor' which informs most contemporary military thinking in South Africa. Africans are seen as inherently incapable of mounting a successful military attack on South Africa and as being continually prone to bungling and internal political divisions. The stereotype is strongly reminiscent of the early years of American involvement in Vietnam and the racist belief in the inferiority of 'gooks'.[16] However, this mythology is strongly rural in its orientation; it emerges in some respects out of previous white involvement in bush wars in Kenya, the Congo, Rhodesia and elsewhere and expresses the traditional Rider Haggard notion of the white man both opening up and preserving civilized values in rural Africa.[17] It thus fails to come fully to grips with the far more damaging urban

12 Yassin El-Ayouty, 'Legitimization of National Liberation: The United Nations and Southern Africa', *Issue*, 2, 4 (Winter 1972), p. 36.

13 *Rand Daily Mail*, 10 January 1980.

14 For the way this symbolic concept of 'the border' has been developed in Afrikaans cinema see Keyan G. Tomaselli, 'Capitalist Penetration: Popular Response—Images in the Cinema', University of the Witwatersrand, History Workshop Paper, February 1981.

15 For an analysis of the political context of this novel see Paul B. Rich, 'Milnerism and a Ripping Yarn: Transvaal Land Settlement and John Buchan's Novel Prester John, 1901-1910', University of the Witwatersrand, History Workshop Paper, February 1981.

16 David Halberstam, 'The Fire to Come in South Africa', *The Atlantic*, (May 1980), p. 88.

17 David Maughan-Brown, 'Myths on the March', paper presented to the Conference on Literature and Society in Southern Africa, University of York, September 1981.

74   *Insurgency, Terrorism and the Apartheid System in South Africa*

phenomenon of sabotage which is visibly on display in the alleged heartlands of white settler power in South African towns and cities which, ever since the 1923 Natives (Urban Areas) Act, have been seen, according to the Stallard dictum, as places where Africans are only to minister to the needs of the white man, that is as temporary sojourners existing as units of labour.[18] 'Stedelike terrorisme in SA gaan toeneem' ('urban terrorism is on the increase') dramatically declared *Die Vaderland* in July 1981 after the wave of attacks on power stations and the paper was forced to admit the existence of ' 'n nuwe radikale jong swart leierskap van die African National Congress' ('a new young radical black leadership of the A.N.C.').[19] Clearly the continued ability of the A.N.C. to mount sabotage assaults right in the South African heartland forces a readjustment in white political perceptions and can, accordingly, sap political morale, reported to be low even amongst young Afrikaner students facing the draft into the army.

The one clear response from within the white power structure to these attacks is to emphasize the shared symbols of racial solidarity at the heart of the 'total strategy' which we will examine more fully in the latter part of this paper. 'Everyone of you is already mobilized' declared the State President Marais Viljoen in October 1979 for 'You and I are fighting for what we hold dearest in life. We are prepared to fight on our own soil and on all fronts in the coming total onslaught on our economy, culture, social system and religion.'[20]

Nevertheless, such a mobilization against the 'total onslaught' needs some form of military reinforcement and this means periodic cross-border raids on the Israeli pattern in order to flush out the encampments of the guerrilla enemies. A classic example of such a counter-offensive against attacks on South Africa itself has been the raid on Maputo in January 1981 to destroy an A.N.C. sanctuary in the suburb of Matola. Here, it has been claimed, there were three main A.N.C. residences out of a total of ten that were selected as targets: *The Solomon Mahlangu Sabotage Unit*, under the leadership of the one white leading A.N.C. cadre, Joe Slovo, who allegedly master-minded the raid on Sasol and the Silverton bank raid of August 1980; the *Matola Castle*, which served as the regional headquarters of the A.N.C. Natal units which had been able to retreat back over the Mozambique border so successfully: and *SACTU House* which served as a base for exfiltrating agents of the South African Congress of Trade Unions out of South Africa for political and ideological indoctrination.[21] The choice of the three centres, if the South African claims are to be believed, indicates the nature of the guerrilla threat as perceived by government intelligence. The Sabotage Unit was an obvious target given the success in the Sasol episode and Joe Slovo has traditionally been seen as 'public enemy number one' by the South African government for a number of years. If he had been either killed or captured in the raid the boost to white political morale would have been considerable.[22] The Matola Castle centre was important given the number of attacks on Natal. In one sense it

[18] P. Rich, 'Ministering to the White Man's Needs: The Development of Urban Segregation in South Africa, 1913-1923', *African Studies*, 37, 2 (1978), pp. 177-91.

[19] *Die Vaderland*, 22 August 1981.

[20] *The Star*, 10 October 1979.

[21] *Sunday Express*, 26 April 1981; *Sunday Times*, 26 April 1981.

[22] 'Joe Slovo—Teddy Bear Terrorist master minding the A.N.C.', *The Star*, March 10 1981.

reflected a desire by the South African government in its counter-insurgency programme to seek to distinguish as far as possible its A.N.C. enemies from the neighbouring African states which have given them sanctuaries. The nature of such a strategy was indicated by the South African Defence Minister, General Magnus Malan, in a speech after the Maputo Raid. Stressing the traditional government objective of seeking 'harmony . . . with our neighbours', Malan emphasized that 'in spite of our neighbours' continued support for terrorists, we shall always try to take action against terrorists only and not against their hosts, unless we are forced to do so'.[23] Clearly the South African government seeks to limit the intensity of its counter-insurgency operations, fearing that too rapid an escalation could lead to an international-ization of the conflict with the possibility of the employment of Cuban or similar forces, as happened in Angola in 1976. Furthermore, in strictly military terms, the A.N.C. is not seen as an organization capable of mounting an offensive on the level of SWAPO in Namibia for a number of years. By July of 1981 the Chief of the Defence Force, General Constand Viljoen, boasted that the A.N.C. 'has not nearly shown itself to be a worthwhile military organisa-tion', echoing in some ways the traditional stereotype of the 'K factor'.[24] Within a week of the speech, though, guerrillas bombed three power stations.

The selection, however, of the third target at Maputo, SACTU House indicates another worry in South African strategists' minds, the longer-term danger of sabotage and guerrilla operations linking up with militant labour organizations. This envisages the possibility of South African insurgency, given the industrialized nature of the society, attaining a level and sophistica-tion far beyond the traditional 'bush war' characterizing the previous phases of conflict in Kenya, Namibia and Zimbabwe. Though it is claimed by South African intelligence that only some 800 out of an estimated 3,000 young blacks who left after the riots of 1976 are still involved in A.N.C. activities, there is undoubtedly some worry that A.N.C. organization is sufficiently sophisticated to implant many of these trained cadres as underground agents inside the black labour movement. In one sense, this reflects the contradictions at the heart of the migrant labour system and influx control in South Africa. With continual movements of workers into and out of the urban, industrial areas there is a potential 'trojan horse' of political and ideological subversion. One of the documents captured in the Maputo raid indicates the depth of the concern. In a letter dated 24 December 1980, one Stan Mthimkulu writes to 'Dear Comrade' (believed to be Joe Slovo) enclosing four sets of photographs along with a false reference book 'which is currently in use in the Natal region'.[25] If genuine, the letter does indicate some form of A.N.C. strategy to filter its agents via false reference books into the migrant labour system and perhaps keep them there as 'sleepers' on the IRA pattern.

iii. Mobilizing Black Political Consciousness

Within the political dimensions of the current A.N.C. sabotage campaign, the third central objective is the desire to link guerrilla activity to the mobilization

---

23 *Rand Daily Mail*, 18 February 1981.
24 *The Star*, 16 July 1981.
25 *Sunday Express*, 26 April 1981.

of black political consciousness. The dramatic impact of the successful bombings both inside South Africa and abroad serves to demonstrate the renewed A.N.C. presence in South African politics after many years spent as an exile organization. The inherent tendency in such a campaign towards military escalation may also serve to enhance the A.N.C.'s political legitimacy if the South African government is driven to over-react. An awareness of this was implicit in a speech of the A.N.C.'s President, Oliver Tambo, in Zimbabwe in August 1981 following the assassination of the movement's representative there, Joel Gqabi. 'Activity cannot stay at the same level and be effective' he warned and prophesied that the conflict would become intensified on both sides.[26]

In some respects, this can be seen to resemble the terrorism identified by David Fromkin as being rooted in a strategy of the indirect approach that depends upon the opponent's response. Arguing from the case of the F.L.N. strategy in Algeria which prompted the French government militarily to over-react and thus drive the bulk of the Algerian population into the arms of the F.L.N., Fromkin concludes that 'terrorism is the indirect strategy that wins or loses only in terms of how you respond to it'.[27] In the case of South Africa, an over-reaction by the South African military machine risks destroying whatever credibility is left in its narrowly-based Homelands political leadership, especially that based on Gatsha Buthelezi's government in Kwazulu, and also risks the hostility of the international community if it engages in too many cross border raids and political assassinations.

Fromkin's analysis though is burdened by an excessive rationality in its depiction of the logic of terrorism, which depends ultimately upon an illogical and highly irrational psychological dimension in its dissemination of fear and disorientation. In the A.N.C.'s campaign at least two major instances of campaigns lapsing into more conventional terrorism can be seen in the killing of two whites in Johannesburg in 1977 by guerrillas who panicked and fled from a bus queue and the January 1980 Silverton bank siege which led to the deaths of the three African insurgents and two white civilians. Both examples illustrate the point that there is a high 'terrorism potential' in any strategy of urban guerrilla warfare.[28]

In the case of the Silverton siege, many of these critical tactical supports were lacking. According to the prosecution in the succeeding trial of nine Africans linked to both the Silverton siege and two other attacks, on the Soekemaar police station in the Transvaal in January and a Port Natal Administration Board Building in Durban in the preceding December, the centres for organization of the attacks lay in the rural areas. After joining the A.N.C. in 1976–7, the men received military training in Angola before eight returned in 1979. Three established a base at Tzaneen in the Northern Transvaal while a further two plus the three who died in the Silverton siege established a base at Ga Rankuwa district in the Bophutaswana Homeland. Two others established a base in the Vryheid district in Natal for the Durban

---

[26] *The Times*, 13 August 1981.
[27] David Fromkin, 'The Strategy of Terrorism', *Foreign Affairs*, 53 (1974–5), p. 697.
[28] Paul Wilkinson, *Terrorism and the Liberal State*, p. 63.

PAUL RICH   77

attack.[29] The pattern seems clear, that the sabotage groups are mainly dependent upon rural supports for launching the urban raids and that no coherent infrastructure yet exists in the urban areas for fully fledged urban guerrilla warfare. Without urban supports, there is a tendency to mount certain *spectacular* attacks to win publicity. In terms of short-term pay-offs this may well be successful, for the three men killed at Silverton were given big funerals leading to, according to Patrick Laurence, 'an uninhibited display of black solidarity which shocked the white establishment'.[30] An opinion poll reported that three blacks out of every four felt strong or qualified sympathy with the Silverton gunmen and 37.9 per cent felt them to be heroes.[31]

This kind of support for the A.N.C. undoubtedly weakens the already fragile base of support for the section of African petty bourgeois leadership which has opted for at least using the Homelands as mechanisms of political mobilization. The 1979–80 sabotage and terror attacks came in the wake of A.N.C. repudiation of Chief Gatsha Buthelezi's Inkatha movement which sought to promote itself as the internal wing of the A.N.C. Despite trying in 1978 to identifying Inkatha with the objectives but not the strategy of the A.N.C., Buthelezi has failed to win any A.N.C. support for his strategy of using the structures of the Kwa Zulu Homeland; and the A.N.C. openly repudiated him in 1979 after secret talks in London.[32] While Buthelezi and Inkatha's move towards the right during 1980 led to the establishment of a steering committee with the white Progressive Federal Party and the eventual publication of a Commission report favouring the creation of a multi-racial state in Natal,[33] the A.N.C. strategy of sabotage and guerrilla action has served to identify it with opposition to the seeming 'co-optation' of Inkatha into the basic structures of the apartheid system. Short of any major new initiatives by the South African government, offering a substantial reform package for the disaffected African petty bourgeoisie, the A.N.C. strategy escalates the pace of political polarization engendered since 1976 and the outlawing of the Black Consciousness movement. It is therefore to the range of responses by the South African state to this new set of circumstances that we now turn.

The Political and Military Response by the South African State

The onset of even limited A.N.C. insurgency over the last four years has led the South African governments of first John Vorster and later P. W. Botha to seek an integration of its political and military responses to the perceived black onslaught upon white power. Since the publication of a Defence White Paper

---

29 *The Star*, 6 August 1980.

30 *Rand Daily Mail*, 28 July 1981.

31 Michael Morris, 'South African Political Violence—A Current Overview in *Terrorisme, Die Strydmetode Van Ons Tyd* (Sentrum Vir Internasionale Politiek, PU vir CHO, 1981), p. 44.

32 Roger Southall, 'Buthelezi, Inkatha and the Politics of Compromise', *African Affairs*, 80, 321 (October 1981), p. 473.

33 Southall, 'Buthelezi, Inkatha and the Politics of Compromise', p. 474. The political 'dialogue' was also with senior members of the Africaner establishment including Piet Koornhof, Minister of Cooperation and Development. For details of the Buthelezi Commission proposals see *The Times*, 12 March 1982.

in 1977, this integration has taken place within the framework of a 'Total National Strategy' which no longer defined the 'defence' of the Republic of South Africa as the preserve solely of the Department of Defence but 'the combined responsibility of all governments'. The role of the Defence Department was also redefined as an 'executive body' which was 'responsible for the achievement of certain national security goals, as directed by the Government'.[34] This has meant, in effect, a growing militarization of all South African policy-making and it was, in some respects, a logical outcome of this that a former Minister of Defence, P. W. Botha, succeeded Dr Vorster as Prime Minister on the latter's resignation in 1978.

The 'total strategy' of the South African government marks, furthermore, an increased concern to balance the alternatives of political and military responses both to the A.N.C. and to hostile international pressures. Hitherto, the presence of A.N.C. insurgency inside South African borders, as in the early 1960s, was seen essentially as a 'security situation' which could be treated as the sole concern of the South African state, though with the occasional entry over the borders of neighbouring states, as in 1961 when Security Police seized the fugitive Anderson Ganyile in Lesotho and brought him back to South Africa.[35] However, since the early 1960s, there have been a number of transformations of this specifically South African definition of 'national security'. The Homelands policy itself represents an attempt by the South African government to internationalize internal political conflict by the establishment of ostensibly 'independent' black nation-states, even if they have gone unrecognized by the rest of the world. The A.N.C., too, has sought international legitimacy of its proclaimed role as 'liberation movement' by its signing of the Geneva Protocol. Furthermore, and most critically, the removal of the buffer states of Rhodesia, Mozambique and Angola and continuing UN pressure to save the independence of Namibia has left South Africa far more exposed in the 1980s to external attack and military intervention.

The significance of 'total strategy', therefore, is that it represents a balancing of political and military initiatives in attempts to both defuse and demobilize A.N.C. insurgency. On the one hand, there is the continuation of the policy of political 'reform' for blacks, coloureds and Indians which has tinged government rhetoric since the period of so-called *détente* after the Portuguese coup of 1974.[36] On the other hand, there has been a growing effort at an active military response to guerrilla activity reflected in the 1981 Maputo raid and the December 1982 raid on Maseru in Lesotho. The exact balance between these two central elements of the 'total strategy' will tend to depend upon both the changing perceptions of the external 'threat' and the balance of civilian and military forces inside the state decision-making apparatus, especially the State Security Council, headed by the Prime Minister, which was established as long ago as 1972.

---

[34] Quoted in M. Hough, *National Security in the RSA: The Strategic Importance of South and Southern Africa: The Pretoria View* (Pretoria, Institute for Strategic Studies, 1981), p. 6.

[35] An account of this episode is in Jack Halpern, *South Africa's Hostages* (Harmondsworth, Penguin, 1965), pp. 3-18.

[36] David Hirschmann, 'Southern Africa: Detente?', *The Journal of Modern Studies*, 14, 1 (1976), 107-26.

i. Political Aspects

As far as the logic of the political 'reform' package is concerned, the South African 'total strategy' remains burdened by the political conservatism of a white settler society.[37] It is probably true, as the two authors John Saul and Stephen Gelb have argued in a recent important essay, that the contemporary state of South African capitalism forbids any complete transformation of the political system in the direction of one man one vote and black majority rule.[38] However, with the increasing internationalization of South Africa's internal political conflict, it has become impossible for the white state to formulate its continuing Homelands programme in isolation from its wider political strategy in the international arena. Thus the government of P. W. Botha has moved towards a policy of political 'reform' as a result of increasing awareness of its link with military security. In an important speech at Durban in August 1979, outlining a '12-point plan', P. W. Botha elaborated on the framework for the 'total national strategy' (TSN) which he expressed, significantly, in the words of an Israeli general: 'We have only one alternative.' The assumptions of this discussion were in many respects updated versions of those lying behind the apartheid discourse of the 1950s and 1960s under the premiership of Dr Verwoerd. The basic premise was the 'multinationalism' of South Africa and 'the acceptance of vertical differentiation with a built-in principle of self-determination at as many levels as possible'. Within this framework, however, there could be a 'division of powers' between whites, coloured and Indians, leading to 'a system of consultation and co-responsibility as far as common interests are concerned'.[39] Thus, whilst the whole position of Africans remained within the basic apartheid tenets of 'Homelands' policy, the Botha administration began moving towards the idea of greater political rights being conceded to the coloured and Indian populations as a means effectively of buttressing white power. As Geldenhuys has argued, 'the 12-point plan is a counter strategy devised within the broad parameters of existing Government policy'.[40]

Even such a limited reform package, however, risks splitting the white power bloc that has grown up over the years since the first major political crisis in the early 1960s at the time of Sharpeville and the A.N.C./P.A.C. bannings. The defection of Andries Treurnicht and 15 National Party MPs from the Botha camp and the growth of extreme right wing pressure by the Conservative Party and the Herstigte Nasionale Party (H.N.P.) on the Botha government illustrate that there is a considerable Verkrampte resistance to such reforms, though it is precisely the need for overall white unity which the government stresses in its 'total strategy' in order to resist the guerrilla attacks.

---

[37] For an analysis of the characteristics of white settler societies in Africa see Kenneth Good, 'Settler Colonialism: Economic Development and Class Formation', *The Journal of Modern African Studies*, 14, 4 (1976), 597–620.

[38] John S. Saul and Stephen Gelb, *The Crisis in South Africa* (New York and London, Monthly Review Press), 1981, p. 44.

[39] *Southern African Record*, 22 (December 1980), pp. 4–6.

[40] Geldenhuys, *Some Foreign Policy Implications of South Africa's 'Total National Strategy'*, p. 11.

80   *Insurgency, Terrorism and the Apartheid System in South Africa*

The point about the 'total strategy', however, as Philip Frankel has pointed out, is that it is rooted in a strongly authoritarian tradition of social engineering and hostility to Westminster-style parliamentary democracy.[41]

As a product of strong state power, it is thus not especially well disposed towards meeting the demands for democratic political rights which have been the basis of the A.N.C.'s programme since at least the time of the passing of the Freedom Charter by the Congress of the people at Kliptown in 1955.[42] The essence of the total strategy's reform proposals is a reappraisal of the political opportunities for alliance formation and co-optation, especially with coloureds and Indians, and an accelerated move towards establishing a black middle class, an objective long pressed by South African liberals as a stabilizing move towards a western pluralistic political system.[43] The nub of the strategy thus lies in enhancing what one observer has previously termed a process of 'authoritarian reform'[44] into a coherent strategy of counter-revolution. As part of this strategy the State Security Council, especially, has been enhanced from its original advisory role at the time of its creation in 1972 into a central co-ordinating body in the total strategy. Military intelligence too has taken over from the Department of National Security as the main gatherer of intelligence information.[45]

This militarization of policy has led to growing government links with corporate business and bodies concerned to enhance the quality of township life, such as the Urban Foundation, and indicates that counter-insurgency criteria are likely to grow in importance in the formulation of policy on the status of South African Asians, coloureds and Africans. In one respect, it makes clear military sense to build up over the next two or three decades an urbanized African population of semi-skilled or skilled workers and a growing business community with enterprises servicing the needs of the townships. This would lessen the likelihood of urban sabotage developing into fully fledged revolutionary guerrilla warfare. An urbanized black population with some economic stake in the existing socio-economic system is likely to be ambivalent in its attitude towards urban guerrillas. It can potentially provide some continuous sources of information to the intelligence gathering military machine as background information for its low intensity operations. Such operations, as Brigadier F. Kitson has pointed out, depend in their effectiveness on the co-ordination between civilian and military intelligence. Given South Africa's present geographical position and the closeness of African states that can serve as base areas for guerrilla operations, the military's co-ordination of *background information* with *contact information* in order to

[41] Philip Frankel, 'Race and Counter Revolution: South Africa's "Total Strategy" ', *Journal of Commonwealth and Comparative Politics*, XVIII, 3 (November 1980), p. 275. See also Saul and Gelb, *The Crisis in South Africa*, pp. 35-8.

[42] For a discussion of the Freedom Charter 'as a unique Statement of A.N.C. ideology in the Fifties' see Janet Robertson, *Liberalism in South Africa, 1948-1963* (Oxford, Clarendon Press, 1971), pp. 172-5.

[43] For an analysis of these liberal hopes see Paul B. Rich, *White Power and the Liberal Conscience; Racial Segregation and South African Liberalism 1921-1960* (Manchester University Press, 1983).

[44] Merle Lipton, 'South Africa: Authoritarian Reform', *The World Today*, (June 1974), 247-58.

[45] Frankel, 'Race and Counter Revolution', p. 279.

engage and defeat its enemy will always be compromised short of continuous and successful cross border raids of the Maputo variety.[46] Growing international reactions render this form of counter-insurgency increasingly costly politically, especially as the terrain involved on the Mozambique and Zimbabwe borders is far less easy to seal off from international media attention than Southern Angola has been in the last few years. Thus additional sources of background information for the military to develop into contact information inside South Africa are likely to become essential. In this sense, therefore, military intelligence may well be a source of pressure in the coming years for an escalation of the pace of reform in urban areas.[47]

However, it is easy to exaggerate the degree to which commitment to the total strategy in ideological terms is actually translated into real policy changes. Frankel, for instance, is premature in his assessment of the Botha government's commitment to genuine reform in urban policy and 'the deep appreciation' in government circles 'of the sense of alienation experienced by urban blacks in the process of being stripped of their South African citizenship'.[48] The present Community Councils Act of 1977 is still rooted in the advisory nature of urban advisory boards that goes back to the Location Advisory Boards established under the Native Affairs Act of 1920. So far the election of representatives to such boards has attracted only a handful of the potential African voters. Of the thirty wards in Soweto only two were actually contested in the first elections in 1979 and 5 per cent of those registered voted: the Council's Chairman, David Thebahali, won a mere 97 votes.[49] Significantly, though, in Dobsonville in 1978 some 42 per cent of the electorate voted in what is generally described as a 'middle class' area of Soweto and acts as a possible portent given a radical change in policy.[50]

The urban policy hinges on crucial reforms in the area of house ownership and access to capital to run businesses, as well as the creation of a skilled and semi-skilled black working class. So far the Botha government has only gazetted a modified version of a 99-year-leasehold plan for urban black housing that was originally introduced under the previous Vorster government. When the scheme first began in 1979, however, it was confined to the middle class suburb of Dube and blacks have not been forthcoming to apply for loans offered by the Urban Foundation with funds from American banks.[51] *South Africa: Time Running Out* concluded rather less optimistically that the leasehold provisions have led to 'uncertainty and suspicion' amongst urban Africans[52] and has so far done little to change the general political climate. On the issue of urban businesses too, the achievement of the National

[46] Frank Kitson, *Low Intensity Operations* (London, Faber & Faber, 1971), esp. chs. 6 and 7.

[47] The study of military intelligence in South Africa is obviously very difficult. For a preliminary study of the role of police control see Philip H. Frankel, 'South Africa: The Politics of Police Control', *Comparative Politics*, 12, 4 (July 1980), 481–99.

[48] Frankel, 'Race and Counter-Revolution', p. 282.

[49] Judy Seidman, *Face-Lift Apartheid: South Africa after Soweto* (London, International Defence and Aid, 1980), p. 17.

[50] Seidman, *Face-Lift Apartheid*, pp. 37–8. Since the elections the Minister for 'Cooperation and Development', Piet Koornhof, has sought to develop greater powers for the 'Community Councils' including the allocation of housing and business licences.

[51] Seidman, *Face-Lift Apartheid*, p. 22.

[52] *South Africa: Time Running Out*, p. 108.

African Chamber of Commerce (NAFOC) in building a R 1,500,000 super-market in Soweto had led to growing pressure by white business for similar opportunities through fear of potential African commercial competition. As a result, a R 21,000,000 supermarket has been planned on white land adjacent to Soweto.

On the issue of black labour, political debate has been dominated by the reports of two commissions: Riekert and Wiehahn. Both have moved generally in the same direction in seeking to entrench the Section 10 rights of those Africans in the urban areas and dividing them off in many ways from the migrant workers whose place of abode are seen as being ultimately in the Homelands reserves. The Riekert Commission recommended that 'qualified' blacks be able to seek employment in a free job market outside the control of labour bureaux. Concomitant with this, it sought to encourage employers to recruit 'qualified' blacks in preference to migrants and to raise wages to a level adequate to cover the costs of permanent urban residence. The general strategy is clearly one of seeking to escalate class divisions within the African popula-tion and so to create an urbanized body of workers with some form of stake in the existing economic system. According to a Fanonist analysis, this is good counter-insurgency strategy; the working class in a situation of a national revolutionary struggle against colonialism is always an uncertain and politically reactionary ally, whilst the key loci of political radicalism lies in sections of the petty bourgeoisie and the lumpenproletarian marginals.[53] This consideration is further reinforced by the general strategy of the Wiehahn Commission on black trade unions which sought their general incorporation into the existing industrial conciliation machinery. The general government response has been to establish a National Manpower Commission and restructure the Industrial Tribunal as an Industrial Court to adjudicate in disputes and create a body of case law. The Commission itself had recom-mended that the black unions should be discouraged from recruiting migrants and the initial government white paper defined 'employees' as only those with the proper urban residence rights. After objections from black trade unions and the 50,000 strong Federation of South African Trade Unions (FOSATU) to this exclusion, the government relented and a ministerial exemption was issued to include migrants in the definition, though it was significantly not included in legislation, thus allowing for its possible later exclusion.[54]

The main strategy of government urban and trade union policy then has been to seek to drive a wedge between the 'qualified' urban African residents and the migrants: a strategy which it believes will assist in any future period of urban insurgency. Already such divisions have been exploited as in the case of Zulu migrants from the Mzimhlope hostel in Soweto going on the rampage against township residents after encouragement from the police and there were allegations that Buthelezi's Inkatha movement was involved in this too.[55] In the longer-term, though, the objectives of the policy may be more sophisticated in that they seek to move beyond simply divide-and-rule towards

[53] Catholic Institute of International Relations, *South Africa in the 1980s* (London, 1981), pp. 26–8.
[54] Saul and Gelb, *The Crisis in South Africa*, pp. 72–3.
[55] Southall, 'Buthelezi, Inkatha and the Politics of Compromise', p. 470.

creating a less disaffected urban African consciousness which will seek political advancement through reformist channels such as the community councils and trade unions.

ii. Military Aspects

The political aspects of the 'total strategy', however, depend upon the South African government being able to ensure an adequate military defence of both the Republic's borders and the insulation of the country's black population from the ideological influences of the A.N.C. To this extent, the loss of the ring of buffer states since 1974 has led the government into greater military intervention than hitherto. The watershed was the Angolan Civil War of 1975–6 following the collapse of Portuguese colonial power and the military intervention of South Africa behind the forces of Jonas Savimbi's UNITA movement in opposition to the Marxist MPLA.[56] The ultimate unwillingness of the American administration to back this South African incursion certainly led to short-term loss of morale in South African governmental circles, but in the longer term it acted as an important guide for further incursions in the politically more favourable climate of President Reagan in the United States and Mrs Thatcher in Britain. The Maputo raid of January 1981, as has been seen, was aimed at destroying the A.N.C. infrastructure in Mozambique and this has been followed up by the more blatant raid in December 1982 by between 50 and 100 commandos on Maseru in Lesotho which led to 37 deaths. Significantly, the strategy of military counter-terror led the following week to the arrest in another small neighbouring state, Swaziland, of some 25 A.N.C. personnel, many of whom had lived in the country for 20 years.[57] The increase in South African military incursions has led to short-term pay-offs first by entrenching South African military domination in the Southern African region and secondly by reinforcing the dependence of the client black states on the Republic's economy at a time when the Southern African Development Coordination Conference (SADCC) (consisting of Angola, Botswana, Lesotho, Malawi, Mozambique, Swaziland, Tanzania, and Zimbabwe) is seeking greater economic autonomy from the Republic.[58] In the longer term, though, the Israeli-style strategy of increased military intervention risks greater international isolation of South Africa economically as well as politically, especially so far as it weakens the political credibility of the government's professed strategy of political reform.

Conclusion: Terrorism or Guerrilla Insurgency?

The nomenclature of 'terrorism' in the South African context disguises the differing ways terror and violence can be employed to further political ends in the region. While the A.N.C. has been careful to seek international legitimacy

---

[56] Colin Legum (ed.), *After Angola: The War over Southern Africa* (London, Rex Collins, 1976), and Tony Hodges, *How the MPLA won in Angola* in Legum, *After Angola.*

[57] *The Times*, December 18 1982.

[58] Michael Hornsby, 'Realistic route to self reliance', *The Times*, August 9 1982; 'South Africa's bad neighbour policy', *The Times*, December 13 1982.

as a 'national liberation' movement and to avoid a strategy of terrorism that runs the risk of escalating into a race war, it confronts a regime that is rooted in a history of violent settler intrusion with only a thin veneer of obeisance to western liberal values. Indeed, South African race relations are distinguished by the fact that they have developed out of a tradition, since the attainment of South African Union in 1910, of authoritarian illiberalism which has followed a pattern of state-initiated social engineering on the basis of ethnic group classification. This process proceeded first under the banner of racial 'segregation' until the early 1940s and then, after 1948, under the ideological umbrella of 'apartheid', now more commonly known as 'separate development' or 'community development'.[59] The significance of this ideological history is that, from at least the time of the Second World War, it has moved directly opposite to the dominant trends of race relations thinking in the rest of the western world. These trends were classically stated by Gunnar Myrdal in his 1944 study of American race relations, *An American Dilemma*, which envisaged the supercession of the minority Southern segregationist ideology by the dominant 'American creed', with its roots in the Enlightenment humanism of the American revolution.[60]

In so far as South African racial ideology has been identified with the authoritarian manipulation of ethnic group identities as part of the entrenchment of white power, it leads logically to the establishment of what E. V. Walter has termed a 'regime of terror',[61] especially given the violent use of state power to divide up large sections of the black population and balkanize the territory of South Africa as a means of defusing united African nationalism. If this employment of terror remains unchecked at the international level, then, with the breakdown of the relative political 'stability' in Southern Africa afforded by the colonial presence in the buffer states, there is the risk of South African military power turning the region into a 'zone of terror' in its attempt to counter insurgency and guerrilla warfare.[62]

Given this systematic state employment of political terror, there is also the continuing possibility of black resistance groups replying in like kind, which could lead to a 'race war' with few or no checks on the use of violence, even genocide, by either side.[63] In a sense, this is a possible implication of the Pan African Congress's programme of black *racial* resistance to white power in

[59] Rich, *White Power and the Liberal Conscience*. For the decline of liberal values in the face of apartheid ideology see also Paul B. Rich, 'Apartheid and the decline of the civilisation idea: an essay on Nadine Gordimer's *July's People* and J. M. Coetzee's *Waiting for the Barbarians*', unpublished paper, African Studies Institute, University of Witwatersrand, June 1983.

[60] Gunnar Myrdal, *An American Dilemma*, (Vol. I), (New York, Pantheon Books, 1962), pp. 3-25.

[61] E. V. Walter, *Terror and Resistance: A Study of Political Violence* (London, Oxford University Press, 1969), p. 7.

[62] Walter, *Terror and Resistance*, p. 6.

[63] Leo Kuper has argued that South African apartheid policies 'have a strong genocidal potential in relation to Africans', though he also notes that 'the genocidal massacre of whole sections, including men, women and children, is not part of government practice, and the murders are on a smaller scale than one would expect from so tyrannical and brutal a regime' such that there 'must be powerful restraints against genocide', *Genocide* (Harmondsworth, Penguin, 1981), pp. 203-4.

South Africa which led in the early 1960s to the rural terrorism of the P.A.C. offshoot *Poqo*.[64] A strategy of guerrilla warfare, on the other hand, would have to be much more patient, eschewing the politically naïve P.A.C. slogan of the late 1950s of 'free by [19]63' in favour of a longer term strategy of popular mobilization, though the geographical terrain of open high veld and firm state control of population movement make this very difficult.[65] However, the continued internationalization of the political and military conflict in the region creates the growing possibility of further superpower involvement beyond the present area of Angola and Namibia. To this extent, the A.N.C. guerrilla strategy may well be subordinated to a wider strategy of Soviet and Cuban military involvement, in which case guerrilla incursions might prove a preliminary for a much wider conflict based upon conventional military warfare.

---

[64] The word *Poqo* is Xhosa for 'pure' and the basis of the movement in the Transkei was migrant workers who had strong connections with local traditions and beliefs but lacked any systematic organizational coherence or unity. Having been deprived of adequate land to form a cohesive peasantry, the *Poqo* activists were not fully proletarianized into working class movements either and the movement, as one analyst has argued, 'was an expression of a general desperation felt both in the reserves and in the locations', Tom Lodge, 'The Rural Struggle: Poqo and Transkei Resistance, 1960-1965', paper presented to the Conference on the History of Opposition in Southern Africa, University of Witwatersrand, Johannesburg, January 1978, p. 8.

[65] In March 1963 Potlake Leballo of the P.A.C. claimed 150,000 members ready for a general uprising, Halpern, *South Africa's Hostages*, p. 26.

[17]

PROSPECTS FOR TERRORISM IN SOUTH AFRICA

Keith Campbell

'TERRORIST' and 'terrorism', contrary to popular belief, are not terms invented by some government's public relations division as propaganda weapons. Rather, they were appelation titles proudly flaunted by the terrorists themselves, presumably to assault social sensibilities (i.e. to induce terror) as violently as their bombs and bullets assaulted the structures of their societies. Thus, Mikhail Bakunin entitled one of his polemics 'Revolution, Terrorism, Banditry'; Nikolai Morozov proclaimed 'The Terrorist Struggle'; G. Tarnovski argued that 'Terrorists . . . have the right to ignore the public conscience . . .'; while Serge Stepniak-Kravchinski, in his sympathetic account Underground Russia, freely described his subjects as 'terrorists'.[1]

TERRORIST WAR AND GUERRILLA WAR

Only later, when it was realized that the blatancy was counter-productive, did the terrorists attempt to confuse the public about the nature of their activities, by seeking to obscure the differences between terrorist war (illegitimate) and guerrilla war (legitimate). What are the differences?

Contemporary war, as a phenomenon, can be divided into three broad classifications: nuclear war, conventional war, and insurgency war. The two branches of insurgency war (guerrilla war and terrorist war) essentially have many similarities: they both employ irregular tactics, strike at weak and vulnerable points, seek safety by hiding in their surrounding environments, appear mysterious and pervasive, and so on. It is these similarities that terrorist propagandists have skilfully played on to obscure the important differences between the two forms of insurgency war.

There are two main distinctions between the two forms of war. Guerrillas almost invariably fight against a recent military conquest and seek to restore the socio-political status quo ante bellum – for example, the contemporary Afghan resistance; elements of the European resistance movements in the Second World War (but not all of them); the Boer commandos (1900-1902); and the Spanish guerrillas (who gave the word 'guerrillas' to the world), against Napoleon's troops in the Peninsula War in (1808-1814).

By contrast terrorists almost invariably fight against their own, or long standing, socio-political structures in order to achieve a revolutionary transformation of society. Thus the platform of the Popular Front for the Liberation of Palestine (PFLP) declares: "The struggle against Israel is first of all a class struggle"; and

Keith Campbell is a lecturer in the Department of International Relations at the University of the Witwatersrand.

398   PROSPECTS FOR TERRORISM IN SOUTH AFRICA

goes on to proclaim revolution against Jordan: "The struggle in east Jordan must take the correct path, that of class struggle";[2] while the political statement of the Weather Underground (a US terror group) stated: 'Revolutionary action generates revolutionary consciousness ... Mass struggle and movements are not mere spectators in revolutionary war ... Militancy and armed struggle are consistent threads in revolutionary movements'.[3] As a result, guerrillas are usually non-ideological, whereas terrorists are always ideological – he seeks to destroy his own community and replace it with something else. As D J C Carmichael puts it: "Terrorism puts each community on trial for its life as a continuing civilisation ... Terrorism implicitly rejects the prior authority of the community ... To adopt terrorist tactics is to reject civilized standards in principle and to enter a jungle of moral savagery ... In the final analysis the essential feature of terrorism is its rejection of civilized standards in principle".[4] By contrast, the guerrilla seeks to restore the 'prior authority of the community' in those situations where it has been violated by foreign invasion.

Resulting from and interwoven with this first key distinction is the second: the nature of the main target of the insurgent operations. The guerrilla invariably directs his prime attention to military targets: not, of course, major concentrations of strength, but isolated outposts, small patrols, vulnerable convoys, lonely sentries, etc. Fixed installations of immediate military value, and regularly employed by the target military, such as fuel depots, bridges, etc. are also attacked. The guerrilla seeks to minimize civilian casualties – for example by blowing up railway lines when the next train will not be a passenger one. Of course, in practice, this care is not always possible, but the intent is there.

The terrorist invariably directs his prime attention to civilian targets: shops, hotels, schools, buses, farms, domestic homes, government buildings – and all their occupants bear the brunt of terrorist attack. Even weak military targets are usually avoided. The intent of the terrorist is to maximize civilian casualties. Fortunately this is not always achieved, but it is the ideal.

This distinction can be clearly illustrated by referring to the totally different attitudes of the Communist Franc-Tireurs et Partisans (FTP) on the one hand, and the Gaullist Maquis and British Special Operations Executive (SOE) on the other: the others sought to stimulate guerrilla war. In the words of M R D Foot:

> "Useful as this (FTP) policy of terrorism was ... it undoubtedly – indeed deliberately – attracted severe reprisals, usually wreaked on the neighbourhood where the killing had taken place and not on the men who had done the job. This did not worry the communists, who believed that they were thus 'precipitating a revolutionary situation', a jargon term carrying conviction to them alone. Many of SOE's sabotage corps were unnerving to German morale in a more sophisticated way, less prodigal of lives".[5]

Max Hastings gives another example: an FTP group that 'was feared and detested throughout most of the surrounding countryside for the ruthless killing of any man suspected of collaboration, and Soleil's orders to his men to seize whatever they needed from whoever possessed it'.[6] The total disregard the terrorist feels for innocent civilians is well illustrated by the words of another FTP leader, code-named Hercules, who, when asked not to place the small town of Terrasson in

SOUTH AFRICA INTERNATIONAL   399

danger, exclaimed: "Terrasson has 3 000 inhabitants and France 40 million! What can these here matter?".[7] By contrast, the Gaullist policy was to minimize civilian casualties.

By using this distinction, it is easy to show that groups such as the Boer commandos and Afghan resistance are guerrillas, while the PLO, ZIPRA, ZANLA, FRELIMO, SWAPO and the ANC are terrorists.[8]

THE STRUCTURE OF TERRORIST ORGANIZATIONS

Terrorist organizations invariably have a dual structure: a political structure and, in parallel, a 'military' structure. This always applies, whether they are urban or rural. Each important level of authority in the 'political' hierarchy is matched by an equivalent level in the 'military' hierarchy; almost always regional political areas are congruent with the various zones of military operation. Schematically:

Political	*Military*
Political Leader	— Military Leader
Political Headquarters	— Military Headquarters
Regional Regional Headquarters	— Regional Headquarters
Local Branches	— Front Line Units

Source: J Paget, 'Counter-Insurgency Campaigning', p. 182.

Neither wing can operate without the other.

The actual process of subversion is, in its classical rural form, a four stage process. Firstly, there is the creation of the underground organizations. This is the function of the party (the political hierarchy), and involves the infiltration, subversion, and intimidation of the local population in the target area. It is a slow process that can take months, if not years. As the underground organization develops and spreads, it destroys the security of the people and disrupts the flow of intelligence to the security forces who are invariably unaware of what is occurring. Once in place, the organization provides logistic support and intelligence for the units of the military wing. Often the infiltrators will focus on real or imagined grievances, felt by the locals, in attempts to gain control over the target population. But such carrots are always accompanied by the stick of terrorism.

Once the party has established this necessary organization, the second stage begins. The 'military' forces begin to come into being with the creation of village squads. These units are often 'part-time' forces, thus making defection and location (and thus destruction) difficult; their function is to reinforce the underground organization, and to eliminate physically the representatives of the central government resident in the villages by assassination. Such governmental representatives have often already had their power and status undermined by the underground organization. These squads can only operate provided the party has already established its organization.

This is followed by stage three: the creation of regional military forces. These, again, act in support of the elements of stages one and two, providing yet greater

400   PROSPECTS FOR TERRORISM IN SOUTH AFRICA

security for the underground organization and virtually eliminating the danger of security force strikes on the village squads, if only by becoming the primary targets for such strikes. But they also act offensively, placing greater pressure on the government and forcing it further on the defensive. In turn, these regional forces can only survive because of the activities of stages one and two, providing them with essential logistical support (especially food) and intelligence (such as locations and strengths of police posts, routes of government patrols, threats from major security force operations, etc.). The police are a special target for these regional units.

The fourth and final stage of the classical insurgency pattern is the formation of regular units. Initially these are small formations established in safe, remote areas or in friendly foreign sanctuaries. Ultimately they reach divisional, even army, strength; their function is to engage and destroy the major units of the government's army. Yet, despite their size and relative power, they are still interlinked with the other levels of the insurgency, which provides the critically needed flow of intelligence, logistics, replacements, and rear area security. Even at this stage all the elements are totally interdependent.[9]

These stages can be schematically illustrated:

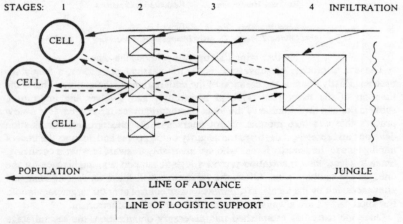

Source: R Thompson, 'No Exit from Vietnam', pp. 32-33.

However, this classic model has rarely been achieved – virtually only in China and Indo-China. In most other cases a hybrid model has come into being, comprising two levels: the underground organization, which functions in exactly the same manner as its namesake in the classic model; and the regional 'military' units, which also have to fulfil some of the roles of the village squads in the classic model. The regular units never occur in these hybrid cases. This hybrid or 'economy' version of terrorist war occurred, for example, in Malaya, Dhofar (Oman), Guinea-Bissau, Angola, Mozambique, Rhodesia (where ZIPRA did create regular units, but these were never deployed as such) and, to date, Namibia.

SOUTH AFRICA INTERNATIONAL   401

In urban terrorist war this 'two level' model – underground organization and terrorist force – is the only applicable one. However, there is a tremendous difference in scale between rural and urban operations: the terrorist units in rural areas can range in strength from 10 to 100 men, with approximately 30 as a good average; in urban areas four to six men and women is a good average size.

But, whatever version of insurgency – classical or hybrid, urban or rural – all have one critically important point in common: all are totally dependent for survival and ultimate success on the underground organization. Without this organization there would be no food, no recruits, no intelligence – the terrorists would be blind, deaf, dumb and starving – and thus easy targets for security forces. In the case of South Africa the primary threat (for reasons that will be made clear later) is urban terrorism; orchestrated by the African National Congress (ANC). The ANC itself provides the underground organization within South Africa, without which its 'military' wing, the Umkhonto We Sizwe (Spear of the Nation), which actually carries out the terrorist attacks, could not function. The ANC underground, like all underground organizations of all terror movements, is itself subdivided into two branches.

There are those who infiltrate the chosen target city to provide the necessary support network to enable the active terrorists, who follow later, to operate. These agents move into (or are recruited within) a chosen district and settle down. They seek employment – regular, unremarkable jobs; they are strictly enjoined to lead a decent, respectable, very definitely law-abiding life; they do nothing that will draw attention to themselves or generate suspicions about their activities. In fact, their neighbours will regard them as good people to have next door.[10] Having established their cover, and rendered themselves above suspicion, they will begin to function. They will seek out suitable dwellings to act as safe houses; recruit local people to strengthen the organization; reconnoitre targets and help decide on the best routes for the attack and subsequent escape; smuggle the active terrorists in; hide, feed, and transport them and, once the attack is completed, smuggle them back to base – in fact, the members of the underground do everything except pull the triggers themselves. The active terrorists would be valueless and incapable without them.

The second branch of the underground infiltrates key institutions of society, in order to undermine society from within. Their targets are the media, churches, universities (both academic staff and the student body). Their job is to disseminate propaganda from positions that are usually accorded respect and credibility, in order to de-legitimize the government and security forces, legitimize the terrorists, confuse the people, and try and turn the young, future elite against their own social and belief system. This branch of the underground is of great, and direct, importance to the terrorists, even though its members will never actually encounter an active terrorist.[11]

These forms of infiltration are occurring now, at this very moment, in South Africa.

What is the ultimate objective of all terrorist forces? Is it to destroy the security forces and so ride victoriously to power? Actually, while there have been a few cases where the terrorists have become powerful enough to inflict military defeats upon

402   PROSPECTS FOR TERRORISM IN SOUTH AFRICA

their enemies (e.g. the Chinese Communists and the Viet Minh) these are very much the exceptions. The actual aim is more subtle, more important: it is to break the political will of the opposing government; to convince it that it cannot win the war; and that it must accede to the insurgents' demands – i.e. that it must surrender. To this end, military victories, in the generally accepted meaning of the term, are unnecessary. Terror groups, as in Aden, Algeria, and Rhodesia, have achieved this while losing virtually every battle they were involved in! For terrorists, it is often forgotten, are thoroughly familiar with the famous dictum of Clausewitz about war being a continuation of politics by other means. The political objective is the target, and everything is directed to it. Operations that are, to the conventional mind, absurd or irrelevant are launched because of their political value. Some terrorists have perceptively described their operations as 'armed propaganda'. The underground and the active terrorists both have key roles in breaking the will of the target government.

The underground organization destroys the sense of security once possessed by the local people, thus destroying the government's support base; it prevents – or greatly restricts – the flow of information to the government, effectively blinding it; it provides the intelligence and support that enable the terrorists to vanish without trace after any contacts, thus frustrating and demoralizing the security forces.

The active terrorists force the agents of local government out, obliging the authorities to evacuate them or relocate them in heavily defended forts (as happened to the British in Palestine), causing the government to lose control of territory, and, even more important, humiliating it. They also draw attention – and thus security force activity – to themselves and, therefore, away from the underground organization, so greatly assisting the latter.

These activities are accomplished by a constant barrage of propaganda for the terrorists, and against the government (this is, in its domestic context, another key responsibility of the underground). Typical themes of such propaganda, as already mentioned, focus on real or imagined grievances, which are cynically exploited by the terrorists, who invariably pose as the means whereby the people's ambitions will be realized, and who, on victory, equally invariably, repudiate and destroy every promise made and action taken.

Thus, in China and Vietnam, land-hunger was endemic among the peasantry; furthermore, few peasants actually owned the land they worked; they rented it – at very heavy rates – from local landlords. In both cases, the terrorists, in the areas they dominated, exploited these grievances by seizing the landlord's ground and distributing it to the peasants, and granting the peasants ownership of the land they worked. And the peasants, in turn (and helped along by the discipline imposed by the underground) supported the terrorists. It was a most successful form of propaganda. But, on coming to power, the terrorists repudiated all their previous policies on land – private ownership was banned, and the peasants forced into collectives and communes against their will. How many died in China is not really known, but this betrayal provoked an uprising in North Vietnam, centred on the province of Nghe An, which had been previously hailed in the revolutionary propaganda as 'The Mother of the Revolution'. This uprising was fiercely

SOUTH AFRICA INTERNATIONAL 403

suppressed by the Communist regime, about 50 000 peasants being killed and at least 150 000 being sent to forced labour camps – Hanoi's own Gulag. Some sources put the number of dead and imprisoned as high as 500 000 – out of a total population of 17 million: in other words, some three per cent of the total population (in South African terms such a proportion would work out at over 700 000 people). It is highly unlikely that many survived their ordeal.[12]

With regard to South Africa the central propaganda thrust is that terrorism is the result of apartheid. Apartheid is held to be both discriminatory and oppressive. Discrimination and oppression are declared 'violence'; therefore, it is argued, it is appropriate that the 'victims' of the 'violence' should themselves resort to 'violence' – terrorism. This argument equates the government with the terrorist, simultaneously legitimizing the terrorists' crimes and de-legitimizing the governments' response. Note that none of these emotive terms – apartheid, discrimination, oppression, violence, etc. – is ever given a clear definition; rather, they are employed loosely, allowing South Africa's enemies the maximum possible capital from their use. This is possible because most people think they know the meaning of these words, when, in fact, they would be hard put to provide logical, coherent and meaningful definitions. And, even if they could, there is no guarantee that their definitions would in any way agree with the concepts behind the use of these terms by terrorist sympathizers.

The purpose of this intentionally confusing propaganda line is to take the responsibility for terrorist outrages off the terrorists who actually perpetrated them, and lay it at the door of the government. This is directly analogous to taking the responsibility for rape off the rapist and placing it on his victim. It is utterly absurd.

Then there is the propaganda directed against the security forces. This uniformly takes the line of claims of atrocities: of massacres in the field; of tortures and murders of prisoners under interrogation; and, if no credible evidence of physical ill-treatment is possible, of 'psychological' damage allegedly arising from interrogation and imprisonment techniques.[13] If the target country possesses a modicum of freedom – as South Africa does – such accusations are voiced from within by front organizations, by agents of the underground infiltrated into legitimate concerns such as newspapers, civic organizations, universities, etc., as well as by sympathizers in such groups recruited by the agents. (Often the sympathizers are so naive, or, as in the case of South Africa, so consumed with a pre-existing hatred, or resentment against the government, that they fail to realize they are being manipulated. They form that group whom Lenin scathingly described as 'useful idiots'.)

Because of the apparent source of these accusations, they are given greater credibility than they would otherwise have received. Occasional lapses by the security forces help this campaign; it being conveniently ignored that such lapses are few and far between, and invariably involve violation of standing orders, in comparison to the (intentionally ignored) purposeful policy of atrocity perpetrated by the terrorists.

Such accusations are routinely directed at the security forces in all insurgency wars; with, usually, no basis in truth. Thus they have been repeatedly directed against the American, British, French, West Germans, Israelis, Italians, Spaniards.

404   PROSPECTS FOR TERRORISM IN SOUTH AFRICA

and Swiss, among many others. The intention is to delegitimize the security forces, and thus the government that employs them: destroy the popularity of both: and to get curbs placed on the operations of the security forces, thus destroying their effectiveness. The more effective the security force unit, the more viciously and constantly it is attacked as criminal. The terrorist's hope is to generate such an effective propaganda barage as to lead to the discrediting or even to the dissolution of the target unit. And it has been known to happen that anti-terrorist units have been disbanded, or rendered totally ineffective, by successful terrorist propaganda.

One does not have to be very perceptive to note that a co-ordinated barrage of anti-security force propaganda is being directed in the pages of some of the country's principal papers, and through the mouths of some of the country's 'leading' academics, focusing especially on the security police. In other words, attempts are being made, at this very moment, to discredit and destroy the effectiveness of the South African Security Forces in order to lay the country open to terrorist attack.

External propaganda, directed to third parties, is disseminated from foreign secure bases by the terrorists' rear headquarters (in the case of the ANC it is London), and is along the same lines as internal propaganda, seeking to legitimize the insurgent as a 'liberator' and delegitimize the government and security forces as 'oppressors' and 'murderers'. Ultimately the target government, apparently unable to protect its supporters, or contain the spread of terrorism, or locate and destroy the terrorist forces, bitterly attacked from within and subject to pressures mobilized by the terrorists' propaganda from without, suffers a collapse in morale, loses the will to continue fighting, and surrenders. Thus it was in Cuba, in Rhodesia, in Nicaragua and in every case where the terrorists won.

What are the ANC's chances of bringing about such a result in South Africa? To answer this we must survey the international, regional and especially domestic environments within which it has to operate.

THE INTERNATIONAL ENVIRONMENT

The ANC enjoys considerable support at the international level, overwhelmingly provided by Third World and Soviet bloc states. This support is made manifest both directly (from the states concerned with the ANC) and indirectly (via the UN system, controlled by the ANC's supporting constituency) and encompasses all the ANC's needs, i.e. training, arms, money, propaganda. Elements within Western countries also support the ANC – with money, and especially propaganda.

Thus the Soviet Union has provided the ANC with training facilities within its own borders since 1964,[14] and, of course, is this organization's main source of arms; as well as arranging for similar assistance from its satellites and clients, including the PLO. The Organization for African Unity (OAU) has passed many resolutions implicitly and explicitly supporting the ANC against the Republic of South Africa and has also sought to generate favourable propaganda throughout the world for ANC activities.

The UN is an especially valuable source of funds and propaganda, granting the ANC observer status at the UN Headquarters, and denying South Africa her membership rights under the Charter. It also provides direct monetary grants – the UN itself provided $9 700 000 for the PAC, and especially ANC, in its 1980-81

SOUTH AFRICA INTERNATIONAL 405

budget, this figure excluding funds provided from the UN Trust Fund for South Africa or the UN Educational and Training Programme for South Africa.[15] Moreover, it is both a forum for, and a prime generator of, ANC propaganda. An example of this latter role was the 'International Conference on Sanctions against South Africa' (20-27 May 1981) organized jointly by the UN and OAU and held at Unesco House, Paris, at which South Africa was repeatedly compared to Nazi Germany.[16]

Then there are the multifarious activities of groups such as the Anti-Apartheid Movement in London, etc. To go into detail on all these groups and activities would be a most repetitive and sterile exercise. However, they cannot be ignored by the Republic, and in counteracting these groups the country has more than one advantage. Firstly, South Africa's opponents are remarkable incestuous – conferences and resolutions are invariably the converted preaching to the converted; arenas in which the 'true believers' refresh their battered and worn faiths by communion with each other, rather than springboards for evangelizing the uncommitted. Nearly 30 years of hostile propaganda has left the average Westerner almost totally unaffected; it also seems to have had little real impact in Asia, or even Africa itself;[17] while, if the attitudes of Polish emigrants are anything to go by, the result in Western Europe seems to have been the creation of a groundswell of sympathy for South Africa.

Thus, considerable scope actually exists for South African overt propaganda, via embassies and consulates abroad, friendly organizations (e.g. the American Legion), etc., using pamphlets, talks, films, books, etc. And Radio RSA is already, and most effectively, reaching areas of the world otherwise inaccessible to the Republic. Of course, it is neither easy to implement such a campaign nor is it swift in its results. But it is necessary that it be waged continuously, consistently, and over many years. It must be seen for what it is: a long, slow, hard struggle that will take years to achieve fruition. But achieve fruition it ultimately will, especially now that the process of reform is under way. South Africa now has something to sell abroad.

Of more direct impact are covert operations: the large, interlinked network in support of the ANC lends itself to infiltration; something the government is, fortunately, well aware of – witness the case of Craig Williamson. And, as Williamson exemplified, one well placed agent can wreak havoc in the ranks of this country's enemies. Nor is this the limit of the potentiality for covert action. Israel, for example, is a most highly experienced and very effective employer of covert action.

THE REGIONAL ENVIRONMENT

This, inarguably, is more important than the international environment. All the support in the world is useless to the ANC if it has no bases to operate from within the subcontinent.

South Africa's neighbours can be conveniently divided into three politico-strategic categories: (i) the active ANC supporters; (ii) the ambivalent neutrals; and (iii) the strict neutrals. The first group comprises Angola, Lesotho, Mozambique, Tanzania and Zimbabwe; the second, Botswana and Zambia; the third, Malawi and Swaziland.

406   PROSPECTS FOR TERRORISM IN SOUTH AFRICA

The active supporters are those countries that provide the ANC with the necessary training and operational facilities for attacks on the Republic. True, Zimbabwe is not yet very active in this role, but past experience with Mozambique, Robert Mugabe's oft-repeated commitment to Marxist-Leninism (or 'Scientific Socialism'), and the fierce propaganda onslaught against this country within Zimbabwe, all indicate that full, active support for the ANC is only a matter of time. As a group they are not entirely identical: three (Angola, Mozambique, Zimbabwe) are self-proclaimed Marxist-Leninist states; one (Tanzania) is a non-Marxist but nevertheless rigidly socialist (and therefore ideologically compatible) state; while the last (Lesotho) is currently a non-ideological state. Note (refer to Map 1) that Tanzania, Mozambique and Zimbabwe form a solid bloc to the North and East of the Republic, whereas Angola and Lesotho are both isolated – the last extremely so.

The ambivalent are those countries – Zambia and Botswana – which allow the ANC appreciable freedom of operation, but have no desire to be drawn into conflict with South Africa and so seek to avoid the establishment of ANC operational bases on their soil. Nevertheless, some infiltration does occur across their borders.

The strict neutrals (Malawi and Swaziland) subject ANC members within their borders to strict monitoring and supervision. Armed ANC members are, *de facto*, regarded as threats to themselves, and are not tolerated.

Of the active supporters, Angola initially appears to be of limited significance, except for the obvious role by virtue of supporting SWAPO, tying down SADF forces in Namibia that would otherwise be available for employment against the ANC. But this is to miss the whole geostrategic significance of the Angola/Namibia war. Should SWAPO win this war, the current geopolitical balance of southern Africa would be upset. Not only would a SWAPO government in Windhoek actively support the ANC (this is clearly stated in the SWAPO programme[18]), but Botswana and Zambia, currently ambivalent neutrals, would be caught in the jaws of a radical pincer. It is simply not credible to believe that they would escape radicalization themselves (if not in terms of internal structures, certainly in terms of foreign relations). They would inevitably become active supporters of the ANC. Malawi and Swaziland, on the other hand, would find it very difficult to uphold their present policies of strict neutrality, and would find themselves forced into ambivalent neutrality. Map 2 graphically illustrates the unfavourable geostrategical situation that would then face the Republic – the whole border from ocean to ocean one huge operational area.

On the other hand, should SWAPO be defeated, and Namibia achieve independence under a government friendly to the Republic (and hostile to the Marxist-Leninist supporters of SWAPO), then the geostrategic balance would swing dramatically in this country's favour. Such a Namibia would be a strict neutral, would act as a base (especially if the two lands were linked by a railway) for Botswana to cling to in the whirlpool of southern Africa, probably resulting in the latter moving from ambivalent to strict neutrality. Zambia would probably follow the same course. Moreover as Angola has invested so much in its support for SWAPO, defeat of the latter organization could easily be accompanied by the total collapse of MPLA control in at least the southern part of the country. This would, *de facto*,

SOUTH AFRICA INTERNATIONAL 407

partition Angola into a UNITA state and an MPLA state, the former almost certainly adopting a strictly neutral approach to the Republic; the latter, desperately fighting to survive and wishing to minimize the dangers facing it, would lapse into an attitude of ambivalent neutrality. This would leave Tanzania, Zimbabwe and Mozambique an isolated bloc. And it is difficult to believe that Lesotho would not also slip into the position of strict neutrality in the face of such a monumental shift in the regional balance of power. This possibility (which is, in fact, the 'best possible case' for South Africa) is illustrated by Map 3. One does not have to be a strategist to realize what a difference this would make to South Africa's security situation.

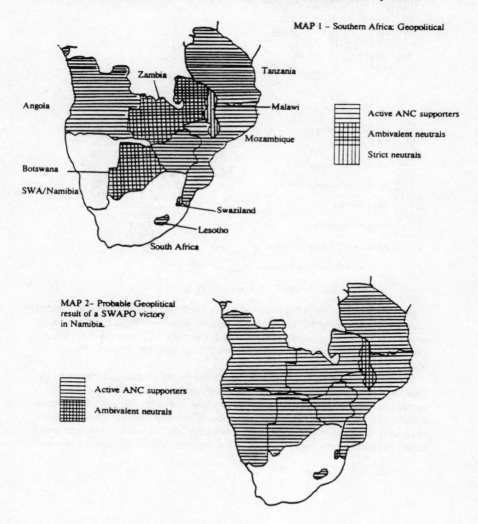

MAP 1 – Southern Africa: Geopolitical

Zambia
Tanzania
Angola
Malawi
Mozambique
Botswana
SWA/Namibia
Swaziland
Lesotho
South Africa

Active ANC supporters

Ambivalent neutrals

Strict neutrals

MAP 2– Probable Geoplitical result of a SWAPO victory in Namibia.

Active ANC supporters

Ambivalent neutrals

408   PROSPECTS FOR TERRORISM IN SOUTH AFRICA

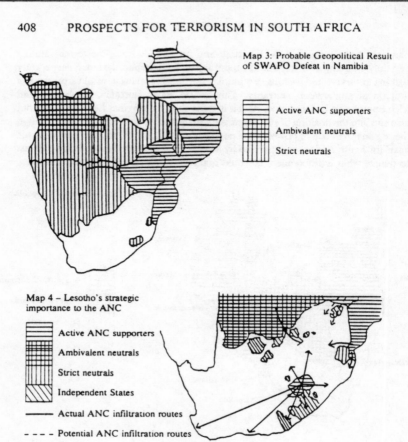

Map 3: Probable Geopolitical Result of SWAPO Defeat in Namibia

Active ANC supporters

Ambivalent neutrals

Strict neutrals

Map 4 – Lesotho's strategic importance to the ANC

Active ANC supporters

Ambivalent neutrals

Strict neutrals

Independent States

——— Actual ANC infiltration routes

- - - - Potential ANC infiltration routes

Source: Paratus, Vol 34, No. 1, January 1983, p. 18.

Thus the Angolan/Namibian war has a very important position within the overall framework of South Africa's own defence against attack – terrorist or otherwise. Of course, the shifts in the geopolitical balance forecast here in the event of the victory or defeat of SWAPO would not occur overnight, but they certainly would come into being.

The actual main base for ANC operations against the Republic is formed by the Tanzania-Mozambique-Zimbabwe bloc. No insurgency can function without a secure base, either located in a remote area within the target country itself or, most usually, in an obliging neighbouring state. This base serves many critically important functions: it is the essential first stop for new recruits en route to training bases; it permits both basic and advanced training; allows the establishment of

SOUTH AFRICA INTERNATIONAL 409

essential munitions depots and supply dumps; and provides a secure environment for headquarters units – including operational command, administration, training, logistics, intelligence and security staffs. Furthermore, it provides a jumping-off base for terrorist infiltration and attack; and, not least, provides the terrorists with an environment in which they can relax and renew their energies for the next mission.

Unfortunately for the ANC their main base area is poorly located *vis-à-vis* the Republic, bordering areas of little importance and remote from key centres. Nor does infiltration from Zimbabwe via Botswana (against Gaborone's wishes) promise any improvement. It is Lesotho which, for the ANC, lightens this grim geostrategical prospect. Lesotho is critically important to the ANC as a forward operating base – a fact which can readily be grasped by referring to Map 4. Because of Lesotho, targets can be reached that would otherwise be unattainable: the country is ideally located for attacks on southern Natal, Transkei, Ciskei, Eastern Cape, Orange Free State, and even the Witwatersrand (under the cover of the heavy flow of people to and from the mines) and the Western Cape. Moreover, it can act as a refuge for terrorists striking at targets elsewhere in Natal from Mozambique, and has long been a favourite escape route for those illegally fleeing the Republic. Without the advanced base facilities provided by Lesotho, the ANC would be crippled.

However, the importance of these base areas renders them very valuable targets from which maximum gain can be achieved from minimum effort by the security forces; while large numbers of security forces are required to track down even a few terrorists once they have infiltrated the country, small numbers of raiders can inflict enormous damage on the terrorist operations and infrastructure through carefully planned strikes against the latter's base areas. This has been illustrated time and again in Asia, the Middle East, and Africa. It is thus essential that South Africa continue the pattern set by the Maputo and Maseru raids. Equally, it is essential for the ANC that these raids be prevented: hence the propaganda campaign, both within and without South Africa, claiming that South Africa is 'destabilizing' her neighbours. (Note that no-one has yet produced a single piece of hard evidence to support these accusations, whereas South Africa has considerable amounts of hard evidence that these neighbouring states are supporting the destabilization of the Republic).

But such cross-border strikes must not be seen as instant panaceas; though dramatic and effective, they are not substitutes for strategy, nor of other (routine) security force activities, nor guarantees of rapid victory. Rather, they are essential elements in a necessarily long term counter-terror strategy. This is clearly illustrated by the Israeli experience.

On independence in 1948, all Israel's borders were subject to extensive terrorist infiltration; today, for all practical purposes, none are. Cross-border raids have played a considerable and probably major role in achieving this impressive security situation. A policy of cross-border raids was instigated in 1952, and has been maintained ever since. Some of these raids have been very small scale; others have been enormous. But the cumulative effects of 30 years of such raids has crippled the Arab's ability to make terrorist attacks on Israel.

410   PROSPECTS FOR TERRORISM IN SOUTH AFRICA

Accordingly the 1956 Suez campaign – launched partially because of Nasser's policies concerning the Suez Canal and the straits at Sharm-el-Sheik, but also because of heavy terrorist attacks from the Gaza Strip – so devastated the terrorist bases infrastructure in the Gaza and Sinai, and so shook the Egyptians, that these frontiers never again experienced any significant terrorist infiltration. And while the 1967 campaign in Judea and Samaria (the West Bank) was not primarily intended to destroy terrorist bases, it nevertheless did so, forcing the terrorist forces to flee across the Jordan, thus greatly reducing their ability to attack Israel. Nevertheless they continued such efforts, resulting in a major Israeli raid on the PLO base areas around the town of Kerama. Though not entirely successful this nevertheless resulted in the PLO moving its base infrastructure deeper into Jordan, rendering even more difficult their attacks on Israel and, arguably, increasing the threat the PLO posed to Jordan, thus helping precipitate the 'Black September' 1971, when the terrorists were expelled from Jordan. A second major Israeli frontier thus became quiet.

As infiltration across the Israeli-Syrian border was impractical, following the 1967 war, this left only the Israeli-Lebanese frontier. Lebanon thus became the main base area for the PLO and, not content with being privileged guests, Arafat's men precipitated the 1975 Civil War, seizing the opportunity to create a 'state within a state' in southern Lebanon. Never has a terrorist organization found itself in such a favourable situation. Yet Israeli strikes forced the PLO to devote more of its resources to defensive purposes, until, at the very height of the PLO's power, for every terrorist intended to engage in offensive operations (anywhere in the world), there were approximately nine others to protect him from Israeli pre-emptive attacks. Even this huge investment in defence, and even assistance from the Syrian army, could not save the PLO from being swept away by operation 'Peace for Galilee' in 1982; the operation that finally secured Israel's northern frontier.

Thus it can be seen that the effects of cross-border raids are long-term, not instantaneous. Though very effective, they are not miraculous; but their cumulative effect can be enormous. It is essential that South Africa engage in such operations as an integral and continuous part of the country's defence strategy. Some will object that such raids will attract Soviet involvement in the subcontinent; but this ignores that such involvement began years ago, long before the Maputo raid. And it is already of impressive scope: 26 150 Soviet bloc troops and 13 200 'civilian' technicians (including Cubans) in Angola and Mozambique alone! Soviet military exports to sub-Saharan Africa reached a record $1 900 million in 1981[19].

Soviet involvement in southern Africa is not in response to any South African actions or policies, but in fulfilment of imperial ambitions of its own. Others will object that Israel is a close ally of the USA, whereas South Africa is not. But this ignores the fact that Israel did not become an American ally until 1968, and forgets that whenever Israel has a choice of straining her relations with the US or abandoning cross-border raids she invariably chooses to strain relations with her ally. Nor must it be forgotten that South Africa is considerably less vulnerable to external pressure than Israel.

There is, however, one massive difference between Israel and the Republic – and

SOUTH AFRICA INTERNATIONAL 411

it is in South Africa's favour. The Arab states are, economically, totally independent of Israel; they depend on Jerusalem for nothing. But South Africa totally dominates her neighbours, both with regard to economic and transport affairs. They are, to a staggering degree, dependent on this country. (Their enmity might very well be not in spite of this dependence but because of it. Envy and jealousy are powerful emotions that are not merely legitimized but elevated as admirable and right by all branches of socialism; there is little South Africa can do about it.)

This opens the door to an integrated political-economic-military strategy, giving the Republic an instrument of policy vastly more flexible, sophisticated and far-reaching than any possessed by Israel. But of the elements of this integrated strategy the military is by far the most important. Economic action can only be effective as an ancillary to military operations – one only has to refer to the poor record achieved by sanctions. As for political action, many will be familiar with Clausewitz's dictum about war and politics, but few will be aware of the important rider he added to it: "War . . . is an act of policy . . . That, however, does not imply that the political aim is a tyrant. It must adapt itself to its chosen means, a process which can radically change it . . ."[20] Thus the politico-military aspects of the strategy become inextricably integrated: they are not two alternatives paralleling each other, rather they are one.

The dramatic rise in the influence of the SADF over the last few years and recent policies towards Lesotho indicates that the government is fully aware of this requirement. Skilfully carried out, such an integrated pre-emptive strategy can severely disrupt the terrorist base infrastructure and force the ANC, like the PLO, to devote the vast majority of its efforts to defending its own bases rather than attacking the Republic, and could very probably also totally deprive the terrorists of their critically important advanced base in Lesotho.

THE DOMESTIC ENVIRONMENT

South Africa is in a very fortunate position with regard to terrorism – it has one of the most hostile environments anywhere in the world for terrorist operations. First, geography is against the attacker. Infiltration across the borders of the Republic is not easy. There are many border areas – if not most – which are semi-arid, possessing only limited supplies of water, which can be controlled relatively easily, making the traditional form of infiltration (groups slipping across the border and moving on foot to their target areas) both difficult and unreliable. In this way the terrorists are, by and large, forced to remain on or near roads, making them vulnerable to random roadblocks and spot-checks.

This applies especially to the western border. On the east the Kruger National Park acts as a huge dead zone or cut-line, a virtually impenetrable barrier for infiltrators – for they are totally dependent on the underground organization for the logistic support and intelligence essential for success, and this underground, by definition, must be embedded in the local populace. And, of course, the Kruger Park has no such populace – except hostile game rangers and SAP patrols. So the terrorists must bypass the Park. In turn, this means that only relatively short stretches of the South Africa-Mozambique frontier are suitable for infiltration –

412   PROSPECTS FOR TERRORISM IN SOUTH AFRICA

allowing the security forces to concentrate their resources for maximum effectiveness.

Nor does the situation improve for the rural terrorist once inside the country. Much of the country remains arid and open, and is incapable of sustaining terror operations: only limited hit and run operations would be feasible. And those areas where rural terrorism is possible are all peripheral and of little importance to the survival of the State. Additionally, these areas are already much employed by dagga (marijuana) growers. So, far from being potential base sites for terror groups, they are already patrolled by the police. Furthermore, it is hard to believe that the drug dealers themselves would permit the ANC to establish itself in their areas for it would bring massively increased security force activity in its wake, totally disrupting their profitable activities. The heart of the country is located on the Highveld, which offers absolutely no cover for the terrorist; no rural based operations are at all possible here (though urban based terrorists might make occasional forays into the countryside).

Added to these natural difficulties are man-made ones: the new call-up system, with the new network of Area Defence Units, coupled with the new legal requirements on the occupancy of border farms, together create a formidable and highly flexible counter to terrorist infiltration. The terrorists – overwhelmingly urban in origin – will be attempting to pass through or operate in totally unfamiliar districts, while the security forces will be literally operating on their home ground, giving them a massive advantage. Nevertheless, there will be some attempts at rural terrorism, if only to try and overstretch the security forces; but they are doomed to failure.

Thus the only manner in which the ANC can strike at the Republic's heartland is by means of urban terrorism. But these main urban centres are nearly all relatively remote from Mozambique (the exceptions are, of course, Pietermatritzburg and Durban – hence the relative frequency of terror attacks in Pietermaritzburg). Even Lesotho – absolutely essential for the urban terror campaign – is not all that close to most of the major centres. Any meaningful attempts at infiltration of the urban areas requires considerable reliance on motor transport, so rendering the terrorists not only vulnerable to the aforementioned roadblocks but also to tighter controls on the Lesotho-South Africa border.

That the ANC's problems do not end with the arrival of the terrorists in the urban areas is clearly shown by the fact that it has been trying to engage in urban terrorism for the past 20 years. Remember the ANC's 'Operation Mayibuye' of 1963, exposed and shattered by the police swoop on Lilliesleaf Farm, Rivonia, and which resulted in the famous Rivonia Treason Trial of 1964. This, arguably, is the most total record of failure in the history of modern terrorism. How had this come about? It was the result of the constant disruption of the ANC's (and South African Communist Party's) underground organization (the two organizations are closely integrated[21]) by the Security Police, thus crippling the Umkhonto We Sizwe. This has been possible because of effective security legislation, allowing for detention without trial. Naturally, this legislation has, because of its effectiveness, been subject to fierce propaganda attacks by the ANC/SACP, its agents, fellow travellers, sympathizers and assorted opponents of the South African government.

SOUTH AFRICA INTERNATIONAL 413

Detention without trial has been a feature of virtually every successful counter-insurgency campaign since 1945, and has been employed by the most impeccably democratic countries. Britain, for example, has resorted to it repeatedly. In Malaya, no less than 10 000 suspects were detained at one time; while in Kenya the total reached 32 000 (in April 1954 alone, 16 500 suspects were detained) and though many were released after processing, many others were not.[22] Both Malaysia and Singapore possess and use special security legislation to forestall and defeat terrorism by the Malaysian Communist Party (MCP), which reactivated itself in the late 1960s. Reportedly, some suspects have been detained in Malaysia for the past 13 years. Yet both are prosperous democracies, while Malaysia is also a multiracial, nonracist state. Note that well; Malaysia is a prosperous, democratic, independent, multiracial and nonracist country – and it is under Communist terrorist attack! The MCP's original justification for its campaign was to bring about the independence of the country. This was achieved 25 years ago, yet the MCP is still attempting revolution. The reason for this is that Malaysia is a capitalist state – it espouses free enterprise. And this is also the real reason underlying the ANC/SACP onslaught on the Republic. For them, apartheid (however defined) is merely a local variation of the real enemy – capitalist imperialism. If ever apartheid could be totally abolished, yet capitalism retained, the ANC/SACP would regard this as a cosmetic reform and, like the MCP after Malaysian independence, continue their attempts at fomenting revolution. Indeed, the ANC has openly stated in its own publications that they do not seek reform but rather the seizure of power for themselves.[23] Fortunately, both the Malaysian government and Police Special Branch on the one hand, and the South African government and Security Police on the other, are both very aware of the threat.

The problem, from a public relations point of view, with detention without trial, is that its achievements are negative: in things that do not happen, rather than those that do. It is therefore impossible to give a definite list of achievements, whereas it is very easy to attack the obvious inroads made into theoretical political freedoms.

The phrase theoretical political freedoms is purposely chosen; while detention does encroach on these, it must never be forgotten that such freedoms can be exercised only if one is alive and free from intimidation. Thus more important than political rights are the fundamental rights of life and security. And it is these often forgotten rights which are protected and strengthened by security legislation.

But surely there have been deaths in detention? True, but they are few in comparison to those who would have died in an effective terror campaign. Let us briefly list the civilian death tolls in some of the terrorist wars, urban and rural, since 1945. In Malaya, in a 12 year period, 2 473 were killed, while another 810 went missing, presumably killed. In Kenya, in eight years 2 000 civilians died; in Aden, over four years 290 died and 922 were wounded; while in the eight-year Algerian War of Independence, more than 69 000 civilians were killed or abducted and presumed killed. Remember these figures are for civilians only – they do not include soldiers, policemen, or the terrorists themselves.[24]

No one can say how many South Africans of all races would have died if an

414   PROSPECTS FOR TERRORISM IN SOUTH AFRICA

effective terror campaign had been allowed to continue over the last 20 years. Foreign experience indicates that it would greatly exceed the total number of terrorist victims and dead detainees that South Africa has suffered to date. And it must be pointed out that deaths in detention are not unique to South Africa. No less than 402 such deaths occurred in the eight years of Mau-Mau in Kenya.[24] Abolition of these detention laws would cripple the security forces, greatly benefit the terrorists, and directly result in the death and maiming of many innocent people.

Owing to government's awareness of the threat, the ANC has only been able to establish a weak and fragmented underground within South Africa to support terror attacks. However, new opportunities for subversion are inevitably opening along with political and economic reforms. Trade unions, with potentially great power to disrupt the economy, are coming into being. They will be – already are – targets for ANC infiltration; And controlled unions could be used to help bring economic chaos to the country. Those who doubt this should be reminded of Lenin's instructions on this point: "We must agree to any sacrifice, and even if need be to resort to all sorts of tricks, slyness, illegal methods, evasion and concealment of truth, only so as to get into the trade unions, to remain in them and to carry on Communist work at all costs.[26] This, after all, is merely a logical extension of the strategy of 'entryism' pursued towards other key institutions of society and, as mentioned above, with the intention of undermining the State from within. In this regard is should perhaps be noted that the ANC/SACP is a multiracial organization. To assume, as the Rhodesians did, that all whites are reliable is a one-way route to disaster: even to assume that all Afrikaners, because they are Afrikaners, are trustworthy is dangerous. All nations have their traitors, opportunists and muddle-headed idealists. South Africa, in general, and Afrikanerdom, in particular, are no exceptions.[27] Some of the ANC/SACP's most effective agents are, and will be, white and white Afrikaners, precisely because they are generally presumed to be above suspicion.

In order to prevent such situations arising, the security police – which is and always will be the main arm of the security forces in the fight against the ANC –must continually monitor all sectors of society regarded as sensitive. Innocent people will, no doubt, be subject to suspicion and observation. But this, in the long run, is for their own benefit. When – it will not be if – infiltrators are discovered, they must be neutralized (unless they are used, unwittingly, to expose the rest of the network), even if this creates a storm of protest without and within the country on the part of people who are totally unaware of the agents' true nature.

For, it must be repeatedly emphasized, conformity is the terrorists' camouflage. They neither act nor appear as they are portrayed by Hollywood and pulp thriller writers. Indeed they, especially the members of the underground, will behave in a perfectly normal manner. As a result the revelation of their true identity invariably comes as a great – indeed, unbelievable – shock to those who thought they knew them. Such incredulous reactions are understandable but meaningless: to be completely above suspicion is the number one aim of any infiltrator; he or she simply cannot function if this level of trust is not achieved. The security police, of course, usually cannot reveal the information upon which an arrest is based. This invariably adds to the public's confusion. But it cannot be helped; anyone, even people one thinks one knows intimately, could be terrorists. For that is how it is in a terrorist war.

It must be stressed that such security police operations are not opposed to, nor interfere with, internal reform; rather, they are the essential pre-conditions to reform. As already indicated, the ANC is opposed to reform and will do everything possible to disrupt or abuse the process for its own revolutionary ends. Placing curbs upon the police will directly undermine the process of reform, endanger the country's security, and thus the security (i.e. the right to life) of everyone within its boundaries.

CONCLUSION

Currently the prospects facing the ANC are bleak. Over 20 years of external propaganda and internal effort have produced no significant impact on either foreign public opinion (even among political elites, denunciation of apartheid is merely a meaningless ritual) or the internal order of the Republic. Except for Lesotho, all of the ANC's actual or imminent base areas are poorly located *vis-à-vis* South Africa. Nor can it be assumed that Lesotho will be permitted to continue in this role by South Africa – all indications are that it will not. Internally, the terrorists face highly trained, well organized, very experienced security forces, who have managed to keep ahead of the ANC at every step, and show every indication of continuing to do so.

The ANC has only three causes for hope: (i) Namibia – which has become the geostrategic pivot of the subcontinent – falls to SWAPO, coupled with the inevitable geopolitical consequences of such an event. But this is highly unlikely, as the costs to South Africa of continuing the status quo in Namibia are far less than those arising from a SWAPO victory.

(ii) Or if the current reform process can be wrecked before the new constitution has a chance to prove itself. This is the ANC's best chance as processes of reform always make the states concerned temporarily more vulnerable to subversion. However, successful implementation of the new constitution will greatly strengthen the State and probably doom the ANC to ultimate defeat.

(iii) Or, finally, if the ANC and its sympathizers are able to get curbs placed on the security forces, to ridicule them, to expose them to contempt, and so to demoralize them, and by so doing, disarm the State. This is why the simple act of expressing support for the security forces is one of the most important contributions that society can make in a terrorist war.

The ANC will seek to become more active in this country; they will strive to give the impression that they are far stronger than they really are; but they will be easily contained provided that the national response and public reaction are appropriate. If they are, then terrorism, on its own, poses no threat to the Republic; it will have no prospects in South Africa.

416   PROSPECTS FOR TERRORISM IN SOUTH AFRICA

FOOTNOTES

1. Laqueur, W. (ed) The Terrorism Reader: A Historical Anthology, Wildwood House, London, 1974, pp. 65-68, 72-78, 79-84, and 84-90 respectively. Bakunin, Morozov, and Tarnovski were prominent and influential advocates of terrorism; Stepniak-Kravchinski a sympathetic chronicler of Russian terror movements. The polemics referred to by the above authors were originally published in 1869, 1880, and 1883 respectively.

2. Ibid, p. 148.

3. Ibid., pp. 173-176.

4. Carmichael, D.J.C. 'Of Beasts, Gods, and Civilized Men' in Terrorism: An International Journal, vol. 6, No. 1, pp. 3-18.

5. Foot, M.R.D. Resistance, Canada, London, 1978, p. 91 italics added.

6. Hastings, M. Das Reich: The march of the 2nd SS Panzer Divison through France, June 1944, Pan, 1983, p. 68. Italics added. Soleil was the group's leader. Guerrilla groups among the Resistance usually confined themselves to killing collaborators who actively informed against the Resistance – and never merely on suspicion. See Lampe, D. The Savage Canary; The story of Danish Resistance, Corgi, 1959, pp. 92-102.

7. Hastings, op. cit., p. 168.

8. The above analysis has been based on (apart from the works already cited): Barber, N. The War of the Running Dogs: How Malaya defeated the Communist guerrillas, 1948-60, Collins, London, 1971; Carver, M. (Lord) War Since 1945, Weidenfeld and Nicolson, London, 1980; Clutterbuck, R. Guerrillas and Terrorists, Faber and Faber, London, 1977; Geraghty, T. Who Dares Wins: The story of the Special Air Service 1950-1980, Arms and Armour Press, London, 1980; Hawes, S. and White, R. (eds) Resistance in Europe 1439-45, Penguin, London, 1976; Horne, A. A Savage War of Peace: Algeria 1954-1962, Penguin, London, 1979; James, H. and Sheil-Small, D. The Undeclared War, New English Library, London, 1973; Lewy, G. America in Vietnam, Oxford University Press, New York, 1978; Luffin, J. The PLO Connections, Corgi, London, 1982; Paget, J. Counter-Insurgency Campaigning, Faber and Faber, London, 1967; Palmer, D. Summons of the Trumpet: US-Vietnam in Perspective, Presizlio, San Rafael, 1978; Schaerf, C. and Carlton D. (eds) International Terrorism and World Security, Croom Helm, London, 1975; Sterling, C. The Terror Network: The Secret War of International Terrorism, Weidenfeld and Nicholson, London, 1981; Stiff, P. and Reid-Daly, R. Selous Scouts: Top Secret War, Gralago, Alberton, 1982; Schmitt, C. Theorie des Partisanen, Duncker and Humblot, Berlin, 1975; Tinnus, D. The Hit Team, Futura, London, 1976; Thompson, R. (Sir) Defeating Communist Insurgency, Chatto and Windus, London, 1966, No Exit from Vietnam, Chatto and Windus, London, 1969. Revolutionary War in World Strategy 1945-69, Secker and Warburg, London, 1970; Wolff, E. Peasant Wars of the Twentieth Century, Faber and Faber, London, 1969.

9. This account has been largely based on the analyses of Paget op. cit., passion and Thompson op. cit. passim.

10. On this, see the Italian Red Brigades' manual Standards of Security and Work-Style, cited by Sterling, op. cit., pp. 300-301.

11. For example, a leading supporter of the German Red Army Faction (Baader-Meinhof gang) was a lawyer, Siegfried Haag; he later became the leader of the RAF; assistance to terrorists resulted in the arrest and conviction of Swiss lawyer Maitre Rambert; while one of the Red Brigades leading agents was the millionaire publisher Giangiacomo Feltrineli – the man who had Pasternak's Dr Zhivago first published in the west! See Sterling, ibid., passim but especially p. 25 ff, p. 77 ff.

12. Wolf, op. cit., pp. 190-191.

13. Perhaps the classic case, in their absurdity, of such accusations were those directed by Italian radicals against the Swiss authorities over the imprisoned German terrorist Petra Krause, as related by Sterling op. cit., pp. 80-81: 'The indomitable committee demanding her extradition to Italy spoke only of a fine and sensitive woman . . . whose experience at the mercy of her Swiss jailers was a 'bloodchilling case of the violation of human rights' . . . reports spoke of her 'slow death . . . under the psycho-physical tortures of rigorous isolation' in the Zurich jail, and the tormenting sound of a nearby 'excessively noisy' hydraulic pump"! Krause was extradited to Italy – and, as her supporters had hoped, acquitted for lack of evidence: there was plenty of evidence for her crimes in Switzerland, however – hence the pressure for her extradition.

14. Grieg, L The Communist Challenge to Africa, SAFF, Sandton, 1977, p. 158 ff.

15. Marais, N. "Effective Action Against the African National Congress" SA Forum Position Paper No. 5, March 1983, vol. 6.

16. du Plessis, J. "The 'Just Struggle' and War of Words in Southern Africa" SA Forum Position Paper No. 7, April 1983, vol. 6.

17. Refer to Naipaul, S. North of South: An African Journey, especially p. 316 ff.

18. von Löwis, H. "SWAPO's design for South West Africa/Namibia" in SA Forum. No. 6, March 1983, vol. 6.

19. The Star, Johannesburg, 4 April 1983: note these are official American figures – despite claims that Pretoria is alarmist, the government is decidedly reticent on the Soviet build-up in neighbouring states.

20. Clausewitz, K. On War, translated and edited by Howard, M. and Paret, P., Princeton University Press, Princeton, 1976, pp. 86-87.

SOUTH AFRICA INTERNATIONAL 417

21. This is openly boasted of by the ANC and SACP – see, for example, the official journal of the ANC, Sechaba, July 1981 and January 1982.
22. Thompson, R. (Sir) (ed) War in Peace: *An Analysis of Warfare Since 1945*. Orbis, London, 1981, p. 83, p. 112.
23. Refer, for example, to Sechaba, October 1979, p. 16.
24. Thompson, R. (Sir) (ed) *op. cit.*, pp. 83, 113, 120; and Horne, A. *op. cit.*, p. 538.
25. Thompson, R. (Sir) (ed) *op. cit.*, p. 113.
26. Lenin, V.I., *Collected Works*, vol. 31, Moscow, p. 37.
27. One must not forget either the Handsoppers or the National Scouts of the Anglo-Boer War: nor more recent examples such as Braam Fischer. The archetype of modern traitors, Vidkun Quisling, was actually a very confused individual who genuinely believed he was a true Norwegian patroit: while Marshal Petain was convinced he was saving France.

[18]

Prospects for Revolution in South Africa

JEFFREY HERBST

The unprecedented violence that has engulfed South Africa's black townships since 1984, the creation of the United Democratic Front, and the emergence of large black trade unions have once again focused attention on the prospects for a revolutionary overthrow of the white government. Speculation has been further fueled by the relatively easy overthrows of dictatorships by popular rebellions in Iran, Haiti, and the Philippines. Indeed, some scholars and many inside the African National Congress now argue, in direct contrast to the strategic thinking of the Congress over the last twenty years, that a quantitative increase in the current form of popular protest may lead to a successful rebellion in South Africa. An examination of the revolutionary opportunities and constraints created by the most recent outbreak of protest is, therefore, necessary if the future evolution of South Africa is to be understood. After arguing that the present protest activities do not pose a threat to the continued existence of the white regime, the article will suggest what developments would indicate that a truly revolutionary situation is developing in South Africa.

THE STRATEGIC DOCTRINE OF THE AFRICAN NATIONAL CONGRESS, 1960–1984.

Since its turn to violence in the early 1960s after decades of peaceful protest, the African National Congress (ANC) — the most important black protest movement in South Africa — has had a relatively clear conception of the struggle it faced in South Africa. The ANC's perspective on revolution has centered around a vanguard party of committed partisans who would lead a guerrilla war. It argued in

JEFFREY HERBST is an assistant professor of politics and international affairs at Princeton University. He has written on political and security affairs in Southern Africa and was also a research associate at the University of Zimbabwe.

its major strategic document that guerrilla warfare was, "the special, and in our case the only form in which the armed liberation struggle can be launched."[1] While it repeatedly stressed the need for support among the people, the ANC rejected popular uprisings as a viable route to revolution in South Africa.

> Untimely, illplanned or premature manifestations of violence impede and do not advance the prospect for revolutionary change and are clearly counter-revolutionary. . . .
> The riot, the street fight, the outbursts of unorganised violence, individual terrorism; these were symptoms of the militant spirit but not pointers to revolutionary techniques.[2]

The ANC argued that mass popular revolt was likely to fail because "Under the modern highly sophisticated police state (which South Africa is) it is questionable whether a movement can succeed in a programme of mass political organisation beyond a certain point without starting a new type of action."[3]

In addition to strategic considerations, the leaders of the ANC rejected popular rebellion as an option because of the dangers it posed to blacks in South Africa. Nelson Mandela, speaking from the dock at the Rivonia trial where he was convicted for sabotage in 1963, said that the ANC sought to "canalize and control the feelings of our people" through organized armed struggle.

> Already small groups had arisen in the urban areas and were spontaneously making plans for violent forms of political struggle. There now arose a danger that these groups would adopt terrorism against Africans, as well as whites if not properly directed. . . . It was increasingly taking the form, not of struggle against the Government — though this is what prompted it — but of civil strife amongst themselves, conducted in such a way that it could not hope to achieve anything other than a loss of life and bitterness.[4]

Mandela also argued that an unorganized mass insurrection would pose insurmountable problems for a post-apartheid South Africa because "there would be outbreaks of terrorism which would produce an intensity of bitterness and hostility between the various races of this country which is not produced even by war."[5]

The ANC, in partnership with the South African Communist Party (SACP), therefore formed Umkhonto we Sizwe (the Spear of the Nation) in the early 1960s to overthrow the white regime. The vanguard party model was kept for over twenty years even though there were occasionally moments when popular revolt seemed to be occurring in South Africa. For instance, even after the violent Soweto uprisings in 1976, the SACP still rejected the strategy of promoting mass insurrection by arming the people.

[1] African National Congress, (ANC), Strategy and Tactics of the African National Congress (Morogoro, Tanzania: African National Congress, 1969), 9.

[2] Ibid., 5–8.

[3] Ibid., 6.

[4] Nelson Mandela, "Rivonia Trial Statement" in *No Easy Walk to Freedom* (London: Heineman, 1983), 164–169.

[5] Ibid., 164.

The events [in Soweto] could not, in themselves, have been transformed into a successful all-round armed uprising even if adequate stocks of weapons had been available. We must not play with the idea of an armed uprising by treating it as a question only of logistics and organisation.[6]

This strategic doctrine was not successful; indeed, the only threats to the regime between 1963 and 1984 were unorganized popular revolts, which the ANC and SACP had warned would not lead anywhere. It was not surprising, therefore, that when unprecedented popular protest engulfed South Africa in 1984 the strategic doctrine of the ANC, and many analysts' understanding of how the revolution would proceed, was thrown into confusion.

THE NEW UPRISINGS

The popular unrest in South Africa that began in 1984 provided those who oppose the white regime with new opportunities and, as is far less well understood, new dilemmas. The protests began with spontaneous boycotts and disturbances at black schools. Violence spread in the run-up to the August 1984 election of coloreds and Indians to a new parliament that ostentatiously excluded blacks. Popular unrest further intensified in September 1984 when there were large-scale protests against rent increases in the Vaal Triangle.[7] The violence spread unevenly through South Africa and there were soon major township disturbances in the eastern and western Cape, the greater Durban area, and the Witswatersrand. Less serious disturbances were reported in parts of Natal, the Transvaal, the Orange Free State, and the northern Cape.[8] On 20 July 1985, the government was forced to declare an indefinite state of emergency throughout large parts of the country, the first such action since the Sharpeville massacre in 1960. Because of continuing unrest including school boycotts, scattered consumer boycotts, and violence in the townships, State President P.W. Botha declared a national state of emergency on 12 June 1986.[9]

The intensity of popular protest can to some extent be understood by examining the development of street fighting in Alexandra, a black township near Johannesburg. Popular protest was ignited in Alexandra in February 1985 with the stabbing of Mukukeng Kumuka, a prominent black politician. After the stabbing,

"The township's teenagers went to war" as the streets were transformed into battle zones, barricades were built, and police vehicles were petrol-bombed and stoned. Troops armed

[6] South African Communist Party, "The Way Forward from Soweto: Political Report of the Plenary Session of the Central Committee of the South African Communist Party, April 1977" reprinted in Brian Bunting, ed., *South African Communists Speak* (London: Inkululeko Publications, 1981), 422.

[7] South African Institute of Race Relations, *Race Relations Survey 1984* (Johannesburg: South African Institute of Race Relations, 1985), 68.

[8] South African Institute of Race Relations, *Race Relations Survey 1985* (Johannesburg: South African Institute of Race Relations, 1986), 536.

[9] Martin Murray, *South Africa: Time of Agony, Time of Destiny* (London: Verso, 1987), 429.

with automatic weapons and gas masks "lined perimeter roads" protecting Sandton, the country's richest white residential area. . . . On 5 March, more than 40,000 people "crammed into the township's dusty soccer stadium" to attend an emotion-laden funeral for seventeen unrest victims.[10]

In late April, after the resignation of the town's mayor and the beginning of a rent strike to protest the presence of troops in the township, a group of "balaclava-clad" men, believed to be off-duty policemen, went on a rampage leaving eight political activists dead and scores of homes firebombed. The next day a crowd estimated at 10,000 confronted the police, and some angry residents directed rounds of AK-47 fire at the security forces. The residents, in a rally attended by 45,000 people in the local stadium, vowed to establish self-defense committees to defend themselves against the regime. The Alexandra Action Committee dug tank traps and all black policemen were forced out of the township. By the beginning of 1985, black militants claimed that they were in complete control of the area and that they had become the de facto government.

The violence that occurred in Alexandra was repeated with numbing regularity in many parts of the country. Between September 1984 and November 1987, more than 2,600 people were killed in the popular protests.[11] The South African Institute of Race Relations estimated that for the period between September 1984 and January 1986 approximately two-thirds of the dead were killed by South African state bodies and that the remainder of the deaths resulted from black-on-black violence.[12] Through January 1986 a total of 3,658 people had also been injured — 2,229 of them by state forces.[13] Damage from the violence up to 27 March 1986 was estimated at $69 million (though probably much higher if the cost to business from stayaways and property damage is included).[14]

More than anywhere else, the violence in the townships was directed against local government structures and the blacks who ran these agencies for the white state. For instance, between September 1984 and the end of March 1985, "there were 243 acts of violence against community councillors, including 66 petrol-bombings which totally gutted 32 homes."[15] Between September 1984 and June 1985, 240 black officials, including 27 mayors, resigned.[16] So few blacks were willing to serve on the discredited local structures that the minister of Constitutional Development, Chris Heunis, had to appoint white civil servants to manage township

---

[10] Ibid., 405–6. Murray is quoting newspaper reports from that period. Descriptions of Alexandra in this paragraph are all from Murray, 404–408.

[11] "Towards a Black Civil War in South Africa," *The Economist*, 7 November 1987, 45.

[12] South African Institute of Race Relations, 1986, 533.

[13] Ibid.

[14] BBC Monitoring Report, 27 March 1986, quoted in *ANC News Briefing* 10, no. 13, 30 March 1986, 3.

[15] Michael Morris, *Soapy Water and Cabinda* (Cape Town: Terrorism Research Centre, 1985), 17.

[16] Murray, *South Africa*, 303.

affairs.[17] In contrast, the first white security officer, a sergeant, did not die in the unrest until January 1986.[18]

The uprisings in the townships coincided with, promoted, and were themselves accelerated by other manifestations of popular protest. One of the most important political developments outside the townships was the establishment of the United Democratic Front (UDF) in 1983 as an umbrella organization for groups opposed in some way to apartheid. It claims to have 650 affiliates with 2.5 million members.[19] While the UDF denies having links with ANC, it is formally committed to abolishing white rule and seeks to promote a nonracial, democratic South Africa.

The period of unrest also saw the consolidation and growth of militant black unions, which sought to confront employers over a wide range of work-related issues. The unions have been growing dramatically over the last few years; in 1985 they formed the 500,000-strong Congress of South African Trade Unions.[20] The most dramatic instance of union development was probably the strike in August 1987 by the National Union of Mineworkers (membership 300,000) against the major mining houses. This biggest strike in the nation's history in the end forced the employers to concede only slightly more than what they originally offered, but the labor action did demonstrate that the unions had an organizational capability and internal cohesiveness far greater than most suspected.

THE HEIGHTENED PROSPECTS FOR POPULAR REVOLT

The new wave of rebellion in the townships, the development of large political organizations with determinedly antigovernment stances, and the precedent of successful and relatively easy popular rebellions in the Philippines, Haiti, and Iran have caused many to revise their estimates about the prospects for revolution in South Africa and the path that revolution will take. As speculation about a post-apartheid South Africa becomes a cottage industry, many now take it for granted that when the present type of revolt increases to a certain level, the South African regime will fall. Barry Buzan and H. O. Nazareth present a typical view:

> The recent upheavals in South Africa almost certainly mark the beginning of the end of white rule. They demonstrate that the blacks are close to acquiring the power to make the country ungovernable and that they already have the ability to disrupt South Africa's international economic position.[21]

More than any other figure, the ghost of the shah of Iran haunts discussions concerning the prospects for revolution in South Africa. While almost all analysts

[17] Ibid.

[18] *Weekly Mail*, 28 February 1986, quoted in *ANC News Briefing* 10, no. 9, 2 March 1986, 2.

[19] South Africa Institute of Race Relations, 1986, 38.

[20] Ibid., 180.

[21] Barry Buzan and H. O. Nazareth, "South Africa versus Anzania: The Implications of Who Rules," *International Affairs* [London] 62 (Winter 1986): 35.

recognize the strength of the South African state that is derived from its over-whelming military superiority, many now hesitate to predict what will happen in South Africa after the shah, possessor of a seemingly omnipotent security ap-paratus and army, was overthrown quickly through popular protest. Xan Smiley captured well the impact of Iran on those contemplating the turbulent South African situation: "And yet, bearing in mind the sort of explosion that overthrew the Shah, there is a nagging feeling that if and when the smouldering anger of the black millions is cleverly stoked up and catches alight, the place could go up in smoke remarkably quickly."[22] Similarly, Tom Lodge, perhaps the leading expert on the ANC, has also been influenced by the ease of the shah's removal:

> In Iran a government was forcibly supplanted without the presence of a revolutionary army. The parallel is not so far-fetched; in particular, South African revolutionaries can point to the demoralisation of a significant section of the security apparatus, the black police, and the apparent inability of the administration in its economic policies to meet the most basic material requirements of the urban black population.[23]

The Iran precedent has not been lost on some within the ANC. Mzala, while discussing the possibility of insurrection, wrote in the official organ of the ANC:

> Let us look at the history of Iran. The Shah's regime collapsed only under the pressure of political uprising of the masses, without this process being preceded by any kind of war or military organisation of the oppressed against the ruling class. What can prevent the apartheid regime in South Africa from collapsing for the same reasons as the Shah's regime?[24]

Others in the ANC also "now believe there is a chance that the whole edifice of white minority rule could collapse as suddenly as the shah's regime in Iran."[25]

In light of the Iranian precedent, many have detected evidence that the ANC is altering its tactics to encourage the new wave of popular rebellion, even though such a stance would mean a virtual abandonment of its traditional strategic doc-trine. One report from South Africa has noted a "radical restructuring in the pat-tern of resistance" by the ANC in order to mobilize the "fighting youth" of the townships.[26] Lodge also argues that "ANC strategical conceptions have in the last few years shifted away from the conventional guerrilla scenario which would as-sign a predominant role to the specialised military force which Umkhonto consti-tutes" and toward "broadening the social base of the armed struggle."[27] Similarly,

[22] Xan Smiley, "A New and Bloodier Image for the ANC?" *The Times*, 27 June 1983, 8.

[23] Tom Lodge, "The Second Consultative Conference of the African National Congress" reprinted in Committee on Foreign Relations, *Situation in South Africa*, 99th Cong., 2nd sess., 22 July 1986, 247.

[24] Mzazla, [pseud.] "Umkhonto we Sizwe: Building People's Forces for Combat War & Insurrec-tion," Part 1, *Sechaba*, [London], December 1986, 20.

[25] Johnathan Steele, "ANC Believes White Majority Rule could Collapse Suddenly," *The Guardian*, 11 August 1985, 7.

[26] "ANC Consultative Conference," *Weekly Mail*, 11 July 1985, quoted in, *ANC News Briefing* 9, no. 28, 14 July 1985, 2.

[27] Tom Lodge, "Mayihlome!-Let Us Go To War!: From Nkomati to Kabwe, The African National Congress, January 1984-June 1985," *South African Review III* (Johannesburg: Raven Press, 1986), 230.

Stephen M. Davis claims that there has been a significant departure from the ANC's previous perspective on evolution in South Africa:

> The Congress's ultimate objective in the 1980s was defined as a cataclysmic insurrection guided by trained units of Umkhonto but carried out by black masses armed with whatever weapons they could find. Apartheid's collapse would be speeded by demoralization in the ruling white community and desertions from police and defense forces. Insurrection itself would be the final thunderclap in a growing storm of labor strikes, township rebellion, and armed attacks.[28]

These assertions have been reinforced by some statements from inside the ANC itself. Mzala, while reviewing the ANC document *Planning for People's War*, gives a clear indication of the impact of the township revolts on some rebels' strategic conception of revolution:

> In 1969, the realistic military perspective was to wage only a protracted guerrilla struggle, but in the 1980s we have seen our struggle take a leap forward, and the situation today has within it the seeds and concrete possiblity for an insurrection. The person who now speaks only of protracted guerrilla war is behind the times. . . .[29]

Joe Modise, commander of Umkhonto we Sizwe, also called in July 1985 for "a people's war . . . by all the oppressed against the oppressors. He called on people to arm themselves with home-made weapons, and ambush security personnel and capture their weapons."[30] Ronnie Kasrils, a member of Umkhonto, has also argued, in direct contrast to the traditional doctrine that was reemphasized after Soweto: "That army of stone-throwers [the people in the townships] has to be transformed into an army with weapons. Our people have the mood and spirit; every stone-thrower wants a gun. We have to put guns in their hands."[31]

At the very least, ANC officials have tried hurriedly to adjust their strategic doctrine to the new outbreaks of violence by arguing that the popular uprisings are an integral part of the ANC's onslaught against South Africa. Oliver Tambo, president of the African National Congress, now declares that the role of Umkhonto we Sizwe is to lead the "mass combat units" that are now forming in the "mass insurrectionary zones" in South Africa's townships.[32] In a demonstration of just how far some in the ANC have moved from their traditional doctrine, ANC radio now urges blacks in South Africa to train themselves in guerrilla warfare in order to promote insurrection.[33] Yet at the same time, Tambo has acknowledged that the pace of the revolutionary struggle will be determined by organized political violence spearheaded by Umkhonto.[34]

---

[28] Stephen M. Davis, *Apartheid's Rebels: Inside South Africa's Hidden War* (New Haven: Yale University Press, 1987), 117.

[29] Mzala, "Towards People's War and Insurrection," *Sechaba*, April 1987, 5.

[30] Quoted in South African Institute of Race Relations, 1986, 532.

[31] Quoted in "People's War, Revolution and Insurrection, " *Sechaba*, May 1986, 4.

[32] Oliver Tambo, "Attack! Advance! Give the Enemy no Quarter!" *Sechaba*, March 1986, 6.

[33] Davis, *Apartheid's Rebels*, 133.

[34] Oliver Tambo, "Render South Africa Ungovernable," *Sechaba*, March 1985, 11.

Given the changes in ANC doctrine and analysts' new uncertainty over the stability of the South African regime, the critical question is what impact the recent events in South Africa will have on the prospects for the overthrow of the white government. If the current type of protest, accelerated by ANC encouragement, could threaten the regime, then those who equate South Africa with other recent instances of popular rebellion are correct in arguing that revolution will happen much quicker than is usually anticipated. The change in ANC rhetoric and perhaps also in tactics would also be justified if the current type of protest can pose a real threat to the white regime. However, if the current type of protest, even at significantly higher levels, cannot threaten the regime, then the analogy with other successful popular revolutions would be incorrect. Correspondingly, if the current type of protests cannot be successful, ANC tactics that use Umkhonto at least partially to encourage popular insurrection will be ineffectual at best and potentially disastrous.

THE NATURE OF THE SOUTH AFRICAN STATE

To understand the actual prospects for revolution it is first necessary to understand the nature of the South African state as it faces the security threat. Unfortunately, far too many have only examined the recent round of popular protest and show no evidence of an informed understanding of the repressive environment that confronts potential revolutionaries in South Africa. The South African state is fundamentally different from the type of state overthrown in Iran, Haiti, and the Philippines. Those states were authoritarian regimes that were led by one man, often with the major goal of enriching the ruler and his relations. In contrast, the South African state is an institutionalized system of repression that is dedicated to preserving the political and economic superiority of an entire racial group. This distinction is important because in an authoritarian regime the leader (be he the shah, Jean-Claude Duvalier, or Ferdinand Marcos) is the glue that holds the whole regime together. When the paramount leader falls, the entire regime, regardless of the strength of the repressive apparatus, dissipates, leading to an unexpectedly early and easy victory for the rebelling forces. Ambassador Jeane Kirkpatrick writes:

> Authority in traditional autocracies is transmitted through personal relations: from the ruler to his close associates (relatives, household members, personal friends) and from them to people to whom the associates are related by personal ties resembling their own relation to the ruler. The fabric of authority unravels quickly when the power and status of the man at the top are undermined or eliminated. The longer the autocrat has held power, and the more pervasive his personal influence, the more dependent a nation's institutions will be on him. Without him, the organized life of the society will collapse, like an arch from which the keystone has been removed.[35]

---

[35] Jeane Kirkpatrick, "Dictatorships and Double Standards," *Commentary* 68 (November 1979): 38.

However, because the South African state is a modern system designed to control the black majority rather than the anachronistic administration precariously centered on the personalistic rule of one family, there is little reason to believe that it will immediately be found to have feet of clay when challenged by rebellious groups.

In this light, the differences between the recently overthrown regimes and the South African state are immediately apparent. For instance, the repression the shah brought to bear on revolutionary forces was, reflecting the different nature of the regimes, far less powerful and unsystematic compared to the capabilities of the South African state. When the opposition to the shah first became public in September and November 1978,

> the monarch made no attempt to destroy the fanatically critical opposition and its highly effective "mosque network" and he refused to countenance an attempt on Khomeini's life. Although the more aggressive military leaders . . . pressed for a much more vigorous campaign aimed at undercutting the dissident's power base and forcing the opposition to be more amenable to compromise, nevertheless both the religious and secular dissidents *were allowed to operate without serious hindrance.*[36]

During the Iranian revolution, troop commanders were only allowed to fire in the air, and security patrols were overwhelmed by attackers who were able to control the streets even in wealthy suburbs.[37] Strikers, whose economic pressure became a significant factor in the shah's fall, continued to receive their wages when they left their jobs, because there was no provision in the law for withholding pay.[38]

In contrast, in South Africa the African National Congress has been outlawed for twenty-five years and is the subject of constant harassment through overt and covert military action. To take only the most recent example, there are now reports of a widespread worldwide assassination campaign against ANC officials that may have resulted in several hundred deaths. Between January and July 1987, eleven ANC officials were killed in Swaziland alone.[39] Among the victims was Cassius Make, the number four man in the command structure of Umkhonto and the youngest member of the ANC executive, who was gunned down outside Mbabane by three whites in a South African-registered car.[40]

The structure of the South African state's security system exemplifies the differences between it and the authoritarian rule of the Pahlavi, Duvalier, and Marcos families. While details are by necessity sketchy, the South African National Security Management System (NSMS) was designed to be a comprehensive response to revolutionary activity. The purpose of the system is to

---

[36] John D. Stemple, *Inside the Iranian Revolution* (Bloomington: Indiana University Press, 1981), 135. (Emphasis added.)

[37] Ibid., 146.

[38] Ibid., 121.

[39] *Business Day*, 17 July 1987.

[40] "Campaign to Assassinate the ANC," *New African*, September 1987, 15.

[1] counter what the state believes is a revolutionary onslaught against it. In practice, this means crushing all popular organisations working for radical political and economic transformation outside official structures; [2] to contain political resistance on an ongoing basis . . . [3] to co-ordinate a far-reaching "hearts and minds" strategy by improving social and material conditions in black areas . . . [4] to act as an early-warning system, spotting potential problems and dealing with them on a military or material level, before they erupt in open revolt.[41]

The NSMS system is under the guidance of the State Security Council (a crucial Cabinet comittee led by the former head of Military Intelligence) and is structured around twelve regional Joint Management Centres (JMCs) which coincide roughly with the country's military command areas. Each of these is staffed by approximately sixty security officials. Below the regional JMCs are sixty sub-JMCs covering the metropolitan regions and consisting of civic, local military, and police officials. Finally, there are 448 mini-JMCs corresponding to municipal councils that are made up of local officials.[42]

While it is always dangerous to simply extrapolate from paper organizational charts to real structures, the resources and capabilities of the NSMS system appear to be formidable. Comrade Ramat, writing in the official organ of the ANC, notes:

> For our cadres operating on the ground inside the country, the Joint Management Centre network, that spread right across the country, poses serious problems. The Intelligence Committee allows the police, military, National Intelligence Service and Military Intelligence to pool information at a local level. This co-ordinated action of all intelligence systems is new, and gives the racist regime an improved capability in identifying individuals and groups that are opposed to it.[43]

Comrade Ramat, quoting South African researcher James Selfe, says that the JMCs "know precisely who was at what meeting and what was said by whom. They also keep tabs on those regarded as important community figures."[44] Comparisons between South Africa and other recent examples of popular rebellion are, therefore, dubious at best. The revolutionary task of the recent popular rebellions — overthrowing a hated leader — is not the problem in South Africa. South African revolutionaries face the much more difficult problem of rebelling against an institutionalized political system.

ACTUAL DANGER POSED BY THE PROTESTS

The recent township protests and other developments in South Africa undoubtedly do represent the beginning of a new era in the country. However, it is impor-

---

[41] Joy Harnden, "The Creeping Coup," *Sash* [Johannesburg] 30 (May 1987): 3.

[42] The above information is all from Ibid., 4.

[43] Comrade Ramat, [pseud.] "Pretoria's Security System: The Network that Spreads Across the Country," *Sechaba*, January 1987, 29.

[44] Ibid.

TABLE 1

Comparative Political Violence

Political Deaths per 1,000 Citizens per Year			
Burundi (1972)	21.58	Madagascar (1948–1952)	.44
Lebanon (1976)	18.91	Kenya (1948–1952)	.38
Nigeria (1968)	18.57	Cameroon (1963–1967)	.32
Pakistan (1971)	4.92	Greece (1948–1953)	.25
Yemen (Sana) (1968)	2.88	Bolivia (1948–1952)	.21
Rwanda (1963–1967)	1.68	Zaire (1963–1967)	.10
Indonesia (1963–1967)	1.10	Colombia (1948–1952)	.08
Uganda (1974)	.90	Argentina (1953–1957)	.07
Hungary (1953–1957)	.81	Chile (1973)	.05
Jordan (1970)	.75	South Africa (1984–1986)	.03
Algeria (1958–1962)	.70	Malawi (1958–1962)	.01
Ethiopia (1975)	.58		

Sources: Political violence data are from *The Economist*, 7 November 1987, 45; and Charles Lewis Taylor and David A. Jodice, *World Handbook of Political and Social Indicators*, 3rd ed., vol. II (New Haven: Yale University Press, 1983), 48–49. Population statistics from United Nations, *Demographic Handbook 1979* (New York: United Nations, 1979); and South Africa Institute of Race Relations, *Race Relations Survey 1985* (Johannesburg: South Africa Institute of Race Relations, 1986).

tant, especially in light of the state's actual repressive capability, to understand systematically the threat posed by the new violence. Table 1 presents comparative figures on political violence, broadly defined, for countries across the world that have been involved in revolutionary situations. While the South African statistics are undoubtedly underestimates, this is also probably true for many of the other countries listed in the table. In addition, all South African deaths from mob violence and security force actions from September 1984 onward were counted as political, even though many resulted from the settling of personal scores or were simply random acts of violence. Indeed, the actual statistics are not that important, because even an order of magnitude increase in the number of South African political deaths would mean that South Africa is only beginning to experience the type of political violence normally associated with attempts to introduce radical change. Political violence is not always a necessary condition for change but, as Table 1 indicates, those who extrapolate from the recent township protests in South Africa and conclude that the country is suffering from violence on a truly revolutionary scale are incorrect if a global perspective is taken. It is particularly striking that the white population, which presumably must be threatened for any change actually to occur in South Africa, has not been touched by the most recent round of protest.

The nature of the conflict, even it it were increased dramatically, also suggests that the present kind of protest cannot threaten the South African state. The townships do not present terrains that are at all amenable to successful revolution. Most of the townships in South Africa were designed to contain black protest and are, therefore, far from white areas and can often only be reached by one road. As the armed vehicles at the gates of so many black urban areas constantly emphasize, these neighborhoods can easily be cut off if a protest threatens to spread beyond the confines of the township. Finally, and perhaps most importantly, the townships are ideal venues for repression, because the regime can easily concentrate security forces in them to forestall popular revolt. For instance, in Sebokeng in October 1984, a joint South African Police-South African Defence Force group consisting of 7,000 men entered the township to quell protests by conducting house-to-house searches for weapons and potential suspects.[45] Similar exercises have occurred in many other townships including Sharpeville and Tembisa.

The poor nature of the townships as spawning grounds for revolution was amply demonstrated by the series of events in Langa, a township near the white town of Uitenhage in the Eastern Cape. The United Democratic Front was strong in Langa, and by February 1985 it had defeated a rent increase and forced fifteen of sixteen black councilors to resign.[46] Conflicts with the police occurred often and during a day of protest on 21 March 1985 the police shot at least twenty-one blacks walking to a funeral. After the funeral, which was attended by 80,000 people, the UDF quickly became the de facto government of the township and established street committees that dealt with all issues facing residents. However, after the state of emergency was declared, the authorities moved in and imprisoned all those who had led the popular protests. In a vivid demonstration of the state's continued ability to shape the terrain of protest, the entire population of Langa was then relocated to a different site. The township today does not, for all practical purposes, exist.

In addition to the townships being poor terrain for revolution, the gross disparities in firepower between the security forces and the population of the townships makes it even more unlikely that township protest will pose a real threat to the South African state. John Saul notes:

> Events since June 1985 suggest that the ANC is still a long way from being able to provide enough of this kind of clout to the resistance movement. Government bullets still tend to be met by sticks and stones; defenseless Africans die while white policemen escape reprisal and the rest of the white population remains cocooned in its comfortable suburban lifestyle.[47]

For instance, in what would become an oft-repeated demonstration of the regime's superior firepower, a combined force of fifty security force vehicles, some of them armored, supported by helicopters and foot patrols in a convoy that stretched 1.2

[45] Michael Morris, *South African Political Violence & Sabotage 1 July 1984–30 June 1985* (Cape Town: Terrorism Research Centre, 1985), 49.

[46] The description of Langa in this paragraph is from Steven Mufson, "The Fall of the Front," *The New Republic*, 23 March 1987, 18.

[47] John S. Saul, "South Africa: The Crisis Deepens" in John S. Saul and Steven Gelb, *The Crisis in South Africa*, rev. ed. (New York: Monthly Review Press, 1986), 231.

miles went through the townships of New Brighton, KwaZakhele, Zwide, and Veeplaas in April 1985.[48]

Firepower alone does not always determine the course of a revolution, and the ANC has always claimed that material strength may not be a decisive factor in its struggle if certain precepts of guerrilla war are followed. The outlawed organization described in 1969 the kind of tactics necessary to confront a nominally more powerful enemy:

> Surprise, mobility and tactical retreat should make it difficult for the enemy to bring into play its superior fire-power in any decisive battles. No individual battle is fought in circumstances favourable to the enemy. Superior forces can thus be harassed, weakened and, in the end, destroyed.[49]

However, the type of guerrilla war needed to overcome superior material resources is the very opposite of what is occurring in the townships. In the townships the white state is able to concentrate its forces and thereby easily defeat the protesters who cannot make a tactical retreat. While it is conceivable that the balance of firepower could change in the future, the ease with which the security forces can seal off and search the townships suggests that it is unlikely that enough weapons can be brought into the townships to present a significantly greater threat to the white state.

An indication of the long-term disutility of township protest has been the large increase in black-on-black violence it has caused among the population of the townships. Nelson Mandela's warning at the Rivonia trial now seems prescient given the black-on-black violence that the township protests have bred. While it is important not to overestimate the scale of nonpolitical (that is, not directed against the state or its puppets) violence and thereby play into the hands of the regime, the dangers posed by random acts of violence spawned by the present form of popular protest have become very clear. *The Sowetean* noted:

> Every so often somebody calls for a stay-away, and more violence follows. After the funerals of those killed during the violence, more violence erupts and more people get killed. We need to seriously consider what we are achieving. Clearly, this cannot go on forever.[50]

Martin Murray, in perhaps the best account of the recent uprisings in South Africa, reached a similar conclusion:

> Without the massive influx of weaponry to the townships, armed insurrection was completely out of the question. In fact, any direct confrontation with the security forces was tantamount to suicide. In some townships, the popular movement turned inward, in effect creating phantom adversaries and striking at available targets of opportunity. This undermined the movement, weakening the resolve of even the most ardent supporters and strengthening the hand of local puppet administrations.[51]

[48] Morris, *South African Political Violence, 1985,* 103.
[49] ANC, *Strategy and Tactics,* 10.
[50] Quoted in John Kane-Berman, "How Black Anger Backfired," *The Guardian,* 7 December 1984, 12.
[51] Murray, *South Africa,* 392–3.

This is not to belittle the achievements of the township protests to date. They have succeeded in destroying the facade of local black government that the white state was trying to establish in order to make its rule more palatable. The actual significance of this action is unclear, however, because most reports from South Africa indicated that these local structures never had much legitimacy. The protests have not, despite claims to the contrary, made the townships ungovernable. They are governed in the most profound sense by the South African security forces who are successfully preventing the population from mobilizing to overthrow the state. Government structures including rent boards, local councils, and other structures have been destroyed, but these bodies do not pertain to the security of the white state.

The other political developments, while of great importance to the pattern of South African politics, also do not seem to promote a long-term threat to the state. The state's ability to decapitate popular organizations by simply imprisoning their leadership and harassing their members will prevent them from becoming security risks in the future. Trevor Manuel, a member of the UDF's national executive, noted the impact of state repression on the UDF:

> Two years and one month after its inception, the UDF finds itself bearing the full brunt of the government's onslaught. Two-thirds of our national and regional executive members are out of action through death, detention or trial. At least 2,000 rank and file members of the UDF are in detention.[52]

For instance, in July 1987 Murphy Morobe and Mohammed Valli were detained, leaving the UDF without even its acting national publicity secretary or its general secretary.[53] Similiarly, in February 1988 the South African government used its powers under the state of emergency to impose harsh restrictions that made it all but impossible for the UDF and other protest groups to operate.

The trade union movement, although a crucial development for black workers trying to improve their welfare, also does not appear to be a security threat to the white state. While the new black trade unionists in South Africa undoubtedly do see their long-term struggle in political terms, the short-term struggle around which their movement revolves is mainly about economic matters and therefore does not present a real threat to the government. For instance, Cyril Ramaphosa, the leader of the South African National Union of Mineworkers, said of the recent mine strike, "As much as we have tried to say that our strike is about wages and conditions of employment, the police intervention and the intransigence of employers are making this strike a political issue."[54] Joe Slovo, leader of the SACP

[52] Saul, "South Africa," 222.

[53] "The UDF: Under Cover but not Underground," *Weekly Mail*, 17 September 1987, 6. Morobe himself was filling in for Patrick "Terror" Lekota who has been imprisoned for the last two years as a defendant in a treason trial.

[54] John B. Battersby, "Mine Union Leader Says Pretoria Politicizes Strike," *New York Times*, 25 August 1987.

and until recently a top official in Umkhonto, argues that trade unions, unless they are somehow integrated into the armed wing of the ANC, cannot become a political threat to the government.

> Left to itself, without the participation and leadership of our revolutionary movement, we cannot expect great things from the great events that are happening in South Africa, i.e. the growth of the organisation of the black workers . . . on its own the trade union movement does not spontaneously generate revolutionary politics. It does not lead to more advanced revolutionary action.[55]

The ANC's analysis twenty-five years ago concerning the prospects for popular struggle now appears to have been substantiated. Despite unprecedented violence, the current round of protest has not and probably cannot pose a serious revolutionary threat to the white state. The exuberance of many scholars and ANC officials who see immediate prospects for popular revolt and, therefore, call for a corresponding change in tactics is ill founded. While continued unrest, even at significantly greater levels, can accomplish some tasks, especially destroying any remaining parts of the local government system and shaking investor confidence in South Africa, it cannot become significant enough to present a security threat to the state or initiate a severe economic crisis that might cause whites to reconsider their commitment to minority rule.

Those who recognize inherent shortcomings of the present type of revolt are now searching for a new avenue of protest that has the potential to threaten the basis of white rule. For instance, Gleb Starushenko of the USSR's Academy of Sciences (Africa Institute) claims:

> There exists a danger, however, that the struggle against apartheid may lose momentum and even bog down at the present pre-revolutionary stage. The historical experience of other countries attests to the fact that if revolution does not go ahead, does not set any new tasks and does not gain appreciable results, it is bound to sustain defeat. Considerable strata of South African society still keeps away from the struggle. . . . The process of the shaping of a revolutionary situation which we now witness in South Africa is far from being completed. Protest demonstrations are largely confined to African townships around big cities. The broad masses of the black population, particularly in bantustans, often stay aloof.[56]

If the current types of protest, which have attracted so much attention, will not pose a security threat to the regime, where should analysts look if we are to detect the truly important aspects of the armed struggle against the South African state?

---

[55] "People's War — The Task is to Make these Words a Reality: Interview with Comrade Joe Slovo," *Sechaba*, April 1983, 12.

[56] Gleb Starushenko, "For Peace, Co-operation and Social Progress," reprinted in *Southern Africa Record* 46 (April 1987): 77–78.

THE COURSE OF ARMED STRUGGLE

The armed struggle waged by the ANC itself is the key to understanding the course of revolutionary activity in South Africa. However, for several reasons the ANC has been notably unsuccessful in its efforts to bring down the white regime through guerrilla warfare. First, the topography of South Africa does not offer impregnable areas that would be conducive to establishing large internal bases for guerrillas of the type that were so important in China, Cuba, Angola, or Mozambique.[57] South African attacks on neighboring states have also prevented the ANC from establishing guerrilla camps near its borders. For instance, by funding antigovernment rebels, the South African government has forced Mozambique to sign the Nkomati Accord, which effectively forced the ANC out of Mozambique. Today all major ANC operations (in Zambia, Angola, and Tanzania) are at least one country (or in the case of Namibia, one colony) away from South Africa's borders. As a result, the ANC has given up the possibility of establishing rear bases that would serve as the launching points for guerrilla attacks.[58] While South Africa no longer has the cordon sanitaire that it possessed before the mid-1970s, the independence of Angola, Mozambique, and Zimbabwe has not caused as much deterioration in its geopolitical position as many had predicted.

The ANC also faces numerous other problems in conducting armed warfare. In sheer size it is overwhelmed by the South African security forces. A recent interview with Joe Slovo suggests that the armed wing of the ANC receives between $8 million and $25 million a year from the Soviet Union and that aid is about matched in logistical and humanitarian contributions from western countries.[59] In contrast, South Africa spends over $2.8 billion on its military alone.[60] The ANC has about 10,000 trained guerrillas of whom approximately 400 are operating in the country at any one time.[61] The South African Army alone, not counting the South African Police and the police and armies of the homelands, has 82,400 men.[62]

As a result, the ANC military campaign has been ineffective in threatening the state. The accompanying chart traces the path of all attacks against South Africa that have not occurred as part of a township disturbance.[63] While the chart almost

---

[57] Tom Lodge, *Black Politics in South Africa since 1945* (London: Longman, 1983), 295–96.

[58] Mzala, "Umkhonto we Sizwe," 22.

[59] Steven Mufson, "Uncle Joe: The White Guru of the ANC," *The New Republic*, 28 September 1987, 20. Davis estimates Umkhonto's budget at $50 million. Davis, *Apartheid's Rebels*, 66.

[60] Jeffrey Herbst, "Political and Economic Implications of South Africa's Militarization," *Jerusalem Journal of International Relations* 8 (March 1986): 45.

[61] Tom Lodge, "State of Exile: The African National Congress of South Africa," *Third World Quarterly* 9 (January 1987): 5.

[62] Herbst, "Political and Economic Implications," 48.

[63] While it is always difficult to systematically retrieve this sort of information, the chart presents the best available evidence of military activity against the South African state. The chart and all subsequent figures cited include all offensive actions against the South African state, some of which may have been conducted by groups other than the ANC. The statistics, therefore, do not include other

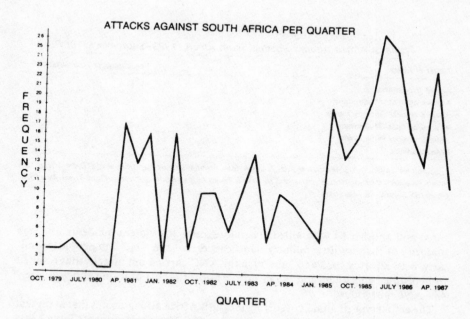

ATTACKS AGAINST SOUTH AFRICA PER QUARTER

Sources: Michael Morris, *South African Political Violence & Sabotage* (Cape Town: Terrorism Research Centre, various years) and Michael Morris, *South African Bomb Summary* (Cape Town: Terrorism Research Centre, various years).

certainly underestimates total ANC activity, the general trends are correct and it includes all significant instances of guerrilla attacks against South Africa. By only including attacks that could not be a part of uncoordinated popular rebellions, the chart is also a more accurate representation of the military threat to the South African state than estimates that simply count all ANC-inspired incidents. The chart shows that there has been a general increase in the number of attacks against South Africa over the last few years. However, the absolute number of attacks is still low. Even in the second quarter of 1986, when the greatest number of attacks ever recorded occurred, there was actually only one new incident every three and one-third days. The ANC has also had to pay a heavy cost for its forays against the white state. For instance, in the period between October 1976 and December 1984, there were 262 ANC attacks while 185 trained Umkhonto men were cap-

ANC-inspired incidents such as shoot-outs with the police when guerrillas are captured. The statisitics also do not include attacks successfully prevented by the South African security forces. All information on the attacks is from a series of reports by Michael Morris, *South African Political Violence & Sabotage* (Cape Town: Terrorism Research Centre, various years); and Michael Morris, *South African Bomb Summary* (Cape Town: Terrorism Research Centre, various years).

TABLE 2

Types of Armed Attacks against South Africa, 1979–September, 1987

Target of Attack	Percentage of Total Attacks
Armed Propaganda	34.1
Attacks against Infrastructure	29.7
Attacks against Security Forces	12.0
Attacks against Government	11.4
Attacks against Businesses	8.0
Assassinations	4.9

Source for Tables 2 & 3: Michael Morris, *South African Political Violence and Sabotage* (Cape Town: Terrorism Research Centre, various years); and M. Morris, *South African Bomb Summary* (Cape Town: Terrorism Research Centre, various years).

tured and another 64 were killed. Therefore, only 262 violent incidents, the vast majority of them of little military significance, cost the ANC 249 people.[64] Similarly, between July 1985 and June 1986 the ANC carried out attacks that resulted in 54 people being killed and 349 injured,[65] but at the cost of losing approximately 489 ANC guerrillas.[66]

The actual type of attacks occurring in South Africa also indicates that at present the ANC has been unable to threaten the South African government. Table 2 lists the frequency of different types of attacks that have occurred in the last few years. "Armed propaganda" (an ANC term) is any type of attack that is not directed against a specific target. The explosive device near Johannesburg Station on 12 February 1982 that scattered ANC and SACP leaflets is an example of armed propaganda.[67]

Table 2 presents strong evidence that the ANC has not been able to mount a significant military threat to the South African government. Over 60 percent of the attacks against South Africa are against infrastructure (such as power line pylons) or done for symbolic purposes.[68] These are the same types of attacks that the ANC was conducting twenty-five years ago when Nelson Mandela was first arrested. There is very little evidence that the ANC is, in the words of Oliver Tambo, "moving from sabotage acts to attack the enemy face to face."[69] While attacks

---

[64] Morris, *Soapy Water and Cabinda*, 38.

[65] Mufson, "Uncle Joe," 20.

[66] "Apartheid Barometer," *Weekly Mail*, 17 September 1987, 4.

[67] Morris, *South African Political Violence & Sabotage 1 January–30 June 1982* (Cape Town: Terrorism Research Centre, 1982), 28.

[68] A similar conclusion has been independently reached by Tom Lodge in his review of ANC activity between 1976 and 1983. Tom Lodge, "The African National Congress in South Africa, 1976–1983: Guerrilla War and Armed Propaganda," *Journal of Contemporary African Studies* 3 (1983/1984): 169.

[69] "Armed Struggle Escalates," *Sechaba*, January 1983, 3.

against infrastructure can occasionally be quite damaging[70] and armed propaganda sometimes results in many injuries.[71] in the main they are of little more than nuisance value. Attacks against businesses that could generate a large amount of damage and cause despondency within the white population are still low. Similarly, attacks against the state itself, especially against its security apparatus, are relatively infrequent.

While the ANC has developed into a more sophisticated military organization in the last few years, its attacks against South Africa do not provide any evidence that it is now capable of inflicting truly significant damage on its opponent. For instance, the type of attack responsible for much of the increase over the last few years—land mines—is relatively unsophisticated and, while undoubtedly having a high probability of success, can never cause significant damage. Joe Slovo himself noted the inadequacy of sabotage attacks ten years ago when reviewing the early military efforts of the ANC:

> Sabotage of property, even on a more sophisticated scale than MK [the abbreviation for Umkhonto we Sizwe] was capable of mounting [in the 1960s], is at best a weapon auxiliary to revolutionary armed struggle. It could neither bring about the downfall of the government, nor draw into action those not already in the fairly small conspiratorial group of activists.[72]

The ANC, therefore, needs both quantitative and qualitative changes in its attacks against South Africa if it is to pressure the South African regime. However, given all the disadvantages that the guerrilla movement faces, is it possible for the ANC to actually mount a significant threat to the South African regime?

IMPORTANCE OF RURAL GUERRILLA WARFARE

The ANC will only present a truly significant threat to the white regime if it is able to conduct an extensive guerrilla war in the rural areas of South Africa. In many ways the new protests in the townships have directed analysts' attention to precisely the wrong area for understanding revolution in South Africa. A true guerrilla presence in the rural areas would be threatening to the South African regime because the state would have to spread its security forces over a vast amount of land. A campaign that caused a dispersion of security forces would make many targets more vulnerable and would pose more dangers to the security forces themselves, because they would be unable to find safety in numbers. Finally, a scat-

---

[70] For instance, the sophisticated ANC attack against the Koeburg nuclear power plant on 17 December 1982 considerably delayed construction of the facility. Michael Morris, *South African Political Violence & Sabotage 1 July-31 December 1982*, 49.

[71] For instance, the bomb placed in a shopping center in Amanzimtoti on 23 December 1985 killed five and injured forty-three. Michael Morris and T. Combrinck, *South African Bomb Summary* (Cape Town: Terrorism Research Centre, 1986), 64.

[72] Joe Slovo, "South Africa-No Middle Road" in Basil Davidson et. al., *Southern Africa: The New Politics of Revolution* (London: Penguin, 1976), 180.

TABLE 3

Location of attacks against South Africa, 1979–September 1987

Type of Location	Percentage of Total Attacks
White Major City[1]	39.4
Rural Area[2]	30.3
White Minor City	14.7
Black Urban Area	6.7
Border Area	8.9

Note: [1] Includes Johannesburg, Pretoria, Cape Town, and Durban.
[2] Includes the "homelands." 6.1 percent of the total atacks occurred in the homelands.

tering of forces would also cost the South African government significant resources above and beyond what it is now paying for security.

The present type of township protest allows the regime to do just the opposite: security forces are easily concentrated in urban areas in a way that does not impose significant costs on the regime. The only way township protests may ever become important security threats in and of themselves is if a large enough part of the security forces is drawn off into protecting the rural areas. Therefore, the surest sign that the security of the white regime is being seriously challenged would be if urban uprisings are not suppressed or are even allowed to spread because the regime has committed a large number of troops to combat the guerrilla war in the rural areas.

The ANC has in fact had a few successes in developing a military campaign in the rural areas. Due in part to the low-level struggle, especially land mines, it is now reported that 43 percent of the white farms on the Botswana border, 39 percent on the Zimbabwe border, and 14 percent on the Mozambique border have been abandoned.[73] However, in general the ANC's rural campaign is still underdeveloped. Table 3 lists the distribution of all attacks that have occurred between 1979 and 1986 for which information on type of location is available.[74] While all of South Africa's border areas are also in rural areas, this category was considered separately, because attacks on the border are of considerably less strategic value to the ANC than attacks in South Africa's vast interior hinterland.

Attacks in rural areas do constitute a significant percentage of total military attacks against South Africa; however, they are not yet high enough to present the kind of rural threat that would require a significant dispersal of South Africa's security forces. The best evidence that the current level of rural warfare is not adequate for the ANC's strategic needs is the large security forces that the South Africans have been able to concentrate in the urban areas. Thousands of troops

[73] Murray, *South Africa*, 210.
[74] Location could not be deduced for 23 of the 350 attacks.

are routinely placed in the townships with no apparent loss of security in other areas of the country. Indeed, in its most recent review of events in South Africa, the ANC admitted that its efforts in the rural areas were inadequate.[75]

However, the ANC faces severe problems intensifying any rural campaign. As noted above, the South African security system now covers the entire country in a comprehensive manner. Beyond its intelligence and command system, the South African military has substantial military assets — especially a powerful air force and well-trained commando units — that will pose substantial obstacles to guerrillas. Even in the "independent" homelands the South African security apparatus is actually quite strong. All the homelands have banned the African National Congress and have implemented security legislation that is at least as harsh as South Africa's.[76] Indeed, the security forces in the homelands have been called "the largest homeland growth industry." In Ciskei, for instance, 66 percent of the total funds allocated to economic development goes to the security forces.[77] Finally, unlike other areas where guerrillas have been successful, there are no forests or mountain ranges in South Africa that could provide sanctuary to guerrillas attacking the government. The prospects for the ANC developing a significant rural presence in the near future are, therefore, dim.

SURVIVAL OF THE WHITE REGIME

The white regime is not threatened by the current type of unrest, even if there is a quantitative increase in the level of popular protest. The South African state is of a fundamentally different nature from other regimes that have recently folded under popular pressure, and the current type of protest is particularly amenable to government repression. The real key to overthrowing the regime, as the ANC recognized twenty-five years ago, is military struggle, especially in the rural areas. However, the ANC has been notably unsuccessful is posing a military threat to the regime and faces an extremely difficult task in developing an armed threat in the rural areas. The prospect, therefore, in South Africa is of continued white rule for the foreseeable future with increasingly violent popular protest that, while not posing a significant threat to the government, will result in repression and suffering. Although the ANC turned to violence twenty-five years ago, the war for South Africa has only just begun.*

---

[75] African National Congress, "Political Report of the National Executive Committee to the National Consultative Conference" in *Documents of the Second National Consultative Conference of the African National Congress* (Zambia: African National Congress, 1985), 21.

[76] Fund for Free Expression, *Human Rights in the Homelands* (New York: Fund for Free Expression, 1984), 6.

[77] Ibid., 129.

* An earlier version of this article was presented at the African Studies Association meeting in November 1987. I am grateful to Henry Bienen, William Foltz, Mark Gersovitz, Peter Johnson, Tom Karis, Christa Kuljian, Steven Mufson, Gideon Rachman, and an anonymous referee for their comments.

THE BASIS OF STRUCTURAL VIOLENCE

Between Verwoerd and the ANC: Profiles of Contemporary Repression, Deprivation, and Poverty in South Africa's "Bantustans"

Eliphas G. Mukonoweshuro

1. The Contemporary Crisis in the "Bantustans"

THE SOUTH AFRICAN NATIONAL PARTY'S DREAM OF TURNING 10 "NATIVE RE-serves"[1] (variously referred to in official jargon as "Bantustans," then "homelands," "national states," "self-governing states," or "emerging black states") into self-sufficient, ethnically defined countries, while simultaneously denying the majority of South Africans the vote in their own country, has turned into a political nightmare. The homelands are falling apart, unable to contain the impact of accelerating political changes since the unbanning of the African National Congress (ANC), the South African Communist Party (SACP), the Pan Africanist Congress (PAC), and other political formations and the release of leading political prisoners such as Nelson Mandela. In particular, the "homeland" governments are now trapped between the Verwoerdian ideology of "separate development" that sustained them and

ELIPHAS G. MUKONOWESHURO teaches Political Science at the University of Zimbabwe, Department of Political and Administrative Studies, University of Zimbabwe, P.O. Box MP 167, Mount Pleasant, Harare, Zimbabwe. He completed his Ph.D. at the University of Birmingham in England in 1982. His main areas of research interest lie in the field of African political economy in general and the southern African region in particular. He has published academic articles in leading international scholarly journals such as *African Affairs, Journal of Social, Political and Economic Studies, Journal of Modern African Studies, Journal of Contemporary Asia,* etc. His two books, *Colonialism: Underdevelopment and Class Formation in Sierra Leone* and *Sierra Leone: The Roots of Dictatorship and Underdevelopment* were accepted for publication by the University Press of America and Africa World Press respectively. They will be published in 1991.

the rapid proliferation of support for the ANC and allied political organizations even in some of their remotest areas.

By legitimizing the ANC, the Pretoria regime has created a political vacuum in which the leadership role that had originally been created for the homeland governments has all but disappeared. Civil administration in these "homeland" apartheid structures has deteriorated so fast that there is a virtual collapse of political leadership.[2] As conditions of undemocratic government, general mismanagement, corruption, and instability continue to escalate in those poverty-stricken areas along with widespread rejection of homeland policy, it is clear that Pretoria faces a serious political problem. The tyranny of some Bantustan leaders, coupled with the use of vicious vigilantes, has led to several coups in all the independent Bantustans: Transkei (1987 and 1988), Bophuthatswana (1988, although South African troops intervened to reverse the coup), Ciskei (1990), and Venda (1990). All except Bophuthatswana are demanding reincorporation into South Africa.[3]

Dramatic changes are also taking place in the "non-independent" Bantustans. The leaders are calling for a total scrapping of the Bantustan system and have invited the ANC, the SACP, PAC, and the United Democratic Front to mobilize freely in their small "states." For instance, Nelson Ramodike, the leader of Lebowa, has called for the restructuring of regional local authorities on a non-racial basis under one government.

The fiscal crisis in the Bantustans has made it impossible to meet some of the homelands' people's most basic demands, such as the need for clean water, electricity, and health and educational facilities. The homeland governments have also failed to achieve economic self-sufficiency and have attempted to retain their ascribed political structures despite the marginalization of the Pretoria-sponsored chiefs' role through the rise of such organizations as the Congress of Traditional Leaders of South Africa (CONTRALESA), which is sympathetic to the ANC. In general, the violence associated with the rejection of these foster "states" should be placed in its proper perspective — the majority of the people for whom the "Bantustan" system was devised are revolting against a system of repression reminiscent of feudal Europe.[4]

2. Lineages of "Bantustan" Absolution

The homeland constitutions, coupled with a corruption of traditional African political practice, conferred upon "homeland presidents" absolute powers last seen in Europe before the onset of the 1789 revolutionary phase.[5] The powers of their immediate subordinates, the chiefs, are entrenched in the constitution, with non-elected chiefs often comprising a majority of those who would exercise supreme authority. The relationship between homeland leaders and subordinate chiefs is analogous to that which existed between 17th–century European kings and their noblemen. As was the case in Europe, the addition of a centralized bureaucracy and security establishment to such a relationship swung the balance of power decidedly in favor of the homeland leaders. Effectively, this enabled the homeland leaders to corrupt traditional African political practice and govern by actions rather than policy.

Apart from this constitutionally sanctioned authoritarianism, to protect themselves against any possible attacks and to quell unrest, the leaders of the four "independent" homelands maintained perpetual states of emergency throughout the 1980s. As for the "non-independent" homelands, they were granted draconian powers to pass their own security legislation, ban and restrict people, ban organizations and publications, and carry out forced removals of settled communities. P.W. Botha[6] handed over to the country's six "non-independent" homelands the same security powers as those enjoyed by the four independent homelands. The effect of the proclamation amounted to a further blurring of the distinction between the powers of "independent" and "non-independent" homelands.

These draconian powers were combined with a strategy of control based on a crude manipulation of four key groups in a given Bantustan: the rural populace, the bureaucracy, the "security" services, and the chiefs and headmen who manipulate, repress, and control the rural populace. The Bantustan constitutions confer on a given president considerable powers to determine the succession of chiefs and headmen and thereby to regulate rural authority. Rebellious chiefs can be isolated and dealt with through security legislation and powers within the bureaucracy, while loyal chiefs are heaped with rewards ranging from trading licences, farms, and other business establishments. However, the major weakness of this strategy is that while it has ensured the loyalty of the chiefs, it has also made a given homeland leader a captive of the "security" forces and the bureaucracy, and thereby increasingly vulnerable to them. The homeland leaders lack any determinate social base for their rulership because the majority of the rural populace has continued to live in abject poverty and massive repression. It is precisely this situation that lies at the root of the current crisis in the Bantustans.

Major challenges to the authority of the Bantustan leaders, therefore, come from the bureaucracy, the intelligentsia, and the security forces. The bureaucracy and intelligentsia are largely interlinked. Most homeland university graduates have joined the bureaucracy since it generally has offered the best opportunities in a given homeland.

As long as the income of civil servants remained on par with those of South Africa and the bureaucracy continued to offer places for new graduates, there were few problems. While a segment of the youth and intelligentsia might strongly question the legitimacy of the homeland system, they could easily be dealt with through the security system, as long as the socioeconomic system offered opportunities for the bulk of the graduates. However, when the growth of the bureaucracy slowed and incomes suffered (as was the case during the second half of the 1980s), dissatisfaction, manifested in an overt defiance of the "Bantustan" system, and open political revolt became evident. In most cases, homeland leaders had to commit ever-increasing budgets to civil service salaries to maintain the cooptation/repression equation. This has resulted in a fiscal crisis that has rendered all the homelands economically nonviable.[7]

A crucial player in the homeland power game is the security establishment. In controlling the security forces, a given homeland leader uses a three-pronged strategy. First, he pays them well, gives them various material fringe benefits, and tries to ensure that they have sophisticated equipment, which confers status and keeps them busy. Second, a given homeland leader generally maintains multiple security forces, such as the police, the army, and the security police, all with separate command structures that report directly to him. Their specific duty is to keep an eye on the populace and on each other. Finally, by frequently moving security force commanders (and/or removing then), a given "president" ensures that no security force commander has the opportunity to build strong loyalty in a given branch of the force or to forge links with other competing branches. As further insurance, a "president" maintains a technically close relationship with South Africa's security forces. However, although the support of the security establishment is critical in controlling the other major support groups, the security forces themselves have been very hard to control, as coups in Transkei, Ciskei, Venda, Bophuthatswana (reversed by South African Forces), etc., have shown. These events suggest that the security paranoia of the homeland presidents is merely an accurate reflection of the realities that their illegitimacy breeds. By the beginning of 1990, resistance to this illegitimacy had assumed almost revolutionary proportions.

For example, in March 1990,[8] there was widespread economic sabotage by the Venda civil servants, causing the Bantustan to grind to a halt. Water and electricity were severely disrupted and, in general, the majority of government departments came to a virtual standstill. Key government employees such as magistrates, prosecutors, and policemen also joined the strike, plunging the homeland into absolute chaos. The same pattern of resistance occurred in Gazankulu, Bophuthatswana, and Ciskei. Only those Bantustan leaders who are well disposed toward reincorporation into South Africa and accept the ANC's mobilization programs in their homelands (e.g., Transkei, KwaNgwane, Lebowa, etc.) seem to have been spared the wave of violent opposition.[9]

In general, then, the changing political climate in South Africa has raised expectations for a better political and material future at a time when most Bantustan regimes have attempted to forge ahead with the same old repressive ways. Most fundamentally, people have simply had enough of decades of extreme impoverishment, unemployment, heavy taxation, and denial of the basic necessities of life. The Bantustans cannot hold up for long. The attempt by the South African government to persuade black people that the "Chief Ministers" and "Presidents" of the Bantustans should represent them in the negotiations for a new constitution is a virtual non-starter. The dismantling of the Bantustan structures is virtually a precondition for negotiations by all the legitimate political groupings, such as the ANC, the PAC, the Mass Democratic Movement (MDM), etc.

Significantly, it is not only the extra-parliamentary groups that hold this view. The Labour Party, which is the ruling party in the House of Representatives, has consistently refused to support any legislation to strengthen the homelands system, for it has opposed Bantustan "consolidation," as well as black spot removals. However, the current political crisis pales into insignificance when placed against the general poverty and deprivation and the draconian program of action that a future government will have to launch to alleviate suffering in the Bantustans.

3. Profiles of Deprivation and Poverty

The Bantustans have proved to be economically unviable.[10] Both the "independent" and "non-independent" homelands have continued to receive over 75% of their revenues from South African subventions, and in Transkei, the largest Bantustan, only 15% of the labor force is internally employed. Indeed, overall, more than 70% of the homelands' economically active population[11] is involved in the migrant labor system, while the rate of homeland job creation fails to absorb more than 10% of those who are newly entering the job market. The result has been vast slums, wrecked by poverty, ignorance, and disease. Thousands of South African babies in the Bantustans are dying of malnutrition and associated diseases; two million children are growing up stunted for lack of sufficient calories in one of the few countries in Africa that exports food.[12] Malnutrition in the homelands has resulted in one of Africa's highest infant-mortality rates and in some areas, illiteracy is as high as 80%.

The homelands are the most densely populated areas of South Africa: in some areas there are up to 329 people per square kilometer as opposed to 17 people per square kilometer in "white" South Africa and 24 people per square kilometer on average throughout South Africa. The majority of the people in the Bantustans do not have access to piped water or electricity, although South Africa produces 60% of the entire continent's energy. In this context, the National Party government has tried over the years to "redress" the situation by providing budgetary support and subsidies to settle industrialists closer to the pools of labor and transport subsidies to settle workers away from "white"

176   MUKONOWESHURO

South Africa.[13] It is precisely this form of support that has been taken to represent the "cost of apartheid"[14] to white South Africa.

(a) Subsidies and Industrialization

The argument that apartheid is costly for the white government in South Africa is largely fictitious. The "cost of apartheid" argument assumes that everything spent on a given homeland would otherwise not have been spent on the same region. However, much of the funds channelled into the homelands directly support South African political and economic interests. In particular, a substantial proportion of the resources is absorbed by the salaries and privileges of the Pretoria-installed political class in the Bantustans and in no way benefit the general populace. In addition, a substantial proportion of the funds is spent on contractors operating as suppliers of goods and services to the Bantustans. The funds therefore flow back to Pretoria.

Most of the formal laborers from the homelands work in "white" South Africa. The taxes that they generate are paid via company profits, Regional Service Councils' business tax, and sales tax on goods bought in South Africa and directly support the "white" fiscus. Consequently, budgetary support and other subsidies can scarcely be called a "transfer" of funds from "white" South Africa to the Bantustans. It is more of a miserly refund to the Bantustans. Consumers from the homelands spend most of their money in the white towns, e.g., KwaNgwane residents buy in Nelspruint, Zwelitsha residents in King Williams Town, while KwaZulu residents shop in Pietermaritzburg or Durban. Pretoria collects taxes directly from the homeland "citizens," because they are not exempt from sales tax in South Africa.

The South African government also collects indirect taxes such as those levied on petrol, excise duties, car parts, etc., which are consumed by homeland residents. In addition, most homelands have major roads running through them that carry up to 80% of South African transit traffic. The vehicle taxes and licence fees are, however, collected by white municipalities. Overall, then, the homelands may in fact be subsidizing South Africa. They also experience a brain drain. Intellectual capital schooled in the homelands departs for South Africa because the economic system applied to the homelands cannot support them.

As for the fortunes of the so-called industrial decentralization program, the experience of Ciskei explodes the myth of homeland improvement through industrialization. The Ciskei spent nine years (since 1981) attracting investment into the territory. Investors flocked from South Africa, Europe, and the Far East, particularly Taiwan, attracted by the much-publicized "tax haven" status of the Bantustan. By 1990, about 204 industries had been established.[15]

The package of incentives designed to attract investors-has resulted in a net loss for Ciskei. First, because of the security forces' brutal implementation of

Repression, Deprivation, and Poverty in South Africa's "Bantustans"   177

the Ciskei's stringent anti-trade union laws, labor-intensive companies have found the investment "climate" quite attractive. The recommended minimum wage, which is not legally enforced, is R120 (about $55.00 in U.S. currency) per month. Companies paying R120 are given R110 by the Ciskei government, which means that their wage bill drops to only R10 per worker per month! Very little, therefore, accrues to Ciskei in the form of labor costs.[16]

In some cases, company taxes have been waived. Apart from this waiver of company tax, personal income tax peaks at only 15%. This effectively means that only 15% is deducted from the money sent out of the territory. In addition, industrialists qualify for 60% transport rebates and harbor duties. Companies relocating to Ciskei from South Africa are given up to R1 million in assistance and they can apply to make their investments in financial rand instead of the commercial rand. This effectively reduces the required initial investment by the potential investor by as much as one-third. In general, therefore, the industrial decentralization program has tended to benefit South African capital more than the ordinary people of Ciskei. Foreign companies have also benefited immensely. Ciskei offers itself as a loophole for companies wanting to invest in South Africa, but in need of getting around the sanctions blockade. "Independent" Ciskei, like the other Bantustans, offers a convenient cover.

(b) Land

The most obstructive myth about the homelands is that the Land Act has left blacks, who comprise 75% of the population, "owning" only 13% of the land. This is an unduly charitable argument. The truth is that blacks own *no* land, not even 13%. Property ownership has been denied homeland residents. Apart from the less than one percent of the residents who, for historic reasons have some freehold title, the rest of the land in the homelands is owned by the homeland governments "in trust" and allocated without secure mortgageable, letable, or saleable title via the chiefs to the residents. Soil erosion, which is currently threatening South Africa's water resources and the entire ecosystem, is one of the physical and measurable disasters of "separate development." Characteristic of the rural black areas are low per capita incomes and high population densities. Soil erosion in the black areas has consequently been caused by poor farming methods forced on people because of high population densities and uneconomic-size plots for agriculture. Black farmers have also lacked subsidized farm inputs, transport to the markets, education, and water-storage facilities. Further, white farmers, who are privileged with these state subsidies, have often caused soil erosion through irresponsible management of cropping and plantation programs.

In these circumstances, a post-apartheid government in South Africa will have to tackle the land question as matter of utmost urgency. Two basic land reform models appear to be under consideration. The obvious options after apartheid are sweeping socialist reforms through state ownership of land, and eventual redistribution under state control or private ownership of land. Redistribution would be aimed at justice and equity with regard to the hitherto deprived, while privatization targets "productivity" and the commercial conservative rural white elite.[17] Either could have severe implications if implemented unwisely.

The land ownership pattern prevailing in South Africa on the eve of redistribution will shape and constrain relocation possibilities. In that context, a broad socialist transformation becomes extremely difficult. Patterns of land rights in South Africa are extremely complex, ranging from freehold to trust land. To assemble any substantial blocks of land for redistribution would be a logistical and administrative nightmare, quite expensive and problematic. Land reform programs that are too complex to administer tend to lose momentum and ultimately collapse.

South African prescriptions for land reform have concentrated on maximum production. Liberal and conservative commentators have not thoroughly considered land options that do not aspire to the yields of mechanized agriculture. The fact remains that South Africa's highly productive white agriculture has reached this level only with massive state assistance against the natural limits of poor soils and scarce water resources. Through these massive, uneconomic, and artificial subsidies, the state has kept many inefficient and marginal farmers on the land. Many argue that marginal or bankrupt white farms could form the core of post-apartheid land reforms based on the model implemented in Zimbabwe. Large tracts of land, especially in Northern Transvaal, are out of production because of land abuse, and some farmers have even abandoned their holdings. Such derelict land would be a dubious asset even for the reformers. Far from markets and suffering from poor soil conditions, these holdings would not make a profit under any system of management devoid of overgenerous, uneconomic subsidies. They cannot provide the launching pad for a realistic agrarian reform. To succeed in any reform program, it seems that the new government would have to disregard all "sacred cows" in policy formulation and implementation.

4. Water Provision

Millions of people live in the homeland areas where no water infrastructure has been provided. This shortage of water weighs heavily against the areas' future viability. Indeed, one of the faces of poverty in South Africa is the lack of clean and easily accessible water. This basic socioeconomic fact is the main reason for the 50,000 infant deaths annually from diarrhea before their first birthday. Outbreaks of cholera and typhoid are also common in areas where in drought or flooding, water becomes contaminated.

Repression, Deprivation, and Poverty in South Africa's "Bantustans"   179

Francis Wilson and Mampela Ramphele[18] have pointed out that the individual daily consumption of water in one part of Ciskei was 9 liters, well below the World Health Organization's goal of 50 liters per person per day. In most black townships the average daily per capita water usage is 19 liters, a tiny fraction of the white consumption of 314 liters a day. In the Mlala district of Gazankulu in the Eastern Transvaal, there is an average of one tap for every 760 people. Middle-class white metropolitan homes have an average two to three taps per inhabitant.

The South African Department of Water Affairs (DWA) estimates[19] that demand for water in the southern African region, including Lesotho and Swaziland, will increase by 58% between 1980 and 2010. The areas with the largest increases in demand are Bophuthatswana (129%), KwaZulu (125%), KwaNgwane (105%), Ciskei (91%), KwaNdebele (88%), and Lebowa (82%). Taking into account the urban drift, DWA estimates are that by the year 2010, the urban complexes of Vryheid–Ulundi in the Eastern Cape will need 869% more water than at present, the Ladysmith–Ezakheni's need will increase by 469%, while that of Tzaneen–Nkowakowa by 55%.

For various obvious historical reasons, the infrastructure serving "white" South Africa was developed first. For instance, engineers sought to develop or build dams that would give the largest storage capacity with the least engineering intervention. Those sites are largely located in areas designated as "white" South Africa. This means that prime sites all over the country have already been used, leaving homeland governments with the most expensive dam sites. These are shallower, allowing water to evaporate more quickly, and each unit of water would therefore be more expensive. For instance, in seeking to redress the development that has passed it by, KwaNgwane is proposing to build a dam on the Komati river for sugar cane production. The dam will eventually yield water costs amounting to R125 per ton of sugar grown, resulting in an overall cost of R1,025 per ton. South African sugar currently costs R900 a ton, which is well above the market price of R450 per ton. KwaNgwane's uneconomic cost of sugar production will have to be subsidized by the South African government. Expenditure on new dams declined in real terms by 8.8% annually between 1970 and 1984. But according to the Department of Water Affairs,[20] this expenditure should rise to 16% by 1992.

South Africa has traditionally regarded the homelands as autonomous members of the southern African region who have to, at least theoretically, manage their own supply and quality of water. Consequently, the South African Department of Water Affairs has formed joint permanent water commissions with each of the 10 homelands and has joint committees with Swaziland, Botswana, Lesotho, Mozambique, and Zimbabwe, thereby bringing to 15 the number of official committees it sits on. In keeping with the Helsinki rules on shared water resources, negotiations on all water issues in a particular catchment area need to be held by countries affected down or upstream. For instance, the Komati river and its tributaries run through "white" South Africa, KwaNgwane, Lebowa, Gazankulu, Swaziland, and Mozambique. Thus, any project on the Komati (or similar) river would involve a process of tedious negotiations involving several commissions.

Apartheid and forced removals have militated against economic rationality. In some cases, where communities have been disadvantaged by forced removals, the South African Department of Development Aid has funded projects that have been less than economically viable. For instance, the Department of Development Aid supplied piped water to Needscamp, a resettlement camp in East London, where the cost to government to supply one kiloliter of water is around R10, compared with the cost of around 50c to urban, white local authorities. Further, the backlog in the black areas is precisely because they are not represented in government. This means that until the constitution makes such provision, the Department of Development Aid will continue to act as a "Member of Parliament" for underdeveloped homeland areas.

Just how much impact a marginal improvement in water supply can have on homelands' living conditions is aptly demonstrated by a recent project in Natal. The Valley Trust in Natal's Valley of a Thousand Hills conducted a survey in 1981 and found that the infant mortality rate was 121 per 1,000.[21] Water supplies and sanitation were poorly developed, with inadequate knowledge of the spread of disease. At the time, the community correctly recognized its major problem as the provision of water and set it as a priority for action. The Trust set out to assist through the provision of appropriate technology, imparting skills in protecting springs, the building of ferro cement tanks to collect water from house roof tops, etc. A follow-up survey[22] conducted in 1988 showed that the community's knowledge, practices, and attitude had changed. Diarrheal disease and improvements in water supply had become a low-priority area in the community's view and the infant mortality rate had fallen to 62 per 1,000.

However, a future government's program to correct these and other problems will be costly. Unfortunately, all too often, homeland governments have been pitted against each other for scarce financial and economic resources. This has resulted in an unviable application of economic resources. This is one of apartheid's policies come home to roost.

5. Health and Social Security

As in other areas of homeland social welfare, the situation in the health and social services is quite critical. The apartheid policy that has fragmented health services in South Africa into 14 departments (10 homeland, 3 "own" affairs, i.e., white, Coloured, and Asian, and one "general" affairs) attempted to redress health issues along racial and ethnic lines rather than geographically.

Repression, Deprivation, and Poverty in South Africa's "Bantustans" 181

This has resulted in an atrocious record of lack of cooperation and duplication of effort. Homelands' health services are further compromised by lack of finance, faulty priorities, and shortage of doctors. Medical professionals in the homelands are competing for South African Treasury funds, while wanting to achieve the same levels or ends — i.e., an efficient health service. That goal is simply unattainable because of the meager resources that are thinly spread because of duplication.

The South African government, through the Regional Health Organizations of South Africa (RHOSA), has started harmonizing the health legislation under each of the 14 ministries. But short of doing away with ethnic structures and replacing the entire legislation with geographical health institutions, it is difficult to understand how the glaring deficiencies and wastages will be resolved.

The health service in the homeland is further compromised by the shortage of doctors. The national average of one doctor to every 2,320 people, while satisfactory by world standards, is whittled down to one doctor for every 10,000 people, and in some cases, to every 40,000 people. There are now 1.6 beds for every 1,000 people in the homelands, but the hospitals admit twice as many patients who have to be accommodated on the floor. Outside the homelands there are 2.5 beds per 1,000 for blacks and 4.8 for whites.

The prevailing socioeconomic conditions in the homelands and not the lack of health facilities as such are the main cause of ill-heath. Ironically, health services in the homelands are heavily subsidized by the state, with more money being spent per capita per annum than elsewhere in Africa. But for its gross national product, South Africa spends very little on the homelands. Poverty-related diseases are widespread in the homelands. Childhood malnutrition is extensive and the major reasons for child admissions to hospitals are diarrhea, malnutrition, pneumonia, typhoid, skin infections, etc. Most child deaths under the age of five are caused by diarrhoea, malnutrition, and tetanus. Outbreaks of cholera are a regular feature throughout the homelands.

In some cases, there has been a marked deterioration in the inadequate services already in place. For instance, tests for cervical cancer have been discontinued in both the black urban townships and the rural homelands, as has been the regular screening for tuberculosis. The tuberculosis figures have consequently risen dramatically, particularly in the Western Cape where the disease reached "epidemic promotions"[23] in 1986, its incidence being among the highest in the world. In 1986, the increase was about 40%, with 22,348 reported cases and 1,288 deaths from tuberculosis in the Western Cape alone.[24] The rural areas of South Africa were free from tuberculosis until the turn of the century. However, the disease was carried to even the remotest areas through the migrant labor system and it flourished there among impoverished living conditions, overcrowding, poor sanitation, and malnutrition.

Of all the health problems afflicting the homelands, malnutrition is the most serious. It is certainly the main cause of infant mortalities in the homelands. Rural areas and the homelands are hardest hit by poverty and hence by diseases. Measles, for instance, is a relatively harmless disease among white South African children. In blacks, however, it is a serious affliction often leading to prolonged suffering, blindness (in combination with vitamin A deficiency), or even death. About 15% of African child mortality (under five) is due to measles.[25]

It seems that nothing short of a united health service will achieve a more equitable distribution of funds. A new government in South Africa would have to urgently consider the introduction of a two-tier unified health system. It would have to speed up the privatization of services for those who can afford it, thereby effecting a massive shift of subsidies to those areas that have until now been neglected. Rural health centers must be developed to admit patients from logical geographical regions rather than from ethnic regions. That process should start with the effective and full utilization of the current infrastructure.

Poverty and disease in the homelands are exacerbated by the absence of a social security system, particularly old-age pensions for retired workers dumped in the Bantustans. The payment of old-age pensions in the homelands has become a random procedure over which the South African government has conveniently turned a blind eye although pension funds originate from the South African treasury. People of pensionable age are left facing poverty, unable to obtain pensions because of sheer bureaucratic inefficiency, corruption, or simple lack of funds. Many families depend on pensions paid to one elderly member of a household as their sole source of regular income.[26] The situation is not peculiar to the homelands, but is a national problem experienced in other rural areas and townships. It would appear that many of the elderly are not getting their pensions either because of identification problems or inadequate documentation and inefficient distribution. In many instances, it takes over one year to register for a pension and then payments are backdated to only six months. Abuse, queuing, and corruption could be reduced if pensioners opened deposit accounts at local post offices and nearby building societies (savings and loans), but then, illiteracy is a forbidding problem. Yet, even for the literate, payment through building society accounts has not provided the ideal solution, since pensioners seldom meet the minimum balance requirements to run an account.

As far as facilities are concerned, white, Asian, and coloured pensions are paid at pay points on an agency basis through the South African post office system. However, the South African post office refuses to distribute black homeland pensions in the same way because they claim staff shortages to cope with greater numbers. Yet distribution is not the only area of discrimination.

There is a huge discrepancy between amounts paid to black and white state pensioners, the former receiving R150 per month while the latter get R251.

One of the major problems that a new government in South Africa would face is the provision of funds for a comprehensive, equitable, and nondiscriminatory pension scheme. The current South African government is hard-pressed to find adequate funds to pay pensions. Consequently, it has attempted to cut costs through various devious devices, such as making homeland governments responsible for administering pensions and then failing to provide enough funds to enable them to pay pensioners who claim. In June 1984, Lebowa simply stopped paying the elderly who applied for pensions after that period, although pensioners already registered continued to receive benefits. During 1984 and 1985, KwaZulu also suspended pension payments.

For any new government in South Africa, the problem with state pensions would have to be conceived as more fundamental than maladministration and discrimination. South Africa is sitting on a time-bomb when one considers the escalating number of state pensioners. For instance, at the end of 1988, there were 790,000 black old-age state pensioners and about 212,000 whites. Over R3 billion was provided to pay all race groups throughout South Africa, including the "non-independent" homelands while the four "independent" homelands, were responsible for their own pension payout.[27] To equalize pension benefits for blacks and whites would cost an additional R1.1 billion. By the year 2005, depending on inflation assumptions, the growing number of the elderly, etc., the pension bill could reach about R17 billion. A new government would have to come up with imaginative schemes, such as contributory pension systems, in order to avoid a possible collapse of the entire system due to shortage of funds.

Conclusion: The Collapse of the Bantustan Strategy

The political turmoil currently ravaging South Africa's Bantustans, coupled with the abject levels of poverty that have been the hallmark of Bantustan living conditions, have led to the collapse of the entire doctrine of separate development. Clearly, the Bantustans are nonviable as a basis for any new political dispensation in South Africa. Economically, they are not self-sustaining entities that could serve as the launching pad for any federalist solution for a post-apartheid South Africa. All the homelands are currently bankrupt.

From the day South Africa gave independence to the Transkei on October 26, 1976, the bankruptcy of the Transkei and all other Bantustans was a virtual certainty. Although the financial agreements between South Africa and the Bantustans at "independence" made provisions for various subsidies, the reasons for the current bankruptcy are easily apparent. A large proportion of homelands governments' expenditure was in the categories where new infrastructures (duplicating those in "white" South Africa) had to be installed and, therefore, expenditure was growing quite fast, e.g., education, health, urban services, and internal "security." In addition, a substantial proportion of the homelands' "budgets" was spent on "administrative expenses," i.e., salaries for the newly created bureaucracies. Very few resources were earmarked for productive activities since the Bantustans were expected to act as labor reservoirs for the South African economy.

Homeland leaders, on opting for "independence," faced a dilemma. They identified the need to prove that they were justified in taking part in the implementation of apartheid structures. Consequently, they invested in "development" projects of dubious economic value, yielding negative rates of economic return — e.g., airports, soccer stadiums, or some grandiose capital-intensive projects. This was dictated by the need for homeland leaders to justify their choice of a phony independence by showing economic "progress." When the time came to pay the debts, the money was simply not available. Thus, being bankrupt both economically and politically, the Bantustans serve no purpose in a post-apartheid South Africa, not even as revamped ethnically neutral administrative structures.

NOTES

1. Significant scholarly research has been carried out on the ideological basis and evolution of the "Bantustan" strategy. For example, Barbara Rogers' *Divide and Rule: South Africa's Bantustans*, London (1976); J. Leewenberg, *Transkei: A Study in Economic Regression*, Africa Publications Trust, London (1976); C. Bundy, "Emergency and Decline of a South African Peasantry," African Affairs 71 (1972: 285).

2. *Weekly Mail* (March 2 to March 8, 1990, Johannesburg).

3. However, in Bophuthatswana, on March 7, 1990, about 50,000 people took to the streets in protest against the regime, demanding reincorporation into South Africa. See *Weekly Mail*, March 2 to March 8, 1990. On April 5, 1990, four Bantustan leaders humiliated South Africa president F.W. de Klerk, when they refused to attend a meeting with him to discuss problems and the future of Bantustans. See "Pretoria's Bantustan Strategy has backfired in its face" (*The Herald* May 29, 1990, Harare).

4. But the position of KwaZulu remains an exception with Chief Buthelezi's government still on friendly terms with South Africa despite never having officially accepted homeland status. KwaZulu's government can rely on significant support from its ethnic organization, i.e., Inkatha, and is therefore spared the degree of rebellion facing other Bantustans.

5. See David Bridgeman, "From Peasants to Parliament" (*Cross Times*, November 1989).

6. *Weekly Mail* (April 4 to April 10, 1986).

7. Michael Savage, *The Cost of Apartheid*, University of Cape Town, Inaugral Lecture August 27, 1986: 3–21).

8. *Weekly Mail* (March 2 to March 8, 1990).

9. *Ibid.*

10. L.G. Abrahamse, "The Economic Consequences of Apartheid." Paper delivered to the 7th Annual Council Meeting of the South Africa Institute of Race Relations, Durban, 1977 (RR 87/76).

Repression, Deprivation, and Poverty in South Africa's "Bantustans" 185

11. J.S. Saul and S. Gelb, "The Crisis in South Africa," *Monthly Review* 33,3 (1981: 49).

12. H. Henning and B. Streck, "Living Off Left-overs," *Cross Times* (January 1990: 19).

13. A. Hirsh, "The Study of Industrial Decentralization in South Africa: Some Comments." In "South African Studies — Retrospect and Prospects." Proceedings of a seminar held in the Centre of African Studies, University of Edinburgh (May 30 to June 1, 1983: 133–152).

14. Michael Savage, *The Cost of Apartheid*, University of Cape Town, Inaugral Lecture (August 27, 1986: 3–21).

15. L. Flanagan, "Taiwan's Tax Haven," *Cross Times* (December 1989).

16. This arrangement was subsequently replaced by the offer of no company tax, although longer-established companies still operate on old concessions.

17. C. Cross and R. Haines, "Toward Post-Apartheid Land Tenure," *Cross Times* (January 1990).

18. F. Wilson and M. Rampbele, *Uprooting Poverty: The South African Challenge*, David Phillip, Cape Town (1987).

19. *Financial Mail* (August 1989).

20. *Ibid.*

21. *City Press* (June 6, 1990).

22. *Ibid.*

23. H. Henning, "Homeland Health Services," *Cross Times* (January 1990: 45).

24. *Ibid.*

25. *Ibid.*

26. F. Wilson and M. Ramphele, *Uprooting Poverty: The South African Challenge* (1987).

27. Pensions in the "independent" homelands are even lower than in South Africa.

[20]

Journal of Southern African Studies. Vol. 15, No. 3, April 1989

Political Violence and the Struggle for Control in Pietermaritzburg[1]

NKOSINATHI GWALA

Introduction

By the end of February 1988 the official death toll in Pietermaritzburg (PMB) townships in the 'confrontation' between Inkatha, on the one hand, and UDF and COSATU on the other hand, stood at about 400. However, unofficial sources estimate the figure at more than the official one. The violence in PMB has been the most publicised in the country during the second half of 1987, and yet the least understood in terms of the political dynamics behind it.

The focus of the paper will be Edendale, the second largest township in PMB. This paper will look into the following aspects. Firstly, a social and economic profile of the PMB townships, with particular emphasis on Edendale, including some administrative aspects of these townships. Secondly, an attempt will be made to explain the social and political interests battling for the control of Edendale. Thirdly, the basis of Inkatha's attempts at establishing its hegemony in PMB townships will be analysed. Lastly, the paper will conclude by drawing some lessons for the struggle against Inkatha in Natal.

The Social and Economic Profile of PMB Townships

According to a recent Development Studies Research Group (DSRG) Survey (1986) on unemployment, PMB has a population of about 400,000 people and it is the second largest city in Natal. More than 80% of this population is black (African, Coloured and Indian). Five major African townshis surround PMB: Sobantu, Imbali, Ashdown (all consisting of standard townships 'matchbox' houses), Edendale and Vulindlela (sprawling townships of mud houses and a sprinkling of brick and block houses). The latter two are the most visibly devastated areas, and capture in a very stark way the poverty that African people are subjected to in South Africa.

PMB is an area with a very high rate of unemployment. Total black unemployment is estimated at 31%, whilst that of whites is just under 5% (DSRG, 1986). However unemployment is lowest at Sobantu, a township which together with Imbali, has always enjoyed Section 10 rights. The two townships with the highest

[1] I would like to thank comrades from 'Maputo' who unselfishly shared some of their experiences with me, and without their contribution this article would not have been possible — 'Heita Maqabane Heita!'

rates of unemployment are Ashdown (39.3%) and Edendale (37.2%). However it is in the age of the unemployed that one begins to appreciate the social basis of political action and why the youth is the most frustrated stratum in contemporary South African society. About 80% of the unemployed are under 35 years of age: 46% less than 25 years old; and 15% are under 20 years of age. The 20 to 24 years group is the age-group with the highest representation among the unemployed (31% of the total). As is increasingly becoming characteristic of South African society, the African youth is the hardest hit by unemployment. This is coupled with another factor, that of the rising level of education of this unemployed youth over the years. The DSRG study also reveals that 42.6% of unemployed persons have at least some secondary school education; 34.2% have reached some level in the primary stage (i.e. Stds 4-6). It is only 5.5% of the unemployed who have no formal education.

There is also a very strong pattern of structural unemployment. For instance it is estimated that 31.9% of male unemployed persons have never been employed, and 56.5% of female unemployed are in the same situation. In addition to this alarmingly high proportion of people never employed, 22.3% of the unemployed have been without employment for periods longer than 18 months.

More than 70% of the African population in PMB townships live in mud houses mainly at Edendale and Vulindlela. In these houses there is neither electricity nor water, and the latter is only available through communal taps, some of them located two kilometres or more from some houses. There is no sewerage system, except in brick or block houses. Pit toilets are used. In the overcrowded areas, where there are about three or four houses within a quarter acre, these pit toilets are only a few metres away from the houses. At Edendale and Vulindlela there are only a few main roads and in some instances there are large stretches of houses with no roads in-between. This factor has also contributed significantly to the difficulty of policing such areas. This degree of social and economic devastation has inevitably become a fertile ground for crime and gangsterism. In fact in 1984 and 1985 Christmas periods, Edendale recorded the highest crime rate in the whole of Natal.

Edendale has historically been a 'multi-ethnic' community. Although it has always been overwhelmingly African, there have been a number of 'Indians' and 'Coloureds' staying and owning land there. However with the tightening of the application of Group Areas Act in the late sixties presssure began building for non-Africans to move out of Edendale into new Indian and Coloured townships on the east of PMB. The pressure for non-Africans, particularly traders and landow-ners, to move out of Edendale, was not unconnected to the collective interests of the African traders and landowners. By the end of the 1970s Edendale was almost 100% African, with the exception of a few Indian traders and one white general dealer.

Edendale as a community has a very long history which dates back to the mid-nineteenth century (about the 1850s). It started as a mission station, initially inhabited by early African christian converts called *amakholwa*. This community came about through the backing of the missionaries whose philosophy was that converted African christians should also be taught and made to fully participate in capitalism ('Christianity and Civilization' as the missionaries would describe this philosophy). (See Etherington [1985], and Lambert [1985] for more details on this grouping and its early economic activities as well as its acquiring of their land). Through these economic ventures there emerged a wealthy African peasantry, whose major business activities were farming and trading. The first highly educated Africans in Natal also came from the *amakholwa* communities of Edendale. It is the direct descendants of this group that have become the current land owners at Edendale.

Land, The Landed Petty Bourgeoisie and the Control of Edendale

a) *Landowners and tenants*

Edendale is one of the very few African areas in the country where Africans have full ownership of the land with freehold titles. Other areas in a similar position in Natal are Clermont and parts of Inanda near Durban. All residents at Edendale, except the landowners themselves, are tenants. The landowning group is dominated by a few well known families who own large tracts of land, some of them as big as 30 hectares. On some of the rented land there are 200 tenant families to one landowner. The tenants do not own anything except their wattle and daub structures. The regulations also do not permit the landowners to allow more than one structure per one-quarter of an acre. Consequently tenants used to have access to large chunks of land on which they used to plant mielies and other crops like beans, peas and pumpkins.[2] There is however still a large percentage of tenants who are landlords, in that they rent out rooms to other people needing accommodation, mainly migrant workers − those who prefer to be in the township rather than hostels. The common practice has been for owners of wattle and daub structures to rent out one or two rooms as a means of supplementing their income, even if they themselves are overcrowded.[3] Another pattern is where those tenants who can afford to build more than one structure rent out these, usually on a one room basis. In many instances this arrangement has created an 'anomalous' situation where some tenants make more money out of their rented houses than their respective landowners on that piece of land.

Permission to build a wattle and daub structure has, in the first instance, to be negotiated with the landowner who then assigns the applicant a site. This is done purely on a personal and informal basis, and even sometimes without a formal written agreement. All that has to be arranged is when and how to pay rent. As a result there is an infinite number of arrangements between landowners and their tenants. The only mediator between the landowner and the tenant are housing inspectors of the Department of Development Aid (DDA − formerly department of Bantu Administration), who have to approve the 'plans' and sites of the houses, and also make sure that the regulations are strictly adhered to. The prospective 'owner' of a wattle and daub structure is also required to pay a certain amount of money in

[2] Due to an increase in the population of Edendale, and consequently more than one house being built on a quarter acre, this activity ceased. The planting of mielies was happening as late as the mid-seventies.

[3] For many people this has been one way of coping with unemployment. In some cases once the owner of a wattle and daub structure becomes unemployed he/she would rent out all the rooms save one or two for the family.

order to get the house registered and get a house number. In order to monitor these regulations the DDA employs a number of spotters whose job is to periodically move around the township to check that there are no unapproved structures being erected. The penalty of building without the necessary approval is demolition of the structure, particularly if it is declared unsuitable by the inspector. Despite these regulations there are many unapproved structures at Edendale. This is usually due to individual landowners themselves, who let people build on their land in order to get more rent. And in such cases the landowners themselves just conclude a deal with prospective tenants and let them build without going through the DDA. In effect, building a wattle and daub structure at Edendale is a matter between the landowner and the prospective tenant. The spotters have not been that active and the DDA has been lax in the application of the rules. Consequently Edendale is becoming very congested and it would not be untrue to say that slum conditions prevail in parts of it.

The irony of the landowner-tenant relationships at Edendale is that the tenants can only occupy the land if they stay in wattle and daub structures and only in so far as they are still tenants. The options available to them are that they either buy those plots which probably more than 90% cannot afford, or seek accommodation in the nearby townships. The latter option really is no option since there is a shortage of the standard township 'matchbox' houses themselves. Whilst the relationship between the landowners and the tenants is potentially a very explosive one, it has remained rather depoliticized, because of its non-bureaucratic character and the 'absence' of state insitutions in the immediate relationship. It has remained depoliticized because the conditions of tenancy itself vary very widely. Ironically, because of tenancy as the major source of income, landowners themselves are also very dependent on their tenants for rent. Nevertheless the politicization of the Edendale community and its recent experiences of mass struggle now hangs ominously over the relationship between landowners and tenants. And it is a relationship that needs to be handled very carefully and strategically by progressive organizations.

b) *The landed petit bourgeoisie and the 'autonomy' of Edendale*

The private ownership of property at Edendale gives the landowners an unusual amount of independence from the state. However the ability of the landed *petit bourgeoisie* to translate this independence into its own expanded reproduction through more profitable use of their land has always been hampered by apartheid and (white) monopoly capital. They have consequently banded together to try and fight against those obstacles to their more profitable use of their land. Up until 1984 they did this through the Edendale Advisory Board (EAB — the official local authority at Edendale), and thereafter through their own mouthpiece, the Edendale Landowners Association (ELA).

However before undertaking an analysis of the LPB it is important to briefly discuss another significant stratum of the African *petit bourgeoisie* at Edendale, the trading African *petit bourgeoisie*. A discussion of this grouping is important because of the overlap of membership between it and the landowners. In fact almost all the main African traders at Edendale are landowners as well, and big landowners at that.

The EAB was representing the interests of both the traders and the landowners, although more of the latter. The trading activities at Edendale have until recently been almost equally shared between one white trader, three African traders and a sprinkling of Indian traders. They have been trading at Edendale for decades now. However there has been a number of small one-shop type African traders as well, mainly in the background of these bigger traders. As a long established community Edendale has been dominated by the same traders. The currently opening trading avenues for new entrants has been largely created by the departing Indian traders who have been pressurized by the EAB through the state to leave the area. As has been the practice in general in South Africa to appeal to the state for reserving trading activities in African areas for Africans only, Edendale has been no exception. The pressure to remove non-african traders at Edendale has been fuelled by the fact that most of the land is owned by Africans. The minutes of the EAB are full of increasing attacks on non-African traders and landowners to get out of the area to such an extent that they have even been appealing to the state to apply the Group Areas Act to get rid of them:

. . . the Department (DDA) had clearly stated that Edendale is a released area which has been set aside for the occupation by Blacks (sic! Africans) only . . . Other racial groups are still residing and operating businesses at Edendale . . . the time now is overdue for the other racial groups to be removed from Edendale and request that the department be asked to define its policy in this regard. (EAB minutes, 25/8/82)
. . . it is the Board's belief that the government has the money to expropriate land belonging to racial groups other than Blacks (sic!) at Edendale . . . (W)here a Black man has to be moved in terms of the Group Areas Act the government has never delayed such action because of funds (EAB minutes, 3/11/82).

This pressure has led to the gradual withdrawal of many Indian traders at Edendale. However in a place like Edendale, the crucial issue is the control of land and its development, upon which all else depends. That is why the major force in attempting to control questions of land and its development has been the landowners.

The mouthpiece of the landowners at Edendale is the Edendale Landowners Association, which was formed on 24 March 1973 in a meeting attended by 171 registered landowners (Constitution of ELA, 1973). Amongst some of the important objectives of the ELA are the following:

* to promote and encourage the development and progress of the community along lines as will naturally evolve out of the Christian life and tradition of the community
* to encourage the founding of trades of whatever kind or nature including the promotion of industries development of vegetable production and the establishment of a market
* to make regulations for the proper control of environment, *tenants*, and livestock and generally for the maintenance of law and order
* to organize and work for the training of persons in local government administration *preparatory for the eventual takeover of the administration from the Local Health Commission.*
* to seek and register a local affairs committee to take the place, *for the time being* of the advisory board (Constitution of ELA, 1973 – emphases added).

These objectives capture both the long term ideals of the landowners and their immediate expectations in 1973, upon which the Edendale of their dreams, as well as that of their forebears, was to be built. The Edendale Landowners Association was formed in anticipation of the handing over of power at Edendale directly to them as the Local Health Commission (LHC − the government administrative body till 1973), was being phased out that year. It was also in anticipation of the abolition of the Advising Board by the state and the giving of Edendale the status of a town board which a 'privately owned' place like Edendale 'deserved', as always argued by the landowners. Their hopes were to be immediately dashed when the government decided to continue with the EAB unchanged, and, as if to rub salt onto the wound, the government took over the administration of Edendale directly through the newly established Drakensberg Administration Board. This forced the landowners to work through the EAB, albeit reluctantly, to continue pushing for these ideals. Hence all the members of the Edendale Advisory Board were landowners who had also played a prominent role in the formation of the Edendale Landowners Association.

The single most important issue for the landowners has always been the development of Edendale as an area with a status of a town board similar to that of the white towns. Such a status would give the landowners the necessary independence to 'develop' and 'improve' the area, as well as protect its freehold status. The first primary concern and the pressure point of the landowners was continued questioning of the status of the Advisory Board which they controlled. Their concern here was around the powerlessness of the Board as an instrument to further their aims. The landowners were always pushing for the abolition of the Advisory Board and its replacement by a town board.

The second major concern of the Advisory Board was the government's treatment of Edendale in the same way as other nearby townships around PMB (EAB minutes, 26/8/81). The landowners always opposed the government's concept of a 'greater Edendale complex', since the landowners see Edendale as fundamentally different from these other townships.

The third concern of the landowners at Edendale is the increase in the rate of crime as well as, ironically, the proliferation of wattle and daub structures. The landowners have been concerned about these two factors mainly because they lower the value of the land, but most importantly because Edendale might turn into a slum area. With respect to the latter they fear that the government might use this as a pretext to take away freehold at Edendale.

The one major thread running through the landowners concerns and actions through the EAB is fear of losing their freehold status, and therefore their land. In fact the preoccupation of the Board for its last ten years, and continued by the ELA thereafter has primarily been the protection of the land from the state. These fears of the landowners may not be unfounded after all. The state's intransigence on a number of requests by the landowners of Edendale has not just been coincidental, but a systematic strategy to undermine them. The state is in a fix about what to do with african freehold land. Legally the state for instance cannot incorporate Edendale into KwaZulu without the consent of the landowners. The state also cannot mediate between the landowners and the tenants since the landowners do not need any bureaucratic mechanism to extract rent from tenants. It is therefore not surprising that the state has been unwilling to give Edendale any measure of autonomous

512   *Journal of Southern African Studies*

administration. For instance whilst the state has gradually given some autonomy to other african townships through, initially the Urban Bantu Councils (1961), community councils (1977) and lately local authorities (1983), the advisory boards have been kept for both Edendale and Clermont.

The resignation of members of the Advisory Board in 1984, which led to its collapse, was in fact not a sign of giving up on the part of the landowners, but was the application of further pressure on the state. However it is the developments after the resignation of the board that have revealed some elements of the state's strategy towards Edendale and the landowners. Between 1974 and 1984 the ELA remained dormant since the interests of the landowners were mainly catered for by the EAB: thereafter it approached the Department of Development Aid for its recognition as the mouthpiece of the 'people' of Edendale.

We ask you to put this resolution into effect please, and also bear in mind, that the Edendale Landowners Association replaces all former organizations as well as the Edendale Advisory Board. Over and above that, it is a REPRESENTATIVE ASSOCIATION with an EXECUTIVE COMMITTEE which has the authority to manage the affairs of the people of Edendale. . . .[4]

What is worth noting here is the fact that the ELA was seeking recognition as the mouthpiece of the people of Edendale, not just the landowners. It is in the DDA's response to this request that the state's intentions are revealed:

As the Edendale Advisory Board has resigned en bloc and other members have not been elected in their stead, your recommendation that the Edendale Landowners Association be recognized as the representatives of the landowners of Edendale is accepted. . . . Kindly inform the Association that the Department recognizes it as being representative of the landowners of Edendale and as their mouthpiece, but that there is no provision for it to be "registered as the mouthpiece for the *people* of Edendale". Nevertheless the Association will be consulted on an ongoing basis with the view to establishing a local authority for Edendale. In fact the first of such discussions already took place on 14 May 1987.[5]

Despite this apparent display of democracy by Pretoria, the ELA in its response still emphasized its representativeness of the *people* of Edendale:

Thank you very much for your advising the Edendale Landowners Association that the Department of Development Aid now recognizes this Association as the mouthpiece for the *people* of Edendale.[6]

These letters in fact capture in a very interesting way the interests at stake in the control of Edendale. Firstly, the state reveals its unwillingness to hand over the control of Edendale to the landowners themselves. The state has always been acutely aware that the landowners hold considerable power through their private ownership of the land. Therefore the alliances that this group enters into have got very serious implications for the balance of power at Edendale. The other nightmare for the state

---

[4] ELA letter to the Edendale township manager dated 17/11/86 (Emphases in original).

[5] Letter from Director-General of DDA to Regional Representative dated 20/5/87 (emphasis and inverted commas in original).

[6] Letter from general secretary of ELA to the Edendale township manager dated 24/7 87. In spite of the Township Manager reacting to this letter by pointing out that the ELA was not recognized as mouthpiece of the people of Edendale, the chairperson of the ELA instructed the secretary to respond as per original reply (From handnotes written on the ELA first reply of 24/7/87).

has been that the landowners neither seek incorporation into KwaZulu nor further subjugation to the government, but want autonomy which they will use independent of the state's and KwaZulu government's (ZG) wishes. It is within this context that, although the interests of Inkatha and those of the state have been developing somewhat 'autonomously', they both coincide on the question of the control of Edendale. For Inkatha it would mean control over a large number of people to maintain its 'dominance' in Natal. For the state subjugation of the people of Edendale under Inkatha would be an ideal situation in that they will be under the control of a collaborative bantustan *petit bourgeoisie*, which is already co-operating with the state at a number of levels e.g. The Joint Executive Authority, and cooperation between KwaZulu Police and the South African Police.[7]

Despite the fact that the landowners have got legal ownership of the land, this alone, without the support of the people of Edendale, is not enough to keep the state away from controlling their land. That is why the ELA also claims to be representing the interests of the people of Edendale as a whole not only the landowners.

It is clear that this 'invisible mass' of 'the people of Edendale' have become the 'bone of contention' to all the contestants at Edendale. Each of the contestants want to be the mouthpiece of these 'people'. For the state, they should be represented by obviously a collaborative local authority; for the landowners they are to be best represented by the ELA itself because these 'people' are 'part of the privately owned property' of Edendale; and for Inkatha they should be represented by them because they are Zulus who are 'naturally' part of the 'Zulu of Edendale'? And how is Inkatha particularly wanting to *become* their representative?

Inkatha, Bureaucratic Clientelism and The Struggle for Hegemony in Pietermaritzburg

Having discussed the social profile of Edendale this section attempts to comprehend the configuration of forces that have produced such political conflict described by some observers as '. . . the most violent upheaval to have taken place in the Natal midlands since the 'Bhambatha' rebellion against colonial rule in 1906' (UDF/ COSATU memorandum on Press coverage of Political Violence in PMB — 1/11/87). Consequently the section will first discuss the political awakening of the people of Edendale in the 1980s. Secondly a detailed analysis of the major contestant in the political battle in PMB — Inkatha — and, arguably, the cause of the current violence.

---

[7] For instance Buthelezi, in a reply to a Comment by Hamilton in the *Sunday Tribune* of 1 11 87, had, amongst other things, this to say about a visit To Ulundi by the Minister of Police: 'Inkatha does not subscribe to mob rule and intimidation and if that means I must consult with the Minister of Law and Order' (bearing in mind that KwaZulu is not a so called 'independent' state) then *I will continue to do so* in the best interests of all the citizens of KwaZulu/Natal . . . (*Sunday Tribune*, 8/11/87 — emphasis added).

a) *'Savumelana!* . . .*':[8] The political awakening of PMB*

Despite the extreme conditions of social and economic depression at Edendale, the place had never really been affected by the major national uprisings characteristic of post-1975 South Africa. Edendale, if not the whole of PMB townships, was never affected by the Soweto uprisings of 1976, nor by the later struggles of the early 1980s. In fact before 1985, Natal as a whole was never as much affected as the Reef and the Eastern Cape.

Edendale has never been a stronghold of any political organization since the banning of the ANC. By as late as 1984 neither Inkatha nor the UDF could claim majority support with confidence. Although the sporadic boycotts by school pupils in places like Sobantu and Imbali at this time were sympathetic or even considered themselves as part of progressive organizations, this was not that organizationally clear-cut. A very broad proposition being made here as to why Edendale has been quiescent for so long, is that it is difficult to pull localities into political action through broad national campaigns, particularly if the basis of such campaigns do not have local resonance or connections. For instance the Soweto uprisings, whose spark was the compulsory use of Afrikaans as a medium of instruction in African schools, was not an immediate issue in Natal where there was no such imposition. Also, to develop radical political consciousness, which does not have a local 'content', does not easily translate into political action. For instance, the township struggles in the eighties have been mainly around the question of local authorities and rent. For Edendale, given the non-bureaucratized, private relationship between landowners and tenants, and the absence of state structures in the collection of rent, rent boycotts did not make an impact at all. In short, the essence of my proposition is that trying to develop organization around national campaigns, unconnected to local issues is a fatal mistake. National campaigns should build from local conditions of oppression and struggle. Whilst the formation of the UDF in 1983 and its immediate campaigns did raise the level of political consciousness of the masses, concrete action only took root in areas that had been involved in previous waves of struggle. This uneven development was never adequately compensated through the building of local structures, primarily on the basis of local realities.

The labour movement, which was in the early eighties more organizationally mature than community political structures, was very instrumental in the political awakening of PMB. Although as early as 1983 there were sporadic school boycotts, and some fairly sustained political resistance in places like Sobantu, these did not spread to other PMB townships in any significant way. The space that was being

[8] This is one of the slogans in the popular toi-toi dance. *'Savumelana'* means 'together we made a vow'. This is usually followed by what they have vowed to do or achieve, which usually is 'communism' or 'soldiers of the struggle'.

[9] In fact this factor makes nonsense of Inkatha Institute's naïve and simplistic explanation of the events in PMB as an outcome of unemployment and poverty (*Daily News*, 11 1/88). The simplicity of this explanation lies in the fact that unemployment and poverty, in themselves, do not automatically lead to uprisings. There are mediating factors that have to be explained, particularly as in the case of PMB. For instance why should poverty and unemployment lead to revolt against the state in some areas, but in others, like PMB, they result in a 'revolt' against Inkatha?

created by the labour movement for mass mobilization can be traced back to the Hulett Aluminium pensions strike of 1981. Despite the fact that this strike resulted in a very costly defeat for the Metal and Allied Workers Union at the time, through vicious suppression by the bosses, it nevertheless left a lasting impact particularly on the people of PMB for one important reason. This company has always been a highly 'visible' employer in PMB, in that it is the biggest factory, and for a community ravaged by unemployment, it was also a very 'prestigious' company, and a 'dream' workplace for people of Edendale who did not have the Section 10 rights. It also drew quite a large percentage of its workforce from Edendale and its environs, although its workers were from all the townships of PMB. The formation of the United Democratic Front (UDF) also provided a platform for community organization, although it took a while before it had an impact in a place like Edendale.

The turning point in the history of resistance and mass mobilization in Edendale and PMB as a whole was the 1985 stayaway demanding the reinstatement of Sarmcol strikers. This was the first major and highly successful mass action by the people of PMB as a whole, and marked a high point of community mobilization by the UDF. This stayaway also saw the emergence of a disciplined alliance between the labour movement and the UDF. This action was then immediately followed by a consumer boycott on the same issue, and by the first major rally since the 1950s — the 1986 May Day rally. The confrontation between Inkatha and the mass democratic movement, was now beginning to raise its ugly head in PMB. Inkatha came out in opposition to both the stayaway and the consumer boycott — claiming that people were being 'intimidated' by the UDF-linked youth. Despite Inkatha's opposition to this historic mass action by the people of PMB, both the stayaway and consumer boycott were very successful. This was definitely an indicator that Inkatha's support in PMB was very low. This must have been the time when Inkatha started seriously considering ways and means of increasing its support in PMB. Evidence to this was the fact that immediately thereafter Inkatha's violent recruitment campaign started. However, it was the 1987 stayaway protesting at the whites-only election that finally laid the basis for the present confrontation, with the now Inkatha-linked Imbali taxi association trying to break the stayaway by defiantly taking passengers to work. In spite of these developments contributing significantly to the politicization, particularly of the youth, it did not translate into any significant progressive political structures at Edendale.

The real spark however which ignited the present conflict was Inkatha's strategy of forcibly recruiting members, which started in a place now known as 'Ulundi' (its real name *Harewood*), under the leadership of a well-known thug, formerly a member of the UDF (Interview with youth, 1/10/87; and affidavits by victims). This started the reign of terror of *Otheleweni* (the Inkatha vigilantes as they are called in Natal townships) in PMB. This terrorization of the Edendale community provided the first common issue ever to unite the people of Edendale and led to the first grassroots structures to emerge, as explained by the youth of Dambuza Road (now 'Maputo'):

Inkatha helped us to achieve what some of us have long been wanting to achieve — the politicization and galvanization of the masses into action. For instance Edendale has for years been a very quiet place politically, but now things are different. . . . At first we thought

Inkatha was part of the struggle. and part of the people. You see Gatsha took the organization and plunged it into the wilderness. We did not agree with him. then he formed *amabutho* (vigilantes). . . . Well Inkatha has given us a lot of problems. We would like to state it clearly that they have tried to attack us. We had to eventually try to defend ourselves from them. taking guidance from people who knew more about Inkatha. As comrades we do not attack. but rather defend our area. and not only ourselves. This struggle is not ours. but also for the people at large. We have also tried to make Inkatha stop attacking us and we encouraged the community to help us. We explained to them. In as much as here in 'Maputo'. many elderly people who were paying (Inkatha membership) fees started to realize the situation and supported us. They realized that we were helping in anyway we could and we were living up to our name (as comrades) [Interview carried out with eight members of a defence committee at Edendale. 1 10/87].

Although it would be interesting to discuss the developments on the ground in terms of mobilization and defence of the township by 'Amaqabane' (comrades). this falls outside the scope of this paper. The comment worth making is that the actions of Inkatha have led to the formation of some of the most resilient and highly organized defence committees ever to emerge in Natal. At the time of writing this paper large areas of Edendale were effectively 'no-go' areas for Inkatha. Also in large parts of Edendale the rate of crime has dropped significantly as 'amaqabane' discipline those thugs who try to exploit the situation and rob people of their belongings in the name of the struggle. This discipline has taken the form of what has been popularly known as 'modelling'. where the culprit is paraded in the streets naked and sometimes carrying whatever he/she might have stolen or robbed. The outcome of this grassroots mobilization has led to the 'taking over' of almost the whole of Edendale by pro UDF/COSATU defence committees. save one small area ('Ulundi'). which is now isolated. Clearly this mass of 'the people of Edendale' have made a choice as to who their true representatives are. They have chosen to be represented by a 'wild card' — the UDF and COSATU — which neither of the other three contesting parties wanted. This has certainly changed the balance of power in the area. These developments and the choices of the people in the area will now begin to have a significant impact on the strategies and alignments of the other interested parties. The reason why both the state and the landowners have been fighting about the representation of the people of Edendale with no response from the community itself has been because of the long quiescence of this community.

b) *Inkatha and hegemony at Edendale*

Inkatha's twelve years of existence can be classified into three broad periods in terms of its strategy and tactics. The first period is 1975-1979/80. It is proposed here that during this period Inkatha's membership was growing quite rapidly. The reason being that when it was formed it did not only get the blessing of the ANC leadership. but was also projecting itself in the image of the ANC. It also emerged at a time when there was general acquiescence in the black communities. save the student struggles waged and largely confined within the black universities (the bush colleges) under the leadership of the South African Students organization (SASO). Buthelezi was also at this time admired by many people for his courage in challenging the state right in the midst of repression.

Inkatha. Political Violence and the Struggle for Control in Pietermaritzburg   517

The major contradiction facing Inkatha during this period was its functioning within the much hated bantustan system and at the same time being a 'liberation movement'. However Inkatha was able to contain this contradiction, at least at the public opinion level, by its avowed anti-independence stance as well as its claim to be using the KwaZulu Legislative Assembly as a platform for consolidating Inkatha itself as a national cultural 'liberation' movement. Beneath this public posturing there were strong class forces and interests developing. Inkatha, like all ruling parties in the bantustans, is an organization whose strength and cohesion centred around the rural bureaucratic *petit bourgeoisie* — the chiefs. In Natal where large urban African areas were also handed over to KwaZulu, Inkatha was given a hold on large urban settlements, like Umlazi, Newcastle, KwaMashu, Hammarsdale, etc. The control, particularly over trading licences in these areas as well as urban bureaucratic structures like community councils, started seeing the cohering of trading and urban bureaucratic *petit bourgeois* interests as well. It was also from this urban bureaucratic *petit bourgeoisie* that the notorious Inkatha warlords were drawn. Inkatha was then beginning to develop a structural dependence on apartheid-sponsored development as well as investment from both local (white) and international monopoly capital. Despite the development of such structural dependence, Inkatha was in many respects different from its 'colleagues' in other bantustans. Inkatha still retained a large working class following. Such an appeal to the Zulu working class has been made possible by the 'availability of a past' of a strongly resilient and warrior Zulu 'nation' that survived longer than any other African resistance to colonialism in the country (Mare and Hamilton, 1987). This tradition is still very strong in the consciousness of many Africans in Natal. Inkatha's growth therefore during this period was largely due to three advantages: 'As a "Zulu" body it was able to mobilize readily, and as a bantustan movement it was protected from the state action . . . (ibid. p. 60)', as well as deriving its political legitimacy from the ANC.

The real turning point in the direction of Inkatha's politics was in 1979/80, when it firstly parted ways with the ANC, and secondly its response to the KwaMashu school boycotts near Durban in 1980. Inkatha clashed with the ANC at the time when the latter was resurfacing very strongly as a political force in the country. Again 1979 saw the formation of Congress of South African Students (COSAS) which spearheaded the school boycotts in 1980. It was Inkatha's response to this challenge by the students which threw into sharp focus its dependence on the bantustan structures. Because Inkatha was now controlling education in KwaZulu, a challenge to Bantu Education also meant a challenge to the KwaZulu Department of Education (DEC) itself. Inkatha's violent repression of student revolt in KwaMashu in 1980 marked a new phase in its strategy.

In addition to this, the growth of the labour movement, though at this stage largely consolidating inside the factories, as well as the resurgence of the congress tradition within the country, signalled a challenge to Buthelezi. The immediate source for Buthelezi to consolidate his power was the 'available' Zulu history which started becoming the primary defining characteristic of Inkatha itself. Though this Zulu lineage ideology was part of Inkatha's original discourse right at its formation, the way it was used in this phase of Inkatha's history was quite different from the earlier period. Whilst in the earlier period the concept of 'Zulu nationalism' was given form around the king (cf Mare and Hamilton, 1987), now it was being given form around Buthelezi and Inkatha. In other words it was ceasing to be a loose 'supra-organizational' concept, but was becoming linked to Inkatha itself. It is also interesting that at this stage the king was being visibly removed from the centre of KwaZulu bantustan politics and being made to be 'above politics'. In effect what all this meant was that Buthelezi became synonymous with Inkatha and the Zulu nation. Therefore political pluralism was being effectively 'delegitimized'. In other words opposition to Inkatha was illegitimate because that meant dividing the 'monolithic' Zulu 'nation'. This was an attempt to define opposition and non-Inkatha politics as divisive and for the Zulu 'nation' to deal with such 'culprits' accordingly. In this way the boycotting KwaMashu students were to be regarded as a 'shame' to the Zulu nation and had to be brought back to line.

Inkatha started becoming a hierarchical organization run from the top, and its membership being increasingly controlled through Zulu cultural affirmations and sanctions. Inkatha also became increasingly centred around Buthelezi as a personalized embodiment of 'the early ANC, the chief of the Buthelezi tribe, prime minister of the Zulu nation, member of the royal family, and, of late, the leader with prophetic powers'.

Inevitably the formation of the UDF in 1983 pushed Inkatha's 'tolerance' for opposition beyond its limits, because this development posed a direct threat to the very existence of Inkatha. The UDF was not only 'competing' for the same membership as Inkatha, but was organizing, at least in Natal, Inkatha's 'reserved' Zulu 'constituency' in a political space belonging to the Zulu 'nation'. The UDF was also a direct challenge to Buthelezi's stature as the 'political leader' of the six million Zulu's. Hence 1983 launched Inkatha into its third phase, that of violent attempts at smashing progressive political organizations. The massacre of the students at Ngoye in 1983 marked the concrete inauguration of this phase. It is also quite significant that the killing of the students was 'justified' on the grounds that it was in defence of Buthelezi's name, as well as dealing with forces of disunity. Buthelezi had this to say immediately after the Ngoye incident:

I must warn South Africa that if the kind of provocation continues which we experienced on Saturday, Inkatha youth will demonstrate their strength and their prowess. . . . The people's (sic) anger is rising and the fervour with which we pursue our objectives will deepen. Nothing will stop us and those forces of disunity which are attempting to do the National Party's dirty work in disrupting our progress will be taught a lesson or two if the denigration of Inkatha continues. . . . The abuse of me must now cease. Continuing to label me a sell-out is going to have ugly repercussions (quoted in Mare and Hamilton, 1987:197).

This was not just a pretext for 'self-defence', but indicated a real perception of the UDF as challenging Buthelezi's leadership − which of course by now was synonymous with Inkatha.

Now as a highly authoritarian and hierarchical Zulu organization controlling the bantustan state machinery, Inkatha is increasingly becoming more reliant on these to maintain its influence and support. It is now being pulled more and more towards the central apartheid state, even in terms of its ideological discourse (e.g. 'ANC wants to make the country ungovernable'; 'UDF and COSATU working in tandem with the ANC'; 'black-on-black violence'; etc. etc. etc). Therefore the deepening of the crisis for the apartheid state invariably means the deepening of the legitimacy crisis facing Inkatha. Hence the narrowing of options available to it to maintain its influence through non-violent and democratic means. Its options are increasingly becoming more bureaucratic and repressive:

* asking the state for the incorporation of 'troublesome townships' into KwaZulu (e.g. Lamontville and Hambanathi).
* Where there is 'trouble' in areas already falling under KwaZulu (e.g. KwaMashu and KwaMakhutha), it seeks more repressive mechanisms e.g. handing over of police stations into KwaZulu, and the passing of legislation on detention without tril by KwaZulu.
* strengthening and widening of bureaucratic-clientelist networks over 'troublesome' group-ings within the ambit of the KwaZulu Government (e.g. Civil servants and student bursary holders to sign 'pledge of loyalty' to the Inkatha controlled Legislative Assembly).

The above constitute what I would call Inkatha's 'bureaucratic entry points' in the control of communities and townships. It is therefore argued here that the conflict in PMB is one moment reflecting a deep legitimacy crisis for Inkatha as a liberation movement. I would even propose that in PMB, where it has had very little support, it is fighting for its very survival.

PMB also captures quite dramatically one other characteristic of Inkatha post-1983, that of being caught in a deep cycle of violence. Because of the trail of hostilities it leaves behind its violent actions, it also can no longer freely mobilize without reprisals from aggrieved communities. This then throws it further into violent action, particularly where its normal bureaucratic entry points are closed. It is against this background that the possibilities of successful peace talks between the mass democratic movement and Inkatha should be assessed, as well as the meaning and implications of peace for an organization like Inkatha. For Inkatha to enter into a peace agreement and observe it, in a place like PMB where it has lost heavily in terms of support, would mean the closing of one of its very few avenues to make its presence felt. Not surprisingly then, it has consistently undermined the peace talks between itself and the mass democratic movement.

It is the absence of Inkatha's normal bureaucratic entry points that has primarily frustrated its attempts at Edendale. Edendale, is not incorporated under KwaZulu. This fact alone severely hampers Inkatha's ability to dominate that community e.g. licenses for traders are not approved by the KwaZulu Government and the allocation of land and houses is not under its control. Obviously the most attractive entry point for Inkatha in a place like Edendale would be through the landowners. Through its winning over of this grouping it would have had a firm 'bureaucratic hold' over the tenants there. There are a number of reasons why this has not, and is unlikely, to happen, despite Inkatha's previous attempts to establish a relationship with this grouping through the EAB before its collapse. It is not in the collective interests of the landowners to align themselves with Inkatha and/or the KwaZulu Government.

One of the most consistent demands of the landowners has been the development of Edendale and a town board status for the area. The Inkatha controlled KwaZulu

Government has proved itself. like all bantustans in South Africa. to be totally incapable of effecting development or significant improvements in people's lives. Instead where the KwaZulu Government has taken over functions from the central government. disaster has ensued. The once highly 'prestigious' and respected Edendale hospital is a living monument. right in the heart of Edendale. of the hopeless failure of KwaZulu to meet even the most basic needs of the people. let alone development. Edendale hospital is now a pale shadow of itself. and is being described by the people of Edendale as a 'source of death' and not health (*'Emtholakufa'* instead of *'Emtholampilo'*). This is worsened by the fact that the shortage of doctors is partly if not largely due to the 'pledge of loyalty' to the Government (and in reality a pledge not to criticize Inkatha). For instance. many doctors who qualify from the University of Natal medical school do not want to go there because of their refusal to sign the pledge. The schools crisis as well as textbook shortage in KwaZulu. is a sad reflection of apartheid's fraud of escaping its responsibility to meet the needs of the people by handing over that responsibility to its hopelessly inept bantustan partners. The landowners are certainly not unaware of this state of affairs.

A related factor which has kept a distance between Inkatha and the landowners is the fact that where areas have fallen under the control of the former through the KwaZulu Government. Inkatha's bureaucratic-clientelist networks become magnified. This is obviously a threat to the 'self-governing' and autonomous status that the landowners want. As discussed above the landowners have been consistently trying to keep the state away from its property and its freehold status. There is absolutely no guarantee that an Inkatha-controlled administration would respect the 'sanctity' of this private property. let alone development.

Perhaps the most serious obstacle to Inkatha's entry at Edendale is that the nature of the landowner-tenant relationship is personal and non-bureaucratic. Therefore the landowners do not need Inkatha's patronage. Inkatha has increasingly controlled and dominated large townships (e.g. Umlazi near Durban). through its control of the most important resources. like allocation of housing. KwaZulu citizenship certificates for purposes of buying land or a house in a KwaZulu township. etc.

The independence and jealous guarding of its private property has not only been expressed by the Edendale landowners. but also by the similarly placed Inanda landowners. For instance the granting of the freedom of Inanda by Inkatha local leaders to Buthelezi in September 1987 drew this response from the Inanda Landowners Association:

This is our own land — it's too high a price to pay for the reconciliation between the Ngcobo brothers (local businessmen instrumental in organizing the ceremony) and Buthelezi. Worse still. was that local residents — as poor as they are — have to foot the bill for the occasion. . . . If they wanted to give the KwaZulu Chief Minister the freedom of their backyards. its fine. they are free to do so. but they must not drag us into this affair (*City Press*. 23/9/87).

The statement continued to say that '. . . . as far as they (the landowners) were concerned the *freedom of their properties* could not be conferred on anyone *without their consent*' (ibid. — emphasis added).

Inkatha. Political Violence and the Struggle for Control in Pietermaritzburg   521

The potential conflict also between Inkatha and the landowners is of an ideological nature. although it still finds its material basis on the freehold nature of the land. The landowners are in fact the direct descendants of *amakholwa*. the first group of Christian converts in Natal. who were well known for their dislike of traditional structures like chieftaincy. as well as ascribed status as opposed to acquired status. as captured by Vilakazi (1965).

Naturally, the early Zulu Christians came together to worship. but the new institution took on other functions. besides those of cohesion. It became the centre of organization for this new group and began to nurture in its members a new way of life. . . . Through this new organization. the missionaries . . . began to demolish systematically old concepts and the old cosmological ideas. . . . Their new religious experiences and their new allegiances to Christ meant that they were set apart from the rest of the tribe. . . . Thus (African) Christians everywhere in Natal and Zululand . . . developed arrogant attitudes towards traditionalists and . . . failed or refused to support or cooperate with the chiefs. . . . *"Sengiyazikholelwa, angikwazi ukukhonza amakhosi amabili"* i.e. *"I* have chosen for myself Christianity. and I cannot serve two kings". (pp. 97-98). This ideology which is still carried by the contemporary landowners sits very uneasily with Inkatha's lineage ideology. This is worsened by the fact that the material reality of Inkatha's lineage ideology is unquestioning subjection to the rule of the accredited (traditional) Zulu leaders.

However what has been pointed out above on the relationship between Inkatha and the landowners does not rule out altogether an alliance between the two. This is even more so because this potential conflict has not been played out in the political arena itself. But the fact that the 'tenants' are now in revolt. as it were — albeit not against the landowners — further makes the alliance between Inkatha and the landowners even more remote. This is because the last thing the landowners would like to see is a revolt by the tenants against them. Any move on the part of the landowners towards an alignment with Inkatha can now certainly lead to a confrontation.

Inevitably, because of the growth of the mass democratic movement and the closure of Inkatha's bureaucratic entry points. the latter was left with no other option to enter Edendale except by force. The propensity of Inkatha to force its way into unsubjected communities is also due to its increasing inability to organize from the bottom up. As it meets more resistance at Edendale it has inevitably sought more 'legal' repressive mechanisms to break its way through by requesting the state to hand over the local Plessislaer police station to Zulu Police (see *City Press*. 1/11/87). As at the time of writing this paper it looked certain that Inkatha has no future in PMB. its last 'hope' now to break into resilient communities is through the Natal KwaZulu *Indaba*. *Indaba* may well be Inkatha's trump card. not because of the support these proposals enjoy in african communities. but because of its potential to widen Inkatha's bureaucratic/repressive domination over African communities. It is contended here that whilst the state is certainly opposed to Indaba's proposals as they stand now, a modified version of these proposals might well be accepted by the state. Whatever the final package will look like, certainly it will include extending Buthelezi's power to all African areas and townships in Natal. That will certainly reopen the currently closed bureaucratic entry points for instance in places like Clermont. Lamontville. Sobantu. etc. The state also needs Buthelezi's cooperation in its national plans. and *Indaba* will certainly enable him to break out of the somewhat restrictive terrain of the KwaZulu bantustan. However such an eventuality will also open new terrains of contestation on the Natal scene, as there is evidence of a groundswell of opposition to *Indaba* within the mass democratic movement. For instance the youth at Edendale had this to say about Indaba:

The *Indaba* thing? It looks like it will divide our country and that is what Inkatha wants . . . maybe we might end up by having to get 'permits' to go to Johannesburg. Indaba will just force us to join Inkatha (Interview, 1/10/87).

Conclusion

PMB is currently Inkatha's big 'ulcer' in Natal. This is because Inkatha, has met determined and wide scale resistance to its attempts at domination. The loss of such a big area for Inkatha would seriously put in doubt its claimed 1.5 million membership as well as its 'leadership' of the Zulu nation. PMB has also exposed on a much larger scale the real basis of Inkatha's 'hegemony' in Natal. The less its bureaucratic access to African communities and townships, the larger is its scale of violent attacks on the people. And this has become a vicious cycle. The less successful it becomes in crushing progressive organizations, the more it relies on the apartheid state for more bureaucratic and repressive apparatuses. This tendency within Inkatha is captured by Velaphi Ndlovu's ('local' Inkatha MP) justification for the local Plessislaer police station to be handed over to KwaZulu Police: 'In Durban townships, where police stations have been taken by KwaZulu, there was no burning of houses and there was peace and order' (*City Press*, 1/11/87). These two strategies (bureaucratic domination and violence) are not mutually exclusive, and are often deployed simultaneously. For the mass democratic movement as well there is obviously a lot at stake in PMB. Isolating and neutralizing Inkatha is crucial in creating space for advancing the struggle in Natal. It is also important for the mass democratic movement to realize that Inkatha has forcibly diverted the struggle away from the main enemy. This needs to be taken much more seriously than it has happened thus far. This entails realizing that the energies of the MDM are going to be increasingly tied to engaging Inkatha in Natal for some time. Therefore it is important to start more serious strategizing on this question than has been done so far. The crucial question now is how to consolidate the gains that have been made through the transformation of the defence committees into permanent structures of the MDM.

The one other lesson that can be drawn from the struggles in PMB, is from the involvement of capital in the peace process. The initial pressure brought about by COSATU local on capital, provides a basis upon which systematic pressure can be applied to capital in future to monitor the activities of its allies, Inkatha. *Indaba* for instance, while it strengthens both the economic and political alliance between Inkatha and capital, it also makes the latter much more immediately vulnerable to pressure, particularly by the labour movement, to control the actions of its allies. For instance capital has deliberately become 'blind' to the actions of Inkatha in the townships, and applying pressure on it at strategic points in time subjects Inkatha's actions to a wider public scrutiny than has hitherto happened.

Inkatha, Political Violence and the Struggle for Control in Pietermaritzburg 523

The last point I would like to make is on the question of class alliances. The case of Edendale raises much more sharply the importance of the alignments of the petty bourgeoisie in the struggle against both the state and Inkatha. One of Inkatha's major bureaucratic entry points is by winning over the local petty bourgeoisie, largely through its clientelist patronage networks, and turn it into their instruments of domination. This then points out the importance of winning over of the local petty bourgeoisie as a means of isolating Inkatha. This question has rather not been given the attention it requires within the Mass Democratic Movement. For instance there are two dominant, if not opposing, positions within the movement on this question, both of which are problematic. The first position is the one which tends to dismiss the African *petit bourgeoisie* as a class whose economic interests are incompatible with the working class. This position tends to treat the African *petit bourgeoisie* as already co-opted by virtue of being a petty bourgeoisie. For instance the Edendale traders and landowners cannot be said to be already co-opted. At best they are 'neutral', and at worst they are co-optible. It is also quite clear that the landowners, in their struggle for an autonomous Edendale, need the people of Edendale, and there is also a convergence of interests between the landowners and the masses in so far as they all do not want Inkatha nor state domination. Despite the well known interests of the landowners, which should be properly understood, they can be brought onto the side of the Mass Democratic Movement, on the basis of a compromise and ultimately under the leadership of the Mass Democratic Movement. For instance progressive organizations can offer a defence against the encroachment of the state on the land in return for guarantees for negotiated rent, non-incorporation into KwaZulu, as well as the kind of development wanted by the people. It is therefore argued here that the ultimate alignments of the landed petty bourgeoisie will largely be determined by the attitude of working class and progressive organizations towards it. A correct strategy at this point in time would not be to alienate this grouping, but wherever possible to actively seek an alliance with it. The consequences of alienating the landowners at this stage are all too clear in that they might be thrown into the hands of the state or Inkatha. The urgency of moving towards that direction is underlined by the fact that, as soon as the state realizes that Inkatha has failed and the Mass Democratic Movement is strong, it might turn around and seek the cooperation of the landowners by conceding to some of their major demands in return for co-operating in the smashing of the Mass Democratic Movement. This possibility is also not too remote because of the state's gradual change on its attitude towards freehold property rights for africans, as part of its reform package. It is therefore dangerous, if not naive, simply to dismiss the landowners as petty bourgeois. This observation also highlights the importance of a conjunctural understanding of the African *petit bourgeoisie*, rather than through a purely abstract and 'structuralist' conception.

The second position on the question of alliances with the African *petit bourgeoisie*, which has tended to gain the upper hand within the Mass Democratic Movement since after 1985, is that of avoiding or even actively discouraging the analysis and exposure of class differences and contradictions within the oppressed. Such an analysis is sometimes treated as if it, in itself, is the creator of these contradictions and tensions within the oppressed, and therefore divisive and delaying the realization of a strong, united anti-apartheid alliance. It is argued here that it is important to analyze and understand the class forces and interests at play within communities-in-struggle. A proper understanding of the class forces and contradictions enables the movement to grasp the nature and content of anti-apartheid alliances in specific localities and situations. Such an understanding starts opening up possibilities for the Mass Democratic Movement to make strategic and well-informed options. For instance there is no doubt that the immediate interest of the landowners is to protect their property as well as convert it into further means of accumulation. No doubt then, for them apartheid is primarily an obstacle in so far as it undermines these goals. Having such an understanding of the landowners gives the concept 'anti-apartheid alliance' a concrete meaning, with the kind of compromises and concessions to be required in such an alliance much more clearer. Resolution of these class differences within an anti-apartheid alliance cannot be postponed until apartheid and exploitation are demolished. Such postponements have in many an African state been the breeding ground for neo-colonialism, reactionary coups, and counter-revolution.

Hopefully this paper has demonstrated that the characterization of what is going on in PMB as an Inkatha − UDF conflict is rather too simplistic and misleading.

References

Bromberger, N. et al (1986) 'Unemployment and Public Works Programmes in the Pietermaritzburg District'. Unpublished Research Report, Development Studies Research Group. University of Natal. Pietermaritzburg.

Etherington, N. (1985) 'African Economic Experiments in Colonial Natal, 19845-1880' in *Guest, B. and Sellers, M (eds): Enterprise and Exploitation in a Victorian Colony*. Pietermaritzburg: University of Natal Press.

Kuper, L. (1965) *An African Bourgeoisie: Race, Class and Politics in South Africa*. London: Yale University Press.

Lambert, J. (1985) 'The impoverishment of the Natal Peasantry' in *Guest, B. and Sellers, M (eds): Enterprise and Exploitation in a Victorian Colony*. Pietermaritzburg: University of Natal Press.

Mare, G. and Hamilton, G. (1987) *An appetite for Power: Buthelezi's Inkatha and the Politics of Loyal Resistance* Johannesburg: Ravan Press.

Vilakazi, A. (1965) *Zulu Transformations: A study of the dynamics of social change*. Pietermaritzburg: University of Natal Press.

[21]

Journal of Southern African Studies. Vol. 13. No. 3. April 1987

*Violence in Inanda, August 1985**

HEATHER HUGHES

Introduction: *situating the study*

Early in August 1985. the urban incendiarism which had been sweeping much of South Africa for some eighteen months erupted in Durban. just at a time when local researchers and other interested observers were trying to understand why Natal was so 'quiet'. Despite much evidence of regionally generated conflict in that province. the widespread anti-government resistance witnessed in the Transvaal and Cape had not manifested itself to anything like the same degree in Natal. When it did break out. sparked by the assassination of Victoria Mxenge outside her Umlazi home on 1 August.[1] many were surprised by both its suddenness and its intensity. Within a week. hardly a shop or government building in African areas of the city was more than a burned-out shell.

Inanda was caught in this upsurge in a way few in the democratic movement could review with anything but regret: events there seemed to culminate in a confrontation between Indian and African people. The media were quick to raise the spectre of the 1949 'race clashes' in Durban. while many denied any racial friction whatever. claiming that to admit such would be to play into the hands of government-confected policies and propaganda.

The analyses which began to appear from November 1985 onwards. dealing either partially or wholly with Inanda. confirmed that the issue of race within the ranks of the oppressed classes was a sensitive one indeed. It is necessary to examine these. in order to justify the appearance of yet another account.

Michael Sutcliffe and Paul Wellings's study. *Attitudes and Living Conditions in Inanda: the Context for Unrest?* is a social survey. based on random sampling of tenants in eight localities in Inanda. The twenty-six questions put to respondents covered four broad areas: life conditions (e.g. 'what do you like most/least about living here?'): attitudes towards landlords (e.g. 'do you have any problems with your landlord?'): future developments (about improvements to living conditions.

---

*I would like to thank David Brown and Omar Badsha for discussing Inanda with me on countless occasions. also my supervisor Shula Marks for valuable guidance and suggestions. and Debby Gaitskell and William Beinart and those at the ICS seminar for helpful comments. All remaining inadequacies are my own.

[1] Victoria Mxenge was a prominent 'political' attorney and treasurer in the Natal executive of the UDF. Her husband Griffiths. jailed for support of the ANC in the 1960s and also a 'political' attorney. was brutally murdered in 1981. His killers have never been found.

removals and so on); and housing and population characteristics.[1] Generally, answers in the first three categories revealed mostly attitudes, opinions and preferences, while those in the last category provided a more 'factual' pool of information. The survey had been initiated in May-June 1985, to 'undertake a study of the whole question of landlord-tenant relations and development' in Inanda.[3] It ended as something rather different: as a comment on reasons for the violence. It concluded,

Prior to the unrest, no deep-seated racist or anti-landlord sentiments existed in the Inanda area. Thus, we believe one cannot build a model of the unrest which paints it as an African-Indian confrontation. Such simplistic analysis only lends credence to the racist explanations provided by the South African government and its mouthpiece the South African Broadcasting Corporation.[4]

Their findings on landlord-tenant relations are not corroborated by any of the other available studies;[5] further, it is difficult to square them with the authors' own suggestion that 'socio-economic, infrastructural and housing conditions' played a part in precipitating open conflict.[6]

One of the more serious problems of the survey is that it takes as its baseline a period of two months prior to the violence, enabling the authors to say,

Normally very quiet, the settlements in Inanda were transformed into places where looting, violence and intimidation became the order of the day. The transformation was extremely rapid and almost beyond comprehension. This was most obvious to us as we had spent the previous two months in the area conducting research.[7]

Some background information, relating to events in the early 1980s, is included, but is incidental rather than integral to their analysis of the conflict. Hobsbawm's general point is pertinent here: 'The danger of this type of study lies in the temptation to isolate the phenomenon of overt crisis from the wider context of a society undergoing transformation.'[8]

The collection of material edited by Fatima Meer, *Unrest in Natal August 1985*,[9] displays much less of this danger. It contains valuable information in eyewitness reports and affidavits from the various townships in Durban and examines some of the deeper roots of the violence. Because of its nature, it is more useful if treated as a source book rather than a sustained analysis. Yet its conclusions on the violence in Inanda need to be questioned, for one is presented with a theory of conspiracy:

Inanda has been earmarked for 'release' to Africans in terms of the 1936 Land Act, but. . . the Government [has not] enough money to buy off privately owned land. How better to short-circuit the whole process than. . . through a racial attack?[10]

[2] M. Sutcliffe and P. Wellings, *Attitudes and Living Conditions in Inanda: the Context for Unrest?* (Durban, 1985), p. 45-7.

[3] Sutcliffe and Wellings, *Attitudes*, p. 7.

[4] *Ibid.*, p. 40.

[5] See for example Surplus People Project (SPP), *Forced Removals in South Africa*, volume 4: *Natal* (Cape Town and Pietermaritzburg, 1983), pp. 393-404.

[6] Sutcliffe and Wellings, *Attitudes*, p. 41.

[7] *Ibid.*, p. 2.

[8] E. Hobsbawm, 'From social history to the history of society', in M.W. Flinn and T.C. Smout (eds.), *Essays in Social History* (Oxford, 1974), p. 17.

[9] F. Meer (ed.), *Unrest in Natal August 1985* (Durban, 1985).

[10] *Ibid.*, p. 40.

African people, in other words, were manipulated by the state in order to attack Indian residents. The study points out correctly that there had been a long history of 'needling Indians'[11] but pushes the argument towards one of conspiracy by emphasising the significance of certain evidence. For example, an Indian shopkeeper whose shop had been destroyed claimed that the day before the attacks there had been a rush to buy empty containers.[12] Further, the research team reported that it had not found a single instance of racial hostility when visiting the area soon after the violence.[13] Also, the presence of white valuators in the area almost immediately after the attacks was viewed as more than coincidence.[14] Leaving aside the difficulties of fitting much of this evidence together, the point remains that for Meer *et al.* the violence was planned, premeditated, and involved deep collusion between state, African landlords and poverty-stricken African tenants. Had more attention been paid to the nature of social class and class interest in Inanda, which have unfolded in racially complex ways, a conspiratorial explanation would have been rendered unnecessary.

The third study to have been published is difficult to deal with, mainly because it was privately commissioned and seemed somewhat sectarian from the start. The reason that it must be noted is that it was widely reported in the local Durban press, particularly in papers catering for an Indian readership.[15] Undertaken on behalf of one side of the Gandhi family by Ken Hill, its brief was quite specific: to establish who had been responsible for the destruction of the Gandhi Settlement — Africans or Indians. Despite the fact that some key eye witnesses refused to participate in the study, Hill concluded that it was Africans who were guilty. It is hard to know why Hill's report received such wide publicity: perhaps its commissioners were hoping to use its findings in negotiations about the future of the Settlement.

In February 1986, a wide-ranging analysis appeared in the *South African Labour Bulletin*. Despite its title, 'Inanda, August 1985', the author, Ari Sitas, draws the constituent parts of the Durban region together into a larger analytical unit in his attempt to explain why it was that 'no major grouping of the oppressed had the capacity to give shape to any explosive conflict in Durban's townships' in 1985.[16] It is an important contribution to debates about, *inter alia*, the nature of the African petty bourgeoisie and its relationship to Inkatha; trade unions and Inkatha; the weaknesses and strengths of the United Democratic Front in Natal; and implications of the violence for the future of the labour movement. It is a key 'ideas piece' for anyone trying to understand regional politics in Natal, but as noted before, is short on detail on Inanda. In many ways, it forms the broader context for the present paper.

Although again dealing only briefly with Inanda, the last of the recent studies deserving mention is Nicholas Haysom's *Apartheid's Private Army*.[17] Focusing as it does on right-wing vigilantes, it is mainly concerned with Phoenix, rather than the

[11] *Ibid.*, p. 43.
[12] *Ibid.*, p. 47.
[13] *Ibid.*, p. 44.
[14] *Ibid.*, pp. 49, 51.
[15] See *Sunday Tribune Herald*, 2 February 1986.
[16] A. Sitas, 'Inanda, August 1985: "Where wealth and power and blood reign worshipped gods"' in *South African Labour Bulletin*, 11, 4 (1986), p. 105.
[17] N. Haysom, *Apartheid's Private Army* (London, 1986).

neighbouring Inanda, for it was there that Indian vigilante groups were organising, in anticipation of some sort of attack from Inanda. (In the week of intense violence in August, vigilantes were relatively unimportant in Inanda itself.) The picture which Haysom provides, of the deep sense of fear in Phoenix as well as in other Indian-designated areas of Durban, and the new-found receptivity to 'protection' from the security forces,[18] are vivid testimonies to the effects of thirty-six years of the Group Areas Act in that city.

There is an important point not made explicit in any of the above studies: the violence in Inanda was not the same as the violence in the townships of Durban and elsewhere. Inanda shares in common with formal townships that it is the consequence of the particular nature of urbanisation in South Africa: it differs markedly in that it has grown without the direct, centralised control of state or local state. In fact, the social engineering of the Nationalist government has ruptured or obliterated the history of very many communities like Inanda precisely to make way for the formal townships. That Inanda has survived so long, as an area housing black people within metropolitan Durban, on privately-owned rather than state-controlled land, is due to a number of circumstances, among them the determination of landowners and tenants alike to remain there. As far as the violence itself is concerned, in Inanda, no less than in any other unenfranchised and economically deprived area of South Africa, there were local causes enough to threaten instability and a breakdown in the social order. It is doubtful whether the onset of violence, finally, would have been so intense or widespread without the stimulus of revived political activity in the country over the past few years; the fact remains, however, that the underlying causes, course and outcome of violence must be sought in Inanda's particular, local history. Whereas one might expect to find a high degree of similarity in the nature of violence in formal townships across the country — due to centralised administration, education and housing[19] — the same cannot be said of areas such as Inanda. In this sense, the pattern of events in Inanda was atypical (but not unimportant), even though certain of its features might have been manifested elsewhere. Since this paper is concerned with the immediate past, the greater part of Inanda's development can be dealt with only briefly. Emphasis is necessarily laid on the period from the 1960s onwards, when Inanda became rapidly incorporated into metropolitan Durban as an 'informal' shanty town.

[18] Haysom. *Apartheid's Private Army*. p. 126.
[19] Regional variation and specific grievances are not of course being ruled out. For the system of township administration, which has been the focus for much resistance activity, see J. Grest and H. Hughes. 'The local state' in South African Research Service (ed.), *South African Review 1* (Johannesburg, 1983) and 'State strategy and popular response at the local level' in South African Research Service (ed.), *South African Review 2* (Johannesburg, 1984).

Violence in Inanda, August 1985   335

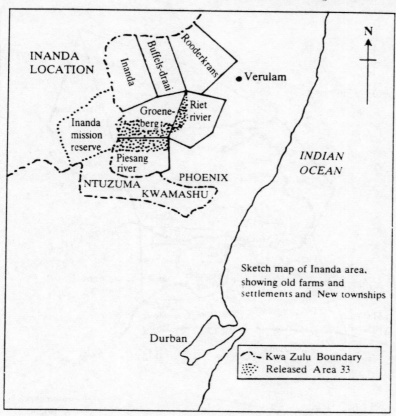

Sketch map of Inanda area, showing old farms and settlements and New townships

⌐⌐⌐ Kwa Zulu Boundary
⠿⠿ Released Area 33

A brief history to the 1960s

The name 'Inanda' applies to several areas or places. whose boundaries sometimes but not always overlap. It was originally given to a farm in the Natalia Republic period. In 1847. the African location to the north-west of Durban was gazetted as the Inanda Location (it shared a border with the farm Inanda). and the stretch of Colony between the location and the sea — some 180 square miles — was known as the Inanda Division of Victoria County. a coastal strip which was to become the centre of Natal's sugar industry. 'Inanda' was also the name given by Daniel Lindley to his mission reserve. at the south-eastern edge of the location. when he moved there in 1857. (See Map 1.) Nowadays. it is the officially designated 'Released Area 33' which is most commonly called Inanda. For the most part. it consists of privately-owned land in the Inanda Division adjoining the eastern side of the old mission reserve. This is the place which is the subject of this paper. (See Map 2.)[20]

[20] For the background on Inanda mission reserve and location (now both part of KwaZulu) see H. Hughes. 'The Inanda district during the colonial period: a preliminary overview'. paper presented to the Conference on the History of Natal and Zululand. University of Natal. July 1985.

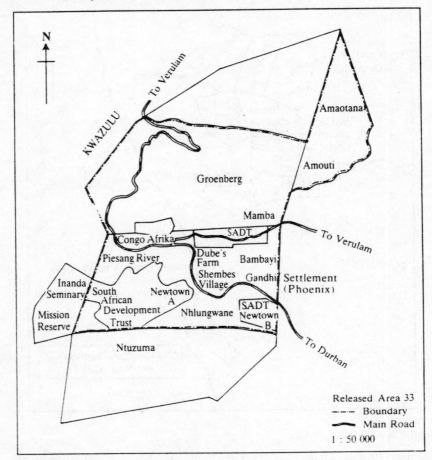

In the nineteenth century, only three farms, or parts of farms, covered the area which would eventually become Released Area 33: Piesang River, Groeneberg and Riet Rivier.[21] All date from the short-lived Natalia Republic. One of them, Piesang River, was for a short time a sugar estate. For a number of reasons, such as that the cane varieties then available could not withstand the inland frost, it went bankrupt in 1869, and was acquired by the Natal Land and Colonisation Company.[22] By the 1870s, all the farms in the area were held by individual or company speculators rather than producers. African people on this land experienced a rapid transformation in their status once colonial rule gave some meaning to the notion of private property: independent producers became tenants, paying cash as rent. In

---

[21] Natal Archives, Pietermaritzburg, Map of Inanda Division, 1873, No. B31.
[22] R.F. Osborne, *Valiant Harvest: the Founding of the South African Sugar Industry* (Durban, 1964), p. 214.

some cases in Inanda. on land owned by individual absentee owners, a labour requirement was attached − if not forthcoming, rent was simply raised. [23]

From the mid-1860s onwards. African tenants began to be displaced by Indian workers who had completed their periods of indenture and had elected to stay in the Colony. a trend foreseen and wholly disliked by Lindley and his Christian band at Inanda:

> The great majority of these imported labourers will never return to their native land. . . they. are indescribably wicked. and seem to me hopelessly lost. now and forever. . . I look upon these Indians as a growing cloud on our social horizon. At present there seems to be no friendly sympathy between the coolies and the Natives. . . [24]

Provision for Indian workers wishing to settle on the land was extremely *ad hoc.* making their entry into agriculture on their own account very different from that of African producers. The first Indian producers were tenants. leasing small plots from absentee landlords in the Groeneberg and Riet Rivier areas. [25] A common adjunct to farming activities was hawking. or keeping small stores. catering particularly for trade with Africans.

In a relatively short while. Indian producers were achieving great success. The Inanda magistrate noted in 1876 that 'but for them maize would be at famine price and vegetables strangers to our table'. [26] Swan. following Bundy. explains the vigour of Indian petty commodity production in terms of easier access to credit. 'which may have appeared to offer them a competitive edge over their struggling African fellow-cultivators'. [27] although this led to bondage relationships very difficult to escape. African producers too were resorting to money-lending to cover rent arrears as well as legal costs against them. [28] By the 1890s, G.H. Hulett noted that 90 per cent of the civil cases in the Verulam magistrate's court were actions for the recovery of rent from African tenants. [29] Apart from possibly differential access to and terms of credit. there is another factor: it seems that Africans in Inanda were charged rent per hut and Indians per acre. The former could well have been the more expensive and restrictive. To bring more hands into the fields would have meant more huts and therefore more rent − and after 1875. more hut tax. [30] In order to try to maintain a foothold on the land. there is evidence of African tenants looking to wage labour (sometimes with Indian agriculturalists). a method which by its very nature tended to undermine their ability as producers.

---

[23] For a fuller treatment of land and labour in colonial Natal. see H. Slater. 'The changing pattern of economic relationships in rural Natal. 1838-1914' in S. Marks and A. Atmore (eds.). *Economy and Society in Pre-industrial South Africa* (London. 1980).

[24] Daniel Lindley. 29 December 1864. cited in E.W. Smith. *The Life and Times of Daniel Lindley, 1801-1880* (London. 1949). p. 378.

[25] J.J.C. Greyling. 'Problems of Indian landownership and land-occupation on the Natal North Coast: a socio-geographic investigation' (Ph.D. thesis. University of Natal. 1969). volume 1. p. 23.

[26] *Natal Blue Book* (Pietermaritzburg. 1876). Inanda Resident Magistrate's Report.

[27] M. Swan. *Gandhi: The South African Years* (Johannesburg. 1985). p. 23: C. Bundy. *The Rise and Fall of the South African Peasantry* (London. 1979). pp. 182-3.

[28] *Natal Native Affairs Commission 1906-7*. Evidence of John Swales. p. 489.

[29] *Ibid.*. Evidence of G.H. Hulett. p. 942.

[30] *Ibid.*. Evidence of John Swales. p. 489.

There were not many African landowners in the Inanda area outside of the mission lands. The Matiwane family owned 281 acres and there were others who owned much smaller acreages — mostly no more than tiny plots.[31] The most important owner was Dr J.L. Dube, who acquired 200 acres of Piesang River — henceforward known as Dube's Farm — in 1901, for his self-help Christian Industrial School, Ohlange. Just before the Land Act of 1913 put a stop to African purchases in 'white' South Africa, Isaiah Shembe also acquired a portion of the old Piesang River Farm in the name of the *Amanazaretha* religious sect. He called his settlement *Ekupha-kameni*, The Elevated Place, a country haven away from the evils of the town.[32]

But it was those few African landowners interested in more secular pursuits who were unsettled by the steady acquisition of land by Indians, untrammelled by legislation such as the Land Act. A member of the Matiwane family complained to the Chief Native Commissioner, when in early 1914 that official came to explain the benefits of the Land Act, that 'the Indians are not like the Natives, because the Indians have the Imperial Authorities to look after their interests. . .'[33] Some small plots were bought by Indian tenant producers, although the major purchases were due to restrictive legislation imposed on Indian traders in town, which left land as one of the few avenues of investment for wealthier immigrants. In the first three decades of this century, the amount of land on the Natal North Coast owned by Indian people increased steadily, as speculators disposed of their holdings.[34] Even by the turn of the century, the Indian population of Inanda was sizeable enough to attract Mahatma Gandhi to establish his Phoenix Settlement there — again, on a portion of the old Piesang River. It is well known that the experiment in a simple, self-sufficient way of life at Phoenix was an important influence in the development of Gandhi's philosophy of *satyagraha* and *bramacharya*.[35] What has never been properly explored are the relationships between Gandhi and his fellow workers at Phoenix and their neighbour Dr Dube, other members of the *Kholwa* (African Christian) community or indeed the Indian tenants or owners in the area. Swan suggests that Gandhi may have been influenced by Dube's prior experiment in self-help,[36] but this is an area still awaiting proper investigation.

From the early 1930s, economic conditions and discriminatory legislation conspired to cause agricultural stagnation in Inanda. Against a background of deep recession, the 1936 Land Act declared Inanda a 'released area' — that is, isolated from 'white' South Africa for incorporation into the neighbouring African reserve at some future date, once the state had acquired the necessary land. The declaration of Released Area 33 can be seen as a direct attack on Indian owners and producers there: in that year, Indian people constituted nearly 52 per cent of the population of the Inanda Division,[37] a substantial proportion of whom would have resided in the

---

[31] *Natal Blue Book on Native Affairs* (Pietermaritzburg, 1894), Inanda Resident Magistrate's Report.

[32] On Shembe, see B. Sundkler, *Zulu Zion* (Oxford, 1976).

[33] Natal Archives, Pietermaritzburg, 1946/13, CNC 147/1913.

[34] A.J. Christopher, 'Natal: a study in colonial land settlement' (Ph.D. thesis, University of Natal, 1969), pp. 331 and 350; Greyling, 'Problems of Indian landownership', p. 29; Swan, *Gandhi*, pp. 67-8.

[35] M.K. Gandhi, *The Story of my Experiments with Truth* (Ahmedabad, 1927).

[36] Swan, *Gandhi*, pp. 59-60.

[37] K. Buchanan and N. Hurwitz, 'The Asiatic immigrant community in the Union of South Africa' in *The Geographical Review*, 39, 3 (1949), p. 444.

released area. Although there were no immediate changes in the pattern of landownership, future purchases of land by Indian people were made extremely difficult. In the future, it would be African landowners, entrepreneurs, churches and those attached to power structures in the reserve who would purchase land from Indian sellers. The state's sluggishness in expanding the holdings of the South African Native Trust was marked all over the country and Inanda was no exception.[38] By 1969, for example, it had acquired only one piece of Piesang River farm.[39]

Alongside of these developments were the increasingly hostile proscriptions of Indian people, embodied in legislation which was 'the result of white demands for effective measures to curb infiltration'.[40] The Asiatic Land Tenure and Indian Representation Act of 1946 applied to rural as well as urban areas, and its effect was 'a sharp decrease in the number of farms acquired by Indians'.[41] Thereafter, the trend was towards intense subdivision of holdings and the consequent decline of productivity and growth of population pressure. Despite the bucolic air of H.I.E. Dhlomo's 1947 poem about Inanda, where 'deer and cattle mingle in the bushes,/ and rustic song and mirth rouse midst the rushes',[42] the agricultural prospect was growing bleaker. In the year before Dhlomo wrote his poem, the Inanda magisterial division contained the second largest number of Indian people after Durban — 24.738 as against 115,833.[43] Again, it is impossible to know exactly how many were living in Released Area 33: it is known, however, that Piesang River, Groeneberg (notably, in an area later to be known as Matikwe) and Riet Rivier formed the southern limit of the largest concentration of Indian-owned farms in Natal, the northern limit being Cotton Lands, an area to the west of Verulam.[44]

The 1950s were years of struggle to maintain footholds on the land, against mounting odds. In the 1960s, a decade of even greater squeeze on small producers with the beginnings of monopolisation in Natal agriculture,[45] when the promise of greater security presented itself in the form of shack farming, landowners willingly allowed human settlements to grow on their properties. In this way, the urbanisation of Inanda began.

The growth of Inanda

It was the clearance of another 'informal' settlement, Cato Manor, that gave a spur to the process. Shanty towns had grown on Durban's peripheries since the 1930s, a product of the acute shortage of more substantial workers' housing and the desire for greater freedom to shape their own lives on the part of residents. It is precisely the

---

[38] SPP, *Forced Removals*, p. 38.
[39] Greyling, 'Problems of Indian landownership', p. 39.
[40] Urban Foundation Natal Region, *Basic Planning Information on Inanda* (Durban, 1980), p. 16.
[41] Greyling, 'Problems of Indian landownership', p. 34.
[42] H.I.E. Dhlomo, 'Inanda' in *Ilanga*, 2 August 1947, reprinted in N. Visser and T. Couzens (eds.), *H.I.E. Dhlomo — Collected Works* (Johannesburg, 1985), pp. 337-8.
[43] M.H. Alsop, *Natal Regional Survey*, volume 2: *The Population of Natal* (Cape Town, 1952), pp. 61-2, 103.
[44] Greyling, 'Problems of Indian landownership', p. 40.
[45] See J. Beall *et al.*, 'The Natal option: regional distinctiveness within the national reform process', paper presented to the conference of the Association for Sociology in Southern Africa, July 1986, p. 19.

tension between these two factors which, according to Paul Maylam, has plagued local urban administration over the decades: the outcome has been a cheap form of housing, requiring little or no capital outlay, but politically and socially uncontrollable.[46]

After numerous civil disturbances in Cato Manor — the 1949 'race riots' and simmering tension over police attempts to curb women's beer brewing, culminating in riots in 1959-60 — the City Council finally decided to opt for political control and to rehouse tenants in the new township of KwaMashu, begun in 1958. Situated to the north-west of the city, KwaMashu itself made a place like Inanda a viable option for daily or weekly commuting to work in the city, since the bus service was extended in this direction. Many either did not qualify for, or refused, housing in the township — they were among the earliest of Inanda's shack dwellers. Others tried KwaMashu but found it unpalatable: 'they stayed here for a few months or six weeks then they jumped off to go and build those "squatters" at Inanda'.[47]

This outward movement, the creation of a new periphery, demonstrated the rate of Durban's metropolitan dilation in a period of 'rapid and unprecedented expansion in the decade 1963-73'.[48] The growth of Inanda changed its social complexion completely. For the few 'big' and several hundred 'small' landowners, tenants brought a steady income. Moreover, for those landlords who were also shopowners, tenants were also consumers. Whereas, before, these had been country concerns with modest turnovers, profitable markets were now growing up around them.

Both African and Indian landlords and traders were represented in this emerging peri-urban class, and their dual source of income was to affect relations with tenant-consumers profoundly. But the class was divided, not only in terms of scale. Especially after the Promotion of Bantu Self-Government Act of 1959, African petty bourgeois interests began to make bids for a share in Inanda. As it was a 'released area', they based their claims on the need for African advancement in African areas. All over Durban, traders in particular couched their class protectionism in explicitly anti-Indian terms. Their leading ideologue was A.W.G. Champion, an active local Inanda resident (his father had been Lindley's assistant and his sister married into the locally influential *Kholwa* family, the Gobas).

Here in Durban, when the Indians were very arrogant, the Africans took sticks to them in 1949. They beat them up and made them close their shops. Yes, the enrichment of Africans from stores and buses started in 1949, it started like that. . .[49]

Not only bantustan policy but also the Group Areas Act affected relations among landlords. At least one African landowner of very long standing in Inanda has had land in surrounding areas expropriated on more than one occasion for the demarcation of Indian Group Areas.[50]

[46] P. Maylam, 'The "black belt": African squatters in Durban 1935-50' in *Canadian Journal of African Studies*, 17, 3 (1983), pp. 413-28.

[47] Interview with Mrs M., cited in SPP. *Forced Removals*, p. 201.

[48] Sitas, 'Inanda', p. 98.

[49] A.W.G. Champion, 'Repetition and indication of years' in M.W. Swanson (ed.), *The Views of Mahlathi* (Pietermaritzburg, 1982), pp. 68-9.

[50] Interview with Dr M.V. Gumede, Inanda, 1 December 1985.

Unlike in the African and Indian townships nearby — the huge City Council housing scheme for Indian people, Phoenix, was constructed in the mid-1970s and the new township of Ntuzuma was begun in 1973 — no group of interests associated with local bureaucracy has arisen in Inanda. This is because until 1979, no authority in the country was willing, or saw it as necessary, to admit responsibility for it, and the ever more populous settlements there grew over two decades without any form of local administration. Moreover, the few controls imposed from the Verulam magistrate's office had 'a rural, rather than an urban orientation'.[51] This situation has given the landlords — or shacklords, as they have been called, signifying their power over the thousands of tenants — added importance, particularly those who have had direct links with the KwaZulu government and Inyanda, the African traders' association which affiliated to Inkatha in 1978. In this way, since there has been no local authority to do it,[52] attempts have been made to protect trading licences against competition — particularly as the licensing authority is the Verulam magistrate and because of administrative red tape, it has been easier for Indian traders to obtain licences.[53]

For many reasons — demographic, social, political, economic — most tenants were to be African people, dotting the hillsides with their shacks, or *imijondolo*. Settlement followed the two main valley systems of the Ohlange and Piesang rivers and tenants depended on these and rainwater for their requirements. Landowners had usually sunk boreholes for their water needs. Basic infrastructural services in Inanda have always been near to non-existent: only the better-off have, for example, been able to connect themselves to the electricity supply, and there is only one tarred road through the whole area.

A substantial proportion of the tenantry is made up of 'people who have spent all or most of their lives in the urban area',[54] unable to find housing in the formal townships, or escaping single-sex hostels to be with family, or perhaps evicted from another shanty settlement. A growing proportion must be coming from rural areas, as conditions there steadily deteriorate: 'conditions in the bantustans are so poor that people are forced to go to urban areas to survive'.[55]

Schlemmer recently calculated that the overall increase in the number of 'informal' dwellings around Durban was 137 per cent between 1966 and 1979:[56] clearly, Inanda, as home of the largest number, was subject to massive pressures with such a rapid growth rate in so short a period. The figures in Table 1 show the increase in Inanda's population over the past decade.

[51] Urban Foundation Natal Region, *Basic Planning Information*, p. 17.
[52] *Ibid.*, p. 50.
[53] Memorandum to the Minister of CAD, 19 February 1982, in Inanda Support Group, *Information Dossier* (Durban, 1982).
[54] SPP, *Forced Removals*, p. 196.
[55] L. Platzky and C. Walker, *The Surplus People* (Johannesburg, 1985), p. 384.
[56] L. Schlemmer, 'Squatter communities: safety valves in the rural-urban nexus' in H. Giliomee and L. Schlemmer (eds.), *Up against the Fences* (Cape Town, 1985), p. 169.

Table 1 — *Population of Inanda. 1977-85*

1977	68.000
1979	88.000
1982	100.000 – 200.000
1985	250.000

Sources: Compiled from Surplus People Project. *Forced Removals*. p. 209: Inanda Support Group estimates. and M. Sutcliffe and P. Wellings, *Attitudes and Living Conditions in Inanda.*[57]

Partly due to the problems of charting the effects of such speeded-up urbanisation. a detailed picture of social structure and relations among the tenantry is difficult to sketch. The vast majority of tenants are semi-skilled or unskilled workers. educational levels are low (about six years of schooling on average). unemployment stands in the region of 45 per cent and there is a sizeable lumpenproletariat — 15 per cent is a recent estimate.[58] The degree of youth unemployment is particularly high. leading to the creation of a 'bitter generation'[59] amongst a tenantry caught in a downward spiral of poverty. due to the severe economic downswing beginning in the early 1980s. and aggravated by inflation and a burdensome general sales tax of 15 per cent on nearly all commodities. To reinforce the trend. opportunities for growing maize or vegetables. or keeping small stock. have diminished rapidly as settlement has become denser. In the early 1980s. densities of 100 to 230 people per hectare could be found.[60] with household size now on average 9.5 people. according to the most recent survey.[61]

For those hopeful of finding work. there have been huge administrative obstacles. Assuming their 'passes' to be in order. those workseekers who came to Inanda after 1968 have not been entitled to register at either the central labour bureau in Durban or at their nearest one in KwaMashu. They have been pushed out to the bureau at Verulam. a small centre where there are few jobs to be had.[62] In order to make ends meet. many have turned to the 'informal sector'. selling goods such as food and clothing. or to 'illegal' employment (that is. bypassing all official allocation channels). so widespread in the Durban area that 'the Administration Board has virtually given up policing it'.[63]

One can readily appreciate the fragility which characterises social relations in Inanda. Levels of crime. especially against the person — mugging. assault. rape. murder — are high. and in this sense at least. Inanda is seriously under-policed. with one small police station in upper Inanda. (In this connection. residents who were consulted in the early 1980s made a distinction between 'ordinary' policemen

[57] Huge discrepancies exist in the population statistics. and these should be taken as indicative of the trend rather than as an accurate reflection of the number of heads in any one year. The method on which most of the figures are based is that of using aerial photographs and estimating population on the basis of the number of structures.

[58] Sutcliffe and Wellings. *Attitudes*. p. 33: Sitas. 'Inanda'. p. 101: SPP. *Forced Removals*. p. 398.

[59] Sitas. 'Inanda'. p. 100.

[60] Urban Foundation Natal Region. *Basic Planning Information*. pp. 27-9.

[61] Sutcliffe and Wellings. *Attitudes*. p. 30.

[62] SPP. *Forced Removals*. p. 188.

[63] S. Greenberg and H. Giliomee. 'Managing influx control from the rural end: the black homelands and the underbelly of privilege' in Giliomee and Schlemmer. *Up against the Fences*. p. 81.

investigating crime, and security policemen, whose job was considered to be to harass people.) Before the violence, most shops were heavily encased in iron grilles at night, and a few of the larger Indian homes ensconced in high barbed-wire fencing and after dark, in glaring spotlight. Particularly in the last few years, gangs have moved into Inanda and staked out areas of influence for themselves. One commentator with a wide knowledge of Inanda has called them 'social bandits turned blood-suckers' — some at least may be traced back to Cato Manor days.[64]

In some areas, tenants cluster together for a specific purpose, such as religion or relation to a landlord. Some of the Indian tenants, numbering about 2,000 individuals before the August violence, would fall in the latter category. The most prominent of the religious centres is that of the *Amanazaretha*, for some years wracked by division over a succession dispute. Other religious groupings include the independent congregationalists around their church in an area called Afrika.

Apart from the collectivities with common linkages, one gains the impression of a generally fractured community, in which welfare and political organisations have found it hard to mobilise support. Since its formation in 1983, the United Democratic Front (UDF) has had a negligible presence in the area, and even Inkatha has not mustered noticeable support. This is another product of the lack of a local authority around which support could cohere. In addition, the most prominent African landlord, Rogers Ngcobo, one of the original central committee members of Inkatha, fell out with the organisation in the early 1980s, claiming that members had not seen any benefits, despite having paid their annual fees.[65] He is now no longer even KwaZulu MP for the area.

Another form of fracture has been an 'ethnic' one, between Pondo and Zulu people. The former, a fairly large minority, have congregated together in shanty towns around Durban (being ineligible for township housing, which is nearly all in KwaZulu). In Inanda there are several groups in areas such as Piesang River and Bambayi. Open conflict such as erupted in shanty towns to the south of Durban over Christmas 1985 has not been witnessed on the same scale in Inanda. However, there is some animosity to Xhosa-speaking people, mostly flaring on the issue of access to scarce resources such as water and fuelled by anti-Pondo statements by leadership elements in KwaZulu.[66]

Crises from 1979

The state has always regarded tenants in 'informal' settlements as 'illegal squatters', and therefore to be removed, since they have settled without official permission. As the Inanda population swelled through the 1970s, so the state took a more active interest in the area and acquired two further blocks of Piesang River from Indian owners, whose properties now housed shanty settlements.[67] Before it took any

---

[64] Omar Badsha provided this information. The father of Thomas Shabalala, a shacklord in Lindelani and widely known to have been involved in the organising of impis in KwaMashu and Inanda (see below), was a gangster in the old Cato Manor.

[65] Interview with R. Ngcobo, Inanda, October 1980.

[66] See for example, Haysom, *Apartheid's Private Army*, p. 83.

[67] Urban Foundation Natal Region, *Basic Planning Information*, p. 52.

further action. a series of local crises. beginning in 1979. brought tenant. landlord and state into a multilateral conflict which served merely to worsen relationships within Inanda.

The first of these was the severe drought which ravaged Natal from 1978 onwards. Over 100.000 head of cattle perished in KwaZulu and grave food and water shortages occurred. Even from the relatively prosperous sugar industry came reports of huge losses and. commented the press. '[N]ow an exodus has started with thousands of people out of jobs moving to the cities'.[68] All sources of water in Inanda dried up and through 1979. some shopkeepers began to sell water. while others gave it away. One storeowner sank a borehole for residents in the immediate vicinity, with financial assistance from Indian businessmen. The KwaZulu government had recently turned down his application for Inanda to be connected to the KwaMashu water supply.[69]

The Urban Foundation had been investigating a bulk water supply too. and calculated that its installation would cost about R1.5 million.[70] The Department of Co-operation and Development (CAD) was unwilling to pursue the idea — to lay on water would be to recognise the permanency of the tenants.

In early 1980. thirty people died of typhoid. Official intervention could be delayed no longer. and an emergency committee was formed. consisting of the Departments of CAD and Health. the South African Defence Force, the Verulam magistrate (who was also the local CAD commissioner) and the Urban Foundation. It organised tankers to bring water to a number of points in Inanda. Only as a result of this crisis did the Department of CAD finally assume responsibility for Released Area 33.

Before water mains were finally laid in 1982. the state used the health/water issue as the pretext for a series of removals. First was a site-and-service scheme. in association with the Urban Foundation. on South African Development (ex-Native) Trust land in Inanda. It was planned in five weeks and aimed at the residents of Amouti. in the northern cone-shaped portion of Released Area 33. For an unexplained reason. Amouti had initially been excluded from the emergency water supply. The Verulam magistrate announced the scheme in July 1980. claiming that 'it gives people an opportunity to own land and to build their own houses. . . to qualify. you must be a resident of Released Area 33. You must also be a citizen of KwaZulu.'[71] Rumours about the scheme began to abound: Africans were being moved to make way for the expansion of Phoenix: Section 10 qualifications would be granted: township houses would be built: free rations would be provided. Arrivals on the scheme found pegged-out sites. each with a pit latrine and one tap for every four or so sites. They were issued with tents until they could erect shacks. in turn an intermediate stage before they were able to construct more substantial dwellings to minimum standards. The only allowance made in terms of people's urban qualifications was permission to seek work at the KwaMashu labour bureau. (The fact surfaced later that those who had possessed Section 10 qualifications were stripped

[68] *Post Natal.* 31 May 1980.
[69] *Daily News.* 9 April 1979.
[70] Inanda Support Group. Minutes. 17 April 1982.
[71] Circular from the Verulam Magistrate. C. Purvis. 17 September 1980.

of these when they moved to the new scheme.)[72] When Newtown was proclaimed a formal township in April 1982, 25,000 people had moved there. A Surplus People Project survey conducted among new arrivals showed that one of the main reasons for leaving their old shacks was that 'tenants (had) found themselves subject to the whims of the landlord'.[73]

The manner in which a committee was formed, purportedly to represent the Newtown community, is instructive for the way in which established local interests moved to protect their positions. Initially, towards the end of 1980, the Verulam magistrate appointed a liaison committee, on which sat Rogers Ngcobo, local indunas and several other landlords.[74] Most of the landlords on the committee were opposed to the scheme, partly for the reason of losing income from departing tenants (whose places they were not supposed to fill) and partly for the more general reason of the state seeming to move against their interests. Rogers Ngcobo was particularly vociferous, accusing first the Department of CAD of having acted improperly in appointing the committee, then the Urban Foundation of having pecuniary motives for its role in Newtown.[75] One analysis explained his response as a 'populist' one — as a Member of the KwaZulu Legislative Assembly, he needed to protect his power base by appearing to act in the interests of 'the people'.[76] Whether or not this was a consideration, his stand earned him the chairmanship of the liaison committee which was elected in early 1981 — though by whom it was elected is unclear, as many Newtown residents did not seem to know about it[77] and had in any case organised their own representative structure in October 1980. Fierce conflict ensued between the two committees over who rightfully represented Newtown, and the residents' committee found the liaison committee in its way whenever it tried to negotiate with the Verulam magistrate.

Other kinds of removals followed. From early 1982, the state began to number shacks, then prosecute tenants on South African Development Trust land, invoking Section 1 of the Prevention of Illegal Squatting Act of 1951. Amidst considerable differences of opinion at various levels in the CAD hierarchy as to which tenants were 'illegal' and which not, and vigorous legal defence raising a myriad of technical arguments, the state backed down on many such cases.[78]

In a second line of attack, and in apparent attempts both to deflect attention away from the Department of CAD and to depoliticise the issue of removals, the Department of Health late in 1981 instructed several Indian landlords either to provide water and sewerage services or to evict tenants. A huge proportion of the Inanda tenantry was thus put at risk. No African landlords were issued with such ultimatums. For some months the instructions were ignored, until in April 1982 random prosecutions began of groups of tenants on Indian-owned land, as well as of

---

[72] *Sunday Tribune*, 22 May 1983.

[73] SPP, *Forced Removals*, p. 396. The fullest available account of the development of Newtown is in ch. 5.

[74] Interview with Newtown fieldworker, 13 October 1980.

[75] Interview with R. Ngcobo, Inanda, October 1980.

[76] G. Seneque, 'The Inanda scheme: a briefing' in *Work in Progress*, 20 (1981).

[77] SPP, *Forced Removals*, p. 401.

[78] Accounts in press; Inanda Support Group, *Information Dossier*.

346   *Journal of Southern African Studies*

the landlords themselves. under the 1936 Land Act. Under such pressure. some landlords began to issue eviction notices and there were angry scenes as tenants in some areas petitioned landlords not to carry these through. Some landlords called in officials to begin demolishing shacks. which led to much bitterness: 'the Indian landlords should bear in mind that they have encouraged the squatters for a number of years to build and improve the dwellings on the said land'.[49] A few tried to withstand the pressure. One. however. after one conviction bowed partially by allowing officials to demolish new shacks. saying at his second trial that he would 'feel awkward' evicting established tenants.[50]

The Indian landlords were being placed in a quite untenable position. for reasons soon made clear. Simultaneous with the first prosecutions was the release of a structure plan for the future of Inanda. which had been commissioned by the Department of CAD and devised by a private Durban consultancy. It acknowledged the logistical necessity of recognising the permanency of the Inanda population. It recommended upgrading accommodation on a planned basis. in a series of 'neighbourhoods'. including some in Released Area 33 but also new ones. stretching well into the less populous Inanda reserve. part of KwaZulu. Judging by the plan. what was being mooted was a huge 'do-it-yourself' township for over half a million people by the year 2000. It also recommended the incorporation of Released Area 33 into KwaZulu as soon as possible. On the very last page of the main report was this advice: 'land owned by non-blacks (i.e. non-Africans) in Released Area 33 should be acquired as necessary in accordance with the approved implementation proposals'.[51] There had been no consultations whatever with tenants and very few with selected landlords. Clearly. the departure of Indian landowners was viewed as a prerequisite for any 'development'. While the plan was sent to the KwaZulu government for ratification. evictions and resentment continued in a climate of increasing uncertainty.

Indian tenants too began to feel isolated and vulnerable. As early as December of 1980. there were reports of friction between Indians and Africans at water points.[52] Many Indian families had apparently accepted that Inanda had become an 'African' area. and began to make application for accommodation elsewhere. In March 1983. the Durban City Council announced that Inanda tenants could not be housed in Phoenix because they were living beyond the Council's jurisdiction.[53] Verulam Town Board declared that it had no housing to offer. and in June. plans were unveiled to rehouse all Indian families in Roodekrans. a new estate near Verulam. yet to be built. In the face of protest. the Department of Community Development decided to undertake a socio-economic survey of the Indian people of Inanda before taking any further action.[54]

Other events fed the general sense of tension and uncertainty in 1983 and 1984. There was a renewed outbreak of cholera in the first months of 1983 (five people had

---

[49] M.T. Mbonambi to H. Hughes. 20 January 1984.
[50] K. Ramnarain. *Daily News*. 5 August 1982.
[51] *Structure Plan for Inanda* (Durban. 1982). p. 65.
[52] *Sunday Tribune Herald*. 28 December 1980.
[53] *Post Natal*. 26 March 1983.
[54] *Daily News*. 27 September 1983.

died of the illness in the previous year) and problems over the supply of water persisted. Also in 1983, a prolonged boycott of PUTCO buses over fare increases occasionally flared into violence between drivers and commuters. [85] There were also isolated incidents of students' protests — for example, towards the end of 1983, police dispersed demonstrations in the vicinity of Ohlange High School. [86] And to exacerbate the deepening divisions between landlords and tenants came a new phenomenon: 'land sharks', going among tenants and 'selling' them their plots, alleging that the Indian owners were disposing of their lands in this way because of the 'Africanising' of the area. When tenants discovered they had been duped and were expected to continue paying rent to the rightful owner, they were understandably bitter — although many turned their anger on the rightful owners rather than on the vanished 'agent'. [87]

At the end of 1984, Inanda's future seemed fixed along the course set for it in the structure plan when the first Inanda township manager was appointed. [88] In January 1985, plaintive letters began appearing in the Durban press: 'Indian residents in Inanda plead that the housing authorities should give us alternative housing immediately, before the problem gets worse and before it's too late for regrets.' [89] Some African landlords appeared to be impatient at the rate of progress in Inanda's conversion into a township. In July, a meeting was held at which one speaker called for a renewed effort to take over Indian lands and shops. Some of those present were so disturbed at the tone that they reported the matter to the Inanda police station. [90] By this stage, the state and its agencies had discovered and forcibly widened every faultline in the social makeup of Inanda.

The events of August 1985

'On Monday, August 5, a rolling school strike and boycott began in most African townships to protest the assassination of Victoria Mxenge. Schoolchildren, especially in KwaMashu, Umlazi, Clermont and Lamontville, started marching from school to school, gathering more and more pupils, until thousands of them were in the streets.' [91]

There were reasons why, all over the country, African secondary school students were in the forefront of resistance to the apartheid policies of the state. Not only were they rejecting an inferior schooling but also 'the closing horizons of their futures'. [92] The added edge in Durban was that, with the important exceptions of Lamontville and Chesterville, all township schools were under the control of the KwaZulu government. In the past, as now, the Minister of Education, Dr O. Dhlomo (also secretary-general of Inkatha), was signalling his government's determination to keep the schools open and 'running normally', despite the boycott calls of the

[85] *Natal Mercury,* 28 January 1983.
[86] *Daily News,* 4 November 1983.
[87] Omar Badsha provided this information.
[88] *Daily News,* 26 October 1984.
[89] *Daily News,* 22 January 1985.
[90] Information from Ela Ramgobin, August 1985.
[91] Sitas, 'Inanda', p. 105.
[92] *Ibid.,* p. 104.

students. Not only was there a heightened ideological conflict here — the students' organisation. the Congress of South African Students, was the backbone of UDF support in the townships — but an overlay of generational conflict as well. as youth came to be identified with the UDF and adults with a more conservative disposition and Inkatha. Over the week beginning on 5 August. in all Durban's African townships students came out on the street (attracting 'fringe' elements whose motives were less clear). attempting to assert their hegemony. They were met by vicious police action. followed by a counteractionary thrust from Inkatha. which seemed. in the bigger townships. to win back the initiative. While these battles left a trail of death. injury and arson in their wake — shops and 'hate' symbols such as administrative offices were the main targets — a more explosive chain of events was touched off in Inanda. For here. two disturbed streams merged into an uncontained torrent. The first was of local origin. the cumulative strife. deprivation and uncertainty of the unorganised poor: the second. the highly politicised revolt of the youth.

On Monday night, 5 August. one group of youths surrounded the house of a policeman in Ntuzuma. He opened fire. killing one of their number. The following morning. the 'rolling strike'. now enraged. reached Inanda. Police dispersed the marchers with tear gas and bullets. but as they scattered. they lost all control of the situation. What can be described as 'lumpen' youth from Inanda took up and led where the students had left off. [93] In the afternoon. two Indian-owned shops and houses were looted and set alight. One of these belonged to one of the most prominent landowners. Laljeeth Rattan. He managed to remove his family before the attack. Police intervened to disperse looters but a crowd regrouped on the main road. where they set up roadblocks and stoned cars and buses. By late afternoon. hundreds of Indian people. having taken fright. had been turned into refugees. They congregated in the Greenbury Hall. Phoenix. [94] where a wrangle began to 'claim' them. involving the House of Delegates and state-sponsored civil defence groups on the one side and more popular housing action groups on the other.

The same pattern — of looting and burning Indian-owned properties. and stoning vehicles on the main road — continued throughout Wednesday. by the end of which approximately twenty Indian-owned premises had been gutted and well over a thousand Indians had found their way to the Greenbury Hall. It was the same again for most of Thursday. on which day one driver was killed and another injured as a result of the stoning. The Indian refugees felt that the police had been of little assistance. In fact. the police seem to have been very thin on the ground. concentrating their attempts on keeping the road clear. At scenes of looting. their response

[93] Accounts concur that students were not in the lead in Inanda. In charting the week's events. it would be tedious to footnote every item. The account has been compiled from the following sources: news coverage in the local press: Meer. *Unrest in Natal*: crisis committee meetings: eyewitness reports: conversations with journalists and photographers. It must be pointed out that the local press. while covering events widely. contained very few firsthand accounts (because of the obvious difficulty of reporting them) although the *Daily News* was better in this respect than the others. Also. one has to be wary of local bias — 'marauding blacks' and 'rampaging mobs' (referring to the protesters) as opposed to 'groups of Inkatha supporters' (referring to the impis). for example.

[94] Not all of those leaving made their way to the hall. although it is safe to conclude that the vast majority did so.

seems to have been very much of a 'hit and run' type: firing on crowds, making arrests and moving off again. [95] Medical evidence confirmed eyewitness accounts that up to Thursday, it was mostly people in their teens and early twenties involved in arson, and police were inflicting the casualties, in the form of bullet wounds. [96]

One account of the unrest in Inanda tells as much about domestic relations and unexpected opportunities as it does of the attack itself. It was gathered by Fatima Meer not many days after the events described:

We spoke to Beatrice, who has taken over the Govender house — six very dark rooms with a verandah. She had rented a room from them for the last fifteen years. That she had been close to them was reflected in her distinctly Indian-accented English. She said she was a member of Inkatha. "When they came to attack. I hid the Indians and I told them that this was my house". After the mob left, the Indians took what they could carry and went away. She says she will buy the house now because the Govenders will not come back. [97]

Late on Thursday afternoon, the character of attacks began to change. Firstly, increasing numbers of adults were caught up in the looting and burning of shops and houses. Secondly, stab and assault wounds were inflicted for the first time. The latter was indicative of a new element in all the African areas of the city: vigilante impis (armed contingents) wielding spears, sticks, knobkerries and the like and acting in the name of Inkatha. From Thursday night, impis were being deployed widely, dispersing youths and searching for stolen goods. In Inanda, their entry caused the violence to spin off in a new direction, as became clear on Friday afternoon.

Meanwhile, as refugees crowded into the hall in Phoenix, panic spread throughout the estate, particularly in those units bordering on Inanda. As rumours spread of a 'repeat of 1949', men began to arm themselves and form into vigilante groups. [98] The Natal Indian Congress (NIC), senior organisation in the Natal UDF and for eighteen months campaigning for the withdrawal of police and army from the townships, found itself in the awkward position of calling upon these same personnel for protection, and a limited army patrol was despatched to Phoenix.

Events reached their pitch in Inanda on Friday, 9 August. Incidents of incendiarism (including the setting alight of sugar cane on the fringes of Inanda) and stone-throwing continued, but the focus was on the area surrounding the Mahatma Gandhi Settlement. Both on the Phoenix and Inanda sides, armed crowds massed early in the morning. A small army contingent made feeble attempts to disperse the opposing factions, then withdrew. The Inanda crowd, estimated at about 300, charged into the Settlement and set numerous buildings alight. The Indian crowd, calling itself the Phoenix Boys, followed. A group of refugees, left homeless after

---

[95] Certainly this is what appeared to be the case judging from aerial media coverage.

[96] Medical report to the crisis committee, 10 August 1985. It is impossible to work out a separate death toll for Inanda. For the whole of Durban, it rose to about seventy, of which around half were police-inflicted fatalities and half the result of spear and assault wounds. The full death toll for Inanda is estimated at between fifteen and twenty.

[97] In Meer, *Unrest in Natal*, p. 50.

[98] See Haysom, *Apartheid's Private Army*, pp. 126-7.

350 *Journal of Southern African Studies*

another township conflict,[99] was caught in the middle. Mewa Ramgobin, a prominent NIC and UDF leader and then standing trial for treason, nearly lost his life at the hands of the Phoenix Boys as he tried to remonstrate with them. In all the violence, Gandhi's home 'Savordaya' and the school which bore his wife's name, Kasturbai Gandhi, were destroyed.

The tragic symbolism of the burning of the Gandhi Settlement went far beyond the immediate act of the violent destruction of a 'place of peace'. It signified also the void of political organisation and ideas, on all sides of the Group Areas divide, which could have allayed, or at least toned down, the confrontations. In the early 1970s, Mewa Ramgobin and Richard Turner (assassinated in 1978) had organised 'peace camps' at the Gandhi Settlement, in an effort to promote nonracial harmony. The Inanda of the mid-1980s was transformed, all of that forgotten. One of the Hambanathi refugees was left to reflect, 'It is a great pity. These people are uneducated and do not know what they are doing.'[100] The other symbolism of the burning of the Settlement is revealed in the case of an Inanda couple, Voice and Bobby Jugdeo.[101] They were married in 1963, she an African domestic servant, he the son of an Indian landowner in Inanda. 'It was a joyous occasion, and there was much merriment in Inanda', Voice recalled. In time, Bobby inherited the four-hectare plot, on which he kept small stock. Later, they rented land to tenants. Their children — boys with Hindi names, girls with English ones — attended Indian schools adjacent to Inanda. In the week of the violence, they were attacked, their house burnt, their livestock stolen. Bewildered as family and friends turned against them, they were forced to flee.[102] An area where some measure of Indian and African co-residence, if fraught in some of its aspects, had continued for more than a century, and the last such area of any significance in the country, had been torn apart.

As the sides were withdrawing on late Friday morning, a large impi from a nearby shanty town, Lindelani, arrived on the scene. It made repeated attacks on Friday and Saturday. They were repulsed, but there were a number of deaths. The effect of this development was to turn the Inanda shanty town against the Lindelani one (whether as part of some competition for dominance on the part of landlords is unclear) and to turn many against Inkatha.

By Saturday, there were 2,000 refugees in Phoenix, while in Inanda isolated incidents continued. Armed vigilantes patrolled the Phoenix side of the border and the atmosphere along it remained tense. The chairman of the House of Delegates, Amichand Rajbansi, paid a brief visit to the area and announced relief measures.

[99] In August 1984 and again in May 1985, the homes of several suspected UDF sympathisers were petrol-bombed in Hambanathi, a township near Tongaat on the Natal North Coast. Many were made homeless and there were a number of deaths. The township authorities threatened the residents concerned with eviction, on the grounds that houses were not being occupied and rent not paid. Many cannot return for fear of their lives.

[100] *Daily News*, 10 August 1985.

[101] Inter-marriage between Indian and African people in Inanda has been extremely rare. While there might be many reasons for this, it is necessary here simply to point out again that conditions have hardly been conducive to a breaking down of cultural, religious or racial distinctions; in fact, quite the reverse has been the case.

[102] *Sunday Tribune Herald*, 25 August 1985.

while in the centre of town, various organisations affiliated to the UDF, as well as church groups, met to form a crisis committee to provide assistance, collect affidavits and to try to restore calm. On Sunday, Inkatha held a 'peace rally' near to the shell of the Gandhi Settlement, to signal reassertion of its position in the townships. In addition, announced Dr Dhlomo, '[W]e have come here to reassure our Indian brothers and sisters of Inkatha's willingness to co-operate with them in all efforts that are aimed at restoring peace, law and order in the area.'[103] Some Indian shopkeepers declared that unless they had a firm guarantee from the KwaZulu government that they would be secure after incorporation, they would not rebuild their premises. Some, however, did venture back — those whose only livelihood and investments had been their land and their buildings. 'My house and farm is worth a lot of money, therefore I decided to return to Inanda,' said one.[104] After the violence, even lower compensations were being offered to them.[105] And after long, drawn-out disputes with authorities, the Indian tenants have been rehoused in Phoenix and Verulam.[106]

At the end of the week of violence, forty-two Indian-owned shops and businesses, as many houses and three surgeries operated by an Indian doctor, had been destroyed by fire. The only Indian shops left intact were in upper Inanda, near the police station, and in the Matikwe area. One of them belongs to the Haffejee family, who have traded there since 1903. It stands opposite the Inanda police station, and their adjoining petrol garage was guarded by police. They had lost four other stores in Inanda.

The last incident of violence in Inanda, identifiable as part of the August upsurge, came exactly a week after it had begun. On Tuesday 13 August, the bodies of three Indian men were found burnt on the Phoenix-Inanda border. They were all from the same family: a father, his son and his brother-in-law. The father had fled his house in Inanda a few days before.[107]

In September, renewed clashes occurred in African townships as Inkatha impis searched out suspected or known UDF supporters and threatened scholars. Inanda escaped this violence, but the more basic economic insecurity persisted. At the beginning of September, clashes over access to water assumed an 'ethnic' dimension. People from Piesang River, allegedly Xhosa-speaking, had been using the taps in Newtown, whose occupants then barred them from the privilege. The shanty dwellers retaliated by preventing buses from entering Newtown. Talks between the leaders of the opposing parties, arranged by members of the KwaZulu Legislative Assembly, averted fresh violence, but the conflict continued to simmer, with Lindelani people also becoming involved in 'anti-Pondo' actions.[108]

[103] *Natal Mercury*, 12 August 1985.
[104] *Natal Mercury*, 23 August 1985.
[105] Meer, *Unrest in Natal*, p. 43.
[106] The refugees, who early on were put in the hands of the House of Delegates, initially refused to move from the hall until they had been allocated council housing. Pressure was put on them to move to a school in Verulam until housing could be arranged, and those who made this move were assured of preferential treatment. The refugees' committee claimed that promises had been made but not kept (such as waiving the normally required deposits). Problems were eventually sorted out and all families were housed by the end of 1985.
[107] *Natal Mercury*, 23 August 1985.
[108] Evidence to crisis committee, 5 October 1985.

In late September 1985. the state released its long-awaited consolidation proposals for KwaZulu. As if to underline its continuing commitment to divisive policies and strategies. its recommendation for the Inanda region was that three more farms to the north of Released Area 33 — Groeneberg. Buffelsdraai and the original Inanda. all housing stable Indian communities — be incorporated into KwaZulu. [109]

Political responses to the Inanda violence

While none of the political organisations directly concerned with the violence had any measurable presence in Inanda. what happened there was critical for all of them. and they responded rapidly. The NIC. senior partner in the Natal UDF. condemned Inkatha for the general unrest and the violence as the work of 'mobs of criminals looting and burning indiscriminately'. and through the crisis committee. called for peace. Yet even those at ground floor level in the UDF had lost control of events. so that the leadership. with its strong commitment to nonviolent change. had little hope of reimposing it. Of greater concern to the NIC itself was a loss of support in its constituency areas. notably Phoenix. A survey conducted by Fatima Meer at the end of August found 'a marked shift towards conservatism on the part of coloured and particularly Indian people'[110] and this observation was echoed in many quarters. In order to try to reattract support. the NIC launched a major press campaign on the weekend of 10 and 11 August.

Chief Buthelezi of Inkatha blamed the malaise on students. the UDF and the ANC. and held that there was 'no anti-Indian sentiment involved in the attacks against Indian homes and shops'. although he added that there was 'a lot of resentment' that some Indians had participated in the new tricameral parliament. Inkatha refused to meet with the crisis committee. probably believing that it could bring the townships under control on its own terms. especially as the police were generally supportive of its endeavours. Its leadership remained equivocal on responsibility for the actions of the impis. asserting only that the movement 'had taken full control of public safety' in the townships. [111]

The Azanian People's Organisation. a black consciousness grouping. felt that the violence had been 'misdirected'. and that black people ought not 'to give any leeway for the enemy to promote ethnicity and division'. [112] Smaller parties. such as those connected to the House of Delegates. also blamed students and the UDF for the violence. Y.S. Chinsamy of the Reform Party believed that it had not been racially motivated because no Indian people had been assaulted or killed. and had been able to leave before the looting of their properties began. [113]

Generally. Inanda was perceived as suffering an overspill of the violence from its epicentres in nearby African townships: there was little that was particular or distinct about it at all. One exception to this view was Ela Ramgobin. a social worker in Inanda. NIC executive member. and grand-daughter of Mahatma Gandhi. who

[109] Full list of recommendations in *Daily News*. 23 September 1985.
[110] Meer. *Unrest in Natal*. p. 77.
[111] *Natal Mercury*. 13 August 1985.
[112] *Natal Mercury*. 10 August 1985.
[113] *Post Natal*. 21-24 August 1985.

placed the responsibility for the events firmly at the door of the state: 'One has to look at the history of Inanda to put it in perspective. People in that area have been asking for help for years. . .'[114]

The explanation for the more general political response is that all these organisations, in different ways, were locked into a political discourse the primary categories of which were racial ones. In the moment of crisis, it would have been inconceivable to admit to any form whatsoever of 'racial hostility', since the implications in the Natal region would have been deeply damaging to them, albeit for very different reasons in each case. In line with the UDF's vision of a nonracial and democratic future, stripped of all legally-enforced segregation, Inanda had been held up as an example of how Indian and African people could live together in harmony. For Inkatha, appeasing racial fears and promising the ability to restore calm and to offer security would earn credibility among Indian people in Natal and cement alliances with reformist groupings against common political foes. In turn, such an option would appeal to the parties in the new Indian house. It would confirm their position that the way to ensure racial harmony was by the separate representation of minority rights.

None was able to go beyond 'African-Indian' relations, to examine instead relations of wealth and poverty and how race had been hitched to vested interest over many years in a place such as Inanda. For the 'Inanda mobs' could not be excused as criminals and hooligans, however obnoxious their behaviour had been. They were local people experiencing ever-increasing degrees of poverty and deprivation, who had identified symbols of wealth and well-being (most certainly without the assistance of the police, as one African landowner had alleged) on the other side of a great divide. That they singled out Indian examples should be seen as the result of the way in which state policies have manipulated racial divisions over a long period, but more thoroughly so in the five years preceding the violence. Two faultlines intersected and with the prompting of student action, the structure gave way.

There was an identifiable pattern to the violence − it had a set of 'rules' and a purpose, 'the use of force being proportionate to that purpose'.[115] That no Indians were hurt or killed on their premises − though when they left in cars and trucks they had stones thrown at them − may perhaps have been good fortune. That nearly all of them left as soon as they could might also have minimised the possibility of injury (although Fatima Meer believed that their departure left their properties completely open to attack).[116] But more likely was the fact that the violence was not the result of any provocative or aggressive action on their part, which might have been interpreted as hostility towards the personal integrity of those of another race. The causes were altogether different, as hopefully this analysis has shown.

[114] *Post Natal*, 21-24 August 1985.
[115] E. Hobsbawm, 'The rules of violence' in his *Revolutionaries* (London, 1977), p. 212.
[116] *Post Natal*, 21-24 August 1985.

354   *Journal of Southern African Studies*

Conclusion: a repeat of 1949?

'A repeat of 1949' was a statement carried in the local media and felt in some
quarters in 1985. Reading Webster's anatomy of the 1949 violence, [117] one can find
some uncomfortable similarities: competition for trading preserves, expressed in
racial form: friction between landlords and tenants in a shanty town: the ambivalent
position of Indians in the South African political order; the lack of synchronisation
between leadership and ground-floor levels in popular political organisations. Then,
as now. Africans had to carry passes and could not proceed beyond a certain level of
skill in the workplace. and urban experiences of Indian and African people differed
in many respects.

One must not be persuaded by the similarities. There were differences, too, most
notably perhaps in the 'rules of violence' on the two occasions. Yet when the events
of 1949 and 1985 are put into their broader context and approached historically, it
becomes clear that superficial comparisons are of little use. In 1949, the Nationalist
government was new: there was no Group Areas Act and therefore no Phoenix and
Chatsworth: there was no bantustan policy and no Inkatha; there was no centralised
urban policy towards Africans and no Umlazi and KwaMashu: there was no heavily
populated Inanda. The conflict in 1949 provided the state with justification to push
ahead with its radical policies of segregation. The conflict of 1985 is an end product
of that process.

---

[117] E. Webster. 'The 1949 Durban ''riots'' – a case study in race and class' in P. Bonner (ed.).
Working Papers in Southern African Studies (Johannesburg. 1977); see also L. Kuper. *An African
Bourgeoisie* (New Haven. 1965). ch. 19.

Legal Dimensions of the Issue

[22]

THE PATHOLOGY OF A LEGAL SYSTEM: CRIMINAL JUSTICE IN SOUTH AFRICA*

SYDNEY KENTRIDGE †

A surprisingly large number of American lawyers visit South Africa or follow closely what is happening in that country. Their fascination with the legal institutions of a small and distant country, whose common law is the Roman-Dutch law, has often struck me as remarkable. I do not complain of it, as one of its agreeable consequences (from my point of view, at least) is that I have been invited to give this lecture. Part of the explanation, no doubt, is that the courts in South Africa deal with laws and institutions that bear an uncomfortably close resemblance to those with which American courts had to deal in the fairly recent past—laws and institutions that permit or even ordain discrimination on grounds of race and colour. Perhaps a more profound reason for American attention to South Africa is that South Africa exemplifies in the most intense form what is possibly the major international issue of the second half of the twentieth century—namely, the correlation between skin colour and enjoyment of political power, civil liberty, and economic affluence. Attention is focused on South Africa not because it has quantitatively less freedom, less justice, or less democratic government than a hundred other countries one could name. Those goods do exist in South Africa, but they are strictly rationed on the sole basis of colour—not on citizenship or birth or merit, but colour alone. Discrimination on the ground of colour in South Africa is not an aberration to be deprecated and remedied, but an institution that is authorised and, frequently, actually commanded by statute. That is the essential difference from the discrimination that undoubtedly continues to be found in the United States, in England, or in New Zealand. It is not discrimination but integration that is expressly forbidden by the Parliament of South Africa.

At the time when *Brown v. Board of Education* [1] was before the United States Supreme Court, and the doctrine of "separate but equal" was on the point of disappearing from American jurisprudence, the same doctrine, which had been blessed twenty years

---

* This Article is based on the Owen J. Roberts Memorial Lecture, delivered 18 October 1979, under the auspices of the Pennsylvania Chapter of the Order of the Coif, the Law Alumni Society, and the University of Pennsylvania Law School.

† Senior Counsel, Johannesburg Bar; Barrister at Law, Lincoln's Inn. B.A. 1941, University of the Witwatersrand; B.A. 1948, M.A. 1953, Oxford University.

[1] 347 U.S. 483 (1954).

604   *UNIVERSITY OF PENNSYLVANIA LAW REVIEW*   [Vol. 128:603

earlier by South Africa's highest court,[2] was also disappearing from South African law. It was, however, disappearing in a different direction. A short statute, known as the Reservation of Separate Amenities Act, 1953,[3] simply and clearly provided not merely that public premises or public vehicles would be set apart or reserved for the exclusive use of persons belonging to a particular race or class,[4] but also that any such setting apart or reservation would not be invalid on the ground that the premises or vehicles reserved for the use of one class were not equal to those reserved for any other race or class.[5]

Another aspect of the South African system makes it a particular subject of interested observation by lawyers in Western countries. Notwithstanding statutes such as that I have just mentioned, and notwithstanding the increasingly authoritarian tone of government in South Africa, the traditional forms of legal process have not been abandoned. Trials, including trials of enemies or critics of the government (two categories which those in high levels of government often have difficulty distinguishing), take place in ordinary courts, open to the press and usually to the public, before the ordinary judges of the land. The accused are entitled to be defended by counsel, and there are always counsel willing to defend them. For many years (and for good reasons into which I need not enter here), we have had no jury trials in South Africa. The judge himself is the trier of fact. Save for this feature, however, a criminal trial in South Africa, up to very recent times at least, was conducted subject to those rules of evidence and procedure that, with the English language and the game of cricket, have been the most beneficent and lasting legacies of the British Empire.

But in very recent times, under the stress of sharpened conflict between the rulers and the ruled that has gone hand in hand with the increasingly authoritarian tone of government to which I have referred, we have witnessed—or, some of us, experienced—a profound distortion of our traditional legal system. A distortion, but not a disappearance. So there is something to be observed, by ourselves as South African lawyers, as well as by foreign lawyers who have a fundamentally similar conception of what constitutes a fair trial: the pathology of a system of criminal justice. This applies largely, although not entirely, to political trials, that is, prosecutions for

---

[2] Minister of Posts & Telegraphs v. Rasool, [1934] App. Div. [A.D.] 167.

[3] Act No. 49 of 1953.

[4] *Id.* § 2.

[5] *Id.* § 3(b).

political offences. It is this pathological condition to which I shall devote most of this lecture. I shall describe it, attempt to define the "philosophy" underlying this departure from previously accepted norms of proper judicial process, and finally say a word about those who participate in it, both judges and lawyers.

There are two preliminary observations to be made. First, by reason of the similarity between the American system and the South African system, one may take this to be an implicit exercise in comparative criminal procedure. Comparative studies, especially in this field, tend to contain a strong moral element, sometimes disquieting but to American lawyers, no doubt, usually satisfying. The procedural novelties—to use a neutral term—that I shall describe have been created not by the judges, but by a sovereign legislature that is unfettered by any such eighteenth-century institution as a bill of rights. Americans may understandably take comfort in the fact that their Constitution, as presently interpreted, does not permit such things to happen. In many Western countries, including the United States, however, there are persons in powerful positions who maintain that existing forms of criminal procedure are weighted too heavily in favour of the accused, and that politically motivated crimes in particular call for special forms of procedure making it easier to obtain convictions. An examination of what may happen to a legal system when these views prevail may therefore be of some general interest.

The second preliminary observation to be made concerns the legitimacy of the criticism of the South African system of political trials. The South African government justifies its security legislation, including those criminal procedure statutes to which I shall refer, on the ground that South Africa faces a serious threat of subversion from within and outside its borders. The existence of this threat may be fully accepted. Persons charged with political offences in South Africa have often been shown to have been engaged in activities that in any country would be regarded as criminal, activities involving actual or potential violence against the state. The question remains, however, whether this undeniable fact justifies the forms of procedure under which those charged with such offences are now tried.

Further, much as the South African government resents criticisms of its laws and practices, it has in a sense invited them. For the South African government firmly maintains that it is a part of the free world and that it is indeed the main, if not the sole, representative in Africa of Western civilization. The distinguished and perceptive judge in whose honour this lecture is presented, in a celebrated address given at Oxford, referred to the rule of law as an idea recognised by what he called "highly civilised nations." Asked what countries he would include in this category, Mr. Justice Roberts replied: " 'My test would be, first, a country that has a representative form of government; second, a country where individual liberty and freedom are protected by law; [and third], where there are bounds and limits to what the government can do to an individual.' " [6] As a South African lawyer, that is the criterion by which I would want my legal system to be judged. I am not impressed when I am told that things are done worse in the USSR or Uganda or, for that matter, in the Comoro Islands. In South Africa we are the inheritors of two of the great legal systems of the world, the Roman-Dutch law of Holland and the common law of England. We should invite and accept judgment by the standards of those systems.

I. Criminal Procedure in South Africa

A. *The Traditional Standards*

In order to understand the pathology of a body, one must know something of its normal functions. It is not necessary for me to describe at length the normal rules of South African criminal procedure, as most of its features will be exceedingly familiar. First, the rules relating to arrest, with or without warrant, are similar in general to those of American law. The arrested person has the right to remain silent and must be warned by the police that he has this right before he is interrogated. He has a right to consult a legal adviser immediately after he has been arrested. He must be brought before a court within forty-eight hours of his arrest. He may apply for bail. Even before the process in court commences, he has (or had in the past) the broad protection of the writ of habeas corpus, or its Roman-Dutch equivalent, the writ *de homine libero exhibendo*.[7] His trial is an adversary proceeding in which he is

---

[6] Discussion by Mr. Justice Owen J. Roberts at Oxford following his lecture, The Rule of Law in the International Community (Nov., 1951), *quoted in* Goodhart, *The Rule of Law and Absolute Sovereignty*, 106 U. Pa. L. Rev. 943, 943 (1958).

[7] *See* 6 J. Voet, The Selective Voet, Being the Commentary on the Pandects 528-29 (P. Gane trans. 1957); Kentridge, Habeas Corpus *Procedure in South Africa*, 79 S. Afr. L.J. 283, 285 (1962).

In the Roman-Dutch law the approach to this writ is entirely without technicality. As stated by one South African judge, the rule is simply that every arrest is prima facie unlawful and must be justified in court by the arresting authority if

protected by the privilege against self-incrimination and in which the burden of proof rests upon the prosecution. He has the right to counsel of his choice (subject, admittedly, to paying the going fee or to finding someone else willing to pay it) and, in general, the right to be confronted with the witnesses against him. The rule against hearsay evidence applies with full, some would even say outmoded, rigour. And no confession is admissible against him that was not in all respects freely and voluntarily made.

Of course, as in all systems, these rules have not always been observed. Confessions made under physical or mental duress do slip past judicial scrutiny; often the requisite police warning of the right to be silent is not given; various statutes alter the burden of proof; the accused cannot always afford counsel, especially the black accused who, in an average year, constitute ninety per cent of all criminal defendants.[8] Nonetheless, these rules, some statutory and some judge-made, have set a standard of due process, the standard by which the fairness of a trial ought to be judged.

The time has now come to examine to what extent these standards still apply in South Africa to trials for political offences. I do not pause to define minutely what is meant by a political offence. It has sometimes been disputed in South Africa, as it has elsewhere, whether such offences exist. It is enough to say that I am referring to crimes committed with the political motive of altering or protesting against the current political dispensation.

South Africa has had an interesting—some would say an over-interesting—history of political turbulence, which has been marked by many series of political trials, including trials for high treason. During the Anglo-Boer War, many Boers living in the British colonies of the Cape of Good Hope and Natal assisted the Boer forces; in 1914 some thousands of diehard veterans of the Anglo-Boer War went into rebellion against the government of what was then the Union of South Africa; in 1922 there was a revolt of white workers on the Witwatersrand; and from 1939 to 1945 a number of Afrikaner nationalists acted in support of the German cause. All these events resulted in trials for treason. In 1958, thirty leaders of the African National Congress and its political allies were charged with con-

called upon to do so. Principal Immigration Officer v. Narayansamy, [1916] Transvaal Provincial Div. [T.P.D.] 274, 276 (quoting the unreported opinion of Wessels, J., in the court below). See also the powerful opinion of Rumpff, C.J., in Wood v. Ondangwa Tribal Auth., [1975] 2 S.A. 294, 310-11 (App. Div.), in which the Appellate Division (South Africa's final appeals court) reemphasised that the remedy should be construed as broadly as possible.

[8] *See, e.g.,* SOUTH AFRICA INSTITUTE OF RACE RELATIONS, A SURVEY OF RACE RELATIONS IN SOUTH AFRICA 66 (1978).

spiracy to overthrow the state by violence. The charge there too was treason. This trial differed in an important respect from previous South African treason trials in that most of the accused were black. After a trial which lasted from August, 1958, to March, 1961, all the accused were acquitted.[9] All these trials were conducted according to the normal rules of South African criminal procedure. Indeed, when the charge was treason, the prosecution had the added burden of complying with a provision that, up to 1977, had always been embodied in the South African Criminal Procedure Acts.[10] These Acts provided that no court would "convict any accused of treason except upon the evidence of two witnesses where one overt act is charged, or where two or more overt acts are so charged, upon the evidence of one witness to each such overt act." [11]

B. *The Terrorism Act*

Possibly because of the highly publicised failure of the prosecution in the treason trial of 1958 to 1961, possibly influenced also by the happenings at Sharpeville in 1960 [12] as well as by disturbances in the Cape in 1962,[13] the South African government adopted a new approach to the prosecution of political offenders. After experimenting with amendments to various other statutes—all designed to facilitate the prosecution and conviction of persons alleged to be carrying on subversive activities against the state—the government, in 1967, put through Parliament an Act that introduced, under the name of "terroristic activities" or "terrorism," a new form of statutory treason.[14] According to this Act, a person is guilty of the

---

[9] The record of this trial is analyzed in T. KARIS, THE TREASON TRIAL IN SOUTH AFRICA (1965).

[10] *E.g.*, Criminal Procedure Act, No. 56 of 1955, § 256(b), *repealed by* Criminal Procedure Act, No. 51 of 1977, § 208.

[11] *Id.* This provision was first enacted in England in the reign of William III in the Statute of Treasons of 1695, 7 & 8 Will. 3, c. 3, § 2. It was repealed in England by the Treason Act, 1945, 8 & 9 Geo. 6, c. 44, § 2, sched. 1, and in South Africa by Criminal Procedure Act, No. 51 of 1977, § 208. It is embodied in U.S. CONST. art. 3, § 3, cl. 1. For a further discussion of this provision, see text accompanying notes 34-40 *infra*.

[12] On March 21, 1960, a crowd of some thousands of blacks gathered at the police station in Sharpeville (about 30 miles south of Johannesburg) to protest against the pass laws. The police fired on the crowd. Sixty-nine blacks were killed, and 180 were wounded.

[13] On 21st November 1972 in Paarl, a small town near Cape Town, a rioting black mob killed two whites and seriously injured three others. They also set fire to shops.

[14] Terrorism Act, No. 83 of 1967. For a thorough, perceptive, and authoritative account of this Act and of other South African security laws generally, see J. DUGARD, HUMAN RIGHTS AND THE SOUTH AFRICAN LEGAL ORDER 250-365 (1978).

offence of participating in terroristic activities if he commits any act whatsoever with the intention of endangering the maintenance of law and order in the Republic of South Africa.[15] Upon conviction he is liable to the penalties appropriate to common law treason, including the death penalty, and subject to a minimum sentence of five years' imprisonment, which may not be suspended.[16]

This Act is a considerable extension of the concept of treason. In the Roman-Dutch law, the crime of treason is limited to acts committed with the intention of overthrowing the state by violence. That element is not essential under the Terrorism Act. On the contrary, the Act, with the aid of presumptions that transfer the burden of proof to the accused,[17] covers a range of offences going well beyond what would ordinarily be regarded as terrorism or treason. For example, the Act prohibits activities that are likely "to cause substantial financial loss to any person or the State." [18] Thus, if it is proved that the accused organised a strike or an economic boycott that was likely to result in such loss, then, unless he can prove beyond a reasonable doubt that that was not his intent, he must be found guilty of terrorism.

The Act's practical effect is greatly extended by the inclusion of a second class of actions that would not ordinarily be regarded as treasonable, namely, actions calculated to create feelings of hostility between the white and black inhabitants of the country.[19] An actual case illustrates the operation of this provision. A young black man wrote a violently anti-white poem. He showed it to only one person, a seventeen-year-old girl. The publication of the poem to this girl was found to have had the likely result of causing her to feel hostile towards whites. The accused could not prove beyond reasonable doubt that he did not intend her to have such feelings. He was consequently convicted of terrrorism and sentenced to five years' imprisonment.[20]

The Act contains many procedural provisions designed to assist the prosecution. The rule against documentary hearsay evidence is modified in favour of the state by an extraordinary, but much used, provision.[21] No court is permitted to grant bail to a

---

[15] Terrorism Act, No. 83 of 1967, § 2(1).

[16] *Id.*

[17] *Id.* § 2(2).

[18] *Id.* § 2(2)(h).

[19] *Id.* § 2(2)(i).

[20] State v. Motsau (Witwatersrand Local Div. Apr., 1974) (unreported).

[21] *See* Terrorism Act, No. 83 of 1967, § 2(3). Under this provision, the prosecutor may produce, not through a witness but from his own file, any document that on

person charged under the Act without the consent of the attorney-general.[22]   Acquittal does not preclude subsequent arraignment on another charge arising out of the same conduct.[23]   Perhaps most remarkable, this statute became law on 12th June 1967, but its substantive, procedural, and evidentiary provisions are all deemed to have come into effect in June, 1962.[24]   That is to say, the Act was made to apply retrospectively to a time five years before it was enacted.   In one leading case, the accused had actually been arrested and in custody for about a year before the Terrorism Act was passed; they were nonetheless charged and convicted under that Act.[25]

These provisions do not in themselves explain the actual work-ing of the Terrorism Act.   The key to its practical operation is to be found in section 6.   This section permits the police, without judicial warrant, to detain any person who any senior police officer has reason to believe either committed an offence under the Act or has any knowledge of such an offence.[26]   The object of the detention is interrogation, and the detention may continue either until the detainee has answered all questions put to him to the satisfaction of the police or until the police are convinced that "no useful pur-pose will be served by his further detention"[27]—a phrase with chilling implications.   It is also expressly provided that no court of law may pronounce upon the validity of a detention under sec-tion 6, nor order the release of a detainee.[28]   Further, no person may have access to a detainee,[29] that is, he is held incommunicado. He may not see or even communicate by letter with a lawyer, a private doctor, or a member of his family.   Habeas corpus is not permitted.[30]   The Act does not authorise physical ill-treatment of detainees,[31] and indeed assault and torture as a means of interroga-

---

its face emanated from any organization of which the accused was at any time a member.   The document is admissible against the accused, and its contents are prima facie presumed to be true.   *See, e.g.,* State v. Malepane, [1979] 1 S.A. 1009, 1015 (Witwatersrand Local Div.) (per Le Roux, J.).

[22] Terrorism Act, No. 83 of 1967, § 5(f).

[23] *Id.* § 5(h).

[24] *Id.* § 9(1).

[25] State v. Tuhadeleni, [1969] 1 S.A. 153 (App. Div.).

[26] Terrorism Act, No. 83 of 1967, § 6(1).

[27] *Id.*

[28] *Id.* § 6(5).

[29] *Id.* § 6(6).

[30] *Id.* § 6(5).

[31] Nxasana v. Minister of Justice, [1976] 3 S.A. 745, 748 (Durban & Coast Local Div.) (per Didcott, J.).   *Cf.* Rossouw v. Sachs, [1964] 2 S.A. 551, 561 (App. Div.) (decided under § 17 of the General Law Amendment Act, No. 37 of 1963, an earlier detention statute).

tion have been officially disavowed by the South African government and by senior police officers. The official attitude is that the only sanction available against a recalcitrant detainee is his continued indefinite detention in solitary confinement, without books, letters, newspapers, or any communication with the outside world.[32] In any country, however, if detained persons have no access to lawyers or to the courts, abuses are bound to occur—as they undoubtedly have in South Africa.

Section 6 detention has a profound effect on the conduct of trials under the Terrorism Act. First, the accused himself will probably have been detained in solitary confinement for weeks, months, or sometimes even years before he is brought to trial. Unless he is a person of extraordinary fortitude, he will probably have made a statement to the police, often in the form of a confession, whether false or true. He is unlikely to understand the rules relating to the admissibility in evidence of his statement. In a disquieting recent development, the police have brought some detainees straight from weeks or months of detention to a court without giving notice to their friends and families. The detainees have then and there been called upon to plead to a complex charge under the Terrorism Act, without the benefit of legal advice or representation. Only after they have pleaded are they able to obtain representation by counsel. Consequently, persons have pleaded guilty to serious charges under this Act without the benefit of legal advice. Perhaps equally important, many of the prosecution witnesses in these trials are persons who have been subjected to prolonged detention in solitary confinement under section 6. Often they too are brought straight from detention to court to give evidence. They will usually have made statements implicating the accused. These statements may be true, but even if they are not, the witness knows that if he retracts, the result may well be either his further detention under section 6 or a charge of perjury.

It is therefore understandable that I have referred to the mode of procedure under this statute as a distortion of South Africa's traditional system of procedure, or as the pathology of a legal system. What has been altered under this new system for trying political offences? To list them briefly: the rules restricting arrest without warrant, the right to be brought before a court speedily after an arrest, the right to bail, the right to legal representation immediately upon arrest, in practice the right to silence, the rule

---

[32] *See, e.g.,* 15 S. AFR. HANSARD cols. 7118-7121 (1978) (statement by Mr. J.T. Kruger, then Minister of Justice, in the House of Assembly in May, 1978).

that the burden of proof is on the prosecution, the rule against hearsay evidence, the court's discretion in sentencing, and along with all of these, the right to habeas corpus. That is to say, a good part of what people in both the United States and South Africa have regarded as essential to a fair trial.

The South African government would justify these departures on the ground that subversion is a real threat in South Africa, that important information about unlawful activities has been obtained by this system of detention without trial, and that many of those convicted under the Terrorism Act were in fact engaged in planning acts of violence against the state. Much of this is true, and the South African government is no doubt entitled to some credit for choosing to try political offenders before the ordinary courts of the land. The reason for this choice may be a residual respect for the judicial process. Or it may be the belief that imprisonment after conviction by a criminal court is politically the most persuasive way of disposing of the accused, and the least likely to provoke internal or international criticism. Either way, the choice is not a discreditable one.

II. The Philosophy Underlying the Terrorism Act

This choice having been made, however, what is the reasoning behind the new, second-class procedure? It is simply that the more serious the crime, the easier it should be to convict the accused. This view has its adherents in all countries. It has often prevailed, especially in the case of political offenders. And it is an understandable view. As Macaulay wrote, in a trial for treason an acquittal must always be considered a defeat of the government.[33] But until recent years, this was not the prevailing philosophy in South Africa any more than it was in the United States of America. For political crime, the traditional view was the opposite one.

I referred earlier to the two-witness rule in treason cases.[34] This has always been an exception in the English law of evidence [35] which, unlike Mosaic law [36] or the canon law,[37] did not require a

---

[33] 7 T. Macaulay, The History of England 313 (Westminster ed., n.d.).

[34] *See* note 11 *supra* & accompanying text.

[35] The only other exception to the English law of evidence in modern times has been perjury, which has a history of its own.

[36] *Deuteronomy* 17:6, 19:15.

[37] According to Professor C.S. Kenny of Cambridge, under canon law no cardinal could be convicted of unchastity without at least 12 witnesses, and a woman could not be a witness. C. Kenny, Outlines of Criminal Law 519 n.6 (19th ed. 1966).

multiplicity of witnesses to prove the commission of a crime. Why should there be this exception in the case of treason? The seventeenth century in England was a century of revolutions and revolutionary plots. Charles II, restored to the throne in 1660, had good reason to fear for his security. Yet one of the first acts passed by the Restoration Parliament was an act requiring proof by two witnesses of certain forms of treason.[38] And in 1695 the Whigs themselves enacted the Statute of Treasons, which reinforced the two-witness rule and provided that persons accused of treason were to be allowed privileges that they had never before enjoyed, such as the right to counsel.[39] This was at a time when the threat of counterrevolution was real and when the only immediate effect of the new law could be to provide the advantages of a fair trial to the government's most intransigent opponents. Perhaps those legislators thought that one day they might again be in opposition. One may nonetheless think that the passage of this law in England in 1695 constituted one of the highest achievements of that Western civilization of which we in South Africa are said to be amongst the heirs and guardians.

Why should anyone think that a person charged with treason required more protection than persons charged with lesser offences? Sir William Blackstone, writing nearly a century after the Statute of Treasons was passed, gave a straightforward answer: "[T]he principal reason undoubtedly is to secure the subject from being sacrificed to fictitious conspiracies, which have been the engines of profligate and crafty politicians in all ages." [40]

The procedure under the South African Terrorism Act represents a complete reversal of the philosophy behind the Statute of Treasons. It embodies a feeling, popular in many places and times, that the more reprehensible an offence is, the easier it ought to be to obtain a conviction, that enemies of the government should not be entitled to the ordinary protection of law, but should be placed at a special disadvantage if accused of a political offence. I do not believe that today special privileges are necessary, but to subject the accused to special disabilities and disadvantages is in a measure to condemn him before he has been tried. The removal of the presumption of innocence is very close to the assumption of guilt.

---

[38] 13 Car. 2, stat. 1, c. 1, § 5 (Treason) (1661).

[39] Statute of Treasons of 1695, 7 & 8 Will. 3, c. 3.

[40] 4 W. BLACKSTONE, COMMENTARIES ° 358. *See* T. MACAULAY, *supra* note 33, at 313-14.

One is reminded of the views of that otherwise humane and enlightened French jurist of the sixteenth century, Jean Bodin, on the crime of witchcraft. He said that persons accused of witchcraft ought to be convicted without further proof unless they could demonstrate their innocence. For, he said, " 'to adhere, in a trial for witchcraft, to ordinary rules of procedure, would result in defeating the law of both God and man.' " [41]

Have the extraordinary rules worked in South Africa? From the point of view of the government, the answer is yes. Information has been extracted from detainees that would probably not have been obtained under the ordinary rules, and persons have been convicted who might have gone free under ordinary procedures. Whether this is worth the price paid is a question of political and moral judgment. One's answer will no doubt depend on the importance one attaches to meeting the criteria for what constitutes a highly civilised nation, as proposed by Mr. Justice Roberts.[42] A South African judge, referring to section 6 of the Terrorism Act, said:

> In providing for the detention for indefinite periods of those who have not been convicted of crimes, for their isolation from legal advice and from their families, and for their interrogation at the risk of self-incrimination, the Legislature has pursued its object by the enactment of measures which are undoubtedly foreign to the ordinary principles of our law. Whether the end justifies the drastic means that have been sanctioned because they are necessary in troubled times for the security of the State, as they are apparently thought by Parliament to be, is a controversial question . . . .[43]

Later in the same judgment he said that effect must be given "to stringent enactments which are positively shown by Parliament's choice of plain words to have been meant, however offensive to conventional legal standards they may be." [44] He described this conclusion as axiomatic in South African law. On this point he is undoubtedly correct.

---

[41] 4 J. Bodin, Démonomanie ch. 4 (1598), *quoted in* C. Kenny, *supra* note 37, at 517-18.

[42] *See* text accompanying note 6 *supra*.

[43] Nxasana v. Minister of Justice, [1976] 3 S.A. 745, 747 (Durban & Coast Local Div.) (per Didcott, J.) (citation omitted).

[44] *Id.* 748.

III. The Attitude of Judges and Lawyers

This brings me to the last part of this lecture, the approach of the judges and lawyers to legislation of this type. South Africa has, as I have said, no bill of rights. Our political system is one of complete parliamentary sovereignty. No court can declare any of the provisions that I have described unconstitutional. Many years ago a South African judge of appeal said that it was the duty of the courts to act as buttresses between the executive and the subject.[45] But how are they to do so in the light of their duty to give effect to parliamentary enactments however draconian and however "offensive to conventional legal standards"? The answer ordinarily given is that their sole power is the power to interpret those enactments. In the judgment previously quoted, the judge put this in clear language:

> Our Courts are constitutionally powerless to legislate or to veto legislation. They can only interpret it, and then implement it in accordance with their interpretation of it. When there is a real doubt about the meaning of a statute, their tradition is to construe it so that it provides for the least amount of interference with the liberty of the individual that is compatible with the language used. The tradition has been observed for so long, and has permeated so many fields of our law, that it is unnecessary to cite authority for its acceptance.[46]

So this too is axiomatic.

No doubt the question will be asked: how have the South African courts performed this function of strict interpretation *in favorem libertatis* in the field of the security and procedural legislation with which I have been dealing? In my—I hope sufficiently—respectful opinion, their performance has been mixed. If I were to mark them by the Oxford method, I would give them a *beta*, query *beta* minus. On the positive side, there has been some attempt to give a restrictive interpretation to those provisions of the Terrorism Act that place the burden of proof on the accused and to ensure that the procedural advantages of the prosecution are not improperly extended. This is at least true of the Appellate Division of the Supreme Court, which has set aside on appeal several verdicts given by trial judges for want of sufficiently con-

---

[45] Rex v. Pretoria Timber Co. (Pty), [1950] 3 S.A. 163, 182 (App. Div.) (opinion of van den Heever, J.A.).

[46] Nxasana v. Minister of Justice, [1976] 3 S.A. 745, 747 (Durban & Coast Local Div.) (per Didcott, J.).

vincing evidence of guilt. In upholding these appeals, it has even reversed the trial judge's findings on the credibility of witnesses.[47] Further, although section 6 (5) of the Terrorism Act states that no court shall pronounce on the validity of any action taken under section 6 or order the release of any detainee, this section does not preclude the court from enquiring into the lawfulness of the treatment that a detainee receives in detention.[48] The court will therefore on suitable evidence enjoin the police from using unlawful methods of interrogation.[49]

On the negative side, however, the courts have shown a marked reluctance to permit evidence of ill-treatment to be given by the person most concerned, namely the detainee himself. In 1964 a case came to the courts under another "security" statute which, like section 6 of the Terrorism Act, provided for detention without access to lawyer or friend for the purposes of interrogation.[50] The wife of a detainee had received a smuggled note from him saying that relays of policemen had interrogated him for twenty-eight hours on end without allowing him to rest or even to sit down. When he fell to the floor out of exhaustion, the police threw cold water over him and dragged him to his feet. The wife applied urgently for an injunction restraining the police from continuing this method of interrogation. The police made affidavits denying the allegations, and the wife's counsel asked the court to order that the husband be brought to court to give evidence himself. This was refused by the judge, and his refusal was upheld by a majority in the Appellate Division.[51] The ground of refusal was that to have the detainee brought to court would interfere with the object of the statute—continuous detention, in isolation, for the purposes of interrogation. Whether this was an inevitable conclusion, having due regard for the terms of the statute, may be judged in the

---

[47] *See, e.g.,* State v. Mdingi, [1979] 1 S.A. 309, 317 (App. Div.); State v. Essack, [1974] 1 S.A. 1, 16-17, 20-21 (App. Div.); State v. ffrench-Beytagh, [1972] 3 S.A. 430, 446 (App. Div.). See also State v. Mushimba, [1977] 2 S.A. 829 (App. Div.), in which the Appellate Division set aside a conviction under the Terrorism Act on the ground that the security police had unlawfully obtained material from the defence files through an agent in the defence attorney's office.

[48] Nxasana v. Minister of Justice, [1976] 3 S.A. 745, 748 (Durban & Coast Local Div.) (per Didcott, J.).

[49] Essop v. Commissioner of South African Police, [1972] 1 Prentice Hall Reports, H. 4 (Transvaal Provincial Div.).

[50] General Law Amendment Act, No. 37 of 1963, § 17.

[51] Schermbrucker v. Klindt, N.O., [1965] 4 S.A. 606 (App. Div.), *aff'g* [1965] 1 S.A. 353 (Transvaal Provincial Div.). *See* Dugard, *The Courts and Section 6 of the Terrorism Act,* 87 S. AFR. L.J. 289 (1970).

light of the fact that two judges of appeal, including the present Chief Justice,[52] wrote powerful dissents.

In a later case the fathers of some young men detained under section 6 of the Terrorism Act applied to the Transvaal court for an injunction to restrain the police from assaulting the detainees during their interrogation. Because of the earlier case, the applicants asked not that the detainees be brought to court but merely that affidavits be taken from them by a government official. The court held that the Act prevented any such affidavit's being placed before it.[53] In other cases also the requirements of the interrogators would seem to have been placed above those of the detainee. It is enough to mention just one more—a much-criticised opinion of the full bench of the Eastern Cape court in which that court held that the threat of further detention did not make the detainee's confession anything but freely or voluntarily made, and thus admissible against him.[54]

These cases give some indication of the judicial approach to the Terrorism Act and to similar statutes. They show judges about their ordinary business of interpreting statutes, evaluating evidence, and reaching varying conclusions. But, it may be asked, what do they feel about these forms of procedure, and especially about indefinite pretrial detention incommunicado, which have so distorted the traditional legal standards they were trained to follow? One may of course ask the same question about the many statutes embodying racial discrimination which the judges are compelled to apply, whatever the hardship those statutes cause. The answer is that on the whole the judges do not say. No doubt some of them regard this legislation as justifiable and proper. Others do not and occasionally hint as much. Some judges who have to enforce these laws emphasise that they are bound by Parliament's law and have no option but to apply it. For example, in a recent case a judge upheld the conviction of an Indian man for unlawfully renting an apartment in a "white" area, and ordered his ejectment although the evidence showed that no habitable accommodation

---

[52] Mr. Justice Frans L. Rumpff.

[53] Cooper v. Minister of Police, [1977] 2 S.A. 209 (Transvaal Provincial Div.) (per Trengove, J.). This case was decided in 1974, but not reported until 1977. More recently, a Natal judge has refused to follow this decision. Nxasana v. Minister of Justice, [1976] 3 S.A. 745, 753-55 (Durban & Coast Local Div.) (per Didcott, J.).

[54] State v. Hlekani, [1964] 4 S.A. 429, 439-40 (Eastern Cape Div.) (decided under General Law Amendment Act, No. 37 of 1963, § 17). The correctness of this decision was left open in State v. Alexander, [1965] 2 S.A. 796, 814 (App. Div.).

was available to him and his family in the "Indian" area of his city. In giving judgment the judge said:

> An Act of Parliament creates law but not necessarily equity. As a judge in a court of law I am obliged to give effect to the provisions of an Act of Parliament. Speaking for myself, and if I were sitting as a court of equity, I would have come to the assistance of the appellant. Unfortunately, and on an intellectually honest approach, I am compelled to conclude that the appeal must fail.[55]

This passage echoes the statement of the great dissenter in *Dred Scott v. Sanford*,[56] Mr. Justice McLean. A lifelong opponent of slavery, Justice McLean excused or explained his enforcement of the fugitive slave laws as follows: "With the abstract principles of slavery, courts called to administer this law have nothing to do." [57] "[T]he hardship and injustice supposed arises out of the institution of slavery, over which we have no control. Under such circumstances, we can not be held answerable." [58]

This reasoning did not go unscathed in the United States, nor has it, entirely, in South Africa. In 1971 a Durban law professor asked, in a public address, whether the time had not come for judges to stand up in defence of the rule of law and to say something about an institution, the Terrorism Act, " 'which they must surely know to be an abdication [*sic*] of decency and justice.' " [59] In particular, he suggested, the judiciary could make the Act less useful to the authorities " 'by denying, on account of the built-in intimidatory effect of unsupervised solitary confinement, practically all creditworthiness to evidence procured under those detention provisions.' " [60] At that time, as the professor knew, a trial under the Terrorism Act was in progress in which allegations had been made that the police had intimidated state witnesses while in detention. The melancholy result, for the professor, was that he was prosecuted on a charge of attempting to obstruct justice. The prosecution's theory was that he was exhorting the judge to disregard admissible evidence and thus to act improperly. On this

---

[55] State v. Adams (Transvaal Provincial Div. Sept., 1979) (unreported).

[56] 60 U.S. (19 How.) 393 (1857) (McLean, J., dissenting).

[57] Miller v. McQuerry, 17 F. Cas. 335, 339 (C.C.D. Ohio 1853) (No. 9,583).

[58] *Id.* 340.

[59] Address by Professor Barend van Niekerk at Durban City Hall (Nov. 9, 1971), *quoted in* State v. van Niekerk, [1972] 3 S.A. 711, 716 (App. Div.). For a discussion of this case, see Dugard, *Judges, Academics and Unjust Laws: The Van Niekerk Contempt Case*, 89 S. Afr. L.J. 271 (1972).

[60] State v. van Niekerk, [1972] 3 S.A. 711, 716-17 (App. Div.).

theory, the professor was prosecuted and convicted.[61] The judge who tried his case said that " 'in a society such as ours' " [62] it was not for judges to take sides in public controversies. Nevertheless, he said, this did not mean that a judge must acquiesce in legislation of a really monstrous kind; his way out would then be to resign.[63]

I know of no South African judge who has in fact found any law so monstrous as to compel him to resign.[64] I do not say this as a criticism of individual judges, least of all as a criticism of those whose minds are troubled by the laws that they have to apply. After all, Justices Story and McLean did not feel called upon to resign from the bench rather than enforce the fugitive slave laws.[65] And one is grateful for those judges who have done what they can to mitigate the harshness of the South African system. The only generalization in which I shall indulge is that if one participates in a system that distorts justice, truisms about the limited functions of a judge will not necessarily save one's soul.

What of the bar? What do they do when they get into court, under the heavily loaded rules of the Terrorism Act? The answer is: the best they can. Lawyers tend to play by the rules of the game; when the rules change, they try to win under the new rules. Indeed, one forgets occasionally that it is a different game. The court looks the same, witnesses are examined and cross-examined, lawyers address the court and cite authority. But the realities break through. A fifteen-year-old boy is called as a state witness. It turns out that he has been in solitary detention for three months before being brought to court. Or the accused are acquitted and discharged by the court, but when they leave the courtroom they are immediately re-arrested and detained.[66] What has the exercise in court been worth?

---

[61] *Id.* 711.

[62] State v. van Niekerk (Durban & Coast Local Div. Dec. 13, 1971) (unreported) (per Fannin, J.), *quoted in* Dugard, *supra* note 59, at 283.

[63] *Id.*

[64] Sir Robert Tredgold, then Chief Justice of the Federation of Rhodesia and Nyasaland, resigned in 1960 in protest against the Southern Rhodesian Law and Order Maintenance Act, No. 53 of 1960. He felt that it "would compel the Courts to become party to widespread injustice." R. TREDGOLD, THE RHODESIA THAT WAS MY LIFE 232 (1968). Whether the provisions of that Act go beyond those of the corresponding South African statutes is a nice point.

[65] *See* R. COVER, JUSTICE ACCUSED (1975), especially chapters 7 & 13.

[66] *Cf.* J. DUGARD, *supra* note 14, at 216 (describing the re-arrest of Mrs. Winnie Mandela and 21 other accused in Pretoria in February, 1970, immediately after their acquittal under the Suppression of Communism Act, No. 44 of 1950).

In this regard South African lawyers, including those who defend in political cases, have, like judges, had to face a fundamental attack on the part they play in the South African system. Mr. Joel Carlson, a South African attorney, who over many years had given service to his clients in political trials in South Africa, eventually went into exile. He considered that his work as a defence lawyer "was assisting the regime to present an overall image, at home and overseas, of judicial integrity and a fair legal system." [67] Others have echoed this view. The question raised, of course, does not apply only to lawyers. What is anyone's duty in a society that he believes to be unjust and that he does not believe can be changed by any effort of his? In *The First Circle* Solzhenitsyn has a character say: "What is the most precious thing in the world? It seems to be the consciousness of not participating in injustice. Injustice is stronger than you are, it always was and it always will be; but let it not be committed through you." [68]

P.W. Botha's South Africa is not by any means Stalin's Russia, but even so this austere imperative is not easy to live by. For judges it may be impossible, and, if Mr. Carlson is right, perhaps for practising lawyers too. Possibly our participation in the distorted legal process I have described does give it some respectability. I hope this is not so, but if so, what is the alternative? Must one refuse to take any part in these trials? A mere practising advocate cannot very satisfactorily explore the ethical and social ramifications of this question, much less offer a generally satisfactory solution. He must fall back on the traditional ethics of his profession, not to answer the question but to evade it.

The answer is one that more appropriately comes from his clients. For the most part the attitude of defendants in South African political trials has been that they wish to be defended—to be acquitted if possible, and, if not, at least to get the minimum sentence. There have been cases, however, in which the defendants have refused to recognize the jurisdiction of the court. These, so far, have been exceptional. This may change. A recent and disquieting tendency in South African political trials has been to exclude the public (although not the press) from the court and to forbid the press from publishing the names of state witnesses. The ground given for these rulings is the fear that those witnesses will be harmed or even killed by the political associates of the accused. In the most recent of the major political trials, in Pietermaritzburg

---

[67] J. CARLSON, No NEUTRAL GROUND 362 (1973).

[68] A. SOLZHENITSYN, THE FIRST CIRCLE ch. 55, at 418 (Fontana ed. 1970).

last September, when the judge ordered the public to be excluded from the court, all the defendants dismissed their counsel and refused to take any further part in the proceedings. This attitude may become more common. But as long as defendants want the services of an advocate, he is not to refuse them. And if it be said that by so doing he is bolstering up an unjust system, that is one more burden of an onerous profession.

By way of summing up, I limit myself to two propositions. One is obvious—in the absence of an entrenched bill of rights, the judiciary is a poor bulwark against a determined and immoderate government. The other is not so obvious, at least in South Africa. It is that legislation such as I have described does more than restrict judges' legal power to protect the liberties of the subject: it increasingly undermines their will to do so, even when it may still be possible. Too soon they accept a position of subordination and unprotesting powerlessness. And this has a reciprocal effect. Judge Learned Hand once said, "[a] society whose judges have taught it to expect complaisance will exact complaisance." [69]

That is the great loss. One day there will be change in South Africa. Those who then come to rule may have seen the process of law in their country not as protection against power but as no more than its convenient instrument, to be manipulated at will. It would then not be surprising if they failed to appreciate the value of an independent judiciary and of due process of law. If so, then it may be said of those who now govern that they destroyed better than they knew.

Is there any hope of restoring what has been lost? It would not be realistic to say so. But realism, however sombre, is not to be confused with silence or acquiescence. "It is not necessary to hope in order to work, and it is not necessary to succeed in order to persevere." [70]

---

[69] L. HAND, *The Contribution of an Independent Judiciary to Civilization,* in THE SPIRIT OF LIBERTY 163 (3d ed. 1960).

[70] Attributed to William of Orange (1533-1584).

[23]

Journal of Southern African Studies, Vol. 14, No. 1, October 1987

The ANC in Court: Towards International Guidelines in Sentencing*

CHRISTINA MURRAY

There is no need to document the fact that South Africa is a divided society nor that state institutions suffer a severe lack of legitimacy. It is also not surprising that, on occasion, political prisoners should refuse to accept the jurisdiction of a South African criminal court. The Escourt treason trial presents a recent example. At the end of 1985, four accused arraigned on charges under the Internal Security Act 74 of 1982 refused to plead, stating that they did not recognise the jurisdiction of the court. One of them, Norbert Buthelezi, read a statement explaining their position. He denied the legitimacy of the courts, claimed prisoner of war status and affirmed the justice of the struggle in which they, as members of the military wing of the ANC, were involved:

> The courts are a loyal and faithful arm of the very government the African National Congress is fighting to destroy. We therefore contend that this court cannot adjudicate in a dispute between ourselves and the government. It is absolutely impossible for the government to be an impartial judge in its own case. We received military training and art of warfare in the people's army 'Umkonto We Sizwe'. In that case we regard ourselves as truly fledged soldiers of our army. The African National Congress is a signatory to the Geneva Convention. We were captured in the process of executing our historical mission of liberating our people. Under the Geneva Convention we must be accorded the prisoner-of-war status. As prisoners-of-war no court of law has power over our case. The Geneva Convention recognizes people who take up arms to fight against national oppression as prisoners-of-war in case of capture by the oppressor's security forces. We refuse therefore to stand trial.[1]

Inevitably, the four accused were convicted. They received sentences ranging from eight to twelve years' imprisonment. In dealing with the claim of prisoner-of-war status Wilson J took the opportunity to assert the independence of the courts using familiar rhetoric:

> The courts of this country are independent of the executive and jealous of the rights of the individual. One of the most important functions of the court is to stand as a bulwark between the citizen and the executive and to guard against the invasion of the rights of the citizen by the executive.

*The author wishes to acknowledge financial support for her research from the Human Sciences Research Council.

[1] *S v Mampumulo and Others*, Natal Provincial Division of the Supreme Court of South Africa, December 1985, Case No. CC 93/85, unreported. The trial took place before the court on circuit in Escourt, Natal.

Of course, as the judge himself seemed aware, no assertion of judicial independence could answer the claims of the accused before him. The target of the ANC's struggle is not merely the white government of South Africa but the full state apparatus established by the white majority in the country. The courts are as much part of this apparatus as, for instance, the police and the army. Nevertheless, the courts are used by South Africans opposed to the government or even determined to overthrow existing state structures. The use that the labour movement has made of courts exemplifies this, as does the extent to which emergency regulations have been tested in court in the last two years.

This note will not examine the various theoretical and political justifications supporting the use of the courts.[2] Instead, taking as its starting point the relative autonomy of legal processes, it examines one argument that lawyers might use to persuade courts to exercise a conciliatory function. The particular question that it looks at is whether the law of the Geneva Conventions of 1949 relating to the treatment of victims of war, raised by Buthelezi in his address to the Escourt court, can play any role in proceedings before a South African criminal court. It argues that it can and should be considered and suggests that this could introduce an element of fairness and objectivity in court procedures that are often perceived as unjust.

In a nutshell the argument based on the law of armed conflict is the following. Subsequent to the conclusion of the 1977 Protocols to the Geneva Conventions of 1949, the law of armed conflict, and more particularly the rules relating to the treatment of prisoners of war, applies not only to wars between states but also to a new class of international war, 'armed conflicts in which peoples are fighting against colonial domination and alien occupation and against racist régimes in the exercise of their right of self-determination'[3] — wars that are known in international law as wars of national liberation. Swapo, the ANC and the PAC are recognised internationally as liberation movements and the conflicts in which they are engaged fall into the extended definition of an international war. The law of the Geneva Conventions and the two 1977 Protocols is, accordingly, directly relevant to South Africa.

Consideration of the law of armed conflict raises two possibilities. The first is at once the most obvious and so unlikely as to be absurd. It is that the Geneva Conventions and the 1977 Protocols should be applied by the South African authorities: captured members of the armed wing of the ANC, for instance, should not be treated as criminals, should not be tried under criminal law applicable to ordinary citizens but should be treated as prisoners of war. This rules courts out entirely. There are many reasons why South Africa will not do this. The most obvious are political. Application of the Geneva Law as developed by the Protocol is seen to mean an admission of the legitimacy of the causes of the liberation movements concerned. In any event it can be argued, and many international lawyers do this, that the adoption of the Protocols with their extended definition of international conflict is irrelevant in South Africa. South Africa, while a party to the

---

[2] For some of the arguments relating to the decision to use the law, see Sheldon Leader's 'Introduction' to the Special Issue on Law and Politics in Southern Africa, *JSAS*, 12, 1 (1985), and the articles that follow it.

[3] See Article 1(4) of Protocol I.

142   *Journal of Southern African Studies*

1948 Conventions, has not ratified the Protocols and therefore. it is said. they do not bind the country. Acceptance of this argument means that there is no international obligation on South Africa to apply the law of the Protocols. Certain writers respond by saying that South Africa's failure to ratify the Protocols is not material: the Protocols reflect principles that have become part of customary international law and which are therefore binding on the country without their being expressly accepted. [4] This argument is probably premature: principles require repeated application in practice before becoming part of customary international law and in this case such practice is absent.

The second way in which the Protocol-based argument might be relevant to South Africa is more subtle and has already had some success in a Namibian court. The second option is simply to argue that. although not formally part of South African law. the law of the Protocols is relevant in the sentencing process. A judge should take into account the international law of armed conflicts. reflected in the Protocols. in determining sentence and. particularly. in deciding whether or not to hand down the death sentence. a competent sentence for both treason and various 'security' offences in South Africa. In South African law an extenuating (or mitigating) circumstance has been defined as 'a fact associated with the crime which serves in the minds of reasonable men to diminish. morally albeit not legally. the degree of the prisoner's guilt'. [5] The range of factors that may mitigate a sentence is wide. The age of an accused. his or her state of health and mental well-being. and the circumstances in which the crime was committed are considerations that are well-known. Political motivation has also been accepted as relevant by South African judges. [6] Thus although a judge sitting in a South African court is bound to convict those accused if their actions constitute a crime in terms of South African legislation. the law grants a wide discretion in sentencing. At this stage of the trial the accused's moral convictions are relevant and the belief that one is involved in a just. international war could operate as a mitigating factor.

The law of the Protocols offers two distinct improvements for the sentencing process. First. article 1 of the first Protocol enables a distinction to be drawn between groups with goals that the international community finds acceptable — struggles against colonial domination and alien occupation and against racist regimes in the exercise of a right of self-determination — and other groups such as secessionist movements and terrorist organisations like Bader Meinhoff and Action Directe. The negotiating history of the Protocols confirms that in this context the term 'national liberation movement' (which is not itself used in the Protocols) must be interpreted narrowly and not be given the wider meaning that political scientists occasionally attach to it. International law practice shows that an organisation will be recognised as a national liberation movement if

---

[4] See. for instance. G. Abi-Saab. 'Wars of National Liberation in the Geneva Conventions and Protocols'. *Académie de Droit International Recueil des Cours*. 165. IV (1979). p. 353.

[5] *R v Biyana*. 1938 Eastern Districts Local Division. 310-11.

[6] For an outline of sentences in political trials in South Africa prior to 1976. see J. Dugard. *Human Rights and the South African Legal Order* (Princeton. 1978). pp. 208-27 and 234-43.

evidence exists of political control over, and organized allegiance of, the people they claim to represent with the support of individual (primarily neighbouring) states and with legitimization by regional and global international organizations. Liberation movements are the expression of cooperative efforts for self-determination undertaken in common by dependent peoples and independent states.

A distinction would be made, for instance, between the ANC, which is engaged in a struggle for self-determination in South Africa and which is recognised as a national liberation movement by the African Liberation Committee of the Organization of African Unity, and the Basutoland Congress Party of Lesotho. In the early 1970s, the Basutoland Congress Party requested the support of the OAU. This was not granted. The Party's struggle against South African-backed Chief Leabua Jonathan might be categorised as a revolutionary struggle for the restoration of democracy but the international community sees it as a domestic struggle for which support would be illegitimate intervention.

Translated into the South African context the concept of national liberation movements used in international law allows a clear legal distinction to be made between the neo-Fascist *Afrikaner Weerstandsbeweging* and the ANC, for instance. Not every organisation which claims to be politically motivated and reaches for arms is given special treatment. To a human-rights lawyer this may present some problems. If, as an American author has commented, compliance by the state with the humanitarian law of armed conflict 'facilitates the eventual restoration of peace and helps to heal the wounds of the nation',[5] one should strive for its widest possible application. The usual exclusion of the IRA from its operation, for instance, is problematic. However, while the standards reflected in international law reflect only the lowest common denominator of consent in the international community, they have not developed in a vacuum. Their applicability to South Africa is a product of that country's failure to allow its people to realise their right of self-determination. Thus they address the most serious conflict in the country. In the words of an American professor:

The criterion is useful because it is often an indicium of a particularly bloody and protracted conflict − precisely the kind of conflict to which the laws of wars should apply. Partisans who believe that they are fighting for their freedom against colonial and racist overlords will not meekly flee the field of battle.[9]

The law of armed conflict not only identifies which movements should receive special treatment, it also circumscribes the means that they can legitimately adopt. The law in this area is substantial and I shall simply give one or two examples which may have a bearing on the activities of national liberation movements. The most important principle in this context is that civilian lives and property should be

[7] K. Ginther, 'Liberation Movements', in N. Bernhardt (ed.), *Encyclopaedia of Public International Law*, Instalment 3 (1981), p. 245.
[8] W.A. Solf, 'Problems with the Application of the Norms Governing Interstate Armed Conflict to Non-International Armed Conflict', *Georgia Journal of International and Comparative Law* (Supplement), 13 (1983), pp. 291, 293.
[9] J.E. Bond, 'Amended Article 1 of Draft Protocol I to the 1949 Geneva Convention: The Coming of Age of the Guerrilla', *Washington and Lee Law Review*, 32 (1975), pp. 65, 72.

protected as far as possible. Here at least two sections of Protocol I are of direct relevance to the activities of national liberation movements. Part IV of the Protocol deals with the civilian population in general and states the basic rule as follows:

In order to ensure respect for and protection of the civilian population and civilian objects. the Parties to the conflict shall at all times distinguish between the civilian population and combatants and between civilian objects and military objectives and accordingly shall direct their operations only against military objectives. (Article 48)

Terms such as 'civilian' and 'civilian objects' are defined in Article 50 and certain special rules are given. Neither the civilian population nor individual civilians should be the object of attack. for instance (Article 51 para 2): indiscriminate attacks are prohibited (Article 51 para 4) and 'an attack which may be expected to cause incidental loss of civilian life. injury to civilians. damage to civilian objects, or a combination thereof. which would be excessive in relation to the concrete and direct military advantage anticipated' is an example of an indiscriminate attack (Article 51 para 5).

The section on Combatant and Prisoner of War Status reinforces the principle that civilians are to be protected. Article 44 requires combatants to distinguish themselves from the civilian population 'while they are engaged in an attack or in a military operation preparatory to an attack'. This requirement is qualified on recognition of the fact that in certain types of conflict it is impractical. In such circumstances combatant status is retained (and thus protection by the law of armed conflict) if arms are carried openly 'during each military engagement' and 'during such time as [the combatant] is visible to the adversary while he is engaged in a military deployment preceding the launching of an attack in which he is to participate'.

Many other principles could be cited. While their application might not be easy — for instance whether an attack is 'excessive in relation to the concrete and direct military advantage anticipated' is unlikely to be self-evident — they provide far more precise guidelines than ordinarily available in the sentencing process. Moreover. as part of the international law of armed conflict. a jurisprudence relating to the way in which they should be enforced has developed around many of them.

The argument that the law of the 1977 Protocols justifies special consideration being given to the fact that an accused is a member of *Umkhonto*. the armed wing of the ANC. was not received sympathetically when presented to Curlewis J sitting in the Transvaal Provincial Division in *S v Mogoerane and Others*. The accused before him were indicted for murder. They were found to have taken part in attacks on three police stations in South Africa which left four dead and eleven injured. Curlewis J declared the argument based on the law of armed conflict to be of 'no relevance at all'. adding:

The interest. perhaps. of Professor Dugard's evidence concerning the prisoner-of-war argument is that. as he told us. the convention was passed with two organisations in mind: the PLO and the ANC. The PLO in my view. is a bunch of thugs who kill Jews. The fact therefore that irresponsible people overseas and elsewhere praise it and give it a status and put a gloss of respectability upon it. does not seem to me to show much right thinking. Over forty years ago another bunch of thugs went around killing Jews and they also had a gloss of respectability put upon them for a long time. That was called appeasement. [10]

Simon Mogoerane, Jerry Mosololi and Marcus Motaung became the third, fourth and fifth members of the ANC to be hanged for taking up arms against the South African government.

Curlewis J's attitude to the ANC and his comment later in his judgment that 'no decent black person' would approve of the acts of the accused underscore the inadequacy of the reasonable man test imported in the definition of an extenuating circumstance. Curlewis J finds no difficulty in determining the moral guilt of the accused and he is confident that reasonable men will agree with him. Like him, reasonable men view the PLO as a bunch of thugs and, by analogy, consider members of the ANC to be thugs. Furthermore, and again like the judge, 'no decent black person' would approve of the acts of the accused.

The discrepancy between Curlewis J's assessment of what might reasonably be seen to diminish the moral guilt of the accused and the view of the community is glaring. An application of the law of the Protocols in this context would not have avoided heavy sentences for the accused. They had relied on civilian guise for the success of their mission and had, inevitably, harmed civilians in their attacks. It could, however, have avoided the imposition of the death penalty which is absolutely prohibited by the law of armed conflict and may have suggested a conciliatory rather than provocative judgment, given the divided view of the actions of the accused within the country. [11]

A plea for the application of the humanitarian law of armed conflict in the sentencing process is not an idealist's dream with no hope of success. An argument similar to that put to Curlewis J was raised in a Namibian court where three members of the armed wing of Swapo were convicted for contraventions of the Terrorism Act 83 of 1967. The presiding judge, Bethune J, treated the argument sympathetically and asserted that the trend in international law to treat combatants in wars of national liberation as prisoners of war was a relevant factor to consider in sentencing. He stated: 'Under all the circumstances it is likely that [the accused] considered their actions to be part of a justified struggle which has enjoyed strong foreign as well as internal support.' [12] A Natal judge, Mr Justice Didcott, while not invoking the law of armed conflict expressly, has shown a similar sensitivity to the position of members of the ANC convicted in his court. In *S v Buthelezi and Others* he described three ANC members as soldiers. He added:

---

[10] *S v Mogoerane and Others*, Transvaal Provincial Division of the Supreme Court of South Africa, August 6, 1982, published in *Lawyers for Human Rights Bulletin*, 1 (February 1983), pp. 118, 124.

[11] Public opinion was revealed in the mobilisation of support for a campaign to stop the execution of Mogoerane, Mosololi and Motaung. It was a campaign that met with a sharp government reaction: the acting Chief Magistrate of Johannesburg banned meetings of the committee established to campaign for the lives of the three men (*The Star*, 10/6/1983). Included in a ban on meetings connected with the hangings was a commemorative service to be held in a Johannesburg cathedral (*The Star*, 11/6/1983). In Durban, on the day of the executions, police made 23 arrests when about 400 people marched through the streets in protest. Police used teargas at an all-night vigil held for the three in a Durban church hall (*The Star*, 10/6/1983). They also intervened when about 700 students demonstrated against the executions at the University of Zululand, a black university (*Rand Daily Mail*, 10/6/1983).

[12] *S v Sagarius and Others*, 1983(1) *South African Law Reports*, 833 (SWA), p. 836. (Author's translation from Afrikaans.)

146   *Journal of Southern African Studies*

That the black people of this country have real and legitimate grievances is widely acknow-ledged today. So is the danger that their grievances may sometimes be expressed in a violent way. Leading South Africans, South Africans of all communities and shades of opinion, South Africans holding responsible office, have said as much time and again. [13]

It is important to emphasise that, at best, consideration of the nature of the struggles in southern Africa and their status in international law might enable judges to determine sentence within a broader perspective. It cannot provide some sort of absolute, objective standard against which crimes could be measured. It means that matters such as the nature of the offence, the means chosen to execute goals and the extent of the harm caused would be highly relevant. But other issues would remain important − the age of the prisoners, their background and upbringing and so on. The discretionary nature of sentencing has to be observed and there are dangers in introducing rigid formulae. Indeed, it is the very flexibility of the sentencing process that leaves space for an argument such as the one put forward here. Were there a rigid list of criteria beyond which a judge could not go, a politically radical suggestion such as this one would surely not appear on it. The point is, however, that humanitarian law is a highly developed branch of international law, designed to limit suffering between antagonistic parties to a conflict. It contains principles which could be used by judges in sentencing to avoid some of the pitfalls that inevitably face the adjudicator of such a bitter struggle.

[13] Durban and Coast Local Division of the Supreme Court of South Africa, September 13, 1982, published in *Lawyers for Human Rights Bulletin*, 1 (February 1983), p. 129.

[24]

MOVEMENT AND STATE STRATEGIES

The Role of International Law in the Struggle for Liberation in South Africa

John Dugard

TODAY SOUTH AFRICA IS A SOCIETY IN TRANSITION FROM RACE-BASED REPRESsion to a non-racial democracy. A combination of factors, both international and national, has produced the present situation. In this article I shall describe and examine the role played by international law, particularly within the framework of the United Nations, in bringing the National Party to the negotiating table. I shall also consider the role of international law in the process of transition.

Apartheid, Domestic Jurisdiction, and Human Rights

South Africa's racial policies have featured on the agenda of the General Assembly since the latter's very inception. In 1946, at the request of the Government of India, the General Assembly first considered the question of the treatment of people of Indian origin in South Africa (Resolution 44[I]); and thereafter this item was examined regularly until 1962 when it merged with the question of apartheid (Resolution 1761 [XVII]). In 1952, the wider apartheid question was raised directly in the General Assembly when 13 countries sought its inclusion on the agenda on the ground that this policy violated Articles 55 and 56 of the Charter of the United Nations, which oblige states to promote respect for human rights and fundamental freedoms. Thereafter, the question of apartheid appeared annually on the agenda of the General Assembly. In 1960, following the shooting of blacks at a peaceful demonstration at Sharpeville, the question was elevated to the Security Council

---

JOHN DUGARD is a Professor of Law and Director of the Centre for Applied Legal Studies at the University of the Witwatersrand, Johannesburg, (P.O. Wits, 2050, South Africa). He is the author of *South African Criminal Law and Procedure* (1977), *Human Rights and the South African Legal Order* (Princeton, 1978), and *Recognition and the United Nations* (Grotius, 1987).

Social Justice Vol. 18, Nos. 1-2   83

(Resolution 134 [1960]), which has continued to consider the matter on a fairly regular basis.

Apartheid was proclaimed at a time when institutionalized racial discrimination was still to be found in the legal order of the United States of America and in most colonial regimes. Not surprisingly, therefore, South Africa found support from many Western governments for its insistence that its racial policies fell within its exclusive domestic jurisdiction. Moreover, the extent to which Article 2(7) of the U.N. Charter protected a state's domestic policies from international scrutiny, and the status of the human-rights provisions in the Charter in the new postwar world order was as yet unresolved. Consequently, South Africa's racial policies became the testing ground for the battle between human rights and domestic jurisdiction.

There is an inherent tension between the human-rights provisions in the Charter and the recognition of the exclusive domestic jurisdiction of states contained in Article 2(7). In the early days of the United Nations, South Africa sought to block any discussion of her racial policies on the ground that Article 2(7) took precedence over the human-rights provisions (Higgins, 1963: 64-65). Encouraged by the support of many Western states, South Africa demanded that an advisory opinion be obtained from the International Court of Justice. However, the General Assembly of the United Nations, unsure of the correctness of its interventionist interpretation of Article 2(7), preferred to keep the matter away from the Court and refused South Africa's request (Ozgur, 1982: 19). Gradually, international opinion changed as apartheid became more brutal, South Africa more intransigent, and decolonization more pervasive. The wisdom of the observation of the Permanent Court of International Justice in the *Nationality Decrees* case that the question of domestic jurisdiction is "relative" and "depends upon the development of international relations" (1923 PCIJ Reports, B4: 23) became apparent with respect to apartheid, as state after state abandoned its support for the South African position. Some states made their concession on Article 2(7) reluctantly and sought to limit their recognition of the precedence of the human-rights provisions over domestic jurisdiction to apartheid. In practice, such a limitation was impossible. Apartheid forced states to choose between the supremacy of domestic jurisdiction and human rights. They chose human rights and, in so doing, took international law into a new era.

Closely related to the debate over domestic jurisdiction was the dispute over the legal status of the human-rights provisions in the Charter. Until 1971, South Africa questioned the legal force of the human-rights provisions, arguing that they were a mere statement of ideals and failed to impose any legal obligation. This controversy was also resolved in the context of apartheid when the International Court of Justice, in the 1971 *Namibia Opinion*, held that apartheid — as extended to Namibia — violated the Charter, a decision

International Law and the Struggle for Liberation in South Africa   85

that necessarily implied that the human-rights provisions imposed legal obligations on member states (Schwelb, 1972: 348-349).

The history of the conflict between the United Nations and South Africa is therefore one of legitimate intervention in the domestic affairs of a member state of the organization. This intervention has taken many forms. The strategies employed by the international community, principally acting through the United Nations, to persuade or compel South Africa to abandon its racial policies illustrate the manner in which international law has evolved to provide the international community with mechanisms for the assertion of human rights.

Strategies Employed by the International Community to Oppose Apartheid

During the 1950s, the General Assembly adopted a conciliatory approach toward apartheid. It established a Commission on the Racial Situation in the Union of South Africa, which recommended the repeal of racist laws and the suggested methods that might be employed "to facilitate the peaceful development of the racial situation in South Africa."[1] Persuasion rather than coercion characterized the policy of the United Nations toward South Africa.

In the early 1960s, the mood of the United Nations changed as a result of the increase in size of the Afro-Asian bloc, the change in attitude toward Article 2(7) and apartheid by many Western states, the shooting of black demonstrators by the South African police at Sharpeville, and South Africa's withdrawal from the Commonwealth of Nations, which resulted in a loss of support from members of that "Club" in the United Nations. Since then, "condemnations" and "deprecations" of apartheid have replaced "appeals" and "invitations" for change and the General Assembly has abandoned conciliation in favor of coercion.

When the Security Council first considered the question of apartheid in 1960 and 1963, it adopted an approach that, in many respects, resembled the initial efforts of the General Assembly.[2] South Africa's intransigence, however, compelled it to adopt a more coercive and confrontational approach.

A. Economic Sanctions

Sanctions Imposed by the General Assembly

In 1961, in Resolution 1598 (XV) the Assembly requested member states to take separate and collective action in conformity with the Charter, without particularizing such action, to bring about an abandonment of apartheid. In 1962, the envisaged action was spelled out in detail in Resolution 1761 (XVII) when member states were requested to break off diplomatic relations with South Africa; to close their ports to all vessels flying the South African flag; to enact legislation prohibiting their ships from entering South African ports; to boycott all South African goods and to refrain from exporting goods, including arms and ammunition to South Africa; and to refuse landing and passage facilities to all South African aircraft.

The measures recommended in Resolution 1761 (XVII) have been endorsed and expanded upon in subsequent years.[3] The wide support for coercive measures in the General Assembly is demonstrated by the fact that in 1986, 126 member states voted in favor of a resolution calling on the Security Council to impose mandatory economic sanctions against South Africa.

Resolution 1761 (XVII) and its successors have their constitutional basis in Articles 10-14 of the United Nations Charter and are thus only recommendatory in nature (Dugard, 1966). These resolutions are not, however, devoid of legal effect. In the first instance, member states are obliged to consider them in good faith with a view to implementing them. Second, as Sir Hersch Lauterpacht observed in the *Voting Procedure Case*, "on proper occasions they provide a legal authorization for members determined to act upon them individually or collectively" (1955 ICJ Reports: 118-119).

Sanctions Imposed by the Security Council

The Security Council first considered South Africa's racial policies in 1960 after the police killings at Sharpeville. On that occasion it labelled the situation in South Africa as one that "if continued might endanger international peace and security" — that is, not a threat to international peace under Article 39 of the Charter — and merely called upon South Africa to abandon apartheid (Resolution 134 [1960]). In 1963 and 1964, the Security Council went further and called on states to cease the supply of arms and military equipment to South Africa.[4] However, as the resolutions were not based on findings under Article 39, but on the lesser determination that the situation "seriously disturbed" international peace under Chapter VI, they were merely recommendatory and not mandatory (Dugard, 1966). Thereafter the Council reaffirmed its non-mandatory calls to states to refuse to supply South Africa with arms and military equipment (Resolutions 282 [1970]; 311 [1972]).

The Soweto uprising of 1976-1977 and the repressive police action taken to suppress it provided the necessary justification for intensified measures by the Security Council. On October 31, 1977, the Council condemned the brutal action taken under the security laws in Resolution 417 and then, on November 4, it imposed a mandatory arms embargo against South Africa under Chapter VII. In Resolution 418 the Security Council determined "that the acquisition by South Africa of arms and related materiel constitutes a threat to the maintenance of international peace and security" and decided that all states should "cease forthwith any provision to South Africa of arms and related materiel of all types."

International Law and the Struggle for Liberation in South Africa 87

This resolution was significant for several reasons. First, it determined the situation in South Africa to be a threat to international peace under Article 39 and ordered states to take action against South Africa under Chapter VII of the Charter. Second, it was the first occasion on which the Security Council had ordered enforcement action to be taken against a member state. Previously the Council had ordered such action to be taken against a non-member only — Rhodesia. Third, it opened the door for further collective action under Chapter VII to be taken against South Africa, as the major hurdle in the way of such action — a finding of a threat to the peace under Article 39 — had been cleared.

In 1977, it was widely believed that further mandatory sanctions would follow the imposition of the arms embargo. But this was not to be. The Reagan administration in the United States and the Thatcher government in Britain used their vetoes[5] in the Security Council to ensure that there was no extension of mandatory sanctions. Only non-binding resolutions, premised on findings falling short of a "threat to the peace," urging states to take selected economic sanctions against South Africa, were allowed to pass (Resolution 569 [1985]).

Sanctions Outside the United Nations

In 1946, India instituted a trade boycott of South Africa. Since then, and particularly since 1962 when the General Assembly first called on states to sever economic ties with South Africa, other states and international organizations have imposed economic sanctions of different types on South Africa. In 1963, the Organization of African Unity called for the imposition of a "total economic boycott" against South Africa; in 1985 and 1986, the Commonwealth agreed to impose a wide variety of sanctions ranging from a ban on air links to bans on the import of agricultural products, uranium, coal, iron, and steel from South Africa; and in 1986, the European Community decided that its member states should place a ban on new investment in South Africa and on the import of iron, steel, and gold coins from South Africa. Many states have unilaterally imposed sanctions. Of special importance is the Comprehensive Anti-Apartheid Act passed by the Congress of the United States in 1986, which imposes limited economic sanctions against South Africa (Hanlon and Omond, 1987).

In some quarters, economic coercion of this kind — that is, not authorized by the Security Council acting under Chapter VII of the U.N. Charter — is viewed as unlawful (Barrie, 1988). Here, reliance is placed on two important resolutions of the General Assembly, the Declaration on the Inadmissibility of Intervention in the Domestic Affairs of States and the Protection of Their Independence and Sovereignty of 1965 (Resolution 2131 [XX]) and the Declaration on Principles of International Law Concerning Friendly Relations and

Co-operation among States in Accordance with the Charter of the United Nations of 1970 (Resolution 2625 [XXV]), which declare that:

> No state may use or encourage the use of economic, political, or any other type of measures to coerce another state in order to obtain from it the subordination of the exercise of its sovereign rights or to secure from it advantages of any kind.

However, even if economic coercion is prohibited by international law, it can hardly be maintained that the collective and unilateral economic measures taken against South Africa are not justifiable under contemporary international law. The doctrine of humanitarian intervention and a host of Security Council and General Assembly resolutions recommending economic sanctions against South Africa provide clear legal authorization for such action (Maddrey, 1981; Szasz, 1988).

B. Exclusion from International Organizations

New methods of communication and transport have led to closer political and economic cooperation between states through the agency of international organizations, with the result that exclusion from these organizations has become an important sanction. The international community has employed this sanction extensively against South Africa.

South Africa's exclusion from international bodies commenced in 1955 when it voluntarily withdrew from the United Nations Educational, Scientific and Cultural Organization (UNESCO). Since 1961, South Africa has "withdrawn" from a number of international bodies, but in most cases the withdrawal has been under pressure and resorted to in order to avoid the ignominy of expulsion. South Africa has "withdrawn" or been excluded from the following organizations: the Commonwealth (1961), the Food and Agriculture Organization (FAO)(1964), the International Labour Organization (ILO) (1964), and the Universal Postal Union (UPU) (1979). It has been obliged to withdraw from participation in conferences of the World Health Organization (WHO), the International Telecommunications Union (ITU), the International Civil Aviation Organization (ICAO), the World Intellectual Property Organization (WIPO), and the International Atomic Energy Agency (IAEA) (Heunis, 1986: 148-175, 486-491).

Although South Africa has been saved from expulsion from the United Nations by the vetoes of the Western Powers, it has been excluded from participation in the proceedings of the General Assembly since 1974. The legality of this action on the part of the General Assembly is questionable as, in the terms of the Charter, only the Security Council and the General Assembly together may suspend a state's membership rights in the United Nations (Article 5) or expel it (Article 6) (Ciobanu, 1976; *sed contra* Suttner, 1984).

C. Non-Recognition of Bantustans

The South African government clearly hoped that its Bantustan "states" would be recognized as independent states, since this would have conferred legitimacy on the policy of separate development as an acceptable form of self-determination. However, although Transkei and other Bantustan states arguably meet the requirements for statehood laid down in the Montevideo Convention, no state except South Africa itself has recognized any of these creations. On the contrary, the sanction of collective non-recognition has been effectively employed to deny statehood to these entities and to deny legitimacy to separate development.

In 1976, two days after the grant of "independence" to Transkei by South Africa, the General Assembly adopted a resolution condemning "the establishment of Bantustans as designed to consolidate the inhuman policies of apartheid" and called on all governments to "deny any form of recognition to the so-called independent Transkei" (Resolution 31/6A). Similar resolutions were adopted in respect of the purported independence of Bophuthatswana, Venda, and Ciskei.

These recommendations have been strictly observed. Probably the best explanation for the collective non-recognition of the Bantustan "states" is that the United Nations has determined their creation to be in violation of emerging norms of *jus cogens* in the field of human rights and self-determination (Dugard, 1987: 98-108).

D. The Denunciation of Apartheid as a Crime against Humanity

Innumerable resolutions of the General Assembly and Security Council have condemned apartheid as a violation of the human-rights provisions of the U.N. Charter. The outlawing of apartheid has, however, been taken several steps further. Since 1966, apartheid has been labelled as a "crime against humanity" (General Assembly Resolution 2202A [XX]) and in 1973, apartheid became a special international crime. The International Convention on the Suppression and Punishment of the Crime of Apartheid of 1973 declares apartheid to be a "crime against humanity" and obliges signatory states to bring to trial and to punish persons found guilty of this crime. The "crime of apartheid" is defined as the denial of basic rights to members of a racial group "committed for the purpose of establishing and maintaining domination by one racial group of persons over any other group of persons and systematically oppressing them" (Article 2). Over 70 states have ratified this Convention.

E. Support for Liberation Movements

The United Nations has given a wide range of support to the two South African liberation movements recognized by the Organization of African Unity — the African National Congress (ANC) and the Pan-Africanist Congress (PAC). The General Assembly sees them as the "authentic representatives of the overwhelming majority of the South African people."[6] As such, they have been invited to attend and address meetings of the principal and subsidiary organs of the United Nations. Indeed, an apologist for the South African government has complained that they "have more rights in the various organs of the United Nations than the South African government" (Heunis, 1986: 307).

In addition, the United Nations has relaxed the prohibition on the use of force contained in Article 2(4) of the U.N. Charter with respect to these liberation movements. Although the Security Council has never expressly authorized states — particularly the "Frontline States" — to use force against South Africa, it has, by its silence, condoned their support to the ANC and PAC, in the form of permission to establish military bases in their territories and to transit their territories. The General Assembly has gone further. On many occasions it has recognized the justness of the struggle waged by the ANC and PAC and called upon states to provide *all* forms of assistance to them.[7] Furthermore, interpretative definitions given by the General Assembly to the unlawful use of force and aggression have carefully excluded the actions of liberation movements (Wilson, 1988: 94-103).

Further legitimacy has been given to the military activities of the liberation movements by the 1977 Protocols Additional to the Geneva Conventions of 1949. Protocol I classifies conflicts involving liberation movements "fighting against colonial domination and alien occupation and against racist regimes in the exercise of their right of self-determination" as *international* and not internal conflicts (Article 1[4]) and thereby categorizes ANC and PAC combatants as soldiers entitled to treatment as prisoners-of-war if captured (Dugard, 1989).

The Impact of International Action on Apartheid and the Role of International Law

Some discount the effectiveness of international action against South Africa. Economic sanctions, they claim, failed to weaken either the economy of the country or the political resolve of its white people. The armed struggle was no more than a painful irritant; the non-recognition of the Bantustan states an exercise in futility; and the International Convention on the Suppression and Punishment of the Crime of Apartheid a mere rhetorical gesture. More-

International Law and the Struggle for Liberation in South Africa   91

over, they argue that the mobilization of international opinion served to harden white attitudes and to delay liberation.

This cynical approach is difficult to sustain in the light of recent developments. The appeals by State President F.W. de Klerk to Western nations to lift sanctions now that negotiations with the ANC have commenced surely indicate a causal link between sanctions and negotiations. It is not idealism and altruism that have brought the National Party to the negotiating table, but rather a combination of international pressure and internal unrest. While economic sanctions have been the most important of the international weapons employed against apartheid, the others should not be discounted. Political and moral isolation have also played their part. South Africans have keenly felt the Republic's exclusion from international political, cultural, and sporting life. The non-recognition of the Bantustan states has destroyed the viability of the territorial fragmentation of South Africa into a collection of ethnic "states" as an acceptable political solution. And the repeated denunciation of apartheid as morally unacceptable to the international community has undermined the moral basis for apartheid that its early ideological architects fought so hard to establish.

International law has evolved under the pressure of apartheid. Without apartheid, it is unlikely that the domestic-jurisdiction clause in the U.N. Charter would have been so completely subordinated to the interests of human rights; or that the prohibition of racial discrimination would have become a fundamental international norm, of the character of *jus cogens*; or that wars of national liberation would have been transformed into international conflicts; or that the concept of a "crime against humanity" would have been extended beyond the Nazi experience. International law has evolved to play its part in the downfall of apartheid, but in the course of this process, international law itself has become a system of law more attuned to the interests of human rights and to the needs of an interdependent world, and less rooted in notions of state sovereignty. South Africa has benefitted from international law, and international law has benefitted from South Africa.

International law will continue to guide and shape South African society. Non-discrimination, respect for human rights, and the right to self-determination have been consistently invoked against apartheid. They are now part of the national consciousness and form the basic principles for the new political dispensation. This is apparent in both the ANC's *Constitutional Guidelines*[8] and the National Party government's guiding principles[9] in which the legal protection of human rights and equality before the law feature prominently. In addition, the prohibition on the fragmentation of a self-determination unit as part of the modern law of self-determination (Dugard, 1987: 161-162) is likely to deter any attempts aimed at territorial partition. The form of Namibian independence was guided by a set of principles approved by the Security Council.[10] Although the United Nations has not attempted to lay down constitutional principles to guide the establishment of a post-apartheid society, there is little doubt that the new South Africa will be shaped by the principles of racial equality and respect for human rights that the United Nations has expounded in its condemnations of apartheid over the past 40 years.

The 1973 International Convention on the Suppression and Punishment of the Crime of Apartheid designates apartheid as a "crime against humanity" and provides for the prosecution before national or international tribunals of persons guilty of this crime. Whether the architects of apartheid or those responsible for the execution of the most brutal features of this policy will be granted amnesty or tried before tribunals applying the principles of Nuremberg is uncertain. The mood of reconciliation that presently pervades relations between the National Party government and the ANC suggests that there will be no such trials, as does the granting of amnesty to members of the ANC convicted of serious crimes. On the other hand, the history of Germany and Argentina shows that a new society cannot be built on ignorance of the past. It must acknowledge the evils of the past and keep the truth of this history constantly before its people to ensure that similar events do not recur (Aspen Institute, 1989). The crimes of apartheid and the illegitimacy of the legal order under which they were perpetrated must not be forgotten. Children in a new South Africa must be fully informed of the past in their history courses. But more may be required. Other societies have demanded an authoritative official denunciation of the past by means of public prosecution or the holding of a commission of inquiry. In South Africa the selective prosecution of those responsible for the planning and execution of population removals and the killing of political detainees might serve to denounce the atrocities of apartheid. But, in addition, there will be a need for a full exposure of the theory and practice of apartheid by means of an impartial enquiry. Reconciliation is essential; but the history of apartheid must not be forgotten.

NOTES

1. The First Report of this Commission appears in 8 U.N. GAOR, Supp 16, U.N. Doc. A/2505 (1953).

2. See resolutions 134 (1960), 182 (1963), 191 (1964).

3. See, for example, resolutions 3151 G(XXVII) and 39/72A (1984).

4. See resolutions 181 (1960), 183 (1960), and 191 (1964).

5. For an account of these vetoes, see *U.N. Chronicle* (No. 4) 29, 35 (1986).

6. See, for example, General Assembly resolutions 3151G (XXVIII); 3411 (XXX); 36/172A (1981); 37/69A (1982); 39/72A (1984).

International Law and the Struggle for Liberation in South Africa 93

7. See, for example, resolutions 35/206A (1980), 36/172A (1981), 37/69A (1982), 38/39A (1983), 39/72A (1984).

8. The text of these *Guidelines* appears in *Columbia Human Rights Law Review* 21 (1989: 235).

9. In 1989, the South African Law Commission, a government-appointed body, recommended the adoption of a Bill of Rights for South Africa that advocates the full recognition of civil and political rights, equality before the law, and the franchise for all adult South Africans. See South African Law Commission, Working Paper 25, Project 58, Group and Human Rights (1989). The text of the draft Bill of Rights is published in *Columbia Human Rights Law Review* 21 (1989: 241).

10. See S/15287 of July 12, 1982.

REFERENCES

Aspen Institute
1989   State Crimes. Punishment or Pardon. Queenstown, Maryland: Justice and Society Program of Aspen Institute.

Barrie, George N.
1988   "Agora: Is the ASIL Policy on Disinvestment in Violation of International Law?" American Journal of International Law 82: 311.

Ciobanu, Dan
1976   "Credentials of Delegations and Representation of Member States at the United Nations." International and Comparative Law Quarterly 25: 351.

Dugard, John
1989   "Human Rights, Humanitarian Law and the South African Conflict." Harvard Human Rights Yearbook 2: 101.
1987   Recognition and the United Nations. Cambridge: Grotius Publications.
1986   "The Conflict between International Law and South African Law: Another Divisive Factor in South African Society." South African Journal on Human Rights 2: 1.
1966   "The Legal Effect of United Nations Resolutions on Apartheid." South African Law Journal 83: 44.

Hanlon, Joseph and Roger Omond
1987   The Sanctions Handbook. Harmondsworth, England: Penguin Books.

Heunis, Jan C.
1986   United Nations versus South Africa. Johannesburg: Lex Patria.

Higgins, Rosalyn
1963   The Development of International Law through the Political Organs of the United Nations. London: Oxford University Press.

Maddrey, W.C.
1981   "Economic Sanctions against South Africa: Problems and Prospects for Enforcement of Human Rights Norms." Virginia Journal of International Law 22: 345.

Ozgur, Ozdemir A.
1982   Apartheid, the United Nations and Peaceful Change in South Africa. Dobbs Ferry, New York: Transnational Publishers.

Schwelb, Egon
1972   "The International Court of Justice and the Human Rights Clauses of the Charter." American Journal of International Law 66: 338.

Szasz, Paul, C.
1988   "Agora: Is the ASIL Policy on Disinvestment in Violation of International Law?" American Journal of International Law 82: 314.

Suttner, Raymond
1984 "Has South Africa Been Illegally Excluded from the United Nations General Assembly?" Comparative and International Law Quarterly of Southern Africa 17: 279.

Wilson, Heather A.
1988 International Law and the Use of Force by National Liberation Movements. Oxford: Clarendon Press.

Terrorism in Southern Africa:
South Africa's Role

[25]

ANNALS, *AAPSS*, 463, September 1982

South Africa and Instability in Southern Africa

By ELAINE A. FRIEDLAND

ABSTRACT: Terrorism and the political use of violence are not necessarily synonymous. Terrorism is the use of violence for the primary purpose of creating a general atmosphere of fear and alarm. Thus, a terrorist organization does not limit its tactical use of violence to military and other such strategic targets but will additionally direct its violent tactics against the public at large. If employed by a government, the objective of such a use of terror can be to create submission to a repressive status quo. If used by an anti-governmental group, the objective may be to create a situation of instability in order to facilitate the overthrow of the existing government. In southern Africa, anti-governmental organizations operating in Mozambique, Angola, and Zimbabwe depend on financial and military assistance from the South African regime which utilizes these organizations as one component of its strategy to destabilize the governments of the former countries. This article demonstrates that (1) these anti-governmental organizations, such as União Nacional de Independência Total de Angola (UNITA) and the Movimento de Resistência Nacional de Moçambique, by their tactics, conform to the definition of a terrorist organization; (2) these anti-governmental organizations could not survive without their linkages to the South African regime; and (3) the South African regime's objective in promoting these anti-governmental organizations is to attempt to continue the status quo inside South Africa.

Elaine A. Friedland is presently on the faculty of the New York Institute of Technology. She received her Ph.D. in political science from the City University of New York in 1980 and has had articles published in the Journal of Southern African Affairs, The African Review *(Dar es Salaam),* Civilisations, *and the* Journal of Black Studies. *Her areas of research specialization are South African politics and the international political economy.*

I N southern Africa, there exists simultaneously an interrelationship between political violence and political conflict, as well as between political conflicts in the international and domestic arenas. First, the primary conflict in the domestic arena is between the South African regime, on the one hand, and the African National Congress of South Africa (ANC) and the South West African Peoples' Organization (SWAPO) on the other hand. Because of this conflict, the South African regime opposes, in the international arena, the Movimento Popular de Libertação de Angola-Partido de Trabalhadores (MPLA-PT), the Frente de Libertação de Moçambique (FRELIMO), and the Zimbabwe African National Union-Patriotic Front (ZANU-PF)—the ruling political parties of Angola, Mozambique, and Zimbabwe, respectively. Moreover, this international conflict has created a domestic conflict in Angola, Mozambique, and Zimbabwe where anti-governmental organizations challenge the legitimacy of the respective ruling political party. In each situation, the conflict has repeatedly involved political violence, and that political violence has commonly entailed terrorism.

This article (1) defines the concept of terrorism; (2) investigates the present situation in Angola, Mozambique, and Zimbabwe in terms of the development and specific activities of the respective anti-governmental organization; (3) examines the relationship between these anti-governmental organizations and the South African regime; and (4) discusses the South African regime's policy goals vis-à-vis Angola, Mozambique, and Zimbabwe, as well as the reason that regime is pursuing those particular goals. From this analysis, it will be demonstrated that the South African regime has a major responsibility for the existence of terrorism and potential instability in the region.

A DEFINITION OF TERRORISM

Currently, in the general press, governmental officials brand as "terrorist" all political opponents—groups or individuals—who accept the legitimacy of using violence as a political tactic. However, these officials simultaneously ignore or condone a similar use of violence by their own bureaucratic institutions or foreign allies. Hence, not only has this popular usage of the word "terrorist" caused it to degenerate into a term employed to vilify one's political opposition but, more importantly, it has obscured the intimate relationship between politics and violence.

Politics, in its essence, is a conflict for power. Namely, political conflict is fundamentally a struggle either to maintain or gain control over an institution, and the primary institution in our present society is the state. Max Weber defines the state as "a human community that (successfully) claims the monopoly of the legitimate use of physical force within a given territory."[1] Consequently, the state as an institution always implies, as a prerequisite, the threat of the use of violence or counterviolence. Thus, when a political struggle's objective is control of the state itself, that struggle will always involve violence.[2] In other

1. "Politics as a Vocation," in *From Max Weber: Essays in Sociology,* eds. H. H. Gerth and C. Wright Mills (New York: Oxford University Press, 1958), p. 78.
2. H. L. Nieburg, *Political Violence: The Behavioral Process* (New York: St. Martins

SOUTH AFRICA

words, "war is . . . a continuation of political commerce, a carrying out of the same by other means."[3] Hence, since "the ultimate kind of power is violence,"[4] political conflict can never be totally divorced from violence in the final analysis.

For this reason, the concept of terrorism should not be equated with political violence in general. To make such an equation would lead to the logical deduction that all struggles pertaining to the issue of control over the state will eventually involve terrorism. Historical data demonstrate that this inference is empirically invalid. Rather, the concept of terrorism must be delimited and defined as involving specific forms of political violence. Since the word "terror" is synonymous with abject fear and horror, terrorism should be defined as the tactical use of political violence for the purpose of creating an atmosphere of fear and intimidation among the public at large. The particular forms of political violence subsumed under the category of terrorism are: arbitrary imprisonment, mass arrest, mutilation, torture, the kidnapping or seizing as hostages of persons lacking in political decision-making authority, massacres and other similar acts of mass murder, and collective punishment directed against sections of the population solely because of the acts of others. In situations of terrorism, political violence is not restricted to military and other such strategic targets. In addition, attacks against

the general population occur more frequently than attacks against strategic targets.[5]

The political actor utilizing terrorism—that is, a terrorist organization—can be either an anti-governmental organization or a ruling political party. When the latter is the case, the target of the terrorism could be the domestic population and/or the population of a foreign state. Hence, terrorism is used to try to deter political activity deemed illegitimate by that regime, as well as to punish those actually involved in such activities. The objective is to maintain an existing political order or to create a new one through forcing the target population to submit to it. In situations where an anti-governmental organization employs terrorism, the purpose would be to obtain one or more of the following objectives: advertise a political cause; gain concessions from a government, that is, using terrorism as a form of "coercive bargaining"; provoke indiscriminate governmental repression; and undermine the legitimacy of the existing regime through creating complete sociopolitical chaos. Moreover, if such an anti-governmental organization became the dominant political force within a geographic region, then that organization would also use terrorism for the same purpose as the ruling political party.[6]

5. Tully, pp. 4-42; United Nations, General Assembly, Ad Hoc Committee on International Terrorism, *Report 1979* (A/34/37), pp. 5, 8; Edgar O'Ballance, *Language of Violence* (San Rafael, CA: Presidio Press, 1979), pp. 1, 11; Brian Jenkins, *International Terrorism: A New Model of Conflict* (Los Angeles: Seminar on Arms Control and Foreign Policy Research Papers, 1975), pp. 1-2.

6. A/34/37, p. 8; Michael Stohl, "Myths and Realities of Political Terrorism," in *The Politics of Terrorism*, ed. Michael Stohl (New York: Marcel Dikker), pp. 3-4, 14.

Press, 1969), p. 11; Charles Tully, "Collective Violence in the European Perspective," in *Violence in America*, eds. Hugh Davis Graham and Ted Robert Gurr (New York: New American Library, 1969), p. 10.

3. Carl von Clausewitz, *On War* (Baltimore: Penguin Books, 1968), p. 119.

4. C. Wright Mills, *The Power Elite* (New York: Oxford University Press, 1956), p. 171.

PROBLEM OF TERRORISM IN ANGOLA, MOZAMBIQUE, AND ZIMBABWE

Angola, Mozambique, and Zimbabwe achieved their independence through a long, protracted military conflict between the nationalist movement and the colonial regime. This military conflict, besides undermining the authority of the colonial regime, destroyed much of the existing socioeconomic infrastructure. Thus, these governments' priority goal has been national reconstruction and economic development.[7] However, there currently exist in each of these countries antigovernment organizations employing political violence to challenge the legitimacy of the ruling political party. Consequently, scarce resources have been diverted from economic development to national defense: in Angola defense expenditures are around 50 percent of the national budget; in Mozambique, nearly 30 percent; and in Zimbabwe, almost 15 percent.[8]

The Angolan situation

Before Angola's independence in November 1975, three nationalist organizations, each having its own military force, functioned in Angola: the MPLA-PT, the Frente Nacional de Libertação de Angola (FNLA), and União Nacional de Independência Total de Angola (UNITA). The MPLA's leadership

aims to industrialize Angola and to provide social benefits for the general Angolan population. In contrast, the leadership of the FNLA and UNITA seeks to gain power without changing the relationship between the government and the general Angolan population from that which existed under the colonial regime. To justify their own political ambitions, their organizations stress regional over national loyalty. During the period of the anticolonial struggle, the leaders of the FNLA and UNITA more frequently directed their armies against the MPLA's army than against the Portuguese army.

Following the April 1974 coup d'etat in Portugal, the military regime's decolonization policy forced the three organizations to form a "tripartite" transitional government. However, in March 1975 the FNLA and UNITA military forces began attacking MPLA supporters and by July 1975, a full-scale civil war raged between the MPLA and an alliance of the FNLA and UNITA. The South African military forces entered the civil war in August to aid UNITA and intensified their intervention at the end of October. After this, the MPLA obtained Cuban military assistance.[9]

Even though the civil war formally ended in March 1976 with the temporary withdrawal of the South African military forces, UNITA continued its campaign of violence against the Angolan government. This campaign has included the bombing of foreign embassies; bombing, or attempted bombing, of hospitals, schools, marketplaces,

7. Elaine A. Friedland, "Regional Cooperation and Development Policy in Southern Africa" (Paper delivered at the Conference on Science, Technology and Development—Association for the Advancement of Policy, Research and Development in the Third World, Washington, DC, Nov. 1981).

8. *Africa Research Bulletin: Economic, Financial, and Technical Series*, 18:6113 (Jul.-Aug. 1981), 18:6280 (Dec. 1981-Jan. 1982).

9. Basil Davidson, "Recent History of Angola," in *Africa South of the Sahara 1980-81* (London: Europa Publications, 1980), pp. 141-47.

SOUTH AFRICA 99

and hotels; killing of foreign mis-- sionaries; kidnapping of foreign technicians; mass abduction of villagers; and stealing of cattle from villagers.[10] Consequently, UNITA has directed most of its political violence against the Angolan civilian population, not militarily strategic targets. Due to these particular tactics, UNITA conforms to the definition of a terrorist organization.

The Mozambican situation

In August 1974 the Portuguese military regime agreed to form, in Mozambique, a transitional government with FRELIMO as the dominant political force. Then the ultraconservative sector of the Portuguese community in Mozambique —allied with a tiny portion of the socioeconomic elite of the African community that had a similar socioeconomic outlook—attempted a coup d'état to block FRELIMO's assumption of power. Although a general strike and FRELIMO's army quashed the coup, this sector never reconciled itself to Mozambique's independence in June 1975, with FRELIMO as the ruling political party.[11] From 1975 to 1979, this

sector functioned through several political organizations. Some of them—such as the Frente Unida de Moçambique—claiming to be nationwide, initially advocated Mozambique's reintegration into a Portuguese federal republic and then joining South Africa's plan for a "constellation of Southern African States," while others—for instance, the Frente de Libertação de Cabo Delgado—stressed regional over national loyalty.[12]

Early in 1979, through the Southern Rhodesian colonial regime's intervention, these various organizations coalesced into the Movimento de Resistência Nacional de Moçambique (MRNM). Before the MRNM's formation, incidents of political violence directed against the civilian population occurred very infrequently. Afterward, however, the occurrence of such incidents vastly increased. The MRNM has been responsible for train robberies, kidnapping and killing foreign technicians, attacking farming villages and burning those villages' granaries, looting stores, mass abductions of villagers, mutilating government supporters, hijacking buses, and an attempted bombing of a Maputo hotel.[13] Because the

10. United States, Department of State, *Foreign Broadcast Information Service: Middle East and Africa* (hereafter cited as *FBIS: Middle East and Africa*), 17 Dec. 1981, p. U2; *Africa Research Bulletin: Political, Social, and Cultural Series* (hereafter cited as *ARB: PSC*) 15:5050-51 (Nov. 1978), 17:5709 (Jun. 1980), 17:5775 (Aug. 1980), 18:6048 (May 1981); Edward F. Mickolus, *Transnational Terrorism: A Chronology of Events 1968-1979* (London: Aldwych Press, 1980), pp. 598, 761, 885.

11. Elaine A. Friedland, "A Comparative Study of the Development of Revolutionary Nationalism in Southern Africa— FRELIMO (Mozambique) and the African National Congress of South Africa" (Ph.D. dissertation, City University of New York, 1980), pp. 445-47; Tony Hodges, "Mozam-

bique: the Politics of Liberation," in *Southern Africa in Crisis*, eds. Gwendolen M. Carter and Patrick O'Meara (Bloomington: Indiana University Press, 1977), pp. 67-69.

12. "Mozambique," *Economist*, Jun.-Jul. 1981, p. 40; Hodges; Victor Ndovi, "FRELIMO's Ruthless Enemies," *New African*, May 1979, pp. 38-40; "Mozambique" in *Africa Contemporary Record 1978-1979*, ed. Colin Legum (New York: Africana, 1980), p. B332; "Mozambique," in *Africa Contemporary Record 1979-1980*, ed. Colin Legum (New York: Africana, 1981), pp. B729-30.

13. Ndovi; David Ward and Martin Plaut, "The True Story behind the Bombing of Mozambique," *New African*, Jan. 1982, p. 24; *British Broadcasting Corporation*, 22 Jan., 2 Feb., 1982; *ARB: PSC*, 16:5198 (Mar. 1979),

MRNM primarily directs its political violence against nonstrategic targets, it constitutes a terrorist organization.

The Zimbabwean situation

European and African supporters of the Southern Rhodesian colonial regime opposed ZANU-PF becoming the ruling political party. It was this colonial regime that was responsible for creating the MRNM, and soon after Zimbabwe's independence in April 1980, the MRNM extended its activity to eastern Zimbabwe, in the region adjoining Mozambique. As a consequence of the MRNM's raids on stores and attacks on travelers, a warlike situation still exists in eastern Zimbabwe. Additionally, the ultraconservative sector of the European community in Zimbabwe twice plotted to assassinate, en masse, the ZANU-PF leadership. This same sector has been implicated in attempting to create a regionalist political organization in southwestern Zimbabwe. Simultaneously, arms caches were found throughout southern Zimbabwe, mostly on the property of persons of European descent, but also on property owned by the other nationalist political party—the Patriotic Front-Zimbabwe African People's Union.[14] Although, as of yet, no direct evidence exists indicating whether these arms were intended to be used against strategic targets or against the civilian population, the political opposition to ZANU-PF has adopted the strategy of political violence. Furthermore, some sectors of this opposition—but not all—have committed acts of political violence that qualify as terrorist actions.

LINKAGES BETWEEN THE SOUTH AFRICAN REGIME AND THE TERRORIST ORGANIZATIONS

The existence of terrorism in Angola, Mozambique, and Zimbabwe is not a symptom of mass opposition to the policies of the respective ruling political party. In each case, the terrorist organization derives its base from a very tiny sector of society. In the cases of Angola and Mozambique, that sector has become a class of emigrés, while it is becoming a class of emigrés in Zimbabwe. Moreover, these organizations primarily attack the public at large in the region in which they operate, thus antagonizing the people of that region. Hence, these organizations depend for their continued operation not upon the local population but upon an outside power—the Republic of South Africa.

UNITA's association with the South African regime began during the Angolan civil war. Since that time, UNITA's army has functioned essentially as an appendage of the South African army. Although the South African military forces try to conceal their recurrent violations of Angolan sovereignty by crediting their own actions to UNITA, UNITA can only attack strategic

16:5475 (Nov. 1979), 17:5909 (Dec. 1980), 18:5969 (Feb. 1981), 18:6027 (Apr. 1981); Mickolus, p. 863; *Facts on File*, 40:565 (Jul. 1980); *FBIS: Middle East and Africa*, 2 Feb. 1982, pp. U4-5; *Quarterly Economic Review: Tanzania and Mozambique*, no. 3, 1980, p. 16; no. 1, 1981, p. 13.

14. Robert H. Taylor, "Zimbabwe 1980: Politicisation through Armed Struggle and Electoral Mobilisation," *Journal of Commonwealth and Comparative Studies*, 19(1):77 (Mar. 1981); *ARB:PSC*, 17:5718 (Jun. 1980), 17:5904 (Dec. 1980), 18:6119 (Jul. 1981); *Brit-*

ish Broadcasting Corporation, 16 Feb. 1982; *FBIS: Middle East and Africa*, 22 Dec. 1981 p U5, 4 Feb. 1982, p. U4.

SOUTH AFRICA   101

targets with the direct assistance of, and in conjunction with, the South African military forces. Furthermore, even the South African regime's military actions inside Angola are not restricted to strategic targets, since villages, towns, and cities in southern Angola have been destroyed as a consequence of these invasions.[15]

When the MRNM was formed, its primary promoter was the Southern Rhodesian colonial regime, providing it with radio transmitter facilities, a military training camp in Bindura—near the city of Umtali—military equipment, and other logistical support, as well as paying its soldiers a comparatively substantial salary and air dropping supplies to units inside Mozambique. However, because the Southern Rhodesia colonial regime obtained most of its financial and military assistance from the Republic of South Africa, the South African regime indirectly sustained the MRNM since its creation. Thus, with Zimbabwe's independence, the South African regime assumed direct responsibility to maintain the MRNM—moving the radio transmitter facilities and military training camp to Phalaborwa, Transvaal, and having the South African air force repeatedly violate Mozambican air space to air drop food and military supplies to units inside Mozambique. Moreover, like UNITA, the MRNM requires direct

logistical aid from the South African military forces in order to attack strategic targets.[16]

In the early 1970s, the Southern Rhodesian colonial regime created an African volunteer military unit, "Selous Scouts," which was particularly ardent in its support of the status quo. Then, in 1978, that regime obtained the collaboration of Bishop Abel Muzurewa, his personal political party, which was the United African National Council, and its military force—the "auxiliaries." Furthermore, during the 1980 election, South African corporate interests financed the United African National Council's campaign. From these two groups—opposed to the ZANU-PF as a ruling political party—have come Zimbabweans allied to the South African regime. By early 1981, the South African military forces were training 5000 Zimbabweans in a camp near Phalaborwa, Transvaal. This strategic-logistical assistance has been implicated in attacks against strategic targets.[17]

The South African regime is the primary promoter of the anti-governmental organizations that employ terrorism, supplying them with military advisers, logistical support, and financial assistance—support without which these organizations could not continue

15. *Rand Daily Mail* (Johannesburg), 8 Sept. 1981; "The Terrible Dilemma of Angola's War Victims: Become Refugees or Die," *New African*, Jan. 1982, p. 25; John Stockwell, *In Search of Enemies* (New York: W. W. Norton, 1978), pp. 154, 164-65, 185-86, 215, 233; *ARB: PSC*, 15:4708 (Jan. 1978), 15:4737 (Feb. 1978), 16:5129 (Jan. 1979), 16:5263 (May 1979), 16:5418 (Sept. 1979), 17:5591 (Feb. 1981), 18:5975 (Feb. 1981); *Facts on File*, 41:620 (Aug. 1981), 41:629 (Sept. 1981); *Manchester Guardian Weekly*, 13 Dec. 1981.

16. Ward and Plaut; *Quarterly Economic Review: Tanzania and Mozambique*, no. 4, 1980, p. 15; Ndovi; *British Broadcasting Corporation*, 22 Jan. 1982; *Star* (Johannesburg), 12 Dec. 1981; *FBIS: Middle East and Africa*, 18 Jan. 1982, p. U1; *ARB:PSC*, 16:5198 (Mar. 1979), 16:5268 (Jun. 1979), 16:5475 (Nov. 1979), 17:5909 (Dec. 1980), 18:6084 (Jun. 1981) 18:6185-86 (Sept. 1981), *Facts on File*, 40:565 (Jul. 1980); *Guardian* (London), 26 Oct. 1981; *New York Times*, 23 Feb. 1982.

17. Taylor, pp. 78-82; *Manchester Guardian Weekly*, 3, 10 Jan. 1982; *Star*, 11 May, 1981; *ARB:PSC*, 18:6258 (Nov. 1981).

102   **THE ANNALS OF THE AMERICAN ACADEMY**

functioning. Consequently, the South African regime completely approves of these organizations' tactics—including terrorism—or else the regime would have used its influence over them to effect a change of tactics. The regime itself has therefore adopted the tactic of terrorism as part of its foreign policy toward neighboring states, and as a result it too complies with the definition of a terrorist organization.

THE SOUTH AFRICAN REGIME'S FOREIGN POLICY OBJECTIVES

The South African regime's foreign policy is closely interconnected with its domestic policy. Since 1912, the South African regime—based on a colonial-type system, restricting political rights to the European population to maintain the Black population, that is, the African, Indian, and Colored communities, in a politically and economically subordinate position—has been in conflict with the ANC, which seeks to replace that colonial-type system by a democratic system. Although the ANC employed a strategy of nonviolent tactics from 1912 until 1961, the South African regime frequently responded with arbitrary imprisonment, mass arrests, massacres of unarmed demonstrators, and torture, both psychological and physical. In essence, the South African regime directed political violence against the Black population in general, thereby aiming governmental terrorism at forcing the population to submit to the existing political order. In 1961, the ANC adopted a military strategy to change the South African system, restricting its political violence to strategic targets. A similar process occurred

in Namibia, with SWAPO choosing a military strategy in 1966.

To the South African regime, an intracontinental conflict exists between nationalist organizations seeking the economic restructuring of their societies and the forces aiming to sustain the economic status quo. In order to isolate the ANC and SWAPO from potential allies, the South African regime first subsidized, financially and militarily, the Portuguese and Southern Rhodesian colonial regimes, and then after independence began aiding African politicians who were sympathetic to the South African status quo. It intervened in the Angolan civil war, continued to support UNITA, sponsors the MRNM, and trains an anti-governmental Zimbabwean military force.[18]

Furthermore, even though the governments of the independent Southern African states are ideologically sympathetic to the ANC's and SWAPO's objectives, these states' present economic dependence on South Africa limits—except for Angola—their effective support of the ANC and SWAPO to statements of solidarity. Simultaneously, though, these states seek to end that economic dependence. Thus, the South African regime considers the economic independence and industrialization of those states as a threat to the South African status quo. The regime's strategy is to use the MRNM to prevent Mozambique's and Zimbabwe's economic development, and UNITA to thwart Angola's and Zambia's economic development.[19]

18. Friedland, "A Comparative Study."
19. Friedland; Ward and Plaut; Julian Burgess, "South Africa's Campaign against SADCC," *African Business*, Jan. 1982, pp. 12-14.

SOUTH AFRICA   **103**

CONCLUSION

Depending on the circumstances, a terrorist organization can be a ruling political party or an anti-governmental organization. However, the use of violence per se does not make a particular political actor a terrorist organization; rather it is its lack of restriction to strategic targets and its utilization of violence against the public at large. It is the employment of the latter that places the MRNM, UNITA, and the ultraconservative opposition groups of Zimbabwe under the classification of terrorist organizations. In reality, these organizations function as an extension of the South African military forces. Thus, the actual opposition to the political and economic policies of the MPLA, FRELIMO, and ZANU-PF is the South African regime that wants—in Angola, Mozambique, and Zimbabwe—regimes more accommodating to the existing South African system and that is attempting to block those countries' industrialization through the use of these organizations to discourage outside foreign investment and disrupt the building of a new economic infrastructure. Lastly, the South African regime's predominant influence over those organizations indicates its approval of their use of terrorism, while that regime employs, inside South Africa and Namibia, political violence against the public at large. Hence, the South African regime, due to its particular tactical use of political violence in its domestic and foreign policies, qualifies as a terrorist organization.

QUESTIONS AND ANSWERS

Q: Dr. Gilson Austrate, Long Beach, New York. I was impressed with Dr. Friedland's statement when she emphasized the role of the Union of South Africa and rather neatly deemphasized the role of the Soviet surrogates in Angola, namely, Cuba, East Germany, and Czechoslovakia. My question is, On what sources do you base your statements on Angola?

A: The issue seems to be where the movements happen to be getting their arms. These movements will take arms from any place that will give them. We talked about SWAPO. However, the United States does not give arms to SWAPO, nor do the ANC. Historically, when it came to the struggle in Mozambique, where did the arms go? To the Portuguese. Where did they go when it came to Southern Rhodesia? Indirectly, the arms went to the status quo, the Southern Rhodesian Colonial Regime. Angola, the same way. My sources happen to be from the Voice of America report.

Q (Austrate): My sources indicate the contrary, that the Soviet surrogates and the Soviet Union were very much responsible for tipping the scale in Angola and putting into power a minority group against the will—

A: Okay. They are not a minority group, first of all, and as I say, in terms of the invasion of Angola, it happened to be that UNITA and FNLA were on the defense. They were being defeated by MPLA and they had no aid from the Soviet Union. When South Africa came in with conventional forces to aid UNITA and the FNLA, Angola had to get conventional aid, and they got it from Cuba. Remember the American Revolution. Where did the Americans get their arms? Not from Britain. They went to France. The conflict, by the way, between Britain and France at that time is equivalent to that between the United States and the Soviet Union today. You have to understand, if you have your opponent using violence against you, you have to get arms. And they had no choice. This is where the ANC gets their arms. If the United States denies them arms, are you going to say they should just lay down and die?

Q: Philip Devine, University of Scranton. My question is also for Dr. Friedland. I was very troubled by your analysis of dissident movements in Mozambique, Angola, and Zimbabwe. You seem to treat them almost as domestically unreal and mere agents of the South African government. It seems to me that this kind of argument is called very nasty things when the target or hate state is other than South Africa. I would therefore like to urge very strongly that people concerned with these issues avoid the temptation to blame whatever conflict may occur in any country in the world on their favorite hate state, whether that should be South Africa, the Soviet Union, or whatever other hate state some particular individual or group may happen to have.

A: As I mentioned, the actions of these groups mean that they are not going to get support from the population. If you are attacking the very people from the area within which you operate, you are alienating those people. Therefore, the group has to get outside support. These are not groups that are based in their region

and that have support from the region. You have to understand these states: the population is very, very small and very spread out. Mozambique, in size, would be the whole West Coast of the United States. Its population is 12 million. So the fact is that you can have groups operating without the support of the people just moving around, and if you are being attacked by these groups, and they are in fact endangering the civilians, people react. They do not support the groups. That is why I say that they are getting support from the Republic of South Africa.

Q (Devine): I cannot believe that in any other context you would make the argument that just because a group is terrorist, it can have no local support.

A: I said there is very little local support.

Q: I am Dr. Gene Ulmer, a geologist at Temple University. I think that what the profile of Africa presented here failed to point out is that things are changing there very rapidly. I would agree with what we heard if we were still back in the mid-seventies, but in the last five to ten years, the situation has become quite different. The build-up of military forces was mentioned. If I may be permitted one personal comment—in 1974, I watched the smoke come up from a village of 200 and some Black people in Mozambique. They were killed by Red Chinese, not by Blacks who were liberated, not by South Africans, and that is the one criticism in a concrete way I would make. I think the one thing that you have left out is the terrible role that the Red Chinese are playing in all this.

SOUTH AFRICA   **105**

A: It happens to be there were no Red Chinese in Mozambique and in fact, in terms of villagers being killed, it was Black soldiers in the Portuguese army who were terrorizing the population.

COMMENT (Ulmer): I am afraid you did not understand me. I saw this happen.

COMMENT (Friedland): You saw this?

COMMENT (Ulmer): Yes, I did.

COMMENT (Friedland): Were you in the village when these people were—

COMMENT (Ulmer): If I had spoken up, I would have been shot.

[26]

THE MOZAMBIQUE NATIONAL RESISTANCE AND SOUTH AFRICAN FOREIGN POLICY

STEVEN METZ

SINCE THE COLLAPSE of the Portuguese empire in southern Africa in the 1970s South African national security policy has undergone a radical evolution. After the initial surprise at the rapidity with which this took place faded, the Pretoria government attempted to frame a *modus vivendi* with the newly independent states.   The basic assumption of this policy was that the black states' commitment to the end of apartheid was primarily rhetorical and was intended more for domestic political consumption than as a framework for foreign policy.   Thus, it was believed in Pretoria, these economically fragile states would be willing to temper their anti-apartheid rhetoric and actions in exchange for financial, managerial and technological assistance from South Africa.

By the 1980s, however, it was clear that this was not true.   As black frustration within South Africa grew, so had regional support for the African National Congress (ANC) and other black nationalist groups.   Since one of the major strengths of the Pretoria government, its economic power, had not proved effective in tempering support for the anti-apartheid movement, a conscious decision was made by the South Africans to turn to their other forte, military power.[1]   Thus, over the past five years, South Africa has pursued an increasingly aggressive and militarized approach towards its neighbours.   This has taken a variety of forms, including direct military incursions and commando raids by the South African armed forces.[2]

Steven Metz is a Visiting Assistant Professor at Virginia Polytechnic Institute and State University, Blacksburg.

1.   The South African armed forces total 83,400 (63 per cent conscripts) with reserves of about 321,000; the air force includes 304 combat aircraft and 10 combat helicopters; there are about 145,500 paramilitary forces, including commandos, police, and police reserves.   On a comparative basis, the major 'Front Line States' in southern Africa (Angola, Mozambique, Zambia and Zimbabwe) have total permanent forces of about 114,250 with 188 combat aircraft and helicopters.   The nations, of course, have no system of military cooperation or joint command. In terms of military expenditures, South African estimates for 1983–84 were $2·7 billion, with the Front Line States' estimated total of $1·77 billion (all figures from *Africa Insight*, 15, (1985), p. 204).   When other factors such as combat organization and proficiency plus the national industrial base (South Africa is the only nation in the region with a well-developed indigenous armaments industry) are taken into account, South Africa's military predominance is even greater.
2.   Robert I. Rotberg, 'South Africa in its Region—hegemony and vulnerability', in Robert I. Rotberg, *et al.*, *South Africa and Its Neighbors: regional security and self-interest* (Lexington, MA: Lexington Books, 1985), p. 5.

While these have, on occasion, proved effective in altering the behaviour of the black nations of the region, direct intervention is always expensive in both economic and political terms, and thus is reserved for extreme situations.[3]   In most instances methods *short* of direct intervention are the preferred way of inflicting punishment on neighbouring states.   Thus, as Christopher Coker has noted, '[t]he destabilization of her neighbours has become one of the most important and persistent South African concerns since 1978'.[4]

For South Africa the solution to this conflict between the efficacy of intervention and its costs has been the funding, training and support of surrogate forces to destabilize the Front Line States.   These surrogates have ranged from relatively unimportant and politically unpromising groups such as Ntsu Makhehle's Lesotho Liberation Army and the dissidents in Zimbabwe's Matabeleland to Jonas Savimbi's UNITA.   All have assisted South Africa both by punishing Front Line support for anti-apartheid forces and by reinforcing and amplifying the economic weaknesses of these nations.   While the effectiveness of these surrogates has varied greatly, among the most persistent and, from the Pretoria's perspective, successful, of these operations has been South African support for an anti-FRELIMO guerrilla movement called the Mozambique National Resistance (MNR).

The Origins of the Mozambique National Resistance (MNR)

Glenn Frankel points out that the MNR is unique among African guerrilla movements in that it was founded by 'white spy masters' rather than indigenous groups.[5]   But while it is certain that the group has always been an element of southern Africa's racial politics, the specifics of its origins are less clear.   Robert Jaster, for instance, argues that the MNR was formed by the Portuguese as a covert anti-FRELIMO organization during the revolution in Mozambique, while Gordon Winter, a former member of the South Africa Bureau of State Security, gives the credit to the South African Military Intelligence.[6]   The general conclusion, however, is that the MNR was 'essentially the creature of the Rhodesian armed forces', and was formed

---

3.   See Thomas M. Callaghy, 'Apartheid and Socialism: South Africa's Relations with Angola and Mozambique', in Thomas M. Callaghy (ed.), *South Africa in Southern Africa: the intensifying vortex of violence* (New York: Praeger, 1983), pp. 267–322; Richard Leonard, *South Africa at War: white power and the crisis in southern Africa* (Westport, Conn.: Lawrence Hill, 1983); and Steven Metz, 'State Terror and South African Foreign Policy', in John H. Morgan (ed.), *Terrorism and Psycho-Politics*, (Wyndham Hall Press, forthcoming 1987).
4.   Christopher Coker, 'South Africa: a new military role in southern Africa, 1969–1982', *Survival*, March/April 1983, 25, No. 2, p. 62.
5.   Glenn Frankel, 'South Africa's Guerrillas', *Washington Post*, 8 October 1984.
6.   Gordon Winter, *Inside BOSS: South Africa's secret police* (London: Allen Lane, 1981), p. 545.   See also Robert S. Jaster, 'A Regional Security Role for Africa's Front-Line States: experience and prospects', *Adelphi Papers Number 180* (London: International Institute for Strategic Studies, 1983), p. 20.

MOZAMBIQUE NATIONAL RESISTANCE & S. AFRICAN FOREIGN POLICY 493

by the Rhodesian Special Branch after the FRELIMO victory in 1974 with the support of former members of the Portuguese secret police (PIDE).[7]

The first real indication of MNR activity came in June of 1976 when the radio station 'Voice of Free Africa' (*Voz da Africa Livre*) began anti-FRELIMO broadcasts from Rhodesia.[8] According to Ken Flower, who was Ian Smith's top security officer, the first military units of the MNR were trained in August and September of 1976 at Bindura, north of Salisbury.[9] The Portuguese were actively involved at this point and provided the files of several disbanded anti-insurgency units, the *flechas* for use as recruitment lists.[10] These had been taken to Rhodesia by the former PIDE agent Orlando Cristina after the victory of the FRELIMO forces. Until he was assassinated in 1983, Cristina was a central figure in the development of the MNR. In addition to his contacts with PIDE and Portuguese anti-insurgency forces, Cristina also served as private secretary to Portuguese millionaire Jorge Jardim. Jardim had close personal contacts with Salazar, and, because of the massive financial losses which he suffered at the time of the FRELIMO victory, was deeply interested in political conditions in Mozambique. Cristina and Jardim also represented a link to Portuguese business interests which served as a valuable source of funding for the MNR.

The Smith government in Salisbury appeared to have two objectives for the MNR. One was that its members should act as interpreters, guides and scouts for Rhodesian excursions into Mozambique in search of ZANU guerrillas. The other objective was to provide an added impetus to the general economic and political destabilization of the areas of Mozambique which were used as basing areas for Robert Mugabe's ZANU. The MNR made no attempt to confront the FRELIMO army directly, but rather operated in small bands which attacked villages and cut transportation and communication lines. At the same time the MNR grew in size through forced conscription during raids and by attracting a wide range of both whites and blacks interested in the overthrow of the FRELIMO government. This latter group included former FRELIMO soldiers dissatisfied with the Machel government, former members of the Portuguese armed

7. 'Mozambique', in Colin Legum (ed.), *Africa Contemporary Record 1979–1980* (New York: Africana, 1980), p. B730. See also Paul Fauvet and Alves Gomes, 'The "Mozambique National Resistance"', supplement to *AIM (Agencia de Informacao de Mocambique) Bulletin*, no. 69, p. 3; Allen Isaacman and Barbara Isaacman, 'South Africa's Hidden War', *Africa Report*, November–December 1982, pp. 4–9; Colin Legum, 'The MNR', *CSIS Africa Notes*, **16**, July 1983, p. 1; and Callaghy, 'Apartheid and Socialism', p. 309.
8. It appears that at this time the Rhodesian aims were quite limited, with the 'Voice of Free Africa' intended as a response to the 'Voice of Zimbabwe' which broadcast from Mozambique. See Fauvet and Gomes, 'The "Mozambique National Resistance"', p. 3.
9. Colin Legum, 'The Southern African Crisis', in Colin Legum (ed.), *African Contemporary Record 1982–1983* (New York: Africana, 1983), p. A14.
10. Legum, 'The Southern African Crisis', p. A15.

494   AFRICAN AFFAIRS

forces and secret police (especially the elite counter-insurgency groups), Rhodesian and South African commandos, and mercenaries.[11]

As the military situation in Rhodesia worsened for the Smith government in 1979, the MNR was ordered to expand its area of operation in Mozambique, and to establish permanent bases.[12] This at first appeared successful. On 23 March 1979 the MNR, in its largest operation to that point, set fire to a fuel depot at Munhara, outside Beira. By August of that year the MNR had succeeded in penetrating even deeper into Mozambique and had established two camps in the Gorongosa mountains. In October, however, the location of the camps was betrayed by local informers employed by the MNR. After a three-day assault, Mozambique government forces captured the lower base; ten days later the upper base also fell.

The next few months represented the nadir of the MNR. Their military leader, Andre Matade Matsangaiza, a former FRELIMO quartermaster who had escaped from Mozambique after having been convicted of stealing military supplies, had died in the assault; the Rhodesians and Cristina then supported different candidates for the leadership position; the succession struggle subsequently led to a bloody gun battle between factions of the group. Guerrillas from the losing faction surrendered to Mozambican authorities, leaving the MNR with less than 500 members.[13] Leadership of the remnants of the MNR was quickly assumed by Cristina's candidate, Afonso Dhlakama (who had also been dishonourably discharged from the Mozambican army for theft), but Rhodesian support ended in 1980 with the Lancaster House agreement and the creation of Zimbabwe.

MNR Operations from 1980 to 1984

At this point South Africa moved to assume full control of the MNR. A few days before the independence of Zimbabwe South African Defence Forces (SADF) transport planes moved the MNR radio station to Phalaborwa in northern Transvaal.[14] At the same time new training and headquarters facilities were established, at first near Phalaborwa in the northern Transvaal, and later at Zoabastad. The South African relationship with the MNR was not a new one: SADF personnel had been present at the Gorongosa base, and an MNR deserter had claimed that South Africa had been involved in supplying arms to the group from its inception.[15]

---

11. Joseph Hanlon, *Mozambique: The Revolution Under Fire* (London: Zed, 1984), pp. 221–224.
12. Fauvet and Gomes, 'The "Mozambique National Resistance" ', p. 5.
13. *African Recorder 1982*, p. 5963.
14. Legum, 'The Southern African Crisis', p. A16.
15. Legum, 'The Southern African Crisis', p. A15; *African Recorder 1981*, p. 5578. The South African government has denied these charges.

MOZAMBIQUE NATIONAL RESISTANCE & S. AFRICAN FOREIGN POLICY 495

When the Gorongosa base was destroyed towards the end of 1979, the South Africans were instrumental in the establishment of the new base at Garagua.

Documents captured by Mozambican forces the next year show that South Africa moved very rapidly to fill the void left by the end of Rhodesian control of the MNR.[16] In October of 1980 an important meeting involving Dhlakama and a South African intelligence officer identified as Colonel van Niekerk took place at the Garagua base. Among the topics discussed were the methods by which South Africa would supply and train the MNR and targets for future operations. In addition, it was agreed that the new strategic objective of the MNR was the total economic destabilization of Mozambique.[17]

In light of this new strategic objective, the tactics of the MNR also changed. The area of operation was enlarged until it eventually included ten of Mozambique's twelve provinces. In order to reinforce the economic dependence of Zimbabwe and Malawi on South Africa the transportation corridor between Mutare in Zimbabwe and the Mozambican port of Beira became the primary target of guerrilla raids. With the independence of Zimbabwe and the formation of the Southern African Development Coordination Conference (SADCC) in 1980, South Africa felt that the chances for the creation of what came to be called a dependent 'constellation of states' were slipping away. Thus any action which could disrupt economic links between Zimbabwe and the outside world served South African foreign policy.

Evidence of this new approach came quickly after the meeting with Colonel van Niekerk. In November of 1980 the Mutare-Beira oil pipeline was cut. This was not re-opened until January of 1983 (and then was immediately cut again), reinforcing Zimbabwe's dependence on oil from South Africa. During the same period the power lines from Cabora Bassa to South Africa were also cut. Since this was an important source of electricity to the northern Transvaal the motives of the MNR are not clear. There is some indication that this was undertaken at Cristina's suggestion to camouflage South African links to the MNR.[18] Throughout 1981 the Beira region remained a favoured target. In November 1981, the buoys in the Beira harbour were sabotaged, briefly closing the port.[19] In December 1982, Beira was again the target of a major attack and a series of storage tanks holding oil intended for Malawi were destroyed causing $35 million in damage.

At the same time the MNR also carried out raids in many of the outlying

16. See *African Recorder 1982*, p. 5920; and Hanlon, *Mozambique*, p. 221.
17. Fauvet and Gomes, 'The "Mozambique National Resistance" ', p. 8.
18. Fauvet and Gomes, 'The "Mozambique National Resistance" ', p. 10.
19. The sophistication and complexity of this attack suggests that it may have been performed directly by South African commandos. See Legum, 'The MNR', p. 3.

regions of Mozambique.   In 1982 it began attacking small towns.   The favoured tactic here was to target areas without army garrisons, mutilate anyone with ties to the government, forcibly recruit young men, destroy health, educational and economic facilities, and leave before Mozambican troops could arrive.   The FRELIMO forces were often little help against such raids, since the guerrilla tactics they had used against the Portuguese had largely been replaced by more conventional Soviet-style tactics.   As Colin Legum notes: 'While . . . modern weapons and conventional battle tactics might be useful if it were ever to come to confronting a direct attack by the South African army, they are of little use in fighting a bush war against guerrillas'.[20]

While under Rhodesian control, the MNR had made some tentative attempts to construct a popular base of support and to create liberated zones.[21]   Under South African direction, however, the MNR's tactics changed to an almost total reliance on random violence, sabotage and intimidation.   Favourite targets included food distribution networks, harvest activities, rail lines and roads, telephone and telegraph facilities, schools, sawmills, cotton and tea processing plants, and state farms.   In 1982 the MNR began to kidnap and kill foreign technicians working in development projects.   In May this caused the Swedish government to withdraw fifty technicians involved in the construction of a wood processing and paper manufacturing facility.[22]   In August two Soviet geologists were executed by the MNR.[23]   By the end of the year twelve foreign technicians had been killed.   By 1983 food supplies to many remote regions had been entirely cut off, thus exacerbating the effects of the drought which had devastated most of the southern Africa region.   From its low point in 1980, the MNR had grown by 1984 to a force numbering between 5,000 and 16,000.

While the MNR appears to have been ordered by the South Africans to improve its political image in 1981, the programme made public in August of that year was extremely vague, and there have been no attempts to implement it since then, even in those regions where the MNR has been strong.   While it is certainly true that the MNR has been able to draw on local discontent with the FRELIMO government, it has never been a coherent, indigenous political movement.   Thomas Callaghy has noted: 'Although it does have some popular support in certain areas, it is, unlike UNITA, the child of external forces without UNITA's autonomous viability'.[24]   The methods used by the MNR have alienated the local population, and, while there were attempts to build a UNITA-type tribal base

20.   Legum, 'The Southern African Crisis', p. A13.
21.   Hanlon, *Mozambique*, p. 227.
22.   Isaacman and Isaacman, 'South Africa's Hidden War', p. 7.
23.   *New York Times*, 24 August 1983, p. A5.
24.   Callaghy, 'Apartheid and Socialism', p. 310.

MOZAMBIQUE NATIONAL RESISTANCE & S. AFRICAN FOREIGN POLICY 497

among the Shona, Makonde and Makua people, the widespread demand for local militia to combat the guerrillas indicated that popular support was never deep.[25] Even if physical evidence of South African ties to the MNR are discounted, the tactics of the group suggest that the MNR can only be understood as a tool of South African foreign policy.

The Nkomati Accord

The Machel government seems at first not to have taken the MNR seriously. Since the group was never able to defeat the Mozambican army in open combat, it was often seen as more of a nuisance than a threat. But by late 1981 the effects of MNR raids had become more damaging. Mozambique attempted to meet the challenge in two ways. The first was through the improvement of its own military capabilities. Many FRELIMO guerrillas who had been demobilized in the late 1970s were called up, and in 1982 village militias were formed and the army was re-organized to emphasize counter insurgency operations.[26] The second method was through defense accords with other Front Line states. A Mozambique–Zimbabwe pact was signed in 1981, and in 1982 Tanzania sent 200 military advisers.

These efforts proved ineffective. By 1982 the MNR had cost the Mozambican government an estimated $3·8 billion dollars through direct damage and increases in defence expenditures.[27] According to official estimates, the MNR had destroyed 840 schools, 12 health clinics, 24 maternity clinics, 174 health posts, two centres for the handicapped and 900 shops while kidnapping 52 foreign technicians and killing 12.[28]

By 1983 it was clear that the only way to stop the MNR was through an agreement with South Africa. South Africa had continually denied support for the MNR, but solid evidence indicated otherwise. In addition to the documentary evidence captured by the Mozambican government, numerous MNR deserters and prisoners told of South African advisers and supply missions. Captured MNR bases often contained heliports or aerial drop zones, and Soviet-made weapons which had probably been seized from SWAPO forces were frequently found. In October 1981 a white man killed during an attempted sabotage attack was later shown to have been associated with the Rhodesian Selous Scouts and the SADF.[29] The MNR itself, in 'Voice of Free Africa' broadcasts, never denied the South African connection. Even the US State Department admitted that the MNR 'receives the bulk of its support from South Africa'.[30]

25. Michael S. Radu, 'Mozambique: nonalignment or new dependency?', *Current History*, March 1984, **83**, No. 491, p. 134.
26. Callaghy, 'Apartheid and Socialism', p. 312.
27. Frankel, 'South Africa's Guerrillas', p. A36.
28. Speech by President Samora Machel, reprinted as a supplement to *AIM Bulletin*, No. 94.
29. Legum, 'The Southern African Crisis', p. A17.
30. Jay Ross, 'Pretoria-Backed Raids Bleed Destitute Country', *Washington Post*, 6 April 1983.

498   AFRICAN AFFAIRS

In late 1983 Mozambique and South Africa opened talks on mutual
security arrangements and the first major meeting between the two
countries' representatives took place in December in Mbabane, Swaziland.
Throughout the first few months of 1984 Mozambique continued the talks,
while opening new offensives against the guerrillas. After a February
meeting in Maputo between Roelof F (Pik) Botha, the South African
Foreign Minister, and Major General Jacinto Soares Velos, economic
adviser to President Machel of Mozambique, it was announced that the two
nations intended to enter into a formal security agreement.

On 16 March 1984 an agreement called the Nkomati Accord was signed by
President Machel and Prime Minister Pieter Botha. According to the
document, both sides agree 'to forbid and prevent in their respective territories the organisation of irregular forces or armed bands' which intend to
attack the other.[31]   Both sides also refused to allow their territory to be used
for the transit, basing or supply of any group planning aggression against the
other.

The Nkomati Accord, however, did not end MNR operations. Attacks
have continued on an almost daily basis since it was signed. Initially the
agreement did appear to drive a wedge between the MNR and South Africa,
as MNR statements became quite critical of South African efforts in
Mozambique.[32] While there was some initial debate over whether the
South African government continued to re-supply the group or whether the
MNR was simply utilizing supplies either stockpiled before the accord or
provided by private sources in South Africa, it was clear that the group
was still a major problem for the financially beleaguered Mozambican
government.   In 1985 papers captured from the MNR (the 'Gorongosa
Documents') showed that Pretoria continued training, supplying and
directing the MNR during and after the negotiations.[33]   A diary captured
during a government attack on the MNR stronghold at Casa Branca suggested that the South Africans never really intended to uphold their part of
the bargain.[34]   Colonel van Niekerk appears to have retained his position as
liaison between the South African Defence Force and the MNR, and to have
continued to orchestrate the training and supply of MNR forces. At most
the Nkomati Accord changed the tenor of South Africa's support for the
MNR, as support was thereafter channeled through Malawi. Despite military assistance to Mozambique from Zimbabwe, the MNR has remained a
serious drain on the Machel government, has caused 42 per cent of all

31.   'Agreement on Non-Aggression and Good Neighborliness Between Mozambique and
South Africa, 16 March 1984', reprinted, *inter alia*, as a supplement to *AIM Bulletin*, No. 93.
32.   See *Johannesburg Star*, 19 January 1984 and 29 May 1984.
33.   Mota Lopes, 'The MNR: opponents or bandits?', *Africa Report*, January–February 1986,
p. 68.
34.   Glenn Frankel, 'War of Attrition Hits Mozambique's Poor', *Washington Post*, 12 May
1986.

MOZAMBIQUE NATIONAL RESISTANCE & S. AFRICAN FOREIGN POLICY 499

government spending to go to defense, and has turned large parts of the country into an economic and political desert.[35]

South Africa and the MNR

It is important to ask why South Africa decided to use the MNR as a tool of its foreign policy. But this in fact involves asking two separate questions: What were South Africa's objectives in using the MNR? Why did South Africa decide that the destabilization of Mozambique by surrogate forces would attain those goals?

There were two basic objectives of South African support for the MNR. The first of these was to discourage Mozambican ties to the African National Congress (ANC) in South Africa. Although Mozambican support for the ANC has never approached the level of support which that country provided for ZANU during the war in Rhodesia, there were important ANC offices in Maputo, and the organization's leader, Oliver Tambo, was treated as a head of state. During the 1980s ANC raids into South Africa, which consisted primarily of terrorist actions by small groups, became increasingly embarrassing for the National Party government since they indicated that the long-range stability of the regime, which was an important attraction for foreign investment, was open to question.[36] The crucial role which outside support played in ANC actions was proved by the increasing sophistication of the raids. Thus it was no coincidence that South Africa assumed control of the MNR just a few months after the spectacular ANC attacks on the crucial oil-from-coal (SASOL) facilities.[37] Since the Mozambique border is only a few hundred miles from the South African heartland around Johannesburg and Pretoria, the clearest reason for support of the MNR was to end Mozambique's ties to the ANC.

The second reason was to disrupt attempts to lessen the region's economic dependence on South Africa. During the colonial period the Portuguese and British territories of southern Africa became linked in an intricate communication and transportation network. The Mozambican ports of Beira and Maputo were used for exports from Rhodesia, Zambia, Malawi and from the northern Transvaal. As South Africa industrialized after World War II, the economies of the region became even more closely intertwined. When external threats to apartheid increased in the early and mid 1970s, it became clear to South Africa that the *laager* approach, which attempted to make the Republic as autonomous as possible, was neither economically nor

35. Allen Isaacman and Barbara Isaacman, 'In Pursuit of Non-alignment', *Africa Report*, May–June 1983, p. 49.
36. See Thomas Karis, 'The Resurgent African National Congress: competing for hearts and minds in South Africa', in Callaghy, (ed.), *South Africa in Southen Africa*, pp. 211–217; and Paul Rich, 'Insurgency, Terrorism and the Apartheid System in South Africa', *Political Studies*, 32, (1984), pp. 68–85.
37. Leonard, *South Africa at War*, p. 21.

politically feasible.   The result was the creation of a policy aimed at forming an economically linked 'constellation of states' in southern Africa.[38] According to this plan, economic ties between South Africa and the black states should be developed beyond simple trade links into a sort of regional division of labour with the Republic providing capital, technology, manufacturing capabilities and managerial expertise, and the other nations of the region contributing labour and raw materials.   This idea was not entirely new.   In the late 1940s Dr H. F. Verwoerd had proposed that a regional commonwealth be formed which would include South Africa, the independent 'tribal homelands', plus the former High Commission Territories (Lesotho, Botswana, Swaziland).   As the imminent independence of the nations of southern Africa became clear in the early 1970s, the notion of a constellation re-emerged; its main proponent became Pieter Botha.   After Botha became Prime Minister, he officially launched the constellation policy at a November 1979 meeting with Johannesburg businessmen.

The rationale behind the constellation plan was clear: by utilizing its economic power for political purposes, South Africa would be playing from a position of strength.   It was assumed that the leaders of the Front Line states were even more interested in economic development than in the end of apartheid.   By promising this development, South Africa felt that it could moderate Front Line support for the ANC while, at the same time, decreasing the chances for Soviet influence in the region.[39]   In addition, the formation of a regional constellation would bring other benefits.   For instance, the participation of the Front Line states in the scheme would represent a *de facto* recognition of the homelands, thus splitting the Front Line states and the rest of black Africa, and muting Western criticism of the homelands policy.[40]

Botha's constellation policy, however, was, for all practical purposes, stillborn.   At a meeting of the Front Line foreign ministers in May of 1979, a proposal was raised to form some sort of regional economic grouping in order to lessen economic dependence on South Africa.   At a summit meeting in Lusaka in April 1980, the Southern African Development Coordination Conference was formed.[41]   So far, though, this group has not

38.   See W. J. Breytenbach, *The Constellation of States: a consideration* (Johannesburg: South Africa Foundation, 1980); W. J. Breytenbach and S. Cleary, *Two Views on South Africa's Foreign Policy and the Constellation of States* (Johannesburg: South Africa Institute of Race Relations, 1980); Deon Geldenhuys, 'Regional Cooperation in Southern Africa: a constellation of states', *International Affairs Bulletin*, **2**, (1979), 36–72; Wolfgang Thomas, 'A Southern African "Constellation of States": challenge or myth?', *South Africa International*, **10**, (1980), 113–128; and C. J. Botha, 'The Constellation of States: peace-in-pieces?', *South African Yearbook of International Law*, **7**, (1981), 105–113.
39.   Christopher Hill, 'Regional Cooperation in Southern Africa', *African Affairs*, **82**, (1983), p. 217.
40.   Robert M. Price, 'Pretoria's Southern African Strategy', *African Affairs*, **83**, (1984), p. 14.
41.   For general background on the SADCC see Richard R. Weisfelder, 'The Southern African Development Coordination Conference: a new factor in the liberation process', in

met the expectations of its founders. Because the SADCC is an economically heterogeneous grouping which ranges from more or less capitalist economies to Marxist ones, it has made only tentative progress in the creation of a formal institutionalized structure to oversee regional economic development. There is also some dispute over the political goals of the SADCC. President Machel has stated: 'Some people have tended to think that we are forming this economic group purely to face South Africa. In our view, this regional grouping is being established despite and not merely because of South Africa and her concept of a regional constellation of states'.[42] But it is clear that, as Reginald Herbold Green argues, 'SADCC is quite overtly part of the Southern African liberation struggle'.[43]

Thus the second reason for South African support of the MNR was the disruption of development plans that exclude it. By destroying pipelines, power lines and transportation links between Zimbabwe and Mozambique, the MNR reinforced Zimbabwe's economic dependence on South Africa and caused Mozambique to divert scarce resources to the military. It should be noted that these two objectives, the desire to strike at the ANC and the reinforcement of economic dependence in the region, are not mutually exclusive; one of the major reasons why South Africa espouses the constellation is that it would modify Front Line support for South African opposition. The overriding objective of South African foreign policy since 1948 has been 'the protection of the country's unique sociopolitical order from external threat'.[44] The two objectives sought by support for the MNR were, then, two sides of the same coin.

The MNR and South Africa's 'Total Strategy'

The second part of the question posed earlier asked why South Africa decided to utilize surrogate forces for the destabilization of neighbouring states. The most obvious answer is that this was the most efficacious solution to a security problem. A full answer, however, lies deeper than that: the South African decision to use the MNR is intrinsically linked with the approach to national security developed in the Republic in the 1970s, the 'total strategy' as it was called, and thus can only be fully understood in that context.

In the early 1970s it was widely assumed that there was no conceivable

Callaghy, (ed.), *South Africa in Southern Africa*, pp. 237–266; John Edlin, 'Key to Southern Africa's Economic Independence', *Africa Report*, May–June 1983, pp. 57–64; and Douglas Anglin, 'Economic Liberation and Regional Cooperation in Southern Africa', *International Organization*, 37, (1983), pp. 617–646. On the relationship of the SADCC to South African national security policy see Gavin G. Maasdorp, 'Squaring Up to Economic Dominance: regional patterns', in Rotberg *et al.*, *South Africa and Its Neighbors*, pp. 91–136.
42. Quoted in Anglin, 'Economic Liberation', p. 620.
43. Reginald Herbold Green, 'Southern African Development Coordination: the struggle continues', in Legum (ed.), *Africa Contemporary Record 1982–1983*, p. A28.
44. Price, 'Pretoria's Strategy', p. 11.

502   AFRICAN AFFAIRS

array of forces which could threaten South African security for at least the remainder of the decade.[45]   In addition to the protection offered by the *cordon sanitaire* of Ian Smith's Rhodesia and the Portuguese colonies, South Africa already had the best army and largest industrial base in the region. Prime Minister Vorster had offered non-aggression pacts to the independent Front Line states in 1970, but the rejection of this offer was not then considered a serious setback for the Republic.   Even the threat of communist advances in Africa was not considered overly dangerous, since it was assumed that the United States would accept responsibility for the defeat of any pro-Soviet forces in the region.

In the mid 1970s, however, a series of events illustrated the 'defeatist and inflexible' nature of the *laager* strategy on which South African security policy had been built.   In addition to growing domestic terrorism and international economic pressure, the independence of the Portuguese colonies created both a conventional military threat and the fear that the ANC and other domestic opposition groups would flourish, given the assistance of the new radical nations.   The failed intervention in Angola proved especially traumatic.   Although the South African military and political leadership was convinced that their forces had performed well in the face of numerically superior MPLA and Cuban forces, they were especially worried by the failure of the United States to come to their assistance.   The South African military elite was also concerned over what they thought to be an inordinate impact on national policy held by 'doves' in the Foreign Ministry. Thus the war in Angola, according to General Mangus Malan of the South African Defence Force (SADF), 'focused the attention on the urgent necessity for the State Security Council [a body directed by the Prime Minister but dominated by the military] to play a much fuller role in the national security of the Republic than hitherto'.[46]   The result was a conscious decision in South Africa to develop a cogent security plan which was not contingent on the political whims of the United States, and to re-structure the internal decision-making procedure in a way which would amplify the impact of the military and the other security-oriented agencies.

The escalating violence in Rhodesia and the inability of the South African expeditionary force to defeat the SWAPO guerrillas in Namibia with finality added new urgency to this.   Rather than interpreting the instability in southern Africa as an inevitable part of the worldwide trauma of decolonization, the South Africans were convinced that they were the target of a massive geostrategic attack by the Soviet Union.   The object, according to

45.   See, for instance, Mohamed A. El-Khawas and Barry Cohen, (eds), *The Kissinger Study of Southern Africa: national security study memorandum 39* (Westport, Conn: Lawrence Hill, 1976).
46.   Quoted in Deon Geldenhuys and Hennie Kotze, 'Aspects of Political Decision-Making in South Africa', *Politikon*, **10**, (1983), 34–35.

MOZAMBIQUE NATIONAL RESISTANCE & S. AFRICAN FOREIGN POLICY 503

the South Africans, was control of the region's vital minerals which would be used to blackmail the West.[47]   What South Africa faced was a 'total onslaught' by world communism operating on many levels.   Thus all three of South Africa's problems (international economic pressure, domestic terrorism, and the external military threat) were thought to be dimensions of the communist onslaught.   Since the 'total onslaught' operated at many levels, the South African response must do likewise.   Thus there arose the idea of the 'total strategy' which would, according to General Malan, consist of an aggressive counter-offensive in the areas of ideology, politics, economics, and technology.[48]

The total strategy was first proposed by the then Defence Minister P. W. Botha in the 1977 White Paper on Defence.[49]   The notion that modern war was inevitably total and included political, economic, diplomatic, and cultural efforts is an old one.   Among the inspirations for the South African version of this idea was Andre Beufre's book *Introduction à la Stratégie* and the writings of Mao Zedong.[50]   The purpose of the total strategy was to mobilize and coordinate all of South Africa's resources.   According to Prime Minister Botha:

> A country which is facing a total onslaught has to have a total strategy to combat it.   This onslaught is not just military but political, economic, and psychological.   Against this background it was essential that South Africa's strategy should be a total one, in which military, political, and economic factors all play a part.[51]

The total strategy was originally to incorporate two strands: the development of the economic constellation of states and an intense military build-up, in effect, a 'carrot and stick' policy.[52]   In practice, however, the 'stick' came to dominate as the Front Line states refused to exchange economic assistance for political concessions on the issue of majority rule and the end of apartheid.   As is true for most nations, South Africa experienced an intra-governmental debate over the general tenor of its foreign policy with

47.   For recent explanations of South African thinking on this see: 'South Africa: target of a destabilization campaign', backgrounder 7/1983 (Washington: South African Embassy, 1983); and Republic of South Africa, Department of Defence, *White Paper on Defence and Armaments Supply 1982*.

48.   General Magnus Malan in a speech to the South African Institute for Strategic Studies, quoted in Deon Geldenhuys, *Some Foreign Policy Implications of South Africa's Total National Strategy, with Particular Reference to the 12-Point Plan* (Johannesburg: South African Institute of International Affairs, 1981), p. 3.

49.   Republic of South Africa, Department of Defence, *Defence White Paper 1977*, reprinted as a supplement to *Paratus*, May 1977.

50.   Leonard, *South Africa At War*, p. 199; 'Republic of South Africa', in Legum (ed.), *Africa Contemporary Record 1979–1980*, p. B766.

51.   Quoted in Callaghy, 'Apartheid and Socialism', p. 270.

52.   Deon Geldenhuys, 'Recrossing the Matola Threshold: the "Terrorist Factor" in South Africa's regional relations', *South Africa International*, **13**, (1983), No. 3, p. 153.

504   AFRICAN AFFAIRS

the representatives of the Foreign Ministry favouring a more conciliatory
policy based on economic leverage while the Defence Department espoused
a more aggressive and martial approach.   Several factors tilted this debate
in favour of the hawks.   The first was the replacement of J. B. Vorster with
P. W. Botha as prime minister in 1978.   Botha had been defence minister
for some time (and continued to hold that portfolio until 1980), and thus
retained close personal and professional ties with the military establishment.
His closest associate and the architect of the total strategy was General
Magnus Malan.   Malan was from a distinguished Afrikaner family with a
long history of involvement in South African politics and with the
Broederbond.   His military background was in guerrilla and counterinsurgency warfare, and included involvement with South African operations in
Namibia, Rhodesia, Mozambique and Angola.   In addition to Malan, who
assumed the Defence portfolio in 1980, Contand Viljoen, the SADF chief,
and Jan Geldenhuys, the Senior Army Command Officer, also began to play
a major role in policy formulation.[53]   Thus, under Botha's direction, the
influence of the military and the intelligence services in South African
foreign policy increased to the point that Kenneth Grundy has noted a
'power realignment' in favour of the national security apparatus.[54]

The second factor increasing the influence of South Africa's hawks was
the Republic's disintegrating security position.[55]   This was largely the
result of the growing violence of the war in Zimbabwe.   As is always true,
the existence of a security threat increases the political power of the military.
Since the instability of southern Africa throughout the 1970s had led to the
diversion of a greater proportion of state resources to the SADF than before,
it was natural that the military would become more involved in policy
making.   In addition, the qualitative and quantitative improvement in
South Africa's military during the 1970s made reliance on a hawkish policy a
more viable alternative than it would have been a decade earlier.[56]

53.   James M. Roherty, 'Beyond Limpopo and Zambezi: South Africa's strategic horizons',
South Africa International, 14, (1983), No. 1, p. 323.   For detail on the South African foreign
policy formulation process, see Robert I. Rotberg, 'The Process of Decision-Making in Contemporary South Africa', *CSIS Africa Notes*, 22, 28 December 1983; and Deon Geldenhuys,
The Diplomacy of Isolation: South African foreign policy making (New York: St Martin's, 1984).
54.   Kenneth Grundy, *The Rise of the South African Security Establishment: an essay on the
changing locus of state power*, Bradlow Series no. 1 (Johannesburg: South African Institute of
International Affairs, 1983); and *The Militarization of South African Politics* (Bloomington:
Indiana University Press, 1986).   See also Robert I. Rotberg, 'Decision Making and the
Military in South Africa', in Rotberg *et al.*, *South Africa and Its Neighbors*, pp. 13–26.
55.   Cornelius van N. Sholtz, First Secretary of the South African Embassy, Washington,
D.C., interview with the author, 31 August 1984.
56.   On the South African military build up see Leonard, *South Africa At War*, pp. 98–130;
Gutteridge, 'South Africa's Defence Posture'; Chester A. Crocker, *South Africa's Defence
Posture: coping with vulnerability*, The Washington Papers, No. 84 (Beverly Hills and
London: Sage, 1981); and Chester A. Crocker, 'Current and Projected Military Balances in
Southern Africa', in Richard E. Bissell and Chester A. Crocker (eds), *South Africa into the 1980s*
(Boulder, Col: Westview, 1979), pp. 71–105.

MOZAMBIQUE NATIONAL RESISTANCE & S. AFRICAN FOREIGN POLICY 505

The final event which helped transform the total strategy into a militarized policy was the formation of the SADCC. The possibility that the Front Line states could break their economic dependence on South Africa made the use of economic leverage much less tenable, and thus eroded the influence of those within the South African government supporting an economically-based policy. The economic approach was not, however, fully jettisoned, but rather merged with the military strategy as the objective of South African military operations became *both* the direct response to security threats and the disruption of attempts to decrease the Front Line states' economic dependence on South Africa. The end result of all of this was that the economic aspect of the Total Strategy was put in abeyance even if not fully abandoned. Toward the end of the 1970s and into the 1980s South African foreign policy came to rely more and more on direct military solutions to perceived threats.

Conclusion: The MNR and The Total Strategy

It is clear that even the most widely optimistic member of the South African political and defence apparatus never fully believed that the MNR would overthrow the FRELIMO government in Mozambique. As Barry Blechman points out, indirect applications of military force can *either* be attempts at direct military victory *or* can be a form of political pressure aimed at affecting decisions within the target state.[57] It is clear that South African support for the MNR falls into the second category. Why then did South Africa pick this particular option among those available? The answer to this has three parts.

The first part of the answer is the overall militarization of South African foreign policy. This was due to some degree to an accident, Botha's assumption of political power, but more directly to the rising perception of threat in South Africa. The demise of the white *cordon sanitaire* left South Africa to rely on its own resources; the failure of the West to rescue the South African expeditionary force in Angola further reinforced this feeling of isolation. This apparent abandonment by the West was so traumatic that there have been discussions within South Africa of developing a 'non-aligned foreign policy'. It is a truism of international politics that insecurity breeds aggression. For South Africa this, plus the rejection of the constellation of states by the Black nations, led to a foreign policy which more readily relied on military measures.

The second part of the answer is a growing belief in South Africa that the threat to the nation's security must be met at its own level, 'fighting fire with fire'. South Africa views world politics as a Manichean struggle between

57. Barry M. Blechman, 'Outside Military Forces in Third-World Conflicts', in Christoph Bertram (ed.), *Third-World Conflict and International Security* (Hamden, Conn: Archon, 1982), pp. 33–34.

two diametrically opposed ideologies, and sees its own security problem as an offshoot of this. According to the South Africans, many of the difficulties faced by the West in the anti-communist struggle have resulted from a refusal to meet threats at their own level. One of the major tenets of Leninism is that the end justifies the means; thus all tactics are acceptable. In any sort of political struggle between groups utilizing diverse value systems, the party most willing to break the rules of conduct is often the winner. South Africa thus feels that it is suicidal to retain Western liberal inhibitions about sponsoring destabilization and revolution when faced with exactly those tactics by the other side. In effect, the 'moral high road' in international politics is laudable either when the stakes of the contest are low or when the threat is weak. According to the South Africans, neither of these conditions are met where their security problems are concerned. Thus all tactics are acceptable to stave off the challenge.

Finally, the resort to destabilization is the direct outcome of a failed intervention in Angola. In most cases nations would prefer to answer security threats directly; after all, the use of surrogates is a tenuous strategy at best. In the case of South Africa, the failed intervention in Angola illustrated the serious constraints on direct intervention from both within the country and from world pressure.[58] This further increased the utility of surrogate operations. The use of surrogates is an especially attractive option because the ties to the surrogate forces can often be feasibly denied if it becomes politically expedient. The difficulty is, though, to make the connection with the surrogates clear enough to send the proper message to the target nation, while camouflaging the connection so that it can be denied if necessary. Judging from the willingness of Mozambique to accede to demands to end support for the ANC, this delicate balance seems to have been accomplished by South Africa.

In fact, though, it is necessary to draw a distinction between surrogates such as the MNR and other forces supported by South Africa such as UNITA. UNITA (and some of the dissident groups in Zimbabwe) appear to be 'secondary surrogates', meaning that they were not created by South Africa, have a more autonomous existence and agenda, and thus are less willing supplicants. UNITA especially rules large parts of Angola as if it were a legitimate government, and would undoubtedly sever its ties to South Africa if that were possible. The ability of the MNR to have survived its early years without direct South African involvement is very questionable; even today the MNR is much more a pliable tool of South African foreign policy than UNITA. In addition to this pliability, the two sorts of

---

58. American support for the 'Contras' in Nicaragua illustrates the same point. See Steven Metz and Jeremy Preiss, 'Fighting Fire with Fire: South Africa, the United States and the use of surrogate forces in Mozambique and Nicaragua', a paper presented at the 1984 meeting of the African Studies Association, Los Angeles.

MOZAMBIQUE NATIONAL RESISTANCE & S. AFRICAN FOREIGN POLICY 507

surrogates are also distinguished by tactics. While UNITA strikes at targets directly related to the strength and survival of the MPLA government, it does not pursue the sort of wholesale economic devastation that has become the MNR's stock-in-trade. Since the long-term objective of Savimbi and UNITA is control of Angola, this would clearly be counter-productive. The use of economic devastation by the MNR illustrates, then, that the objectives of this group are not stability, democracy and development in Mozambique, but the preservation of Mozambique's network of dependency on South Africa. The MNR, in other words, can accurately be labelled a puppet of South Africa, while UNITA cannot.

From South Africa's perspective, though, surrogates of the puppet variety are the more useful tool. The South Africans undoubtedly realize that their ties to Savimbi represent a marriage of convenience to be severed when possible. Because the MNR owes its existence to South Africa, it is a more subtle tool of Pretoria's foreign policy, and can be turned on and off to a greater extent than UNITA or other regional rebel movements. Thus it can be concluded that South Africa will continue to make moderate use of UNITA-type surrogates, but will place greater reliance on MNR type movements for some time. The threat which originally instigated support for the MNR may recede, but is not likely to disappear. While South Africa may face future security threats so pressing that the constraints on direct intervention are ignored, these will continue to be extreme circumstances, especially given the growing readiness of the Western nations to implement sanctions against Pretoria. There will also continue to be situations such as that dealing with Lesotho where the costs of direct intervention are low, and thus it is a feasible option. Cases like that of Mozambique, where the threat is important enough to require action but not important enough to require acceptance of the domestic and international costs of a direct large-scale intervention, are also likely to persist. Most of all, South Africa is likely to resort to surrogates in the future simply because such a policy has worked in the past. This is especially true of surrogates of the second, or MNR-type, which aim more at dislocation rather than political and economic development since, as Joseph Hanlon has noted, 'destabilization works'.[59] Just as the lessons of a failed intervention become deeply etched in the collective consciousness of a nation's policy-makers, so do the successes. Thus, so long as the advantages that accrue from support of surrogates for regional destabilization appear to outweigh the costs, such a policy will remain a part of the political landscape in southern Africa.

59. Hanlon, *Mozambique*, p. 252.

Name Index